For Reference

Not to be taken from this room

Novels
for Students

National Advisory Board

Novels for Students

Presenting Analysis, Context, and Criticism on Commonly Studied Novels

Volume 10

Michael L. LaBlanc
and Ira Mark Milne, Editors

Carol Jago, Santa Monica High School, Advisor
Kathleen Pasquantonio, Novi High School, Advisor

Foreword by Anne Devereaux Jordan, Teaching and Learning Literature

GALE GROUP

Detroit
New York
San Francisco
London
Boston
Woodbridge, CT

Novels for Students

Staff

Series Editors: Michael L. LaBlanc and Ira Mark Milne.

Contributing Editors: Elizabeth Bellalouna, Elizabeth Bodenmiller, Reginald Carlton, Anne Marie Hacht, Polly Rapp, Jennifer Smith.

Research: Victoria B. Cariappa, *Research Team Manager.* Maureen Eremic, Barb McNeil, Cheryl Warnock, *Research Specialists.* Andy Malonis, *Technical Training Specialist.* Barbara Leevy, Tamara Nott, Tracie A. Richardson, Robert Whaley, *Research Associates.* Scott Floyd, Nicodemus Ford, Sarah Genik, Timothy Lehnerer, *Research Assistants.*

Permissions: Maria Franklin, *Permissions Manager.* Margaret A. Chamberlain, Edna Hedblad, *Permissions Specialists.* Erin Bealmear, Shalice Shah-Caldwell, Sarah Tomasek, *Permissions Associates.* Debra Freitas, Julie Juengling, Mark Plaza, *Permissions Assistants.*

Manufacturing: Mary Beth Trimper, *Manager, Composition and Electronic Prepress.* Evi Seoud, *Assistant Manager, Composition Purchasing and Electronic Prepress.* Stacy Melson, *Buyer.*

Imaging and Multimedia Content Team: Randy Bassett, *Image Database Supervisor.* Robert Duncan, Dan Newell, *Imaging Specialists.* Pamela A. Reed, *Imaging Coordinator.* Dean Dauphinais, Robyn V. Young, *Senior Image Editors.* Kelly A. Quin, *Image Editor.*

Product Design Team: Kenn Zorn, *Product Design Manager.* Pamela A. E. Galbreath, *Senior Art Director.* Michael Logusz, *Graphic Artist.*

Copyright Notice

ISBN 0-7876-3829-3
ISSN 1094-3552
Printed in the United States of America.

10 9 8 7 6 5 4 3 2 1

Table of Contents

The Informed Dialogue: Interacting with Literature

When we pick up a book, we usually do so with the anticipation of pleasure. We hope that by entering the time and place of the novel and sharing the thoughts and actions of the characters, we will find enjoyment. Unfortunately, this is often not the case; we are disappointed. But we should ask, has the author failed us, or have we failed the author?

We establish a dialogue with the author, the book, and with ourselves when we read. Consciously and unconsciously, we ask questions: "Why did the author write this book?" "Why did the author choose that time, place, or character?" "How did the author achieve that effect?" "Why did the character act that way?" "Would I act in the same way?" The answers we receive depend upon how much information about literature in general and about that book specifically we ourselves bring to our reading.

Young children have limited life and literary experiences. Being young, children frequently do not know how to go about exploring a book, nor sometimes, even know the questions to ask of a book. The books they read help them answer questions, the author often coming right out and *telling* young readers the things they are learning or are expected to learn. The perennial classic, *The Little Engine That Could, tells* its readers that, among other things, it is good to help others and brings happiness:

"Hurray, hurray," cried the funny little clown and all the dolls and toys. "The good little boys and girls in the city will be happy because you helped us, kind, Little Blue Engine."

In picture books, messages are often blatant and simple, the dialogue between the author and reader one-sided. Young children are concerned with the end result of a book—the enjoyment gained, the lesson learned—rather than with how that result was obtained. As we grow older and read further, however, we question more. We come to expect that the world within the book will closely mirror the concerns of our world, and that the author will *show* these through the events, descriptions, and conversations within the story, rather than *telling* of them. We are now expected to do the interpreting, carry on our share of the dialogue with the book and author, and glean not only the author's message, but comprehend how that message and the overall affect of the book were achieved. Sometimes, however, we need help to do these things. *Novels for Students* provides that help.

A novel is made up of many parts interacting to create a coherent whole. In reading a novel, the more obvious features can be easily spotted—theme, characters, plot—but we may overlook the more subtle elements that greatly influence how the novel is perceived by the reader: viewpoint, mood and tone, symbolism, or the use of humor. By focusing on both the obvious and more subtle literary elements within a novel, *Novels for Students* aids readers in both analyzing for message and in determining how and why that message is communicated. In the discussion on Harper Lee's *To Kill a Mockingbird* (Vol. 2), for example, the mockingbird as a symbol of innocence is dealt with, among other things, as is the importance of Lee's use of humor which "enlivens a serious plot, adds depth to the characterization, and creates a sense of familiarity and universality." The reader comes to understand the internal elements of each novel discussed—as well as the external influences that help shape it.

"The desire to write greatly," Harold Bloom of Yale University says, "is the desire to be elsewhere, in a time and place of one's own, in an originality that must compound with inheritance, with an anxiety of influence." A writer seeks to create a unique world within a story, but although it is unique, it is not disconnected from our own world. It speaks to us *because* of what the writer brings to the writing from our world: how he or she was raised and educated; his or her likes and dislikes; the events occurring in the real world at the time of the writing, and while the author was growing up. When we know what an author has brought to his or her work, we gain a greater insight into both the "originality" (the world of the book), and the things that "compound" it. This insight enables us to question that created world and find answers more readily. By informing ourselves, we are able to establish a more effective dialogue with both book and author.

Novels for Students, in addition to providing a plot summary and descriptive list of characters— to remind readers of what they have read—also explores the external influences that shaped each book. Each entry includes a discussion of the author's background, and the historical context in which the novel was written. It is vital to know, for instance, that when Ray Bradbury was writing *Fahrenheit 451* (Vol. 1), the threat of Nazi domination had recently ended in Europe, and the McCarthy hearings were taking place in Washington, D.C. This information goes far in answering the question, "Why did he write a story of oppressive government control and book burning?" Similarly,

it is important to know that Harper Lee, author of *To Kill a Mockingbird,* was born and raised in Monroeville, Alabama, and that her father was a lawyer. Readers can now see why she chose the south as a setting for her novel—it is the place with which she was most familiar—and start to comprehend her characters and their actions.

Novels for Students helps readers find the answers they seek when they establish a dialogue with a particular novel. It also aids in the posing of questions by providing the opinions and interpretations of various critics and reviewers, broadening that dialogue. Some reviewers of *To Kill A Mockingbird,* for example, "faulted the novel's climax as melodramatic." This statement leads readers to ask, "Is it, indeed, melodramatic?" "If not, why did some reviewers see it as such?" "If it is, why did Lee choose to make it melodramatic?" "Is melodrama ever justified?" By being spurred to ask these questions, readers not only learn more about the book and its writer, but about the nature of writing itself.

The literature included for discussion in *Novels for Students* has been chosen because it has something vital to say to us. *Of Mice and Men, Catch-22, The Joy Luck Club, My Antonia, A Separate Peace* and the other novels here speak of life and modern sensibility. In addition to their individual, specific messages of prejudice, power, love or hate, living and dying, however, they and all great literature also share a common intent. They force us to *think*—about life, literature, and about others, not just about ourselves. They pry us from the narrow confines of our minds and thrust us outward to confront the world of books and the larger, real world we all share. *Novels for Students* helps us in this confrontation by providing the means of enriching our conversation with literature and the world, by creating an *informed* dialogue, one that brings true pleasure to the personal act of reading.

Sources

Harold Bloom, *The Western Canon, The Books and School of the Ages,* Riverhead Books, 1994.

Watty Piper, *The Little Engine That Could,* Platt & Munk, 1930.

Anne Devereaux Jordan
Senior Editor, TALL
(Teaching and Learning Literature).

Introduction

Purpose of the Book

The purpose of *Novels for Students (NfS)* is to provide readers with a guide to understanding, enjoying, and studying novels by giving them easy access to information about the work. Part of Gale's "For Students" Literature line, *NfS* is specifically designed to meet the curricular needs of high school and undergraduate college students and their teachers, as well as the interests of general readers and researchers considering specific novels. While each volume contains entries on "classic" novels frequently studied in classrooms, there are also entries containing hard-to-find information on contemporary novels, including works by multicultural, international, and women novelists.

The information covered in each entry includes an introduction to the novel and the novel's author; a plot summary, to help readers unravel and understand the events in a novel; descriptions of important characters, including explanation of a given character's role in the novel as well as discussion about that character's relationship to other characters in the novel; analysis of important themes in the novel; and an explanation of important literary techniques and movements as they are demonstrated in the novel.

In addition to this material, which helps the readers analyze the novel itself, students are also provided with important information on the literary and historical background informing each work. This includes a historical context essay, a

box comparing the time or place the novel was written to modern Western culture, a critical overview essay, and excerpts from critical essays on the novel. A unique feature of *NfS* is a specially commissioned overview essay on each novel, targeted toward the student reader.

To further aid the student in studying and enjoying each novel, information on media adaptations is provided, as well as reading suggestions for works of fiction and nonfiction on similar themes and topics. Classroom aids include ideas for research papers and lists of critical sources that provide additional material on the novel.

Selection Criteria

The titles for each volume of *NfS* were selected by surveying numerous sources on teaching literature and analyzing course curricula for various school districts. Some of the sources surveyed included: literature anthologies; *Reading Lists for College-Bound Students: The Books Most Recommended by America's Top Colleges;* textbooks on teaching the novel; a College Board survey of novels commonly studied in high schools; a National Council of Teachers of English (NCTE) survey of novels commonly studied in high schools; the NCTE's *Teaching Literature in High School: The Novel;* and the Young Adult Library Services Association (YALSA) list of best books for young adults of the past twenty-five years.

Input was also solicited from our advisory board, as well as educators from various areas.

From these discussions, it was determined that each volume should have a mix of "classic" novels (those works commonly taught in literature classes) and contemporary novels for which information is often hard to find. Because of the interest in expanding the canon of literature, an emphasis was also placed on including works by international, multicultural, and women authors. Our advisory board members—educational professionals—helped pare down the list for each volume. If a work was not selected for the present volume, it was often noted as a possibility for a future volume. As always, the editor welcomes suggestions for titles to be included in future volumes.

How Each Entry Is Organized

Each entry, or chapter, in *NfS* focuses on one novel. Each entry heading lists the full name of the novel, the author's name, and the date of the novel's publication. The following elements are contained in each entry:

- **Introduction:** a brief overview of the novel which provides information about its first appearance, its literary standing, any controversies surrounding the work, and major conflicts or themes within the work.

- **Author Biography:** this section includes basic facts about the author's life, and focuses on events and times in the author's life that inspired the novel in question.

- **Plot Summary:** a factual description of the major events in the novel. Lengthy summaries are broken down with subheads.

- **Characters:** an alphabetical listing of major characters in the novel. Each character name is followed by a brief to an extensive description of the character's role in the novel, as well as discussion of the character's actions, relationships, and possible motivation.

  Characters are listed alphabetically by last name. If a character is unnamed—for instance, the narrator in *Invisible Man*–the character is listed as "The Narrator" and alphabetized as "Narrator." If a character's first name is the only one given, the name will appear alphabetically by that name.

- Variant names are also included for each character. Thus, the full name "Jean Louise Finch" would head the listing for the narrator of *To Kill a Mockingbird,* but listed in a separate cross-reference would be the nickname "Scout Finch."

- **Themes:** a thorough overview of how the major topics, themes, and issues are addressed within the novel. Each theme discussed appears in a separate subhead, and is easily accessed through the boldface entries in the Subject/Theme Index.

- **Style:** this section addresses important style elements of the novel, such as setting, point of view, and narration; important literary devices used, such as imagery, foreshadowing, symbolism; and, if applicable, genres to which the work might have belonged, such as Gothicism or Romanticism. Literary terms are explained within the entry, but can also be found in the Glossary.

- **Historical Context:** This section outlines the social, political, and cultural climate *in which the author lived and the novel was created.* This section may include descriptions of related historical events, pertinent aspects of daily life in the culture, and the artistic and literary sensibilities of the time in which the work was written. If the novel is a historical work, information regarding the time in which the novel is set is also included. Each section is broken down with helpful subheads.

- **Critical Overview:** this section provides background on the critical reputation of the novel, including bannings or any other public controversies surrounding the work. For older works, this section includes a history of how the novel was first received and how perceptions of it may have changed over the years; for more recent novels, direct quotes from early reviews may also be included.

- **Criticism:** an essay commissioned by *NfS* which specifically deals with the novel and is written specifically for the student audience, as well as excerpts from previously published criticism on the work (if available).

- **Sources:** an alphabetical list of critical material quoted in the entry, with full bibliographical information.

- **Further Reading:** an alphabetical list of other critical sources which may prove useful for the student. Includes full bibliographical information and a brief annotation.

In addition, each entry contains the following highlighted sections, set apart from the main text as sidebars:

- **Media Adaptations:** a list of important film and television adaptations of the novel, including source information. The list also includes stage adaptations, audio recordings, musical adaptations, etc.

- **Topics for Further Study:** a list of potential study questions or research topics dealing with the novel. This section includes questions related to other disciplines the student may be studying, such as American history, world history, science, math, government, business, geography, economics, psychology, etc.

- **Compare and Contrast Box:** an "at-a-glance" comparison of the cultural and historical differences between the author's time and culture and late twentieth-century Western culture. This box includes pertinent parallels between the major scientific, political, and cultural movements of the time or place the novel was written, the time or place the novel was set (if a historical work), and modern Western culture. Works written after the mid-1970s may not have this box.

- **What Do I Read Next?:** a list of works that might complement the featured novel or serve as a contrast to it. This includes works by the same author and others, works of fiction and nonfiction, and works from various genres, cultures, and eras.

Other Features

NfS includes "The Informed Dialogue: Interacting with Literature," a foreword by Anne Devereaux Jordan, Senior Editor for *Teaching and Learning Literature* (*TALL*), and a founder of the Children's Literature Association. This essay provides an enlightening look at how readers interact with literature and how *Novels for Students* can help teachers show students how to enrich their own reading experiences.

A Cumulative Author/Title Index lists the authors and titles covered in each volume of the *NfS* series.

A Cumulative Nationality/Ethnicity Index breaks down the authors and titles covered in each volume of the *NfS* series by nationality and ethnicity.

A Subject/Theme Index, specific to each volume, provides easy reference for users who may be studying a particular subject or theme rather than a single work. Significant subjects from events to broad themes are included, and the entries pointing to the specific theme discussions in each entry are indicated in **boldface**.

Each entry has several illustrations, including photos of the author, stills from film adaptations (if available), maps, and/or photos of key historical events.

Citing Novels for Students

When writing papers, students who quote directly from any volume of *Novels for Students* may use the following general forms. These examples are based on MLA style; teachers may request that students adhere to a different style, so the following examples may be adapted as needed.

When citing text from *NfS* that is not attributed to a particular author (i.e., the Themes, Style, Historical Context sections, etc.), the following format should be used in the bibliography section:

"Night." *Novels for Students*. Ed. Marie Rose Napierkowski. Vol. 4. Detroit: Gale, 1998. 34–5.

When quoting the specially commissioned essay from *NfS* (usually the first piece under the "Criticism" subhead), the following format should be used:

Miller, Tyrus. Essay on "Winesburg, Ohio." *Novels for Students*. Ed. Marie Rose Napierkowski. Vol. 4. Detroit: Gale, 1997. 218–9.

When quoting a journal or newspaper essay that is reprinted in a volume of *NfS*, the following form may be used:

Malak, Amin. "Margaret Atwood's

"The Handmaid's Tale' and the Dystopian Tradition," in *Canadian Literature* , No. 112, Spring, 1987, 9–16; excerpted and reprinted in *Novels for Students*, Vol. 4, ed. Marie Rose Napierkowski (Detroit: Gale, 1998), pp. 61–64.

When quoting material reprinted from a book that appears in a volume of *NfS*, the following form may be used:

Adams, Timothy Dow. "Richard Wright:

"Wearing the Mask," in *Telling Lies in Modern American Autobiography* (University of North Carolina Press, 1990), 69–83; excerpted and reprinted in *Novels for Students*, Vol. 5, eds. Sheryl Ciccarelli and Marie Napierkowski (Detroit: Gale, 1999), pp. 59–61.

We Welcome Your Suggestions

The editor of *Novels for Students* welcomes your comments and ideas. Readers who wish to suggest novels to appear in future volumes, or who have other suggestions, are cordially invited to contact the editor. You may contact the editor via e-mail at: **mark.milne@galegroup.com.** Or write to the editor at:

Editor, *Novels for Students*

Gale Group

27500 Drake Road

Farmington Hills, MI 48331–3535

Literary Chronology

1812: Charles Dickens is born in Portsmouth, England, on February 7.

1828: Leo Tolstoy is born to an upper-class Russian family on September 9 at the family's estate in Tula province, Russia. His father is Count Nikolay Tolstoy, a nobleman and prestigious landowner.

1843: Charles Dickens's *A Christmas Carol* is written in a six-week period in October and November and then published. The novel is the first of five short Christmas books published by Charles Dickens.

1869: Leo Tolstoy's *War and Peace* is completed.

1870: Charles Dickens dies, and is buried in Poet's Corner in Westminster Abbey, an honor reserved for England's most notable literary figures.

1879: Edward Morgan Forster is born on January 1 in Coventry, England.

1905: Ayn Rand, also known as Alice Rosenbaum, is born on February 2 in St. Petersburg, Russia.

1910: E. M. Forster's *Howards End* is published. Critics generally agree it surpasses Forster's earlier novels. Fourteen years would elapse before the publication of *A Passage to India*, Forster's last novel.

1910: Leo Tolstoy dies of pneumonia on November 20.

1923: Norman Mailer is born on January 31 in Long Branch, New Jersey, to Isaac (an accountant) and Fanny (owner of a small business) Mailer.

1924: James du Maresq Clavell is born on August 10 in Sidney, Australia, to British colonists Richard Charles and Eileen (Collis) Clavell.

1927: Hannah Green is born in Cincinnati, Ohio. Her father is a foreign copyright and trademark agent, like his fictional counterpart in *The Dead of the House*, and her mother is a homemaker.

1928: Gabriel Garcia Marquez is born in Aracataca, Colombia, on March 6, to poor parents, Gabriel Eligio Garcia and Luisa Santiaga Marquez Iguaran.

1934: N. Scott Momaday is born on the Kiowa Reservation in Lawton, Oklahoma, on February 27. His father, Alfred Morris, is an artist and teacher (in fact, his artworks are used to illustrate several of Momaday's books, including his history of the Kiowa people, *The Way to Rainy Mountain*). His mother, Mayme Natachee Scott, is a teacher and a writer of children's books.

1934: Bette Greene is born in Memphis, Tennessee, on June 28.

1941: Anne Tyler is born on October 25 in Minneapolis, Minnesota, to parents who are liberal activists and members of the Society of Friends.

1948: Norman Mailer's *The Naked and the Dead* is published and earns overwhelming popular and critical acclaim. Most reviewers have deemed the novel to be one of the best war stories ever written.

1955: Barbara Kingsolver is born in Annapolis, Maryland, on April 8, but grows up in rural Kentucky.

1957: Ayn Rand's *Atlas Shrugged* is published. It is the final novel written by Russian-born American philosopher and author. It is a controversial and widely popular work. According to a 1991 Library of Congress report, it is considered the second most influential book after the Bible in the lives of its readers.

1968: N. Scott Momaday's *House Made of Dawn* is published and garners little critical and commercial attention in the United States. Yet within a year, it wins the prestigious Pulitzer Prize for fiction, and receives international critical acclaim.

1970: E. M. Forster dies on June 7 in Coventry at the home of friends.

1971: Hannah Green's only novel, *The Dead of the House*, is published in book form after originally appearing in the *New Yorker* as a series of shorter fictional pieces. It is reprinted in 1996.

1973: Bette Greene's first novel, *Summer of My German Soldier*, is published and becomes her best-known novel. Chronicling one summer in the life of a twelve-year-old Jewish girl in the rural South, the novel becomes an overwhelming critical success and has gone on to become a classic of juvenile literature. The book has been nominated for the National Book Award, and has won the New York Times Outstanding Book Award, the Golden Kite Society's children's book writer's award, and the American Library Association's Notable Book Award. In 1978 a sequel by Greene is published, entitled *Morning is a Long Time Coming.*

1975: James du Maresq Clavell's *Shogun: A Novel of Japan* is published. Although not considered great literature by most critics, *Shogun: A Novel of Japan* makes its author one of the most widely read twentieth-century novelists. In the first five years of its printing, 7 million books are sold. NBC sponsors a film extravaganza as 130 million people watch the 12-hour miniseries *Shogun*. The miniseries prompts the sale of another 2.5 million books. Since the movie, even more people have read the book or watched the shorter 2.5-hour-long film.

1982: Ayn Rand dies on March 6; ironically, the author who used the cigarette as a symbol of glowing human intellect in her last novel lost a lung to cancer shortly before her death.

1982: Gabriel Garcia Marquez's novel *Chronicle of a Death Foretold* is first published in English.

1988: Anne Tyler's *Breathing Lessons*, her eleventh book, is published. It becomes the winner of the 1989 Pulitzer Prize for fiction as well as *Time* magazine's Book of the Year.

1993: Barbara Kingsolver's *Pigs in Heaven* is published. Barbara Kingsolver is already a well-established and successful author. This novel, her third, garners critical and popular success and earns her a nomination for an ABBY award, the American Library Association award, the *Los Angeles Times* Fiction Prize, and the Cowboy Hall of Fame Western Fiction Award.

1994: James du Maresq Clavell dies from a combination of cancer and stroke at his home in Vevey, Switzerland.

Acknowledgments

The editors wish to thank the copyright holders of the excerpted criticism included in this volume and the permissions managers of many book and magazine publishing companies for assisting us in securing reproduction rights. We are also grateful to the staffs of the Detroit Public Library, the Library of Congress, the University of Detroit Mercy Library, Wayne State University Purdy/Kresge Library Complex, and the University of Michigan Libraries for making their resources available to us. Following is a list of the copyright holders who have granted us permission to reproduce material in this volume of *Novels for Students (NfS)*. Every effort has been made to trace copyright, but if omissions have been made, please let us know.

COPYRIGHTED MATERIALS IN *NfS*, **VOLUME 10, WERE REPRODUCED FROM THE FOLLOWING PERIODICALS:**

American Literature, v. L, January, 1979. Copyright © 1979 by Duke University Press, Durham, NC. Reproduced by permission. *The American Scholar*, v. 21, Winter, 1951-52. Copyright © 1952, renewed 1980 by the Phi Beta Kappa Society. Reproduced by permission of the publishers. *Best Sellers*, v. 38, December, 1978. Copyright 1978, by the University of Scranton. Reproduced by permission. *Book World—The Washington Post*, February 27, 1972 for "An Accumulation of Time Past" by L. J. Davis © 1972 by L.J. Davis. Reproduced by permission of Sterling Lord Literistic, Inc./ May 8, 1983 for "Adolescent Heroines" by Michele Slung; June 13, 1993 for "The Mother and the Tribe" by Wendy Smith. © 1983, 1993, Washington Post Book World Service/Washington Post Writers Group. Both reproduced by permission of the respective authors. *The Cambridge Quarterly*, Spring, 1971 for "Mr. Forster's Fine Feelings" by Duke Maskell. Copyright © 1971 by the Editors. Reproduced by permission of the author. *The Christian Science Monitor*, October 10, 1957. © 1957, renewed 1985 The Christian Science Publishing Society. All rights reserved. Reproduced by permission from *The Christian Science Monitor*. *College English*, v. 40, November, 1978 for "On 'Atlas Shrugged'" by Judith Wilt. Copyright © 1978 by the National Council of Teachers of English. Reprinted by permission of the publisher and the author. *Commentary*, v. 75, May, 1983 for "How Good is Gabriel Garcia Marquez?" by Joseph Epstein. Copyright © 1983 by the American Jewish Committee. All rights reserved. Reproduced by permission of the publisher and the author. *Commonweal*, v. CXVI, February 24, 1989. Copyright © 1989 Commonweal Publishing Co., Inc. Reproduced by permission of Commonweal Foundation. *Critique*, v. XIV, 1972. Copyright © 1972 Helen Dwight Reid Educational Foundation. Reprinted with permission of the Helen Dwight Reid Educational Foundation, published by Heldref Publications, 1319 18th Street, N. W., Washington, DC 20036-1802. *English Journal*, v. 69 for "Children of the Holocaust" by Judy Mitchell. Copyright © 1980 by the National Council of Teachers of English. Reproduced by

B. From *The Radical Novel in the United States, 1900-1954: Some Interrelations of Literature and Society*. Harvard University Press, 1956. Copyright 1956 President & Fellows of Harvard College. Copyright renewed © 1984 by Walter Bates Rideout. All rights reserved. Reproduced by permission of the author. Scott Trimble, Martha. From *N. Scott Momaday*. Boise State College, 1973. Copyright 1973 by the Boise State College Western Writers Series. All rights reserved. Reproduced by permission of the publisher.

PHOTOGRAPHS AND ILLUSTRATIONS APPEARING IN *NFS*, VOLUME 10, WERE RECEIVED FROM THE FOLLOWING SOURCES:

A triptych showing all the shoguns who ruled Japan during the Tokugawa period, 1875. © Asian Art & Archaeology, Inc./CORBIS. Reproduced by permission.—Chamberlain, Richard, from the movie "Shogun," 1981, photograph. NBC-TV. The Kobal Collection. Reproduced by permission.—Cherokee girl in costume, Blue Jay on her wrist, photograph. Bettmann. Reproduced by permission.—Clavell, James, photograph. AP/Wide World Photos. Reproduced by permission.—Drug summit site, Cartagena, Colombia, 1990. AP/Wide World Photos. Reproduced by permission.—Forster, E. M., photograph. AP/Wide World Photos, Inc. Reproduced by permission.—Garcia Marquez, Gabriel (looking right, in dark shirt), 1982, photograph. AP/Wide World Photos. Reproduced by permission.—Greene, Bette, photograph. Reproduced by permission.—Hepburn, Audrey, Mel Ferrer, in the movie "War and Peace," 1956, photograph. Paramount. The Kobal Collection. Reproduced by permission.—Hoover Dam, Nevada, photograph. Nevada Commission on Tourism. Reproduced by permission.—Kingsolver, Barbara, photograph. AP/Wide World Photos. Reproduced by permission.—Mailer, Norman, photograph. Archive Photos, Inc. Reproduced by permission.—Momaday, N. Scott (waving to crowd), photograph. AP/Wide World Photos. Reproduced by permission.—Rand, Ayn (standing on city streets), 1962, photograph. AP/Wide World Photos. Reproduced by permission.—Russian Revolution (Petrograd), photograph. AP/Wide World Photos. Reproduced by permission.—Section of Baltimore, Maryland. Archive Photos, Inc. Reproduced by permission.—Seven Dials Slum, Dudley Street in the Seven Dials (Covent Garden) area of London, engraving by Gustave Dore. Hulton-Getty/Tony Stone Images. Reproduced by permission.—Stewart, Patrick, Joel Gray in the movie "A Christmas Carol," 1999, photograph by Oliver Upton. CBS-TV. The Kobal Collection. Reproduced by permission.—Strzhelchik, Vladislav (standing on battlefield), in the film "War and Peace," 1968, photograph. The Kobal Collection. Reproduced by permission.—Thompson, Emma, Anthony Hopkins, in the movie "Howard's End," 1992, photograph. Mayfair. The Kobal Collection. Reproduced by permission.—Tyler, Anne, photograph. Courtesy of Knopf. Reproduced by permission.—Woodward, Joanne, in the television film "Breathing Lessons," 1994, photograph. The Kobal Collection. Reproduced by permission.

Contributors

Jane Elizabeth Dougherty: Freelance writer, Medford, MA. Original essay on *Howards End*.

Jeremy Hubbell: Freelance writer; M.Litt., University of Aberdeen. Entries on *Atlas Shrugged*, *Breathing Lessons*, and *Shogun*. Original essays on *Atlas Shrugged* and *Shogun*.

David J. Kelly: Professor of English, College of Lake County (IL). Entries on *A Christmas Carol*, *House Made of Dawn*, and *War and Peace*. Original essays on *A Christmas Carol*, *House Made of Dawn*, and *War and Peace*.

Jeffrey M. Lilburn: Writer and translator specializing in twentieth-century American and Canadian literature; M.A., University of Western Ontario. Original essay on *Chronicle of a Death Foretold*.

Nancy C. McClure: Educational consultant and freelance writer, Clarksburg, WV; Ed.D., West Virginia University. Entry on *Chronicle of a Death Foretold*.

Tabitha McIntosh-Byrd: Freelance writer; M.Litt., University of Aberdeen. Entries on *The Dead of the House* and *Summer of My German Soldier*. Original essays on *Breathing Lessons*, *The Dead of the House*, and *Summer of My German Soldier*.

Wendy Perkins: Assistant Professor of English, Prince George's Community College, Maryland; Ph.D. in English, University of Delaware. Entries on *The Naked and the Dead* and *Pigs in Heaven*. Original essays on *The Naked and the Dead* and *Pigs in Heaven*.

Rita Schweiss: Freelance writer, Roanoke, VA. Entry on *Howards End*.

Atlas Shrugged

Ayn Rand
1957

The final novel written by Russian-born American philosopher and author Ayn Rand, *Atlas Shrugged* is a controversial and widely popular work. According to a 1991 Library of Congress report, it is considered the second most influential book after the Bible in the lives of its readers. A complex combination of mystery, love story, social criticism, and philosophical concepts, the 1,100-page novel embodies the author's passionate celebration of individualism, free will, capitalism, logic, and reason.

Set in an imaginary America in a communist world, *Atlas Shrugged* is a sharp critique of a corrupt communist system and its damaging effects on areas as various as love, science, and industrial productivity. The novel's main protagonists, Dagny Taggart and Hank Rearden, are capitalist-minded industrialists, "Atlases" who carry the collapsing national economy on their backs. Things change, however, when the mysterious John Galt begins a revolution against the existing order, believing that the parasitic society would destroy itself if its competent and hard-working members would simply stop working. But first, the protagonists must learn how to let go of the ties of obligation, responsibility, and guilt connecting them to the abusive community in all aspects of their lives.

As Rand said to her biographer, Nathaniel Branden, the novel explains her philosophical principles in a dramatic action story combining "metaphysics, morality, economics, politics and sex." Rand wrote *Atlas Shrugged* with a sense of mission; she said, "[A]fter *Atlas* I was no longer pres-

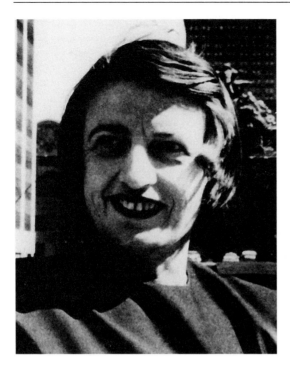

Ayn Rand

sured, my lifelong assignment was over." Despite tremendous popular success—the novel sold over 5 million copies by 1984—Rand believed she had explained her philosophical views clearly enough and did not write another word of fiction for the rest of her life

Author Biography

Ayn Rand, a.k.a. Alice Rosenbaum, was born on February 2, 1905, in St. Petersburg, Russia. Her family was relatively wealthy; Rand's father was a self-made man who owned a pharmacy. According to her biographer, Barbara Brandon in *The Passion of Ayn Rand,* Rand was a precocious child who spent much time among adults, gathering information about the world around her. At the age of nine, she had already developed a strong fascination about the battle between good and evil, as well as her notion of the characteristics of the ideal man. "Intelligence, independence, courage. The heroic man," she described him to her biographer. Rand later recreated this model in many of her fictional characters, including the mysterious John Galt in *Atlas Shrugged.*

Rand's keen awareness of her ideological and political surroundings easily detected the problems that would begin to plague Russia in her childhood; she grew to despise the communist rule of Lenin's Bolsheviks, who came into power with the 1917 revolution. Under communism, her family was forced to give up her father's business, leave their home under the threat of ongoing internal conflicts, and almost starve to death. In her biography, Rand remembers that she "began to understand that politics was a moral issue" and that she detested any "government or society or any authorities imposing anything on anyone."

While working on a bachelor's degree in history in St. Petersburg, by then named Leningrad, Rand studied American history. She told Branden that she found it incredible: "I saw America as the country of individualism, of strong men, of freedom and important purposes. I thought, 'This is the kind of government I approve of.'" In 1926, Rand got a chance to visit relatives in America; even before she took off, she had decided not to return from her trip.

As a struggling writer in America, Rand went from summarizing works to be adapted as Hollywood scripts, to writing plays (one of which was produced on Broadway), to publishing a semi-autobiographical first novel. However, it was not until the publication of her later novels, *The Fountainhead* and *Atlas Shrugged,* that she achieved fame on a grand scale. Her novella *Anthem* served as an outline for both of these works; in her fiction, Rand described the threat and immorality of communism while developing her own strictly capitalist philosophy of Objectivism. In *Atlas Shrugged,* her self-proclaimed masterpiece of Objectivist theory, she proposes the destruction of a parasite communist society as the only way to achieve the capitalist utopia. In the postscript to *Atlas Shrugged,* she described the essence of Objectivism and the novel's major theme as "the concept of man as a heroic being, with his own happiness as the moral purpose of his life, with his productive achievement as his noblest activity, and reason as his only absolute."

Rand's later theoretical pieces—*The Virtue of Selfishness, a New Concept of Egoism,* her newsletter *The Objectivist,* and other works—further develop the principles of her philosophy. Although her novels became bestsellers worldwide, Rand did not write fiction after *Atlas Shrugged.* She died on March 6, 1982; ironically, the author who used the cigarette as a symbol of glowing human intellect in her last novel lost a lung to cancer shortly before her death.

Plot Summary

Part 1: Non-Contradiction

Atlas Shrugged opens in a devastated New York City with crumbling buildings, empty stores, and closed businesses. It is a vision of an impoverished country in a communist world system, which slowly but surely destroys national and foreign economy alike. As capable, productive workers and business owners are devastated by bureaucratic machinations, they begin to abandon the existing order one by one and mysteriously disappear. In the meantime, the political and industrial parasites support each other and live off of the creative and productive "giants" who remain and must support them on their shoulders. The apathy of the people is summed up in a new slang expression, "Who is John Galt?" which conveys hopelessness, fear, and a sense of futility, as well as everything unachievable and imagined.

In the first part of the novel, Rand introduces several industries that keep the weakened communist system from failing. Taggart Transcontinental, the economic artery of the United States on which all the other industries depend, is the largest and most reliable railroad in the country. Although Jim Taggart is the official president, it is his competent and capitalist-minded sister Dagny Taggart who actually runs the business. When a part of the railroad collapses, Dagny decides to rebuild it with the new and publicly condemned Rearden Metal, a revolutionary alloy lighter and stronger than steel. Hank Rearden, the inventor, is the self-made owner of Rearden Steel and several other related companies, and a fellow capitalist businessman who shares Dagny's work philosophy. The new line is planned to connect the rest of the country to Colorado's Wyatt Oil, the only flourishing refinery on the continent. Wyatt, Dagny, and Hank are united in their battle to preserve competition and productivity in the nation's economy, so their own businesses can survive. The establishment, however, regards them as cruel and selfish businesspeople who only care about their work and the money they make from it.

Although the project seems to be doomed from the start due to governmental censure, the line is completed and has a successful first run; Dagny names it the John Galt line to spite her opponents.

In the meantime, Dagny and Hank fall in love and begin a secret affair (secret because Hank is married). While on a vacation together, the two stumble upon a revolutionary model of a motor in an abandoned factory. Dagny begins a quest to find the engineer who invented it, but the search is a dead end; instead, she hires the promising physicist Daniels to try to finish the motor.

In the meantime, with the passing of a new communist law of equal opportunity, the successful businesses in the country are forced to reduce their production. The governmental excuse for this restriction is that the rest of the businesses cannot compete with them. Dagny, Hank, and Wyatt all take a serious financial blow; in his final protest before he disappears (like many before him), Wyatt burns down his refinery.

Part 2: Either-Or

In the second part of the novel, the decay of the national economy continues. Francisco d'Anconia, Dagny's childhood friend and former lover, seems to be running the family business of d'Anconia Copper straight into ground after many generations of flourishing success. Francisco befriends Hank and leads him to a conclusion that, in an unjust and abusive society, his work is worthless because it can only be used by parasites for their own survival and further exploitation. When Hank is put on trial for selling more Rearden Metal to a customer than the state regulations allow (in efforts to keep a supplier in business), he clearly understands the idea of a noble man's guilt used as a weapon of obligation against him. However, the society still holds some reins on Hank: when his wife Lillian finds out about Dagny, she uses the information to establish herself higher in the hierarchy of corruption. Hank is blackmailed into giving all the rights to Rearden Metal to the State Science Institute, to be used in Project X—a destruction device based on sound waves and as powerful as the atomic bomb.

In the meantime, another set of laws is passed that takes away almost all the rights of individuals in the community; however, by this time even those who decide which laws to pass are becoming anxious because the resources are running out. Under the new pressure imposed by the laws, Dagny quits her job and goes to a cabin in the countryside. In her absence, a terrible accident occurs on the railroad: due to the establishment's incompetence, the Taggart Tunnel caves in on one of the trains. Dagny rushes back to work, followed by Francisco, who tries in vain to persuade her to abandon the lost cause and quit the railroad she loves too much.

Upon her return, Dagny continues to try to salvage the railroad, cutting off some lines to make up for the others. On one of her trips across the deteriorating country, she meets a tramp sneaking on her train. The tramp tells her he used to work with a man called John Galt, a worker who abandoned the factory declaring he would stop the motor of the world before he would participate in the unjust system. With an ominous premonition, Dagny heads out to reach Daniels and prevent him from quitting his work on the motor, but she arrives only to see him taking off in a plane with "the destroyer"—a strange man who persuades the capable members of society to desert what they are doing. Dagny flies after them and ends up crashing in the Rocky Mountains.

Part 3: A Is A

Dagny awakens in a damaged plane after a rough landing into a well-hidden valley in the mountains; the valley is the seat of Galt's new world. Galt takes her on a tour of the place: all of the capable social "dropouts" gather here to establish their own free-enterprise system. Ragnar Danneskjold, a notorious pirate on the outside, works as the new world's internal revenue service with the goal of returning to the competent all the wealth they have lost to the corrupt system. The motto of the valley is "I swear by my life and my love of it that I will never live for the sake of another man, nor ask another man to live for mine." The members of this community are on a strike of the mind, denying the most precious human resource to the outside society which opposes it. However, Dagny cannot stay in the new paradise, although she feels that she has fallen in love with Galt; instead, she returns to the decaying outside world to continue fighting alongside Hank for its preservation.

The country is falling into despair due to the overwhelming economic crisis; Lillian tries to use Hank's affair to blackmail Dagny into reassuring the nation in a radio address, but Dagny turns the tables and instead reveals the blackmail on the radio. Another national broadcast is scheduled, this time to be given by the head of the state, but the airwaves are taken over by Galt who, in a lengthy speech, explicates his philosophy and beckons those remaining to escape and never let their strength be used by the weak.

Galt gets caught; the government, by this time in panic over the impending world collapse, tortures him to make him take over and restore the failing economy. Dagny, Francisco, and Hank manage to find and rescue him, but just then the old world crumbles: the lights of New York City go out, the motor of the world stops. The novel ends with Galt's little army looking at the civilization they will rebuild under the sign of the dollar.

Characters

Hugh Akston

A famous philosopher, "the last advocate of reason" and a renowned teacher at the Patrick Henry University; John Galt, Francisco d'Anconia, and Ragnar Danneskjold were his students. Galt persuades him to leave the society that rejects reason and to join his cause, and Akston accepts, moving deep into the countryside and opening a small diner. In Galt's utopian refuge, Akston dedicates all of his intellectual power to educating others in the philosophy of reason.

Orren Boyle

The president of Associated Steel, Boyle works closely with the government to ensure his success in business. He bribes politicians to eliminate his competition, especially the steel industry owned by Hank Rearden. Boyle can sell defective steel because it is the only product on the market; however, constructions of his material collapse and people get killed. Boyle is an illustration of corruption in industry.

Cherryl Brooks

A salesgirl at a dime store who catches Jim Taggart's eye because she naively considers him a national hero. Before Cherryl realizes that Jim has been taking credit for all of Dagny's visionary achievements at the railroad, the two are married. Her husband uses her to gain popularity as a man of the people who embraces the working class.

Kip Chalmers

A petty politician whose arrogance and ignorance leads to the disaster in the Taggart Tunnel.

Ken Danagger

The last competent producer of coal in the country nearing economic collapse. He secretly purchases much-needed Rearden Metal from Hank, because the portion assigned by the government is not enough to keep his business running. The illegal sale is discovered and the two of them are sued, but before the trial, John Galt pays Danagger a visit and persuades him to join the revolution.

Francisco d'Anconia

In his conversations with Hank Rearden (whom he eventually converts to Galt's revolution), Francisco serves as the author's mouthpiece, preaching the Objectivist philosophy in many areas of human life, from industry to sex to psychology. He is a brilliant businessman and heir to the largest and oldest company on earth, d'Anconia Copper, which originated in Argentina but has expanded over several generations to all the parts of the world. Superbly intelligent, ingenious, energetic, and determined, Francisco is Dagny's childhood friend and first lover; the two of them share the concept of a world of invention and productivity, and both believe in the inherent morality of capitalism.

About his family, Francisco says, "None of us has ever been permitted to think he is born d'Anconia. We are expected to become one." In that sense, Francisco is also a self-made man: he worked in the mines since childhood and independently acquired his first copper mine at the age of 20, parallel with his college degree. At the Patrick Henry University he befriends two brilliant students with whom he forms a trio of prodigies, the future leaders of the John Galt revolution. As part of his fight, Francisco has the difficult task of sacrificing his family business so that it does not become a tool in the communist system of corruption. He conducts a gigantic cover-up to present his company as still successful, while he invests in dry copper mines and even sabotages the productive ones.

Quentin Daniels

A young physicist who used to study at the Utah Institute of Technology, but now works at the deserted institute as a night watchman. Dr. Stadler recommends him to Dagny when she asks for someone who would be able to recreate the innovative motor. Daniels accepts the assignment, but John Galt discovers his work and persuades him to quit before the motor is finished.

Ragnar Danneskjold

A member of the brilliant trio from the Patrick Henry University, who participates in Galt's fight by becoming a pirate and sabotaging the communist world's ocean trade.

Media Adaptations

• Ayn Rand had begun adapting Atlas Shrugged as a television miniseries in 1981, but the project was never completed. She died in 1982.

Dr. Floyd Ferris

Stadler describes Ferris as "the valet of science" who once used to be a biologist, but has become a politician. Ferris supports the immoral communist rule, publishes a scientific book on the meaninglessness of reason, and gets a lot of money from the government to devise the secret project X—a deadly weapon similar to the atomic bomb. Ferris is the representative of corruption in science.

John Galt

The identity of this character is the element of mystery in the novel from the first line: "Who is John Galt?" As the existing world order collapses, Galt arrives as a mythological figure, the savior with a master plan: he is the leader of the movement that works to destroy corrupt communist rule in America. Long before Galt appears in the novel and his revolution announces itself, his name becomes a part of the slang, popularized among everyday people: it represents apathy, fear, and the futility of their life in the status quo.

A self-made man and a brilliant student of science and philosophy at the Patrick Henry University (along with Francisco d'Anconia and Ragnar Danneskjold), Galt realizes that his world can only be saved through the destruction of communism and reinvention of capitalism. After he persuades his aforementioned school friends to join his cause, Galt and his small but quickly growing army get to work to find and "convert" as many people as possible to their revolutionary ideology.

The rebels gather the competent and the creative members of the society into a sabotage operation: Galt's disciples simply leave their work and get petty jobs instead, thus making once productive resources, factories, and industries absolutely useless for the political parasites. Then, Galt forms a new world under the sacred sign of the dollar, a capitalist Atlantis where everything is earned by one's own work.

Galt is the man of the mind, superbly rational, intelligent, brave, perfectly self-confident, and serene. Rand intended her hero to be somewhat abstract and symbolic, almost god-like. She stated, "One does not approach a god too closely—one does not get too intimate with him—one maintains a respectful distance from his inner life." Galt is the embodiment of Rand's Objectivist philosophy (which he explains in a sixty-page speech near the novel's end), her "ideal man," and the perfect counterpart for the novel's heroine, Dagny Taggart.

Richard Halley

The composer of music that celebrates individual achievement; Dagny remains a fan of his concertos long after they are dismissed by the public as old-fashioned.

Hank

See Henry Readen

Jim

See James Taggart

Owen Kellogg

A competent young engineer who used to run the Taggart Terminal. Dagny offers him a better job with more responsibility on the railroad, but he quits to join Galt's revolution.

Paul Larkin

Hank Rearden's devotee who depends on his charity for living. When the government passes the law that prohibits one person to own more than one business, Hank has to sell his iron ore mines to his friend. Larkin, unable to do business well, lets the mines disintegrate; eventually, he openly joins the communal majority, which defends the weak and unable like himself, and turns against his benefactor.

Wesley Mouch

Rearden's lobbyist in Washington, although he sells out his services to the highest bidder. He works with Orren Boyle and Jim Taggart until he gains true political power with presiding assignments to various committees. One of his new positions is the Top Coordinator of the Bureau of Economic Planning and National Resources, which "kills" Ellis Wyatt's oil business and seriously harms Hank Rearden's company. Mouch is also

one of the people behind the creation of the deadly Project X.

Midas Mulligan

A banker who deserts the old world, which judges him as selfish; he is one of the originators of Galt's valley.

Henry Rearden

Henry Rearden (also known as Hank) is a self-made businessman, the embodiment of the rags-to-riches American dream who starts at the societal bottom and reaches the top with hard work and dedication. Hank begins to work in steel mills at the age of fourteen, and makes rapid progress thanks to his sense of leadership, responsibility, and skill. At the age of forty-five, he owns Rearden Steel and several related businesses; also, he spends ten years of his life in experiments for Rearden Metal, which promises to revolutionize modern metallurgy. Hank has the society working against him, however, including his parasitic family and his manipulative wife, Lillian, who lives to control him. He allows their abuse because they manage to persuade him that his ascetic devotion to business is inhuman; Hank is told all of his life that desire, be it professional or physical, is the lowest of all vices. Also, he believes that his enemies are harmless and that it does not bother him to carry a few social parasites on his back.

Hank falls in love with his business associate Dagny Taggart and befriends the libertine businessman Francisco d'Anconia, who slowly prepares him to stop supporting the society that abuses him. As the communist regime begins to feel the approaching economic collapse of the country, the so-called looters begin to rely more and more heavily on the work of the competent individuals, including Hank. Rearden Steel is decimated through various directives that take away Hank's accomplishments and production and distribute them to the "public" in the name of equality. Hank becomes increasingly devastated by the situation in the country and the world through his encounters with the sinister looters, who have all the power. Gradually, Hank realizes that the parasites can only have the power he is willing to give them with his work, and joins Galt's revolution.

Lilian Rearden

Lillian is Hank's cold and calculating wife, whose aim in life is to have as respectable a social standing as possible. She is an expert in manipulating people by offering them what they want; Hank marries her because she appears fascinated by the purpose of his life, his work, and his business. Coming from an old family with a distinguished social position and a modest financial standing, Lillian had access to the top layer of New York's society, where she met Hank, a newcomer industrialist. She is graceful, elegant, always in control; also, she enjoys using her high-class charm and eloquence ironically at parties and family gatherings to put down her husband's dedication to his work as something low-class and indecent. Although she lives off of Hank's money, she maintains strong relations with the movers and the shakers of the corrupt system and supports their ideology. Lillian's ultimate goal is to control her husband socially; she gets a chance to do so when she discovers that he has a lover, but her plan fails.

Dr. Robert Stadler

Founder of the State Science Institute, an establishment of scientific research which was supposed to be free of governmental influence; however, this changes in the corrupt society. Stadler, once famous for saying, "Free scientific inquiry? The first adjective is redundant," used to teach physics at the Patrick Henry University and had the same three brilliant students who later started the rebellion against the corrupt system. In fact, Stadler and Akston used to compete for the three students, but Akston won with his philosophy of logic and purpose. In turn, Stadler eventually gets caught in the compromise between his Institute work and the governmental corruption, which uses his research facility to create a deadly weapon, proportionate to the atomic bomb. He rationalizes his participation in it until the end.

Dagny Taggart

Dagny, in Rand's words, is both her epitome of an ideal woman, and "[her]self, with any possible flaws eliminated." She is resolute, intelligent, ambitious, adventurous and strong; in her thirties, she is the vice president in charge of operation who actually runs Taggart Transcontinental, the family business inherited by her weak and indecisive brother. In the existing social system, Dagny is a threat because she functions on the principle of capitalism: she works for her money, takes chances on new and possibly profitable inventions (such as Rearden Metal), and values her workers and business partners on the sole basis of their job performance. The railroad is Dagny's purpose, her life's work, and her pride, but although her competence

and toughness earn her respect of her workers, the communist supporters (including her brother) condemn her as selfish, unfeeling, unfeminine, and materialistic. At the same time, however, they rely on her skill to provide the services they are not capable of carrying out.

Since her childhood, Dagny was aware that the family railroad was to be her life; she excelled in her engineering studies and worked her way up in the company, where nobody expected her to be so successful in running the place. An uncompromising capitalist with firm moral beliefs, Dagny can only love men who share her views: her childhood friend and first lover, Francisco d'Anconia; her business associate Hank Rearden; and finally the leader of the revolution and her ideological soulmate, John Galt.

As the country begins to falter, Dagny fights courageously not only for her railroad, but for everything good and productive in human civilization. When she becomes aware that there is a "destroyer" who talks all the competent businesspeople into quitting, she goes after him and even crashes into his secret headquarters; she is the only person to succeed in finding John Galt. Dagny is the last person Galt manages to recruit from the decaying old world.

James Taggart

Dagny's older brother James Taggart (also known as Jim) is an example of a failed individual by Rand's standards. Jim is the president of the railroad who got the position on the basis of tradition instead of merit. He is a weak, indecisive, malevolent man who fears change and responsibility. Therefore, the ideology of the existing political order works for him, and he supports the directives that make him better off than his competitors. The corruption ultimately hurts his company along with the rest of the country's economy, but he does not mind as long as nobody blames him.

Jim hates and fears his sister and her friends and considers them cruel users of the people, but he is also aware of their powerful ability to make the industry work, which he cannot do. He joins the communist majority and takes pleasure in seeing Dagny suffer under the legislative regime he supports; the degradation of others is his only source of self-confidence. He even marries a poor salesgirl to have someone who would always look up to him.

Nathaniel Taggart

Dagny's famous ancestor, the founder of Taggart Transcontinental, whose life is a hard-core declaration of laissez-faire capitalism. Dagny often finds inspiration in his larger-than-life statue in the concourse of the Taggart Terminal.

The Wet Nurse

A nickname given to a boy fresh out of college who is government-appointed to oversee Rearden Steel and make sure that Hank's business runs according to the regulations. Although he espouses the current ideology, the boy begins to admire Hank and his work ethics. He is the example of the social corruption in education, which apparently can be reversed with hands-on experience of "honest work."

Eddie Willers

Dagny's assistant at the Taggart Transcontinental, he is an efficient and dedicated worker, extremely loyal to his childhood friend Dagny. Eddie unknowingly reveals all of her plans and business secrets to an anonymous railroad worker, who turns out to be John Galt.

Themes

Individual vs. Society

The very title of *Atlas Shrugged* illustrates the rebellion of one person against the system. It evokes the image of the mythological giant whose job in the universe is to hold the world on his shoulders—until he shrugs and lets it fall. Likewise, the revolutionary John Galt exemplifies the conflict of one against many when he starts a rebellion against the entire system of corruption that has taken over the world.

Several characters—who eventually end up on Galt's side—experience the feeling of fighting society alone. Dagny Taggart and Hank Rearden often perceive their position as that of solitary crusaders, trying to prevent the collapse of the world by gathering as many capable industrialist leaders as possible for their struggle. Rand makes it quite clear that her celebration of individualism requires her heroes and heroines to become isolated: Dagny is the only effective executive at the Taggart Transcontinental, always fighting with her brother and the board of directors to let her keep the railroad running. Hank faces the same prospect as he tries to preserve his business from the industrial

looters; when he is put on trial for selling more metal to one of his customers than regulations allow, he stands up to the judicial system alone.

Isolation is another requirement in the struggle, since the secret of the revolution must remain among the people already devoted to the cause. Thus, the new world must be carefully hidden from intruders in the depth of the mountains. With the individualist aspects of the revolution comes a necessary sacrifice of one's social ties. None of the rebels can share their knowledge with their friends and family members, unless those individuals are deemed ready for the conversion to Galt's cause.

Guilt

Hank Rearden is the most guilt-ridden character in the novel. In the process of his conversion to Galt's revolution, Rand develops the Objectivist theory of guilt and explains how this emotion is used by the establishment as a means of social control. Guilt is isolated as a tool that keeps individuals tied to the parasitic elements of the community. According to the establishment, since "people" in general are not as skilled and capable as the novel's successful capitalists, it is the duty of those who can produce goods and services to take care of the needy—because they should feel guilty for being successful in the first place.

At the beginning of the novel, Hank feels guilty because he does not have any interest in his family's pastimes and opinions. To redeem himself, he lets them live in his house and spend his money. When his mother asks him to give his incompetent brother a job at the mills, however, Hank refuses to be drawn into a family obligation that would jeopardize his business. Although he is not ashamed of his business, Hank still feels guilty for his apparent lack of compassion. His friendship with Francisco d'Anconia eventually takes away his sense of guilt, as Francisco teaches him to apply the same standards he has in business to the relationships in his life.

Hank also struggles with guilt about sexuality. After the first night he spends with Dagny Taggart, Hank reproaches both his lover and himself for the base desire of their bodies (which he has learned to despise in his marriage); his guilt almost makes him destroy the relationship with the only woman he loves. When Hank's wife finds out about his mistress, she denies him divorce. Instead, she plans to stay in his life to remind him how depraved and dishonorable he really is whenever he feels any pride for his business achievements. According to

Galt, however, the perception of body and soul as separate is another myth produced by the establishment: "They have taught man that he is a hopeless misfit made of two elements, both symbols of death. A body without a soul is a corpse, a soul without a body is a ghost—yet such is their image of man's nature."

During his trial for the illegal sale of Rearden Metal to Ken Danagger, Hank finally pinpoints the purpose of guilt in the judicial system, which needs his cooperation to victimize him. Once he refuses to cooperate, the society is powerless and cannot harm him.

Morals and Morality

According to Rand, the question of what is moral when the individual functions in a corrupt system is problematic. This is illustrated in the ideological conflict between Dagny Taggart and John Galt, who appear to be on the same side according to their beliefs and emerging love for each other, although they oppose each other throughout the novel. The battle between these two characters is parallel to the larger struggle of Galt's revolution against the parasitic world; however, the communist principles described in *Atlas Shrugged* are ideologically contrary to those espoused by Galt and Dagny. These two kinds of conflict illustrate Rand's understanding of morality, as determined by social and individual standards.

Atlas Shrugged praises capitalist work ethics as inherently moral, since (as Rand's protagonists often point out) the capitalist workers gain profit that is proportionate to their labor, skill, and merit. On the other hand, Rand criticizes communism as a corrupt system, which gives undeserved chances to the unworthy workers on the basis of human equality and compassion for those in need. In the communist system Rand depicts, the damage to the economy caused by the needy's lack of skill and responsibility must be ameliorated from another source: the productive, successful businesses that function according to capitalist standards. The society uses the capitalists' own guilt as a tool of control; at the same time, the legislature implements a number of laws and directives compelling them to participate in the system. Rand also argues that the legislative apparatus allows for many loopholes, used by incompetent businesspeople to eliminate competition and to profit from the work of economic "Atlases" who keep supporting the parasitic society. This is the center of hypocrisy in *Atlas Shrugged:* while pretending that the existing social order is concerned with the benefit of the entire

Topics for Further Study

- Rand was the originator of Objectivist philosophy, embodied in *Atlas Shrugged.* Did Objectivism ever gain acceptance in mainstream philosophy? Why or why not?

- Compare and contrast the Objectivist principles, listed in John Galt's radio address, to those of prominent communist philosophers such as Karl Marx. What are the main differences between these two ideologies? How does each view the purpose of human life and work?

- Research the political systems of the 1950s United States and the Soviet Union and compare the differences between the two countries in their government's regulations of businesses. How do these governmental approaches compare to the establishment's directives in *Atlas Shrugged?*

- Research the life of a well-known and successful businessperson in today's America, for example Donald Trump, Bill Gates, or Madonna. Compare and contrast his or her path toward success, attitudes, and professional ethics to those of Rand's protagonists, Dagny Taggart and Hank Rearden. Do today's entrepreneurs function by the same standards as Rand's heroes? What are the differences? Do you think they are justified?

- Compare the utopia of John Galt's valley to present-day capitalist America, citing specific examples. Would Rand approve of the United States economy of today? Why or why not?

population, the administrative ruling class lets the community sink into decay while the looters are getting rich.

Dagny and Galt oppose the described social establishment; they both believe in the morality of capitalism. Dagny remains in the existing system and struggles to prevent its collapse, out of concern for the people and businesses who would be hurt. Galt, however, abandons the country in decay and embarks upon its complete destruction so that the new world can be born. Although both Dagny and Galt operate according to capitalist principles, the effects are different: because Taggart Transcontinental is trapped in the corrupt civilization, all of Dagny's efforts ultimately only serve the social looters she is trying to fight. Galt's work, on the other hand, exists in his utopian world and is untouched by the problems of society. Although both characters are portrayed as moral according to their work ethics, they will consider each other's activities harmful until they agree on the necessary death of one world for the benefit of the other.

Style

Point of View

In *Atlas Shrugged,* Rand efficiently uses a third-person narrative that most often comes from the limited omniscient perspective of one of her protagonists. Thus, the reader knows everything that is going on in the life and mind of one character, until the focus shifts to another. The two characters on whom Rand focuses most often are Dagny Taggart and Hank Rearden: the story evolves around their memories, impressions, thoughts, and feelings, and the plot follows their actions. This approach helps lead the readers to understand and identify with the character whose life they perceive in such intimate detail. Moreover, through third—instead of first-person point of view—these major characters seem to be presented objectively. This device makes the author's claims about the novel's social systems seem more effective: readers who identify with Dagny and Hank are compelled to agree with their (and Rand's) opinions in the novel, and to experience their "conversion" to John Galt's revolution in their own beliefs.

For the sake of contrast, Rand occasionally shifts the point of view to let the reader in on the thoughts of less central characters (e.g., Eddie Willers, Jim Taggart, Dr. Robert Stadler) to represent different attitudes towards the political issues discussed in the novel. The portrayal of the "villains" in the novel is markedly condescending and negative; however, their perspective shows how seductive the ruling communist ideology can be and why it poses such a threat.

Symbolism

The symbols in *Atlas Shrugged* are abundant starting from the title: Atlas, the mythological giant who carries the world on his shoulders, symbolizes the class of capitalist workers whose work carries the weight of national and global economy, while the parasitic communist system reaps the fruits of their achievements. The prominent symbol of the capitalist order that recurs in the novel is the dollar sign: it is repeatedly cited by the corrupt communist characters in the novel as the emblem of evil. Capitalist industrialists are condemned by the society because they only believe in money and do not think that those capable of producing have an obligation to support those who are not.

The dollar sign is also the official symbol of John Galt's revolution: he makes the sign in the sky when his fight is over. Dagny even attempts to track him down by following his mysterious brand of cigarettes with the sign of the dollar stamped by the filter. The cigarette is another symbol in the novel: the author describes it as "fire, a dangerous force, tamed at [man's] fingertips" and compares it to "a spot of fire alive in [a thinker's] mind." Another spot of fire in the novel, Wyatt's torch, symbolizes the rebellious spirit of the individual reigning over the darkness of a society that opposes reason.

Critic Ronald E. Merrill notes Rand's use of Jewish symbolism throughout the novel. According to the Talmudic doctrine, thirty-six just men are the minimum needed to keep Sodom and Gomorrah from divine wrath. Interestingly, the great sin of Sodom was not sexual perversion but collectivism—just like the communist world in *Atlas Shrugged*. The exact number of "just men" withdrawn from the world and named in the description of Galt's valley is thirty-six. Similarly, Hank's gift of a precious ruby necklace to Dagny echoes the proverb "Who can find a virtuous woman? For her price is far above rubies" (Proverbs 31:10).

Allusion

Using the technique of allusion, or indirect reference, Rand evokes the concept of utopia—a notion created by Sir Thomas More in the sixteenth century to present an alternative society as a means of critiquing one's own society. The communist society in the novel represents a failed utopia: ideally a perfect system that grants happiness to all through to the equal distribution of goods, instead the communist society collapses in its own ineptitude and becomes hell instead of the promised paradise. John Galt's new world, however, suggests the possibility of another utopia, outside the boundaries of the existing corrupt order where competent individuals can create and produce freely, without being exploited by their peers.

Early descriptions of the new world allude to characters and places from myths and legends. One of the rumors about Galt's identity is a mythological allusion to the man who has discovered the lost island of Atlantis, but had to desert all his worldly possessions in order to live there in perfect happiness. Another fantastic rumor claims that Galt was a man who discovered the fountain of youth, but realized that he could not bring it to the people: they had to reach it themselves. The third calls Galt a Prometheus who changed his mind: after giving people the gift of fire and being punished for it, he withdrew the fire until they withdrew the punishment. Each of these references, rooted in the legendary, depicts Galt as a heroic, mythical character; they also symbolize parts of his philosophy and sacrifices needed in his quest. Like the lost island of Atlantis, Galt's new world cannot be reached until one leaves behind everything that is trapped in the decaying old world. Likewise, as the fountain of youth is immovable, the reborn capitalist establishment is only available to those who can reach it themselves. Finally, Promethean fire is symbolized by the offering of everything that an individual produces, but the offering ends up withdrawn from the vultures of corruption until the punishment for capitalist success stops.

Historical Context

The Red Scare

Atlas Shrugged, although clearly set in the imaginary communist equivalent of the United States, lacks orientation in time. As Ronald E. Merrill notes, "The American economy seems, structurally, to be in the late nineteenth century, with large industrial concerns being sole proprietorships run by their founders. The general tone is however that of the 1930s, a depression with the streets full of panhandlers. The technological level, and the social customs, are those of the 1950s. And the political environment, especially the level of regulation and the total corruption, seems to anticipate the 1970s. We are simultaneously in a future in which most of the world has gone Communist, and the past in which England had the world's greatest navy."

Nonetheless, the novel's clear warning against the economic and political immorality of communism reflects the America's fear of the growth of the Communist Party in the 1950s, which resulted in the Red Scare. After World War II, the Soviet Union went from being an American ally to being an undeclared enemy due to the threat of a nuclear war. The two countries, weighed against each other as the only remaining world superpowers, kept a tentative political balance in a period known as the Cold War. As a reaction to the growing fear of everything Russian, the Wisconsin senator Joseph McCarthy formed the House Un-American Activities Committee, a council whose purpose was to investigate anything and anybody suspected for any reason of communist beliefs or connections to the Soviet Union. The result was an ample number of interrogations, blackmails, arrests, and threats, and the extreme censorship of individual freedom. Although Rand stated her support for the House Un-American Activities Committee in 1947 and openly spoke against communism, she later condemned the committee members as intellectually deficient headline chasers who had forgotten the ultimate importance of individual rights in their blind pursuit.

America's (A)moral Crisis

In her review of the 1950s in the United States, Stacey Olster describes the nation's intellectual mood as culturally anemic: although opposed to the communist ideology of the Soviet Union, the country's intellectuals accepted the American alternative merely as a "lesser evil." The country's thinkers, including Rand, feared that the complacent nation would incline toward conformism. As one of the responding voices to the 1952 "Our Country and Our Culture" symposium stated, the 1950s were the period of "waiting in darkness before what may be a new beginning and morning, or a catastrophic degradation of civilization," quotes Olster.

At the time Rand was working on *Atlas Shrugged,* her greatest fear was the aforementioned catastrophe: that the United States would succumb to dangerous collectivism and end up letting in socialist ideas through the back door of its weak, if not non-existent, cultural ideology. According to Rand, America of the 1950s did not have a social backbone. In *Capitalism: An Unknown Ideal,* she said the country's conservatism and liberalism were loosely defined concepts that "could be stretched to mean all things to all men." Rand's theoretical writings of the time describe capitalism in the United States as lacking a philosophical base, because the country did not have an original culture.

Compare & Contrast

- **1950s:** Mao Zedong starts the Great Leap Forward in the People's Republic of China, placing more than half a billion peasants into "people communes." They are guaranteed food, clothing, shelter, and child care, but deprived of all private property.

  Today: China is one of the few nations in the world whose government is still modeled on Marxist ideology. China has reformed its economy and applied for inclusion in the World Trade Organization.

- **1950s:** The Treaty of Rome removes mutual tariff barriers, uniting Belgium, France, West Germany, Italy, Luxembourg, and the Netherlands into the European Economic Community. The EEC is planned to promote the European economy and make it more competitive with Britain and the United States.

  Today: The EEC has become the European Union (EU), with seven additional members: Austria, Denmark, Finland, Greece, Ireland, Portugal, Sweden, and the United Kingdom. The Euro is the shared monetary unit this market.

- **1950s:** The Soviet Union launches Sputnik I, the world's first human-made Earth satellite. A month later, Sputnik II is launched with a live dog on board. *The New York Times* correspondent in Moscow hears a Russian say, "Better to learn to feed your people at home before starting to explore the moon."

  Today: The United States is exploring the possibility of water on the moon in order to support colonization. A probe has been launched to observe an asteroid in order to gain knowledge about how to deflect one should it head towards Earth.

- **1950s:** First seen in an Easter march at Aldermaston, England, the symbol for total nuclear disarmament introduced by English philosopher Bertrand Russell will become a universal peace symbol. However, Washington does not accept the plan for a denuclearized zone in central Europe, and Britain follows suit in May.

  Today: Despite the growing number of generals and scientists who are calling for the abolishment of nuclear weapons, the United States shows no sign of considering this idea or even ratifying a non-proliferation treaty.

In response to this lack, Rand declared she would invent these missing cultural foundations in her fiction. As a result, *Atlas Shrugged* became her ultimate expression of the Objectivist logic which she saw as the only salvation for America; in fact, Rand would reply to the critics who questioned her about Objectivism that all they wanted to know was in the novel.

Anxiety and Affluence

With Europe still rebuilding from World War II and using the funds from the Marshall Plan, America was the number one manufacturing power in the 1950s. The country's financial stability, as well as its pride over the defeat of the Nazi powers, created a national attitude characterized by a mix of contentment with material comforts and altruism. Inflation was low, the suburbs were expanding, and the Interstate Highway Act (1956) made touring in the car far more pleasurable—Howard Johnson's made eating on the road better too. When *Atlas Shrugged* was published, several reviewers criticized Rand's vision of a decaying America as absurd at a time of national prosperity; others also condemned her scorn of charity as non-Christian and inhuman.

Critical Overview

The publication of *Atlas Shrugged* was eagerly awaited by Rand's fans, who adopted Objectivism

The Russian Revolution in Petrograd, 1917. Growing up in Russia during the Bolshevik Revolution engendered in Rand a loathing for Communist politics.

with her previous work, *The Fountainhead,* but it seems that her critics expected her next novel with equal anticipation. *Atlas Shrugged* produced more written commentary than any of Rand's other publications; like the rest of Rand's work promoting Objectivism, the novel inspired rather heated responses. When *Atlas Shrugged* was published in 1957, it was immediately established as a highly controversial literary work: while some critics labeled it downright fascist, others praised its scope and philosophical depth. Rand was accused of writing in caricatures and oversimplifications, and trying to pass her political views poorly masked in an

unrealistic story; her work was called hateful, destructive, and un-Christian. Patricia Donegan wrote for *Commonweal* that "whatever power Miss Rand has as a writer is expressed in an immense hostility, a real malevolence that takes joy in the sight of destruction." Another critic, Granville Hicks for the *New York Times Book Review,* suggested that the massive size of Rand's novel served "as a battering ram" to crush the "enemies of [her] truth."

Perhaps Rand's most fervent critic, Whittaker Chambers reviewed *Atlas Shrugged* in his essay "Big Sister Is Watching You," calling the novel "remarkably silly," "primitive story-telling," "a soapbox for delivering her Message" (which, he notes, Rand got from Aristotle and Nietzsche), and a work that yells to its readers to head for the gas chamber. Chambers deconstructed each facet of the novel, calling it simplistic, naive, incongruous, and condescending in the tone it uses to lecture its readers.

A more moderate attack came from John Chamberlain in the *New York Herald Tribune Book Review,* who praises the novel as "vibrant and powerful" but admonishes Rand for her opposition to altruism. Chamberlain's appreciation for the book's main political parable and its intense, purified characters is clouded by Rand's lack of Christian compassion.

Some critics disapproved of Rand's disturbing view of the United States. "[O]ne tries in vain to project the world of *Atlas Shrugged* from the familiar world of contemporary America. There is no connecting link. On what grounds, for example, does Miss Rand postulate a failing economy?—the American economy today is booming. She does not say," objected Ruth Chapin Blackman in an article for the *Christian Science Monitor.* Blackman also criticized the novel's melodramatic and unconvincing plot.

On the other hand, *Atlas Shrugged* also received an abundance of positive criticism. In her essay for *College English,* Mimi R. Gladstein called the book "philosophically feminist" and praised the character of Dagny Taggart: "She is the head of a railroad. She has sexual relationships with three men and retains their love and respect. She is not demeaned or punished for her emancipation, sexual or professional.... She is a rarity in American fiction—a heroine who not only survives, but prevails." Gladstein explored the relationships in the novel and the logic Rand infused into the description of each romance, especially the author's refusal to accept sacrifice as a positive aspect of love. The novel's protagonists are also lovers that defy the division between body and mind/soul, another aspect of Rand's philosophy that Gladstein commended.

In his book on Rand's ideas, Ronald E. Merrill praised *Atlas Shrugged* for its manifold literary construction and compelling character portrayal: "A complete, radically new philosophy is expounded, and with astonishing clarity. The practical implications of philosophical ideas are illustrated on every level, from metaphysics to epistemology to ethics to politics to economics to esthetics. The novel's plot is a miracle of organi-

zation. And with all this, the book is a thrilling page-turner." Merrill also noted that, in 1957, it was a truly radical notion to make a business entrepreneur a fictional hero; Rand lived in an environment that regarded businesspeople with some contempt. As for the book's richness of issues, Merrill suggested that *Atlas Shrugged* should be regarded "as a sort of magical box full of tightly folded intellectual origami, each of which should be carefully opened, contemplated, and cherished." He also analyzed the construction and plot placement of each major character, pointing out the intricate web of connections between ideas and consequences throughout the novel.

Finally, Stacey Olster questioned Rand's feminism but emphasized her sensitivity to the issues of the times, especially the fear of communism and the national sense of dispirited complacency. Having noted a few historical slip-ups in *Atlas Shrugged* (e.g. the dollar sign, far from being originally American, was taken from the Spanish milled dollar), Olster's essay concludes with a quote from one of Rand's former disciples on the controversial issue of Objectivist influence: "Look how much she had to offer! Look at how much I was learning! If she got a little berserk now and again, *so what?*"

Criticism

Jeremy W. Hubbell

Hubbell is a graduate student in History at the State University of New York, Stony Brook. In the following essay, he explores how Rand's technique of dialogue and character development support the philosophy of Objectivism.

Ayn Rand was extremely proud of *Atlas Shrugged:* she often said that her last novel was a perfect fictional presentation of her philosophy of Objectivism, and even directed inquisitive critics to read the novel if they had any questions about her theories. Indeed, the protagonists of Rand's "Bible of Objectivism" embody and thoroughly explain the principles the author considered sacred: individualism, morality, reason, judgment, self-sufficiency, and freedom from guilt. The most complete explanation of Rand's philosophy in *Atlas Shrugged* is undoubtedly John Galt's 60-page speech, but the ideas that support and expand the scope of the Objectivist outlook onto other aspects

What Do I Read Next?

- Every utopian text draws, if only a little, from Sir Thomas More's classic original. *Utopia,* published in the sixteenth century at the bloom of English Humanism, criticizes the existing social, political, and religious order in Europe from the viewpoint of an imaginary perfect society based on reason.

- *Anthem,* Ayn Rand's 1938 novella, served as a basis for her further publications. A parable of Objectivist philosophy, it presents the ideology and the basic plot of *Atlas Shrugged* in a nutshell.

- In her first critically acclaimed novel, *The Fountainhead,* Rand's hero Howard Roark explores and celebrates the morality of individualism and egoism in the world of architecture. The novel, published in 1943, ensured Rand's principle of Objectivism a cult following.

- *We the Living* was Rand's semi-autobiographical first novel, published in 1936. Begun only four years after her arrival in the United States, it is Rand's fulfillment of a promise given to the friends she left behind that she would tell the world about Russia's slow death. Kira, the young woman in the story and Rand's alter ego, struggles for love and survival under the communist regime.

- *The Virtue of Selfishness,* Rand's 1964 nonfictional publication consisting of several of her theoretical essays, spells out her philosophical principles from selfishness and ethics to purpose and morality, as described in her novels.

- Another writer who dared to make a business entrepreneur his fictional hero in the 1950s was Cameron Hawley. His 1952 novel, *Executive Suite,* tells the story of a man's struggle to maintain a major company after the CEO's sudden death.

---

of life are presented gradually by her other characters. Francisco d'Anconia, Dagny Taggart, Hank Rearden, and many minor characters contribute to the construction of the Objectivist outline in the novel; they teach, learn, discover, and struggle with Rand's principles, growing through interactions with each other as well as through conflicts with their enemies in the society. While Hank and Dagny are the most prominent "learners" among the novel's characters, Francisco and Galt serve primarily as teachers. The process of the characters' budding awareness of the social, psychological, and philosophical factors in their lives is illustrated in Rand's effective use of dialogue.

Often called one of Rand's most appealing fictional personalities, Hank Rearden is a man without much introspection at the beginning of *Atlas Shrugged:* he heads the group of characters who have to go through much learning before they embrace the novel's Objectivism. Hank has a good basis for his further Objectivist development: he is a self-made and self-educated industrialist, with enviable abilities, an inventor's spirit (he creates the miraculous Rearden Metal himself), and a perfectionist attitude towards his work. From the start, Hank is an example of Rand's heroic business entrepreneur, a proponent of the capitalist system and the justly earned triumph such a system enables. He enjoys his possessions, because they are the results of many years of hard work, but his pride in personal achievements is marred by his self-imposed guilt, upheld by his parasitic family and a manipulative wife. Because the closest people in his life keep telling him that his attention to business rather than to people is evil and selfish, Hank develops a deeply rooted sense of deficiency as a human being, convinced that he lacks compassion.

As Galt will eventually point out, however, Hank's real guilt lies in the fact that he does not question the rational impulse of injustice that he feels whenever a member of his family calls him egotistic and unfeeling. In the Objectivist doctrine, reasoning and judgment are imperative in one's self-awareness. Instead, Hank accepts the guilt they

" Some of the most striking moments of philosophical awakening in the novel occur in conversations between the protagonists and their social enemies. As Hank notices early on, the very process of dialogue is one of the weapons of the corrupt system: the faults of the establishment and its criminal activities are never named, because the power of the uttered word could shake up the illogical foundations of communist ideology."

impose on his lack of interest and respect for their lives, and does not question whether he is right in dismissing their concerns as unimportant. The novel eventually reveals that each of his family members is a useless ingrate, feeding off of Hank's own sense of obligation to the bond of blood rather than the Objectivist bond between people of same values. According to Rand, a person is what a person does: one's values are inextricable from one's work ethics, which is why Hank can only feel love for the businesspeople he can trust.

The theme of guilt imposed by one's family appears in Dagny's biography as well, although she does not accept it. Mrs. Taggart tries to make her daughter "normal" by motherly advice on femininity, and the rest of her relations mourn the girl's unnatural aspirations and development, but Dagny never falters in her single determination: to run the family railroad. The only relative she respects is Nathaniel Taggart, her ancestor who built the railroad business with extraordinary determination. Dagny's dedication to the railroad is not inspired by its family tradition; rather, she loves the business because of its nature of human inventiveness, production, and motion. If family were important

to Dagny, she would be concerned about Jim Taggart's opinions; luckily, Rand's heroine never pays attention to her inept brother's reactions to her threatening adequacy.

In fact, both Dagny and Hank become aware of greater social evils through their arguments with family members. Hank shocks his mother when he refuses to hire his incompetent brother only because he is a human being who needs a job, but the national legislature eventually legalizes the hiring on the basis of need. As Dagny realizes in one of her confrontations with Jim, he supports the censuring directives that eliminate the competitive market because he is weak himself and does not like to compete, especially with his sister. Nonetheless, the government passes a law that cuts down the production of successful businesses so that the smaller ones will not be destroyed by the competition, even though there is a greater demand for goods and services than the legislature allows. In both cases, Rand bases the faults of the communist system on personal failings: individual immorality, exemplified in Hank's mother's claim of brotherly obligation and in Jim's need to restrict his environment to his own level, is at the root of the political evil that eventually destroys the country.

As the pressure increases and industrial entrepreneurs begin to see the organization of their elusive social enemy, Dagny and Hank are offered alternatives. Francisco, Galt's revolutionary who operates against the system under the guise of a reckless playboy, steps on the stage and confronts the social parasites with the contradictions of their own beliefs. When Jim attacks him for the disaster at the San Sebastian copper mines in Mexico, which cost his investors a fortune, Francisco replies that the catastrophe was actually a blessing: workers were employed and paid for months without much work to do; the contractor, although unqualified, really needed the job; and the wealth of the investors was distributed to the needy poor. Plus, Francisco adds, they should be thanking him from liberating them from the root of all evil—money. He continues by questioning this assertion, however, and concludes that there is nothing evil about money, because it is only a symbol used for exchange. The evil is the shame people feel when they are making money, shame caused by unjust social condemnation. Thus, Francisco's logic teaches those who actually listen to him about the faults in the so-called altruistic approach, which dismisses the value of work and glorifies the virtue of need. Rand thus explains the Objectivist principle of self-sufficiency and honest labor as inherently moral.

Nevertheless, neither Dagny nor Hank (although they both feel a bond with Francisco) is ready to accept completely the philosophy behind the secret revolution. Hank, already preconditioned to feel guilt, is bound by his love for Dagny; when his wife uses the information about their affair to blackmail Hank, he succumbs. However, between the beginning of the affair and the blackmail incident, Hank's feelings about Dagny gradually change: he starts the relationship almost against his own wishes, tortured by guilt for what he perceives as depravity in himself, and thinking that his physical desire is base and vilifying. Dagny, on the other hand, has never considered mind and body as separate; she enjoys the pleasures of their relationship fully and does not see sex as detached from the rest of her personality. The change in Hank's attitude and his full acceptance of his sexuality happens in another conversation, another lecture with Francisco, who explains Rand's Objectivist application to sex. According to Francisco, people only want the lovers who exemplify what they are striving for in life. Thus, Hank's desire for everything that Dagny is transcends the mere limitations of bodily lust.

According to Rand and Objectivism, a person's pursuit of happiness is the top priority in life. Dagny realizes early on that the joy she was expected to feel at parties in her youth does not come from the lavish interiors, beautiful music, and expensive food; instead, the only true joy is that of the creative human spirit, and the only people who enjoy parties are those who have some accomplishment to celebrate. Of course, the happiness must be of the right kind. Jim's happiness at finding a poor girl to marry so that he'll always have someone to look down upon is abusive and destructive. However, Rand makes another differentiation: when Hank feels exhilarated after Wyatt burns down his refinery so that it does not fall into the parasites' hands, he is also aware of the danger of feeling joy at the sight of destruction. But the destruction of an achievement which, in the corrupt system, can only be used against its creators, is actually a constructive act, Rand suggests. This lesson is the hardest one to learn: Dagny is the last to join the revolution, because she is too devoted to the railroad and cannot bear to see it destroyed. But her final awareness comes when the old world literally collapses in panic, and the world leaders use brute force to try to persuade Galt to salvage their economy.

Some of the most striking moments of philosophical awakening in the novel occur in conversations between the protagonists and their social enemies. As Hank notices early on, the very process of dialogue is one of the weapons of the corrupt system: the faults of the establishment and its criminal activities are never named, because the power of the uttered word could shake up the illogical foundations of communist ideology. Also, words are actions in the lives of executives, and in the decaying world of *Atlas Shrugged,* only the competent are capable of making decisions.

Another way in which language is used by social parasites is to make the issues as elusive as possible. Repeatedly Hank and Dagny confront contractors who offer excuses and collectivist slogans rather than completed work; the state institutes condemn, in vague terms, new inventions that could shake up the economy by advancing specific companies; the government agents who threaten business operations avoid clearly presented ultimatums; and even blackmailers do not name the threat they want to impose. Hank challenges the system that requires the victim's verbal participation in his own execution: in his trial for the sale of illegal quantities of steel to a customer, Hank refuses to admit guilt as such on the basis that the definition of guilt is wrong. The disabled system, which needs his capable business to leech on, sets him free. Through sometimes tiring repetition of clear versus ambiguous language, Rand depicts the all-pervading nature of immorality by Objectivist standards; her heroes, however, convey the clarity and simplicity of her philosophy in the end.

Atlas Shrugged describes with painstaking detail the deterioration of a political system whose faults are rooted in personal shortcomings. Through her protagonists, Rand makes a binding connection between the individuals in society who wish to preserve their creative and productive freedoms, and the members of the same society whose immorality (whether they are aware of it or not) causes destruction.

Source: Jeremy W. Hubbell, in an essay for *Novels for Students,* Gale, 2000.

Ronald E. Merrill

In the following excerpt, Merrill praises Atlas Shrugged *for its complex literary style and compelling characterizations.*

With the publication of *Atlas Shrugged* in 1957 Rand reached the destination of her intellectual journey—the Taggart Terminal. She had purged the last vestiges of Nietzsche's errors from her thinking, and completely integrated her ideas into her

> " The practical implications of philosophical ideas are illustrated on every level, from metaphysics to epistemology to ethics to politics to economics to esthetics. The novel's plot is a miracle of organization. And with all this, the book is a thrilling page-turner...."

own philosophical system, Objectivism. The great question of her life, the dilemma of the rational person in an irrational society, at last was solved to her satisfaction. The concept of the "sanction of the victim" provided her answer—and provided also the key plot device, the strike of the men of the mind, for her greatest novel.

Atlas Shrugged, from a purely stylistic or literary point of view, is inferior to *The Fountainhead.* But as an intellectual achievement, it is far superior. A complete, radically new philosophy is expounded, and with astonishing clarity. The practical implications of philosophical ideas are illustrated on every level, from metaphysics to epistemology to ethics to politics to economics to esthetics. The novel's plot is a miracle of organization. And with all this, the book is a thrilling page-turner....

Rand described her fiction style as 'Romantic Realism'. She regarded herself as a Romantic in that her fiction dealt with ideal people and their pursuit of important values; and a Realist in that the settings of her stories and the issues they dealt with were those of real life rather than fantasy. This description is quite appropriate to most of her work. However, *Atlas Shrugged* marks somewhat of a departure. Stylistically, it represents a considerable change from *We the Living* and *The Fountainhead,* Building on the techniques with which she had experimented in *Anthem,* Rand made *Atlas Shrugged* a more abstract, conceptual, and symbolic work than her earlier novels; it might best be described as a work of Romantic Surrealism. The cover painting by George Salter accurately conveys the mood and style of the novel.

Atlas Shrugged takes place in the United States, and cities such as New York and Philadelphia are recognizable. But Rand goes to considerable pains to create an ambiance that is far from realistic. The United States of the novel has no President, but a "Head of State"; no Congress, but a "National Legislature". Most of the world is Communist, but this word does not appear in the book at all; instead, Communist countries are referred to as "People's States". The story takes place in no particular time, and in 'realistic' terms is a tissue of anachronisms. The American economy seems, structurally, to be in the late nineteenth century, with large industrial concerns being sole proprietorships run by their founders. The general tone is however that of the 1930s, a depression with the streets full of panhandlers. The technological level, and the social customs, are those of the 1950s. And the political environment, especially the level of regulation and the total corruption, seems to anticipate the 1970s. We are simultaneously in a future in which most of the world has gone Communist, and the past in which England had the world's greatest navy.

With a subtle choice in literary technique Rand adds to the effective mystery of the story. In *The Fountainhead* Rand adopts the universal viewpoint; we see inside the head of almost every significant character and many very minor ones. (The only important exception is Henry Cameron.) In *Atlas Shrugged* Rand uses what might be called a 'half-universal' viewpoint. We are told the thoughts of nearly every significant character, hero or villain—except the strikers.

In further contrast to Rand's other works, *Atlas Shrugged* is permeated with symbols—from Atlantis to Wyatt's Torch, from Galt's motor, which draws on the power of the lightning, to Nat Taggart's statue. The symbolic theme of the stopping motor provides a powerful motif throughout the book. And of course there is the famous dollar sign....

One of the paradoxes in Rand's style is her combination of extremely serious philosophical themes and a sense of humor that occasionally verges on the literary equivalent of the practical joke. In *Atlas Shrugged* one of her puckish tricks involves the sly use of Jewish symbolism and myth. For instance, considerable emphasis is laid on Rearden's gift to Dagny of a ruby necklace. It is hard to escape the allusion to the famous biblical quotation:

Who can find a virtuous woman? for her price is far above rubies. [Proverbs 31:10]

But more interesting is her use of a Talmudic doctrine to provide the basic device of the book: The doctrine of the 36 Just Men. The idea of the 36 Just Men derives from the story, in Genesis, of the destruction of Sodom and Gomorrah. Lot, who resided in the former city, was warned by God to leave, as the place was condemned to destruction because of the evil of its inhabitants. Lot attempted to avert the catastrophe, promising to find other good men in the place; when he failed, he and his family left and the cities were destroyed.

It is interesting to note that—contrary to the popular misconception—the great sin of the Sodomites was not sexual perversion but collectivism. According to the Talmudic account, Sodom's egalitarian government institutionalized envy, even forbidding private charity because some recipients might get more than others. The judicial system was perverted into an instrument for expropriating the wealthy and successful. The ultimate crime for which the Sodomites were destroyed was placing envy and equality above benevolence and justice.

From the biblical account of Sodom and Gomorrah, Jewish scholars evolved the idea that God would destroy the earth if ever it lacked some minimum number of good people. The exact number needed to avert His wrath was hotly debated, and finally settled, for numerological reasons, as 36.

In *Atlas Shrugged,* Rand (who was Jewish by background, though not religious) takes as her theme the destruction of civilization when its 'just men' are withdrawn. The analogy with the 36 Just Men is striking, particularly when one notes that exactly 36 strikers are specifically identified in Galt's Gulch. An incident near the end of the story convinces me that the symbolism is intentional.

As Dagny, Galt, and the other strikers are returning to the valley after rescuing Galt, they pass over New York City. (This in itself is suggestive of some special significance, since New York is nowhere near the great circle route between New Hampshire and Colorado.) As they fly over, the lights of New York go out. Dagny gasps, and Galt orders, "Don't look down!"

What?!

Can this be the same John Galt who said, "Nobody stays in this valley by faking reality in any manner whatsoever."? The incident is totally out of character. And that's Rand's little joke; Galt is saving Dagny from being turned into a pillar of salt....

The plot of *Atlas Shrugged* is marvelously constructed, an intricate machine that meshes smoothly with the novel's philosophical themes.

There are, it must be conceded, some notable flaws. For instance, during his affair with Dagny, why does Francisco not tell her about his college friends—Galt and Danneskjold? Obviously this would make hash of the mystery element of the plot, so Rand simply makes Francisco behave out of character. Later she is forced to make Hugh Akston lie to Dagny for the same reason.

A more serious problem is Galt's refusal to let Rearden learn that Dagny is alive, after her crash in the valley. As Nathaniel Branden has pointed out, this gratuitous cruelty does not reflect well on Galt—nor on Dagny. Apparently Rand regarded this incident as essential to the plot; Rearden's loyalty to values, as demonstrated by his continued search for Dagny, is a major factor in her motive for leaving the valley. But surely the dilemma could have been dealt with otherwise.

These are minor problems. Overall, the plot of *Atlas Shrugged* is one of the greatest accomplishments of world literature. Not only is it a masterpiece of logic in itself, but it integrates perfectly the needs of the story with Rand's exposition of a series of philosophical principles. And, with an absolutely insolent arrogance, as if to show off, Rand neatly organizes this extraordinarily complex book into three tidy, cleanly structured sections of ten chapters each.

To analyze the plot of *Atlas Shrugged* thoroughly would require far too much space. But we may consider the main strands.

The primary sequence is the story of how Dagny and Rearden discover the secret of the strike and are led to join it. On the political level, this is integrated with the account of the final destruction of statist society. On the personal level, it is integrated with Dagny's romantic involvement with Francisco, Rearden, and finally Galt. These three strands are braided into the primary plot-line of the novel.

Half-a-dozen subplots are woven into the structure. One is Francisco D'Anconia's Monte-Cristo-like crusade of destruction. Two follow the fates of minor heroes, Eddie Willers and Cherryl Brooks. Three more describe the degradation and destruction of the villains James Taggart, Lillian Rearden, and Robert Stadler. Is this pleasing symmetry intentional? Quite possibly....

The unifying principle of *Atlas Shrugged* is the connection between philosophical ideas and their consequences. It is worth examining one passage in detail to study Rand's technique. The primary incident in the chapter, 'The Moratorium on Brains', is the catastrophe at the Taggart Tunnel in which an entire passenger train is annihilated. At least one critic has cited this passage as evidence that Rand took a malicious, sadistic pleasure in killing (fictional) people. What is really involved here?

Rand makes the tunnel accident play an important role in the novel's plot mechanics. It brings Dagny back from her self-imposed exile so that she can receive Quentin Daniels' letter. It interrupts Francisco's explanation of the strike at a crucial point, and sets up the confrontation between Francisco and Hank Rearden in Dagny's apartment. The disaster also necessitates the journey that will put her on a frozen train and propel her into her meeting with John Galt.

The sequence also plays an important part in a more subtle aspect of the plot, by beginning the process of final preparation for Dagny to be confronted with the secret of the strike. The first step is Directive 10-289. Dagny's instinctive rejection of this irrational horror results in her resignation from Taggart Transcontinental. But this, to Rand, could not be a satisfactory resolution; Dagny must reach this stage of emotional revulsion, but she could not be Rand's heroine if she made her decision on the basis of emotion. What has been accomplished however is that Dagny (and the reader) have been presented with the solution to the novel's dilemma—the strike.

Dagny's resignation is followed by a month of meditation in the woods, in which for the first time her basic dilemma is made explicit. Then the pressure is turned up. Francisco appears to present her with the key concept of the sanction of the victim. It is at this point that the tunnel catastrophe intervenes. Francisco fails to recruit Dagny—because Dagny, having quit due to emotional revulsion, returns due to emotional revulsion.

It is important to understand that Dagny's emotional reaction to the disaster plays a critical role. She is not merely annoyed by a sublime piece of incompetence. She is not just outraged by the destruction of an important item of her railroad's property. She is horrified by the human destruction, the loss of life. Rand is building up here to a major, dual climax in the novel's plot: Dagny's discovery of the secret of the strike, and her meeting with John Galt. The tunnel catastrophe plays a key role in building the tension that will be (partially and temporarily) resolved in Galt's Gulch.

During this chapter Dagny is put under increasing emotional stress, until she nears the breaking point. Directive 10-289 drives her from her job in disgust—and separates her from Rearden (on whom it also puts pressure). Her month in the woods wrestling with an insoluble problem focusses her emotional state. Then there is the astounding revelation that Francisco is in fact faithful to her—a scene interrupted by the report of the tunnel catastrophe. The sequence continues with the confrontation between Rearden and Francisco, which raises the tension of Dagny's sexual relationship with Rearden to a maximum. We can begin to see how masterfully Rand pulls these two strands of the plot together in preparation for Dagny's encounter with Galt.

But the Taggart Tunnel catastrophe is not merely an incident in the plot; it also functions as a demonstration of an important principle: the relationship between political oppression and the breakdown of social responsibility—and the consequent destruction of social function. Rand in this chapter provides us with a vivid picture of the way even everyday activities disintegrate when the men of ability and rationality are driven underground. This is the function of the scene on the book's philosophical or intellectual level.

Rand begins preparation for this scene early and carefully ties it into the other events of the plot. Early in the story we learn of the bad condition of the Taggart track near Winston, Colorado. Accidents happen on this stretch of the road. The need to repair it is casually mentioned. But it is merely a nuisance, a potential problem.

With Dagny's resignation, Rand begins her demonstration. First, the repairs at Winston are cancelled; the rail instead is used on the Florida line, which is more frequently travelled by politicians. This decision is allowed to stand—because Dagny is gone. Then the spare diesel at the Taggart Tunnel is withdrawn, again to please a politician. Eddie Willers attempts to stop it, but with Dagny gone he is helpless.

The process by which the accident happens is, to anyone acquainted with industrial safety principles, entirely realistic. It is exactly the sort of sequence which creates real-life disasters such as the Bhopal and Chernobyl accidents.

The petty politician Kip Chalmers, inconvenienced by a derailment near Winston, insists on immediate continuation of his journey—through the tunnel—though no diesel engines are available. The men of intelligence and integrity, who could prevent the ensuing catastrophe, are gone because of Directive 10-289, just as Dagny is. The best of those who remain are, like Eddie, of insufficient rank to intervene successfully. One by one, the safeguards set by rational men are violated by political appointees, driven by their fear of political reprisals.

It would take only one man to prevent the tragedy—but that one man is not present any more. The Superintendent of the Division has been replaced by an incompetent. Higher management, with Dagny gone, evades all responsibility. The one man who fights the disaster, Bill Brent, lacks authority. The physical order is signed by a boy who lacks knowledge.

So the inexorable march to disaster continues. The dispatcher knows he is sending men to their deaths. But he no longer cares; his beloved brother committed suicide, his career ruined by Directive 10-289. It appears that disaster may be averted when the chosen engineer walks out rather than take a coal-burner into the Tunnel—but a replacement is found, an alcoholic who kept his job by political pull and union corruption. The conductor, who might have warned the passengers, has become embittered and cynical; he limits his action to saving himself. Even the switchman might have averted the wreck at the last minute. But in the new environment of the railroad, he fears for his family if he disobeys orders, even to save lives.

So the Comet proceeds into the tunnel. And with magnificent irony Kip Chalmers, having succeeded in scaring the Taggart employees into sending him to his death, proudly proclaims, "See? *Fear* is the only effective way to deal with people!" ...

By her own account, in *Atlas Shrugged* Rand finally succeeded in portraying her ideal man, John Galt. And indeed, she has met the challenge of showing completely moral persons in a way that she did not achieve in *The Fountainhead,* Dominique and Wynand are, as we have seen, contaminated by Nietzschean morality and the corresponding despair. Roark is morally perfect, but he is not a full ideal because he is naive. He is good without knowing fully why he is good. John Galt, however, has moral stature and philosophical knowledge.

Atlas Shrugged has a complex plot involving a number of major and minor heroic characters. Rand takes as her primary heroes the giants of intellect and productivity, particularly business entrepreneurs. The basic fabric of these characters derives from the hero of one of her favorite books, Merwin and Webster's *Calumet K,* Charlie Bannon, an engineer and construction supervisor, a natural leader and compulsive worker who solves problems with effortless ingenuity, is described as skeletally thin. Appropriately, Rand fleshes out this skeleton with full personalities to create her business heroes.

The modern reader may not realize how radical it was, in 1957, to make a businessman a hero. It should be kept in mind that Rand wrote this book in an environment in which 'entrepreneur' was almost a dirty word. It is interesting to note, however, that there was one other significant writer of the period who defended businessmen, and who may have influenced Rand: Cameron Hawley.

In Hawley's second novel, *Cash McCall* (1955), the theme is ethical conflicts in business, and the author comes down squarely for the position that commerce is an honorable activity. McCall is what would now be called a 'corporate raider', and Hawley skillfully depicts his economic value and productiveness.

Even more interesting for our discussion is the theme of Hawley's first novel, *Executive Suite* (1952). This is the story of a struggle for control of a major company after its CEO, Avery Bullard, suddenly dies. Here is the scene in which the hero, looking out over the company town, decides it is his responsibility to take over the leaderless corporation:

> They were his ... all of them ... the uncounted thousands, born and unborn. If he failed them there would be hunger under those roofs ... there had been hunger before when the man at the top of the Tower had failed them. Then there would be no food ... and the belongings of the dispossessed would stand in the streets ... and a man in a black coat would come to take the children to the orphans' home ....

> ... Did the people under those roofs know what Avery Bullard had done for them? Did they realize that if it had not been for Avery Bullard there would be no Tredway Corporation ... that the Pike Street plant would never have been built ... that the Water Street factory would have rotted and rusted away like the steel mill and the tannery and the wagon works ... that there would be no Tredway jobs, no Tredway paychecks?

> No, they did not know ... or, if they did, they would not acknowledge their belief ... or, if they believed, they were not willing to pay the price of gratitude. Had any man ever thanked Avery Bullard for what

he had done? No. He had died in the loneliness of the unthanked.

Don Walling accepted his fate. He would expect no thanks … he would live in loneliness … but the Tredway Corporation would go on. There would be jobs and pay checks. There would be no hunger. The belongings of the dispossessed would not stand in the streets. No children would be sent to the orphans' home.

Though the motives of Hawley's character are hardly those of an Objectivist, the theme of the entrepreneurial businessman as an unappreciated hero who gives society far more than can ever be repaid clearly prefigures Rand's use of the same theme. There is no external evidence to support it, but she may well have been influenced by Hawley's heroes. (She would certainly, however, have been disgusted by *The Lincoln Lords* [1960], which idealizes a man who bears no small resemblance to Peter Keating.)

Into the gray-suited bodies of her business executive heroes Rand poured the souls of her childhood idols from the melodramas she devoured as a girl. There resulted those extraordinary characters who have inspired so many of her young readers—especially the central heroes of *Atlas Shrugged,* Dagny Taggart and the three men who become her lovers: Francisco D'Anconia, Hank Rearden, and John Galt.…

In Dagny Taggart Rand creates her ideal woman. Her earlier female protagonists are mostly Nietzschean and, as such, tragic figures. Dominique Francon, it is true, renounces her allegiance to Nietzsche, but this decision does not come until nearly the end of *The Fountainhead,* so that we can only project what her life and personality will be like as an Objectivist. Gaia, the teenaged heroine of *Anthem,* is not a well-developed character. It is only with the appearance of Dagny that we can see how Rand visualizes the 'ideal' woman.

Dagny, like the other heroes of *Atlas Shrugged,* is an incarnation of the virtue of competence. In her mid-thirties she is the de facto CEO of the country's largest railroad. Intelligent, decisive, self-confident, she embodies the prime characteristic of the natural leader: she is the person who knows what to do.

As one might expect from Rand's literary technique, Dagny's characterization is rooted in a seeming paradox. On the one hand, she appears neuter, if not masculine, in her aggressiveness and career dedication. Lillian Rearden describes her as "an adding machine in tailored suits". When Cherryl Taggart claims her place as the woman of the Taggart family, Dagny responds, "That's quite all right. I'm the man."

On the other hand, Dagny is an intensely feminine woman. (She is, in fact, the kind of woman who wears a dress and stockings to explore an abandoned factory!) She is attracted to strong, dominant men, and desires to play an explicitly submissive role in her sexual relationships.

The key to the seeming contradiction is that Dagny has repressed her sexuality in the hostile society in which she exists. Dagny's air of coldness and unemotional, pseudomasculine behavior are a consequence of her immersion in a society which contains nobody to whom she can respond naturally. This is hinted at in Rand's depiction of the Rearden anniversary party, at which Dagny is described as presenting a challenge which nobody can perceive. There is a vivid contrast between Dagny's unexpressed personality in the statist world and her temperament in Galt's Gulch, where she happily becomes—a housewife! That this was Rand's conscious intention is shown by her notes for *Atlas Shrugged:*

> Dagny, who is considered so hard, cold, heartless, and domineering, is actually the most emotional, passionate, tender, and gay-hearted person of all—but only Galt can bring it out. Her other aspect is what the world forces on her or deserves from her.

Rand herself was profoundly ambivalent on the issue of feminism. She was a strong advocate of careers for women, of course, and said (in her *Playboy* interview), "There is no particular work which is specifically feminine." She endorsed (with some political reservations) Betty Friedan's *The Feminine Mystique.* She was contemptuous of 'housewives' in general. On the abortion issue, Rand took a vigorously 'pro-choice' position.

Yet Rand could scarcely be classified as a feminist. Though most of her heroines lack interest in marriage and family life, there are exceptions. Gaia, in *Anthem,* shows no ambition beyond following her man, and is pregnant at the end of the novel. Rand sympathetically portrays the anonymous young woman who chooses motherhood as a 'profession' in Galt's Gulch, as well as Mrs. William Hastings, who appears to be a 'mere' housewife. Rand's notorious statement that a woman ought not to aspire to be President of the United States hardly sounds like feminism. And, in response to a question about her position (at her 1981 Ford Hall Forum appearance) she said, "I'm a male chauvinist."

Rand could hardly have meant by this—in a literal dictionary sense—that she exhibited "unreasoning devotion" to the male sex and contempt for the female sex. She did not say that men in general are superior to women. What, then, did she mean? Consider this:

> Hero-worship is a demanding virtue: a woman has to be worthy of it and of the hero she worships. Intellectually and morally, i.e., as a human being, she has to be his equal; then the object of her worship is specifically his masculinity, not any human virtue she might lack.

Later in the same essay, Rand says, "[the feminine woman's] worship is an abstract emotion for the metaphysical concept of masculinity as such". It appears that Rand would attach a special, exceptional value to 'masculinity' as 'the fact of being a man', and that she was a 'male chauvinist' in this sense. Rand is explicit that the feminine woman's desire to look up to man "does not mean dependence, obedience or anything implying inferiority".

When we examine Rand's fictional heroines, we find that they certainly exhibit this intense admiration for the masculinity of their lovers. But, despite Rand's stated opinions, her fiction suggests that she regarded men as being inherently superior to women. Gaia, for instance, is far from being an intellectual equal of her mate. For that matter, Dominique does not seem to be quite a match for Howard Roark in ability, nor Dagny for John Galt.

All Rand's heroines are explicitly submissive in a sexual sense. Indeed, it is hard to avoid the suggestion of a certain degree of masochism in the physically vigorous couplings of Dagny and Rearden, in Faulkner's burning Karen Andre with hot platinum, and of course in Dominique's first sexual encounter with Roark.

Rand herself married a man who was far from being a John Galt in intellectual stature. Frank O'Connor, protective, nurturing, and pliable, gave her the emotional support of a husband without the inconvenient demands. She could pursue her career as she wished, and he accommodated her. Like Dagny, she was the man in her family.

But she really didn't want to be a man. Her struggle over the decades compelled her to become mannish in many ways; a 'womanly' woman could never have waged the war Rand fought. Yet through it all she battled to remain a woman. The desire to reclaim and assert her femininity, contends Barbara Branden, impelled her into the affair with Nathaniel Branden.

One can find a psychological explanation for Rand's portrayal of the sexes in her personal conflict. As a woman she longed for a mate who could match or even surpass her ability, a hero who would fill her need for romance and passion, a man who would dominate her sexually. Yet hero-worship has its obligations as well as its privileges; a marriage with a real-life John Galt, even if she could have found one, would have imposed demands she could never have accepted. Nothing could be allowed to interfere with her intellectual growth or achievements. Devastating as this paradox was to her personal happiness, its tension contributed to her art, in which she portrayed a series of fascinating man-woman relationships.

From a more abstract point of view, Rand's vision of men and women reflects her uncritical acceptance of the twentieth-century cliché that human behavior has no genetic component. Accepting that humans are born "*tabula rasa*"—blank slates—she could not develop a theory of sexuality that accounted for the inherent differences between the sexes in a coherent manner. As we will see, this contradiction also had its effect on the Objectivist ethics.

Rand may not have understood what made the male sex an ideal for her, but she knew what she liked, and the heroes of *Atlas Shrugged* demonstrate her vision of man at his best....

Francisco Domingo Carlos Andres Sebastian D'Anconia is the favorite character of many readers of *Atlas Shrugged.* Like Dagny, he embodies a paradox: He is at once a man of extraordinary *joie de vivre,* gay, lighthearted, sophisticated; and a man of tragedy, frozen, unemotional, implacable.

The light side of Francisco embodies the sense of life that Rand aspired to, the unobstructed, effortless achievement of joy in a totally benevolent universe. As the young boy who can do anything, and do it superbly, who fears nothing and hates nobody, he presents an extraordinarily attractive figure.

The other side of the coin is the tortured but self-controlled man who allows no feeling or suffering to affect him, much less deflect him. His relentless pursuit of his terrible purpose invokes our awe and admiration.

We love Francisco precisely because of the union of these aspects of his personality. It was a stroke of artistic genius to create a character paradoxically embodying these disparate traits; and it is a tribute to Rand's literary skill that she could integrate them into a convincing personality....

Hank Rearden is older than the other major heroes of *Atlas Shrugged*. (He is 45 as the novel opens.) He also presents a different sort of inner conflict. Unlike Dagny, he feels a fundamental sense of guilt, which has been carefully nurtured over the years by his wife, the despicable Lillian. He has responded by emotional withdrawal.

It is critical to emphasize that Rand does not present Rearden's obsessive fixation with his business as an ideal. On the contrary, his struggle with emotional repression is a key thread of the plot.

We see Rearden, when he is first introduced, as a man who is interested in nothing but steel. He literally falls asleep when forced to deal with any other topic. The only hint that he is anything beyond a stereotypical workaholic is a jade vase in his office.

But this is not the real Rearden. As his affair with Dagny flowers, he expands as a person. Without losing his passionate commitment to his career, he begins to develop the full personality that he had so long repressed. He takes an interest in ideas, begins to express his love of beauty, becomes more relaxed and gay. As this process unfolds, his emotions open up. He finds himself able to love Dagny. He also responds more effectively to his coworkers; his relationship with his secretary, Gwen Ives, visibly expands and becomes more personal as his affair with Dagny progresses. And he is able to de-repress his resentment of, and contempt for, his worthless family.

Much of the novel is devoted to showing Rearden's gradual emotional blossoming, as he responds to Dagny and to Francisco D'Anconia. This is a vital factor in the plot; before he can join the strikers, he must not only deal with his unearned guilt, but he must establish new, interpersonal values so that his mills are not the be-all of his life—otherwise he could not abandon them....

To depict an ideal man in a work of literature is a difficult assignment for any author. Few have attempted it; none have attempted such an ambitious ideal as does Rand.

John Galt, by the nature of the novel's plot, carries a heavy burden to start with. As the leader of the strikers, and the core of the novel's mystery element, he does not even appear on stage (except in disguise) until the last third of the book. We see him for two chapters; then he again disappears until the book's climax. Galt receives so little exposure to the reader that only Rand's superb technique can make him real at all.

Unfortunately, it is not quite sufficient to fully expand his character. John Galt, like Howard Roark, is too perfect to sustain a convincing internal conflict. Indeed, Galt was explicitly intended to represent man-become-god, and Rand deliberately avoided any details of characterization that might have made him seem more 'human' in the usual, self-deprecatory sense of the word. John Galt is Rand's ultimate answer to Nietzsche; he is an assertion that we need not evolve any 'superman', that man can become godlike himself if he so chooses.

But of course, the Randian paradox appears as always. John Galt, the ideal man, the pinnacle of the human species, is condemned to work underground, as a greasy laborer in the Taggart tunnels. This idea, that in a corrupt society the best men will be found at the bottom, plays a part in all of Rand's novels. Kira encounters Leo in a redlight district. In *The Fountainhead* Dominique discovers Howard Roark working, like a slave or a convict, in a quarry. The hero of *Anthem* is assigned as a streetsweeper and does his illicit scientific work in an abandoned subway tunnel—underground.

(An interesting inversion takes place in the strikers' valley. Galt, the lowly trackworker, becomes the revered leader of society. And Dagny, the wealthy executive, finds herself penniless and must find work as a maid.)

Galt was not merely Rand's ideal man; he was the projection of Rand herself. He verges on pure intellect; he is a philosopher and teacher; he is the leader of an intellectual movement; and he is, through most of his life, frustrated by the inability to find a partner worthy of him.

If John Galt sometimes seems more a symbol than a person, it reflects Rand's difficulty in visualizing her ideal man. When she tried, she ran up against the contradiction implicit in her *tabula rasa* model of humanity: to be an ideal man, John Galt would have to be inherently different from a woman. He would have to be distinctively male, not just a pure intellect happening to inhabit a male body. Just as Rand could not make herself fully female, so she could not make her ideal hero fully male. Her concept of humanity, for all its novel and perceptive insights, was incomplete....

Rand also creates an incredible rogues' gallery of villains, and provides them with some beautifully appropriate names: Wesley Mouch, Tinky Holloway, and Cuffy Meigs are classics. Floyd Ferris has just the right ring for the handsome, slick, and vicious scientist-bureaucrat. Robert Stadler's name gives a hint of the statist views which make him a villain. Perhaps best suited of all is that undistinguished politician Mr. Thompson, an old-fashioned gangster very similar in style to the weapon suggested by his name.

Though Rand has been criticized for creating two-dimensional villains, the fact is that she devotes considerable effort to digging into the psychology of evil. Three villains are analyzed in considerable depth: James Taggart, Lillian Rearden, and Robert Stadler.

Jim Taggart is visualized by most readers as short, fat, and ugly; some critics have even attacked Rand for making all her villains physically unprepossessing. This is a tribute to her skill; the actual description of Jim Taggart in the book is as tall, slim, and aristocratic in appearance. It is the reader who unconsciously visualizes him as ugly, giving him a physical appearance to fit his character.

For ugly he is—psychologically. A man of mediocre talent, he inherits control of Taggart Transcontinental. At the opening of the story, he is 39 and a neurotic whose response to the problems of the railroad he nominally heads is, "Don't bother me, don't bother me, don't bother me." Gradually we watch his psychological disintegration, until he ends up as a catatonic. He is unable to face the fact that he is "a killer—for the sake of killing", and psychosis is ultimately his only escape.

Lillian Rearden is a marvelous portrayal. She is a fitting foil for Dagny: intelligent, capable of shrewd psychological insight, and completely dedicated to relentless pursuit of a single goal. Her campaign to destroy Hank Rearden is masterfully conceived and flawlessly executed. It is only his extraordinary inner strength, and some timely help from Dagny and Francisco, that saves him.

In the story of Dr. Robert Stadler, Rand achieves a Trollopian depiction of temptation and the consequences of surrender to it. When we first see Stadler, he is a great mind, a brilliant scientist, who has compromised with statism to get the money to continue his research. This initial sin inexorably presents him with a series of moral dilemmas, and each failure to turn back leads him deeper into the morass.

In his first crisis, the State Science Institute issues an attack on Rearden Metal. Though Stadler knows it is false, he dares not contradict it, for fear that the Institute's funding might be reduced. Later Floyd Ferris attacks science and reason explicitly, and even uses Stadler's name in doing so. This time Stadler protests—but not publicly. Ferris goes on

to create Project X, using Stadler's discoveries to forge a weapon of terror. And now, under Directive 10-289, the consequences of rebellion are more serious; Stadler faces not mere embarrassment but the threat of starvation. Under compulsion, he publicly praises his tormentors and commends them for their perversion of the knowledge he had created. By the novel's end Stadler has surrendered utterly to corruption, and his last act in life is an undignified scuffle with a drunken criminal for possession of the murderous weapon he had once scorned.

Most of Rand's villains fill bit parts. The mystic Ivy Starnes, the whining Lee Hunsaker, the pretentious Gilbert Keith-Worthing, and many others are portrayed with a few deft strokes and used as needed. Each, however, is used to make a unique point.

Rand is careful, despite her 'black and white' moral code, to avoid any hint of moral determinism. One villain, the "Wet Nurse", demonstrates that it is possible to turn away from evil. Another, the labor racketeer Fred Kinnan, shows a certain blunt honesty that makes him more sympathetic than his colleagues....

Perhaps the most neglected characters in discussion of *Atlas Shrugged* are what one might call the 'lesser heroes'—people who are morally good, but lack the immense ability of Dagny and the other strikers. Rand treats sympathetically such tiny roles as the police chief of Durrance (who helps Dagny locate the Starnes heirs) and Mrs. William Hastings. Another such character, the hobo Jeff Allen, supplies a key piece of information in the main mystery of the plot. Three of these characters, however, receive considerable attention: Tony (the "Wet Nurse"), Cherryl Brooks, and Eddie Willers.

Tony, the young, amoral bureaucrat who is sent to supervise Rearden's production under the "Fair Share Law", represents the human potential for moral redemption. At his first appearance, he is a total cynic. The very concept of morality has been educated out of him, so that he finds Rearden's integrity disturbing and incomprehensible. Gradually, in the productive environment of the Rearden mills, he develops a desire for an ideal to believe in. Tony begins to feel admiration and sympathy for Rearden. He offers assistance in bribing the bureaucracy to obtain higher quotas, which Rearden of course rejects. Later, when Rearden defies the State Science Institute's order for Rearden Metal, Tony is concerned for Rearden's safety and chides him for taking such a risk. His commitment to Rearden becomes progressively stronger: he

A favorite novelist of Rand's youth, Victor Hugo later influenced her writings.

cheers Rearden's triumph at his trial; he fails to report Rearden's violations of regulations, and later volunteers to actively conceal them; he asks Rearden to let him quit the bureaucracy and work for the mill, even if only in a menial job. In the end he has accepted Rearden's ideals and fights to defend them; Tony's murder is the final straw before Rearden joins the strike.

Cherryl Brooks is the most tragic character of *Atlas Shrugged*. She is a slum girl determined to rise. (Had the book been written ten years later, Rand might well have made Cherryl a Black.) She is not brilliant, not an intellectual, has no career ambitions. But she is fiercely honest, idealistic, and courageous. Finding herself married far "above her station" to James Taggart, she applies her limited ability to the task she considers appropriate to her: becoming a high-society "lady." Zealously she studies etiquette, culture, and style to become the kind of wife Taggart, in her vision of him, deserves. And she succeeds; the slum girl from the five-and-dime transforms herself into a sophisticated member of the aristocracy of wealth. Again we see a classic Randian cliché-reversal. Taking off from Shaw's *Pygmalion,* Rand invents an Eliza Doolittle who transforms herself into a lady on her own initiative and by her own efforts—against the op-

position of her 'benefactor', who wants her to remain a slum girl. But Cherryl's effort to become a worthy consort for her husband goes for nothing; Taggart is not a hero but a rotter; he has married her, not to ennoble her, but to destroy her.

The most important of the lesser heroes is Dagny's assistant, Eddie Willers, the very first character to whom we are introduced as the novel opens. It is easy to underestimate Eddie Willers. Standing beside Dagny Taggart or Hank Rearden he seems ordinary, not very competent, almost a bit wimpish. This, however, is due merely to the contrast with Rand's extraordinary heroes, as the moon seems dim in sunlight. Hank Rearden, who ought to know, says that Eddie has the makings of a good businessman. In fact, he is a highly able executive. Toward the end of the book, he bribes his way onto an Army plane and flies into a city torn apart by civil war. In the space of a few days, single-handed, he negotiates immunity with three separate warring factions, reorganizes the Taggart terminal, revitalizes its personnel, and gets the trains running again. Some wimp!

All three of these lesser heroes come to bad ends. Tony is murdered when he defies his masters and attempts to warn Rearden of the plot against his mills. Cherryl commits suicide when she discovers the horrifying truth about her husband. Eddie strands himself in the desert, sobbing at the foot of a dead locomotive. Why is there no happy ending for these characters?

Mimi Gladstein suggests that Eddie's fate is punishment for his refusal to accompany Dagny to Galt's Gulch. Certainly it is a consequence of that decision, but it is wrong to see it as punishment for a moral failing.

In her treatment of the lesser heroes Rand expresses an important truth. The essence of statism is the destruction of all that is good in the human spirit. The ablest heroes frequently escape, to make new lives for themselves elsewhere. Such people as Rachmaninoff and Sikorsky and Rand escaped from the Bolsheviks. Such people as Einstein and Fermi and von Mises escaped from the Nazis. It was mostly the people of more ordinary intellect that perished at Vorkuta or Auschwitz. These were the people who attempted to fight, but lacked the ability to do so effectively—like Tony. Or they were the people who died of sheer despair, facing a horror beyond their conception—like Cherryl. Or, they were those who might have escaped, but could not bring themselves to give up their old life and start over again with no capital but their own minds—like Eddie. Rand had known such people; her own father died under the Soviet regime, unwilling to leave Russia and give up the hope that he might somehow get his business back. She pities them, does not condemn them.

It should be evident to the reader that a great deal more could be said about *Atlas Shrugged*. This book is one of the most complex novels ever written, and its analysis poses hundreds of fascinating problems which will occupy scholars for decades.

I lack the space to properly cover the many concepts that Rand developed in this novel: 'sanction of the victim' and the impotence of evil; envy and the hatred of the good for being good; the 'individual surplus' of the great innovators; the intimate connection of philosophical premises and personal and social character; and many others.

Atlas Shrugged is not merely a novel to be read for entertainment, enjoyable though it is. Nor is it a treatise to be read for enlightenment, instructive though it is. The reader will benefit most who regards the book as a sort of magical box full of tightly folded intellectual *origami,* each of which should be carefully opened, contemplated, and cherished.

Source: Ronald E. Merrill, *The Ideas of Ayn Rand,* Open Court, 1991, pp. 59–74, 74–78, 85.

Whittaker Chambers

An American memoirist, journalist, and critic, Chambers is best known for his involvement in the 1948 trial that led to State Department official Alger Hiss's conviction for passing government documents to Soviet Agents. Once a member of the Communist Party, Chambers later became an editor and coumnist for the staunchly conservative journal National Review, *an evolution he chronicled in his autobiography* Witness *(1952). In the following essay, which was originally published in 1957, Chambers finds it difficult to take seriously the plot and philosophy of* Atlas Shrugged, *and maintains that the work is more a tract than it is a novel.*

Several years ago, Miss Ayn Rand wrote *The Fountain-head.* Despite a generally poor press, it is said to have sold some four hundred thousand copies. Thus, it became a wonder of the book trade of a kind that publishers dream about after taxes. So *Atlas Shrugged* had a first printing of one hundred thousand copies. It appears to be slowly climbing the best-seller lists.

> The news about this book seems to me to be that any ordinarily sensible head could possibly take it seriously, and that, apparently, a good many do. Somebody has called it: "Excruciatingly awful." I find it a remarkably silly book."

The news about this book seems to me to be that any ordinarily sensible head could possibly take it seriously, and that, apparently, a good many do. Somebody has called it: "Excruciatingly awful." I find it a remarkably silly book. It is certainly a bumptious one. Its story is preposterous. It reports the final stages of a final conflict (locale: chiefly the United States, some indefinite years hence) between the harried ranks of free enterprise and the "looters." These are proponents of proscriptive taxes, government ownership, Labor, etc. etc. The mischief here is that the author, dodging into fiction, nevertheless counts on your reading it as political reality. "This," she is saying in effect, "is how things really are. These are the real issues, the real sides. Only your blindness keeps you from seeing it, which, happily, I have come to rescue you from."

Since a great many of us dislike much that Miss Rand dislikes, quite as heartily as she does, many incline to take her at her word. It is the more persuasive, in some quarters, because the author deals wholly in the blackest blacks and the whitest whites. In this fiction everything, everybody, is either all good or all bad, without any of those intermediate shades which, in life, complicate reality and perplex the eye that seeks to probe it truly. This kind of simplifying pattern, of course, gives charm to most primitive story-telling. And, in fact, the somewhat ferro-concrete fairy tale the author pours here is, basically, the old one known as: The War between the Children of Light and the Children of Darkness. In modern dress, it is a class war. Both sides to it are caricatures.

The Children of Light are largely operatic caricatures. In so far as any of them suggests anything known to the business community, they resemble the occasional curmudgeon millionaire, tales about whose outrageously crude and shrewd eccentricities sometimes provide the lighter moments in Board rooms. Otherwise, the Children of Light are geniuses. One of them is named (the only smile you see will be your own): Francisco Domingo Carlos Andres Sebastian d'Antonio. This electrifying youth is the world's biggest copper tycoon. Another, no less electrifying, is named: Ragnar Danesjöld. He becomes a twentieth-century pirate. All Miss Rand's chief heroes are also breathtakingly beautiful. So is her heroine (she is rather fetchingly vice-president in charge of management of a transcontinental railroad). So much radiant energy might seem to serve an eugenic purpose. For, in this story as in Mark Twain's, "all the knights marry the princess"—though without benefit of clergy. Yet from the impromptu and surprisingly gymnastic mattings of the heroine and three of the heroes, no children—it suddenly strikes you—ever result. The possibility is never entertained. And, indeed, the strenuously sterile world of *Atlas Shrugged* is scarcely a place for children. You speculate that, in life, children probably irk the author and may make her uneasy. How could it be otherwise when she admiringly names a banker character (by what seems to me a humorless masterstroke): Midas Mulligan? You may fool some adults, you can't fool little boys and girls with such stuff—not for long. They may not know just what is out of line, but they stir uneasily.

The Children of Darkness are caricatures, too; and they are really oozy. But at least they are caricatures of something identifiable. Their archetypes are Left Liberals, New Dealers, Welfare Statists, One Worlders, or, at any rate, such ogreish semblances of these as may stalk the nightmares of those who think little about people as people, but tend to think a great deal in labels and effigies. (And neither Right nor Left, be it noted in passing, has a monopoly of such dreamers, though the horrors in their nightmares wear radically different masks and labels.)

In *Atlas Shrugged,* all this debased inhuman riffraff is lumped as "looters." This is a fairly inspired epithet. It enables the author to skewer on one invective word everything and everybody that she fears and hates. This spares her the plaguy business of performing one service that her fiction might have performed, namely: that of examining in human depth how so feeble a lot came to exist at all, let alone be powerful enough to be worth hating and fearing. Instead, she bundles them into one undifferentiated damnation.

"Looters" loot because they believe in Robin Hood, and have got a lot of other people believing in him, too. Robin Hood is the author's image of absolute evil—robbing the strong (and hence good) to give to the weak (and hence no good). All "looters" are base, envious, twisted, malignant minds, motivated wholly by greed for power, combined with the lust of the weak to tear down the strong, out of a deep-seated hatred of life and secret longing for destruction and death. There happens to be a tiny (repeat: tiny) seed of truth in this. The full clinical diagnosis can be read in the pages of Friedrich Nietzsche. (Here I must break in with an aside. Miss Rand acknowledges a grudging debt to one, and only one, earlier philosopher: Aristotle. I submit that she is indebted, and much more heavily, to Nietzsche. Just as her operatic businessmen are, in fact, Nietzschean supermen, so her ulcerous Leftists are Nietzsche's "last men," both deformed in a way to sicken the fastidious recluse of Sils Maria. And much else comes, consciously or not, from the same source.) Happily, in *Atlas Shrugged* (though not in life), all the Children of Darkness are utterly incompetent.

So the Children of Light win handily by declaring a general strike of brains, of which they have a monopoly, letting the world go, literally, to smash. In the end, they troop out of their Rocky Mountain hideaway to repossess the ruins. It is then, in the book's last line, that a character traces in the air, "over the desolate earth," the Sign of the Dollar, in lieu of the Sign of the Cross, and in token that a suitably prostrate mankind is at last ready, for its sins, to be redeemed from the related evils of religion and social reform (the "mysticism of mind" and the "mysticism of muscle").

That Dollar Sign is not merely provocative, though we sense a sophomoric intent to raise the pious hair on susceptible heads. More importantly, it is meant to seal the fact that mankind is ready to submit abjectly to an elite of technocrats, and their accessories, in a New Order, enlightened and instructed by Miss Rand's ideas that the good life is one which "has resolved personal worth into exchange value," "has left no other nexus between man and man than naked self-interest, than callous 'cash-payment.'" The author is explicit, in fact deafening, about these prerequisites. Lest you should be in any doubt after 1,168 pages, she assures you with a final stamp of the foot in a postscript: "And I mean it." But the words quoted above are those of Karl Marx. He, too, admired "naked self-interest" (in its time and place), and for much the same reasons as Miss Rand: because, he believed, it cleared away the cobwebs of religion and led to prodigies of industrial and cognate accomplishment.

The overlap is not as incongruous as it looks. *Atlas Shrugged* can be called a novel only by devaluing the term. It is a massive tract for the times. Its story merely serves Miss Rand to get the customers inside the tent, and as a soapbox for delivering her Message. The Message is the thing. It is, in sum, a forthright philosophic materialism. Upperclassmen might incline to sniff and say that the author has, with vast effort, contrived a simple materialist system, one, intellectually, at about the stage of the oxcart, though without mastering the principle of the wheel. Like any consistent materialism, this one begins by rejecting God, religion, original sin, etc. etc. (This book's aggressive atheism and rather unbuttoned "higher morality," which chiefly outrage some readers, are, in fact, secondary ripples, and result inevitably from its underpinning premises.) Thus, Randian Man, like Marxian Man, is made the center of a godless world.

At that point, in any materialism, the main possibilities open up to Man. 1) His tragic fate becomes, without God, more tragic and much lonelier. In general, the tragedy deepens according to the degree of pessimism or stoicism with which he conducts his "hopeless encounter between human questioning and the silent universe." Or, 2) Man's fate ceases to be tragic at all. Tragedy is bypassed by the pursuit of happiness. Tragedy is henceforth pointless. Henceforth man's fate, without God, is up to him, and to him alone. His happiness, in strict materialist terms, lies with his own workaday hands and ingenious brain. His happiness becomes, in Miss Rand's words, "the moral purpose of his life." Here occurs a little rub whose effects are just as observable in a free enterprise system, which is in practice materialist (whatever else it claims or supposes itself to be), as they would be under an atheist Socialism, if one were ever to deliver that material abundance that all promise. The rub is that the pursuit of happiness, as an end in itself, tends automatically, and widely, to be replaced by the pursuit of pleasure with a consequent general softening of the fibers of will, intelligence, spirit. No doubt, Miss Rand has brooded upon that little rub. Hence, in part, I presume, her insistence on "man as a heroic being" "with productive achievement as his noblest activity." For, if Man's "heroism" (some will prefer to say: "human dignity") no longer derives from God, or is not a function of that godless integrity which was a root of Nietzsche's anguish, then Man becomes merely the most consuming of animals, with glut as the condition of his happiness and its replenishment his foremost activity. So Randian Man, at least in his ruling caste, has to be held "heroic" in order not to be beastly. And this, of course, suits the author's economics and the politics that must arise from them.

For politics, of course, arise, though the author of *Atlas Shrugged* stares stonily past them, as if this book were not what, in fact, it is, essentially—a political book. And here begins mischief. Systems of philosophic materialism, so long as they merely circle outside this world's atmosphere, matter little to most of us. The trouble is that they keep coming down to earth. It is when a system of materialist ideas presumes to give positive answers to real problems of our real life that mischief starts. In an age like ours, in which a highly complex technological society is everywhere in a high state of instability, such answers, however philosophic, translate quickly into political realities. And in the degree to which problems of complexity and instability are most bewildering to masses of men, a temptation sets in to let some species of Big Brother solve and supervise them.

One Big Brother is, of course, a socializing elite (as we know, several cut-rate brands are on the shelves). Miss Rand, as the enemy of any socializing force, calls in a Big Brother of her own contriving to do battle with the other. In the name of free enterprise, therefore, she plumps for a technocratic elite (I find no more inclusive word than technocratic to bracket the industrial-financial-engineering caste she seems to have in mind). When she calls "productive achievement" man's "noblest activity," she means, almost exclusively, technological achievement, supervised by such a managerial political bureau. She might object that she means much, much more; and we can freely entertain her objections. But, in sum, that is just what she means. For that is what, in reality, it works out to. And in reality, too, by contrast with fiction, this can only head into a dictatorship, however benign, living and acting beyond good and evil, a law unto itself (as Miss Rand believes it should be), and feeling any restraint on itself as, in practice, criminal, and, in morals, vicious—as Miss Rand clearly feels it to be. Of course, Miss Rand nowhere calls for a dictatorship. I take her to be calling for an aristocracy of talents. We cannot labor here why, in the modern world, the pre-conditions for aristocracy, an organic growth, no longer exist, so that impulse toward aristocracy always emerges now in the form of dictatorship.

Nor has the author, apparently, brooded on the degree to which, in a wicked world, a materialism of the Right and a materialism of the Left, first surprisingly resemble, then, in action, tend to blend each with each, because, while differing at the top in avowed purpose, and possibly in conflict there, at bottom they are much the same thing. The embarrassing similarities between Hitler's National Socialism and Stalin's brand of Communism are familiar. For the world, as seen in materialist view from the Right, scarcely differs from the same world seen in materialist view from the Left. The question becomes chiefly: who is to run that world in whose interests, or perhaps, at best, who can run it more efficiently?

Something of this implication is fixed in the book's dictatorial tone, which is much its most striking feature. Out of a lifetime of reading, I can recall no other book in which a tone of overriding arrogance was so implacably sustained. Its shrillness is without reprieve. Its dogmatism is without appeal. In addition, the mind, which finds this tone natural to it, shares other characteristics of its type. 1) It consistently mistakes raw force for strength, and the rawer the force, the more reverent the posture of the mind before it. 2) It supposes itself to be the bringer of a final revelation. Therefore, resistance to the Message cannot be tolerated because disagreement can never be merely honest, prudent or just humanly fallible. Dissent from revelation so final (because, the author would say, so reasonable) can only be willfully wicked. There are ways of dealing with such wickedness, and, in fact, right reason itself enjoins them. From almost any page of *Atlas Shrugged,* a voice can be heard, from painful necessity, commanding: "To a gas chamber—go!" The same inflexibly self-righteous stance results, too (in the total absence of any saving humor), in odd extravagances of inflection and gesture—that Dollar Sign, for example. At first, we try to tell ourselves that these are just lapses, that this mind has, somehow, mislaid the discriminating knack that most of us pray will warn us in time of the difference between what is effective and firm, and what is wildly grotesque and excessive. Soon we suspect something worse. We suspect that this mind finds, precisely in extravagance, some exalting merit; feels a surging release of power and passion precisely in smashing up the house. A tornado might feel this way, or Carrie Nation.

We struggle to be just. For we cannot help feel at least a sympathetic pain before the sheer labor, discipline and patient craftsmanship that went to making this mountain of words. But the words keep shouting us down. In the end that tone dominates. But it should be its own antidote, warning us that anything it shouts is best taken with the usual reservations with which we might sip a patent medicine. Some may like the flavor. In any case, the brew is probably without lasting ill effects. But it is not a cure for anything. Nor would we, ordinarily, place much confidence in the diagnosis of a doctor who supposes that the Hippocratic Oath is a kind of curse.

Source: Whittaker Chambers, "Big Sister is Watching You," in *Ghosts on the Roof: Selected Journalism of Whittaker Chambers, 1931–1959,* Edited by Terry Teachout, Regnery Gateway, 1989, pp. 313–18

Nathaniel Branden

In the following excerpt, Branden discusses the climax of Atlas Shrugged *and the novel as the climax of Ayn Rand's novels.*

Just as, within each novel, the climax sums up and dramatizes the meaning of all the preceding events, raised to the highest peak of emotional and intellectual intensity—so, as a total work, *Atlas Shrugged* is the artistic and philosophical climax of all of Ayn Rand's novels, bringing the full of her dramatic, stylistic and intellectual power to its most consummate expression.

Ayn Rand has proudly referred to *Atlas Shrugged* as a "stunt novel"—proudly, because she has made the word "stunt" applicable on so high a level. By the standard of sheer originality, the idea of a novel about the minds of the world going on strike is as magnificent a plot-theme as any that could be conceived. If Ayn Rand has scorned the Naturalists who write about the people and events next door, if she has declared that the purpose of art is to project, not the usual, but the *unusual,* not the boring and the conventional, but the exciting, the dramatic, the unexpected, the rationally desirable yet the astonishingly new—then she is, preeminently, a writer who practices what she preaches.

Atlas Shrugged is a mystery story, "not about the murder of a man's body, but about the murder—and rebirth—of man's spirit." The reader is presented with a series of events that, in the beginning, appear incomprehensible: the world seems to be moving toward destruction, in a manner no one can identify, and for reasons no one can understand.

There are no "red herrings" in the story, no false clues. But the mystery is to be solved by *philosophical* detection—by identifying the philosophical implications of the evidence that is presented. When the reader is finally led to the solution, the meaning and inescapable necessity of all the things he has been shown seems, in retrospect, simple and self-evident.

It is epistemologically significant that *Atlas Shrugged* is written in the form of a mystery. This is consistent with the philosophy it propounds. The reader is not given arbitrary assertions to be taken on faith. He is given the facts and the evidence; his own mind is challenged to interpret that evidence; he is placed, in effect, in the position of the people in the novel, who observe the events around them, struggle to understand their cause and meaning, and are told the full truth only when they have seen sufficient evidence to form a reasoned judgment.

The most impressive feature of *Atlas Shrugged* is its integration. The novel presents the essentials of an entire philosophical system: epistemology, metaphysics, ethics, politics (and psychology). It shows the interrelation of these subjects in business, in a man's attitude toward his work, in love, in family relationships, in the press, in the universities, in economics, in art, in foreign relations, in science, in government, in sex. It presents a unified and comprehensive view of man and of man's relationship to existence. If one were to consider the ideas alone, apart from the novel in which they appear, the integration of so complex a philosophical system would be an extraordinarily impressive achievement. But when one considers that all of these philosophical issues are dramatized through a logically connected series of events involving a whole society, the feat of integration is breathtaking.

If one were told that an author proposed to dramatize, in a novel, the importance of recognizing the ontological status of the law of identity—one could not be blamed for being skeptical. But it is of such startling dramatizations that the virtuosity of *Atlas Shrugged* is made....

Tremendously complex in its structure, presenting the collapse of an entire society, the novel involves the lives, actions and goals of dozens of characters.... Yet every character, action and event has a dramatic and philosophical purpose; all are tied to the central situation and all are integrated with one another; nothing is superfluous, nothing is arbitrary and nothing is accidental; as the story moves forward, it projects, above all, the quality of the implacably, the irresistibly logical....

The climax of *Atlas Shrugged* is singularly typical of the spirit of the novel as a whole: the integration of the unexpected and the utterly logical—

> By the standard of sheer originality, the idea of a novel about the minds of the world going on strike is as magnificent a plot-theme as any that could be conceived."

of that which starts by appearing shocking and ends by appearing self-evident. One reader has described *Atlas Shrugged* as having the quality of "cosmic humor." It is written from the perspective of a mind that has discarded the conventional categories, standards and frame of reference—and has looked at reality with a fresh glance....

No other climax could sum up so eloquently the thesis and the meaning of *Atlas Shrugged*. The men of ability have all gone on strike, the world is in ruins, and the government officials make a last grotesque effort to preserve their system: they torture Galt to force him to join them and save their system *somehow*. They order him to *think*. They *command* him to take control. Naked force—seeking to compel a mind to function. And then the ultimate absurdity of their position is thrown in the torturers' faces: they are using an electric machine to torture Galt, and its generator breaks down; the brute who is operating the machine does not know how to repair it; neither do the officials; Galt lifts his head and contemptuously tells them how to repair it.

The brute runs away in horror—at the realization that they need Galt's help even to torture him. The officials flee the cellar also—"the cellar where the living generator was left tied by the side of the dead one." ...

There are persons to whom clarity and precision are the enemies of poetry and emotion; they equate the artistic with the fuzzy, the vague and the diffuse. Seeking in art the reflection and confirmation of their sense of life, they are psychologically and esthetically at home only with the blurred and the indeterminate: that which is sharply in focus, clashes with their own mental state. In such persons, Ayn Rand's literary style will invoke a feeling of disquietude and resentment; Ayn Rand's use of language is best characterized by a line concerning Dagny Taggart: "she had regarded language as a tool of honor, always to be used as if one were under oath—an oath of allegiance to reality and to respect for human beings." Because her writing is lucid, such persons will tell themselves that it is crude; because her writing conveys an unequivocal meaning, and does not suggest a "mobile" to be interpreted by the subjective whim of any reader, they will tell themselves that it lacks poetry; because her writing demands that they be conscious when they read it, they will tell themselves that it is not art.

But the specific trademark of her literary style is its power vividly to re-create sensory reality and inner psychological states, to induce the most intense emotions—and to accomplish this by means of the most calculated selection of words, images and events, giving to logic a poetry it had never had before, and to poetry a logic it had never had before....

In *Atlas Shrugged,* Ayn Rand has created more than a great novel. By any rational, objective literary standard—from the standpoint of plot-structure, suspense, drama, imaginativeness, characterization, evocative and communicative use of language, originality, scope of theme and subject, psychological profundity and philosophical richness—*Atlas Shrugged* is the climax of the novel form, carrying that form to unprecedented heights of intellectual and artistic power....

Just as in philosophy Ayn Rand has challenged the modern doctrines of neo-mysticism and epistemological agnosticism, so in literature she has challenged the view of man as an impotent zombie without intellect, efficacy or self-esteem. Just as she has opposed the fashionable philosophical dogmas of fatalism, determinism and man's metaphysical passivity, so she has opposed the fashionable literary projections of man as a stuporous puppet manipulated by instinct and socio-economic status. Just as she has rejected the mystics' theories of Original Sin, of man's depravity and the misery of life on earth, so she has rejected the presentations of unfocused, whim-worshipping neurotics staggering along a trail of hysterical destruction to the abyss of whimpering defeat. Just as she has rescued philosophy from the cult of the anti-mind and the anti-man, so she has rescued literature from the cult of the anti-novel and the anti-hero. As an artist, she has brought men a new sense of life. As a philosopher, she has brought them the intellectual implementation of that sense of life: she has shown what it depends upon and how it is to be earned.

When one considers the quality of enraptured idealism that dominates her work, and the affirmative view of the human potential that she projects, the most morally corrupt of the attacks leveled against her—and the most psychologically revealing—is the assertion that she is "motivated by a hatred of humanity."

It is culturally significant that writers who present dope addicts and psychopaths as their image of human nature, are *not* accused of "hatred for humanity"—but a writer who presents men of integrity and genius as her image of human nature, *is.*

In Ayn Rand's novels, the heroes, the men of outstanding moral character and intellectual ability, are exalted; the men of conscientious honesty and average ability are treated with respect and sympathy—a far more profound respect and sympathy, it is worth adding, than they have ever been accorded in any "humanitarian" novel. There is only one class of men who receive moral condemnation: the men who demand any form of the unearned, in matter or in spirit; who propose to treat other men as sacrificial animals; who claim the right to rule others by physical force. Is it her implacable sense of justice—her loyalty to those who are *not* evil—her concern for the morally innocent and her contempt for the morally guilty—that makes Ayn Rand a "hater of humanity?" If those who charge Ayn Rand with "hatred," feeling themselves to be its object, choose to identify and classify themselves with the men she condemns—doubtless they know best. But then it is not Ayn Rand—or humanity—whom they have damned....

The most tragic victims of the man-degrading nature of contemporary literature are the young. They have watched the progression from the boredom of conventional Naturalism to the horror of nightmare Symbolism—the progression from stories about the folks next door to stories about the dipsomaniac next door, the crippled dwarf next door, the axe-murderer next door, the psychotic next door. *This,* they are now informed, is what life is "*really*" like.

In projecting the artist's view of man's metaphysical relationship to existence, art explicitly or implicitly holds up to man the value-goals of life: it shows him what is possible and what is worth striving for. It can tell him that he is doomed and that *nothing* is worth striving for—or it can show him the life of a Howard Roark or a John Galt. It is particularly when one is young, when one is still forming one's soul, that one desperately needs—as example, as inspiration, as fuel, as antidote to the sight of the world around one—the vision of life as it might and ought to be, the vision of heroes fighting for values worth achieving in a universe where achievement is possible. It is not *descriptions* of the people next door that a young person requires, but an *escape* from the people next door—to a wider view of the human potentiality. This is what the young have found in the novels of Ayn Rand—and that is the key to the enormous popularity of her novels.

Source: Nathaniel Branden, *Who Is Ayn Rand?: An Analysis of the Novels of Ayn Rand,* Random House, 1962, pp. 118–21, 126–27, 129, 140–44.

Judith Wilt

In the following essay, Wilt discusses Atlas Shrugged *as a feminist work.*

I *could* wish that the cancer-causing cigarette were not the ultimate symbol of glowing mind controlling matter in the book, I could wish that the rails which reflect the self-assertion of the heroine were not envisioned running to the hands of a man invisible beyond the horizon—most of all I wish the author had resisted the temptation to have her hero trace the Sign of the Dollar over the devastated earth before his Second Coming. But yes, I agree with Mimi Gladstein, there is a feminist element in Ayn Rand's *Atlas Shrugged,* and it's on my ideal Women's Studies reading list too.

It made a deep impression on me at nineteen and now I can see at least two feminist reasons why. First, the book's opening sections on Dagny Taggart's childhood and adolescence depict with great power the most shattering discovery the awakening womanmind makes—this world is not the one the vigorous confident girlchild expected to find and to help run when she "grows up." And second, the book's middle and final sections depict with still greater power, nay satisfaction, the destruction of that false usurpers' world.

Rand's extended invocation of catastrophe feels astonishingly like the 1970's: "On the morning of September 2 a copper wire broke in California, between two telephone poles.... On the evening of September 7, a copper wire broke in Montana, stopping the motor of a loading crane.... On the afternoon of September 11, a copper wire broke in Minnesota, stopping the belts of a grain elevator.... On the night of October 15, a copper wire broke in New York City, extinguishing the lights ..." In fact, *Atlas Shrugged* partakes of the general post-nuclear apocalypticism of the 1950's. But there is also a special quality of *feminine* rage

> ... the book's opening sections on Dagny Taggart's childhood and adolescence depict with great power the most shattering discovery the awakening womanmind makes—this world is not the one the vigorous confident girlchild expected to find and to help run when she "grows up."

discernible not only in the analysis of the Originating Sin behind the usurping world—"altruism," selflessness, the worship of "the other" and his need before one's own—but in the nature of the destruction.

According to her vision of the great age of progress (the nineteenth century, that is—not, I admit, perfectly recognizable to the historian in Rand's form), humanity civilized, indeed organicized, material nature by infusing it with its own purposeful creativity—metal plus mind equals the living copper wire, the bridges and motors and lights which are, so to speak, the mystical body of the human mind, the "material shapes of desire" as Rand phrases it. When mind goes astray or is withdrawn, the enterprise collapses upon itself, and the plot of *Atlas Shrugged* is predicated upon the desire of the best minds in the world to "go on strike," to destroy the old shapes of desire because they have been appropriated, usurped. Thus in the novel destruction of what is outside the self becomes the measure of greatness, purposefulness, authenticity, even more than construction or preservation of what is inside the self. The heroine's adolescent lover, Francisco D'Anconia, devotes his life to "destroying D'Anconia Copper in plain sight of the world." The hero, John Galt, who organizes the strike and convinces the suppliers of oil, then coal, then steel to withdraw just as the national economy, swinging wildly about in its search for a savior, needs them most, is the hated "Destroyer" to Dagny before she actually meets him. Even after she meets him and knows him, complicatedly, as the full shape of her desire, that desire remains destructive to the measure of its authenticity. Before entering his Atlantis she understands that she would have destroyed the Destroyer if she could—but not until she had made love to him; after she leaves it to go back and try to halt the world's self-destruction, she goes to see him in his hideout in New York despite the risk that she will lead his enemies to him. He describes, to her horror, the trap she has probably enclosed them both in, and urges

> "It's our time and our life, not theirs. Don't struggle not to be happy. You are."
>
> "At the risk of destroying you?" she whispered.
>
> "You won't. But—yes, even that.... Was it indifference that broke you and brought you here?"
>
> "I—." And then the violence of the truth made her pull his mouth down to hers, then throw the words at his face: "I didn't care whether either one of us lived afterwards, just to see you this once!"

This subterranean commitment to a cleansing violence, an ethic of destruction, is evident in Rand's vision of both work and sex, is indeed what makes the two functions of the same desire. What attracts Rand, and Dagny, to the industrial barons of the nineteenth century, is unmistakably the sense of their successful smashing of opposition. What brings Dagny back to her job after one early frustration is the disastrous train wreck which destroyed the Taggart tunnel through the Rockies— she cannot accept that destruction and wants to mitigate it. The test of her ethical adulthood at the end of the novel is her willing desertion of the railroad she runs just as the Taggart bridge across the Mississippi, the last link to the West, is destroyed. Leaving, she sanctions this and all following destruction. Dagny first comes to John Galt by crashing her plane into his private mountain retreat; when they return to the city he follows her, running, into the dark tunnel of the terminal, and they share a love scene not easily distinguishable from mutual rape: "she felt her teeth sinking into the flesh of his arm, she felt the sweep of his elbow knocking her head aside and his mouth seizing her lips with a pressure more viciously painful than hers."

At the root of all this eager violence is an equivocal passion for the display of *will* in a world where will seems to Rand's heroine to have either utterly rotted away or else become so devious in its operations as to be unrecognizable, a world "feminized" in the worst sense of the word. "Oh, don't ask me—do it!" she prays at seventeen when Francisco, too, "seizes" her, and she receives his

violence thankfully as an anodyne for the disappointment of the formal debut party months before, where "there wasn't a man there I couldn't squash ten of." What she doesn't realize then, what Francisco and Galt are about to learn, is that the power to create *or* to squash that comes from will is not in fact equal to the power to expropriate or squash that comes from will-lessness, not only because there is more of the latter than the former in the world, but more because the people of will have accepted the chains of certain moral systems which short circuit or diffuse their desires.

Dagny suffers from the quantity of will-lessness opposed to her will. Gaining the position she requires, Operating Vice President of the Taggart railroad, was "like advancing through a succession of empty rooms," deathly exhausting but productive of no violence, cleansing or otherwise. Her disgust and near despair are in this respect interestingly like that of an ambitious *man.* Indeed, at the wedding of her wealthy brother and the energetic little shop girl he marries, the bride challenges the sister-in-law she has heard of as a cold and unfeminine executive: "I'm the woman in this family now," and Dagny replies, "That's quite all right, I'm the man." At the same party Francisco, the self-proclaimed womanizer who is actually one of the Destroyers, answers Hank Rearden's contemptuous "Found any conquests?" with "Yes—what I think is going to be my best and greatest." Rearden is himself the conquest Francisco is after; Dagny's first lover wants her second lover not for explicitly sexual purposes, of course, but for the Cause. And yet, in several senses Rearden is the female to Francisco and Dagny in the novel:

> "I'm saying that I didn't know what it meant, to like a man, I didn't know how much I'd missed it—until I met him."
>
> "Good God, Hank, you've fallen for him!"
>
> "Yes, I think I have."

This is more than the love of one man for another, though it is certainly that too, and eloquently described by Rand, and welcome. It is the love of one being whose desire has been short-circuited, "hooked to torment instead of reward" as Rand describes it, for another whose desire is direct and confident of its ends. And it is this kind of frustration, desire short-circuited, will "contravened," as Lawrence would say, that makes Rearden a kind of female icon. It is the archetypal female plight that Rand explores in his story, displacing it cleverly from her heroine, whom she values too much to subject to it, to her middle-rank hero, whom she loves and pities.

Rearden's existence at book's opening is a schizophrenic shuttling between an unendurable dead family and marriage, and a profoundly satisfying work life whose very satisfaction is a guilty torment because all his love is concentrated there among the machines, mill schedules, and metals which are, inexplicably and "shamefully" to the usurpers of altruism, alive and lovable to him. He makes the classic "female" adjustment: he accepts the world's definition of his work-life, love, and productivity as guilt and his withdrawal of pure love from his family as shame. He hates and tries to eliminate the sexual desire which is at the heart of the corrupt world of marriage and family and relies on sheer strength, doubled and redoubled, to support both sides of his existence and the conflicts between them. "Well, then, go on with your hands tied, he thought, go on in chains. Go on. It must not stop you." When he finds himself desiring Dagny Taggart, the mind and spirit his working soul most admires, it is a catastrophe to his split self—"the lowest of my desires—as my answer to the highest I've met.... it's depravity, and I accept it as such." Dagny does not challenge his definition, knowing that their living experience as lovers will teach him the truth, but it is Francisco who actually tells him the truth. In this novel it is still true that women, even the heroine, mainly exist and demonstrate, while men develop and articulate. "Only the man who extols the purity of a love devoid of desire, is capable of the depravity of a desire without love," Francisco argues; only "the man who is convinced of his own worthlessness will be drawn to a woman he despises." Led by Francisco and Dagny, Rearden emerges from the schizophrenia, reconnects the circuits of his sexual and productive desire to his sense of self-worth, and achieves in the end, like Dagny, that act of abandonment-destruction which, again, is Rand's rite of passage from the usurpers' world to the "real" one. Only it is not just the mills which, like Dagny's railroad, must be destroyed: it is also Rearden's family—mate, mother, brother—which, deprived of his coerced strength, must be let slide into poverty and degradation and madness before the new beginning is possible.

Finally, interestingly, Rearden's reward for making his passage does not include a mate, as Dagny's does. Discovering that Francisco, whom he loves, was Dagny's first lover, Rearden "seized" the woman (again) and consummated an act of love that included, through the woman's body, "the act of victory over his rival and of his surrender to him," just as Dagny too "felt Francisco's presence through Rearden's mind." When Dagny chooses John Galt, the purest shape of her desire and the full expression of her sense of self-worth, Rearden is left, as Francisco was before him, with only his maturity, his recaptured sense of being. Solitary, but not alone, for all three men and the woman are "in love—with the same thing, no matter what its forms." And in Rand's world, which is above all Aristotle's and Euclid's world, "A is A," as the title of her last section proclaims, all movement arises from the unmoved mover of legitimate self-love, and four people who are equal to the same first principle are equal to each other, as long as they live.

Essentially, Rand's novel portrays the victory of Aristotelian and Euclidean thought over Platonic and Planckian relativism. For them, as for John Galt, "reality" stays put and yields its truths to human observation. Only the villains celebrate, only the psychotic accept, the message of much twentieth-century physics and psychology, that matter is not solid nor perfectly predictable and that the mind is at some level simply "a collection of switches without shape." In this respect, in addition to being, as Mimi Gladstein argues, both a science fiction romance and a feminist model, *Atlas Shrugged* is genuinely a "novel of ideas," and it belongs, all 1,100 pages of it, on that reading list too.

Source: Judith Wilt, "On 'Atlas Shrugged,'" in *College English,* Vol. 40, No. 3, November, 1978, pp. 333–37.

Ruth Chapin Blackman

In the following excerpt, Blackman briefly looks at the America that Rand portrays in Atlas Shrugged.

In a statement published as a postscript to *Atlas Shrugged,* Ayn Rand has defined her philosophy, "in essence," as "the concept of man as a heroic being, with his own happiness as the moral purpose of his life, with productive achievement as his noblest activity, and reason as his only absolute."

Atlas Shrugged is [a] ... polemic inadequately disguised as a novel and designed to dramatize these views. The result is an astonishing mixture of anti-Communist manifesto, superman, and the lush lady novelist Ethel M. Dell—a novel that does its own purpose a disservice through caricature and oversimplification.

"

American political history is the history of struggle between individualism and the collective good, yet Miss Rand would, at the stroke of her wand, eliminate the whole area of working compromise, make an absolute of either extreme, and pit them against each other. It takes the heart out of her story."

Miss Rand postulates an America in a time of waning strength and production. The government is being delivered into the hands of the "looters," despicable men whose plundering is rationalized by mouthing the concept that the fruits of the strong belong to the weak: from every man according to his ability, to every man according to his need....

As the looters perpetrate increasingly repressive and senseless measures on the economy, chaos grows and the able men, frustrated at every turn, take to deserting their jobs and disappearing. Their establishment of a Shangri-la in the Colorado mountains is a neat but unconvincing aspect of a story that already has too little contact with reality.

For one tries in vain to project the world of *Atlas Shrugged* from the familiar world of contemporary America. There is no connecting link. On what grounds, for example, does Miss Rand postulate a failing economy?—the American economy today is booming. She does not say.

To be sure, her two types are familiar minorities at either end of the political scale, neither one of them as important as the great middle ground between. American political history is the history of struggle between individualism and the collective good, yet Miss Rand would, at the stroke of her wand, eliminate the whole area of working compromise, make an absolute of either extreme, and pit them against each other. It takes the heart out of her story.

Miss Rand properly condemns the whining mentality which demands handouts as its natural

right. But she minimizes the philanthropy that is not a gesture of moral weakness but of strength; and she completely ignores the fact that brilliant intelligence and achievement may not always be accompanied by conscience, that the figures of the past whom she most admires have been called by others—and with reason—robber barons....

Had Rearden and the other men of integrity in the book exercised their political responsibilities with the devotion which they gave to their jobs, whether industry, philosophy, or science, the looters would not have taken over. This is the drama that Miss Rand's melodramatic fabrications lack.

Source: Ruth Chapin Blackman, "Controversial Books by Ayn Rand and Caitlin Thomas: 'Atlas Shrugged,'" in *Christian Science Monitor,* October 10, 1957, p. 13.

Sources

Branden, Barbara, *The Passion of Ayn Rand,* Doubleday, 1986.

Branden, Nathaniel, *Judgment Day: My Years with Ayn Rand,* Houghton Mifflin, 1989.

———, *Who Is Ayn Rand? An Analysis of the Novels of Ayn Rand,* Random House, 1962.

Chamber,Whittaker, "Big Sister Is Watching You," in *National Review,* December 28, 1957, pp. 594-96.

Chamberlain, John, "Ayn Rand's Political Parable and Thundering Melodrama," in *New York Herald Book Review,* October 6, 1957, pp. 1, 9.

Chapin Blackman, Ruth, "Controversial Books by Ayn Rand and Caitlin Thomas: *Atlas Shrugged,*" in *The Christian Science Monitor,* October 19, 1957, p. 13.

Donegan, Patricia, "A Point of View," in *Commonweal,* November 8, 1957, pp. 155-56.

Gladstein, Mimi R., "Ayn Rand and Feminism: An Unlikely Alliance," in *College English* Vol. 39, No. 6, February 1978, pp. 25-30.

———, *The Ayn Rand Companion,* Greenwood Press, 1984.

Hicks, Granville, "A Parable of Buried Talents," in *New York Times Book Review,* October 13, 1957, pp. 4-5.

Merrill, Ronald E., *The Ideas of Ayn Rand,* Open Court, 1991.

Olster, Stacey, "Something Old, Something New, Something Borrowed, Something (Red, White, and) Blue: Ayn Rand's *Atlas Shrugged* and Objectivist Ideology," in *The Other Fifties,* ed. Joel Forman, Villard, 1997, pp. 288-306.

For Further Study

Branden, Barbara, and Nathaniel Branden, *Who Is Ayn Rand?* Random House, 1962.

Rand's disciples and close associates get a glimpse at the author's private life. The book was later repudiated as too limited by only the information Rand authorized for publication.

Davis, L. J., "Ayn Rand's Last Shrug," in *Washington Post,* December 12, 1982, p.7.

The article reviews Rand's non-fiction work, *Philosophy: Who Needs It?* and its resonance in her final novel, *Atlas Shrugged.*

Ellis, Albert, *Is Objectivism A Religion?* Lyle Stuart, Inc., 1968.

Ellis finds faults in Rand's philosophy and challenges her views, at the same time critiquing Objectivism's cult-like following.

Machan, Tibor, "Ayn Rand: A Contemporary Heretic?" in *The Occasional Review,* Vol. 4, Winter, 1976, pp. 133-50. Machan outlines Rand's heretical opinions in five philosophical areas: metaphysics, ethics, epistemology, politics, and aesthetics.

O'Neill, William F., *With Charity Toward None: An Analysis of Ayn Rand's Philosophy,* Philosophical Library, 1971. One of the very few even-handed reviews of Rand's work. The book explores the rationality of Objectivist principles and empirically tests their validity.

Wilt, Judith, "On *Atlas Shrugged,*" in *College English,* Vol. 40, No. 3, November, 1978, pp. 333-37. In this essay, Wilt discusses *Atlas Shrugged* as a feminist work of self-awareness and rebirth and praises its passion.

Breathing Lessons

Anne Tyler

1988

A highly regarded author of short stories and novels, Anne Tyler is known for her fiction that explores the vicissitudes of human existence in late twentieth-century America. Tyler's readers readily identify with her complex characters and see their own experiences mirrored in her fiction. She often makes her readers laugh out loud, but she also makes them think—about life, loss, family, death, and all aspects of the human condition.

Breathing Lessons is Tyler's eleventh book. Winner of the 1989 Pulitzer Prize for fiction as well as *Time* magazine's Book of the Year, it is the story of the "run-of-the-mill marriage" of Ira and Maggie Moran. The story explores the joys and tribulations of marriage, as Maggie and Ira travel from Baltimore to a funeral and home in one day.

Author Biography

On October, 25, 1941, Anne Tyler was born in Minneapolis, Minnesota. Her parents were members of the Society of Friends and liberal activists, and the family lived in a series of Quaker communes across the Midwest and South of the United States. Anne read voraciously as a child and began write stories at the age of seven. When she was eleven, the family moved to Raleigh, North Carolina, where she attended public school for the first time. The alienation she experienced at that time became a recurring theme in her writing.

Tyler attended Duke University on academic scholarship. During her time there, she studied creative writing and Russian. Although she wrote simply for "something to do," she received the Anne Flexner award for creative writing twice. Her short stories were published throughout her college years. At nineteen, Tyler graduated from Duke after three years, with a B.A. in Russian.

In 1961, after a year of graduate studies at Columbia University, Tyler returned to Duke. There, she worked as a Russian language bibliographer until 1963. She married and moved to Montreal, Quebec, where her husband studied medicine. While there, she worked as an assistant librarian and wrote her first and second novels, *Morning Ever Comes* (1964) and *The Tin Can Tree* (1965).

In 1967 Tyler and her family moved to Baltimore, Maryland. Once the girls were in school, Tyler began writing full time. In 1970 she published *A Slipping-Down Life,* followed by *The Clock Winter* in 1972. Her 1985 novel, *The Accidental Tourist,* was made into the film of the same name in 1988.

Anne Tyler

Plot Summary

Part One: The Funeral

The novel opens with Ira reflecting on the amount of waste in the world, including his own life. Ira runs his father's picture framing business in Baltimore, while Maggie works as a nurse in a nursing home. On this Saturday they are preparing to go to a funeral, and Maggie is picking up their car from the mechanic's shop. As she drives home, she listens to a call-in radio program, and is convinced that the woman announcing her impending marriage is former daughter-in-law, Fiona. She collects Ira and they set out for the funeral in rural Pennsylvania.

Ira and Maggie argue in the car as he grows increasingly impatient with her wish to drop in and see Fiona and their granddaughter, Leroy. Nearly lost, they stop to buy a map and get coffee in a small town. While Ira checks the map, Maggie confides her family woes in a waitress—much to her husband's disgust. They start driving again, but Maggie becomes so upset that she demands to be let out at the side of the road. A half an hour passes while she constructs an imaginary new life and remembers a brief infatuation with a distinguished nursing home resident. Ira picks her up and they continue their journey.

The Morans are the first to arrive at the church for the funeral. The widow—Maggie's oldest friend, Serena—arrives, and informs them that she wants them to recreate her wedding service as a memorial. This will involve singing the songs from the wedding; in Maggie and Ira's case, a duet of "Love is a Many Splendored Thing." In a key scene, Serena advises Maggie to "throw it all away": to allow things and people to pass out of her life. As other mourners arrive, they either agree or refuse to recreate Serena's wedding ceremony.

Later, Serena shows a film of her marriage ceremony from many years ago. The crowd watches the soundless images and there is much amusement as well as sorrow. Maggie recalls how she first met Ira. Suddenly in love with him all over again, she goes to find him and they begin to make love. Serena catches them at it and throws them out of the house.

Part Two: Breakdown

As in the beginning of the novel, Ira reflects on the opportunities he has missed and the regrets he has about his life. This section is narrated from Ira's perspective, as the couple begins the drive home and Maggie tries to convince him to visit Fiona. On the way, they become stuck behind an erratic driver who nearly runs them off the road.

Maggie gets revenge by motioning that the car's wheel is about to come off, but instantly regrets her actions when she sees that the driver is an elderly black man. Remorseful, she forces Ira to turn back to see what happened.

The driver, Mr. Otis, has pulled over; Ira and Maggie pull over to help him. Nothing they say can convince him that his car is okay. The Morans take him to a gas station while he awaits his nephew's tow truck. As Maggie falls into a comfortable familiarity with Mr. Otis, Ira reflects on the emotional "waste" his wife has caused him. The nephew arrives, and the Morans prepare to leave. As they do Mr. Otis comes out with his words of advice, similar to that of Serena's: "Spill it! Spill it all, I say! No way *not* to spill it!" Ira agrees to pay a visit to Fiona.

Part Three: Homecoming

Maggie reflects on her life: the absence of her granddaughter, then her cat, and her humidifier. It seems that she can't keep anything in perspective. She remembers Fiona's pregnancy—her "breathing lessons." When they arrive at Fiona's house, Leroy doesn't recognize them. While Ira teaches his granddaughter how to play Frisbee, Maggie tries to make Fiona agree to try again with her ex-husband. Maggie invents a story to persuade Fiona how much her son, Jesse, still loves her: she claims that he takes Fiona's old soapbox with him wherever he goes. Fiona, still in love with him, agrees to come to Baltimore for the rest of the weekend. Leroy is overjoyed; she is fascinated by her father, who hasn't visited her in several years.

In an extended flashback sequence, Maggie remembers Jesse and Fiona's courtship and marriage. After Jesse joined a band and dropped out of high school, Fiona was one of his "groupies." After she got pregnant, Maggie persuaded her to give him a chance. Maggie lied to Fiona, therefore establishing a pattern of deception with Fiona. The marriage proves rocky, but everyone loves Leroy as soon as she is born. A shaky peace holds until all of Maggie's lies are revealed. Fiona leaves with Leroy and never comes back.

Back in the present, the travelers stop in at a grocery store and buy Leroy's favorite food. As they return home, Jesse arrives. Fiona asks him where her soapbox is, and of course he doesn't remember a soapbox; it is clear that Maggie has made this up too. Ira tells her the truth: Jesse is already living with a woman, and that he is incapable of sustaining a relationship. Furious, Jesse walks out.

Fiona and Leroy leave too. Shocked and numb, Maggie goes upstairs with ice cream. Her daughter is packing to go away to school. Ira plays solitaire. In denial, Maggie begins a scheme to have Leroy come and live with them and go to school in Baltimore. Ira hushes her and she calms down, asking him what they will have to do for the next twenty years. They hold each other until she becomes peaceful, and then she goes to bed. Tomorrow, like today, they have "a long car trip to make."

Characters

Durwood Clegg

Durwood is one of the few people with whom Maggie has kept in touch from high school. She turned down a date with him because, like her own father, Durwood is "too pliant … too supplicating." When Ira refuses to sing with Maggie at the memorial service, Durwood volunteers to help.

Ben Gabriel

Former owner of a power-tool company, Mr. Gabriel is a patient at the Silver Threads Nursing where Maggie works. For a short time she develops an infatuation with him, until she realizes that he reminds her of her husband.

Serena Gill

Serena is a childhood friend of Maggie's. When her husband dies, Maggie and Ira embark on a road trip to attend the memorial service. An eccentric woman, Serena displays her own *gypsy* style of dress at the service: sandals, a red dress with a v-neck cut and rhinestone sunburst, and a black shawl. In addition, she decides to reenact her wedding at the funeral. Most of the original participants are present, and she asks each to perform the same duties as they did at the wedding. This is ridiculous to everyone, but they indulge her.

Lamont

Lamont is Mr. Otis' earnest nephew. He is responsible and careful young man. When he comes to help his uncle after his automobile mishap, he warns him that he has to be more careful and less trusting.

Daisy Moran

Daisy is youngest of the Moran children. She exemplifies the overachiever: she toilet-trained herself and began waking up early in first grade to lay out her own clothes. Daisy wants to be a quantum physicist and has a scholarship to an Ivy League school. She criticizes her mother, and sometimes seems to barely put up with her.

To her father, Ira, Daisy is far from being normal or, in some sense, human. She seems to have skipped her own youth, never joining in any childish mischief. Ira sees Daisy's "pinched-faced" expression of disapproval as a reflection of his own, and as a sign that Daisy has voluntarily taken on heavy responsibilities prematurely. Daisy is her father's daughter and Ira is painfully aware of it. She proves to be the opposite of her brother, Jesse.

Dorrie Moran

Ira's other older sister, Dorrie, suffers from seizures that momentarily paralyze her left leg. She is also mentally challenged. Dorrie carries around a suitcase full of her most prized possessions.

Fiona Moran

Fiona is Jesse's ex-wife who now lives in Cartwheel, Pennsylvania with her daughter, Leroy. She is a pretty blonde who fell for Jesse, even knowing that he was a musician without prospects or a high school diploma. Tired of living with the Morans and tired of Jesse's incompetence, she divorced him. Now living on her own, she works as a beautician and is studying electrolysis in order to diversify her skills.

Ira Moran

Ira is Maggie's husband. He is a responsible husband and father, and supports his father and two sisters in addition to his family. Ira represents a man in the midst of a mid-age crisis: he regrets some of the choices he has made, and mourns the opportunities that he missed. In a sense, he feels trapped. He deals with these feelings by playing the game of Solitaire.

Ira loves his wife Maggie. Still, he wishes she wouldn't intervene in other people's lives. When she does, he becomes the harsh voice of reason and truth. When he interferes, it is to save Maggie from being blamed for the failure of her schemes.

Jesse Moran

Jesse is the oldest child of Maggie and Ira. Loved and resented by his father, who constantly points out his shortcomings, he is indulged by his mother. He is a high school dropout, and the lead singer of a rock band, Spin the Cat. Like Maggie, Jesse is a dreamer; he is also wild and irresponsi-

Media Adaptations

- The television film adaptation of *Breathing Lessons* was released in 1994. Under the direction of John Erman, the movie starred James Garner, Joanne Woodward, Paul Winfield, and Kathryn Erbe.

---

ble. He is a poor father and was an unfaithful husband to Fiona.

Junie Moran

Junie is Ira's older sister. She suffers from agoraphobia, but is able to momentarily overcome these feelings when she accepts Maggie's idea to go out in public wearing a red wig. The wig enables Junie to momentarily escape the limitations of her condition.

Leroy Moran

Seven-year-old Leroy is Fiona and Jesse's daughter. Much to Maggie's dismay, she hardly remembers her grandparents.

Maggie Moran

Maggie is an impulsive woman who is married to Ira. A middle-class American housewife, she also works as a geriatric nurse and considers herself a natural caregiver. She knows that people consider her flighty and a bit foolish sometimes, especially in comparison to her sensible and predictable husband. A very sensitive and caring woman, tends to put the needs of other people in front of her own; in a sense, she neglects herself and concentrates on everyone else around her.

In her concern for others, she has made many mistakes. For example, she lies to Fiona in order to save her son's marriage, not realizing that she is hurting others in the process and ignoring the truth. Moreover, when she realizes how lucky she is to have Ira at the funeral, she tries to express her love in a physical manner. Obviously this is inappropriate at a funeral, and she hurts the feelings of Serena, the widow.

Sam Moran

Sam is Ira's elderly father. He sits in his rocking chair above the frame shop all day.

Daniel Otis

Mr. Otis is an elderly African-American man who almost drives the Morans off the road with his car. In response, Maggie prompts Ira to pass the car so she can pull a prank on the driver: she signals that he is losing one of his wheels. When she realizes that he is an older man, Maggie regrets her actions and begs Ira to stop and help him. They cannot convince him that his car is okay; instead, he contacts his nephew to come out and get him.

Anita Palermo

Anita is Serena's mother. Maggie always knew her as a proud woman, until they day she helps Serena move her to the nursing home.

Mrs. Stuckey

Mrs. Stuckey is Fiona's mother. She is a harsh and judgmental woman. Maggie is jealous of her close relationship with Leroy.

Sugar

See Elizabeth Tilghman

Elizabeth Tilghman

Elizabeth Tilghman (also known as Sugar) was the class beauty and an old friend of Serena's. She is concerned with appearances and looks "more like a widow than the widow herself."

Themes

Family

The central theme of Tyler's novel is the dynamic of modern American families. Within that theme, Tyler focuses on the fact that an individual's initial sense of identity derives from his or her relationship with his or her family. For Tyler, the family acts as force on an individual, in both positive and negative ways. In *Breathing Lessons,* each character has an individual interpretation of the concept of family that coincides with their understanding of their own identity. For example, Ira feels trapped by his family to the point where he felt that "his sisters' hands dragged him down the way drowning victims drag down whoever tries to rescue them." This view of the family extends from Ira's perception of himself as someone cheated out of his dreams. One of those dreams is that a family is loving, loud, boisterous, and fun. Ira's view of his own family as a trap is mirrored in his job as a picture framer. For Ira, the image never changes and it never matches his envisaged ideal portrait.

Maggie's idealized family is busy, exciting, and flexible: she believes that the family can be created with whomever she chooses to make family. In her frenetic and endless family creation, she resembles a mother hen more worried about her extended brood than about herself. Maggie's meddling in the affairs of Jesse and Fiona exposes her concern not so much with marriage, but with keeping her family together. Unlike Ira, Maggie does not give much thought to her own blood relations. Thus, it is ironic that she cites bloodline as her reason for stealing her granddaughter away from Mrs. Stuckey, stating "we're Leroy's grandparents till the day we die."

Marriage

The question of what an ideal marriage recurs in the novel. Everyone has a theory about marriage. Serena married because it was time to marry. Maggie married because she thought she had found her soul mate. Jesse thinks of marriage as a bad habit, the "same old song and dance." As the novel points out, there are rituals and a repetitive pattern to marriage—"the same jokes and affectionate passwords"—and the same "abiding loyalty and gestures of support and consolations."

The title of the novel metaphorically captures the answer to the question, according to Maggie and Ira. Regular breathing, the exchange of gases or the giving and taking of breath, is life. Similarly, the life of marriage is full of giving and taking. During the novel's one day, Maggie and Ira reveal the many layers of their twenty-eight years together. They are constantly arguing and making up, remembering petty feuds and wondrous delights. When they speak aloud they are not "bickering" but "compiling our two views of things." Marriage is all about sharing the everyday feel of life with another person, and it is this aspect that most bothers the widowed Serena. As she tells Maggie over the phone, she is realizing that Max is not present for discussions about "what the plumbing's up to, and how the red ants have come back in the kitchen." When Maggie offers to discuss the mundane, Serena answers, "but they're not your red ants too, don't you see? I mean you and I are not in this together."

Mr. Otis and his wife, Duluth, present another view of marriage. As their nephew Lamont describes it, their marriage consists of childish bickering. Mr. Otis corrects him, insisting that his marriage with Duluth is full of life and passion. To Mr. Otis, marriage should be something you can look back on fondly from the nursing home. Mr. Otis says he will remember his partnership with Duluth as "a real knock-down, drag-out, heart-and-soul type of couple." Anything else would be dull and worthless, and liable to fall apart like Lamont's marriage.

Human Condition

Tyler's characters negotiate their lives and their relationships with one another in what critic Alice Petry has described as "a messy chaotic world of happenstance." For Tyler, happenstance is what life is all about, and her characters deal with situations many readers will understand. The ways in which Tyler's characters carry out their negotiation through everyday life differ. These disparate ideas and ways of managing give rise to the humor and the tension of the novel.

The clearest example stems from a comparison of the Morans. Ira is very serious, as he tries to play with the "hand" he has been dealt in the form of a full house: crazy siblings, "ailing" father, incompetent son, and an introverted daughter. On the other hand, Maggie is playing games. As Ira reflects:

> And his wife! He loved her, but he couldn't stand how she refused to take her own life seriously. She seemed to believe it was a sort of practice life, something she could afford to play around with as if they offered second and third chances to get it right. She was always making clumsy, impetuous rushes toward nowhere in particular—side trips, random detours.

Serena (a play on the word serene) and Mr. Otis suggest that people have to step back and look at themselves once in a while. Doing this enables the individual to see his blind spots. Mr. Otis offers this lesson in self-improvement through the parable of his dog, Bessie. Bessie was a smart dog, but nevertheless when she played fetch and the ball landed on a chair, Bessie would go after it through the spindles of the back of the chair. All she had to do was go around, but she insisted on getting the ball her way. Bessie was "blind in spots." Humans do the same thing; everyone desperately wants to have things their way. Mr. Otis believe that if people would stop a moment and examine their own situation, they could then see the obstacle which

Topics for Further Study

- The legal issues of child custody and visitation rights have become more complex recently. What rights have the courts awarded to grandparents? What is your view on the issue?

- What is the role of game playing in the novel? How do games demonstrate the motif of breathing lessons or support Tyler's large themes?

- Considered to be a triumph of urban revitalization, how is Harborplace doing today? Locate some pictures or film of the area and provide a description. Has it exceeded the hopes of the city planners in Baltimore?

- Tyler's novel returns to the topic of the nursing home repeatedly. Research the quality of nursing home care across the United States in the late 1980s. How does it compare with the care given in today's nursing homes? What does the placing of senior citizens in nursing homes say about the value our society places on the elderly, then or now?

---

prevents them from getting what they most want in life.

Style

Point of View

Breathing Lessons utilizes a third-person omniscient narrative, with the middle section told from Ira's point of view. The first and last sections are Maggie's interpretations of events. The two viewpoints allow both character to provide their perspective on their lives and long marriage.

Comedy of Manners

Works that are considered "comedy of manners" are witty and cerebral. In such works, the characters struggle to uphold appearances and social standards. The plot normally revolves around a sexual affair, or another sort of scandal. Like all comedies, the comedy of manners uses humor to teach a lesson. The greatest modern artist who wrote such works was the French playwright, Moliere. He pokes fun of society's morality, especially in terms of the religious hypocrisy that marked the seventeenth century. A more recent example in English is Oscar Wilde. His *Importance of Being Earnest* (1899) is a brilliant examination of the hypocrisy in British society.

Tyler uses comedy throughout her fiction. Much of the comedy in *Breathing Lessons* develops out of embarrassing situations that occur as a result of bad manners. It is not proper on any occasion to sneak into your host's bedroom and have sex there with your husband. It is especially improper to do so during a funeral dinner. Tyler pulls this off, in part because the reader will believe that Ira and Maggie have given up sex. The subtle touches are the key; Serena stares at Ira with "his open zipper and his shirttail flaring out." Yet the scene doesn't simply end; Maggie tries to put a good face on it, and says, "well, bye now!" to everyone.

Tyler's humor is often tragicomic; the situations are funny because no one is hurt. The best example occurs in the beginning of the novel. Maggie's absent-minded collision with the Pepsi truck is comedic only because no one was injured or died. Other moments of humor are due to unusual associations and juxtapositions. A love song is written on a coupon, which Maggie later hands to a store clerk. Religion is mocked when a billboard with a spiritual message is given the same attention as a billboard with an advertisement.

Time

One of the original sources for dramatic theory in Western European literature is Aristotle's *Poetics,* composed around 330 BCE. In this study, he establishes rules to govern the construction of a comedy or tragedy. One area of the Aristotelian rules gives us the "unities": unity of action, unity of place, and unity of time. According to the rule of the unity of time, the action of a drama should take place in just one day. Tyler's use of Aristotle's rule frames the action: the novel begins when Maggie and Ira oversleep, and it ends with them going back to sleep.

Another way time is used by Tyler is the flashback. This technique disrupts the chronology of the day with episodes of reminiscence on the parts of Maggie or Ira. A flashback differs from the narrative stories that, for example, Mr. Otis tells. Flashbacks, in this novel, are internal to Maggie or Ira's mind. Moreover, a flashback can be interrupted by someone and then returned to, sometimes more clearly. This happens to Ira when he remembers the infamous trip to Harborplace, both during and after the run-in with Mr. Otis. It is during the second flashback that he has his benevolent epiphany, which he soon forgets.

Picaresque

In its early form, the picaresque novel resembles the loosely structured tales of romance, such as the stories from the Arthurian cycle, *Tristram and Iseult,* or *Gargantua and Pantagruel.* Essentially a first-person narrative, the picaresque novel chronicles the accidental adventures and rewards experienced by a knight-errant while on his quest. The adventures often include conflicts with other knights or dragons, and the reward ranges from wisdom to money or gold. Since *Don Quixote,* which was written in the early seventeenth century, the picaresque hero typically has a less serious sidekick, acting as comic relief. The story form from that time on begins to take on humorous overtones, until it becomes downright bawdy, with Henry Fielding's eighteenth-century tale of *Tom Jones.*

Breathing Lessons employs many picaresque elements. The serious protagonist is Ira, on a quest to get to the funeral and back home. He wants to follow the map from point A to point B. Maggie is not so linear and would prefer to go with the flow, "all we've got to do is watch the road signs." Maggie is the Sancho Panza to Ira's Don Quixote—an amusing, light-hearted companion. She is in charge of navigation, but she didn't bring "that map." Instead, she dreams up a map of adventure: to rescue the fair Leroy from her imprisonment in Cartwheel. Accidents and distractions lead to many smaller adventures. Like all good picaresque tales, the reader is sure that tomorrow's journey with daughter Daisy will be anything but uneventful.

Historical Context

Political Apathy

Poor economic conditions at the end of the 1970s led to a change in the political landscape of America. In 1980 Ronald Reagan won the presidential election with only 51.6 percent of the popular vote. His "landslide victory" resulted from a turnout of only fifty-four percent of the voting-age population. In other words, only twenty-seven percent of all eligible voters elected Reagan to office. Many commentators expressed disappointment over voter apathy and the lack of democratic participation.

The Decade of Greed and the Working Class

In 1981 Reagan restructured the tax code. His theory that deep tax cuts would be offset by an increase in employment rates and tax revenue through greater capital investment—known as trickle-down theory—was proven false, just as Nobel Prize-winning economist Wassily Leontief guaranteed. According to *Forbes Magazine,* the richest one percent of Americans gained a combined total of one trillion dollars between 1979 and 1990. In other words, a greater stratification between rich and poor was the result of early 1980s economic policy.

Race Relations

In a 1988 *Newsweek* poll, seventy-one percent of African Americans concurred with the statement that the United States government was not doing enough to help blacks in the United States. The year before, neo-Nazis and Ku Klux Klan members assaulted civil rights marchers celebrating the recently established Martin Luther King Jr. holiday in Forsyth County, Georgia. The Klanwatch Project of the Southern Poverty Law Center documented forty-five arson cases and cross burnings, as well as hundreds of acts of vandalism against African Americans between 1985 and 1987.

Meanwhile, although the numbers of new recruits to the Klan increased, so did the number of people that attended counter-Klan rallies. Louis Farrakhan, who represented a minority of the African American community, antagonized many people with his speeches against Jews and whites. In 1989, David Duke, a former Grand Wizard of the Klan, won a seat in the state legislature of Louisiana, much to the embarrassment of the Republican Party.

The Reverend Jesse Jackson encouraged a policy of racial harmony. He challenged the democratic establishment by mounting a second presidential campaign. While not endorsed by the Democratic Party, he became a hero to many black Americans. Under his leadership, the Rainbow Coalition became a political force on behalf of the "rejected and despised." In response, the Republican Party attempted to attract new minority members and put forth the idea of the party as a "big tent" tolerant of differing opinions.

World Affairs

Peace initiatives all over the world were prevalent in 1988. The Iran-Iraq war ended in a tentative cease-fire in August. Soviet troops began to withdraw from Afghanistan. In December of 1988, PLO Chairman Yasser Arafat gave an address to the United Nations in which he rejected military violence, recognized the existence of Israel, and declared that only a political solution will resolve the Palestinian-Israeli conflict. His words were greeted warmly by all sides, but Arafat lost this initiative when he publicly supported Iraqi leader Saddam Hussein during the Gulf War.

In Burma, a period of hope known as the "Burmese Spring" seemed to be softening the dictatorial powers ruling the country. From March to September, hundreds of thousands of students and young people demonstrated in favor of democratic reforms. Finally, the army cracked down on the demonstrators in a gruesome display of force beginning September 18. Hundreds of people were killed, dissidents were jailed, and the country's name was changed to Myanmar.

Critical Overview

It wasn't until after her fifth novel and Gail Godwin and John Updike wrote positive reviews of her work that Tyler garnered critical and commercial attention. Since then, she has attracted a large following. While Tyler is considered an excellent writer and novelist, her work does not fit with current academic interest and her long-term reputation is uncertain.

Breathing Lessons received the Pulitzer Prize in 1989. Initial reviews of the novels derided the comparison of Maggie to Lucy, the character portrayed by Lucille Ball on *I Love Lucy.* Critics felt that the comparison with television's favorite comedic character was not appropriate in a work of complex literature. Another focus of early reviews was the many digressions from the main movement of the story.

Many critics fail to move beyond the subject matter of Tyler's novels. They have difficulty getting past the fact that Tyler writes about domesticity. However, many critics are captivated by Tyler's techniques. Gene Koppel found Tyler's game theory approach to domestic manners intriguing. He asserted that *"Breathing Lessons* makes an unambiguous point about the need for the

Joanne Woodward and James Garner in the 1994 TV adaptation of Breathing Lessons.

game-spirit to be accompanied by a sense of responsibility and by the ability to endure through adversity."

Several commentators have focused on Tyler's employment of African American characters in her novels. Alice Hall Petry addressed this issue; she surveys the ways in which black characters in other Tyler novels embody practical knowledge that the main white characters are looking for:

> Perhaps Mr. Otis, that angel bearing a message of survival, could ascertain these truths precisely because he, as an elderly black man, had always been an outsider. As someone excluded from the mainstream of southern white society for decades, he did not have the luxury of falling into the counterproductive lifestyle of those with more opportunities, more education, and more money. He had to learn to see things aright in order to survive.

Petry concluded: "thanks to the wisdom and dignity of her black characters, Anne Tyler's novels—full of sudden death, dysfunctional families and disappointment—are indeed ultimately bright books of life."

Barbara A. Bennett focused on Tyler's humor. Bennett maintained that Tyler's use of humor makes ordinary times and ordinary people interesting. She went on to reveal the four categories of

humor, "each of which serves a specific purpose in extending the theme of miscommunication."

> (1) Linguistic errors that characters make either consciously or subconsciously; (2) The psychological shift or attempt to divert attention away from the real issue; (3) Inadequate words in communication; and (4) Non-traditional means of communication.

She then surveyed the comedic techniques Tyler utilizes, particularly an example of Freudian slips as well as a spoonerism in "You're just a twick!"

In his review, Richard Eder asserted that "Tyler only seems to be a realist." He means that though her style leads one to think that she is simply describing events and people in them, Tyler is actually imparting lessons about life to the readers and the characters. For example, Eder maintained that "weddings are Tyler's moments of truth, equivalent to Hemingway's hunting and fishing exploits, though funnier." Characteristically, these moments of truths and lesson learning are brought about by physical moments, similar to Henry Fielding's picaresque stories. "Tyler does not condemn her characters to stasis. She lets them move, though never as much as they think they are moving. She teaches them to blunder into the art of letting life subvert them." There are risks to Tyler's methods, according to Eder:

Subversion—the parade that brings clowns, the clowns that bring a parade—is her art too, and the risk that goes with it. Pick up too many outriders, particularly if they are dedicated to slipping spokes in the wheel, and your vehicle slows. Momentum is Tyler's difficulty; even in her best novels there are moments when vitality flags and things bog down.

Eder hinted that this may be part of Tyler's technique: her novels imitate the automobile, constantly being renewed and bashed up again.

Criticism

Tabitha McIntosh-Byrd

Tabitha McIntosh-Byrd is a doctoral candidate and English literature instructor at the University of Pennsylvania. In the following essay, she analyzes the use of formal, biological, and "game" narratives of time in Anne Tyler's Breathing Lessons.

When Maggie Moran hears the question, "What Makes an Ideal Marriage?" on the radio, it causes her to crash her car. This question recurs throughout the novel, and is asked and answered by multiple characters at key stages of the day. It also brings together the novel's central imagery and motifs. The car is the "vehicle" through which both the plot and the Morans' marriage will be propelled—a literal mode of travel and a metaphoric representation of life itself. Maggie's relationship to time, odometers, and topography mirrors her personal journey to an ambiguous destination, while Ira's obsession with speed and efficiency works in an opposite, though equally revelatory, manner. In the final analysis, both Morans must realize that there is no "final destination" that can be reached by either shortcuts or circumnavigation. Like Ira's interminable card playing, there is only the random chance of the game.

The structure of Tyler's novel acts as a metacommentary on these major thematic concerns. The book is organized by an extremely rigid chronological framework that is undermined and interrupted by flashback sequences. It thus conforms to and deviates from the dramatic "Unity of Time"—Aristotle's rule that establishes that the action of a drama should take place in a single day. *Breathing Lessons* begins when the Morans awake to go on a journey and ends with them falling asleep in expectation of another journey; this structure neatly

> Ira searches for a map—a formal structure composed of grids and squares through which to interpret the nonlinear landscape. He must "frame" the journey in the same way that he creates frames for his customers, elevating the "random" to the status of the "meaningful." Maggie, on the other hand, becomes obsessed by the *process* of their journey—watching the odometer to make sure that it corresponds with the road markers."

frames the narrative just as Ira literally provides "frames" in his job.

Within this framework lies a confused picture of a marriage. The narrative is told from both Maggie and Ira's perspective, tracing their memories and experiences as current events recall past ones. Like the chronological rigidity of the "present" story, the past is equally structured—organized as a series of layered versions of events that repeat and restate themselves until they arrive at a denouement in the final pages of the novel.

In this way, Maggie plays and replays her memories of Jesse, delaying her final recollection of events until circumstances force her to remember the traumatic end of his marriage in full. At the same time, this sequence of memories is directly mapped onto the unfolding of the present. Maggie's impulsive "white lie" that brought Jesse and Fiona together parallels her creation of a new lie to reunite them: the crib that Jesse was supposed to be building, and the soapbox which he is supposed to be keeping for Fiona's sake. The pressures of these two lies build in tandem within each storyline, reaching a head in both Maggie's present and past tenses at the same time.

What Do I Read Next?

- Star employee of Baltimore's Rent-a-Back, Inc., Barnaby Gaitlan is the protagonist of Tyler's most recent novel, *A Patchwork Planet* (1998). At the age of thirty, Barnaby is divorced and still not finished with college or free of a debt to his parents. He helps senior citizens sort out their attics and basements while they fend off attempts to put them in nursing homes.

- In Mary Pipher's study, *Another Country: Navigating the Emotional Terrain of Our Elders* (1999), she turns her attention to the psychological trauma and emotional difficulty surrounding what has become the last phase of life in America: the nursing home.

- Tyler's *Dinner at the Homesick Restaurant* (1982) relates the family history of the Tull family. Pearl is abandoned by her traveling salesman husband and has to raise three children on her own.

- *The Accidental Tourist* (1985) remains a favorite of many of Tyler's fans. The story concerns recently divorced travel writer Macon Leary, who hates travel. Macon moves home with his temperamental dog, Edward, and has a relationship with the dog's trainer.

- If anyone can be considered Tyler's inspiration, it is Eudora Welty. Her collection of short stories, *The Golden Apples* (1949), is Tyler's favorite collection. Most of the stories are set in Morgana, a town on the Mississippi Delta, and contains elements of Greek mythology.

- Flannery O'Connor's sense of the absurd and the gothic has been an influence on many writers. Her posthumous collection of short stories, *Everything That Rises Must Converge* (1965), focuses on a series of flawed characters with comic detachment.

Despite Ira's role as a vehicle of revelation in Maggie's repressed memories, he too is subject to repetition of the past until true recollection is achieved, as shown in his expanding versions of the infamous trip to Harborplace, both during and after the run-in with Mr. Otis. It is during the second flashback that he has epiphany—that "the real waste" of his life lies in not realizing how much he loves his family. For Ira, as for his wife, such revelations are both painful and traumatic, disrupting the extremely fixed chronological stories they tell about themselves. Both Morans experience the past as a disruption of their present myths of selfhood—transforming Maggie from a helper to a meddler, and Ira from a martyr to a willing victim. Indeed, both Morans literalize the homonymic relationship between time and nerves—the two meanings of the word "tense."

The insistent use of direct repetition—including whole pages of reproduced text as well as reiterated allusions and textual echoes—adds a rather different interpretive angle to this neat parallel of time and action. Instead of artistic satisfaction, the structural shadowing acts as a signifier of oppression, emphasizing the trapped lives of the characters contained within the pages of the text. Maggie and Ira are locked into a rigidly formal sequence of behavior. Ira is obsessed with maps and waste—his favorite books are mariner narratives. As Fiona says, these are just a more sophisticated version of the "How to get from A to B" stories "that men love so much."

What Ira does not understand is that he is as stuck in the endless dance of repetition and restatement as his wife is. Nowhere is this made clearer than in the first page of Part Two—a word for word recapitulation of the novel's opening page: "For the past several months now, Ira had been noticing the human race's wastefulness." The restatement transforms Ira's words from insight into a symptom of blindness: rather than "noticing," Ira is merely repeating himself. His words become the literal embodiment of the "waste" he decries: a surfeit of repeated language that empties out all inherent meaning from itself, carrying his character and the plot nowhere. Ira's thoughts become through this restatement, not so much valid self-analysis, but the lack of it—a pattern no more or less progressive than the "dance" of Jesse's arguments with his parents that he is impelled to repeat with Fiona.

This habituated behavior is exemplified by Ira's rigid habits: his endless games of Solitaire and his self-revealing whistling. Again, Tyler's use of chronology literalizes both metaphors and homonymic relationships between terms. Ira's moments of crisis and revelation are juxtaposed with his games so that a gradual picture emerges of him "playing the hand he has been dealt" in life as well as Solitaire. His "full house" of challenging and challenged family members requires as much ceaseless shuffling and reshuffling as his card games, and—like those card games—has been ritualistically complicated through his own choice. Ira's understanding that both are just "games" of his own devising is as delayed and hidden from him as is his habit of revealing his thoughts by whistling songs whose lyrics can be applied to the situation. Indeed, his chief irritation with Maggie is that *she* acts as the game playing interrupter of his linear rationalism. As he reflects:

> And his wife! He loved her, but he couldn't stand how she refused to take her own life seriously. She seemed to believe it was a sort of practice life, something she could afford to play around with as if they offered second and third chances to get it right. She was always making clumsy, impetuous rushes toward nowhere in particular—side trips, random detours.

In fact, Maggie is just as serious as he is, and just as unable to accept that the events into which she is thrust are as random and nonsequential as a hand of cards. Serena makes this controlling metaphor explicit when she advises Maggie to let go of her emotional attachments to the past with the words, "Discard! Discard!" Though Ira considers his wife full of "clumsy, impetuous rushes," and though Maggie's narrative persona appears to fulfill this by shifting with seeming random through experiential time, it is Serena who realizes that her old friend's mind is as bound by formal structure as Ira's. Maggie's "side-trips" to the past occur for deliberate reasons, triggered by specific stresses and functional needs. Like Ira, she is obsessed with "end games." For Ira, these are shortcuts and navigation. For Maggie they are destinations, deaths, and happy endings.

Nowhere is this division between the spouses more apparent than in their relationship to traveling. Ira searches for a map—a formal structure composed of grids and squares through which to interpret the nonlinear landscape. He must "frame" the journey in the same way that he creates frames for his customers, elevating the "random" to the status of the "meaningful." Maggie, on the other hand, becomes obsessed by the *process* of their journey—watching the odometer to make sure that it corresponds with the road markers. The tension of waiting for the gauges to synchronize causes her to reach the point of exhaustion. As she says, "This is making me a nervous wreck.... I feel like I've been through a ringer." Her own ritualistic pattern formation is neatly uncovered in this small vignette—Maggie is a woman obsessed with resolutions and synchronicities. Her nearly hysterical need to make the miles and markers correspond is a displacement of her equally hysterical need to make the milestones of her family correspond to the rhythm of the imagined "Ideal Marriage" of the opening pages. Like Ira, she refuses to accept that there is no overarching pattern to life, and that she must "discard" half of her hand in order to achieve peace.

Less obvious, but no less formally significant, is the use of biological time as a structural device both in Tyler's novel and in her presentation of Maggie's self-awareness. Maggie is a woman standing at a very specific point in her physiological chronology: menopause. As Virginia Schaefer Carroll points out, Tyler's heroine is in the middle of the "climacteric"—"a sequence of emotional and physiological transitions experienced by women from age thirty-five to sixty." The essential, unstated fact that lies at the heart of *Breathing Lessons* is Maggie's approaching menopause.

When this is taken into account, her random "dashes" and side trips attain central points of departure and arrival—the need to create a stable identity that is not based on motherhood. The apparently random digressions attain new meaning: all of Maggie's memories can be seen to be specifically tied to her need to be needed, evidenced in her remembered or imagined roles as a nurse's aide, a wife, a lover, and a mother. As in so many key motifs of the novel, this revelation into character motivation is given in part through literalized metaphors: in Maggie's career as well as her sense of self-worth she can only understand herself as a "care giver."

The fact that all of these issues are tied together in one central sense of loss is made clear in Maggie's pivotal conversation with Serena at the funeral. In the only direct reference to menopause in the novel, Serena advises her friend to:

Let it all go! … You don't have any choice…. That's what it comes down to in the end." You start shucking off your children from the day you give birth. Throw out the toys in the basement. Move to a smaller house.

Though menopause "delights" Serena, Maggie is horrified at the thought of letting go, and her response lays bare her sense of herself as "career carer":

I don't feel I'm letting go; I feel they're taking things away from me. My son's grown up and my daughter's leaving for college and they're talking at the nursing home about laying off some of the workers.

Maggie is afraid of being made "redundant"—both literally (in her job), and metaphorically (as a mother). When this biological chronology is factored into an understanding of the rest of the chronological devices at play in *Breathing Lessons,* the repetition and restatement of the novel's formal structure become suddenly clear. Like Maggie herself, the text experiences itself and is experienced as a series of repeated gatherings and purges—ritualistic reenactments of events, memories, and words that mirror the repeated motions of Maggie's menstrual cycle. When Maggie finally acknowledges the end of that cycle, the novel, like her motherhood, ends on a note as uncertain and ambiguous as her final question: "Oh, Ira … what are we two going to live for, the rest of our lives?"

Source: Tabitha McIntosh-Byrd, in an essay for *Novels for Students,* Gale, 2000.

Gene Koppel

In the following essay, Koppel discusses the game playing in Tyler's Breathing Lessons *and the assertion that a balance between game playing and responsibility is necessary to live successfully.*

When Maggie Moran, a nursing assistant in a home for the elderly and the central character of Anne Tyler's novel *Breathing Lessons,* tries to locate a favorite patient during a fire drill, the resulting fiasco bears more than a coincidental resemblance to a slapstick scene from an *I Love Lucy* episode. Maggie ends up in a part of the home off-limits to her and leaps into a laundry cart to conceal herself when she thinks she detects the approach of a supervisor:

Absurd, she knew it instantly. She was cursing herself even as she sank among the crumpled linens. She might have got away with it, though, except that she'd set the cart to rolling. Somebody grabbed it and drew it to a halt. A growly voice said, "What in the world?"

It is not a supervisor, but a fellow employee. The latter, however, having discovered Maggie inside the cart, mischievously calls over another attendant standing nearby and together the two noisily and rapidly push the cart down the corridor. At the end of Maggie's ride stand, of course, the two people who can embarrass her the most, Mrs. Inman, "the director of nursing for the entire home," and the man Maggie was seeking, Mr. Gabriel. The latter is a dignified gentleman whom Maggie admires and who (she believes) had admired Maggie for her competence and self-command. He will think of her this way no longer.

That Anne Tyler expects the reader to compare Maggie Moran's laundry-cart episode to television situation comedy is clearly indicated one page later:

Maybe [Mr. Gabriel] could view her as a sort of *I Love Lucy* type—madcap, fun-loving, full of irrepressible high spirits. That was one way to look at it. Actually, Maggie had never liked *I Love Lucy.* She thought the plots were so engineered—that dizzy woman's failures just built-in, just guaranteed. But maybe Mr. Gabriel felt differently.

But Mr. Gabriel is not amused by his real-life Lucy; his idealization of Maggie ends with this incident. The reader's interest in Maggie, however, continues. Unlike Mr. Gabriel, the reader has never had illusions about Maggie. That aspects of her character are similar to Lucy Ricardo's has probably occurred to him before. For example, in the opening scene of the novel Maggie calls for the family car at the body shop; the moment she pulls into the street she collides with a truck [she had turned on her radio to a local talk show and mistakenly thought she heard the voice of her former daughter-in-law announcing an approaching second marriage]. Hearing the crash, the manager of the body shop rushes out; when he yells,

"What the…? Are you all right?" she stared straight ahead in a dignified way and told him, "Certainly. Why do you ask?" and drove on before the Pepsi driver could climb out of his truck, which was probably just as well considering the look on his face.

Maggie's resemblance to Lucy has been implicit since the beginning of the novel.

If a reader wishes, it would be easy to argue that the above Lucy-passages work to undercut the positive elements in Maggie's character; some of the early reviewers of *Breathing Lessons* disapproved of Tyler's associating her heroine with a popular television character. Still, I do not believe that most readers will respond to Maggie's failures with the easy, condescending laughter that they give to the shallow farce of a typical television comedy. For both Maggie's games and the textual world which contains them are related to actual life in complex ways which Lucy's games are not.

While many of the pursuits and activities of our everyday world are often casually referred to as "games," most people (not only book reviewers) look askance at those, like Maggie, who seem to have difficulty distinguishing "real life" from actual games. Ira Moran clearly disapproves of Maggie's confusion of life and play:

> And his wife! He loved her, but he couldn't stand how she refused to take her own life seriously. She seemed to believe it was a sort of practice life, something she could afford to play around with as if they offered second and third chances to get it right. She was always making clumsy, impetuous rushes toward nowhere in particular—side trips, random detours.

The truth is—if we judge him by our society's standards of financial and social success—Ira Moran has fared no better than Maggie in the real world. Both were highly intelligent, promising high-school students. After high school, however, Ira reluctantly took over his family's picture-framing shop to support his hypochondriac father and two agoraphobic sisters instead of pursuing his plan to become a doctor. Maggie more willingly gave up her chance to go to Goucher College, becoming instead a nurse's aid in a retirement home. Both are quite aware that they are, in the usual sense of the word, failures. Ira laments that he "was fifty years old and had never accomplished one single act of consequence." And, during a depressed moment, Maggie makes an assessment of their lives that is even more depressing than Ira's:

> What Maggie's mother said was true: The generations were sliding downhill in this family. They were descending in every respect, not just in their professions and educations but in the way they reared their children and the way they ran their households.

Thus the Morans realize that the great majority of their contemporaries must consider them to be almost completely inept at the game of success—a game which many believe is the most serious thing in life.

On the other hand, Maggie and Ira are also aware that the game of material success is not "the only game in town." During a rare family outing to the Baltimore harbor, when he seriously considers the value of the commitment she has made, Ira's regrets disappear:

> He hugged [his sister Dorrie's] bony little body close and gazed over her head at the *Constellation* floating in the fog.... And Junie had pressed close to his other side and Maggie and [his father] Sam had

> While many of the pursuits and activities of our everyday world are often casually referred to as "games," most people (not only book reviewers) look askance at those, like Maggie, who seem to have difficulty distinguishing "real life" from actual games."

watched steadfastly, waiting for him to say what to do next. He had known then what the true waste was: Lord, yes. It was not his having to support these people but his failure to notice how he loved them.

Ira is only human and thus cannot sustain this intense awareness of his love for these helpless, difficult people for more than an "instant," but there is no doubt that this love plays an important role in authenticating his existence. And the reader also does not doubt that Maggie finds in her work and in her efforts (wise and otherwise) to love and help her family what she needs to consider her life worthwhile.

Ira's disapproval of Maggie's less-than-serious approach to life might lead the reader to suppose that Ira himself has little room in his life for playing games, but this would not be true. There are two pastimes that Ira holds dear. The first is an elaborate form of solitaire in which he indulges as often as possible; the second is losing himself in books which center on the adventures of lonely explorers: "It struck [Maggie] as very significant that Ira's idea of entertainment was those interminable books about men who sailed the Atlantic absolutely alone." These books obviously provide Ira with vicarious adventures which give him relief from his daily routines and responsibilities, but Maggie is correct about the significance of his preference for solitary heroes. Earlier we learned that "Ira didn't have any friends. It was one of the things Maggie minded about him." And we also learn that Ira cannot cope with life's grimmer contingencies (which is rather ironic, when one remembers that he had longed to be a doctor):

How peculiar [Ira] was about death! He couldn't handle even minor illness and had found reasons to stay away from the hospital the time she had her appendix out.... Whenever one of the children fell sick, he'd pretended it wasn't happening.... Any hint that he wouldn't live forever—when he had to deal with life insurance, for instance—made him grow set-faced and stubborn and resentful.

Perhaps, then, Ira's favorite game of solitaire, which he plays with a deck of cards he keeps in his pocket (he even carries it on the funeral journey that takes up the first section of the novel), provides him with a framework within which he can cope with and even enjoy the element of contingency which terrifies him in the actual world. And as there is nothing in our lives that is either more important or more undependable than our fellow human beings, it is clear why Ira's imaginings are most comfortable when they center on vicarious voyaging with men whose isolation makes them impervious to the unreliability of any other person. The books about solitary explorers and the games of solitaire provide him with frameworks within which he can confidently face the unpredictable element in life—as his making and selling of picture frames provide him and his family another kind of "framework" to order life in a way they find tolerable. (There is a roughly parallel situation in *The Accidental Tourist* with Macon Leary and his family; the latter are also more terrified of the unpredictable world and even more irrationally compulsive in their routines than Macon himself.)

The readers of *Breathing Lessons,* like the viewers of *I Love Lucy,* know that the heroine's game-strategies are comically doomed from the beginning. And Maggie—as Lucy would be in her place—is pathetically sincere about her devious, far-fetched scheme of reuniting her terminally immature son, Jesse, with his former wife, Fiona, and his daughter (and Maggie's only grandchild), Leroy. First, on their way back from the funeral, Maggie persuades Ira to detour to the small town where Fiona is living with her mother. Next, she manipulates Fiona and Leroy into riding back with her and Ira to their home in Baltimore where (through a surreptitious telephone call from Fiona's home) she has arranged for Jesse to appear at dinner.

The reunion dinner proves to be a fiasco. Jesse, fearful that his ex-wife and his family view him as a "loser" (the word that game-players dread hearing above any other), is too tense and defensive to control his childish ego and his temper long enough to establish any kind of meaningful communication with his wife and daughter. But it is Ira who brings the dinner to a sudden end with a brutally frank condemnation of his son. He reveals to Fiona that Jesse is living with another woman and then describes what he believes is his son's permanent inability to overcome his inadequacies:

This is the way things *are* ... [Jesse] never was fit husband material! He passes from girlfriend to girlfriend and he can't seem to hold the same job for longer than a few months; and every job he loses, it's somebody else's fault.

As a result of this speech, Jesse (rapidly followed by Fiona and Leroy) walks out on Maggie's reconciliation dinner.

What conclusion is the reader supposed to draw from this incident—that Ira sees Jesse and others as they really are and Maggie sees them as she would like them to be? As Ira had explained to Fiona earlier, "It's Maggie's weakness: She believes it's all right to alter people's lives. She thinks the people she loves are better than they really are, and so then she starts changing things around to suit her view of them."

Is the reader, then, to conclude that Maggie views life as a game she can play according to her own rules and for her own amusement, in the course of which she is free to manipulate others? And, of course, to treat people as objects to be manipulated is unKantian, unChristian, and generally inhumane. This is certainly a possible interpretation of Maggie, but other factors are present in the text to qualify or even to reverse these conclusions. Maggie's rose-tinted glasses can be seen partly as weakness, partly as charity towards others. Similarly to Miss Bates in *Emma,* Maggie actually *sees* those she loves as better than they are: she is convinced that Jesse is *nearly* the young man she wants him badly to be and that he *could* be happily reunited with his family:

She was in trouble with everybody in this house, and she deserved to be; as usual she had acted pushy and meddlesome. And yet it hadn't seemed like meddling while she was doing it. She had simply felt as if the world were the tiniest bit out of focus, the colors not quite within the lines—something like a poorly printed newspaper ad—and if she made the smallest adjustment then everything would settle perfectly into place.

If Maggie's inability to see life in all its grim reality can be considered, at least in part, a positive side to her character, Ira's clear-headed realism has its negative aspect. Ira has a deep fear, it will be recalled, of life's contingencies. Since his mother's death when he was fourteen, he has tried to avoid all thoughts of sickness or death or any other of life's unpleasant surprises. He refuses to make friends, obviously because friends, more often than family, disappoint one or prove unreliable. Thus there is a distinct possibility that his unchanging, bleak view of his son owes as much to his fear that hope will lead to disappointment as it does to the presence of an inner strength which always leads him to see things realistically. When Maggie interferes in the lives of Jesse and Fiona, it is to reunite them. When Ira interferes, it is to end the suspense associated with the shaky relationship of his son and Fiona. In this way Ira brings about the sad but secure state of a defeated relationship; Ira need no longer be disturbed by the insecure hope that his son will make a success of his marriage. It is a fear of life as much as the courage to face reality that underlies Ira's refusal to entertain illusions. On the other hand, Maggie is open to life in all its unpredictabilities: "Oh, Ira, you just don't give enough credit to luck," she says at one point. "Good luck or bad luck, either one." But giving credit to luck, to the unpredictability of life, is what Ira fears most.

Since Ira and Maggie are so different in their attitudes toward the contingencies of life, it might appear at first glance that the success of their marriage is either poorly conceived fiction or outright miracle. How somber, defensive Ira, with his rigidly ordered approach to life can tolerate, much less love his outgoing, recklessly playful wife is not an easy problem to resolve. There is no doubt, however, that Ira does love Maggie: "Well, face it, there were worse careers than cutting forty-five-degree angles in strips of gilded molding. And he did have Maggie, eventually—dropping into his lap like a wonderful gift out of nowhere." This unexpected development in his life Ira accepts without regret! I believe that the insight of Tony Tanner into the happy relationship of Jane Austen's stuffy hero, Fitzwilliam Darcy, and her light-hearted heroine, Elizabeth Bennet, in *Pride and Prejudice* will also serve for Anne Tyler's contrasting couple:

> … in their gradual coming together and Darcy's persistent desire for Elizabeth we do witness the perennial yearning of perfect symmetry for the asymmetrical, the appeal which 'playfulness' has for 'regulation', the irresistible attraction of the freely rambling individual for the rigidified upholder of the group. Indeed it could be said that it is on the tension between playfulness and regulation that society depends, and it is the fact that they are so happily 'united' by the end of the book which generates the satisfaction produced by the match.

The insight that successful relationships and successful societies need both the spirit of the game

and the spirit of discipline not only explains Maggie and Ira Moran's satisfying marriage, it also explains why their son Jesse, who as a child loved to make up stories that "had in common the theme of joyousness, of the triumph of sheer fun over practicality," fails at every relationship and every task he attempts. What Jesse does not have, as Ira pointed out above, is perseverance, a sense of duty or responsibility which is necessary to sustain any relationship. Without this even Jesse's potential for love, which is very real, is largely wasted. As important as love is in Anne Tyler's fictional world, it cannot survive unless those who love are willing to adjust to and often simply to endure the complexities and strains which are always present in adult relationships. Ira's love for his emotionally maimed father and sisters is an obvious example of how much strength and sustained sacrifice can be demanded by those whom one loves. And in the central relationship in the novel, Ira and Maggie had to make drastic changes in their romantic expectations of each other. In the bedroom of Serena's house after the funeral Maggie discovers Ira alone, playing his game of solitaire, and reminisces with him about the early days of their marriage:

> He pondered a king, while Maggie laid her cheek on the top of his head. She seemed to have fallen in love again. In love with her own husband! The convenience of it pleased her—like finding right in her pantry all the fixings she needed for a new recipe.

> "Remember the first year we were married?" she asked him. "It was awful. We fought every minute."

> "Worst year of my life," he agreed, and when she moved around to the front he sat back slightly so she could settle on his lap. His thighs beneath her were long and bony—two planks of lumber "Careful of my cards," he told her, but she could feel he was getting interested.

Of course, Maggie and Ira both have their moments of regretting the lost dreams of youth, the dreams of the perfect mate. Maggie realizes that her nursing-home friendship with Mr. Gabriel (before the Lucy-side of her emerged and destroyed his image of her) was a subconscious attempt to revive her (and Ira's) youthful romantic fantasies: "All Mr. Gabriel was, in fact, was Maggie's attempt to find an earlier version of Ira. She'd wanted the version she had known at the start of their marriage, before she'd begun disappointing him." But Maggie and Ira's love has survived the rough journey into reality. Jesse's love for his wife, Fiona, is capable of little more than beginning the trip.

Thus *Breathing Lessons* makes an unambiguous point about the need for the game-spirit to be accompanied by a sense of responsibility and by the ability to endure through adversity. Without this "rule" of an underlying stable commitment the marriage-game has little chance of lasting long enough to bring fulfillment to the players. But there is also no doubt that the main emphasis of the novel is on the need of a spirit of play if a person is to be truly fulfilled.

The very form of the work itself attests to this. Ira Moran, it will be recalled, is frequently exasperated by Maggie's refusal to recognize that life is a deadly serious business; instead of living in dread of making wasteful errors, "She was always making clumsy, impetuous rushes toward nowhere in particular—side trips, random detours." And at the center (both literally and figuratively) of Anne Tyler's plot there is such a side trip, a seemingly random—and quite lengthy—detour with no apparent purpose. It comes about on the Morans' return trip from the funeral. Irritated by the erratic driving of an elderly African-American in front of them, Maggie shouts at the driver as Ira finally manages to pass him that his wheel is coming off. Then, guilt stricken, Maggie forces Ira to return to where the old man has stopped and gotten out of his car to contemplate his (falsely) suspect wheel. After some consideration, Mr. Otis (the name of the old man) gets into the Moran Dodge and Ira detours off the main highway and drives him to a Texaco station managed by his nephew, Lamont. There, while waiting for Lamont to return from a service call, Mr. Otis describes how his wife threw him out of the house because she had dreamed that he stood on her needlepoint chair and trampled on some of her embroidery. After Lamont arrives and learns what has happened, he castigates his old uncle both for his erratic driving and his childlike marital conduct (although ironically Lamont, like Jesse Moran, is divorced). Mr. Otis's reply to Lamont, which comes at the approximate center of the novel, is so important that both men's speeches are worth quoting at length:

> "You two act like quarrelsome children," Lamont told him.
>
> "Well, at least I'm still married, you notice!" Mr. Otis said. "At least I'm still married, unlike certain others I could name!"
>
> Ira said, "Well, at any rate—"
>
> "Even worse than children," Lamont went on, as if he hadn't heard. "Children at least got the time to spare, but you two are old and coming to the end of your lives. Pretty soon one or the other of you going to die and the one that's left behind will say, 'Why did I act so ugly? That was who it *was*; that person

was who I was with; and here we threw ourselves away on spitefulness,' you'll say."

"Well, it's probably going to be me that dies first," Mr. Otis said, "so I just ain't going to worry about that."

"I'm serious, Uncle?"

"*I'm* serious. Could be what you throw away is all that really counts; could be that's the whole point of things, wouldn't that be something? Spill it! Spill it all, I say! No way *not* to spill it. And anyhow, just look at the times we had. Maybe that's what I'll end up thinking. 'My, we surely did have us a time. We were a real knock-down, drag-out, heart-and-soul type of couple,' I'll say. Something to reflect on in the nursing home."

Lamont rolled his eyes heavenward.

Lamont doesn't understand his uncle's musings on the essential importance of appreciating the non-essential, apparently foolish or wasteful aspects of life, and during a first reading perhaps the reader also doesn't understand why Anne Tyler has "thrown away" the central portion of her novel on an episode apparently unrelated to the main plot and characters. (Random House's recent cassette-recording condensation of *Breathing Lessons,* read by Jill Eikenberry, omits the entire Mr. Otis episode.)

But the detour to Lamont's station is no more wasted than the "unsuccessful" lives of Maggie and Ira Moran. *Breathing Lessons'* irregular form, as well as its characters and events, is a warning against taking the games of life and of art too seriously, or more accurately, against trying to make all women and men and all artists play the same kind of game, devoted to achieving the same kind of goal. At the same time, of course, Anne Tyler is providing us with a game; she eschews the obvious tight plot or transparently coherent form in which important, organic developments neatly fall into place without too much effort from the reader, and provides us instead with an eccentric, episodic plot which invites us to experience and evaluate the chain of events not in the spirit of a tight artistic logic but of adventure, of creativity.

Thus the psychology and spirit of game-playing permeate *Breathing Lessons,* shaping its characters, events, themes, and basic form. And in its central concern with game-playing the novel explores the nature of art itself. Hans-Georg Gadamer has based a large part of his philosophy on the assumption that art is a kind of game; thus a literary work such as *Breathing Lessons* accomplishes its purposes by stimulating us to enter the playing field of its textual world. We become players, responding to fictional events as though they were real. At the same time we are aware that the world of the novel is not real. Thus our experiences as readers both insulate us from the real world and its dangers and yet constantly draw on our experiences in that real world. Gadamer forcefully argues that we must never let the game-like apartness of a work of art, the discontinuity of our experiences of art from our everyday existences, tempt us to consider those experiences as purely aesthetic, unrelated to our understanding of the rest of our lives, or to the understanding of the culture that has shaped us.

In all of his discussions of the arts, Gadamer holds to both sides of the paradox that art, as a kind of game, is set apart from real life and at the same time vitally and necessarily related to actual existence. Concerning the first part of the paradox, he states: "Beautiful things are those whose value is of itself apparent. You cannot ask what purpose they serve. They are desirable for their own sake ... and not, like the useful, for the sake of something else." But, again, there is always the emphasis that when one enters upon the playing-field of a work of art and gives oneself up to its game— "Play fulfills its purpose only if the player loses himself in his play"—the world of that work of art will reveal its structure to the participant. The result is an increase of knowledge, an Aristotelian "recognition" which has significant relationships to the reader's life:

> The being of all play is always realisation, sheer fulfillment, energeia which has its telos within itself. The world of the work of art, in which play expresses itself fully in the unity of its course, is in fact a wholly transformed world. By means of it everyone recognises that that is how things are.

This paradox that the game of art is at the same time separated from real life and yet meaningfully related to our actual lives is obviously at work in the form of *Breathing Lessons* and in the fictional world revealed through that form. And as neither the novel's world nor ours is simple and unambiguous, the insight that we gain from the novel that "that is how things are" can not be reduced to a tidy little moral about the nature of happiness— or, for that matter, about the nature of Maggie Moran.

Near the end of the novel Maggie has severe doubts about her own basic character: perhaps her lack of practical sense has prevented her from accomplishing anything for those she loves. Immediately after her Fiona-and-Jesse reunion plot collapses, she has "a sudden view of her life as circular. It forever repeated itself, and it was en-

tirely lacking in hope." And later that night, after describing to Ira another of her dreadful miscalculations which years before had badly embarrassed her friend Serena and Serena's ill, aged mother, Maggie comments, "I don't know why I kid myself that I'm going to heaven." At this point the reader might conclude that the textual world in which Maggie lives has thoroughly discredited any pretensions that either she or the reader has held that her character and her life should be viewed positively.

But another interpretation is possible. When Maggie contemplates her poor chances of getting into heaven, the reader might recall that during a Moran family trip to the Pimlico race track Maggie had advised (with what success isn't certain) the women of the family to bet on a horse named Infinite Mercy. Infinite mercy is, of course, what we all need from God if we are to get to heaven, and as much of it as possible from our fellow human beings, if we are to get through life. Further, Maggie's depressed mood clears away by the time she is ready for bed. She becomes quite cheerful again as she begins to generate another plot— which will be immediately shot down by Ira—to convince Fiona to send Leroy to live with them for the sake of Leroy's education, and she watches Ira enjoying his favorite game of solitaire:

> He had passed that early, superficial stage when any number of moves seemed possible, and now his choices were narrower and he had to show real skill and judgment.

Similar to Ira's game, Ira's and Maggie's lives are now at a mature stage, and to play them out satisfactorily will demand their best efforts. Maggie's best efforts will involve her adapting her spirit of play, her vivid imagination, to human relationships as they really exist—to realize that her grown son and her almost grown daughter (not to mention her separated daughter-in-law and granddaughter) will be playing their own games, on their own fields, all unrelated to Maggie's own fantasies and desires. As part of this realization, Maggie must also more fully grasp what the author who created her has always (from her first novel, as a matter of fact) known: loving, understanding relationships between men and women are difficult to achieve, but they are possible; romance, however, is always an illusion. Occasionally, Maggie has realized this:

> Why did popular songs always focus on romantic love? Why this preoccupation with first meetings, sad partings, honeyed kisses, heartbreak, when life was also full of children's births and trips to the shore and

longtime jokes with friends? … It struck Maggie as disproportionate. Misleading, in fact.

But this kind of hard look at the shallowness of the rules and roles demanded of those who play at romance has been too unpleasant for Maggie to sustain. It is more typical of her to give way to the kind of sentimental, gushing emotions that caused her to sentimentalize Mr. Gabriel or to believe that even where Jesse and Fiona were concerned, love would conquer all:

> Then Jesse wrapped his arms around [Fiona] and dropped his head to her shoulder, and something about that picture—his dark head next to her blond one—reminded Maggie of the way she used to envision marriage before she was married herself.… She had supposed that when she was married all her old problems would fall away.… And of course, she had been wrong. But watching Jesse and Fiona, she could almost believe that that early vision was the right one. She slipped into the house, shutting the screen door very softly behind her, and she decided everything was going to work out after all.

But, of course, it didn't.

This growing, painful realization of the futility of the sentimental aspects of her vision of life causes Maggie to exclaim despairingly, "Oh, Ira … what are we two going to live for, all the rest of our lives?" Ira embraces her, giving her the loving, supportive response that she needs:

> "There, now, sweetheart," he said, and he settled her next to him. Still holding her close, he transferred a four of spades to a five, and Maggie rested her head against his chest and watched. He had arrived at the interesting part of the game by now, she saw. He had passed that early, superficial stage when any number of moves seemed possible, and now his choices were narrower and he had to show real skill and judgment. She felt a little stir of something that came over her like a flush, a sort of inner buoyancy, and she lifted her face to kiss the warm blade of his cheekbone. Then she slipped free and moved to her side of the bed, because tomorrow they had a long car trip to make and she knew she would need a good night's sleep before they started.

On this positive note the novel ends, and it is up to the reader to decide whether it is ironic (as I believe the optimistic final paragraph of *Morgan's Passing* is) or whether the text as a whole encouragesus to believe that Maggie has gained enough insight, and that she and Ira share enough love, to continue their lives successfully. Of course, any growth Maggie experiences will certainly not involve her losing the spirit of play that lies at the core of her personality. For those like Maggie Moran and (as Tony Tanner pointed out) Elizabeth Bennet view life in much the way that the rest of

us think of a game: it is there to be enjoyed. After all, one chooses to play a game; if one "plays" mainly out of a sense of duty or obligation then one's participation becomes mechanical and the essence of the game is destroyed. Of course, all aspects of life cannot be approached in the spirit of play. Jesse Moran and (again in *Pride and Prejudice*) Lydia Bennet do themselves and others a great deal of harm by not realizing this. And at times Maggie Moran also goes too far in "playing with" people's lives without their consent or knowledge. Most of the time, however, Maggie understands and honors the central relationships of life and the duties that belong to them. And when she does blunder and end up looking like a fool, her resulting fits of futility and self-loathing are soon swept away by her innate love of living, her underlying certainty that life is basically good and that the games *she* chooses to play are worth playing for their own sakes—not for the social and financial prizes that our popular materialistic culture awards to the winners of *its* favorite games. Maggie's wisdom clearly reveals to her (and to us) that the most important goals of life, loving relationships, are certainly not damaged or lost by one's possessing a joyful spirit.

What all of this amounts to, this peculiar mixture of optimism, futility, charity and irony which *Breathing Lessons* brings to a reader, will depend upon the total response to the text (and to his own life) of each reader. In spite of the apparently light, breezy nature of this novel, each reader will become aware, as he experiences his day with the Morans, that he, like Ira during that final game of solitaire, is being challenged, and as he advances in his solitary pursuit of the text his interpretive skill is increasingly important. For playing games of life and art to human beings is like friendship or marriage or even breathing. These activities come naturally to us, yet at times, as Maggie tries to convince the pregnant Fiona when they discuss childbirth classes, they demand all of our effort, all of our skill if we are going to successfully play our "natural" roles. As Maggie does with Fiona and Jesse, Anne Tyler can lure us into the game, and keep us playing until the end. However, Tyler, unlike Maggie, knows that when each reader decides, "That's how things are," the exact nature of "that" must be decided by the reader. In determining the final effect of a work of art, in contrast to the outcome of a competitive game, or one of Maggie's elaborate schemes, Anne Tyler knows that relinquishing ultimate control is the way in which an artist wins.

Source: Gene Koppel, "Maggie Moran, Anne Tyler's Madcap Heroine: A Game-Approach to *Breathing Lessons*," in *Essays in Literature,* Vol. XVIII, No. 2, Fall, 1991, pp. 276–87.

Elizabeth Beverly

In this excerpt, Beverly examines Tyler's characterization in Breathing Lessons.

Walking into the wide but comfortable expanse of an Anne Tyler novel can feel like settling down into a porch swing on a late summer evening. The neighbors on the porch next door begin to talk as the swing easily glides....

Imagine the ease of sitting in a porch swing and hearing not only the neighbors' conversation, but overhearing the minds of the neighbors as they sit in silence, unable or unwilling to speak, yearning to make sense of their particular lot.

The minds we overhear in Tyler's eleventh novel, *Breathing Lessons,* belong to Maggie and Ira Moran on a late summer Saturday, as the middle-aged couple drive out of their ordinary suburban Baltimore life to the funeral of Maggie's best friend's husband in rural Pennsylvania. The trip to the mid-morning service should be easy enough, Ira should even be back in time to open his framing shop for afternoon business, but before departure, on page five, as Maggie drives out of the auto body shop, she hears a voice on the radio that sends her lurching into the street, into a new minor accident that seems to loosen everything: the previously intact fender, the past, hopes for the future, faith in her marriage, longing for the grandchild whom the couple haven't seen in years. Just as the car can't stay fixed, the day's tidy plans crumble, and a quest begins.

Breathing Lessons is the story of that quest, modest by the standards of imaginative literature, but deeply felt. As Maggie and Ira undertake this rather haphazard daylong journey, we realize from their cascading memories and hopes that they are both in search of nothing less than the meaning of family. But even as I write these words, I sense that I am making Tyler's novel sound much more earnest than it really is. In fact, the narrative ambles easily, delightfully, at times preposterously. The sure prose, the wonderful telling details, the concerns of busybody Maggie and silent, kind Ira create a world in which we can remain interested, intrigued perhaps, but undisturbed....

Should this bother us? Does the novelist owe the reader a kick in the pants? Should a reviewer criticize a gifted novelist for seeming to refuse the

> " The problem is not that the book veers to whimsy, but more that the easy, whimsical tone creates a false sense of peace and thereby devalues the actual longing which rips through the hearts of the characters for whom we care."

high moral charge of art? No, no, and no! But what about the characters whose lives we've followed so faithfully? What does the novelist owe them? Should they exist simply for our amusement and then be put cozily to bed at day's end before the novelist has even begun to engage in the heartfelt pain they've expressed?

There are no answers to these questions, but if it occurs to a reader to raise such questions at all, to imagine that characters are trapped by the very form that creates them, then we're in the presence of an oddly skewed work, one which raises expectations it has no intention of meeting. The problem is not that the book veers to whimsy, but more that the easy, whimsical tone creates a false sense of peace and thereby devalues the actual longing which rips through the hearts of the characters for whom we care.

I believe that the skewing begins with the conceptualization of Maggie, in whose mind we ride throughout two of the three major sections of the novel. As soon as we meet her on her unsteady way to the body shop, we suspect we shall like her. As soon as we meet her, we learn to laugh with her and at her....

Chunky little Maggie wheels right through the day; she's more scatterbrained than eccentric, more endearing than downright lovable, more "inventive" than simply dishonest. We stick with her because she's funny, always on the verge of amazement, and takes herself half seriously. But not seriously enough, if we're to believe Ira. And we do believe Ira. By the time we are allowed into Ira's head, we find that "he loved her, but he couldn't stand how she refused to take her own life seri-

Baltimore, Maryland, where Tyler makes her home, is also the setting for many of her novels.

ously. She seemed to believe it was sort of a practice life, something she could afford to play around
with as if they offered second and third chances to
get it right."

Ira's insight evolves from his conviction that
human life is full of waste, particularly poignant
since Ira's youthful ambition to become a doctor
was swallowed years earlier by the obligations he
assumed for his family, not only for Maggie and
their children, but also for his weak father and two
dependent sisters, one developmentally disabled,
the other emotionally so. The fact that Ira's section
occupies the physical center of the novel seems to
be no accident. The more sober of the two main
characters, he provides the weight to hold the narrative on course. Or he ought to. But the novel itself is Maggie's own crazily conceived course. She
is the one who sees what to do, where to go, proceeds through the day and, we suspect, through life,
with the only authority this family knows.

This authority gets her into trouble, makes her
appear ridiculous: to Ira, to her children, to us.
About her kindly meant deceptions, Ira asserts,
"It's Maggie's weakness: She believes it's all right
to alter people's lives. She thinks the people she
loves are better than they really are, and so then

she starts changing things around to suit her view
of them."

Certain novelists could be described in the
same way as Maggie, but I suspect that Tyler agrees
with Ira about the suitability of such imaginative
whim. I think she believes that the lives she has invented for Maggie and Ira are simply what they are.
There is no changing them. It's as if Maggie,
Tyler's creation, has more faith in herself and in
the world than Tyler herself does. Tyler's world,
full of the wonders of language and the tenacity of
hope, is an insistently secular world. During the
course of the novel, we sit through a funeral designed to make a widow feel better, a wedding re-
hearsal, a film of a wedding, some choir practice,
a few moments in church. But nothing sacred dis-
turbs the quality of these lives. It's no surprise that
Maggie's longing for family union seems at moments almost monstrous. There is no promise of
any greater union than that expressed in amicable
silence....

And so the novel closes with Ira playing solitaire on his side of the bed, and Maggie settling
down on her side of the bed. Perhaps Tyler wants
us to believe this cozy separation is happiness, that
Maggie's ambition is unrealistic, therefore laugh-
able. Perhaps she wants us to recognize that com-

fort doesn't depend upon how such a day ultimately turns out, but upon the fact that such a day can happen at all, that past, future, and present can occasionally stream through us all at once, and make life appear full and rich and possible.

If this is the case, then it is a mercy that Maggie can so simply close down and go to sleep. But I feel bad that by the end of Maggie's novel I can take her no more seriously than Ira or even Tyler. For she is a neighbor who would want to make my life better if she could, if only I could let her words reach me, disturb me, wake me from my nightlong, easy swing.

Source: Elizabeth Beverly, "The Tidy Plans That Crumbled," in *Commonweal*, Vol. CXVI, No. 4, February 24, 1989, pp. 120–21.

Robert Towers

In the following excerpt, Towers focuses on the unconventional qualities in Breathing Lessons.

[In] Anne Tyler's novels, sympathetic recognition of her characters comes almost too easily, even as their expected oddity holds out the promise of small surprises. Like the *Rabbit* novels of John Updike, her books expertly render a familiar world in which our own observations are played back to us, slightly magnified, and with an enhanced clarity. Anne Tyler seems to know all there is to know about the surfaces of contemporary middle-middle-to lower-middle-class life in America, and if she chooses not to explore the abysses, she is nonetheless able to dramatize—often memorably—the ordinary crises of domestic life, of marriage and separation, of young love, parenthood, and even death. Though her style lacks Updike's metaphoric glitter, it has a strength and suppleness of its own. She can also be very funny.

In her recent novels—*Dinner at the Homesick Restaurant* and *The Accidental Tourist*—she has seemed at her best. The latter novel, particularly, is a luminous book. Beginning with the senseless murder of a twelve-year-old boy, it traces, with psychological cunning and humor, the steps of the boy's eccentric and obsessive father as he blunders his way toward a new life. Her eleventh novel, *Breathing Lessons,* strikes me as less substantial, more susceptible to the tendencies to whimsicality and even cuteness that sometimes affect her work. It is nonetheless shrewd in its insights and touching in its tragicomic vision of familial hopes and disappointments.

Breathing Lessons begins in absurdity. A middle-aged housewife, Maggie Moran, goes to a re-

> **Anne Tyler seems to know all there is to know about the surfaces of contemporary middle-middle-to lower-middle-class life in America, and if she chooses not to explore the abysses, she is nonetheless able to dramatize—often memorably—the ordinary crises of domestic life, of marriage and separation, of young love, parenthood, and even death."**

pair shop to pick up their car so that she and her husband Ira can drive from Baltimore to a funeral in Deer Lick, Pennsylvania.

> She was wearing her best dress—blue and white sprigged, with cape sleeves—and crisp black pumps, on account of the funeral. The pumps were only medium-heeled but slowed her down some anyway.... Another problem was that the crotch of her panty hose had somehow slipped to about the middle of her thighs, so she had to take shortened, unnaturally level steps like a chunky little wind-up toy wheeling along the sidewalk.

As she is leaving the body shop, Maggie hears on the car radio what she takes to be the voice of Fiona, her ex-daughter-in-law, announcing on a talk show her intention to remarry—this time for security instead of love. Meaning to brake, Maggie accelerates instead and runs in front of a Pepsi truck that smashes into her left-front fender—"the only spot that had never, up till now, had the slightest thing go wrong with it."

Such is the start of what turns out to be a very full day in the lives of the warm-hearted and scatterbrained Maggie and cranky, taciturn Ira....

I can think of no one who captures the flavor of car travel in America today better than Anne Tyler—the attempt to pass an oil truck, disputes over directions, a stop at a roadside grocery-café

("The café lay at the rear—one long counter, with faded color photo of orange scrambled eggs and beige link sausages lining the wall behind it"), where Maggie, who loves to spill out her life's story to strangers, engages in a heartfelt conversation with a sympathetic waitress and in a long flashback recalls an elegant old man whom she had loved in the nursing home where she now works. The couple finally arrives at the church in Deer Lick where they are informed by the widowed Serena that she has invited to the funeral all of the old friends who had attended her wedding and that they are all expected to sing the same 1950s songs that they had sung then. When Maggie and Ira are asked to sing "Love is a Many-Splendored Thing," Ira balks. What follows is a comical set piece, including, after the funeral, the showing of a movie of Serena and Max's wedding years ago, and the attempt, which is interrupted, of Maggie and Ira to have a "quickie" in Serena's bedroom while the funeral reception is going on downstairs.

It was at this point that I felt that Anne Tyler had allowed her novel to slip into whimsy and slapstick. While the unconventional Serena, with her mixed feelings about her husband's illness and death, is carefully drawn, the funeral itself and its aftermath are simply preposterous. I was relieved to get back onto the highway, to see things from Ira's cooler point of view for a change, and to move on to the family drama involving Fiona, Jesse, and Leroy that occupies the final hundred and fifty pages of *Breathing Lessons*. We do not know until nearly the end whether Maggie's irrepressible determination to make everything work out is doomed or not.

Maggie is presented as a meddler in other people's lives but a lovable one. Tyler invites the reader to participate in Maggie's schemes, to laugh at her misadventures and miscalculations, but also to admire her resiliency. And for the most part one goes along. But Maggie sometimes seems too broad in relation to the much subtler handling of the other characters—she is too awkward, too silly, to carry the burden that has been assigned to her. The sentimentality in the conception of her character becomes an irritation.

Ira, on the other hand, displays that firmness of outline and richness of specification that we associate with Anne Tyler's most successful characters—especially her quirky men. Ira is presented as a gruff failure, frustrated in his ambitions, exasperated by his "whifflehead" wife, disappointed in his feckless son, saddened by the humorlessness of his over-achieving daughter. He had wanted to be a doctor but has ended up running a framing shop which he had to take over when his father, declaring himself disabled by heart trouble, gave up the attempt to support himself and his two incapacitated daughters. Ira now supports all three of them as well as his immediate family. He makes fun of Maggie's vagaries, plays solitaire, and maintains long silences. Yet he is shown to be capable of complex feelings of tenderness even when most irritated by his family.

> He had a vivid memory of Jesse as he'd looked the night he was arrested, back when he was sixteen. He'd been picked up for public drunkenness with several of his friends—a onetime occurrence, as it turned out, but Ira had wanted to make sure of that and so, intending to be hard on him, he had insisted Maggie stay home while he went down alone to post bail. He had sat on a bench in a public waiting area and finally there came Jesse, walking doubled over between two officers. Evidently his wrists had been handcuffed behind his back and he had attempted, at some point, to step through the circle of his own arms so as to bring his hands in front of him. But he had given up or been interrupted halfway through the maneuver, and so he hobbled out lopsided, twisted like a sideshow freak with his wrists trapped between his legs. Ira had experienced the most complicated mingling of emotions at the sight: anger at his son and anger at the authorities too, for exhibiting Jesse's humiliation, and a wild impulse to laugh and an aching, flooding sense of pity.

It is writing of this authority and delicacy that justifies the admiration accorded to Anne Tyler's work—and redeems *Breathing Lessons* from the excesses of its whimsy.

Robert Towers, "Roughing It," in *New York Review of Books,* Vol. XXXV, No. 17, November 10, 1988, pp. 40–41.

Hope Hale Davis

Davis compares some of Tyler's other works to Breathing Lessons *in this passage.*

Up to now Tyler has given us irresistible "idiosyncratic characters who amble about in Chekhovian fashion," as a reviewer of *The Clock Winder* described them. Fantastic as these endearing oddballs may be, the world they live in is no never-never-land. Unequipped to manage in it, they can sometimes be saved by meeting the right unlikely person. We exult in the happy ending, which seems almost too good to be true. And indeed it may be. An amazingly bountiful one is offered Jeremy, the preoccupied artist who strives to cope with real-life demands in *Celestial Navigation,* but it is taken away again, through simple and unbearable human misunderstanding. In *Dinner at the Homesick*

Restaurant Ezra tries time after time to put on a festive family reunion, but concludes in the end, "I really, honestly believe I missed some rule that everyone else takes for granted; I must have been absent from school that day."

The readers who so quickly made *Breathing Lessons* a best seller must have expected some similar memorably loving hero. They had recently read *The Accidental Tourist,* laughing while taking in its message (running like a warm undercurrent through all the earlier works) that nobody can be too off-beat to win some discerning soul. Looking forward to her next novel with such anticipation, have they been a little let down by *Breathing Lessons?* Here the eccentrics are only minor characters acting in small comic set pieces along the way, not moving spirits like James in *Tin Can Tree* or Morgan in *Morgan's Passing,* who spends not only his life but even his pseudo-death impersonating.

For all its incidental flashes of inspiration and comedy, [*Breathing Lessons*] gave me a sense of slackening, even of retreat. It opens, in fact, with a stale, statistically way-off male chauvinist cliché. In a farcical scene where Tyler's humor is surprisingly labored, Maggie retrieves the car from the body shop that has just repaired the latest of her crumplings, and (distracted by a voice on a call-in radio show that she thinks is her daughter-in-law's) promptly heads out into the path of a passing truck.

The sexist slander becomes worse: Maggie makes an irresponsible escape, and then within minutes is pretending to search in her hopeless handbag for a map she doesn't dare admit she has left at home. (This is an almost identical repeat of a scene in *Searching for Caleb.*) A few miles farther on, at a stop for a snack, to the distress of Ira, Maggie confides to the café waitress a detailed family history. Though she sometimes slips out of character and exposes the brain of her author, here Maggie is exactly what her husband calls her, a whiffle-head.

Tyler clearly is no feminist, seeing half of humanity good and the other half villainous. This is mostly a virtue, except that female subjugation is merely one of the monstrous social facts and threats of which Tyler has seemed virtually oblivious throughout her writing. In *Breathing Lessons* Maggie prevents Fiona's abortion at a clinic where patients are harassed by a mob of Right-to-Lifers, whose behavior and dubious propaganda show Tyler as close as she has ever come to taking a social position. Yet Maggie is there for strictly personal reasons, preoccupied by the fibs she must tell

> **For all its incidental flashes of inspiration and comedy, [*Breathing Lessons*] gave me a sense of slackening, even of retreat."**

to make sure her grandchild will be born. Tyler presents a black in this novel, but only in one of her comic divertissements, and he is a sweetly subservient oldtimer with an IQ of 50.

The lives of Tyler's characters, including the better-educated ones, are affected solely by other individuals. She does know that when they make up a family, the change is qualitative, the family group becomes a force, sometimes malign. She demonstrates this so well that she captures—yes, captivates—us within her smaller world. What she reveals is how rare and precious goodness is, in man or woman, how fragile its carriers. And how someone of either sex can be an exploiter, or a victim, for reasons that are more complex than gender.

Breathing Lessons is mainly Maggie's story, but she is presented as a questionable heroine. Maddening as Ira's withholding can be (it has crushed the development of his son), Tyler shows his life of quiet sacrifice, running his father's framing shop to support his inadequate sisters. For a few brief minutes she takes us into his mind:

> He was fifty years old and had never accomplished one single act of consequence. Once he had planned to find a cure for some major disease and now he was framing petit point.

He is as disappointed in his over-achieving daughter heading toward Ivy-land as in his under-achieving son, a failing rock singer much like Drumstrings Casey, the anti-hero of *A Slipping-Down Life.* We see Maggie also from Ira's painful point of view:

> He loved her, but he couldn't stand how she refused to take life seriously. She seemed to believe it was a sort of practice life, something she could afford to play around with as if offered second and third chances to get it right. She was always making clumsy, impetuous rushes toward nowhere in particular—side trips, random detours.

Actually, what Maggie is trying to get right on the day of this story is their current life. With the unwilling Ira she carries out a scheme meant to end the separation of their son from his wife and retrieve the lost relationship with Leroy, the granddaughter. Maggie's campaign is Tyleresque, precipitating unexpected comedy. But it involves a problem that is far from comic, one Tyler's characters have struggled with before: Do you dare to take action that affects the course of other people's lives?

In *Celestial Navigation* a spinster who rooms in hapless Jeremy's house overcomes her inhibition and takes a step that permits the happy turn of events, yet can't bring herself to intervene again, thus letting it fail. In *Searching for Caleb* Justine tries to get the 17-year-old daughter to ride in the U-Haul truck with her father, whom the girl can't forgive for this restless move that is wrenching her away from her school only months before graduation. Justine castigates her own lack of tact or subtlety: "She never would let a quarrel wind up in its natural way.... She always had to be interfering."

Meddling is by no means the ruling theme in Tyler's novels, however. Within the limits she has set herself, watching ordinary people anyone might meet, she has also set a goal—the goal of all great writers—to show that even the most infuriating of humans, closely observed, from within and without, can become important, essential, precious. In *Dinner at the Homesick Restaurant* Ezra is faithfully taking care of his difficult mother who has alienated her other sons and daughters. Blind and lonely, she requires him to read aloud from her old diaries. I can't remember encountering a more poignant scene than the one in which he reads an entry revealing her ecstasy and promise at age 18.

So perceptive is Tyler's ear that within their context inarticulate responses like "I see," "Not at all," or "Huh?" can carry deep foreboding. We feel a sense of irreparable loss from a quiet voice saying, "Oh."

Not all Tyler's effects come from hints and auguries. She allows her characters sudden rare conclusions, direct and sweeping. During one flashback in *Breathing Lessons* Maggie recalls the widow Serena as a highly practical bride, buying a wedding dress that could be dyed purple to wear later, and considering whether she could rent (like a bartender) a man to stand in for her unknown father. When Maggie protests at her lack of romanticism about the groom Serena says calmly, "Of course I love him. But I've loved other people as much. I

loved Terry Simpson in our sophomore year—remember him? But it wasn't time to get married then, so Terry is not the one I'm marrying."

Tyler permits a pause for reflection, then continues: "So there again, Serena had managed to color Maggie's view of things. 'We're not in the hands of fate after all,' she seemed to be saying. 'Or if we are, we can wrest ourselves free any time we care to.'"

True or false? This may be Tyler's mischievous game.

Source: Hope Hale Davis, "Watching Over the Ordinary People," in *New Leader,* Vol. LXXI, No. 20, November 28, 1988, pp. 19–21.

Richard Eder

Eder considers Breathing Lessons *as Tyler's "funniest book," although perhaps "not her best" in the following review.*

No Olympian or high-flying view for Anne Tyler's art and the people it invents. She is a low-flyer, a crop-duster, zooming in at head-height and lifting hats; skimming the ordinary because it provides certain essential kinds of humanity, sometimes catching a wing tip on it or blowing its dust into her engine; and finally, with all the risks, accomplishing a gleeful astonishment.

Her people are arrayed in comic eccentricity. But Tyler waives the preservative chill customary to such a thing. They perform as close as possible to life temperature. They are soft, sometimes too soft.

In almost any Tyler novel there are moments when the reader worries about the low altitude, wonders whether the humor and sentiment are getting perilously close to shtick, suspects that the characters are becoming so comfortable in their quirks as to forfeit movement.

It is Tyler's idiosyncratic form of authority. She gives her people no freedom to be anything but themselves. She never stops imagining them or listening for their possibilities. Sometimes she can't hear them and improvises—we sense a kind of shuffling—but it's not long before they are back in her ken and under orders: Your soil will not change; grow in it. Grow any way you want.

And how they grow. *Breathing Lessons* turns a fraying middle-class household into a mixture of picture palace and puzzle palace; a familiar place made new.

It is set in the 28-year marriage of Maggie and Ira Moran and told in the course of a day trip from their Baltimore home to the funeral of the husband of an old school friend. The marriage is the soil I mentioned, more thin than fertile, and seared by dry spells.

The story is about what grows there: a man and a woman who are two versions of the human condition, two different stories in the same story, like the old tales in which a father sends two children out in opposite directions to seek their fortunes and misfortunes. But Ira and Maggie are never apart. It is their opposite spirits that make their common life a painful, provident slog for the one; and a painful, cloudy passage of dragons and treasures for the other.

We start with what in another author's hands might be two stock figures. Ira is careful and methodical and conceals his warmth beneath a mystique of competence; Maggie is emotional, impulsive, interfering and sloppy.

Each is in a kind of mid-life anguish; Ira, because he gave up his hopes of being a doctor to run the family picture-framing business on behalf of his half-invalid father and two sisters; Maggie, because her two children are grown up and her granddaughter lives with her son's former wife.

Maggie's stock figure is only a starting point. When a friend counsels Maggie to learn to let go, she retorts: "I don't feel I'm letting go. I feel they're taking things from me." In her quixotic and farfetched efforts to fight life's depredations; and in the repercussions these have on Ira's effortful equanimity, we get not only some of Tyler's most exuberant humor but two of her most moving and penetrating portraits.

The trip to Deer Lick, Pa., begins as it is to continue—in a comedy that, based as it is on a mixture of misadventure, misapprehension and unregenerate originality, is invariably a comedy of character.

Dressed to the nines, but already beginning to come unfastened, Maggie picks up the family car at the auto body shop. Hitting the accelerator instead of the brake, she has her fender mashed by a passing truck. Maggie, and everything she possesses or attempts, will always have dents....

Eventually, [she and Ira] get to the funeral. Serena, the widow, has arranged it to be a replay of her youth and that of her former classmates. Each is assigned to sing one of the pop songs of their day; later, at the reception, a movie of her wedding is shown. The sequence is a remarkable blend of farce and poignancy beneath which we are made

> "Her people are arrayed in comic eccentricity. But Tyler waives the preservative chill customary to such a thing. They perform as close as possible to life temperature. They are soft, sometimes too soft."

to feel the bareness of time and its dwindling choices.

The funeral scenes are intercut with the recollection of Maggie's and Ira's courtship, a phenomenon largely precipitated by another chain of Maggie's misapprehensions and impulses. It was a successful chain, as it happened....

There are moments when Maggie's klutziness seems overloaded, when she is just too funny and inept. But they are minor defects in a portrait that is triumphant because Tyler neither judges Maggie and Ira nor indulges them. Comedy of her sort is the supreme form of kindness; it brings out an extraordinary depth of feeling.

Maggie and Ira—whose portrait is more sparing but equally vivid and compassionate—are not heroes, but they are, in a sense, heroic. It is the heroism of enduring. Each does a number of unforgivable things, but in a marriage that lasts, forgiveness is not the point. Going on to the next day is.

Breathing Lessons may not be Tyler's best book; it is not a comparison I am easy with. The flashbacks sometimes slow down her matchless way with the present tense. The softness is sometimes too noticeable.

On the other hand, it may be her funniest book. Maggie's extraordinary encounter with an old black motorist whose flamboyant disassociations outbid her own is one of the funniest sustained sequences of contemporary writing that I can think of. And there are moments when the struggle among Maggie, Ira, and the melancholy of time passing forms a fiery triangle more powerful and moving, I think, than anything she has done.

Source: Richard Eder, "Crazy for Sighing and Crazy for Loving You," in *Los Angeles Times Book Review,* September 11, 1988, p. 3.

Sources

Bennett, Barbara A., review, in *South Atlantic Review,* Vol. 60, No. 1, January, 1995, pp. 57-75.

Eder, Richard, "Trying on a New Life," in *The Los Angeles Times Book Review,* May 7, 1995, p. 3.

Hall Petry, Alice, "Bright Books of Life: The Black Norm in Anne Tyler's Novels," in *The Southern Quarterly,* Vol. 31, No. 1, Fall, 1992, pp. 7-13.

Koppel, Gene, "Maggie Moran, Anne Tyler's Madcap Heroine: A Game-Approach to *Breathing Lessons,*" in *Essays in Literature,* Vol. XVIII, No. 2, Fall, 1991, pp. 276-87.

Rowe Willrich, Patricia, "Watching Through Windows: A Perspective on Anne Tyler," in *The Virginia Quarterly Review,* Vol. 68, No. 3, Summer, 1992, pp. 497-516.

For Further Study

Bail, Paul, *Anne Tyler: A Critical Companion,* Greenwood Press, 1998.

> Not only does Bail provide a survey of the plots, structures, characters, and themes of Tyler's novels, he also offers a comprehensive biography.

Croft, Robert W., *An Anne Tyler Companion,* Greenwood Press, 1998.

> An A-Z guide of characters in Tyler's fiction, as well as brief summaries of her novels, essays, and short stories.

Voelker, Joseph C., *Art and the Accidental in Anne Tyler,* University of Missouri Press, 1989.

> Voelker explores the role of accident in Tyler's fiction.

A Christmas Carol

Charles Dickens
1843

It is hard to believe that there is anyone on the planet who is not familiar with the story of *A Christmas Carol*. Written in a six-week period in October and November of 1843, the novel was the first of five short Christmas books published by Charles Dickens. Obviously, it was the most successful novel in the series. In fact, he was so certain that people would like his story that he refused to sell the rights to his publisher and instead paid to publish it himself. His instincts proved correct, and soon after its publication all of the copies were sold.

In his later years, Dickens would read an abridged version of *A Christmas Carol* at public readings for which he charged a fee. Often, that fee went to the several charitable organizations that he was involved with throughout his lifetime. The book itself was instrumental in raising people's awareness of poverty.

Since its publication, the story has been told many times in all imaginable forms. Despite the thousands of times that *A Christmas Carol* has been adapted to stage, radio, movies, and television, the novel remains the most popular and poignant telling of the tale.

Author Biography

Dickens was born in Portsmouth, England on February 7, 1812. His family moved to London be-

Charles Dickens.

fore he was two, but his father had trouble making enough money to feed his large family. In 1824 Dickens' father was sent to debtor's prison, along with most of his family. Charles, who was twelve years of age, did not have to go to prison because he was already working at Warren's Blacking Factory. In later life he remembered the factory bitterly and would only talk about it with a few close friends.

The family was released from debtor's prison a few months later, thanks to an inheritance that Dickens' father, John, received when his mother died. His mother wanted Charles to continue on at the factory, but his father made provisions for him to attend school. Dickens attended school until he was fifteen, and then worked as a clerk in a lawyer's office, studying Latin at night.

Dickens became a freelance reporter at Doctors' Commons Courts in 1829. In 1834 he started publishing sketches of London life using the pseudonym "Boz." In 1836 these short pieces were collected in a book called *Sketches by Boz.* Soon after the publication of these sketches, William Hall, of the publishing firm Chapman and Hall, approached him to write humorous text to accompany a series of plates by the illustrator Robert Seymour. Immediately, Dickens conceived of Mr. Pickwick.

When Seymour committed suicide, Dickens went on to turn his ideas into *The Pickwick Papers.* That was the start of his career as a novelist.

By 1843 he had completed four books and was in the middle of the next, *Martin Chuzzlewit,* when he took time out in October and November to write *A Christmas Carol.* He continued to write novels, most of them being published in serial form before being bound as novels.

The list of Dickens' books are familiar to any casual reader: *David Copperfield, A Tale of Two Cities, Oliver Twist,* and *Great Expectations,* to name just a few. Dickens also did charitable work, managed a theater company, and edited magazines. When he died in 1870, he was buried Poet's Corner in Westminster Abbey, an honor reserved for England's most notable literary figures.

Plot Summary

Stave I: Marley's Ghost

As *A Christmas Carol* opens, readers are introduced to Ebenezer Scrooge, the epitome of a tight-fisted miser: he is too cheap to heat his office, too cheap to give his clerk Christmas Day off without demanding he come in early the next day, and too cheap to care about the suffering of the poor people all around him. The tale begins on Christmas Eve, and Scrooge is visited by his nephew Fred, a good-natured man who tries to celebrate the holiday with his uncle, but is rebuked:

> "If I could work my will," said Scrooge, indignantly, "every idiot who goes about with 'Merry Christmas' on his lips, should be boiled with his own pudding, and buried with a stake of holly through his heart. He should!"

Yet Fred is not discouraged by his uncle's crankiness and wishes him well. As he leaves, two men from a charitable organization enter and ask Scrooge for a donation to help the poor. He suggests that the poor should go to prisons and workhouses, and the man points out that many would rather die than live under those wretched conditions.

> "If they would rather die," said Scrooge, "they had better do it, and decrease the surplus population."

When he goes home that evening, Scrooge sees the face of his long-dead business partner, Jacob Marley, in the knocker on his front door. Going upstairs to his flat, he thinks he sees a hearse riding up the stairs. Dozing in a chair by a dim fire, he hears chains in the cellar coming nearer, until Marley's ghost enters the room.

Marley's ghost explains that he is required in death to wander the earth, walking among humanity as he never did in life. The chain around him is "the chain I forged in life." He has come to warn Scrooge that he must change his ways, and he foretells that three spirits will come to Scrooge over the next three nights. When he leaves through the window, Scrooge sees hundreds of ghosts in chains wandering out in the street below his window.

Stave II: The First of the Three Spirits

The next morning, Scrooge is visited by the Ghost of Christmas Past. The ghost walks to the window and orders Scrooge to accompany him, but Scrooge asserts that he will fall.

"Bear but a touch of my hand *there*," said the Spirit, laying it upon his heart, "and you shall be upheld in more than this."

Scrooge finds himself at the school that he attended as a boy, watching all of the other children leaving for Christmas. He is shocked to see a young Scrooge, a lonely but imaginative boy that daydreams about characters out of Ali Baba and Robinson Crusoe. Suddenly it is the same scene a few years later, when Scrooge's little sister, Fan, excitedly tells him that their father said he can come home this year.

The next stop is the shop where Scrooge was an apprentice as a young man. It was run by Fezziwig, a ruddy, jovial man who tells his clerks to put away their work to prepare for the holiday festivities. All of the business equipment is put away and food and musicians and guests come in, and Fezziwig and his wife lead the dancing. Scrooge starts to realize the benefit of kindness, telling the Spirit:

He has the power to render us happy or unhappy; to make our service light or burdensome; a pleasure or a toil. Say that his power lies in words and looks; in things so slight and insignificant that it is impossible to add and count 'em up; what then? The happiness he gives, is quite as great as if it cost a fortune.

In the next scene, a woman named Belle breaks off her engagement to young Ebenezer Scrooge. He has changed, she explains: he has become obsessed with money and fearful of poverty. Although heartbroken, he eventually he agrees. Scrooge is then taken to Belle's house several years later, where she is surrounded by a happy, laughing family. Her husband returns home and says that he heard that Marley was dying, and that Scrooge would then be left all alone in the world. Distraught, Scrooge begs the Spirit to take him home.

Stave III: The Second of the Three Spirits

Back in his room, Scrooge is awakened by the Ghost of Christmas Present, a jolly giant carrying a torch. His room is decorated with wreaths and holly and delicious-smelling foods. This spirit takes Scrooge through London, where shopkeepers are joyfully setting out baskets of food and happy people are doing last minute shopping. As people pass with their dinners, the Spirit sprinkles some kind of seasoning on it with his torch, and they become even happier.

He takes Scrooge to the home of his clerk, Bob Cratchit. Mrs. Cratchit and some of the children are preparing the Christmas dinner. Bob Cratchit comes in from church carrying their son, Tiny Tim, who has a crutch. There is little to eat, but it is prepared well, and the family is glad for what they have. Bob Cratchit raises a toast to Scrooge, but Mrs. Cratchit and the children cannot find it within herself to say anything nice about him:

Scrooge was the Ogre of the family. The mention of his name cast a dark shadow on the party, which was not dispelled for full five minutes.

Before leaving the Cratchit house, Scrooge asks the spirit if Tiny Tim will live. He is told that if things do not change, the young boy will die.

Next, they visit an impoverished mining camp. There, they see cheerful people celebrating Christmas despite heart-wrenching poverty. They go to a ship out at sea to find the ship's crew also making the best of the holiday. They observe a party at the house of Scrooge's nephew and see Fred's family playing games, eating, and laughing. When Scrooge's name is brought up, Fred expresses his pity for him. Yet most of his guests think of Scrooge as a nasty, foolish old man.

Before leaving, the Ghost of Christmas Present opens his gigantic robe to show Scrooge two pathetic-looking young children: Ignorance and Want. Scrooge asks if there isn't someone who could take care of them, and the spirit responds:

"Are there no workhouses?" said the Spirit, turning on him for the last time with his own words. "Are there no workhouses?"

Stave IV: The Last of the Spirits

Scrooge is visited by the Ghost of Christmas yet to Come, which is shrouded in black and does not speak. This mysterious apparition takes him out into the town. They pass a group of businessmen standing on a street corner, talking about a death and laughing about how cheap the funeral will be.

Another group of people on the street mentions a death in passing and then go on to talk about the weather. In the cheap, dingy part of town they observe a pawnbroker buying things that two women have stolen from the room where a dead man was laid out. They have spoons and clothes and the curtains from his bed, complete with rings, and even the shirt that had been left on the body. Scrooge recognizes the things as his.

When Scrooge asks to see anyone in town who felt emotions over this man's death, the Spirit takes him to a couple who owe the dead man money. They are relieved to hear of the death, hoping that their debt will pass to someone more understanding. When he begs to find someone grieving, he is taken to the Cratchit house, where the family is devastated by the loss of Tiny Tim. With a sinking feeling, Scrooge demands to know who the dead man is. The Spirit takes him to a churchyard and shows him a grave with his own name on it. Scrooge falls to his knees and begs for the chance to change, and when he grabs the Spirit's hand his cloak collapses into a pile of bed linen.

Stave V: The End of It

Elated that he is alive and has a second chance at life, Scrooge goes to the window and calls down to a boy in the street and asks what day it is. When he finds out that it is Christmas, he tells the boy to go to the poultry shop and have them bring the big prize-winning turkey, which he sends anonymously to the Cratchit house. He then dresses in his best clothes and goes out.

In the street he meets the man from the charitable organization that he chased from his office the day before. He gives him money and promises more. Then he visits Fred's house and recognizes all of the party guests who were there when he saw it with the Ghost of Christmas Present. The next morning, Bob Cratchit arrives for work eighteen minutes late; for a moment, Scrooge acts like his old self, but then he breaks into a smile and tells Cratchit that they will sit down with a bowl of warm punch that afternoon and talk about raising his salary.

Eventually, Scrooge becomes like a second father to Tiny Tim, taking care of his medical bills so that he regains his health. In future years he is aware that people find his change of personality strange, but he realizes how fortunate he is to have a second chance.

Characters

Belle

Belle is Scrooge's old girlfriend. Years ago, she broke her relationship off with him because she felt that he had changed for the worse. In a vision of Christmas past, Scrooge sees her married and surrounded with laughing, happy children who love her.

Bob Cratchit

Cratchit is Scrooge's assistant, a loyal and diligent employee. After leaving the gloom of the Scrooge and Marley office on Christmas eve, Cratchit "went down a slide on Cornhill, at the end of a lane of boys, twenty times, in honour of its being Christmas eve, and then ran home to Camden Town as hard as he could pelt, to play at blindman's bluff." A child at heart, Cratchit truly enjoys carrying Tiny Tim around town, and is a loving family man.

Martha Cratchit

Martha is the Cratchit family's oldest daughter.

Peter Cratchit

Peter is Bob Cratchit's oldest son.

Tim Cratchit

See Tiny Tim

Mrs. Dilber

In Scrooge's vision of his own death, he sees Mrs. Dilber sell some of his belongings: "sheets and towels, a little wearing apparel, two old-fashioned silver teaspoons, a pair of sugar tongs, and a few boots."

Fred

Fred is Scrooge's nephew and only living relative. A genial man, he stops by on Christmas Eve to wish Scrooge a Merry Christmas and ends up thoroughly rebuked. Yet the young man does not seem to let his uncle's nasty demeanor bother him or affect his relationship to his uncle.

The Ghost of Christmas Past

The first spirit to visit Scrooge is The Ghost of Christmas Past. Wearing a white tunic trimmed with summer flowers and carrying a sprig of holly, the ghost has rays of light emanating from its head and carries a candle extinguisher to wear as a cap and snuff the light. Scrooge is able to travel with him to long-ago times and places; in this way, Scrooge is able to see himself as a younger man and remember a time when he was more open and hopeful about life.

The Ghost of Christmas Present

The second spirit is loud and boisterous, a large man who shows up with a mountain of food and drink. His purpose is to show Scrooge how his friends and family are celebrating Christmas without him. For example, Scrooge's nephew, Fred, is throwing a lavish party for a large group; and Bob Cratchit is enjoying his time with his family, even if the Christmas dinner is modest and the presents few.

The Ghost of Christmas Yet to Come

This ghost does not speak, but shows Scrooge a bleak future. Resembling the popular conception of the Grim Reaper, The Ghost of Christmas Yet to Come is enshrouded in a long black robe. From this future, Scrooge learns that Tiny Tim will not survive because Cratchit could not afford adequate medical help. Also Scrooge learns that when he dies, no one really cares. His passing is a relief to some and ignored by others.

Joe

Joe is the disreputable fence who buys Scrooges old clothes and linens. He will eventually sell them for a big profit.

Jacob Marley

Marley is Scrooge's late business partner. Dead for seven years, he comes back to haunt Scrooge and warns him that he is wasting his life. Moreover, he tells him that if he doesn't change soon, he'll end up like Marley: a restless old ghost. Initially, Marley's face appears in the knocker of Scrooge's front door, but then the ghost appears in full. His appearance is shocking: his jaw is tied together with a rag, which drops when he takes the rag off; he is bound around the waist with a chain, "the chain I forged in life," made of "cashboxes, keys, padlocks, ledgers, deeds, and heavy purses wrought in steel." He informs Scrooge that he will be visited by three ghosts.

Old Fezziwig

Fezziwig is Scrooge's old employer. A large and genial man, he throws a huge Christmas party, with food and music and dancing and drinks and good cheer all around. He provides a contrast to

Media Adaptations

- One of the most highly regarded versions of *A Christmas Carol* stars Alistair Sims as Scrooge, directed by Brian Desmond Hurst. Released in 1951, it is available from VCI Home Video.

- Another praiseworthy version of the novel is the 1984 made-for-television movie with George C. Scott, David Warner, and Edward Woodward. It was released on video by Twentieth Century Fox in 1999.

- In December of 1999, TNT and Hallmark Entertainment premiered a new movie version with Patrick Stewart, Richard E. Grant, and Joel Grey starring. It was directed by David Jones.

- Michael Caine plays Scrooge, Kermit the Frog plays Bob Cratchit, and the Great Gonzo plays Charles Dickens in *The Muppet Christmas Carol,* released on video in 1997 from Jim Henson Video Co.

- *Scrooged* (1988) is a humorous adaptation of Dickens' novel, with Bill Murray as a television executive. The movie was directed by Richard Donner and is available from Paramount Home Video.

- This story has been adapted to the stage, screen, and television so many times that there is an entire book on the subject. *A Christmas Carol and its Adaptations,* written by Fred Guida, includes scenes from old kinescope films and foreign productions. It was published by McFarlane and Co. in 1999.

the kind of employer Scrooge turns out to be: parsimonious and cold.

Ebenezer Scrooge

Scrooge is the protagonist of the story and is one of the best-known characters in all of literature. He is described as a miserly man; for example, he is so stingy that he won't pay to keep his own apartment heated. It is never fully explained why he has become such a miserable old miser, but some clues are given in the scenes of past Christmases. The reader learns that Scrooge had a strict and distant father—he made him stay at school during Christmas break and only let him come home one year because his sister asked if he could come home. Maybe as a result of such childhood rejection, Scrooge later withdraws from his friends and loved ones. As his girlfriend notes: "You fear the world too much.... All your other hopes have merged into the hope of being beyond the chance of its sordid reproach."

Throughout the course of the story, Scrooge learns to treasure humanity through the glimpses that the ghosts of Christmas Past, Present, and Future give him into his own life. Also he realizes the impact one person can have, as with Tiny Tim. After the spirits leave, Scrooge is relieved to find that he still has a chance to change the course of his life. This he promptly does: he becomes generous and good-humored, a positive force in the community, and good friends with Tiny Tim.

Fan Scrooge

Fan is Scrooge's deceased sister. She seems to have been a loving and supportive presence in his youth.

Tim Cratchit

Tim (also known as Tiny Tim) is Bob Cratchit's youngest son. He is physically challenged, as he must use a crutch to get around. As a result, he is often carried from place to place by his father. Tiny Tim never complains about his handicap, and his emotional strength and positive attitude impress everyone around him. After being shown a version of the future in which Tiny Tim is dead, Scrooge vows to help the boy. In fact, Scrooge does donate money for Tiny Tim's medical treatment.

Themes

Guilt and Innocence

Often in ghost stories, the ghostly apparitions function to remind the main character of something evil he or she has done in the past. In other words, ghosts act as the character's conscience. Scrooge certainly has enough to feel guilty about: he is mean and tight-fisted with his assistant, Bob Cratchit; dismissive of his nephew, Fred; miserly and cold with the men from the local charity association; and

nasty to the little caroler that he chases away from his keyhole with a ruler. Each of these people are associated with some form of innocence, a reminder of the less fortunate or the love of family and friends.

Marley's ghost raises the question of guilt directly, explaining that he himself is forced to walk the earth as a ghost because he was a heartless, self-involved man. The ghosts of Christmas Past, Present and Future make no accusations toward Scrooge about his behavior—but with the warning that Marley has given him, Scrooge interprets the visits to mean that unless he changes his life and learns to value the people around him, he will end up like Marley. Moreover, by revisiting events and people from his past, he realizes just how much he has missed by shutting himself off from family, friends, and coworkers. With the help of the ghosts, he resolves to change his life.

Fear

"You fear the world too much," Belle tells Scrooge as she is breaking off their engagement. It is implied by his sister's visit to his school that the roots of these fears can be found in a problematic and dysfunctional relationship with his father. Although we don't know the details, it was an obviously unhappy relationship that impacted Scrooge's relationships with others the rest of his life. It figures that his withdrawal from Belle, his growing interest in financial dealings, his lack of companions, and his unhappiness is a result of this early trauma. The ghostly intervention makes him see that the loneliness and neglect he has brought upon himself is even worse than the general fear of the world that he developed from the neglect suffered during his childhood. Beside the fear of his own death, Scrooge is very affected by the realization of Tiny Tim's death, which he inquires about with "an interest he had never felt before." When he finds out that the boy's fate could be avoided, he finds an opportunity to reach out and help someone other than himself. His emotional and financial support saves Tiny Tim's life and provides the true emotional connection that Scrooge desired all along.

Wealth and Poverty

A recurring theme in the work of Dickens is the tremendous gap between the rich and poor. In fact, he portrayed the gritty world of the working class and lower class of London at a time when most novelists—most of them educated and from

Topics for Further Study

- Write a synopsis for an updated version of *A Christmas Carol,* using people who are in the news or who are famous in your community.

- Try to find out about music that would have been popular at the time of the novel. In particular, try to get a copy of "Sir Roger de Coverley," which Fezziwig dances to. Pick a popular song that you think is like the old music, and explain the relationship between the two songs.

- Research the significance of Christmas to charitable organizations, explaining how much their income from donations increases during December and what they do to prepare for it.

- Write a short story about Tiny Tim as a grown-up, explaining how the crippling disease he had as a child was cured because of his father's rich benevolent employer.

- Examine the traditional use of ghosts in Victorian writing and write a paper explaining how their use here is common or uncommon.

---

the upper class—had no sense of what poverty or its victims were like.

In this story, Bob Cratchit's meager earnings can barely feed his family. In spite of this, the members of the Cratchit household are a cheerful and happy bunch. When Scrooge looks in on them with the Ghost of Christmas Present, he hears about the tiring jobs that the children work or will work, and he notes the little they have to eat, with the meager plum pudding being a great treat. As Scrooge observes, "They were not a handsome family; they were not well dressed; their shoes were far from being waterproof; their clothes were scanty; and Peter might have known, and very likely did, the inside of pawnbroker's. But they were happy, grateful, pleased with one another's company, and contented with the time.... "

By contrast, the wealthy Scrooge lives in miserable circumstances in a cold abandoned building that is dark because he does not want to spend money on candles ("darkness was cheap, and Scrooge liked it"). His wealth is not bringing him any more happiness—it only perpetuates the fear that one day he will lose it.

A Christmas Carol does not equate poverty with cheer and wealth with misery, however. The party at Fred's house shows people who are wealthy having a good time, while two children revealed to him by the Ghost of Christmas Present—Ignorance and Want—make it clear that even though people like the Cratchits can laugh in their poverty, it still a serious and life-threatening matter.

Style

Point of View

Mainly, this novel is narrated in the third person; that is, the story is usually told as "he said" or "she said" or "Scrooge watched them," etc. In the beginning, though, there is a little touch of a first-person narrator, as someone talking directly to the reader, referring to himself as "I." This narrator is the type of personality who will use a phrase and then mull over its appropriateness ("I might have been inclined, myself, to regard a coffin-nail the deadest piece of ironmongery ... ") and to make humorous satirical remarks.

This first-person voice fades away once the characters in the book start interacting with one another, leaving the characters and the action of the novel to keep the readers' attention. The last time this first-person narrator is heard from is when it remarks on how strange it is that Scrooge, who had not thought of Marley since hours earlier, would see his face on the door knocker ("let any man explain to me, if he can, how it happened that ... ")

Setting

London is the setting of this novel, as it is for many of Dickens' works. The character of the city does not come into play much except in the gloomy darkness on the afternoon of Christmas Eve, caused by London's legendary fog. It is also present during the scene on Christmas morning presented by the Ghost of Christmas Present, with the city coming alive. Dickens gives long lists of the objects associated with Christmas (baskets of chestnuts, Spanish onions, tea, coffee, raisins, mistletoe, etc.), a bounty and richness that Scrooge has rejected in favor of his lonely, solitary existence.

Compare & Contrast

- **1843:** The world's first Christmas cards are sent out by Henry Cole, a director of a London museum.

  Today: Millions of Christmas cards are sent out each year by families and business, but many people are replacing paper cards with animated Internet cards.

- **1843:** The squalid courts and cheap food shops of a London area dubbed "Porridge Island" are cleared away for a development area called Trafalgar Square, in honor of Lord Nelson's victory at the Battle of Trafalgar.

  Today: Trafalgar Square is one of London's main tourist attractions; unfortunately, it is also famous for its enormous pigeon population.

- **1843:** Samuel B. Morse begins construction of a telegraph wire between Washington, D.C. and Baltimore using money appropriated by Congress.

  Today: Telephone communication is instantaneous, but millions of miles of wires are being replaced with fiber-optic cables for even quicker Internet transmission.

- **1843:** Documents are copied by hand. The first prototype of a typewriter is invented, but is not very practical.

  Today: Computers can accurately turn printing or spoken words into typed documents and then alter their appearance in countless ways before they are printed.

- **1843:** A new child labor law in Britain prohibits employment of boys or girls under the age of ten in coalmines. In Massachusetts, a new law limits children under twelve to working no more than ten hours a day.

  Today: Developed countries pressure third-world countries to enforce child labor laws, while at the same time taking advantage of their cheap production costs.

- **1843:** Cologne authorities suppress the newspaper published by socialist Karl Marx, which decries the exploitation of the working class. The following year Marx meets Friedrich Engels, with whom he was to write *The Communist Manifesto* in 1847.

  Today: Many of the Marxist governments of the twentieth century, based on communist ideas from Marx and Engels, have moderated their views and adapted some capitalistic practices.

The one other notable setting in the novel is the cold, dark house where Scrooge lives, which had been occupied by Jacob Marley before his death. Among its more individual characteristics are the wide staircase and the fireplace, which is decorated with carvings of scenes from the Bible. It is also symbolic of his isolation that Scrooge would live in such spare, dark surroundings.

Historical Context

Victorian Christmas

At the time when Dickens was writing, the Christmas tradition was not nearly as important as it is today. Celebrating Christmas started in the fourth century, incorporating many of the symbols of pagan holidays such as the Roman Saturnalia and the Saxon Yule holiday, such as holly and wreaths. The date of December 25th was borrowed from pagan cultures—it was the date of the Winter Solstice, the shortest day of the year.

For centuries Christmas grew in importance slowly, but treating it as a celebration was looked upon suspiciously because of its pagan origins and because it made a festive celebration out of one of the most solemn days on the Christian calendar, the birth of Jesus. During the Protestant Reformation of the sixteenth century that sought to turn the church away from worldly and materialistic concerns, celebrating Christmas was actually outlawed for a short time. Yet it wasn't long before the symbolic, festive aspects of the holiday started showing up again as people carried on the traditions they had been taught.

During the reign of Queen Victoria in England, the Christmas tradition gained popularity. One reason for this was that the monarchy supported it: Prince Albert, Queen Victoria's husband, brought the German tradition of decorating the Christmas tree when he came to England. Another reason was economic, as the Industrial Revolution was creating a population shift from rural areas to cities, where new manufacturing techniques required workers. This growing urban population found comfort in the Christmas traditions. As the city became more crowded and dirty, the citizens looked forward to celebrations, especially Christmas.

Urban Life

In the mid-nineteenth century, London was a crowded, dirty place, a fact that no one did more to publicize than Dickens himself. Industries were not regulated, and widespread pollution and exploitation of the work force resulted. Laborers, many of them children, were required to work fourteen-hour days in order to help their families pay bills; if a family was unable to make ends meet, they might end up in Debtor's Prison—as Dickens' family did when he was twelve.

Dickens described the squalid, dirty condition of London in vivid detail. Yet, some historians believe that the actual conditions of Victorian London might not have been as gruesome as described. Because the reign of Victoria was a time of increased social concern in England, there probably is much exaggeration in the reports of squalid poverty.

Critical Overview

A Christmas Carol has never been considered Dickens' finest work by literary critics, but from its first publication it was a popular favorite. It sold an impressive six thousand copies at its first printing in 1843, and was quickly reprinted in numerous authorized and unauthorized editions.

Today, critics seldom discuss *A Christmas Carol,* in part because of its universal popularity. Also this short novel is considered not emblematic of Dickens' work in general. Although critical reaction to his novels has been favorable, commen-

Patrick Stewart as Ebenezer Scrooge in the 1999 TV adaptation of A Christmas Carol.

tators tend to deride the length of the books he produced. David Cecil, for example, was critical of Dickens' novels when he commented in his book *The Victorian Novelists: Essays in Reevaluation:* "He cannot construct, for one thing. His books have no organic unity; they are full of detachable episodes, characters who serve no purpose in furthering the plot."

It is a criticism that did not apply to the development of ideas in this short novel. Cecil went on to point to Dickens' finest quality: his ability to fill every scene he wrote with exact, convincing details. Famed novelist Anthony Trollope had it wrong, according to Cecil, when he charged that Dickens' writing was "exaggerated." He emphasized that what might seem excessive was actually Dickens' strength: "Scott's imagination and Emily Bronte's were of a finer quality, Jane Austen's was more exactly articulated, but they none of them had an imagination at once so forceful, so varied and so self-dependent as Dickens."

In addition, commentators often focus on the characters in Dickens' work. Some critics quickly dismiss them as being broadly written in order to play upon readers' emotions; moreover, it has been charged that they are designed more as sentimental caricatures than well-rounded psychological portraits. On the opposing side are those critics who concede that his characters are drawn broadly, but then go on to point out that even a character with one exaggerated trait can be real. On this point, Julian Symons asserts: "It would be nearer to the truth to say that they are pathological distortions of human egoism, in which a thwarted radical enacts forbidden scenes of violence through the mouths and bodies of characters labeled *wicked.*"

Scrooge is not violent, but that is only because he is old and decrepit. His attempts to threaten Bob Cratchit for wanting coal for warmth, or his harsh treatment of the little caroler at his door, are done with the spirit of evil that Symons says audiences identify with as "forbidden scenes." It is clear to any new reader of Dickens that he is trying to manipulate his audience's emotions, and the critical debate hovers around whether or not he has a right to do that.

One of the great writers of the twentieth century, G. K. Chesterton, summed up the effectiveness of Dickens' manipulations this way: "A Dickens character hits you first on the nose and then in the waistcoat, and then in the eye and then in the waistcoat again, with the blinding rapidity of some battering engine.... " While other critics consider Dickens' emotional manipulation as dishonest and even cheap, Chesterton believed that this was the business of the novelist.

> Dickens was often called a sentimentalist. In one sense he sometimes was a sentimentalist. But if sentimentalism be held to mean something artificial or theatrical, then in the core and reality of his character Dickens was the very reverse of a sentimentalist. He seriously and definitely loved goodness. To see sincerity and charity satisfied him like a meal. What some critics call his love of sweet stuff is really his love of plain beef and bread.

It makes sense that critics are usually suspicious of a novel that the general public likes too much, especially one that uses such emotion-wringing devices as Christmas and a physically-challenged child. However, despite critical condemnation, the short novel has remained a well-loved Christmas classic for people around the world.

Criticism

David Kelly

Kelly is an instructor of Creative Writing and Literature at Oakton Community College and College of Lake County, in Illinois. In this essay, he examines the question of whether Charles Dickens' A Christmas Carol is effective because of its adept manipulation of readers' sentiments, or if it earns its popularity with powerful storytelling.

I guess I would have to agree with Charles Dickens' detractors who say that he was too long-winded, that he should have learned to cut to the point of almost anything he was writing about a little quicker. I agree with them—but then, so would Dickens himself. There is a story about him, told by Kate Douglas Wiggin, the author who grew up to write *Rebecca of Sunnybrook Farm.* She was only twelve when she approached him on the train between Portland, Maine and Boston and started a discussion about his books, listing what she liked and then mentioning that he should have cut "some of the very dull parts." In response, Dickens roared with laughter and pressed for further thoughts on the subject of what she might think dull. Now, it could be considered just common politeness for a grown man to give a twelve-year-old critic his full attention, patronizing to let her call him dull; on the other hand, when a child could see what was excessive, he would have no choice but to take heed.

Fortunately, he was able to avoid the problem of wordiness in his novellas by working in a form so short that it never has time to be excessive. This is never truer than in *A Christmas Carol,* which lends itself to quick scene changes. Still, this book brings up the next most common charge levied against Charles Dickens: that of cold, manipulative sentimentality. He has been called the Norman Rockwell of literature, a technical stylist who says the things that he (rightly) thought his audience wanted him to say.

For those like myself who think that critics have no business blaming a book for being popular, Dickens was a good, interesting, vivid writer first. Yet I can see the other side's point—that too much of what he did was driven by popular opinion and not by artistic standards.

I think that what saves Dickens from the charge of excessive sentimentalism, in *A Christmas Carol* and in general, is the fact that he was always willing to balance life's joy against its misery. This would be an easier point to support with the life stories presented in the longer books, such as *David Copperfield* and *Great Expectations* or especially *Bleak House,* but it stands even with a commercial enterprise like the story of Scrooge. He took risks that were clearly not popular in order to round out his vision of the world.

Considering the charge of sentimentality, the first thing to get out of the way is the simple, obvious fact that nobody had or has any deeply held hatred for Charles Dickens. Not only are those who raise questions about his work too sensible to try to dismiss him as a fraud, but they probably don't even feel good about taking sides against him. As G. K. Chesterton, himself a powerful and interesting novelist, noted, "In everyone there is a certain thing that loves babies, that fears death and that likes sunlight: that thing enjoys Dickens."

Ironically, *A Christmas Carol* happens to play off of all of the elements Chesterton mentioned. It has the baby—Tiny Tim—who, though able to verbalize his saintly philosophy in whole paragraphs, still has to be carried around on his father's shoulders like an infant. It teases readers' thirst for sunlight throughout from the foggy afternoon at the start to the beams shining from the head of the Spirit of Christmas Present to the sooty darkness of the coal mines to, at last, the "Golden sunlight" that pours down on the reformed Scrooge when he throws open his shutters on Christmas morning. Moreover, it clearly has death—other figures of death through the years have matched the frightening quietude of the Ghost of Christmas Future, but none has surpassed it as a representative of fate's no-nonsense certainty.

There are certainly some grim moments presented in this story, the kinds of details that are avoided by true commercial sentimentalists who today cheapen our sense of the time by using phrases like "Victorian Christmas" or, worse, "Dickensian Christmas" to hawk their merchandise. For one thing, Scrooge is really pretty evil. Adaptations have made him a comical cranky grouch, characterized with the quaint, faintly Biblical epitaph "covetous old sinner"; his crabbing about Bob Cratchit's use of coal might remind readers of their own grandfather or father's battle to control the thermostat in order to hold off poverty. The fact is, though, that the Scrooge of the book is nearly as mean and dangerous as he would like to think he is.

Aside from his interactions with Cratchit— who, after all, toasts Scrooge's health on Christmas and so just may be a glutton for his abuse—the clearest view readers get of his business practices is from the young couple, Caroline and her unnamed husband. They find themselves on the verge of ruin at Scrooge's hand, and are only saved by his death; as a creditor, Scrooge was "merciless."

This sort of urban despair became Dickens' hallmark, his strength as a social activist, waking the public to the miseries that come from forcing uneducated, angry people into crowded, unsanitary conditions."

In his personal life, too, Dickens paints Scrooge's heartlessness more sharply than is necessary to establish the idea of the cranky old miser who has a heart of gold deep within. The strength of his iciness comes through when Belle surprises him by breaking off their engagement on the grounds that he idolizes only money. He has no argument to raise, forced to admit in the face of her well-stated rationality that she is right.

It could be argued that these disturbing aspects of Scrooge's personality cannot be considered true looks at life's dark side because they serve a function in the story: they are things to be overcome to make his final conversion truly triumphant. So they are not about reality, but about good storytelling. I think of it from the other perspective, though, considering how easily it would have been for Dickens to make Scrooge just nasty, not evil, leaving out the extreme details, which show human nature as being a little less disturbing as mass audiences would like to think of it. A book that was only playing off of popular sentiment could easily have done without the young couple celebrating Scrooge's death, or could have had a younger Scrooge snarl "good riddance" when his woman leaves him instead of having him stand awestruck.

Scrooge is the story's protagonist; therefore, Dickens had to necessarily keep him likable to some extent, positioning Scrooge close enough to the border of evil to make him redeemable in the end. With other aspects of *A Christmas Carol* he could be freer to show the world as he saw it, or to show a world that his readers wanted to believe in, if that was what he was trying to do. For every bad in the novel's world there is a good, and for every good a bad: the question becomes whether Dickens was sentimentalizing or manipulating

What Do I Read Next?

- One of the most poignant Christmas stories ever written is Truman Capote's "A Christmas Memory" (1966), which is often included in fiction anthologies and included in his collection *A Christmas Memory, One Christmas [and] The Thanksgiving Visitor* (1996), available from Modern Library.

- Charles Dickens was the author of several commercially and critically popular novels. One of his best is *The Tale of Two Cities,* originally published in 1859. Set against the background of the French Revolution, the story follows the adventures of Sydney Carton, and his eventual self-sacrifice for the sake of his friends. It is also available on CD-ROM from Quiet Vision in 1999.

- Published in 1999, Patricia Davis' novel *A Midnight Carol* chronicles the story of how Dickens' novel came to be: thirty-year-old Charles Dickens, his debts piling up and a fifth child on the way, somehow writes his most popular work.

- Daniel Poole's *What Jane Austen Ate and Charles Dickens Knew* (1993) describes the trials and tribulations of daily life in nineteenth-century England in an informative and amusing way.

---

emotions with these valleys and peaks, creating the proverbial "emotional roller coaster" that leaves readers drained but satisfied, or if this balance of extremes is just an honest way of presenting life.

Among the grimmest sights presented is the back street that the final Ghost takes Scrooge to, a presentment of the only place where his life will matter after his death—the "obscure part of town." The people there are "half-naked, drunken, slipshod and ugly"; the whole area "reeked with crime, with filth, with misery." Unlike the poverty of the Cratchit house, or the dingy coal mine or the lonesome ship at sea, there is no joy in the misery here, and there is going to be no ray of sunshine coming into this quarter once Scrooge has lightened up and started loving his fellow human beings. The foul-smelling street populated by cretins has its reverse image in the joyful Christmas morning scene the Ghost of Christmas Present shows Scrooge, and it is meant to inspire Scrooge's (and, presumably, the reader's) fear of extreme poverty. Yet what it does not have is any comforting sense of hope.

This sort of urban despair became Dickens' hallmark, his strength as a social activist, waking the public to the miseries that come from forcing uneducated, angry people into crowded, unsanitary conditions. This could only be considered manipulative if the author overstates the case to elicit sympathy for a condition that doesn't really exist: historians may argue Dickens' accuracy in recording urban blight in other novels, but here, and throughout *A Christmas Carol,* the short form keeps him from going too far past the truth.

The pawnshop that is located in this slum also has a reverse image—in that cheeriest of all workplaces, Fezziwig's warehouse. In the pawnshop, one encounters "old rags, bottles, bones and greasy offal"; the other has its floors swept and its lamps trimmed by eager employees, encouraged by their boss, so that "the warehouse was as snug, and warm, and dry, and bright a ballroom, as you would desire to see on a winter's night." It is in his portrayals of these two places that critics might be able to find the most fault in Dickens' characterizations, which tend to be on the broad side, so that no one could miss their significance to the story.

The benevolent Fezziwig might have been a credible character if only he hadn't taken up the dance, or danced so well, or had a few more lines of dialogue so that readers could get to know him as something more than a contrast to the figure Scrooge cuts as he presides over his counting house. It makes its point too well, making too memorable in his larger-than-life gusto, straining our imaginations just a little too much by asking us to believe that Scrooge could ever forget what happened there.

Old Joe, the pawnbroker, shows the similar defect of being given too little space within the text of the book to really act out the function he has been assigned. Dickens is not above taking the easy way out—that of having the character tell the audience exactly what conclusion they should reach themselves. "You couldn't have met in a better place," Joe tells the people who have picked the dead man clean of his possessions, reinforcing our impression of the people and the rotten location.

Later he actually says, "We're all suitable to our calling, we're well matched."

Does Dickens have to tell us this? As obvious as it is, would Joe have been conscious if it? As with Fezziwig, this is not so much a case of populist sentimentality, because such people do exist and they do have their place within this story. It is more a case of underdevelopment, of having the characters acting too obviously for functional purposes, which is only slightly different than the unearned emotion that causes critics to charge him with sentimentalizing.

A Christmas Carol has been adapted to the stage, radio, television, and movies thousands of times since it was first printed. Like many things associated with Christmas, these adaptations are meant for children. The weirdly Scrooge-like logic here, that Christmas is something to be put away as one gets older, poses an obvious irony. The result of these adaptations, though, is that many people in our non-reading world only know the story in its sanitized version, from scenes and lines that scriptwriters find acceptable for children.

There is a difference between a well-crafted story that leaves readers feeling good and one molded to be a feel-good piece, and Dickens, with *A Christmas Carol,* stays well within his artistic bounds. There will always be questions about whether particular lines or characterizations or even certain books were made with no better purpose than to yank at the public's heartstrings, but this book, which has a unique place in popular imagination, is more about reality than popularity.

Source: David Kelly, in an essay for *Novels for Students,* Gale, 2000.

Craig Buckwald

Buckwald examines the theme of restriction and containment in A Christmas Carol, *as exemplified by the description of Scrooge as "solitary as an oyster."*

> Oh! but he was a tight-fisted hand at the grindstone, Scrooge! a squeezing, wrenching, grasping, scraping, clutching, covetous old sinner! Hard and sharp as flint, from which no steel had ever struck out generous fire; secret, and self-contained, and solitary as an oyster.

If at the beginning of *A Christmas Carol* Ebenezer Scrooge apparently lacks a heart, he is at all times the undisputed heart of the story he inhabits. It is thus entirely fitting that this formal introduction to the miser's objectionable qualities, occurring in the piece's sixth paragraph, anticipates

> ... "self-contained" points to a condition best summarized thus: what there is inside a thing is kept under wraps, prevented from finding its way to the outside, and what might be larger is kept smaller."

much in the narrative fabric that follows. We could, for example, profitably begin an interpretation of the tale with the first two figures in the description—the "tight-fisted hand" and the unproductive "flint"—for from them spring the images of closed and open and clasped and touching hands; feeble and potent fires; and brightness and darkness through which Dickens' Christmas message palpably appeals to the imaginations of its readers. And yet, the centrality of hand and flint notwithstanding, I want to focus on the culminating simile in which Scrooge is compared to an oyster. The oyster image, I argue, despite its unassuming character, is really a kind of master-trope for the story, one that casts new light not only on Scrooge but on imagery, structure, and meaning in the *Carol* as a whole.

To assess the oyster image's importance in the story, we need to begin with the simile's three-part characterization of Scrooge: "secret, and self-contained, and solitary." That the Scrooge of the first "stave" is "solitary as an oyster," isolated from his fellow creatures as an oyster's body is by its enclosing shell, needs only acknowledgment here. This fact is both generally evident in the story and specifically remarked by the narrator: "To edge his way along the crowded paths of life," we are told, "warning all human sympathy to keep its distance, was what the knowing ones call 'nuts' to Scrooge." By identifying reclusiveness and misanthropy with miserliness, the story characterizes Scrooge's habitual shunning of other people as the denial of the human commerce upon which a healthy society depends.

Unlike the accusation of reclusiveness, the charge that Scrooge is "secret ... as an oyster" seems suspect. "Secret," if it is not to be confused with the other terms, implies in this context that there is not only something hidden inside of Scrooge but something *good,* some equivalent to an oyster's tasty flesh or cradled pearl. We might well be puzzled by such a notion because beneath the miser's outward chilliness, there seems to be, as the narrator says, more "cold within him." But true to the simile, Scrooge does have something better deep inside of him, though for the most part it is kept hidden even from us. Two earlier incarnations comprise the first part of his secret: once there was a Scrooge who, craving love, longed to leave school to join his family for Christmas just as later there was a Scrooge who gratefully, gleefully partook of the Fezziwigs' abundant and caring Christmas hospitality. Like the rooms in his present house that are now let out as offices, the younger Scrooge once belonged to a home; and like the house itself, which once "play[ed]" with other houses, the older Scrooge belonged to a festive community. The second part of Scrooge's secret is that, beneath his rough shell, something of his earlier incarnations still lives and can even on occasion be glimpsed, though by now, with respect to his daily life and outward behavior, it has been rendered as feeble as the small fire he allows his clerk; nearly as contained as fire within flint; and as incapable of issuing forth on its own as is his house, which, during its game of hide-and-seek, must have hidden itself "where it had so little business to be … and … forgotten the way out again." It is only granting this surviving inner warmth that Scrooge's feeling response to the ghostly visions, at first guarded but soon afterwards engaged-in openly, is at all probable.

It is the narrator's claim, however, that Scrooge is "self-contained … as an oyster" that proves the most fruitful, only partly because it addresses both the miser's solitariness and secrecy. If we take into account the way the adjective is colored by the oyster image—an image of a crusty shell "containing" an organism quite shut-off from the world around it—"self-contained" points to a condition best summarized thus: what there is inside a thing is kept under wraps, prevented from finding its way to the outside, and what might be larger is kept smaller. It is in this dual sense that the simile speaks expressively of Scrooge.

The narrator's first pointed words about Scrooge, "Oh! but he was a tight-fisted hand at the grindstone," prepare us for the extreme containment of his physical self. "The cold within him," we are told, "froze his old features, nipped his pointed nose, shrivelled his cheek, stiffened his gait"; we hear of his "thin lips" and "wiry chin." When, a few paragraphs later, we learn of Scrooge's predilection "to edge his way along the crowded paths of life, warning all human sympathy to keep its distance," it is impossible not to imagine him keeping to the edge of the sidewalk when he must venture out onto the London streets. In short, restriction defines, literally or imaginatively, not only Scrooge's physique and physiognomy but his stiff gait, the area trodden by that gait, and his bodily activity in general. In case we fail to notice these physical containments, we are given a foil in Bob Cratchit, who, when finally released from the dungeon-like counting-house for the holiday, emblematically celebrates his freedom in a burst of bodily kinesis. Cratchit, we are told, "went down a slide on Cornhill, at the end of a lane of boys, twenty times, in honour of its being Christmas-eve, and then ran home to Camden Town as hard as he could pelt, to play at blindman's-buff." The active expansiveness of the clerk's physical presence, his body now vertical, now horizontal, his legs kicking out in front of him as he races home, is matched by the extravagance of his movement over land, twenty trips downhill when one would have been out of his way.

But later we are also given foils with an added dimension. When the Ghost of Christmas Past shows Scrooge the vision of Belle as a grown woman, she is at home with her daughter, and both are surrounded by activity personified—more children than Scrooge can count, and "every child … conducting itself like forty." The narrator, however, enviously sexualizes the "young brigands'" "ruthless" "pillag[ing]" of Belle's daughter. He confesses that though he longs to be "one of them," he could never take such liberties with the daughter's person:

> And yet I should have dearly liked, I own, to have touched her lips; to have questioned her, that she might have opened them; to have looked upon the lashes of her downcast eyes, and never raised a blush; to have let loose waves of hair, an inch of which would be a keepsake beyond price: in short, I should have liked, I do confess, to have had the lightest licence of a child, and yet been man enough to know its value.

Later, Scrooge witnesses a game of blindman's-buff played by the company at his nephew's house, during which the narrator disingenuously deplores the conduct of the young man called Topper, who somehow manages to pursue "that plump sister in the lace tucker" wherever she goes, and finally traps her in a corner where he engages in conduct "the most execrable." Whether in the horde of rampant children freely touching Belle's daughter, or in Topper's pursuit and braille identification of Scrooge's niece, the dimension of sexuality is admitted into the expansive physical activity which in the story counterpoints the unredeemed Scrooge's "stiff gait."

Scrooge's self-containment, of course, is more than physical. His obsession with business and wealth not only occupies his time and energy but constitutes the frame of reference by which he judges everything and everyone in his world: "can even I believe that you would choose a dowerless girl," says Belle to Scrooge in one of the first spirit's vision, "—you who, in your very confidence with her, weigh everything by Gain …?" Proving Belle's appraisal, Scrooge earlier reacts harshly to his nephew's greeting of "merry Christmas":

> Merry Christmas! What right have you to be merry? what reason have you to be merry? You're poor enough.

> What's Christmas time to you but a time for paying bills without money; a time for finding yourself a year older, and not an hour richer; a time for balancing your books and having every item in 'em through a round dozen of months presented dead against you?

In addition to an idolization of wealth, Scrooge betrays in these lines a problem of *comprehension,* an inability to see beyond the containment of his own perspective and understand his nephew's opposing values: "what reason have you to be merry? You're poor enough," he cries in the second of his three questions. The fact that Scrooge concerns himself with his nephew's fortunes at all reveals that more than self-concern is at work here: he attempts to purge Fred of his Christmas spirit precisely because *it makes no sense to him* that Fred should keep it. In other words, Scrooge's anti-Christmas speech is, oddly enough, his least selfish moment in the first stave, for it is an attempt to disabuse Fred of unprofitable behavior for Fred's own good. The attempt is feeble, however, due to the very philosophy that Scrooge champions. As he says later to the "portly gentlemen" who urge him to know the conditions and suffering of the poor, "It's not my business…. It's enough for a man to understand his own business, and not to interfere with other people's. Mine occupies me constantly. Good afternoon, gentlemen!" Even Scrooge's unself-conscious use of the word "business" here for "responsibility" reveals that his perspective is contained by his miserly occupation, just as his lonely

living quarters are surrounded by offices, or as an oyster's body is by its shell.

It is perhaps remarkable that Scrooge says as much as he does to Fred about the irrationality of the Christmas spirit, for speech is apparently another activity he prefers to curb. The scene with Fred is of great importance to the story because we witness in it the sparring of opposite philosophies of Christmas. Thus it is necessary that Scrooge, then Fred, each have his say, though Cratchit's applause from the next room after Fred's humane, eloquent utterance ensures that not even the most Scrooge-ish of readers will fail to recognize which philosophy the story sanctions. But once the positions are stated, little more is said, mostly because Scrooge closes his mind to any further discussion and shuts off his flow of words with a resounding "Good afternoon!"—an utterance that he repeats four times, until his nephew is convinced of the impasse and leaves the office. Scrooge also condescends to a brief and unpleasant exchange with the gentlemen who ask him for a Christmas contribution for the poor—an exchange also ended by an unambiguous "Good afternoon …!"—and two briefer ventings of spleen directed toward his clerk. We know of no other words he shares with anyone of flesh and blood until Christmas morning.

Marley's ghost clearly emblematizes an oyster-like containment of body and bodily activity when he laboriously drags up to Scrooge's sitting-room the heavy chain of "cash-boxes, keys, padlocks, ledgers, deeds, and heavy purses wrought in steel" which "wound about him like a tail." That his condition also represents containment of mental activity is revealed in the Ghost's declaration, "My spirit never walked beyond our counting-house—mark me!—in life my spirit never roved beyond the narrow limits of our money-changing hole." Leaving nothing to chance, the phantom makes the connection that hardly needs making: "would you know," he asks Scrooge, "the weight and length of the strong coil you bear yourself? It was full as heavy and as long as this, seven Christmas Eves ago. You have laboured on it, since. It is a ponderous chain!" Scrooge has, we might remember, just "double-locked" himself into his chambers for the night.

Which brings us to the message of the *Carol,* only part of which, in accordance with Marley's appraisal of his own oyster-against-the-"ocean" life, has traditionally been grasped. Responding to the Ghost's lamentations, Scrooge says, "But you were always a good man of business, Jacob":

"Business!" cried the Ghost, wringing its hands again. "Mankind was my business. The common welfare was my business; charity, mercy, forbearance, and benevolence, were, all, my business. The dealings of my trade were but a drop of water in the comprehensive ocean of my business!"

If Scrooge's notion of his life has been limited by too narrow a focus on financial gain, Marley's appraisal of his past life is similarly limited by too narrow a focus on social responsibility. While the story unequivocally prefers reformed Marleyism to unreformed Scroogism, it advocates the former philosophy as only part of a more inclusive program for existence.

A good life, the story tells us, is a vitally *excursive* one. Such a life requires, first, that the individual go beyond the containing limits of the merely self-concerned self to benevolent participation with one's proper society—that is, with humanity or, in Fred's words, with one's "fellow-passengers to the grave." Of course, this participation includes the guardianship of "the common welfare" that Marley outlines, and the love and festivity that he fails to mention, but also more-mundane behaviors such as walking full in the center of a busy sidewalk; frank and honest communication with members of one's family; spontaneous snow-sliding with neighborhood boys; knowledge and sympathetic understanding of other people, ideas, and things; friendly conversation with relatives, solicitors, and employees; even romance and physical sexuality. A "good man" or woman, according to the *Carol* if not to Marley, is social in a very wide sense of the word.

And yet, the story tells us, a properly excursive life also means that the individual, by engaging in the benignly expansive behavior that is all of our nature, realize *for his or her own benefit* the manifold possibilities of being, mental and physical. To put it another way: Scroogism not only damages society but the self that, through action and interaction, could be much more. It is this concern for the self's potential that accounts for the persistent and disturbing imagery of individual impairment and thwarted development in the story: the flint unproductive of fire to which Scrooge is compared; Scrooge's "shrivelled" cheek; the gold and coals in Scrooge's care that are not turned to the human comfort that is their purpose; Belle's daughter who figures to Scrooge the daughter he might have fathered; the Cratchits' threadbare and meager existence; and most pointedly, Tiny Tim, who is in the first scheme of things both lame and destined for a childhood grave. A concern for the self,

independent of any concern with social justice, also accounts for the sympathy which the story encourages in us for Scrooge in his manifestly unhappy humbug existence and which is articulated by the *Carol*'s spokesperson for the Christmas spirit. As Fred says regarding his uncle's refusal to join him for Christmas dinner:

> the consequence of his taking a dislike to us, and not making merry with us, is, as I think, that he loses some pleasant moments, which could do him no harm. I am sure he loses pleasanter companions than he can find in his own thoughts, either in his mouldy old office, or his dusty chambers. I mean to give him the same chance every year, whether he likes it or not, for I pity him.

The story, insisting again and again that self-interest and social good coincide, refuses either to choose or to distinguish between them. In the *Carol,* really one of the most optimistic of all possible worlds, self-interest (properly defined) and social good are quite simply the same thing. It is precisely this identity that is figured in the mutual pleasure-taking/pleasure-giving between Topper and the "plump sister" during blindman's-buff as well as in the nameless phantoms' misery over not being able to help others when Scrooge glimpses them from his own window; and it is precisely this identity that the miser Scrooge, setting his interest at odds with others', cannot see.

Appropriately, the final stave shows that Scrooge-the-oyster has opened his shell, or had it opened, or lost it altogether, as a condition of his redemptive humanization. Where initially he is unrelentingly "solitary," at the end he turns up at the door of his nephew and niece's where he is made to feel at "home" amid the Christmas company; in coming years, he becomes "a second father" to Tiny Tim and "as good a friend ... as the good old city knew, or any other good old city, town, or borough, in the good old world." Similarly, where Scrooge initially keeps his surviving warmth of heart "secret" beneath a wintry exterior, fellow-feeling, sympathy, and joy cascade out of him when he wakes on Christmas morning.

To be sure, his gift to the Cratchits is anonymous. But rather than betraying a division between self and others, his anonymity demonstrates a selfless generosity apparently common enough in the world of the story that the collectors for charity readily assume Scrooge means this when he tells them to "put [him] down for" "Nothing!" But there is a further distinction to be drawn as well. The anonymity of Scrooge's gift, as well as similar instances of "secret" behavior in the story, socializes and thus redeems secrecy by making it a condition of festive surprises. We have seen such surprises when, on Christmas day, Martha is playfully hidden from, then revealed to, Bob Cratchit in the spirit of holiday merriment and when Topper seems to be blindfolded and disinterested, but inexplicably pursues the "plump sister" until he uncovers his matrimonial design with gifts of ring and necklace. In the final stave, playful surprise explains Scrooge's side-"splitting" glee that Bob Cratchit "shan't know who sends" his family the large prize Turkey, and is perhaps partly behind the miser's unannounced poking of his head into Fred's dining room when, for the first time ever, he has come to join the holiday celebration. And such surprise is triumphantly seen in Scrooge's reversal of manner, from "feign[ed]" surliness and displeasure to joyful fellow-feeling, when Bob arrives at the office late on the day after Christmas:

> "Now, I'll tell you what, my friend," said Scrooge, "I am not going to stand this sort of thing any longer. And therefore," he continued, leaping from his stool, and giving Bob such a dig in the waistcoat that he staggered back into the Tank again: "and therefore I am about to raise your salary!"

Scrooge also escapes his various self-containments. Where the "old" Scrooge is contained in person and activity, the "new" Scrooge, like Bob Cratchit on Christmas Eve, explodes with joyful, expansive physical activity, flailing his arms as he wildly attempts to dress himself, "running to the window" and "put[ting] out his head," and then dancing while he shaves. When he gets out "into the streets," instead of keeping to the edge of the sidewalk, literally or figuratively, Scrooge meets passersby "with a delighted smile," heartily shakes hands with one of the "portly" men who visited his office the previous day, and "pat[s] children on the head." "He had never dreamed that any walk—that anything—could give him so much happiness." Scrooge never gets to engage in the sexual fondling that the narrator earlier envies, but he does show a decided, and joyful, inability to keep his hands to himself on the day after Christmas, playfully giving his clerk a powerful "dig in the waistcoat" as he offers him a raise and a clap on the back while he says—"with an earnestness that could not be mistaken"—"A merry Christmas, Bob!" In the same way, where the "old" Scrooge suffers from a containment of perspective, the "new" Scrooge clearly shows that he understands the importance of the Christmas spirit when, for instance, he unreflectingly chooses to enhance the Cratchits' meager celebration or decides to join the festivity at his nephew's home. Finally, where Scrooge at first seems intent on restricting his speech, he now exhibits a positive delight in it. Waking on Christmas morning, he spontaneously "Whoop[s]" and "Hallo[s]" to "all the world" his new-found Christmas spirit. He reveals a fondness for conversation when he shouts from his open window to a boy on the street below:

> "Do you know the Poulterer's, in the next street but one, at the corner?" Scrooge inquired.
>
> "I should hope I did," replied the lad.
>
> "An intelligent boy!" said Scrooge. "A remarkable boy! Do you know whether they've sold the prize Turkey that was hanging up there? Not the little prize Turkey: the big one?"
>
> "What, the one as big as me?" returned the boy.
>
> "What a delightful boy!" said Scrooge. "It's a pleasure to talk to him. Yes, my buck!"

Scrooge is so filled with Christmas spirit that even the boy's "smart" response is to him an "intelligent" one, and a simple question is "delightful"—so welcome is any conversation now to a man who has just found the joy of what lies beyond himself, that "everything could yield him pleasure." The identity of self-interest and social interest that the earlier staves so optimistically assert is also asserted in the final stave, most clearly in Scrooge's interaction with the poulterer's man and the boy when they return with the prize turkey: for every coin paid, there is at least one "chuckle" as Scrooge is giddy with the privilege of making expenditures that will bring the Cratchits happiness.

Scrooge, in short, finally passes beyond his shell. And yet, if we stopped here, we would be ignoring the peculiar resonance that the oyster image has for the larger structure of the story. To perceive it, we need to begin with a couple of facts about the *Carol*.

The first pertains to the "old" Scrooge. Though initially he is far from being another mobilely malignant Iago, neither is Scrooge the innocuous stay-at-home that a shut oyster is. If he were only this, people and dogs would not fear to meet him on the street as they do, nor would we be so sure in our disapproval of him. The truth is that Scrooge is a positive source of pain to others, though only if they have the misfortune of crossing his path, or in some other way rubbing against his immovable, "abrasive" character. When Fred wishes him, "A Merry Christmas, uncle! God save you!" Scrooge snaps back, "Bah! ... Humbug!" Later, when an unlucky caroller stops at Scrooge's keyhole, the miser chases him away with a ruler. Of course, the best example is Bob Cratchit, who suffers in Scrooge's presence but whose spirits soar when he leaves the office. Interestingly, other characters can feel Scrooge's unpleasantness when his presence has merely been invoked. Bob's family feels it when, in the vision of Stave Three, he bids them toast his employer with their holiday concoction of gin and lemon, and, we are told, "the mention of his name cast a dark shadow on the party, which was not dispelled for full five minutes." Scrooge's niece, in another of the second spirit's visions, also finds the festivity of her evening disrupted by talk about her uncle. Scrooge's "abrasiveness," his power to cause discomfort through no special effort of his own, is surely one of the ways in which he is "hard and sharp as flint."

The second fact concerns nearly everybody in the story *except* Scrooge. The "old" Scrooge is unique in the sense that he lacks the Christmas spirit nearly all of the world of the *Carol* possesses so wholeheartedly. If Scrooge is "hard and sharp as flint," the other characters can be seen as "soft"—a word appropriate anyway to the human compassion and lack of severity comprising the Christmas spirit. Softness also inspires the words of the engagingly intrusive narrator. When, for example, the Ghost of Christmas Present reveals the power of his torch to placate angered dinner-carriers, the narrator enthusiastically explains, "For they said, it was a shame to quarrel upon Christmas Day. And so it was! God love it, so it was!" Even the narrator's active disapproval is expressed with appropriate softness—with lightness, even affection: "Oh! but he was a tight-fisted hand at the grindstone, Scrooge! a squeezing, wrenching, grasping, scraping, clutching, covetous old sinner!" The colloquial ring of the initial metaphor, and the participial *tour de force* that follows—both in charged exclamation—are simply too gleeful to allow us to feel the narrator is repulsed, alarmed, or even greatly disturbed by Scrooge's example. There is an amusement and relish in these lines reminiscent of the oral storyteller each time he or she introduces an eccentric character who has taken the polish of time and become a favorite. Perhaps nothing, however, so well articulates the dual attitude of the narrator toward Scrooge as the final "old sinner!"—a label expressing both disapproval and warm familiarity. To sum up, we can see how the story's fictional world and the words of the narrator are consonant, enveloping the "hard," "sharp," "abrasive" Scrooge with concentric layers of "soft" matter.

My point, of course, is that Scrooge is lodged within his world, and his story, as an irritating grain

of sand against the fleshy part of an oyster. A benefit of this analogy is that it not only describes the state of things in the first stave but also how the rest of the story works: Scrooge, undergoing a process of transformation through the visits of the three spirits, finally emerges as the story's "pearl."

There is some sense in regarding Scrooge's transformation as the result of a destructive process. If we see him as an oyster within a crusty shell, closed to the world, Marley's ghost and the three spirits force their way into his mind and heart just as they force their way into his locked apartments. They either pry open his shell bit by bit, or neutralize its hardness through the bombardment of pathetic visions: thus, sounds accompanying a childhood scene "fell upon the heart of Scrooge with a softening influence," and "he softened more and more" when his niece plays on the harp "a simple little air" once familiar to his sister. As a result of the visitations, Scrooge is able to pass through his containing shell as easily as he and the first spirit "passed through the wall" of his solitary dwelling en route to the place of his boyhood.

But the problem with this view of the transforming process is that it does an injustice to Scrooge. Is he defeated by the spirits who come to him for his benefit? Compared with his old humbug self, does the Scrooge of Christmas morning seem diminished in stature or completeness? The answer to both questions is clearly, no. The first spirit increases Scrooge by bringing into his everyday consciousness Christmas memories long-stored in some secret, lost place within him. The second and third spirits augment this consciousness with knowledge of the present and predictions of the future. Together, Marley's ghost and the spirits give Scrooge the wisdom of a new perspective, which then branches out in the qualities of love, compassion, altruism, and joyfulness that he previously lacked. Many of the visions, like that of the Fezziwigs' ball, are a pleasure to Scrooge, but even when he is most plagued by what the spirits show or say to him, he is only set back briefly, the pace of his travels allowing him little time for grief or self-reproach.

In fact, generally speaking, Scrooge's own spirit is unmistakably ascendent during the night. His curiosity, and desire to benefit from the unpreventable visitations, soon supply their own momentum. Vision after vision holds his attention and provokes his questions and comments; "the game of How, When, and Where" that is played at his nephew and niece's Christmas gathering even provokes guesses which none of the company can hear. By the time Scrooge meets the second spirit, it is clear that he accepts the entire supernatural enterprise as his own: "'Spirit,' said Scrooge submissively, 'conduct me where you will. I went forth last night on compulsion, and I learnt a lesson which is working now. Tonight, if you have aught to teach me, let me profit by it'." With the appearance of the third spirit, whose "mysterious presence filled him with a solemn dread," Scrooge's determination and eagerness seem still greater: "'Lead on!' said Scrooge. 'Lead on! The night is waning fast, and it is precious time to me, I know. Lead on, Spirit!'" Because he does possess this momentum, which aligns his will with that of the spirits, we see again how the story is both unequivocally critical of Scrooge's attitudes and behaviors, and merciful to Scrooge the man. Holding him up to rebuke and humiliation and blame is not the story's intent. Rather, the dissociation of the man from his sins allows Dickens to make his point doubly: Dickens condemns Scroogism while he exemplifies an un-Scrooge-like mentality by showing Scrooge authorial kindness.

If Scrooge may be considered ascendent during the night, he emerges positively triumphant on Christmas morning when, among other robust exuberances, he shouts from his window to the street below, adding his joyful noise to the general peals of church bells, "the lustiest peals he had ever heard." Scrooge's expansive vocalizing and bodily movements on Christmas morning are appropriate to a character who seems not to diminish but to grow stronger and more complete before our eyes.

A better way to regard the movement of the story is to discern the "abrasive" anti-Christmas Scrooge made compatible with the "soft" pro-Christmas company comprised of nearly all of the fictional world surrounding him and the narrator as well. Indeed, Scrooge finally joins the others in Christmas spirit and activities. And yet, we have to realize that Scrooge is not so much remade *in* the others' image as he is remade *according* to it. In no other character are Christmas qualities given such a dazzling embodiment as in Scrooge on Christmas morning: "I am as light as a feather, I am as happy as an angel, I am as merry as a schoolboy. I am as giddy as a drunken man," he cries. Scrooge is so charged here with seasonal energy that he takes on multiple identities—another way in which he is "more" or greater at the end of the story than at the beginning. *Too* charged is more precise, for the "new" Scrooge ceases to be merely mortal: he is really the Christmas spirit personified,

its pure essence, and an embodiment more important to the story's meaning than the allegorical and spooky Ghost of Christmas Present because he provides us with a human model of behavior, if also an exaggerated one. It is Scrooge's super-Christmas spirit which gives the story such a satisfactory climax (how less exciting if Scrooge awoke merely to become like Fred!) as well as dictates the brevity of the final stave—such dazzle cannot be prolonged without devaluation. Scrooge's dazzle is the appropriate end-product of the story, a treasured moment revealed only after the necessary processes of generation are complete. Dickens' story, it might be said, finally opens in the last stave to offer us this treasure, this "pearl." When Thackeray praised the *Carol* as "a national benefit, and to every man or woman who reads it a personal kindness," he implicitly paralleled its writing and publication with the giving of a gift [*Fraser's Magazine* 29 (February 1844)]. More Christmas present than mere gift, the story proceeds, even as it obeys the dynamic of a pearl-generating oyster, from the concealment of Scrooge's inner goodness to a climactic unwrapping of that goodness that involves each reader with Dickens in a personal enactment of a Christmas ritual. And so author and reader participate in the excursive sociality that *A Christmas Carol* celebrates.

We can never know, of course, the extent to which Dickens conceived of the structure of his story according to the image of a pearl-generating oyster. But there is some reason to conclude that he would have welcomed such an interpretation as consonant with his own sense of how his story works and of the nature of his authorial role. The careful mothering of supernatural agents effects Scrooge's change, accreted wisdom making Scrooge both more than what he was and better. But behind these spirits is the narrator—certainly an alter-ego of Dickens himself—who really presides over the re-creation. Thus, we should not be surprised to hear the narrator's comment on Scrooge's Christmas laugh: "Really, for a man who had been out of practice for so many years, it was a splendid laugh, a most illustrious laugh. The father of a long, long line of brilliant laughs!" In Genesis we hear of another Creator who, once the work was done, looked down with approval on his Creation. Just what is created in *A Christmas Carol* is glimpsed in the newly awakened Scrooge's own words: "I don't know anything. I'm quite a baby. Never mind. I don't care. I'd rather be a baby. Hallo! Whoop! Hallo here!" In an oyster's experience, the nearest thing to a baby is a pearl.

Source: Craig Buckwald, "Stalking the Figurative Oyster: The Excursive Ideal in *A Christmas Carol*," in *Studies in Short Fiction,* Vol. 27, No. 1, Winter, 1990, pp. 1–14.

William E. Morris

In the following essay, Morris examines Ebenezer Scrooge's "conversion" in A Christmas Carol. *According to Morris, "Dickens does not intend Scrooge's awakening to be a promise for all covetous old sinners, but only a possibility to be individually hoped for."*

As everyone knows, being called a "scrooge" is bad. When labeled like this, one is considered "a tight-fisted hand at the grindstone.... Hard and sharp as flint, from which no steel had ever struck out generous fire; secret, and self-contained, and solitary as an oyster." In reality, and in short, one is a party-pooper, afflicted with general overtones of inhumanity.

This is the popular definition of the word *Scrooge,* and it is unfairly the usual description of Charles Dickens' Ebenezer Scrooge, of *A Christmas Carol.* Scrooge's conversion to a permanent goodness, which is every bit up to those impossible standards met by the totally admirable Cheerybles and Mr. Brownlow, seems to have been utterly forgotten, or ignored. Popularly lost is Dickens' last word on Scrooge: "… it was always said of him that he knew how to keep a Christmas well, if any man alive possessed the knowledge." By common consent Scrooge has been a villain at every Christmas season since 1843. Indeed, that reformed old gentleman might well answer, "'It's not convenient, and it's not fair.'"

What "we" remember about *A Christmas Carol* is the flinty employer, the humbly simple (and sentimental) clerk, and sweet Tiny Tim. If the general reading public remembers Scrooge's conversion at all, it sees the alteration as a punishment brought about and maintained through fear. The conversion is seen as only a part of the story, when in fact it is what the story is *all* about. *A Christmas Carol* is not, as some readers seem to think, "The Little Lame Prince" or "The Confidential Clerk." It is the reawakening of a Christian soul, although (as Edgar Johnson makes clear [in *Charles Dickens, His Tragedy and Triumph,* 1952]) it is not a religious conversion. Religious or not, the story is a celebration of an important conversion, the sort of conversion on which Dickens pinned his hopes for social, moral, economic, and even political recovery in England. The carol sung here is a song of celebration for a Christmas birth that offers hope; it is not a song of thanks for revenge accomplished or for luck had by the poor. To be an "old Scrooge" is, in the final analysis, a good thing to be. And with careful rereading of the tale the clichés of a hasty public would surely disappear.

What is more damagingly unfair than the popular mistake is the critics' treatment of Scrooge's conversion, which ranges from Edgar Johnson's insistence that Scrooge is "nothing other than a personification of economic man" to Humphry House's assertion [in *The Dickens World,* 1941] that "his conversion, moreover, seems to be complete at a stroke, his actions after it uniform." At the critics' hands the enlightenment of Scrooge is not individual, believable, real, or even interesting. Perhaps the most surprising comment is this one by Chesterton [in *Charles Dickens,* 1906]:

> Scrooge is not really inhuman at the beginning any more than he is at the end. There is a heartiness in his inhospitable sentiments that is akin to humour and therefore inhumanity; he is only a crusty old bachelor, and had (I strongly suspect) given away turkeys secretly all his life. The beauty and the real blessing of the story do not lie in the mechanical plot of it, the repentance of Scrooge, probable or improbable; they lie in the great furnace of real unhappiness that glows through Scrooge and everything round him; that great furnace, the heart of Dickens. Whether the Christmas visions would or would not convert Scrooge, they convert us.

It is my contention that the story records the psychological—if overnight—change in Scrooge from a mechanical tool that has been manufactured by the economic institutions around him to the human being he was before business dehumanized him. His conversion is his alone, not that of "economic man"; Dickens does not intend Scrooge's awakening to be a promise for all covetous old sinners, but only a possibility to be individually hoped for. Further, if the visitations by Marley and the three spirits be accepted as dreams ("Marley was dead, to begin with. There is no doubt whatever about that."), their substance, as well as their messages and their effects, must have come from the recesses of Scrooge's own mind. And finally, if the conversion comes from within Scrooge, it could have been effected at a stroke, for surely it had been subconsciously fermenting for a long time. Of such things Christmas miracles, or epiphanies, may very well be made. Scrooge explains it: "'I haven't missed it. The spirits have done it all in one night. They can do anything they like. Of course they can!'"

From the Marley-faced doorknocker to the third Phantom's hood and dress shrinking, collapsing, and dwindling down to the bed post, Scrooge is dreaming, awake and asleep. The entire substance of the dreams has been all of Scrooge's own making; he has, in an agitated state, conjured up those things that he has until now hidden from himself but has not been unaware of: his own compounded sins, and Marley's; his happy and sad boyhood; his small sister and the memory of an unkind father; the gay times working under old Fezziwig on a Christmas long ago; Scrooge's denial of Belle, the girl he was to have married; the supposed or heard-of later happiness of the same girl (at Christmas, of course), married to another man; the eve of Marley's death; the Christmas gaiety of common people at the present Christmas season (which he had known, for he spoke harshly of it at his place of business only that afternoon); the happy Cratchit home this Christmas, with its touching sight of Tiny Tim and the blight of the subdued Cratchit opinion of Scrooge; Christmas present with miners, lighthouse keepers, and seamen—all more content than Scrooge despite their condition; the bright games at the Christmas home of his nephew, a place to which he was invited and angrily refused a few hours ago; the sight of the two tattered children under the Spirit's robes—the boy Ignorance, the girl Want; his own cheap funeral and the theft of his possessions; the scorn of him among business men; the death of Tiny Tim and the view of Scrooge's own tombstone. All these would have been known to him, through experience, imagination, or the public press or gossip.

The dream visions are connected, as dreams, not only to what he knew or feared or imagined, but to each other through recurring scenes, motifs, verbal expressions, and physical props. They are believably motivated—that is, if dreams are ever believably motivated.

In Stave One, before Scrooge goes to sleep, Dickens presents several clues to what trouble his dreams; we can infer the other clues from the dreams themselves. First the reader learns that this afternoon is cold, foggy, and dark. And during the dreams cold, fog, and darkness persist and dominate until they are the atmosphere of the dreams. Cold, which dominates the day, runs through the dreams, relieved only by and for persons who share each other's company. It is not relieved for Scrooge, who in his dreams can no longer use the imagination which Dickens says he relied upon to defeat cold at his counting-house. Cold is the most persistent element in the story—more pervasive than even the fog and darkness. It is the temperature of the world that cannot be shed or blown away

> Religious or not, the story is a celebration of an important conversion, the sort of conversion on which Dickens pinned his hopes for social, moral, economic, and even political recovery in England."

by anyone but must be lived with and among. It is triumphed over only by the philanthropy of fellowship (which might be more specifically called kindness, love, tolerance, and sympathy between individual persons), not by the misanthropy of solitaries or the collective bargaining of institutions ("'I help to support the establishments I have mentioned—they cost enough: and those who are badly off must go there,'" explains Scrooge). Here is that assertion dramatized:

> The cold became intense. In the main street, at the corner of the court, some labourers were repairing the gas-pipes, and had lighted a great fire in a brazier, round which a party of ragged men and boys were gathered: warming their hands and winking their eyes before the blaze in rapture. The water-plug being left in solitude, its overflowing suddenly congealed, and turned to misanthropic ice.

The great fire in the brazier of the workmen is the exact opposite of Scrooge's "very small fire" and the one he allows his clerk ("it looked like one coal"); their rapture is not at all like Scrooge's grouchiness and gloom. In contrast to the laborers', Scrooge's overflowings are congealed and turned to misanthropic ice, like the water-plug left in solitude. It is the solitude of Scrooge that has congealed him so that no outside force of weather knows where to have him. It could not be less open to the warmth that in this story is equated to human companionship.

And yet Scrooge does feel the cold, in spite of what people thought. He has caught cold in the head; he does bundle up; he does sit close to the small fire in his chambers and brood over it. The denial of cold as an economic hindrance is part of a public role that he has taken on as he has slipped into isolation. Fuel costs money just as warmth costs human feeling; and human feeling leads into a world which he has come to foreswear. "What shall I put you down for?" asks one of the gentlemen who come in the spirit of charity to collect money for the needy on Christmas Eve. "'Nothing!' Scrooge replied. 'You wish to be anonymous?' 'I wish to be left alone,' said Scrooge." What Scrooge comes to see (and thus the reason for his conversion) is that if one is left alone he does become anonymous.

Over and over in the dreams, this is Scrooge's fear: that he will be left and forgotten, that he will die and no one will care. This fear grows as the suggestion of anonymity recurs more frequently during the course of the dreams. Defense against cold is the first demand Scrooge makes of Bob Cratchit on the day after Christmas, for a fully awakened Scrooge says, "'Make up the fires and buy another coal-scuttle before you dot another i, Bob Cratchit!'" At last Scrooge has determined to keep human warmth about him.

Fog and darkness become symbols for incommunication and isolation in the dreams; their opposites become symbols for communication and integration with mankind. Light and clarity of vision are subdued, except in flashes of Christmas past when Scrooge is a schoolboy at play, or a young man at old Fezziwig's party, or an onlooker at Belle's happy home. These flashes are only glimmers in a usually dark atmosphere. One of the few bright outdoor scenes is the one in which Scrooge is shown himself playing as a boy: "The city had entirely disappeared. Not a vestige of it was to be seen. The darkness and the mist had vanished with it, for it was a clear, cold, winter day, with snow upon the ground." But, as the Spirit of Christmas Past reminds him, "These are but shadows of the things that have been." Fog and darkness dominate until the last section of the story, when Scrooge awakes on Christmas morning and puts his head out the window to find, "No fog, no mist; clear, bright, jovial, stirring cold; cold piping for the blood to dance to; golden sunlight; heavenly day; sweet fresh air; merry bells. Oh, glorious! Glorious!" Throughout the dreams Scrooge's mind has kept the real weather of the day on which he retired.

Part of the darkness motif is figured in the games hide-and-seek and blindman's-buff. It may be paraphrased as "none are so blind as those that will not see." Apparently in the recent past Scrooge has noticed the blind men's dogs pulling their masters from his path, and then wagging their tails as though they said, "'No eye at all is better than an evil eye, dark master!'" The observation must have been Scrooge's. Perhaps, too, was the plight of his house, "up a yard, where it had so little business to be, that one could scarcely help fancying it must have run there when it was a young house, playing at hide-and-seek with other houses, and forgotten the way out again." Even Scrooge on this evening is being buffeted like a blind man in trying to find his house amid the fog and dark. His flight of fancy about the house ("one could scarcely help fancying it") must surely reflect his unformulated yet subconscious worry about his own state, which the personification of the lost house parallels. Whether Scrooge knew that Cratchit hurried home to play blindman's-buff we do not know, though his dreams and his Christmas actions in behalf of the Cratchits indicate that he knew a great deal about his clerk's family. In any case, in his dreams Scrooge imagines a game of blindman's-buff at his nephew's home, and he also imagines Martha Cratchit playing a game of hide-and-seek with her father. The blind men are buffeted out of love; their awakenings are joyous—in Scrooge's dreams, in his yearnings. It must be the case with Scrooge that he is lost yet struggling to be found.

Cold, fog, and darkness afflict Scrooge's sight and feeling. The sound of bells also plagues him. It is significantly recurrent. At his counting-house it has long disturbed him: "The ancient tower of a church, whose gruff old bell was always peeping slyly down at Scrooge out of a Gothic window in the wall, became invisible, and struck the hours and quarters in the clouds, with tremendous vibrations afterward, as if its teeth were chattering in its frozen head up there." In his chambers, "his glance happened to rest upon a bell, a disused bell, that hung in the room, and communicated for some purpose now forgotten with a chamber in the highest story of the building." This is the bell that starts ringing mysteriously, then stops, and is followed by the clanking noise of Marley's ghost. This bell, as well as the others, symbolizes the mystery of what is lost to Scrooge—the proper use of time and service, of a call to human beings. Bells toll the coming of the spirits, though Scrooge's sense of time causes him to doubt their relevance ("The clock was wrong. An icicle must have got into the works.") Bells call happy people to church; they punctuate parties and other human assembly. At last Scrooge responds to bells without fear, but happily to "the lustiest peals he had ever heard." He has found the purpose for which the bell communicated with a chamber in the highest story of the building. He has had bells on his mind since the evening before, not merely because they marked time's passing but also because they connected people in warmth, worship, play, death, and love. This last would have a special tug upon Scrooge: the girl he was to have married long ago was named Belle.

The hardware of life haunts Scrooge, too—the forged metals which he has depended upon in place of human relations to secure, lock up, and insure what he will possess of existence. He has replaced with metal "solidity"; he has forged a chain, has relied on steel. But the hardware is unsubstantial. On Christmas Eve it melts into the hallucination of a doorknocker that comes alive in the likeness of Jacob Marley. And, though Scrooge doublelocks himself in, the hardware of Marley clanks to him, as does that of numerous other phantoms. Hardware reappears several times more as an undependable tool of life. The last of the Spirits takes Scrooge to a filthy den, a junk heap. "Upon the floor within, were piled up heaps of rusty keys, nails, chains, hinges, files, scales, weights, and refuse iron of all kinds. Secrets that few would like to scrutinise were bred and hidden in mountains of unseemly rags, masses of corrupted fat, and sepulchres of bones." It is here that the dreamed-of charwoman, laundress, and undertaker's man bring to sell for hard cash the only effects of dreamed-of dead Scrooge. And his imagined effects belong here, among the junk. For these, material possessions, Scrooge has traded human love. In the dreams his fear of losing them has emerged. Spirits from the outside world have come into Scrooge's counting-house this afternoon—his nephew, the charity gentlemen, the lad who sang through the keyhole:

'God bless you, merry gentleman! May nothing you dismay!'

They have asked for his money and love. Worse, they have threatened his only security: the belief in only material possession. In the dreams their invasion is reasserted by magnification into phantoms who would take away his wealth.

Selling Scrooge's possessions in the dream, the women say, "'Who's the worse for the loss of a few things like these? Not a dead man, I suppose?' 'No, indeed,' said Mrs. Dilber, laughing. 'If he wanted to keep 'em after he was dead, a wicked old screw,' pursued the woman, 'why wasn't he natural in his lifetime?'" Scrooge, like an old screw—a piece of hardware himself—has not been natural. This he has known subconsciously. He is struggling through metaphor to make himself aware

of it; for he is not yet, in spite of appearances, inhuman. He is not yet as dead as a doornail, which, as Dickens observes at the outset, is considered "the deadest piece of ironmongery in the trade." It was what Marley was as dead as, but not Scrooge, thanks to his submerged conscience.

It is easy to see why several other motifs should run through Scrooge's dreams—the many references to death and burial, to the passage of time, to the poor, to persons unhappy alone and happy gathered together. They are life that Scrooge has tried not to live by.

One motif, marriage, needs exploration, however. The Christmas Eve of the dreams was not only the seventh anniversary of Jacob Marley's death—of Scrooge's last connection with a true fellow misanthropist—but it was also the afternoon he had replied to his nephew's invitation to dinner by saying he would see the nephew in hell first, then had blurted out as rationale: "'Why did you get married?'" Love, to Scrooge, was the only symptom nearer insanity than the wish for a merry Christmas. Scrooge had built a wall of scorn against happy married life, and in the dreams we see his return to the problem, before and after the wall was built. In Stave Two, Belle sums up the problem: "You fear the world too much,' she answered, gently. 'All your hopes have merged into the hope of being beyond the chance of its sordid reproach. I have seen your nobler aspirations fall off one by one, until the master-passion, Gain, engrosses you.'"

But why does gain obsess him? Why has he given up Belle for gold? And why does marriage appall him? The answers may be revealed in the dreams. Taken back to his solitary and unhappy days as a schoolboy, Scrooge sees his old imagined friends of those days, characters from *The Arabian Nights,* and he cries: "'And the Sultan's groom turned upside down by the Genii; there he is upon his head! Serve him right. I'm glad of it. What business had *he* to be married to the Princess!'" The groom is not good enough to marry the Princess, for he is poor. In the next scene of the dream Scrooge appears as a boy left at school while his classmates have gone home on holiday. He is discovered by his sister Fan (later to become mother of Scrooge's nephew), who announces her errand to take Scrooge home:

'To bring you home, home, home!'

'Home, little Fan?' returned the boy. 'Yes!' said the child, brimful of glee. 'Home, for good and all. Home for ever and ever. Father is so much kinder than he used to be, that home's like Heaven! He spoke so gently to me one dear night when I was going to bed, that I was not afraid to ask him once more if you might come home; and he said Yes, you should; and sent me in a coach to bring you. And you're to be a man!' said the child, opening her eyes, 'and are never to come back here; but first, we're to be together all the Christmas long, and have the merriest time in the world.'

We can conjecture the relationship between Scrooge and his father; surely the father had been a tyrant, and possibly he had shaped the ideal of marriage for his son. Or, if one guesses, perhaps the father's cruelty resulted from money worries so that Scrooge felt marriage was possible only if the husband were secure financially. This at least seems to have led to the rift between Scrooge and Belle, which could very well have stemmed from the example of Scrooge's father. The simple fictional childhood of *Arabian Nights* and *Robinson Crusoe* ("Poor Robinson Crusoe, where have you been, Robinson Crusoe?") has been lost, cut in upon by the harsh facts of economic life. Obsession with wealth for its own sake has begun as a desire to build a platform on which to base married life. The obsession has made love for anything but gold impossible. This is what ailed Scrooge—this and the submerged struggle against the master-passion, Gain at the expense of humanity and in the interest of dehumanization.

Scrooge has observed and evidently thought kindly upon the marriages of the Fezziwigs and Cratchits. But the former was overshadowed by fear of insecurity in marriage; Scrooge's youthful sympathy for the Fezziwigs' union was submerged. Similarly, Scrooge's reveling in the happy-and-threatened Cratchit family remained under his flinty consciousness until the dream conversion. Of his sister's marriage we learn only that it resulted in Fan's death; apparently Scrooge cannot think upon it further. He has believed the only safe road is the one to personal economic security. Travel along that road, as Scrooge takes it, necessitates avoidance of human love.

No change can come from without his mind. His emergence must originate in his mind, for that is where he has locked everything up. The dreams are remembrances and imaginings based on remembrance. They are subconscious fears. Moreover, they have been so tightly, inhumanly, pressed that they must burst forth, and Scrooge must either in his crisis reform totally or not at all. There is no degree of inhumanity. It is true that he overcompensates and becomes a ridiculous countercaricature. But then he has shocked himself severely. The

understanding of self has been huge; so its early manifestations were bound to be foolish. If it is difficult to imagine such overnight conversion, it is even more difficult to imagine a gradual one. He is being smothered by his isolationist creed; so he must throw it off violently. Scrooge is either a human being and must understand it, or become a thing. On this fateful Christmas Eve he has denied all he has had of human life—family, friendship, love, charity—indeed, all fellow-feeling. He can no longer find life enough to breathe in isolation; he must break out into the world. The dreams—inner explosions of conscience—are the last resort.

They are not reform theory. They do not echo pamphlets, or legislation, or sermons from the public pulpit, but individual human conscience. They come from the effects of a lifetime at last asserted. Thus they can, apparently at a stroke, overset the habits of many misled years.

Source: William E. Morris, "The Conversion of Scrooge: A Defense of That Good Man's Motivation," in *Studies in Short Fiction,* Vol. III, No. 1, Fall, 1965, pp. 46–55.

Edgar Johnson

Johnson is a major Dickens scholar whose Charles Dickens: His Tragedy and Triumph *(1952) is considered the definitive biography of the novelist. In the following essay adapted from that work, Johnson expounds on the social importance of* A Christmas Carol.

Everyone knows Dickens' *Christmas Carol* for its colorful painting of a rosy fireside good cheer and warmth of feeling, made all the more vivid by the contrasting chill wintry darkness in which its radiant scenes are framed. Most readers realize too how characteristic of all Dickens' sentiments about the Christmas season are the laughter and tenderness and jollity he poured into the *Carol.* What is not so widely understood is that it was also consistently and deliberately created as a critical blast against the very rationale of industrialism and its assumptions about the organizing principles of society. It is an attack upon both the economic behavior of the nineteenth-century business man and the supporting theory of doctrinaire utilitarianism. As such it is a good deal more significant than the mere outburst of warmhearted sentimentality it is often taken to be.

Its sharper intent is, indeed, ingeniously disguised. Not even the festivities at Dingley Dell, in *Pickwick Papers,* seem to have a more genial innocence than the scenes of the *Christmas Carol.* It is full of the tang of snow and cold air and crisp green holly-leaves, and warm with the glow of crimson holly-berries, blazing hearths, and human hearts. Deeper than this, however, Dickens makes of the Christmas spirit a symbolic criticism of the relations that throughout almost all the rest of the year subsist among men. It is a touchstone, revealing and drawing forth the gold of generosity ordinarily crusted over with selfish habit, an earnest of the truth that our natures are not entirely or even essentially devoted to competitive struggle.

Dickens is certain that the enjoyment most men are able to feel in the happiness of others can play a larger part than it does in the tenor of their lives. The sense of brotherhood, he feels, can be broadened to a deeper and more active concern for the welfare of all mankind. It is in this light that Dickens sees the Spirit of Christmas. So understood, as the distinguished scholar Professor Louis Cazamian rightly points out, his "philosophie de Noël" becomes the very core of his social thinking.

Not that Christmas has for Dickens more than the very smallest connection with Christian dogma or theology. It involves no conception of the virgin birth or transubstantiation or sacrificial atonement or redemption by faith. For Dickens Christmas is primarily a human, not a supernatural, feast, with glowing emphasis on goose and gravy, plum-pudding and punch, mistletoe and kissing-games, dancing and frolic, as well as open-handedness, sympathy, and warmth of heart. Dickens does not believe that love of others demands utter abnegation or mortification of the flesh; it is not sadness but joyful fellowship. The triumphal meaning of Christmas peals in the angel voices ringing through the sky: "On earth peace, good will to men." It is a sign that men do not live by bread alone, that they do not live for barter and sale alone. No way of life is either true or rewarding that leaves out men's need of loving and of being loved.

The theme of the *Christmas Carol* is thus closely linked with the theme of *Martin Chuzzlewit,* which was being written and published as a serial during the very time in which the shorter story appeared. The selfishness so variously manifested in the one is limited in the other to the selfishness of financial gain. For in an acquisitive society the form that selfishness predominantly takes is monetary greed. The purpose of such a society is the protection of property rights. Its rules are created by those who have money and power, and are designed, to the extent that they are consistent, for the perpetuation of money and power. With the growing importance of commerce in the eighteenth cen-

> " With the growing importance of commerce in the eighteenth century, and of industry in the nineteenth, political economists—the "philosophers" Dickens detested—rationalized the spirit of ruthless greed into a system claiming authority throughout society."

tury, and of industry in the nineteenth, political economists—the "philosophers" Dickens detested—rationalized the spirit of ruthless greed into a system claiming authority throughout society.

Services as well as goods, they said, were subject only to the laws of profitable trade. There was no just price. One bought in the cheapest market and sold in the dearest. There was no just wage. The mill owner paid the mill hand what competition decreed under the determination of the "iron law of wage." If the poor, the insufficiently aggressive, and the mediocre in ability were unable to live on what they could get, they must starve— or put up with the treadmill and the workhouse— and even these institutions represented concessions to mere humanity that must be made as forbidding as possible. Ideally, no sentimental conceptions must be allowed to obstruct the workings of the law of supply and demand. "Cash-nexus" was the sole bond between man and man. The supreme embodiment of this social theory was the notion of the "economic man," that curiously fragmentary picture of human nature, who never performed any action except at the dictates of monetary gain. And Scrooge, in the *Christmas Carol,* is nothing other than a personification of economic man.

Scrooge's entire life is limited to cash-boxes, ledgers and bills of sale. He underpays and bullies and terrifies his clerk, and grudges him even enough coal in his office fire to keep warm. All sentiment, kindness, generosity, tenderness, he dismisses as humbug. All imagination he regards as a species of mental indigestion. He feels that he has discharged his full duty to society in contributing his share of the taxes that pay for the prison, the workhouse, the operation of the treadmill and the poor law, and he bitterly resents having his pocket picked to keep even them going. The out-of-work and the indigent sick are to him merely idle and useless; they had better die and decrease the surplus population. So entirely does Scrooge exemplify the economic man that, like that abstraction, his grasping rapacity has ceased to have any purpose beyond itself: when he closes up his office for the night he takes his pinched heart off to a solitary dinner at a tavern and then to his bleak chambers where he sits alone over his gruel.

Now from one angle, of course, *A Christmas Carol* indicts the economic philosophy represented by Scrooge for its unhappy influence on society. England's prosperity was not so uncertain—if, indeed, any nation's ever is—that she needed to be parsimonious and cruel to her waifs and strays, or even to the incompetents and casualties of life. To neglect the poor, to deny them education, to give them no protection from covetous employers, to let them be thrown out of work and fall ill and die in filthy surroundings that then engender spreading pestilence, to allow them to be harried by misery into crime—all these turn out in the long run to be the most disastrous shortsightedness.

That is what the Ghost of Christmas Present means in showing Scrooge the two ragged and wolfish children glaring from beneath its robes. "They are Man's," says the Spirit. "And they cling to me, appealing from their fathers. This boy is Ignorance. This girl is Want. Beware them both, and all of their degree, but most of all beware this boy, for on his brow I see that written which is Doom, unless the writing be erased." And when Scrooge asks if they have no refuge, the Spirit ironically echoes his own words: "Are there no prisons? Are there no workhouses?"

Scrooge's relation with his clerk Bob Cratchit is another illustration of the same point. To say, as some commentators have done, that Scrooge is paying Cratchit all he is worth on the open market (or he would get another job) is to assume the very conditions Dickens is attacking. It is not only that timid, uncompetitive people like Bob Cratchit may lack the courage to bargain for their rights. But, as Dickens knows well, there are many things other than the usefulness of a man's work that determine his wage—the existence, for example, of a large body of other men able to do the same job. And if Cratchit is getting the established remuneration for his work, that makes the situation worse, not bet-

ter; for instead of an isolated one, his is a general case. What Dickens has at heart is not any economic conception like Marx's labor theory of value, but a feeling of the human value of human beings. Unless a man is a noxious danger to society, Dickens feels, a beast of prey to be segregated or destroyed; if he is able and willing to work, whatever the work may be—he is entitled at least to enough for him to live on, by the mere virtue of his humanity alone.

But the actual organization that Dickens saw in society callously disregarded all such humane principles. The hardened criminal was maintained in jail with more care than the helpless debtor who had broken no law. The pauper who owed nobody, but whom age, illness or industrial change might have thrown out of work, was treated more severely than many a debtor and jailbird. And the poor clerk or laborer, rendered powerless by his need or the number of others like him, could be held to a pittance barely sufficient to keep him and his family from starvation.

Against such inequities Dickens maintains that any work worth doing should be paid enough to maintain a man and his family without grinding worry. How are the Bob Cratchits and their helpless children to live? Or are we to let the crippled Tiny Tims die and decrease the surplus population? "Man," says the Ghost, "if man you be in heart, not adamant, forbear that wicked cant until you have discovered What the surplus is and Where it is.... It may be, that in the sight of Heaven, you are more worthless and less fit to live than millions like this poor man's child. Oh God! to hear the Insect on the leaf pronouncing on the too much life among his hungry brothers in the dust!"

Coldhearted arrogance and injustice storing up a dangerous heritage of poverty and ignorance— such is Dickens' judgment of the economic system that Scrooge exemplifies. But its consequences do not end with the cruelties it inflicts upon the masses of the people or the evils it works in society. It injures Scrooge as well. All the more generous impulses of humanity he has stifled and mutilated in himself. All natural affection he has crushed. The lonely boy he used to be, weeping in school, the tender brother, the eager youth, the young man who once fell disinterestedly in love with a dowerless girl—what has he done to them in making himself into a money-making machine, as hard and sharp as flint, and frozen with the internal ice that clutches his shriveled heart? That dismal cell, his office, and his gloomy rooms, are only a prison within which he dwells self-confined, barred and close-locked as he drags a chain of his own cashboxes and dusty ledgers. Acting on a distortedly inadequate conception of self-interest, Scrooge has deformed and crippled himself to bitter sterility.

And Scrooge's fallacy is the fallacy of organized society. Like his house, which Dickens fancifully imagines playing hide-and-seek with other houses when it was a young house, and losing its way in a blind alley it has forgotten how to get out of, Scrooge has lost his way between youth and maturity. Society too in the course of its development has gone astray and then hardened itself in obdurate error with a heartless economic theory. Scrooge's conversion is more than the transformation of a single human being. It is a plea for society itself to undergo a change of heart.

Dickens does not, it should be noticed, take the uncompromising position that the self-regarding emotions are to be eradicated altogether. He is not one of those austere theorists who hold that the individual must be subordinated to the state or immolate himself to the service of an abstract humanity. Concern for one's self and one's own welfare is necessary and right, but true self-love cannot be severed from love of others without growing barren and diseased. Only in the communion of brotherhood is it healthy and fruitful. When Scrooge has truly changed, and has dispatched the anonymous gift of the turkey to Bob Cratchit as an earnest of repentance, his next move is to go to his nephew's house and ask wistfully, "Will you let me in, Fred?" With love reanimated in his heart, he may hope for love.

There have been readers who objected to Scrooge's conversion as too sudden and radical to be psychologically convincing. But this is to mistake a semi-serious fantasy for a piece of prosaic realism. Even so, the emotions in Scrooge to which the Ghosts appeal are no unsound means to the intended end: the awakened memories of a past when he had known gentler and warmer ties than in any of his later years, the realization of his exclusion from all kindness and affection in others now, the fears of a future when he may be lonelier and more unloved still. And William James in *The Varieties of Religious Experience* provides scores of case-histories that parallel both the suddenness of Scrooge's conversion and the sense of radiant joy he feels in the world around him after it has taken place. It may be that what really gives the skeptics pause is that Scrooge is converted to a gospel of good cheer. They could probably believe easily enough if he espoused some gloomy doctrine of intolerance.

But it is doubtful whether such questions ever arise when one is actually reading the *Christmas Carol*. From the very beginning Dickens strikes a tone of playful exaggeration that warns us this is no exercise in naturalism. Scrooge carries "his own low temperature always about with him; he iced his office in the dog-days." Blind men's dogs, when they see him coming, tug their masters into doorways to avoid him. The entire world of the story is an animistic one: houses play hide-and-seek, doorknockers come to life as human heads, the tuning of a fiddle is "like fifty stomach aches," old Fezziwig's legs wink as he dances, potatoes bubbling in a saucepan knock loudly at the lid "to be let out and peeled." Scrooge's own language has a jocose hyperbole, even when he is supposed to be most ferocious or most terrified, that makes his very utterance seem half a masquerade. "If I could work my will," he snarls, "every idiot who goes about with 'Merry Christmas' on his lips should be boiled with his own pudding, and buried with a stake of holly through his heart. He should!" Is that the accent of a genuine curmudgeon or of a man trying to sound more violent than he feels? And to Marley's Ghost, despite his disquiet, he remarks, "You may be an undigested bit of beef, a blob of mustard, a crumb of cheese, a fragment of an underdone potato. There's more of gravy than of grave about you, whatever you are!"

All these things make it clear that Dickens—as always when he is most deeply moved and most profound—is speaking in terms of unavowed allegory. But the allegory of Dickens is in one way subtler than the allegory of writers like Kafka or Melville. Kafka is always hinting the existence of hidden meanings by making the experience of his characters so baffling and irrational on a merely realistic level that we are obliged to search for symbolic significances. And Melville, too, by a score of devices, from those rolling, darkly magnificent and extraordinary soliloquies to the mystery of Ahab's intense and impassioned pursuit of the White Whale, forces us to realize that this is a more metaphysical duel than one with a mere deep-sea beast.

Dickens, however, leaves his surface action so entirely clear and the behavior of his characters so plain that they do not puzzle us into groping for gnomic meanings. Scrooge is a miser, his nephew a warmhearted fellow, Bob Cratchit a poor clerk—what could be simpler? If there is a touch of oddity in the details, that is merely Dickens's well-known comic grotesquerie; if Scrooge's change of heart is sharp and antithetical, that is only Dickens'

Mid-nineteenth century engraving of "The Seven Dials Slum in London."

melodramatic sentimentality. Surely all the world knows that Dickens is never profound?

But the truth is that Dickens has so fused his abstract thought and its imaginative forming that one melts almost entirely into the other. Though our emotional perception of Dickens' meaning is immediate and spontaneous, nothing in his handling thrusts upon us an intellectual statement of that meaning. But more than a warm-hearted outpouring of holiday sentiment, the *Christmas Carol* is in essence a serio-comic parable of social redemption. Marley's Ghost is the symbol of divine grace, and the three Christmas Spirits are the working of that grace through the agencies of memory, example and fear. And Scrooge, although of course he is himself too, is not himself alone: he is the embodiment of all that concentration upon material power and callous indifference to the welfare of human beings that the economists had erected into a system, businessmen and industrialists pursued relentlessly, and society taken for granted as inevitable and proper. The conversion of Scrooge is an image of the conversion for which Dickens hopes among mankind.

Source: Edgar Johnson, "The Christmas Carol and the Economic Man," in *American Scholar,* Vol. 21, No. 1, Winter, 1951, pp. 91–8.

Norman Berrow

In the following essay, which was originally presented as a lecture in May, 1937, Berrow reacts negatively to A Christmas Carol.

There has been much said this evening in praise, I might almost say in adulation, of Charles Dickens. Just by way of a change I want to offer a few words of criticism. In case some of you might consider these words as something of the nature of an attack, I should like to point out, though there is really no need to do so, that a man who stands in such an impregnable position as Dickens does not fear attack. But a little criticism may not be amiss.

I should like to give some honest opinions on *the* Christmas Book; and by *the* Christmas Book I mean *A Christmas Carol,* the best known of all the Christmas Books, the one that everybody knows—Dickens readers and others—the one on which young people so often cut their Dickens-teeth.

You will understand that these are my personal opinions. It is probable that a large number of you will disagree with me; if you do I hope you will get up and say so. Discussion is the life-blood of study, and we are a study-circle. Discussion is as good for the intellect as confession is for the soul.

Well, my candid opinion of *A Christmas Carol* is that it is the best of a rather poor lot of stories. In fact, when I consider that it was written by a giant and a genius like Charles Dickens, I think it is the poor best of an exceedingly poor lot.

To begin with, it is humourless. By that I do not mean that it isn't funny or witty—although it most decidedly isn't either—but I mean that it is, to my mind, devoid of that impalpable flavour that may permeate any book, grave or gay, serious or frivolous; that impalpable flavour that almost instantly puts the reader on good terms with himself and with the author. Humour is that quality in literature that gives content.

Humour has nothing to do with farce or wit. If you look up the word in any good dictionary you will find that it gives some such definition as this: "Disposition of mind or feeling; frame of mind;" and so forth. It is the quality in a book that gains your immediate sympathy with the author, the aims and objects of his writings, and all that he stands for as expressed in his work. In a word, humour, in a book, makes you good-humoured.

But *A Christmas Carol* does not give me content, and it does not make me good-humoured; I'm afraid it only irritates me. I have the queerest impression that, though Dickens set himself to write a happy story, he was not altogether a happy man when he wrote it.

My second grievance is that it is childish. The story may not be, but the style is. The opening paragraphs, for instance, give me the impression that Dickens was not writing for intelligent grown-ups, but for rather backward children. In the first page or two he seems to be hammering home a few points into the fickle and wandering mind of a backward child. By the time he has finished with the matter, it is quite clear to even a half-witted Troglodyte that, firstly, Marley was dead, and, secondly, that Scrooge was aware of the fact.

In this opening Dickens is, of course, making a bid for the reader's sympathetic attention to his tale; he is striving for that humour I have just spoken of. But honestly, he does not get my sympathetic attention. I think he fails lamentably.

This is very strange when we consider the glorious openings to some of his other books. Consider, for example, that brilliant discourse on the Chuzzlewit family tree; the account of that meeting that is our introduction to the Pickwick Club; the swing and the rhythm of the account of Veneering's first dinner-party. Veneering's dinner-parties were actually rather dreary affairs to attend;

> "Well, my candid opinion of *A Christmas Carol* is that it is the best of a rather poor lot of stories. In fact, when I consider that it was written by a giant and a genius like Charles Dickens, I think it is the poor best of an exceedingly poor lot."

but to read about them is sheer delight, a delight which brings a smile to our lips and a sudden gush of warmth to our hearts whenever we come upon the name of Veneering. And that smile is not a smile of sympathy and affection for Veneering and Company, but a smile of sympathy and affection for Dickens and his handling of Veneering and Company. I have to admit that the name of Scrooge brings me no such joyous glow of recognition. I have no smile to summon up for his handling of the firm of Scrooge and Marley (deceased).

But my chief quarrel is with the story as a story. It has, of course, a moral, as I well know. But I hate morals hurled at my defenceless head with the vigor and mercilessness with which this one has been hurled. I prefer to extract the moral from a story for myself. And, having decided to write a moral story for Christmas, Dickens decided also to lay it on with a trowel. You don't gild lilies. You paint 'em. You gild refined gold—see Bible. He painted the lily.

A Christmas Carol is a story about Christmas and the awakening of the Christmas spirit in the stony breast of a miser and a skinflint through the medium of supernatural agencies. It is saturated with an exaggerated Christmas fervour; it is larded with soggy and indigestible lumps of sickly sentiment; and it is—or, rather, it is meant to be—made terrible and hair-raising by the introduction of three ghostly apparitions. Of these I say simply this: they may have raised the hair of our fathers and mothers, but I do not think they curdle the blood in our veins to any great extent. In these days we are, to use a colloquialism, more hard-boiled. And there is the inevitable impossible and sanctimonious infant in the person of Tiny Tim. I am sympathetic towards Tiny Tim because he was a cripple, but had he been a hale and hearty child I should have looked almost with kindness on any person who had made away with him.

Dickens, by the way, was never very happy with children. Look at Little Nell, with her graveyard complex; Paul Dombey, with his philosophical discourses on the subject of the wild waves' conversation; Kit Nubbles, with his unnatural conscientiousness; and others. To say the least of it, his child characters were more than a little smug They were angels. We all know very well that children are most decidedly not angels. I have not any children, but if I had and they started speaking and acting like Little Nell, or Little Paul, or Tiny Tim—even if they were cripples—I should have a doctor in right away, and suggest a good hearty blood-letting.

These harsh words are not directed against an author who struggled and fought and passed on to have his place taken by others who came after him. They are directed against the gigantic, irreplaceable figure of the greatest man in English literature, probably the greatest man in the literature of the world. Consequently they are spoken more in sorrow than anger, and without prejudice. They are the candid opinions of one who knows very well that there are those who will spring to the defence of a man, who, incidentally, does not need any defending.

Feeling as I do about the *Christmas Carol,* I rather wonder how Dickens ever came to write it. I have a theory about that, but first I should like to digress a little. I am, in my way, a very humble member of Charles Dickens's profession, and I have often been asked the question: Why does a man write books? Well, there are several answers. He may write a book for money. He has only to write two or three to see the fallacy of that particular answer. He may write a book to gain fame. But there again, apart from a few literary giants, the average author's literary fame—if any—is terribly evanescent and lost in the multitude.

As a matter of fact, the real reason why a man, or a woman, writes fiction is that there is a sort of poison in the blood that wells up and demands outlet in the form of literary expression. The man has to get rid of it or burst. That is a rather forceful way of putting it, but that is the idea. And if he is a born story-teller, no sooner does he get rid of one lot of poison than another wells up inside him. There are, of course, people who feel the urge to write but who never do write. In their case the poison is not so virulent. It wells up, simmers for a time, giving them a kind of mental indigestion, and then dies down

again, and they go on with their jobs as usual. There are also pangs in mental creation....

But there are also pleasures. I personally get a lot of fun in concocting those slight, if bloodthirsty, yarns of mine. True, the mechanical process of typing three hundred or so pages is apt to grow rather wearisome, but the pleasure is there. A man writes what pleases him, and his writing gives him pleasure. That, of course, I need hardly point out, does not mean to say that it will necessarily please his readers. On the other hand, in my short experience, I have found out that there is a great deal of truth in Emerson's dictum: that a man who writes to please himself, pleases everybody; and a man who writes to please other people, pleases nobody.

Now, in the case of *A Christmas Carol,* I feel that Dickens set out to please other people, and not altogether to please himself. The writing of the *Carol* was not so much a pleasure to him as a task. Christmas had come round again, the next issue of his magazine was to be a Christmas number, therefore a Christmas story had to be written. And he wrote it, not because he wanted to write it, but because convention demanded that it should be written. And so he did not do himself justice.

I put forward another point to be considered at the same time. Dickens was in the hey-day of his production—I do not say powers, because his powers never waned—in the flood-tide of his popularity.

He was, I feel sure, an eminently modest man, as all truly great men are, but he was beginning to realise that he was a force in the land. The whole country was laughing uproariously at the antics of Pickwick and his disciples. It had wept over Oliver Twist, followed with breathless interest the adventures of Nicholas Nickleby, devoured *The Old Curiosity Shop* and *Barnaby Rudge,* and had plunged into *Martin Chuzzlewit.* Dickens had discovered that he could sway the nation, and so, when Christmas time of 1843 came round, he decided to sway the nation with a Christmas Moral Story. I can see him in his study, at the well-known desk with the sloping surface, driving a dogged pen and muttering:

"I'll make them feel good-will to all men; by Heaven, I will!"

He did the same the following Christmas, with *The Chimes,* and again I get that impression of dogged determination, of the accomplishment of a task. He begged for sympathy—not for himself, but for others—and at the same time, to give force to his message—I might almost say his lecture, his sermon—he made the flesh creep. Or he tried to.

And in placing this condition upon himself, in writing to order, as it were, the creating of a moral story containing nothing that would bring the semblance of a blush to the cheek of the young person and a vast amount of what was good for that same young person, I think we find something of the reason why these Christmas Books, again to my mind, fall far short of his usual brilliantly high standard.

There is not an atom of bitterness in what I have said. These books detract in no way from the huge enjoyment we all get in reading his other works. But I want to remind you, by way of conclusion, that we are Dickens students, and not just blind Dickens worshippers. We should never forget that, though he was a giant, a genius, a mob in revolt, as Chesterton once so aptly and pithily described him, he was also a very human man, subject to very human faults and frailties.

Source: Norman Berrow, "Some Candid Opinions on *A Christmas Carol,* " in *Dickensian,* Vol. XXXIV, No. 425, December, 1937, pp. 20–4.

Sources

Cecil, David, "Charles Dickens," The Bobbs-Merrill Company, Inc., 1935, pp. 37-74.

Chesterton, G. K., "'Great Expectations'," in *Appreciations and Criticisms of the Works of Charles Dickens,* E. P. Dutton and Co., 1911, pp. 197-206.

———, *Charles Dickens: the Last of the Great Men,* The Press of the Readers Club, 1942, p. 79.

Pool, Daniel, *Dickens' Fur Coat and Charlotte's Unanswered Letters: The Rows and Romances of England's Great Victorian Novelists,* HarperCollins Publishers, 1997, p. 178.

Potter, Dale H., *The Thames Embankment: Environment, Technology, and Society in Victorian London,* University of Akron Press, 1998.

Symons, Julian, *Charles Dickens,* Arthur Barker Ltd., London, 1951.

For Further Study

Hardy, Barbara, "The Change of Heart in Dickens' Novels," in *Victorian Studies,* Vol. V, 1961-62, pp. 49-67.
    Examines the recurring theme of change in Dickens' works

Kaplan, Fred, *Dickens: A Biography,* The Johns Hopkins University Press, 1988.
    Among the many biographies of the author available, this is clearly one of the most insightful and readable.

Page, Norman O., *A Dickens Companion,* Schocken Books, 1984.
    Page, a specialist in Victorian literature, offers a cornucopia for students of Dickens: plot synopses, character listings, and chronologies.

Poole, Mike, "Dickens and Film: 101 Uses for a Dead Author," in *The Changing World of Charles Dickens,* edited by Robert Guiddings, Barnes [and] Noble Books, 1983, pp. 148-62.
    Because this book has been adapted to film so often, it is interesting to look at how Hollywood has interpreted his work.

Stone, Harry, "*A Christmas Carol:* Giving Nursery Tales a Higher Form", in *Dickens and the Invisible World: Fairy Tales, Fantasy and Novel-Making,* Indiana University Press, 1979, pp. 119-45.
    Stone explores the fairy tradition of Victorian England, and his reading of this novel is interesting in its depth of social and biographical background.

Chronicle of a Death Foretold

Gabriel García Márquez

1982

Gabriel García Márquez's novel *Chronicle of a Death Foretold,* first published in English in 1982, is one of the Nobel Prizewinning author's shorter novels, but past and current critics agree that the book's small size hides a huge work of art. According to Jonathan Yardley in *Washington Post Book World, Chronicle of a Death Foretold* "is, in miniature, a virtuoso performance."

The book's power lies in the unique way in which García Márquez relates the plot of a murder about which everyone knows before it happens. A narrator tells the story in the first person, as a witness to the events that occurred. Yet the narrator is recounting the tale years later from an omniscient point of view, sharing all of the characters' thoughts. García Márquez's use of this creative technique adds to the mystery of the murder. In addition, the repeated foretelling of the crime helps build the suspense. Even though the murderers' identities are known, the specific details of the killing are not.

Besides its unusual point of view, the book's themes also contribute to its success. The question of male honor in Latin American culture underlies this story of passion and crime. As in other García Márquez works, there is also an element of the supernatural: dreams and other mystical signs ominously portend the murder. García Márquez's artistry in combining these elements led critic Edith Grossman to say in *Review,* "Once again García Márquez is an ironic chronicler who dazzles the reader with uncommon blendings of fantasy, fable, and fact."

Author Biography

Best known as the author of the prizewinning *One Hundred Years of Solitude,* Gabriel García Márquez began life in Aracataca, Colombia, on March 6, 1928. The son of poor parents, Gabriel Eligio Garcia and Luisa Santiaga Márquez Iguarán, García Márquez lived with his grandparents for the first eight years of his life. According to Márquez, this is a common practice in the Caribbean. In his case, though, his grandparents offered to raise him as a reconciliatory gesture towards their daughter after opposing her marriage to García Márquez's father. As a result, García Márquez grew up in a house with his grandparents, aunts, and uncles and hardly knew his mother. His extended family regaled him with stories: the women told tales of superstition and fantasy, while the men—especially his grandfather—kept him grounded in reality.

In 1947, García Márquez entered the National University of Colombia, in Bogota, to study law. He had to transfer to the University of Cartagena when civil war erupted and closed the University of Bogota. There he began his work as a journalist. He dropped out of college to work as a reporter for the daily paper, *El heraldo,* in Barranquilla and began writing short stories. He had published his first short story, "The Third Resignation," in 1946. The editor of the Bogota newspaper that had published it, *El Espectador* hailed García Márquez as the "new genius of Colombian letters." García Márquez himself, however, was not satisfied with his writing, until a visit back to Aracataca, which was, according to García Márquez, a crucial turning point in his writing. He said in a 1983 *Playboy* interview with Claudia Dreifus, "That day, I realized that all the short stories I had written to that point were simply intellectual elaborations, nothing to do with my reality." García Márquez's writing from that point on reflects the influences of his grandmother's storytelling as well as the myths, superstitions, and lifestyle of the people in Aracataca. *Leaf Storm* introduced the fictional setting, Macondo (named for a banana plantation he saw on his trip back to Aracataca), and its inhabitants. Reviewers think the setting resembles William Faulkner's Yoknapatawpha County.

Even though García Márquez started his most celebrated novel, *One Hundred Years of Solitude,* when he was only twenty, he did not feel that he knew what he really wanted to say in it until about thirteen years later. García Márquez says in the *Playboy* interview that he was driving to Acapulco

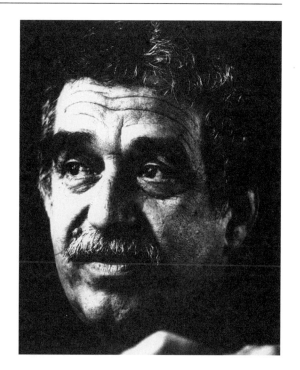

Gabriel García Márquez

when he suddenly had an "illumination" of the tone and everything in the story. Upon his return home, he began writing for six hours a day over the next eighteen months. His wife, Mercedes—whom he married in 1958—cared for their two young sons and supported him.

The resulting book established García Márquez as "one of the greatest living storytellers," according to *Time* magazine correspondent R. Z. Sheppard. He has written several critically acclaimed novels and short stories since then. *Chronicle of a Death Foretold,* published in English in 1982, further developed his reputation as political novelist, and he later wrote both fictionalized and nonfiction accounts of Latin American history. García Márquez's works have won numerous awards, including the 1982 Nobel Prize for Literature.

Plot Summary

Chronicle of a Death Foretold relates the events leading up to and, to a lesser degree, those that follow the murder of Santiago Nasar, a twenty-one year old Colombian of Arab descent. He is killed by the Vicario brothers to avenge the loss of their sister's honor. Told twenty-seven years after the crime by an unnamed narrator (arguably García Márquez himself) who returns to the village where he once lived to put back together "the broken mirror of memory," the story is constructed from the fragmented and often conflicting versions of events as they are remembered by the townspeople and by the narrator himself.

Chapter 1

On the morning after the wedding celebrations for Angela Vicario and Bayardo San Román, Santiago Nasar, son of Plácida Linero and the late Ibrahim Nasar, wakes to greet the bishop who is arriving by boat early that morning. When he enters the kitchen, both the cook, Victoria Guzmán, and her daughter, Divina Flora, know what Santiago Nasar will not learn for some time—that two men are waiting outside the house to kill him. They, like many others Santiago will cross in the short time before his death, do not warn him.

When Santiago leaves the house, he passes the milk shop owned by Clotilde Armenta where the twins, Pedro and Pablo Vicario, are waiting to kill him. It is Clotilde Armenta's plea to "leave him for later, if only out of respect for his grace the bishop" that keeps the twins from killing him immediately. The bishop, however, never gets off his boat and departs after drifting past the crowd gathered on the pier. Santiago then joins Margot, the narrator's sister, and their friend Cristo Bedoya, two of the only people who still do not know about the twins' intentions. Santiago accepts an invitation to breakfast with Margot but wishes first to return home and change.

Meanwhile, Margot learns that Angela Vicario has been returned to her parents by her husband because he discovered that she wasn't a virgin. She does not know how Santiago is involved, only that two men are waiting for him to kill him. When Margot's (and the narrator's) mother hears the news, she immediately sets out to warn Plácida Linero that her son is in danger, but is stopped in the street and told that "they've already killed him."

Chapter 2

Bayardo San Román arrived in the town for the first time in August of the year before looking for someone to marry. According to the narrator, it was never well established how he and Angela Vicario met. One version has Bayardo deciding to marry Angela after first seeing her pass by his boarding house; another has the pair meeting for the first time on the national holiday in October. According to the latter version, Bayardo wins a music box which he has gift-wrapped and delivered to

Angela's home. He soon wins the family with his charms and, despite Angela's protests, succeeds in making her his fiancée.

Prior to the wedding, Angela comes close to telling her mother that she isn't a virgin but is dissuaded from her good intentions and follows the advice of two confidantes who teach her how "to feign her lost possession" so that, on her first morning as a newlywed, she can display the sheet with the stain of honor. When her wedding night arrives, however, she is unable to carry out the "dirty" trick and is returned to her parents' house by her husband. At home, Angela is beaten by her mother and is confronted by her brothers, to whom she reveals the name of the man responsible: Santiago Nasar.

Chapter 3

After completing their gruesome task, the Vicario brothers surrender themselves to their church and announce that although they killed Santiago Nasar openly, they are innocent because it was a matter of honor. Despite their lack of remorse, the narrator tries to demonstrate that the twins did all they could to have someone stop them.

In the meat market where the twins go to sharpen their knives, Pedro and Pablo take every opportunity to announce their intentions. "We're going to kill Santiago Nasar," they say repeatedly. Later, at Clotilde Armenta's, they even reveal their plans to a policeman who passes on the information to the mayor. The latter takes away the twins' knives, but Clotilde Armenta believes the twins should be detained to spare them "from the horrible duty that's fallen on them." She says this knowing that the Vicario brothers are "not as eager to carry out the sentence as to find someone who would do them the favor of stopping them."

Although Pedro thinks his and his brother's duty fulfilled when the mayor disarms them, Pablo insists they carry out their deed. "There's no way out of this," Pablo tells his brother, "it's as if it had already happened." They return to Clotilde Armenta's with a new set of knives and wait while "fake customers" come in to see whether what they have heard is true.

Chapter 4

Following Santiago Nasar's death, an autopsy is performed and determines that the cause of death was a massive hemorrhage brought on by any one of seven major wounds. The autopsy, a "massacre" performed by Father Amador in the absence of Dr. Dionosio Iguarán, makes it impossible to preserve the body and Santiago is buried hurriedly at dawn the next day.

On that day too the entire Vicario family, except the imprisoned twins, leaves town "until spirits cool off." They never return. The twins remain imprisoned for three years awaiting their trial but are eventually absolved of the crime. Pablo then marries his longtime fiancée and Pedro re-enlists in the armed forces and disappears in guerrilla territory.

For many, the only real victim in this tragedy is Bayardo San Román. He is found in his home on the Saturday following the crime, unconscious and in the last stages of ethylic intoxication. He recovers and is later taken away by his family. Angela, for her part, goes "crazy" for her husband following her rejection on her wedding night. For years she writes him a weekly letter until, one day, he shows up at her door, fat and balding, but wearing the same belt and saddlebags he wore in his youth. He carries with him a suitcase with clothing in order to stay and another filled with the almost two thousand unopened letters that she'd written him.

Chapter 5

According to the narrator, Santiago Nasar dies without understanding his death. It is only after parting from Margot and Cristo Bedoya, when Santiago enters the home of his fiancée, Flora Miguel, that he is finally told that the Vicario brothers are waiting for him to kill him. Flora Miguel has heard the news and, fearing that Santiago will be forced to marry Angela Vicario to give her back her honor, returns to him his letters, crying, "I hope they kill you."

When Santiago leaves his fiancée's house, confused and disoriented, he finds himself amid crowds of people stationed on the square as they do on parade days. He begins to walk towards his house and is spotted by the twins. Clotilde Armenta yells to Santiago to run, but Santiago's mother, believing that her son is already up in his room, locks the door seconds before he would have reached safety. Instead, the twins catch up to him and carve him with their knives. The watching crowd shouts, "frightened by its own crime." When the twins are done, Santiago is left "holding his hanging intestines in his hands," walks more than a hundred yards to the back door of his house and falls on his face in the kitchen.

Characters

Colonel Aponte

See Lazaro Aponte

Lazaro Aponte

The head of the police, Lazaro Aponte (also known as Colonel Aponte) first hears of the twins' plot to kill Santiago a little after four o'clock that morning. He has just finished shaving when one of his officers, Leandro Pornoy, tells him. He does not take the threat too seriously, because when he sees the twins, they seem fairly sober. He takes their knives away and feels assured that they will not carry out their plan.

Clotilde Armenta

Owner of the milk shop where the killers slept and awaited Santiago, Clotilde Armenta claims that Santiago already looked like a ghost when she saw him early on the morning of the murder. She makes a mild attempt to convince the twins not to kill Santiago.

Cristo Bedoya

Cristo is a friend of Santiago and of the narrator. The three young men spend the night before the murder attending Angela Vicario's wedding. The next morning, Cristo is with Margot and Santiago on the pier awaiting the bishop's arrival. Cristo and Santiago go their separate ways when they reach the village square. When Cristo hears of the murder plot, he tries, to no avail, to catch up with Santiago to warn him.

Maria Cervantes

Maria owns the brothel, or "house of mercies," where Santiago Nasar, Cristo Bedoya, Luis Enrique, and his brother, the narrator, continue their partying after the wedding. Maria has the reputation of having helped all of them lose their virginity. She is tender and beautiful, yet strict about her house rules.

Purisima del Carmen

Purisima is the mother of Angela and the twins, Pedro and Pablo. A former schoolteacher, Purisima is married to Poncio and has dedicated her life to being a wife and mother. She has raised her daughters to be good wives and mothers and her sons to be men.

Media Adaptations

- Graciela Daniele adapted *Chronicle of a Death Foretold* as an on-Broadway musical performed at the Plymouth Theater in New York City in July, 1995. The theater production received mixed reviews, but was nominated for a Tony award in the Best Musical category.

Divina Flor

A young woman just entering adolescence, Divina Flor is Victoria Guzmán's daughter. Seeing Santiago always overwhelms Divina with emotions she can not yet define. Santiago touches her in ways she does not like and seems to want to harm her. She knows of the plot to kill Santiago, but like her mother, she tells him nothing. She is too young to decide to tell him on her own and is frightened enough by him to want to keep her distance.

Victoria Guzmán

Victoria Guzmán cooks for the Nasar family. Formerly Ibrahim Nasar's mistress, Victoria views Santiago with as much disdain as she does his late father. She still hates Ibrahim for keeping her as his mistress and then making her his cook when he tired of her. She thinks Santiago is exactly like his father and works diligently to keep Santiago away from her daughter, Divina Flor. Victoria learns early on the morning of the murder that Santiago is destined to die, but she says nothing to him.

Plácida Linero

Santiago's mother, Plácida Linero, interprets people's dreams. On the day of her son's death, however, she fails to recognize the significance of Santiago's dream of birds and trees the night before. She regrets that she paid more attention to the birds, which signify good health. Trees, on the other hand, are an omen. In her later years, Plácida suffers from chronic headaches that started on the day she last saw her son. Her knowledge that she unwittingly closed the main door of the house

against Santiago, where his killers caught up with him, haunts her.

Flora Miguel

Flora is Santiago's fiancée through their parents' arrangement. Her family never opens the doors or receives visitors before noon. Flora learns early on the morning of the murder that Santiago is going to die. Because she is afraid that if Santiago lives he will have to marry Angela to save her honor, Flora invites Santiago into her home and vents her frustration and rage. Flora's father, concerned about his daughter, comes to check on her and is the one who tells Santiago of the plot.

Narrator

The narrator never gives his name, but he is a member of the Santiaga family, son to Luisa and brother to Margot. He is also a friend of Santiago Nasar. The narrator has returned to his village twenty-seven years after Santiago's murder and is trying to piece together the events of the day.

Ibrahim Nasar

Ibrahim Nasar, Santiago's father and Plácida Linero's husband, has been dead for three years when the story opens. His memory lives on in Santiago, however, who has his good looks and runs his ranch. Nasar had come to the Caribbean village with the last group of Arabs who arrived after the civil wars ended. A relatively wealthy man, he had purchased the warehouse—in which Plácida and Santiago live—and brought his mistress, Victoria Guzmán, to live with them as their cook. Victoria despises Ibrahim for his womanizing and hates Santiago because he so much behaves like his father.

Santiago Nasar

The son of the recently deceased Arab, Ibrahim Nasar, Santiago Nasar lives with his mother, Plácida Linero, in a small Caribbean village. Twenty-one-year-old Santiago resembles his father. He has his father's Arab eyelids and curly hair. He also possesses his father's love for horses and firearms as well as his wisdom and values. Having inherited the family ranch, The Divine Face, Santiago enjoys a comfortable life and has money to spare. From his mother, Santiago has received a sixth sense about things. On the day of his death, Santiago tells his mother of dreams that he has been having about trees and birds.

Slim and pale, Santiago wears his clothes well—typically a khaki outfit and boots when he is working. On special occasions, such as the day of the Bishop's arrival at the beginning of the story, Santiago looks especially handsome in his white linen shirt and pants. Women appreciate Santiago's good looks and fortune as well as his pleasant disposition. They consider him a man of his word. Men, too, admire Santiago. When his father dies, Santiago has to leave his studies to manage the family business, yet he never complains and is always willing to join with his friends in celebrations of any kind. They know Santiago to be a man who is careful with his guns and ammunition and who has no reason to arm himself except when he is working in the country.

Santiago is to marry Flora Miguel at Christmas time. He seems happy with the arrangement and is content to live life as it is. He appears to have no enemies. Santiago's happy-go-lucky lifestyle ends, however, when Angela Vicario accuses him of taking her virginity.

Pura

See Purisima Del Carmen

Bayardo San Román

The insulted bridegroom Bayardo San Román returns Angela Vicario to her parents' home when he discovers that she is not a virgin. San Román acts very much the gentleman whom people have come to know since he appeared in their small community. Having only been a resident for six months, San Román still has people guessing about his background. The women, however, love his looks and do not worry about who he is. He arrives dressed in a short calfskin jacket, tight trousers, and gloves to match, with silver decorating his boots, belt, and saddlebags. His physique matches that of a bullfighter's, and his skin glows with health. When Bayardo's family arrives for the wedding, the townspeople discover that Bayardo is the son of a wealthy civil war hero.

General Petronio San Román

Bayardo's father, the General, arrives for the wedding in a Model T Ford with an official license. Famous for his leadership in the past century's civil wars, he is immediately recognizable. The General wears the Medal of Valor on his jacket and carries a cane that bears the nation shield. The people of the village no longer question Bayardo's honor and understand that because of who he is, Bayardo can marry anyone.

Luisa Santiaga

Luisa, the narrator's mother, typically knows everything that is going on. On the morning of the killing, however, she goes about her business at home without any inkling of Santiago's fate. When her daughter, Margot, arrives home and begins to relate what she has heard on the docks, however, Luisa suddenly knows before Margot has finished telling her. Luisa is Santiago's godmother but is also a blood relative of Pura Vicario, Angela's mother; therefore, the knowledge of the plan to kill Santiago poses a problem for Luisa.

Margot Santiaga

The narrator's sister and Luisa's daughter, Margot envies Santiago's fiancée. To spend time with Santiago, Margot often invites Santiago to breakfast at her parents' home. Having felt a premonition about Santiago on the day of the murder, she urges Santiago to go home with her immediately. Later, she learns about the plot to kill Santiago while she is awaiting the arrival of the bishop. She is distressed by the news and hurries home to tell her mother.

Angela Vicario

The sister to twins Pedro and Pablo, Angela suffers great humiliation when her newlywed husband discovers that she is not a virgin. Angela is the youngest daughter of the Vicario family, who have raised her to marry. Even though she is prettier than her sisters, she somewhat resembles a nun, appearing meek and helpless. The Vicarios have watched over her carefully, so Angela has had little chance to develop social skills or to be alone with men. Everyone expects Angela to be chaste. When they discover Angela's secret, the family reacts violently to the knowledge that Santiago Nasar is responsible for her disgrace.

Pablo Vicario

Even though twenty-four-year-old Pablo is the older of the Vicario twins by about six minutes, he assumes the role of the obliging younger brother. When Pedro leaves for the military, Pablo stays home to mind the business and take care of the family. Upon Pedro's return, however, Pablo is happy to depend on his brother's leadership. Pedro claims the responsibility for making the decision to kill Santiago. Pablo, however, actually gets the knives and convinces Pedro to carry out his plans after the mayor has disarmed them once.

Pedro Vicario

Pedro Vicario, pig slaughterer by trade, is the twin to Pablo. Pedro and Pablo are responsible for Santiago's murder. Pedro is the "younger" of the twins, having been born about six minutes after Pablo. Twenty-four years old, Pedro and Pablo have lived a hard life. They have a reputation for heavy drinking and carousing. Pedro started their slaughtering business after his father lost his eyesight. While Pedro is the more sensitive of the two, his time in the military has made him hard. He likes to give people orders. Pedro claims to have made the decision to kill Santiago. In addition to acquiring in the military his tendency to command, Pedro also contracted blennorrhea, a medical condition that makes urination difficult and painful.

Poncio Vicario

Poncio Vicario heads the Vicario household. As a former goldsmith who spent years doing close work, he has lost his eyesight. While the family still holds him in high esteem, he is not accustomed to being blind and appears confused and anxious most of the time.

The Widower Xius

Bayardo convinces the widower Xius, an old man living alone in the prettiest house in town, to sell it. He does not decide to relinquish his home, though, until Bayardo offers him ten thousand pesos. Although extremely sentimental about his home and unhappy to be put in such a position, the widower gives in. He dies only two months later.

Themes

Honor

The motive for the murder of Santiago Nasar lies undetected until halfway through *Chronicle of a Death Foretold*. While everyone knows that Nasar will be murdered, no one knows the reason. Then, after a night of carousing, the Vicario twins, Pedro and Pablo, return home at their mother's summons. The family presses a devastated Angela, the twins' sister, to tell the reason for her humiliated return from her marriage bed. When Angela says, "Santiago Nasar," the twins know immediately that they must defend their sister's honor. The twins' attorney views the act as "homicide in legitimate defense of honor," which is upheld by the court. The priest calls the twins' surrender "an act of great dignity." When the twins claim their innocence, the priest says that they may be so before God, while Pablo Vicario says, "Before God and before men. It was a matter of honor."

Revenge

While the twins say the murder was necessary for their sister's good name, and the courts agree with them, many disagree, viewing the murder as a cruel act of revenge. The manner in which they kill Santiago appears to be much more vicious than what a simple murder for honor would entail. The twins first obtain their two best butchering knives, one for quartering and one for trimming. When Colonel Aponte takes these knives from them, the twins return to their butchering shop to get another quartering knife—with a broad, curved blade—and a twelve-inch knife with a rusty edge. Intent on making sure Santiago is dead, the twins use the knives to stab him over and over again. Seven of the wounds are fatal; the liver, stomach, pancreas, and colon are nearly destroyed. The twins stab him with such vengeance that they are covered with blood themselves, and the main door of Plácida Linero's house, where Santiago was killed, must be repaired by the city. Further supporting the view that the twins acted in revenge is the fact that they show no remorse for the murder.

After the murder, the twins fear revenge from the Arab community. Even though they believe they have rightfully murdered Santiago for their sister's honor, the twins think that the tightly knit community of Arabs will seek revenge for the loss of one of their own. When Pablo becomes ill at the jail, Pedro is convinced that the Arabs have poisoned him.

Sex Roles

Purisima del Carmen, Angela Vicario's mother, has raised her daughters to be good wives. The girls do not marry until late in life, seldom socializing beyond the confines of their own home. They spend their time doing embroidery, sewing, weaving, washing and ironing, arranging flowers, making candy, and writing engagement announcements. They also keep the old traditions alive, such as sitting up with the ill, comforting the dying, and enshrouding the dead. While their mother believes they are perfect, men view them as too tied to their women's traditions.

Purisima del Carmen's sons, on the other hand, are raised to be men. They serve in the war, take over their father's business when he goes blind, drink and party until all hours of the night, and spend time in the local brothel. When the family

Topics For Further Study

- Pedro Vicario suffers from a medical condition he acquired while in the military. What is the condition? Research its causes, symptoms, and treatments. Assume the role of a medical practitioner and create a presentation to inform your colleagues about the illness.

- In *Chronicle of a Death Foretold,* the narrator tells the story from a first-person omniscient point of view. Study the various literary points of view and explain why this is an unusual technique.

- Literary critics often credit García Márquez with reviving Latin American literature. Why is this? Research the changes in Latin American literature from the 1920s through the 1980s and make reference to Márquez's contributions.

- Critics have called García Márquez a master of the literary genre magical realism. What is magical realism? Where and how did it originate? Compare and contrast this Latin American genre with other genres or styles, such as science fiction/fantasy or prose poetry.

- García Márquez refers to "the civil wars," particularly when he introduces Santiago Nasar's father, Ibrahim. Investigate the political history of Latin America to determine whether this reference is fact or fiction. Write a paper supporting your findings.

- García Márquez is included in a group of writers referred to as the "Boom generation" in Latin America. Investigate Latin American culture to determine the following: Why do these writers have this distinction? When was the "Boom generation" prominent? Make a comparison to similar times and events in the United States' history, for example, the Harlem Renaissance.

- Investigate Latin American culture to gain an understanding of the idea of "male honor." What is the view of male image in Latin American culture today? How has this affected the treatment of women in Latin America?

---

insists on Angela's marrying Bayardo, a man she has seldom even seen, the twins stay out of it because, "It looked to us like woman problems." "Woman problems" become "men's problems" when the family calls the twins home upon Angela's return. She feels relieved to let them take the matter into their hands, as the family expects them to do.

Deception

Angela Vicario is not a virgin when she marries Bayardo, but no one would suspect otherwise. Her mother has sheltered her for her entire life. Angela has never been engaged before, nor has she been allowed to go out alone with Bayardo in the time they have known one another. Angela, however, is concerned that her bridegroom will learn her secret on their wedding night, and considers telling her mother before the wedding. Instead, she tells two of her friends, who advise her not to tell her mother. In addition, they tell Angela that men do not really know the difference and that she can trick Bayardo into believing that she is a virgin. Angela believes them. Not only does Angela wear the veil and orange blossoms that signify purity, she carries out her friends' plan of deception on her wedding night.

Supernatural

Throughout of *Chronicle of a Death Foretold,* Márquez weaves elements of the supernatural. From the dreams that Santiago has the night before his death to the signs that people note foretelling his death, a sense of an unseen force prevails. For example, Santiago has inherited his "sixth sense" from his mother, Plácida. Margot feels "the angel pass by" as she listens to Santiago plan his wedding. Supernatural intervention pervades all aspects

---

of the characters lives. For example, Purisima del Carmen tells her daughters that if they comb their hair at night, they will slow down seafarers.

Style

Point of View

One of the most outstanding features of *Chronicle of a Death Foretold* is the point of view García Márquez uses to tell the story. Narrating the story from the first-person point of view is the unnamed son of Luisa Santiaga and brother of Margot, Luis, Jaime, and a nun. Having returned to the river village after being gone for twenty-seven years, the narrator tries to reconstruct the events of the day that ends in the murder of Santiago Nasar. Typically, a first-person narrator gives his own point of view but does not know what other characters are thinking: an ability usually reserved for the third-person omniscient, or all-knowing, point of view. In this novel, however, García Márquez bends the rules: the narrator tells the story in the first person, yet he also relates everything everyone is thinking.

Setting

Chronicle of a Death Foretold takes place in a small, Latin American river village off the coast of the Caribbean sometime after the civil wars. Once a busy center for shipping and ocean-going ships, the town now lacks commerce as a result of shifting river currents.

The events of the story evolve over a two-day time period. A wedding has taken place the night before between a well-known young woman from the town and a rich stranger who has been a resident for only six months. On the day of the murder, most of the townspeople have hangovers from the wedding reception. Because a visit from the bishop is expected, however, a festive air prevails.

Foreshadowing

Foreshadowing is typically achieved through an author's implication that an event is going to occur. García Márquez adds a twist to foreshadowing by telling exactly what is going to happen but not why it will happen. The entire story builds on the foretelling of Santiago's murder. The twins do not hide their plot; they tell everyone they meet of their plans. Each village person who hears about the scheme tells the next person. Santiago himself dreams of birds and trees the night before he dies, which his mother later interprets as the foretelling

of his death. In the end, even Santiago knows that he is going to die.

Dream Vision

Throughout *Chronicle of a Death Foretold*, the characters refer to dreams and visions they have that are related to Santiago's impending death. Santiago's mother, for example, though well-known for her interpretations of dreams, fails to understand Santiago's dream of his own death. He tells her of his dream of traveling through a grove of trees and awakening feeling as if he is covered with bird excrement. She remembers later that she paid attention only to the part about the birds, which typically imply good health. Clotilde Armenta claims years after the murder that she thought Santiago "already looked like a ghost" when she saw him at dawn that morning. Margot Santiaga, listening to Santiago boast that his wedding will be even more magnificent than Angela Vicario's "felt the angel pass by." The author's many references to dreams and visions contribute to the surrealistic tone that is characteristic of magical realism.

Magical realism

Latin American culture gave birth to the literary genre magical realism. While critics attribute its beginnings to the Cuban novelist and short story writer Alejo Carpentier they agree that García Márquez has continued its tradition. The hallmark of magical realism is its roots in reality with a tendency toward the fantastic. That is, while everything a magic realist writes has a historical basis, it also has fictitious elements throughout. Emphasizing this point, García Márquez said in an interview with Peter H. Stone in *The Paris Review,* "It always amuses me that the biggest praise for my work comes for the imagination while the truth is that there's not a single line in all my work that does not have a basis in reality."

Historical Context

The Birth of Latin American Culture

The term "Latin America" refers to the area that includes all of the Caribbean islands and the mainland that stretches from Mexico to the southernmost tip of South America. Latin America has a very long history, dating back to Columbus' discovery of the territory in 1492. Settled mostly by Spanish and Portuguese immigrants, Latin American culture is derived from both its European newcomers and its native inhabitants' traditions. Márquez blends elements from both cultures in *Chronicle of a Death Foretold.*

When the Spanish and Portuguese arrived, they easily overcame the native populations. The colonists destroyed native architecture, replaced the native religions with Catholicism, and strengthened the class system that already existed. As the natives died from diseases brought to them by the European immigrants, they were replaced by a new generation that resulted from an intermixing of the male immigrants and the female natives. The new population, known as mestizos, makes up the greatest part of Latin American society today. The mestizos, along with the remaining natives and African slaves, made up the lower class of Latin Americans. They and the mixed-blood mulattos worked as slaves or in the mines. The upper class included whites from Spain and Portugal known as peninsulares. The peninsulares were the only Latin Americans who could hold public office or work as professionals. Between the upper and lower class were the Creoles, European whites who were born in the colonies. The Creoles, although really equal to the peninsulares, were not permitted to hold government positions or to work as professionals. The struggles between the peninsulares and Creoles contributed to the wars for independence.

Colombian Civil Wars

In *Chronicle of a Death Foretold,* Ibrahim Nasar comes to the village after the end of the civil wars. The wars to which García Márquez refers are the Colombian wars for independence. Colombia, called New Granada at the time, experienced a separatist movement in the 1700s as a result of taxation and political and commercial restrictions placed on the Creoles. While independence was assured with Simon Bolivar's victory at the Battle of Boyaca, disagreement between Conservatives and Liberals arose over the issue of separation between church and state. Conservatives stood for a strong centralized government and the continuation of traditional class and clerical privileges. The Liberals believed in universal suffrage and the complete separation of church and state. The conflicts have continued throughout the years.

Post-Colonial Latin America

By 1830, most of the Latin America colonies had gained independence from their mother countries. While they continued to trade with Spain, Portugal, and Great Britain, they began to establish themselves as exporters of raw materials to the rest of the world. In addition to experiencing economic growth, Latin America also gained population. Immigrants poured into Latin American from less prosperous or politically unstable European countries. The growth in population and economic development has continued through the twentieth century. In the late 1990s, the Latin American economy was about the same size as the economies of France, Italy, or the United Kingdom.

Latin American Literature

Latin American literature aligns itself with the history of the region. Literary experts typically delineate four periods of Latin American literature: the colonial period, the independence period, the national consolidation period, and the contemporary period. During the colonial period, the literature reflected its Spanish and Portuguese roots and consisted primarily of didactic prose and chronicles of events. The independence movement of the early 1800s saw a move towards patriotic themes in mostly poetic form. The consolidation period that followed brought about Románticism—and later, modernism—with essays being the favorite mode of expression. Finally, Latin American literature evolved into the short story and drama forms that matured in the early twentieth century. The mid-twentieth century saw the rise of magical realism, for which García Márquez is best known. García Márquez was part of the "boom" trend, the growth of novel writing, that occurred in the 1960s and 1970s. During the boom trend, male voices and masculine themes dominated Latin American writing. Recently, female writers have been recognized for their early works as well as their current achievements.

Critical Overview

Critics credit García Márquez with bringing attention to Latin American literature. When García Márquez first appeared on the literary scene with his popular *One Hundred Years of Solitude,* reviewers praised not only his style but also his ability to tell a story to which everyone can relate. According to John Sturrock in the *New York Times Book Review,* García Márquez is "one of the small number of contemporary writers from Latin America who have given to its literature a maturity and dignity it never had before." David Streitfeld adds this sentiment in the *Washington Post,* "More than any other writer in the world, Gabriel García Márquez combines both respect (bordering on adulation) and mass popularity (also bordering on adulation)." Following on the success of this first novel, García Márquez has continued to build his reputation as a writer and storyteller.

By the time Jonathan Cape Limited of London published the English translation of *Chronicle of a Death Foretold* in 1982, García Márquez had established himself as a master of magical realism, a literature genre born in Latin America. Magical realism, a unique blending of fantasy and reality, evolved out of a culture that has been shaped by a combination of ethnic and religious populations that practice animism, voodoo, and African cult traditions. García Márquez credits his life experiences and his heritage with his ability to present the magical as part of everyday life. He says in a *UNESCO Courier* interview with Manuel Oscorio, "the area is soaked in myths brought over by the slaves, mixed in with Indian legends and Andalusian imagination. The result is a very special way of looking at things, a conception of life that sees a bit of the marvelous in everything."

Throughout García Márquez's long writing career, critics have commended his unique style. Besides his mastery of magical realism, García Márquez also possesses a talent for applying to his stories unconventional narrative styles, universal themes, and an unusual journalistic style that is often a commentary on social and political issues. *Chronicle of a Death Foretold* contains all of these. First, García Márquez has the narrator tell the story in the first person, but from an omniscient point of view. As Ronald De Feo says in a review in the *Nation,* "This narrative maneuvering adds another layer to the book." Next, the themes in *Chronicle of a Death Foretold* touch on universal concerns including male honor, crimes of passion, loyalty, and justice. Finally, most critics agree that *Chronicle of a Death Foretold* provides a snapshot in time of a society that remains captured by its own outmoded customs, beliefs, and stories.

While *Chronicle of a Death Foretold* retains a fairly widespread popularity, some reviewers have not been as accepting of its unusual form. The very characteristics of García Márquez's novel that most critics applaud have prompted others' scorn. Keith Mano, for example, says in the *National Review,* "In general, I wish García Márquez hadn't surrendered so many of the devices and prerequisites that belong to fiction: subjectivity, shifting POV, omniscience, judgment, plot surprise." Anthony Burgess has even harsher criticism in his review in *The New Republic.* He calls the book "claustrophobic" and goes on to say, "It does not induce a

view, as better fiction does, of human possibilities striving to rise out of a morass of conservative stupidity. The heart never lifts. All that is left is a plain narrative style and an orthodox narrative technique managed with extreme competence. Perhaps one is wrong to expect more from a Nobel Prizeman."

Recognized for his revival of Latin American literature, García Márquez receives credit, too, for reinvigorating the modern novel genre. Overall, critics maintain that García Márquez deserves international acclaim for his unique style, plots, themes, and blending of fantasy and realism. In a review in *Tribune Books,* Harry Mark Petrakis describes García Márquez as "a magician of vision and language who does astonishing things with time and reality." Readers all over the world who await García Márquez's books would concur.

Criticism

Jeffrey M. Lilburn

Lilburn, a graduate student at McGill University, is the author of a study guide on Margaret Atwood's The Edible Woman *and of numerous educational essays. In the following essay, he discusses the narrator's attempt to construct a chronicle that recaptures the past.*

Gabriel García Márquez's *Chronicle of a Death Foretold* is a seemingly simple story about the murder of a young man in a small Colombian town. Written in a factual, journalistic style, the novel is told by an unnamed narrator who returns to his hometown twenty-seven years after the crime to "put the broken mirror of memory back together from so many scattered shards." Assuming the role of detective, or investigative reporter, the narrator compiles and reports the information that he collects from the memories of the townspeople he interviews. What he finds, however, is a town full of people with varying and often conflicting memories of the events he is investigating. Consequently, what begins as an attempt to fill the gaps, to find out once and for all what really happened that dark and drizzly morning—or was it bright and sunny?—becomes instead a parody of any attempt to recapture and reconstruct the past.

At first glance, the narrator does what appears to be a very thorough job of finding and compiling information relating to the crime. He speaks to a great many people who knew Santiago Nasar, who were present on the evening of the wedding celebrations, and who were out to greet the bishop on the morning of the murder. Still, new information contradicts and undermines more often than it clarifies. Throughout the narrator's chronicle, for example, we hear varying accounts of the weather on the morning of the crime. According to some, it was a beautiful sunny morning; to others, the weather was drizzly and funereal. To the individuals reporting this information, the memory of that morning's weather is a fact—it is the reality they remember. Or it may simply be the reality they choose to report at that time since facts, or the reporting of facts, change over time. Victoria Guzmán, for example, initially reports that neither she nor her daughter knew that the Vicario brothers were waiting to kill Santiago, yet "in the course of her years" admits that both of them did, in fact, know about the twins' plans.

Memories are problematized further by the fact that the entire town was, on the night before the murder, celebrating Angela Vicario and Bayardo San Román's wedding. To begin, the narrator, before deciding to "rescue" the events of the festival "piece by piece from the memory of others," has "a very confused memory" of those events. Yet there is no indication that the memories of the individuals on whom the narrator relies to construct his narrative are any more reliable than his own. On the contrary, most of the townspeople seem equally confused. The narrator's brother, for example, who returns home in the early hours of the morning and falls asleep sitting on the toilet, also has "confused" memories of an encounter he has with the Vicario brothers on his way home. Similarly, the narrator's "sister the nun" has an "eighty-proof hangover" on the morning of the crime and doesn't even bother to go out to greet the bishop. These fuzzy, alcohol-drenched memories of events that happened twenty-seven years earlier not only help explain the varying reports about the weather, but they cast doubt on the entire narrative that uses these memories as its foundation.

According to Mary G. Berg, the narrator's failed attempt to find consensus among the varied accounts of the past reveals both the subjectivity of memory and the "inherent fallibility of journalistic report or written history." In short, it demonstrates the "insufficiency of words to depict (or reflect) human experience." It also, as John S. Christie writes, undermines the notion of a single narrative authority, since the ambiguity that results from the multiple perceptions and points of view reveals that no one version of the truth exists. Within the world

> " ... by telling the story, by selecting and carefully arranging the conflicting versions of events into a highly structured narrative, the narrator creates the illusion that his version of the events succeeds in recapturing the reality of the past."

represented in the novel, however, ambiguities and uncertainties are not so closely scrutinized. Santiago Nasar is murdered not because it is proven beyond a reasonable doubt that he was the man responsible for stealing Angela Vicario's honor, but because he is accused of doing so. It is the telling, Christie argues, that "creates the reality." The same might be said about the narrator's chronicle: by telling the story, by selecting and carefully arranging the conflicting versions of events into a highly structured narrative, the narrator creates the illusion that his version of the events succeeds in recapturing the reality of the past.

It is, however, only a temporary illusion. The narrator himself suggests that written reports can conceal more than they reveal when he mentions that the original report prepared by the investigating magistrate left out certain key facts. The fact that the twins started looking for Santiago at Maria Alejandrina Cervantes' house, for example, where they and Santiago had been just a short time earlier, is not reported in the brief. If this event is not reported, one must therefore ask what other information was also left out. Similarly, information that could significantly alter how events are understood and interpreted is also missing from the narrator's chronicle; he was only able to salvage "some 322 from the more than 500" pages of the original, incomplete brief from the flooded floor of the Palace of Justice in Riohacha. Moreover, some of the people whose testimony might have proven enlightening either refused to talk about the past, as did Angela's mother, or were unable to do so because they were dead, namely officer Leandro Pornoy.

The narrator's chronicle is complicated even more by the fact that he was himself a resident of

What Do I Read Next?

- Translated from Spanish to English in 1970, *One Hundred Years of Solitude* stands as García Márquez's best-known novel. It combines historical and fictional elements to tell the story of the rise and fall of a small, fictitious town—Macondo, Colombia. Many critics claim that while the novel reflects the political, social, and economic ills of South America, it actually depicts a more universal worldview.

- Many reviewers rate García Márquez's 1975 novel, *The Autumn of the Patriarch,* as his second-finest work. He attempts different stylistic techniques in this story of a political tyrant who has ruled for so long no one can remember his predecessor. García Márquez writes stream-of-consciousness-like sentences and uses a great deal of color and imagery to tell this tale.

- While the main character in *The Autumn of the Patriarch* lives in great isolation and never knows love, the main characters in *Love in the Time of Cholera* experience all kinds of love. Published in 1988, the book tells the story of star-crossed lovers who find themselves back together after over fifty years of separation.

- García Márquez writes about Simon Bolivar in his historical fiction, *The General in His Labyrinth.* This 1990 novel depicts General Bolivar, the liberator of Latin America, leaving for exile in the face of his former admirers' derision.

- Author Bill Boyd produced a nonfiction biography that reads like a novel with 1998's *Bolivar, Liberator of a Continent: A Dramatized Biography.* This accessible text tells the story of Simon Bolivar with both personal and political detail; Boyd also gives some attention to Bolivar's relationship with the United States.

- A rabid dog bites a nobleman's twelve-year-old daughter in García Márquez's *Of Love and Other Demons.* This 1995 story becomes more complicated when an exorcist falls in love with the girl.

- Another author who has successfully combined magical realism with historical detail and political commentary is Isabel Allende. Her 1982 debut novel (first published in the United States in 1985) *The House of Spirits* tells the story of a Chilean family through multiple generations, touching on themes of pride, class, power, sexuality, and spirituality.

the town. He grew up with Santiago and, in later years, they along with other friends spent their vacation time together. Moreover, he was with Santiago on the evening before his murder and, at the moment the crime was committed, was in the arms of Maria Alejandrina Cervantes, a woman with whom Santiago was once obsessed and whom the narrator was seeing without Santiago's knowledge. What's more, the narrator is related to Angela Vicario. According to Carlos Alonso, these ties between the narrator and the community put "in check the objectivity that his rhetorical posturing demands" and may even serve to "nurture the secret at the core of the events." At the very least, they add yet another layer of uncertainty to an already questionable narrative.

Central to an investigation of the events surrounding the crime is the code of honor which leads the Vicario brothers to arm themselves with pig-killing knives and take the life of a man with whom they were drinking and singing just a few short hours before. The code of honor is one which, Christie explains, derives from a paternal authority associated with the "mythic past of some religious or moral order which has now dissipated." Still, the code remains sufficiently relevant in the community that an entire town stands by and watches as Pedro and Pablo brutally kill Santiago Nasar in the street. Years later, the townspeople who could have done something but didn't turn to the code for consolation, believing that "affairs of honor are sacred monopolies, giving access only to those who are part of the drama." The comment made by Prudencia Cotes, Pablo Vicario's fiancée, is also suggestive of the pressure the Vicario brothers were under as a result of the code: "I knew what [Pablo and Pedro] were up to and I didn't only agree, I never would have married [Pablo] if he hadn't done what a man should do."

The structure of the narrative seemingly supports this code by giving the impression that Santiago's death was inevitable. His imminent demise is announced on the very first page of the novel and is announced several times again throughout the chronicle. Even the Vicario brothers are said to think of the murder "as if [it had] already happened." Yet opportunities to prevent the crime are plentiful. By the time Santiago reaches the pier to greet the bishop, for example, very few of the townspeople do not know that the Vicario brothers are waiting for him to kill him. Even the town's mayor and priest are aware of the twins' intentions and do nothing. In the end, William H. Gass writes, "one man is dead, and hundreds have murdered him." And indeed, everyone who knew of the twins' intentions and did nothing to stop them shares responsibility for the crime.

One of the few characters who does try to intervene and prevent the twins from carrying out the duty that has befallen them is Clotilde Armenta. That she fails in her attempt, Mark Millington writes, emphasizes the difficulty that female characters have in trying to move out of the passivity enforced by the male-dominated society. Indeed, the community is very much one characterized by a gender divide. In Angela Vicario's family, for example, boys are "brought up to be men" and girls are "reared to get married." Of her daughters, Angela's mother says that any man would be happy with them because "they've been raised to suffer." Moreover, it is not Angela who chooses to marry Bayardo San Román but rather her family who, like the widower Xius, falls prey to Bayardo's charm and money and obliges Angela to marry him.

Millington argues that the murder of Santiago Nasar encapsulates much of the structure of power in the town. The murder, he writes, involves only male characters who act in defense of an honor code that "safeguards the dominant position of male characters." Female characters, Millington continues, are "peripheral to the main actions of the narrative just as they are peripheral to the structures of power in the society represented." Yet Millington offers a reading of the novel that focuses on what he describes as "the untold story," namely that

of the marginalized and powerless Angela Vicario. Her story, Millington contends, would trace her relationship with Bayardo and culminate with their reconciliation—a reconciliation that undermines the dominant system by annulling their separation. Millington's reading not only draws attention (once again) to the selective nature of the information used to construct the chronicle (the narrator chooses to focus on Santiago's story, rather than Angela's), but also to the multiple truths lurking behind and within it. This reading also highlights the subversive power implied by Angela's refusal to feign her virginity on her wedding night. To do so, Millington explains, would have acknowledged the importance of the honor code.

More importantly, Angela's refusal to feign her virginity provides her with a way out of an arranged marriage to a man that she does not love and eventually allows her to break free of the authority that forced her into the marriage. Later, when Angela discovers that she does indeed have feelings for Bayardo, she begins to write him letters and discovers that she has become "mistress of her fate for the first time." In the version of events constructed by the narrator, however, the details of her story remain largely untold. Trapped and represented in another's chronicle, she is once again subjected to male authority by a narrator who uses pieces of her story to tell the inevitable-seeming story of a death foretold.

Source: Jeffrey M. Lilburn, in an essay for *Novels for Students,* Gale, 2000.

William H. Gass

According to Gass, "Chronicle of a Death Foretold, like Faulkner's Sanctuary, *is about the impotent revenges of the impotent.*

Chronicle of a Death Foretold does not tell, but literally pieces together, the torn-apart body of a story: that of the multiple murder of a young, handsome, wealthy, womanizing Arab, Santiago Nasar, who lived in the town where Gabriel García Márquez grew up. The novel is not, however, the chronicle of a young and vain man's death, for that event is fed to us in the bits it comes in. It is instead the chronicle of the author's discovery and determination of the story and simultaneously a rather gruesome catalogue of the many deaths—in dream, in allegory, and by actual count—that Santiago Nasar is compelled to suffer. Had he had a cat's lives, it would not have saved him.

It is his author who kills him first, foretelling his death in the first (and in that sense final) sen-

> One man is dead, and hundreds have murdered him. The consequences of the crime spread like a disease through the village. Or, rather, the crime is simply a late symptom of an illness that had already wasted everyone."

tence of the novel: "On the day they were going to kill him …" We are reminded immediately of García Márquez's habit of beginning his books in an arresting way, perhaps a by-product of his long journalistic practice. "Many years later, as he faced the firing squad …" *One Hundred Years of Solitude* commences, and *The Autumn of the Patriarch* is no less redolent with death or its threats. "Over the weekend the vultures got into the presidential palace by pecking through the screens on the balcony windows." Santiago Nasar's death is first foretold in the way any fictional fact is, for the fact, of whatever kind, is already there in the ensuing pages, awaiting our arrival like a bus station.

Santiago Nasar also dies in his dreams— dreams that could have been seen to foretell it, had not his mother, an accomplished seer of such things, unaccountably missed "the ominous augury." Before the day is out, his mother will murder him again. Unwittingly, and with the easy fatality we associate with Greek tragedy, Santiago dons a sacrificial suit of unstarched white linen, believing that he is putting it on to honor the visit of a bishop, just as he has celebrated the day before, along with the entire town, the wedding that will be his undoing. So attired, he stands before his mother with glass and aspirin and tells her of the dreams she will misunderstand. Santiago Nasar is then symbolically slain and gutted by the cook as he takes a cup of coffee in her kitchen and has another aspirin for his hangover. His father has mounted this woman, and she is remembering Santiago's father as she disembowels two rabbits (foretelling his disembowelment) and feeds their guts, still steaming, to the dogs.

The cook's daughter does not tell Santiago that she has heard a rumor that two men are looking to kill him, for he continually manhandles her, and she wishes him dead; the town, it seems, knows too, and participates in the foretelling. Attempts to warn Santiago are halfhearted: People pretend that the threats are empty; that the twin brothers bent on his death are drunk, incapable, unwilling; that it is all a joke. But Orpheus has his enemies in every age. Dionysus was also torn to pieces once, Osiris as well. The women whose bodies Santiago Nasar has abused (the metaphor that follows him throughout, and that appears just following the title page, is that of the falcon or sparrow hawk) await their moment. They will use the duplicities of the male code to entrap him. The girl whose wedding has just been celebrated goes to her bridegroom with a punctured maidenhead, and he sends her home in disgrace, where she is beaten until she confesses (although we don't know what the real truth is) that Santiago Nasar was her "perpetrator." And had not her twin brothers believed that the honor of their family required revenge, Nasar would not have been stabbed fatally, not once but seven times, at the front door of his house, a door his mother, believing him already inside, had barred.

The coroner is out of town, but the law requires an autopsy—the blood has begun to smell—so Santiago Nasar is butchered again, this time while dead. The intestines he held so tenderly in his hands as he walked almost primly around his house to find a back door he might enter in order to complete the symbolism of his life by dying in the kitchen he had his morning aspirin in—those insides of the self of which the phallus is only an outer tip—are tossed into a trash can; the dogs who wanted them, and would have enjoyed them, are now dead, too.

Santiago Nasar's mother's last sight of her son, which she says was of him standing in her bedroom doorway, water glass in hand and the first aspirin to his lips, is not, we learn, her last. Her final vision, which she has on the balcony of her bedroom, is of her son "face down in the dust, trying to rise up out of his own blood."

One man is dead, and hundreds have murdered him. The consequences of the crime spread like a disease through the village. Or, rather, the crime is simply a late symptom of an illness that had already wasted everyone. Now houses will decay, too, in sympathy. Those people—lovers, enemies, friends, family—who were unable to act now act with bitter, impulsive, self-punishing foolishness, becoming old maids and worn whores, alcoholics and stupid recruits, not quite indiscriminately. The inertias of custom, the cruelties of a decaying society, daily indignities, hourly poverty, animosities so ancient they seem to have been put in our private parts during a prehistoric time, the sullen passivity of the powerless, the feckless behavior of the ignorant, the uselessness of beliefs, all these combine in this remarkable, graphic, and grisly fable to create a kind of slow and creeping fate—not glacial, for that would not do for these regions, but more, perhaps, like the almost imperceptible flow of molasses, sticky, insistent, sweet, and bearing everywhere it goes the sick, digested color of the bowel....

Chronicle of a Death Foretold, like Faulkner's *Sanctuary,* is about the impotent revenges of the impotent; it is about misdirected rage; it is about the heart blowing to bits from the burden of its own beat; yet the author, Santiago Nasar's first murderer, goes patiently about his business, too, putting the pieces back together, restoring, through his magnificent art, his own anger and compassion, this forlorn, unevil, little vegetation god, to a new and brilliant life.

Source: William H. Gass, "More Deaths Than One: 'Chronicle of a Death Foretold,'" in *New York,* Vol. 16, No. 15, 1983, pp. 83–84.

Joseph Epstein

In the following excerpt, Epstein examines if Garcia Marquez is as talented as popular opinion seems to think he is.

How good is Gabriel García Márquez? "Define your terms," I can hear some wise undergraduate reply. "What do you mean by *is?*" Yet I ask the question in earnest. Over the past weeks I have been reading García Márquez's four novels and three collections of stories—all of his work available in English translation—and I am still not certain how good he is. If I were to be asked how talented, I have a ready answer: pound for pound, as they used to put it in *Ring* magazine, Gabriel García Márquez may be the most talented writer at work in the world today. But talent is one thing; goodness, or greatness, quite another.

Valéry says somewhere that there ought to be a word to describe the literary condition between talent and genius. In writing about García Márquez, most contemporary American literary critics have not searched very hard for that word. Instead they have settled on calling him a genius and knocked off for the day...

> " Valéry says somewhere that there ought to be a word to describe the literary condition between talent and genius. In writing about García Márquez, most contemporary American literary critics have not searched very hard for that word. Instead they have settled on calling him a genius and knocked off for the day...

In sum, no novelist now writing has a more enviable reputation. His is of course an international, a worldwide reputation—one capped by the Nobel Prize, won in 1982 at the age of fifty-four. The Nobel Prize can sometimes sink a writer, make him seem, even in his lifetime, a bit posthumous. But with García Márquez it appears to have had quite the reverse effect, making him seem more central, more prominent, more of a force....

In Latin America, Gabriel García Márquez has been a household name and face since 1967, when his famous novel *One Hundred Years of Solitude* was first published in Buenos Aires. This novel is said to have sold more than six million copies and to have been translated into more than thirty languages.... I thought it quite brilliant and stopped reading it at page 98 (of 383 pages in the paperback edition). A number of intelligent people I know have gone through a similar experience in reading the book. All thought it brilliant, but felt that anywhere from between eighteen to fifty-one years of solitude was sufficient, thank you very much. I shall return to what I think are the reasons for this....

Short of going to Latin American countries on extended visits, how does one find out anything about them? Whom does one trust? New York *Times* reporters capable of prattling on about fifty new poetry workshops in Nicaragua? American novelists—Robert Stone, Joan Didion—who have put in cameo appearances in one or another Latin

American country and then returned to write about it? Academic experts, the kernels of whose true information are not easily freed of their ideological husks? Perhaps native writers? On this last count, I have recently read a most charming novel set in Lima, Peru, *Aunt Julia and the Scriptwriter,* by Mario Vargas Llosa, which gives us a portrait of daily life—corrupt, incompetent, sadly provincial though it is—very different from that which Gabriel García Márquez supplies. Whom is one to believe?

So many oddities crop up. How, for example, explain that García Márquez had his famous novel, *One Hundred Years of Solitude,* a book that he has claimed is an argument for change in Latin America, published in Argentina, universally regarded—to hear Jacobo Timerman tell it—as the most repressive of Latin American countries? How for that matter explain the emergence of Latin American literature to a place very near contemporary pre-eminence? How does one reconcile these various paradoxes, contradictions, confusions? It may be that finally, in reading about Latin America, one has to settle for the virtue which Sir Lewis Namier once said was conferred by sound historical training—a fairly good sense of how things did *not* happen.

Such a sense becomes especially useful in reading a writer like Gabriel García Márquez, who is continually telling us how things did happen. What he is saying is not very new. He speaks of the depredations upon the poor by the rich, upon the pure by the corrupt, upon the indigenous by the colonial—standard stuff, for the most part. But how he says it is new and can be very potent indeed. So much so that Fidel Castro is supposed to have remarked of him, "García Márquez is the most powerful man in Latin America." …

None of this power would exist, of course, if García Márquez were not a considerable artist. Literary artists make us see things, and differently from the way we have ever seen them before; they make us see things *their* way. We agree to this willingly because in the first place they make things interesting, charming, seductive, and in the second place they hold out the promise of telling us important secrets that we would be fools not to want to know....

Sweep and power are readily available to García Márquez; so, too, are what seem like endless lovely touches, such as a man described as "lame in body and sound in conscience." In *"The Handsomest Drowned Man in the World,"* a charming

tale about a time when people had hearts capacious enough for the poetic, the way is prepared for a man "to sink easily into the deepest waves, where fish are blind and divers die of nostalgia." The movements of a woman in the story *"There Are No Thieves in This Town"* have "the gentle efficiency of people who are used to reality." A man in the story *"One Day After Saturday"* is caught at an instant when "he was aware of his entire weight: the weight of his body, his sins, and his age altogether." García Márquez's stories are studded with such charming bits: a woman with "passionate health," a man with a "mentholated voice," a town "where the goats committed suicide from desolation," another man with "a pair of lukewarm languid hands that always looked as if they'd just been shaved." García Márquez, as Milton Berle used to say of himself, has a million of them.

This fecundity of phrase was not always so readily available to García Márquez. Today his fame is such that his very earliest works are being reprinted and translated—most of them are in the collection *Innocent Eréndira and Other Stories*—and these early stories are dreary in the extreme: dryly abstract, bleak, cut-rate Kafka, without the Kafkaesque edge or the humor. As a novelist, García Márquez seems to have come alive when he began to write about the coastal town he calls Macondo and—the two events seem to have taken place simultaneously—when, by adding the vinegar of politics to his writing, he gave it a certain literary tartness.

García Márquez has claimed William Faulkner as a literary mentor, and the two do have much in common. Each has staked out a territory of his own—Yoknapatawpha County for Faulkner, Macondo and its environs for García Márquez; each deals lengthily with the past and its generations; and finally, each relies on certain prelapsarian myths (Southern grandeur before the American Civil War, Latin American poetic serenity before the advent of modernity and foreign intervention) to bind his work together. There is, though, this decisive difference between the two writers: Faulkner's fiction is almost wholly taken up with the past, while that of García Márquez, as befits a politically minded writer, generally keeps an eye out for the future.

Immersion in the work of such writers provides one of those experiences—perhaps it might be called moral tourism—exclusive to literature. By reading a good deal about a place rendered by a powerful writer, in time one comes to feel one has walked its streets, knows its history and geography, the rhythms of its daily life. Only certain writers can convey this experience through the page: Balzac did it both for Paris and French provincial towns; Faulkner did it; Isaac Bashevis Singer does it for Jewish Poland; and García Márquez does it, too.

Viewed in retrospect, the Macondo stories—they are found in *Leaf Storm and Other Stories* and *No One Writes to the Colonel and Other Stories,* and the town is also the setting for the novel *In Evil Hour*—appear to be an elaborate warm-up for the novel *One Hundred Years of Solitude.* They seem to be sketches, trial runs, dress rehearsals for the big novel ahead. In these stories names will appear in passing—like Colonel Aureliano Buendía, one of the heroes of *One Hundred Years*—almost as if they were coming attractions. Then, working the other way around, incidents occur in *One Hundred Years* that have been the subjects of whole stories in the earlier volumes. To know fully what is going on in García Márquez one has to have read the author in his entirety. In these stories the stages in García Márquez's literary development are on display, rather like specimens inside formaldehyde-filled jars showing progress from zygote to fully formed human. One reads these stories and witnesses his talent growing, his political ardor increasing. In these stories, too, García Márquez shows his taste for that blend of fantasy and hyperbole, exhibited in a context of reality, that is known as magic realism....

"What I like about you," says one character to another in the García Márquez story *"The Incredible and Sad Tale of Innocent Eréndira and Her Heartless Grandmother,"* "is the serious way you make up nonsense." Serious nonsense might stand as a blurb line for *One Hundred Years of Solitude.* E. M. Forster remarked that at a certain age one loses interest in the development of writers and wants to know only about the creation of masterpieces. Certainly *One Hundred Years of Solitude* has everywhere been so acclaimed. The novel is a chronicle of six generations of the Buendía family, founders of the village of Macondo. It recounts such extraordinary happenings as Macondo's insomnia plague, its thirty-two civil wars, banana fever, revolution, strikes, a rain that lasts five years, marriages, intermarriages, madness, and the eventual extinction of the Buendía line with the birth of an infant who has a pig's tail and who is eventually carried off by ants.

"One Hundred Years of Solitude is not a history of Latin America," García Márquez has said, "it is a *metaphor* for Latin America." With that quo-

tation we are already in trouble. What can it mean to say that a novel is a metaphor for a continent? Before attempting to ascertain what it might mean, tribute must be paid to the sheer brimming brilliance of *One Hundred Years of Solitude.* "Dazzling" does not seem to me in any way an imprecise word to describe the style of this novel, nor "epic" any less imprecise a word to describe its ambitions. Its contents cannot be recapitulated, for in its pages fireworks of one kind or another are always shooting off. Disquisitions on history, memory, time wind in and out of the plot. Yellow flowers fall from the sky marking a man's death; a heart-meltingly beautiful girl ascends to heaven while folding a sheet, a girl whose very smell "kept on torturing men beyond death, right down to the dust of their bones." Everything is grand, poetic, funny, often at once. A man suffers "flatulence that withered the flowers"; a woman has "a generous heart and a magnificent vocation for love." ...

And yet—why do so many readers seem to bog down in this glittering work? Part of the difficulty seems to me technical, part psychological. *One Hundred Years of Solitude* is peculiarly a novel without pace; it is, for its nearly four-hundred pages, all high notes, service aces, twenty-one-gun salutes. In a novel, such nonstop virtuosity tends to pall. To use a simile to describe a novel that its author describes as a metaphor, reading *One Hundred Years* is like watching a circus artist on the trampoline who does only quadruple back somersaults. At first you are amazed to see him do it; then you are astonished that he can keep it up for so long; then you begin to wonder when he is going to be done, frankly you'd like to see something less spectacular, like a heavy-legged woman on an aged elephant.

Unless, that is, you sense a deeper meaning beneath all this virtuosity. And here it must be said that there has been no shortage of deep readings of *One Hundred Years of Solitude,* a novel which, if critics are to be consulted, has more levels than a ziggurat. There are those who think that the true meaning of the novel is solitude, or, as Alastair Reid puts it, "We all live alone on this earth in our own glass bubbles." There are those who think that the novel is about writing itself.... There are those who are fascinated with the book's allusiveness.... There are those who believe that the stuff of myth ought not to be looked at too closely.... Then there is García Márquez himself, who has given a clear political reading to his own novel, commenting, in an interview, "I did want to give the idea that Latin American history had such an oppressive reality that it had to be changed—at all costs, at any price!" …

Along with magic realism, Gabriel García Márquez has given us another new literary-critical label, "political realism," which, in its own way, is itself quite magical.

If *One Hundred Years of Solitude* leaves any doubt about the political intent of García Márquez's mature work, *The Autumn of the Patriarch* wipes that doubt away. When García Márquez says that *One Hundred Years* is a metaphor for Latin America, he is of course putting a political interpretation on his own novel. But *The Autumn of the Patriarch* is neither metaphor nor symbol but a direct representation of a strong political point of view.…

The dictator in *The Autumn of the Patriarch* lives for more than two hundred years, his demise, *à la* Mark Twain, being often reported but much exaggerated. He has been in power—he has been *the* power—longer than anyone can remember, and his is the greatest solitude of all: that of the unloved dictator perpetuating his unearned power. This man, who himself can neither read nor write, is described, examined, and prosecuted with the aid of a novelistic technique as relentlessly modernist as any in contemporary fiction.

The Autumn of the Patriarch is divided into six chapters, but that is the only division in the novel, and the only concession to the reader's convenience. The book has no paragraphs, and while the punctuation mark known as the period may show up from time to time, the novel's sentences are not what one normally thinks of as sentences at all. A sentence might begin from one point of view, and before it is finished include three or four others.

One of the small shocks of this novel is to see the most complex modernist techniques put to the most patent political purposes. Now it must be said that García Márquez did not invent the Latin American dictator. Trujillo, Batista, Perón, Hernández Martínez, Duvalier (dare one add the name Fidel Castro?)—one could put together a pretty fair All Star team, though these boys are bush league compared with what Europe and Asia in this century have been able to produce.

García Márquez's portrait of the dictator in *The Autumn of the Patriarch* is an amalgam of Latin America's dictators, minus … Fidel and with a touch or two of Franco added. As a picture of squalor, rot, and bestiality, it is devastating. The devastation is in the details, of which the endlessly inventive García Márquez is never in short supply.…

The Autumn of the Patriarch is about more than politics alone—time and the nature of illusion are motifs played upon artfully throughout—but politics give the novel its impetus and are finally its chief subject. These politics are highly selective, predictable, more than a trifle clichéd. Octavio Paz has said that García Márquez, as a political thinker, "repeats slogans." As a novelist, he can make these slogans vivid, even funny, but they remain slogans. For example, the attacks on the United States in this novel come through the dictator's continuous dealings with a stream of U.S. ambassadors of perfectly Waspish and quite forgettable names—Warren, Thompson, Evans, Wilson—who in the end succeed in swindling him out of the very sea. Americans, the Catholic Church, politicians, all, in the mind and in the novels of Gabriel García Márquez, are swindlers. Liberals or conservatives, it does not matter which, they are crooks, every one of them. Which leaves—doesn't it?—only one solution: revolution.

So talented a writer is García Márquez that he can sustain a longish tale on sheer storytelling power alone, as he does in his most recent book, *Chronicle of a Death Faretold*. It has been said of García Márquez that he combines the two powerful traditions of Latin American writing: the left-wing engagé tradition of the Communist poet Pablo Neruda and the modernist mandarin tradition of Jorge Luis Borges. In this slender novel it is the Borges side that predominates. The book is about a plot on the part of twin brothers who are out to avenge their family's honor against a young man who they mistakenly believe has deflowered their sister, thus causing her husband to return her in shame to her family the morning after the wedding night.…

The tale is told with such subtle organization and such complete fluency that García Márquez can insert anything he wishes into it; and indeed the narrator does insert mention of his marriage proposal to his own wife and a brief account of his youthful dalliances with prostitutes. Such is the easy mastery of this novel that the reader is likely to forget that he never does learn who actually did deflower the virgin. *Chronicle of a Death Foretold* is a handsomely written and inconsequential book of a kind that offers ample leeway for deep readings, and one that could have been composed only by a hugely gifted writer. "Intellectuals consider themselves to be the moral conscience of society," García Márquez is quoted as saying in the New York *Times Magazine,* "so their analyses invariably follow moral rather than political channels. In this sense, I think I am the most politicized of them all." Yet, oddly, in García Márquez's fiction morality is rarely an issue; García Márquez himself seems little interested in moral questions, or in the conflicts, gradations, and agonies of moral turmoil. The reason for this, I suspect, is that for him the moral universe is already set—for him, as for so many revolutionary intellectuals, there are the moral grievances of the past, the moral hypocrisies of the present, and, waiting over the horizon, the glories of the future, when moral complexity will be abolished. The moral question is, for García Márquez, ultimately a political question. Outside of his politics, García Márquez's stories and novels have no moral center; they inhabit no moral universe. They are passionate chiefly when they are political; and when they are political, so strong is the nature of their political bias that they are, however dazzling, flawed.

Thus, to return to where I set out, a short answer to my question—how good is Gabriel García Márquez?—is that he is, in the strict sense of the word, marvelous. The pity is that he is not better.

Source: Joseph Epstein, "How Good is Gabriel Garcia Marquez?," in *Commentary,* Vol. 75, No. 5, May, 1983, pp. 59–65.

Anthony Burgess

In this brief excerpt, Burgess addresses the problems of reading a translation, and of expressing an opinion different from "a world consensus." In this second situation, "dare one [the reviewer, in this case] be wholly frank?"

I have two problems in assessing this brief work [*Chronicle of a Death Foretold*] by the latest Nobel Prizeman. The first relates to the fact that I've read it in translation, and any judgment on the quality of García Márquez's writing that I would wish to make is necessarily limited. Mr. Rabassa's rendering is smooth and strong with an inevitable North American flavor, but it is English, and García Márquez writes in a very pungent and individual Spanish. The second problem is the one that always comes up when a writer has received the final international accolade: dare one be wholly frank? Dare one set one's critical judgment up against what, though it is really only the verdict of a committee of literati in Stockholm, is accepted as a world consensus? I note, in [the publisher's] publicity handout, that we are to regard García Márquez as "South America's pre-eminent writer"—a view I cannot give accord to so long as Jorge Luis Borges is alive. I think, as is often the

> **Now here is a new brief novel that is decent, assured, strong, but indubitably minor. I am not seduced by García Márquez's reputation ... into thinking it anything more."**

case with officially acclaimed writers of fiction, that the imputation of greatness has more to do with content—especially when it is social or political—than with aesthetic values. *One Hundred Years of Solitude,* a book which impressed me rather less than it seems to have impressed others, has undoubted power, but its power is nothing compared with the genuinely literary explorations of men like Borges and Nabokov. Now here is a new brief novel that is decent, assured, strong, but indubitably minor. I am not seduced by García Márquez's reputation ... into thinking it anything more.

The minimal distinction of the novella lies in the exactness with which its author has recorded the mores of a community in which machismo is the basic ethos. The bishop is coming on a river boat to give his blessing, and sacks of cockscombs await him to make his favorite soup. The town swelters in morning heat and hangover. Sex is a weapon, not a gesture of tenderness. The atmosphere is visceral. Rabbits are being gutted by the beginning of the story; at the end the dying Santiago Nasar enters his house "soaked in blood and carrying the roots of his entrails in his hands." There is also an element of debased hidalgo refinement.

Before we get to the end, which is less an end than an initial theme to be embroidered with the views of citizens locked in a tradition that they see no reason to break, we are given a sufficient anthropological survey of a society that has never known the benefits of aspirant Protestant materialism and ambiguous matriarchy. It is the world of *Martin Ferrol,* the Argentine epic that glorified machismo and helped to keep South American literature out of the real world. The little novel is an honest record, cunningly contrived, but it seems to abet a complacent debasement of morality rather than to open up larger vistas. It is, in a word, claus-

> In other words, whereas Rivera, the conscious artist, succeeded at what he set out to do—horrifying his readers—García Márquez, the unconscious artist and the better one, creates a realm that gives delight."

trophobic. It does not induce a view, as better fiction does, of human possibilities striving to rise out of a morass of conservative stupidity. The heart never lifts. All that is left is a plain narrative style and an orthodox narrative technique managed with extreme competence. Perhaps one is wrong to expect more from a Nobel Prizeman.

Source: Anthony Burgess, "Macho in Minor Key," in *New Republic,* Vol. 188, No. 17, May 2, 1983, p. 36.

Selden Rodman

In the following passage, Rodman looks at García Márquez's message in Chronicle of a Death Foretold.

In much of his work [Gabriel García Márquez] has turned his hometown into a dream kingdom of shattered expectations built on nostalgia; Macondo is bereft of idealism, visions of a better world, calls to arms. These attitudes are seen as part of an old order that must be stripped away to get at the long-concealed truth....

Before [*Chronicle of a Death Foretold*] came *The Autumn of the Patriarch,* a monologue of a dying tyrant based on the life of Juan Vicente Gómez of Venezuela, whose crimes had been magnified into myth in the mouths of refugees to Aracataca during the novelist's childhood. The book's highly praised style was baroque and convoluted. García Márquez implausibly defends his method by citing the supposed unreadability of *Ulysses* when it first came out, and claiming that "today children read it." Although an intellectual tour de force, *Autumn* lacks the endearing magic of the author at his best.

Chronicle of a Death Foretold, fortunately, brings García Márquez back on track. The setting is Macondo again, with many of the old faces reappearing in minor roles, including the author himself, his family and his wife. The mood is somber and tragic, for this is an account of a horrifyingly brutal and senseless crime....

Part morality tale, part fairy tale, *Chronicle of a Death Foretold* unfolds like a Greek tragedy. We know everything essential to the plot from the opening page, and yet García Márquez fills in the details with such masterful skill that we hang on breathlessly to the final paragraph, where the murder is described. As in all this writer's strongest work, the writing is lucid, factual, almost literary except for an occasional word or phrase in the vernacular ("rotgut," "eighty-proof hangover") to remind us that this is our world.

What is García Márquez trying to say in his books? I can hear him answer, amiably or scornfully depending on his mood, that he isn't trying to say anything, that he writes because he must, that the words come out this way, virtually trancelike, dictated by his memory and edited by the sum of his parts. Which would be the truth.

Still, one searches for *some* connection between the public man and the artist. A typical Latin American liberal, the public man supports all Leftist causes, while shying away from justifying the Soviet Union's domestic atrocities and its more barefaced sandbagging of its weak neighbors. He hates Augusto Pinochet and reveres the memory of Salvador Allende, regardless of what Allende did in Chile during his reign. García Márquez excuses Latin America's political infantilism on the grounds that democratic institutions did not have centuries to mature as in Europe—ignoring the United States, which broke away from colonialism at the same time....

As for the artist, Octavio Paz once tried to persuade me that García Márquez has not changed the language the way Pablo Neruda, Cesar Valléjo and Jorge Luis Borges have. "They started a new tradition, he comes at the end of an old one—the rural, epic and magic tradition of Ricardo Guïraldes, Horacio Quiroga, José Eustacio Rivera." I disagreed, comparing the Colombian Rivera's horrendous penetration of Amazonia with his successor's recreations of the past. One emerges from Rivera's desperate journey in *The Vortex* with a sense of suffocating depression, from García Márquez' strolls through Macondo with a reassuring conviction that a world so full of lusty adventurers, irrepressible louts and unconscious poets cannot be as bad as he says it is. The artist triumphs over the public man, over the sociologist.

In other words, whereas Rivera, the conscious artist, succeeded at what he set out to do—horrifying his readers—García Márquez, the unconscious artist and the better one, creates a realm that gives delight. His characters have lives of their own and they refuse to be manipulated. They may fulfill their tragic destiny, but they behave with so much spontaneity and good humor that we remember them as the better parts of ourselves and accept their world of irrational "happenings" as the real one.

Source: Selden Rodman, "Triumph of the Artist," in *New Leader,* Vol. LXVI, No. 10, May 16, 1983, pp. 16–17.

D. Keith Mano

Mano discusses the problems he found with Chronicle of a Death Foretold.

[*Chronicle of a Death Foretold*] is, at one level, a simile for the fiction-making process. Here we are given events that, in some genuine sense, exist—lie formed by history—*before* they occur. And a townful of people—through their action, thought, custom, laziness, pride, willful negligence, through their unconscious art—create this plot-which-was-real. The irony is: that having created it, they cannot avert it. No second draft is possible: even in art, where free will would seem to be most free, a determinism, a manifest destiny, still presides....

A nameless narrator has come back. (Some 27 years, mind you, after Santiago Nasar was turned to human piecework.) Neither he nor the town can stop riding this hobbyhorse.

> For years we couldn't talk about anything else. Our daily conduct, dominated then by so many linear habits, had suddenly begun to spin around a single common anxiety. The cocks of dawn would catch us trying to give order to the chain of many chance events that had made absurdity possible, and it was obvious that we weren't doing it from an urge to clear up mysteries but because none of us could go on living without an exact knowledge of the place and the mission assigned to us by fate.

Now that formulation, with all respect to García Márquez, is somewhat self-propelled. I don't believe it. No matter what the event, populations don't lie awake for a quarter-century grave-robbing their moral reminiscence. The linear habit will reassert itself. García Márquez's narrator—who previously has employed splendid sparse, aromatic, and elliptical prose—is indulging himself here. For one moment at least García Márquez doesn't trust the event, its portentousness or imagic value.

> **"** Now that formulation, with all respect to García Márquez, is somewhat self-propelled. I don't believe it."

Otherwise his attack is stark and, given García Márquez's purpose, proper enough. Because the narrator is examining an essentially novelistic occurrence, he has been sequestered as a juror might be. He cannot comment or probe: and this rather kiln-dries the novel. Angela, Bayardo, Santiago are left without development or chiaroscuro. They seem cryptic and surfacehard: film characters really. And there must be no surprise—art here lies in the event itself. That, to start with, is García Márquez's conceit. Angela, we don't know, might have taken her own virginity. Nor will we ever understand why rich Bayardo came to this unmarked burial of a town. *Chronicle* has become myth: as you don't ask for the psychohistory of Parsifal or Gawain, you must accept Angela, Bayardo, Santiago. But beyond García Márquez's glass-brick-hard style (redone brilliantly, as usual, by Greg Rabassa in English), beyond a Warren Report-meticulous detective reconstruction, it is hard to care much for these people. Emotion, you see, might skew our clarity. No character—even when he or she is presumed real—should elude an author's control.

The trial record will be introduced. An investigating judge "never thought it legitimate that life should make use of so many coincidences forbidden literature, so that there should be the untrammeled fulfillment of a death so clearly foretold."

García Márquez, I think, is over-indicating here. The events, though pretty sensational, aren't full of unbelievable coincidence. Life often has taken greater poetic license. What will distinguish this happening is the intensity of examination both by his townspeople and by his narrator. Intensity that seems somewhat forced. At one point the narrator, obsessive, will claim that he must put a "broken mirror of memory back together again from so many shards." But memory doesn't just reflect. In general, I wish García Márquez hadn't surrendered so many of the devices and perquisites that belong to fiction: subjectivity, shifting POV, omniscience, judgment, plot surprise. Form is, of course, an artistic choice. García Márquez has given his choice excellent service. But more might have been essayed. After all every death is, to some degree, foretold.

Source: D. Keith Mano, "A Death Foretold," in *National Review,* Vol. XXXV, No. 11, June 10, 1983, pp. 699–700.

Gregory Rabassa

In the following essay, Rabassa looks at the structure of Chronicle of a Death Foretold.

When Gabriel García Márquez announced that he was abandoning literature for journalism until the Pinochet dictatorship disappeared from Chile, people expected him to keep his word, and many were surprised when he published *Crónica de una muerte anunciada (Chronicle of a Death Foretold).* He was not really breaking his pledge, however, as can be seen from what he said in an interview with Rosa E. Peláez and Cino Colina published in *Granma* (Havana) and reprinted in *Excelsior* of Mexico City (31 December 1977). In the interview he is asked what aspect of journalism he likes best, and his answer is reporting. He is subsequently asked about the *crónica* genre and answers that it is all a matter of definition, that he can see little difference between reporting and the writing of chronicles. He goes on to say that one of his ultimate aims is to combine journalism and fiction in such a way that when the news item becomes boring he will embellish it and improve upon it with inventions of his own. So when he wrote this latest book of his, a short, tight novella, by his lights he was not returning to fiction but carrying on journalism as usual, even though his uncramped definitions could well apply to everything that he had written previously and supposedly had put in abeyance.

The chronicle has long been the primitive method of recording events and people and passing them on into history. Most of what we know about medieval Europe has come from chronicles, and in Africa history has been kept through the oral chronicles of the griots. In Latin America, Brazil in particular, the "chronicle" is a recognized and broadly practiced form, offspring of the more ancient variety, that lies somewhere between journalism and "literature." In the United States certain newspaper columns of a more subjective and personal nature correspond to the Latin American chronicle, which almost inevitably makes its first appearance in the press before going into book form. Therefore García Márquez is correct when he says that it is all a matter of definition in the question of whether or not he has abandoned literature and whether or not he has returned.

This new book shows many aspects of life and literature and how one is essentially the same as the other; life imitates art. It starts off in good journalistic style with the "when" and the "what."

> On the day they were going to kill him, Santiago Nasar got up at 5:30 in the morning to wait for the boat the bishop was coming on....

This use of the temporal to begin the narration reminds one immediately of *One Hundred Years of Solitude,* which begins in a similar if not identical vein and sets the stage for the necessary retrospect.... The difference is that *One Hundred Years of Solitude* begins in medias res, in good epic fashion, while this "chronicle" opens almost at the end of the action, not quite so far as the end of life as in *The Autumn of the Patriarch,* but close to it. This might well show the influence of journalism in the direction that García Márquez's style has been taking through these last three longer works. The first is more legendary and historical as it develops toward its inevitable and fated climax, while the last two depend on journalistic investigation for their development.

Julio Cortázar has spoken about that nightmare for authors (and typesetters) in Spanish: *casualidad/causalidad* (chance/causality). There is no need to worry about such a slip in the interpretation of this story, as the two elements coincide quite neatly. It is known from the beginning of the tale that the Vicario twins are planning to kill Santiago Nasar for having deflowered their sister Angela, thus ruining her marriage to the strange but wealthy newcomer Bayardo San Román. Many people in the town are aware of the Vicarios' intentions, but through a concatenation of quite normal, even banal, bits of happenstance, nothing is ultimately done to stop them. Indeed, one gathers that even they have little heart for the dirty job that honor is forcing them to do and are only waiting for the authorities or someone to prevent them from bringing it off, since they are prevented by the code from backing down themselves. The title is quite fitting, therefore, in that the death in question has been announced and is foretold. García Márquez has managed to keep the shock and horror of surprise, however, by seeing to it also that the one person who is blithely unaware of what has been ordained, almost until the moment of the act itself, is Santiago Nasar. In the end chance has become the cause of the inexorable deed: *casualidad/causalidad.*

The format used for the narration of the tale is quite journalistic. The narrator, García Márquez himself, perhaps genuine, perhaps embellished, as he mentioned in the interview cited above, is investigating the murder some twenty years later in order to ascertain how such a thing could have happened, how in the end no one was in a position to stop what nobody, including the perpetrators, wanted to happen. The matter of imperfect memory (there are great discrepancies as to the weather) helps lend uncertainty to a tale or event that had become certain because of uncertainty itself. The narrator also relies upon his own memory; he was home from school at the time of the killing and was a friend and contemporary of Santiago Nasar, having caroused with him the night before the murder. In addition, he interviews the participants and several observers, tracking some of them down to more remote places. The narration is a kind of complicated act of turning something inside-out and right-side-out again in that it resembles the application of fictive techniques to the narration of true events in the manner of Norman Mailer and Truman Capote, but here fiction is treated like fact treated like fiction. This swallowing of his own tale by the snake gives a very strong feeling of authenticity to the story....

Instead of giving us a linear narration of the episodes leading up to the final tragedy, García Márquez divides the novella into chapters, each of which follows the trajectory from a slightly different angle and involves a different combination of characters. The fictive structure is therefore a web of crisscrossed story lines, and in the center (or on the bias) is the hole of solitude and impotence where the killing takes place, uncrossed by any of the lines that would have plugged it and prevented the tragedy. This reminds one of the suicide attempt by Colonel Aureliano Buendia in *One Hundred Years of Solitude* when, in emulation of the poet José Asunción Silva, he asks his doctor friend to make a dot on his shirt where his heart is. We later find that the wily physician, on to the colonel's intentions, has designated the one spot in the area of the heart where a bullet can pass without being fatal. As in so many other aspects of this book when compared to the others, and as García Márquez does so many times with a technique that links all of his tales but at the same time differentiates among them, we have mirror images, reverse and obverse.

There is a richness of characters, as one would expect from this author. While he borrows some from his other books, as is his wont, he invents new

> The chronicle has long been the primitive method of recording events and people and passing them on into history. Most of what we know about medieval Europe has come from chronicles, and in Africa history has been kept through the oral chronicles of the griots."

ones that have great possibilities for expansion into tales of their own, the same as innocent Eréndira and her heartless grandmother, conceived in *One Hundred Years of Solitude* and developed at length in their own novella. As it is, García Márquez is adept at weaving different and seemingly unconnected stories together in order to make the webbing of his complete tale, and any of the tangents that he uses to devise the whole chronicle could be followed off into a separate narrative. There are also intriguing characters on the fringes that we hope to see more of. The wedding and the murder coincide with the bishop's passage up the river (there are always rivers in García Márquez). This episcopal worthy was passing through early in the morning on the day after the abortive wedding and on the day of the killing. The atmosphere, rather than being tetric in advance of the slaughter (the brothers were butchers and killed him with their pig-sticking knives), is ludicrous; for it seems that the bishop's favorite dish is cockscomb soup, and the townspeople have gathered together hundreds of caged roosters as an offering to his grace. At dawn a cacophony ensues as the captive creatures begin to crow and are answered by all the cocks in town. As it so happened, and as predicted by Santiago Nasar's mother, the bishop did not even deign to stop, and his paddlewheeler passed by as he stood on the bridge and dispensed mechanical blessings to the sound of the congregated roosters. This was the comic atmosphere that would surround the death foretold.

What unites so much of García Márquez's writing is the sense of inexorability, of fatefulness.

Things often come to an end that has been there all the while, in spite of what might have been done to avoid it, and often mysteriously and inexplicably, as with the death of José Arcadio, the son, in *One Hundred Years of Solitude.* Here the hand of doom is unavoidable, but the path is tortuous, as it would logically appear that there were ever so many chances to halt the assassination. There is a ouch of mystery too, however, in the fact that the narrator-investigator was never able to find out if Angela Vicario and Santiago Nasar had been lovers. All evidence and logic said that the dashing young rancher, already betrothed to the daughter of one of his Arab father's compatriots, could not possibly have been interested in a brown bird like Angela Vicario. She had her own mystery, however, because in the end, years later, she and Bayardo San Román come back together again as strangely as they had been joined the first time. He appears one day at her new home in "exile" beyond Riohacha with a suitcase full of the letters she had been writing him—all unopened.

From the beginning we know that Santiago Nasar will be and has been killed, depending on the time of the narrative thread that we happen to be following, but García Márquez does manage, in spite of the repeated foretelling of the event by the murderers and others, to maintain the suspense at a high level by never describing the actual murder until the very end. Until then we have been following the chronicler as he puts the bits and pieces together ex post facto, but he has constructed things in such a way that we are still hoping for a reprieve even though we know better. It is a feeling that makes us understand why *King Lear* was altered in the nineteenth century in order to spare those sentimental audiences the ultimate agony of Cordelia's execution. García Márquez has put the tale together in the down-to-earth manner of Euripides, but in the final pathos he comes close to the effects of Aeschylus.

The little slips of fate that seem so unimportant until they end in tragedy are the blocks that he builds with. Coincidence or lack of it is not so patently contrived as in Mario Vargas Llosa's novel *The Green House,* where we have the same characters wearing different masks on different stages. Instead, the epiphanies mount up and reveal the characters and the circumstances (never completely; there is always something unknown) by a succession of banal delights and contretemps....

Chronicle of a Death Foretold might well be the book that García Márquez was projecting in his Havana interview when he said that he wanted to write the false memoirs of his own life. He is not the protagonist of the story, but he is not only the author; he is the narrator. He even tells how he first proposed marriage to his wife and mentions her by name. In this way he is following the tradition of Cervantes, who mingled the real and the fictional to the degree that all levels came together in a time that only Proust could understand, and he is also very close to what Borges is up to in his story "The Other Borges." When Gabriel García Márquez said that he was abandoning literature for journalism, he probably did not realize the ambiguity of his statement, and since then, as he has done in his reportage, he has come to the conclusion that in technique at least—and possibly in many other ways as well—they are the same.

Source: Gregory Rabassa, "Garcia Marquez's New Book: Literature of Journalism?," in *World Literature Today,* 1982, Vol., 1982, No. 1, Winter, pp. 48–51.

Salman Rushdie

In the following review, Salman Rushdie discusses Garcia Marquez's works; the opening sentence of Rushdie's essay purposely imitates Garcia Marquez's writing style.

We had suspected for a long time that the man Gabriel was capable of miracles, because for many years he had talked too much about angels for someone who had no wings, so that when the miracle of the printing presses occurred we nodded our heads knowingly, but of course the foreknowledge of his sorcery did not release us from its power, and under the spell of that nostalgic witchcraft we arose from our wooden benches and garden swings and ran without once drawing breath to the place where the demented printing presses were breeding books faster than fruitflies, and the books leapt into our hands without our even having to stretch out our arms, the flood of books spilled out of the print room and knocked down the first arrivals at the presses, who succumbed deliriously to that terrible deluge of narrative as it covered the streets and the sidewalks and rose lap-high in the ground-floor rooms of all the houses for miles around, so that there was no one who could escape from that story, if you were blind or shut your eyes it did you no good because there were always voices reading aloud within earshot, we had all been ravished like willing virgins by that tale, which had the quality of convincing each reader that it was his personal autobiography; and then the book filled up our country and headed out to sea, and we understood in the insanity of our possession that the phenomenon would not cease until the entire surface of the globe had been covered, until seas, mountains, underground railways and deserts had been completely clogged up by the endless copies emerging from the bewitched printing press, with the exception, as Melquiades the gypsy told us, of a single northern country called Britain whose inhabitants had long ago become immune to the book disease, no matter how virulent the strain....

It is now 15 years since Gabriel Garcia Marquez first published *One Hundred Years of Solitude*. During that time it has sold over four million copies in the Spanish language alone, and I don't know how many millions more in translation. The news of a new Marquez book takes over the front pages of Spanish American dailies. Barrow-boys hawk copies in the streets. Critics commit suicide for lack of fresh superlatives. His latest book, *Chronicle of a Death Foretold*, had a first printing in Spanish of considerably more than one million copies. Not the least extraordinary aspect of the work of 'Angel Gabriel' is its ability to make the real world behave in precisely the improbably hyperbolic fashion of a Marquez story.

In Britain, nothing so outrageous has yet taken place. Marquez gets the raves but the person on the South London public conveyance remains unimpressed. It can't be that the British distrust fantasists. Think of Tolkien. (Maybe they just don't like good fantasy.) My own theory is that for most Britons South America has just been discovered. A Task Force may succeed where reviewers have failed: that great comma of a continent may have become commercial at last, thus enabling Marquez and all the other members of 'El Boom', the great explosion of brilliance in contemporary Spanish American literature, finally to reach the enormous audiences they deserve....

It seems that the greatest force at work on the imagination of Marquez ... is the memory of his grandmother. Many, more formal antecedents have been suggested for his art: he has himself admitted the influence of Faulkner, and the world of his fabulous Macondo is at least partly Yoknapatawpha County transported into the Colombian jungles. Then there's Borges, and behind Borges the *fons* and *origo* of it all, Machado de Assis, whose three great novels, *Epitaph of a Small Winner, Quincas Borba* and *Dom Casmurro,* were so far ahead of their times (1880, 1892, and 1900), so light in touch, so clearly the product of a fantasticating imagination (see, for example, the use Machado makes of an 'anti-melancholy plaster' in *Epitaph*),

> " ... that great comma of a continent may have become commercial at last, thus enabling Marquez and all the other members of 'El Boom', the great explosion of brilliance in contemporary Spanish American literature, finally to reach the enormous audiences they deserve...."

as to make one suspect that he had descended into the South American literary wilderness of that period from some Dänikenian chariot of gods. And Garcia Marquez's genius for the unforgettable visual hyperbole—for instance, the Americans forcing a Latin dictator to give them the sea in payment of his debts, in *The Autumn of the Patriarch:* 'they took away the Caribbean in April, Ambassador Ewing's nautical engineers carried it off in numbered pieces to plant it far from the hurricanes in the blood-red dawns of Arizona'—may well have been sharpened by his years of writing for the movies. But the grandmother is more important than any of these. She is Gabriel Garcia Marquez's voice.

In an interview with Luis Harss and Barbara Dohmann, Marquez says clearly that his language is his grandmother's. 'She spoke that way.' 'She was a great storyteller.' Anita Desai has said of Indian households that the women are the keepers of the tales, and the same appears to be the case in South America. Marquez was raised by his grandparents, meeting his mother for the first time when he was seven or eight years old.... From the memory of [their] house, and using his grandmother's narrative voice as his own linguistic lodestone, Marquez began the building of Macondo.

But of course there is more to him than his granny. He left his childhood village of Aracataca when still very young, and found himself in an urban world whose definitions of reality were so different from those prevalent in the jungle as to be virtually incompatible. In *One Hundred Years of*

Solitude, the assumption into heaven of Remedios the Beauty, the loveliest girl in the world, is treated as a completely expected occurrence, but the arrival of the first railway train to reach Macondo sends a woman screaming down the high street. 'It's coming,' she cries. 'Something frightful, like a kitchen dragging a village behind it.' Needless to say, the reactions of city folk to these two events would be exactly reversed. Garcia Marquez decided that reality in South America had literally ceased to exist: this is the source of his fabulism.

The damage to reality was—is—at least as much political as cultural. In Marquez's experience, truth has been controlled to the point at which it has ceased to be possible to find out what it is. The only truth is that you are being lied to all the time. Garcia Marquez (whose support of the Castro Government in Cuba may prevent him from getting his Nobel) has always been an intensely political creature: but his books are only obliquely to do with politics, dealing with public affairs only in terms of grand metaphors like Colonel Aureliano Buendia's military career, or the colossally overblown figure of the Patriarch, who has one of his rivals served up as the main course at a banquet, and who, having overslept one day, decides that the afternoon is really the morning, so that people have to stand outside his windows at night holding up cardboard cut-outs of the sun.

El realismo magical, 'magic realism', at least as practised by Garcia Marquez, is a development of Surrealism that expresses a genuinely 'Third World' consciousness. It deals with what Naipaul has called 'half-made' societies, in which the impossibly old struggles against the appallingly new, in which public corruptions and private anguishes are more garish and extreme than they ever get in the so-called 'North', where centuries of wealth and power have formed thick layers over the surface of what's really going on. In the work of Garcia Marquez, as in the world he describes, impossible things happen constantly, and quite plausibly, out in the open under the midday sun. It would be a mistake to think of Marquez's literary universe as an invented, self-referential, closed system. He is not writing about Middle Earth, but about the one we all inhabit. Macondo exists. That is its magic.

It sometimes seems, however, that Marquez is consciously trying to foster the myth of 'Garcialand'. Compare the first sentence of *One Hundred Years of Solitude* with the first sentence of *Chronicle of a Death Foretold:* 'Many years later, as he faced the firing squad, Colonel Aureliano Buendia was to remember that distant afternoon when his father took him to discover ice' (*One Hundred Years*). And: 'On the day they were going to kill him, Santiago Nasar got up at five-thirty in the morning to wait for the boat the bishop was coming on' (*Chronicle*). Both books begin by first invoking a violent death in the future and then retreating to consider an earlier, extraordinary event. *The Autumn of the Patriarch,* too, begins with a death and then circles back and around a life. It's as though Marquez is asking us to link the books. This suggestion is underlined by his use of certain types of stock character: the old soldier, the loose woman, the matriarch, the compromised priest, the anguished doctor. The plot of *In Evil Hour,* in which a town allows one person to become the scapegoat for what is in fact a crime committed by many hands—the fly-posting of satiric lampoons during the nights—is echoed in *Chronicle of a Death Foretold,* in which the citizens of another town, caught in the grip of a terrible disbelieving inertia, once again fail to prevent a killing, even though it has been endlessly 'announced' or 'foretold'. These assonances in the Marquez oeuvre are so pronounced that it's easy to let them overpower the considerable differences of intent and achievement in his books.

For not only is Marquez bigger than his grandmother: he is also bigger than Macondo. The early writings look, in retrospect, like preparations for the great flight of *One Hundred Years of Solitude,* but even in those days Marquez was writing about two towns: Macondo and another, nameless one, which is more than just a sort of not-Macondo, but a much less mythologised place, a more 'naturalistic' one, insofar as anything is naturalistic in Marquez. This is the town of *Los Funerales de la Mama Grande* (the English title, *Big Mama's Funeral,* makes it sound like something out of Damon Runyon), and many of the stories in this collection, with the exception of the title story, in which the Pope comes to the funeral, are closer in feeling to early Hemingway than to later Marquez. And ever since his great book, Marquez has been making a huge effort to get away from his mesmeric jungle settlement, to *continue.*

In *The Autumn of the Patriarch,* he found a miraculous method for dealing with the notion of a dictatorship so oppressive that all change, all possibility of development, is stifled: the power of the patriarch stops time, and the text is thereby enabled to swirl, to eddy around the stories of his reign, creating by its non-linear form an exact analogy for the feeling of endless stasis. And in *Chronicle of a Death Foretold,* which looks at first sight like a reversion to the manner of his earlier days, he is in fact innovating again. The *Chronicle* is about honour and about its opposite—that is to say, dishonour, shame....

The manner in which this story is revealed is something new for Garcia Marquez. He uses the device of an unnamed, shadowy narrator visiting the scene of the killing many years later, and beginning an investigation into the past. This narrator, the text hints, is Garcia Marquez himself—at least, he has an aunt with that surname. And the town has many echoes of Macondo: Gerineldo Marquez makes a guest appearance, and one of the characters has the evocative name, for fans of the earlier book, of Cotes. But whether it be Macondo or no, Marquez is writing, in these pages, at a greater distance from his material than ever before. The book and its narrator probe slowly, painfully, through the mists of half-accurate memories, equivocations, contradictory versions, trying to establish what happened and why; and achieve only provisional answers. The effect of this retrospective method is to make the *Chronicle* strangely elegiac in tone, as if Garcia Marquez feels that he has drifted away from his roots, and can only write about them now through veils of formal difficulty. Where all his previous books exude an air of absolute authority over the material, this one reeks of doubt. And the triumph of the book is that this new hesitancy, this abdication of Olympus, is turned to such excellent account, and becomes a source of strength: *Chronicle of a Death Foretold*, with its uncertainties, with its case-history format, is as haunting, as lovely and as true as anything Garcia Marquez has written before.

Source: Salman Rushdie, "Angel Gabriel," in *London Review of Books,* September 16 to October 6, 1982, pp. 3–4.

Bill Buford

In the following essay, Buford focuses on García Márquez's "demythologizing of romantic love" related to the murder and murderer as well as on the "unabsolved guilt" of the community that allowed the murder.

Gabriel García Márquez has repeatedly expressed his surprise at being so insistently regarded as a writer of fantastic fiction. That exotic or "magical" element so characteristic of his work is, by his account, not really his own achievement. It is merely the reality of Latin America, which he has faithfully transcribed in more or less the same way that he might write about it in, say, an ordinary article written for a daily newspaper. On a number of occa-

> In many ways, then, the novel offers itself as an icy demythologizing of both romantic love and the romantic folly it inspires; it is a debunking of dream and sentiment hinted at by the book's epigraph: "the hunt for love is haughty falconry".

sions, in fact, Márquez has said that for him there is no real difference between the writing of journalism and the writing of fiction—both are committed to the rigours of realistic representation—and his own ideal of the novel involves as much reportage as imagination. Viewed in this way, Márquez can be seen as an inspired tropical reporter for whom the strange Columbian world—with its prescient prostitutes, benevolent ghosts, and an eccentric magician who refuses to die—is just his everyday journalist's "beat". The image is not entirely fanciful. In an interview published in last winter's *Paris Review,* for example, he says that the non-fiction account of contemporary Cuba that he is currently writing will prove to his critics "with historical facts that the real world in the Caribbean is just as fantastic as the stories in *One Hundred Years of Solitude.* " What he is really writing, he says, is good old-fashioned "socialist realism".

Chronicle of a Death Foretold is very close to Márquez's ideal fiction. Written in the manner of investigative journalism and in a conspicuously flattened, unadorned prose, the novel sets out to reconstruct a murder that occurred twenty-seven years before.

From the outset of Márquez's chronicle, everybody—including the reader—knows that the Vicario brothers intend to kill Santiago Nasar. Everybody knows how they mean to do it—with a pair of butcher's knives—and why. And they know so much because the brothers are dedicated to telling their plans to everyone they meet. The original Spanish title, lost in English translation, is important here. In *Una crónica de una muerte anunciada, anunciada* signifies not so much "foretold" as "announced" or "advertised" or "broadcast"—none

> **"** One of the book's great virtues is self-containment. It presents a large world *in parvo,* without being selfconsciously a microcosm, framed in noble if miniature proportions, viewed by an aristocrat of letters whose attitude to the human lot mingles contempt and compassion in a witty blend."

of which, admittedly, makes for a very poetic title. The idea of an announced or broadcast death, however, is crucial. The brothers are committed to a course of action that has been determined for them—honour can only be redeemed publicly by their killing of Santiago—and they can only be relieved of their duty by the people around them. Once they have broadcast their intentions to the whole community, everyone, to some extent, by failing to stop them, participates in the crime....

It is ... obvious that this murder, for all the simplicity with which it is narrated, is no simple crime. Part of its significance is evident in the way it is understood by those of Santiago Nasar's generation, for whom the murder seems to mark the end of their youth and render illusory so much that was once meaningful. Flora Miguel, Santiago Nasar's fiancée, for example, runs away immediately after the crime with a lieutenant from the border patrol who then prostitutes her among the rubber workers in a nearby town. Divina Flor—the servant meant for Santiago's furtive bed—is now fat, faded, and surrounded by the children of other loves. And, finally, after more than twenty years, Angela Vicario is reunited with the husband whose affronted masculine pride was the cause of the crime. Overweight, perspiring and bald, he arrives still carrying the same silver saddlebags that now serve merely as pathetic reminders of his ostentatious youth. Márquez's chronicle moves backwards and forwards in time, and views the participants in a senseless murder long after the passion that contributed to it has died. In many ways, then, the novel

offers itself as an icy demythologizing of both romantic love and the romantic folly it inspires; it is a debunking of dream and sentiment hinted at by the book's epigraph: "the hunt for love is haughty falconry".

But the real significance of the murder is much greater, and is felt by the entire community whose uncritical faith in its own codes of justice and spectacle is responsible for the crime. The weight of this responsibility is felt most, though, by the unnamed narrator; he returns because he is bothered not by an unsolved mystery but an unabsolved guilt, and the chronicle he produces is a document charting the psychology of mass complicity. It is interesting that Márquez, in developing a simple tale fraught with obvious political implications, chose not to fictionalize an actual political event— Latin America provides more than enough material—but to treat instead a fictional episode with the methods of a journalist. In so doing he has written an unusual and original work: a simple narrative so charged with irony that it has the authority of political fable. If not an example of the socialist realism Márquez may claim it to be elsewhere, *Chronicle of a Death Foretold* is in any case a mesmerizing work that clearly establishes Márquez as one of the most accomplished, and the most "magical" of political novelists writing today.

Source: Bill Buford, "Haughty Falconry and Collective Guilt," in *Times Literary Supplement,* No. 4145, September 10, 1982, p. 965.

David Hughes

In the following excerpt, Hughes praises the accuracy of García Márquez's description of details as well as his originality for implicating the whole community in the murder through their foreknowledge of the murder plan.

One hundred pages of quality make [*Chronicle of a Death Foretold*] a fiction that reverberates far beyond its modest length. The story is a mere incident. In a waterfront town on the Caribbean a self-contained youth called Santiago Nasar will be, was, and indeed is being, stabbed to death with meat knives. This event takes place in gory detail on the last few pages. It is the sole preoccupation of the pages in between. And on the first we more or less know that it has already happened. So the suspense is not acute....

Not so much marching forward as marking time, the narrative continuum continually drifts more back than forth, rescuing the story piece by piece from the memory of policemen, gossips, officials, shopkeepers, whores, whose 'numerous marginal experiences' are humanly unreliable. They can't even agree about the weather when the blows were struck. And that is the element that melts this strictly factual document (as it pretends to be) into delicious fiction: everyone in town regards his or her personal evidence as fact, whatever the contradictions. By exploiting the fallibility of his characters Marquez arrives at nothing but the truth.

The book's original touch is that these townspeople, deftly sketched without a word or image wasted, know before Santiago does, but without warning him, that he is on the point of being murdered. All have ostensibly cast-iron excuses, loss of nerve, forgetfulness, failing to take the threat seriously, not wishing to become involved. In their variety of selfish responses to foreknowledge, they bring on Santiago's death, as if secretly savouring it in prospect and relishing its aftermath. We are all to blame, mutters Marquez with good humour, because we all brainlessly share the eccentricity of common human feeling.

The book vindicates its brevity by an exactitude of detail that snaps a character to life without recourse to long or even direct description. To visualise a visiting bishop, all we need to be told is that his favourite dish—he discards the rest of the fowl—is coxcomb soup. The mayor's character is purely and simply conveyed when we are casually informed that a policeman is collecting from the shop the pound of liver he eats for breakfast. In these two images all authority, religious and civil, is nicely confounded, just because no heavy weather is made of confounding them. The reader is paid the compliment of being asked to respond imaginatively to the most delicate of hints and indeed to make his own moral structure from the ins and outs of the lack of narrative: to decide for instance, who is lying for good reasons, who being honest for bad.

One of the book's great virtues is self-containment. It presents a large world *in parvo*, without being selfconsciously a microcosm, framed in noble if miniature proportions, viewed by an aristocrat of letters whose attitude to the human lot mingles contempt and compassion in a witty blend. Nobody shows up either well or badly under the microscope. People are seen as wayward but pitiable cells in the body politic, preventing it from functioning properly but at the same time breathing an outrageous life into it.

Some days after reading this novella I am still in several minds as to what it is about. Just a faith-

ful picture of a community living off shopsoiled machismo? An author's obsession with the dramatics of sudden death? The last drop of blood squeezed out of material better suited to a thriller? A neurotic treatise on the erotic corollaries of murder? Any or all of these perhaps—and more. And that's a healthy feeling of perplexity. If good books do furnish the imagination, they also echo on and on in its rooms.

Source: David Hughes, "Murder," in *Spectator*, Vol. 249, No. 8044, September 11, 1982, p. 24.

Sources

Alonso, Carlos, "Writing and Ritual in *Chronicle of a Death Foretold*," in *Gabriel Garcia Marquez: New Readings*, edited by Bernard McGuirk and Richard Cardwell, Cambridge University Press, 1987, pp. 151-68.

Berg, Mary G., "Repetitions and Reflections in *Chronicle of a Death Foretold*," in *Critical Perspectives on Gabriel Garcia Marquez*, edited by Bradley A. Shaw and Nora Vera-Godwin, Society of Spanish and Spanish-American Studies, 1986, pp. 139-56.

Burgess, Anthony, review in *The New Republic*, Vol. 188, No. 1, May 2, 1983, p. 36.

Christie, John S., "Fathers and Virgins: Garcia Marquez's Faulknerian *Chronicle of a Death Foretold*," *Latin American Review*, Vol. 21, No. 41, June, 1993, pp. 21-29.

De Feo, Ronald, review in *Nation*, December 2, 1968.

Elnadi, Bahgat, Adel Rifaat, and Miguel Labarca, "Gabriel García Márquez: The Writer's Craft," interview in *UNESCO Courier*, February, 1996, p.4.

García Márquez, Gabriel, in an interview with Claudia Dreifus, in *Playboy*, February, 1983.

Gass, William H., "More Deaths Than One: *Chronicle of a Death Foretold*," *New York Magazine*, Vol. 16, No. 15, 11 April, 1983, pp. 83-4.

Grossman, Edith, review, in *Review*, September/December, 1981.

Mano, Keith, review, in *National Review*, Vol. 35, No. 2, June 10, 1983, p. 699.

Millington, Mark, "The Unsung Heroine: Power and Marginality in *Chronicle of a Death Foretold*," *Bulletin of Hispanic Studies*, Vol. 66, 1989, pp. 73-85.

Petrakis, Harry Mark, review, in *Tribune Books*, April 17, 1988.

Sheppard, R. Z., review, in *Time*, March 16, 1970.

Stone, Peter H., interview, in *Paris Review*, Winter, 1981.

Streitfeld, David, review in *Washington Post*, October 22, 1982.

Sturrock, John, review in *New York Times Book Review*, September 29, 1968.

Yardley, Jonathan, review in *Washington Post Book World,* November 25, 1979.

For Further Study

Bell-Villada, Gene H., *García Márquez: The Man and His Work,* University of North Carolina Press, 1990.
Followed by an extensive bibliography, this book puts Márquez in the company of other authors whose readers appreciate their ability to combine the commonplace with pioneering philanthropic political trends.

Donoso, Jose, *The Boom in Spanish American Literature,* translated by Gregory Kolovakos, Columbia University Press, 1977.
While this author asserts that the term "the Boom Generation" is misleading, he acknowledges that the novels and novelists coming out of the period deserve their notoriety. In addition, Donoso explains the origin of the term.

Gonzalez Echevarria, Roberto, *Myth and Archive: A Theory of Latin American Narrative,* Cambridge University Press, 1990.
Echevarria provides an extensive bibliography from which he has culled his ideas for his theory of how and where the Latin American narrative started and how it fits in with the modern novel.

Gabriel García Márquez and the Powers of Fiction, edited by Julio Ortega, University of Texas Press, 1988.
A book of critical essays on the works of Gabriel García Márquez, this collection provides insight on Márquez's style through various scholars' viewpoints.

Landmarks in Modern Latin American Fiction, edited by Philip Swanson, Routledge [and] Kegan Paul, 1990.
The "Boom" period in Latin American literature provides the backdrop to this compilation of essays that pertain to key texts written during the era.

Martin, Gerald, *Journeys Through the Labyrinth: Latin American Fiction in the Twentieth Century,* Verso, 1989.
Beginning with the 1920s and continuing through the 1980s, the author presents a view of Latin American literature seen through the perspective of themes and historical periods. He presents new works and authors as well as a list of primary texts and a critical bibliography.

Wolin, Merle Linda, "Hollywood Goes Havana: Fidel, Gabriel, and the Sundance Kid," in *The New Republic,* Vol. 202, No. 16, April 16, 1990, p. 17.
This article describes the internationally known Foundation for New Latin American Cinema and film school located in Cuba that are headed by García Márquez. The school receives contributions from such recognizable people as Robert Redford and offers the typical courses needed to learn the art and craft of filmmaking.

The Dead of the House

Hannah Green
1972

Hannah Green's only novel, *The Dead of the House* (1972), has been praised for its evocative language and lyrical prose. The novel originally appeared in the *New Yorker* as a series of shorter fictional pieces. It was published as a novel in 1971 to critical and commercial praise; when it was reprinted in 1996, the novel was discovered by a new generation of readers.

The novel is the story of a girl's passage from childhood through adolescence and into adulthood. Moreover, it is a much broader history of her entire family. *The Dead of the House* also paints a rich picture of an older American family and its place within the history of America. In addition, it hearkens back to the mythology of the American West.

Author Biography

A native of Cincinnati, Ohio, Green was born in 1927. Her father was a foreign copyright and trademark agent, like his fictional counterpart in *The Dead of the House,* and her mother was a homemaker. She attended Wellesley College, studying with Wallace Stegner and receiving her Bachelor of Arts degree in 1948. She later went to Stanford University, receiving a Master's degree in 1956. While at Stanford, she studied with the celebrated Russian writer, Vladimir Nabokov.

In the early 1960s she began writing what would ultimately become *The Dead of the House.*

In 1970, she was hired as a professor by Columbia University, a position that she held until her retirement. Initially *The Dead of the House* was published in a shorter form in *The New Yorker;* in 1972 it came out in novel form and attracted critical and commercial attention. In 1985 *In the City of Paris,* a juvenile novel about French culture and the wonders of Paris, was published.

Green died of lung cancer on October 16, 1996, in New York City. At the time of her death, she had completed *Golden Spark, Little Saint: My Book of the Hours of Saint Foy,* which has never been published.

Plot Summary

Section One: In My Grandfather's House

The first part of the novel is concerned with the events of Vanessa's childhood, but also with the stories and history of her family. As the name of the section implies, nearly all of this portion of the novel takes place in Grandpa Nye's house located in Cincinnati, Ohio.

While the story is told from a mix of voices filtered through Vanessa's memory, certain events fit within the narrative at the time they are happening. Vanessa's grandmother dies. After the funeral, her grandfather marries Janice, his housekeeper. She is then referred to as Aunt Janice, as the age gap between Grandpa Nye and her seems too large for her to be called grandmother. Vanessa relates much of the history of the family through remembered conversations with her grandfather.

Grandpa Nye and Vanessa's father tell her about her late Uncle Joab. She also takes possession of a book of Joab's poetry; besides reading and memorizing the poems, she adorns the book with flowers, as if it were his grave or even the man himself.

Grandpa Nye tells her many stories: some about his family history, or things that happened to people he knew. He has a skull tattoo and crossbones on his chest, done himself when he was only a boy. He also tells her of the wonders of his many canoe trips across the wild waterways of Canada, and his friendship with an Indian guide.

Section Two: Summer Afternoon, Summer Afternoon

This section takes place primarily at the Nye family's vacation home in Neahwantah, Michigan. An exploration of Vanessa's adolescence and young adulthood, it chronicles her gradual sexual and mental awakening. She explores her love for Dirk Monroe, as well as her intense love for and jealousy of her sister, Lisa.

Vanessa returns again and again to one event. She remembers arriving early for dinner at her grandfather's house to hear him read the DeGolyer family manuscript to her. The oldest piece of written history relevant to the family, he tells her about it and promises it to her several times before she at last has it. She also finds herself increasingly drawn to the story of Tecumseh.

Upon returning from Michigan, the narrative shifts forward in time. After December 7, 1941, there is a focus on World War II. Vanessa works after school rolling bandages for the Red Cross. Dirk comes to visit, and he kisses her. In 1943, Isabel, Vanessa's mother, begins working for the Draft Board. Vanessa is still doing her after-school work for the Red Cross. Dirk comes once more to visit. Their passion nearly overwhelms them as they become more physically intimate in the Nye family parlor. Three weeks after shipping out, Dirk Monroe is killed. On May 7, 1944, he is buried at sea. Upon hearing the news, Vanessa feels that she should cry, but does not.

Section Three: And Here Tecumseh Fell

This section begins with Vanessa stepping off an airplane. It is December 22, 1954, and she is returning home after a year at graduate school in California. Besides the holidays, she is returning home because of her grandfather's illness. Her sister, Lisa, is in an unhappy marriage to a doctor, and has a daughter of her own. Grandpa Nye is in the hospital, suffering the effects of multiple strokes. Vanessa suddenly finds that her parents have grown old.

When she visits her grandfather in the hospital, he is uncommunicative and nearly comatose. She is struck by how hideous and horrible Aunt Janice, her grandfather's second wife, seems to have become. All Aunt Janice talks about is the death of her dog, Calvin. Yet she giggles nervously when talking about it, and does not say anything about the impending death of her husband.

Vanessa visits her grandfather's house for the last time, since it is being sold and he and his wife have long since moved out. A gradual narrative of the events leading up to the sale of the house is revealed. Vanessa and her sister search the house for the last of her grandfather's wine but find none.

As Vanessa gathers with her family for the holiday dinner, the truth of the Nye family past is revealed to her by her father. He tells her that her grandfather never really knew how to manage his money, and that he made some very bad business decisions. He also reveals his own feelings of insecurity that plagued him when Vanessa was young.

In the final scene, the family is gathered at the dinner table reminiscing about the family when the phone rings. Vanessa's father, Morgan, comes into the room and announces, "Papa is dead." The novel ends with these words.

Characters

Eugenie

Eugenie is the family's African American housekeeper. Known only by her first name, Eugenie takes care of the family, and helps clean Grandfather Nye's house when they move out.

Aunt Janice

See Janice Nye

Uncle Joab

See Joab Nye

Dirk Monroe

Dirk is Vanessa's first love. She doesn't seem to be truly in love with him; he just seems fated for her, in much the same way her parents met and seemed destined for each other. He is killed three weeks after setting off for boot camp. Vanessa does not express particular sadness over his death.

Grandfather Nye

See Nathaniel Nye

Isabel Nye

The mother of Vanessa and Lisa, Isabel Nye is a comfortably privileged woman who does not always know quite what to do with her children. Raised in relatively wealthy circumstances, she is accustomed to having things naturally her way.

Janice Nye

Janice is not the aunt of Vanessa and Lisa; she is Nathaniel's second wife. She is known as Aunt Janice because of the great age difference between her and Nathaniel. Originally his housekeeper, she becomes a caregiver after their marriage. Her role is making sure her husband does not fall down the stairs, shopping, and entertaining people. In Vanessa's eyes, Janice is a shallow and insensitive person who cares more about her dog than her husband. Janice sells the Nye family house, claiming that the age and upkeep are too much for them to handle. This sends Nathaniel into a depression; he eventually has a stroke and ends up in hospital.

Joab Nye

Joab Nye is the late son of Nathaniel Nye, brother of Vanessa's father. After dying during a hernia operation at the age of twenty-three, Nathaniel collects his verse into book form to immortalize his son.

Lisa Nye

Lisa is Vanessa's younger sister and is described as beautiful like their mother, Isabel. While Lisa and Vanessa spend a lot of time together, they are not particularly close. Lisa is like her mother in more ways than just her beauty. She is fawned over by boys, while the older Vanessa is usually ignored. She seems much more comfortable with her role of beautiful and feminine woman than Vanessa would be.

Lisa and Vanessa have several strange and long-standing conflicts based on sibling rivalry. In the final section of the novel, the sisters finally discuss and resolve these episodes. The end of novel finds Lisa unhappily married with a daughter, Amy.

Morgan Nye

Morgan is Vanessa's father, as well as the son of Nathaniel Nye. He is a copyright and patent agent, like Green's own father. Through the recollections of Morgan and his wife, Isabel, as well as Nathaniel, it is apparent that Morgan is raising his daughters in much the same way he himself was raised. He too spent summers at the family's home at Neahtawantah, on Traverse Bay in Michigan. During his summers there, he met his wife.

Morgan's occasional loudness and exuberance suggest that he drinks too much. His bouts of melancholy regarding his dead brother Joab are melodramatic. Morgan says of Joab, "if *he* had only lived, I would have loved him more than any human being." While otherwise a quiet man, episodes like these give a sense of both passion and immense sadness to Morgan Nye.

Nathaniel Nye

Nathaniel (also known as Grandpa Nye and Papa Nye) is the patriarch of the Nye family and is grandfather to both Vanessa and Lisa. Nathaniel is a former reporter, editor, professional speaker, and retired businessman. He is a man given to expounding freely about history, both that of the family and historical figures. He is also willing to tell the tales of his own life, with Vanessa being his favorite audience. Nathaniel's most cherished image of himself is as an outdoorsman and naturalist. Until his the end of his life, Nathaniel is an active man. He climbs trees to get the grapes for his wine. He makes the wine himself, and cuts wood for his fireplace. He longs for one last grand canoe trip across the wild rivers of Canada.

Papa Nye

See Nathaniel Nye

Vanessa Nye

The protagonist of the novel, Vanessa relates the story of her life from her childhood to adulthood. As a young girl, she is curious and asks her grandfather to repeat stories she has already heard, because she wishes to remember his stories. Most of the first section of the book is made up of recalled conversations or observations she has heard from others.

As the story progresses, Vanessa becomes more proactive and less of a passive observer. She is also a very insecure girl: she is concerned with whether or not boys like her, and if her father likes her sister better. Growing up, she becomes more aware of her body and explores the feeling of sun and water on her skin. She has her first stirrings of sexual feeling when she begins dating Dirk Monroe, her childhood friend.

As an adult, Vanessa is less self-absorbed and more concerned about the feelings of others. Her academic success and independence has led to a sense of security and confidence.

Themes

Man Against Nature

The ambiguous relationship between man and his environment is explored in *The Dead of the House*. Nathaniel Nye, Vanessa's grandfather and the idealized representation of man, is the character most associated with this thematic concern. The veteran of many canoeing expeditions through the rivers and untouched regions of Canada "before the white man found it," Nathaniel is constantly torn between his need to civilize and conquer nature and his desire to live in harmony with it. He tells Vanessa several stories of his boyhood, when he and his friends would camp next to the river and spy out on the ships just as the Native Americans had before them. As an older man, he hires Native American guides to take him to isolated, untouched areas.

When Vanessa's story begins, Nathaniel is an old man. He lives his life within the boundaries of civilization in a large house in a nice neighborhood in Cincinnati. Still clinging to his desire to somehow have contact with nature, he goes on missions to harvest the wild grapes, which he crushes to make his wine. In this way, he fulfills his desires: he takes the wild fruit and makes it into something himself.

Writing

Writing is used as a thematic device—both to connect the events and histories within the story with the characters, as well as to connect the whole with the novel itself. Writing, as a form as well as a narrative device, takes many forms within the novel.

Writing something down implies permanence. By publishing his written histories of the family, Nathaniel has made them immortal. When his son Joab dies, Nathaniel has his book of poetry published. Thus, though his son his dead, he still lives through his writing and need never die; he will also exist for those, like Vanessa, who never knew him. While many of the anecdotes and events of his own life would seem to be lost with Nathaniel when he dies, the existence of Vanessa's own narrative makes sure that this is not so. Green transcends the limits of the text and transfers them from within to without. The fact that the reader has the book to read implies that her narrative—and thus the history of the family and those within it—do and will exist.

The idea of the written word and the fact that it becomes written history once it is written down makes the idea of the book into a complete circle. While it begins in Vanessa's childhood when her grandfather is old and ostensibly ends when he dies, this is not the case. The last line of the book is "Papa is dead." Yet the very completion of the novel, and the writing of Vanessa's story, makes this meaningless. Having set down the last words of the story, the story has been written and is permanent. That the story has an end means that Papa is not dead. He is immortal.

Lineage versus Heredity

The concepts of lineage and heredity play important roles in the book. Within a family, it is typical for some amount of a person's self-identity to be shaped both by the reality of inheritance of traits, known as heredity, as well as by the perceived notion of such, known as lineage. The difference between the two ideas of lineage and heredity is fairly straightforward, and is often referred to as nature versus nurture. Heredity implies inheritance, or the direct passage of traits through a parent to a child. Lineage is much broader and harder to quantify. It can be as simple as the idea of "coming from a good family," or something more abstract, like the idea of someone somehow being the "black sheep of the family."

Vanessa's heredity complicates her life. She does not look like her mother, while her sister Lisa does. Because her father loves her mother, Vanessa assumes that since she does not resemble her and her sister does, her father naturally loves her sister more. This is further complicated by the fact that she looks like her grandmother, who eventually went insane. She naturally fears this connection to her heredity, as well as her disappointment at not simply being beautiful like her mother.

Her lineage is something else altogether. She is descended from orators, preachers and explorers. This sort of lineage would imply an adventurous nature, and Vanessa is true to it. While she does not literally explore things with a canoe and Indian guide, she does explore the history of her family, with her questions as the vehicle of exploration and her grandfather as her guide. She is outspoken and is never afraid to ask questions or speak her mind; this ties in with her natural desire for exploration, making her quests for knowledge and identity easier to come by.

Her grandfather tells Vanessa many times that "you take after your pirate ancestor on your grandmother Nye's side of the family." This particular implication of her lineage implies that Vanessa is not possessed of a nature willing to follow within the bounds of convention. Vanessa, whether through her true lineage or her own nature, follows this idea. Rather than marry and have children—as her mother, grandmother, and sister have done—she makes her own way. She goes to college and then to graduate school, at a time when it was not

common for many women to do so. She is, in her own way, a rebel—or even a pirate, when it is considered that she has plundered her grandfather's life and stories for her own.

Topics for Further Study

- Research the history of Native American cultures in the Ohio Valley. Write a history of the Nye family from the perspective of the people whose land was taken.

- Read the first chapter of James Joyce's *Portrait of the Artist As A Young Man* and compare it to the first section of *The Dead of the House*. How do Joyce and Green convey the experience of childhood through their narrative techniques?

- Apart from Eugenia, African Americans are invisible in this novel. Read Toni Morrison's *Beloved* and compare her version of Ohio history with Green's.

- *The Dead of the House* is a semi-autobiographical novel that contains many autobiographical and biographical texts. Write an autobiography of yourself that includes the texts of your family's lives.

- In a 1972 *New York Times Review of Books* article, critic Richard Elman said that reading *The Dead of the House* was "like falling in love." What do you think he meant by this?

Style

Stream of Consciousness

Much of *The Dead of the House*—especially the first part—is told in a stream-of-consciousness style. The term was coined by William James in *Principles of Psychology* (1890) to describe the flow of thoughts experienced by the waking mind. It is now used to describe a narrative method by which novelists can convey the unspoken thoughts and feelings of their characters without using the conventions of explicatory dialogue and narrative voice. The most famous novelists that utilize this technique are James Joyce and Virginia Woolf. In fact, Woolf's technique is very similar to Green's in that her novels attempt to convey the thoughts and perspectives of multiple characters through the lens of a single narrative voice.

Green uses this technique to allow Vanessa's narrative to skip from current events to recollected conversations with her grandfather and back again at random. This frees the story from traditional literary linear narrative technique, and represents Vanessa's evolving relationship with her family. The degree to which the novel is told in stream of consciousness is tied directly to Vanessa's age. The novel is divided into three parts. In the first, she is a child, and events are much more likely to be freed from the constraints of traditional narrative. In the second part, as she is an adolescent and the narrative is more structured. She is developing a more solid consciousness, and is more aware of the things around her as her world expands. By the third part of the book, Vanessa is a young adult and the narrative is "concrete." This follows naturally on both theories of psychology and the nature of memory. As her mind develops and matures, she sees things in an increasingly mature and logical fashion. On the other hand, it would be natural for the memories of her childhood and youth to grow less focused as she moves further away from them in time.

In this way, the early events of the novel and her recollections of them are both less clear and less focused, while her adult recollections, being told in the true narrative present, are more focused and follow a naturalistic chronology. As a first-person narrative in the form of a memoir, *The Dead of the House* structures itself as a continuous act of recollection, rather than a story which develops over time. Many of the earlier recollections of the book are drawn from subconscious or dimly remembered parts of her childhood, and therefore seem disjointed and random. The closer the story moves to the present, the more "real" and more immediate the events become.

Oral History

Oral history is made up of stories about real people and events that are passed down from one generation to another within cultures that lack a written language. While important for recounting past events that occur both within the culture and to the historian and his own family, the purpose of oral history is much more important to the nature of family itself. In certain African tribes, all families have a member who serves the purpose of of-

ficial oral historian; this person is known as a *griot,* and the concept of oral history itself is sometimes called *griot.*

The *griot* is responsible for not only the knowledge and history of the family or culture and the events which have transpired, but also for the names of every relative past and present, and their actual relation to each other. This effects other members of *griot* cultures, so that it is very common for everyone to be able to name hundreds, if not thousands, of their relatives. To do this is a source of pride. Thus, oral history enables cultures and families to have much closer bonds than one would find in written language cultures. History, culture, and lineage are very real and immediate within cultures that rely on oral history.

Much of *The Dead of the House* is told through a stylized, written version of oral history. Many of Vanessa's conversations with her grandfather, parents, and others are recounted not as text, but as dialogue. This differs from standard dialogue in that it is not told as it is happening, but rather is recounted at a later date. Being a first-person narrative told in the present tense, the insertions of conversations of the past into the story that do not follow the linear narrative makes them a literal form of "oral history," rather than a further narrative within the story.

Like the *griot* cultures of Africa, the use of oral history within *The Dead of the House* makes history and relatives real to both the keeper of the knowledge and the one who has the knowledge imparted to them. While Vanessa has access to the books about her family and the poems of her Uncle Joab, the oral recollections of her grandfather and father make them all the more real to her. While her grandfather does not speak much of him, she receives the knowledge—the oral history—of her Uncle Joab from her father, giving her insights into his life and personality that his poems never could. Oral history makes history real, and personal. It comes from those familiar with the person or situation, and gives one intimate knowledge. The oral history of the Nyes is the constitutive basis of their family, and brings Vanessa closer to those around her and those who lived before.

Historical Context

The Mid-1960s

The 1960s were a decade of great cultural upheaval and change. The beginning of the decade

Compare & Contrast

- **Late 1940s:** The Indian Relocation program uses government money to move Native Americans off of the reservations. The aim is to assimilate them into mainstream culture and provide economic and social opportunities.

- **1970s:** The American Indian Movement (AIM) stages protests for the rights of native peoples, including marches on Washington, the occupations of the BIA (Bureau of Indian Affairs) Offices, and the sieges at Wounded Knee and Alcatraz Island.

- **Today:** Government efforts strive to make Native American groups economically self-sufficient. After concerted counterintelligence operations by the Federal government, American Indian protest movements have been considerably weakened. Leonard Peltier, an AIM member, is still imprisoned on what many to believe to be false charges.

- **1950s:** In the postwar housing boom, suburbs begin springing up around major urban areas.

This is fueled by the building of the national highway system.

- **1970s:** America's major cities see large population drops as migration to the suburbs becomes epidemic. Further roads and highways are built, and the reliance on cars becomes a major issue with the OPEC gas crisis.

- **Today:** Urban renewal schemes and public transport are key issues in many U.S. cities. Two decades of cheap gasoline have caused a resurgence in large, inefficient vehicles, even as the nation's highway infrastructure slowly crumbles.

- **1972:** After more than a decade of civil rights protests, the fight for equality turns violent on a national scale in the mid-1960s, with race riots in major cities across America.

- **Today:** Federal laws against discrimination are generally enforced, and abusers are subject to civil suits.

saw landmark legislation to outlaw racial discrimination in any form. Rock-and-roll music, which had been growing in popularity since the 1950s, became a full-blown phenomenon in the early 1960s. Many social commentators viewed the increasing popularity of this kind of music as a sign of impending cultural collapse. This new music was considered fast-paced, bass-heavy, and immoral. It was also viewed as connected to music that had its origins in African American communities, such as rhythm and blues and jazz. The combination of popularized "black music" and desegregation with its attendant effects seemed to be tearing down the walls between white culture and black culture.

The moral decay of American society was thought to be reinforced by the introduction of the birth control pill, which was developed in the late 1950s and widely available by 1962. Many perceived the concept of sexual intercourse outside

marriage as another sign of the moral collapse of society; the pill certainly took away the most feared consequence of sexual behavior—unwanted pregnancy. With more control of one's own body and the increasing number of women entering the workforce and colleges, divorce rates exploded, concerning conservative elements even more. At the same time, feminist groups appeared, and women become a forceful, politically active group. The last line of *The Dead of the House*— "Papa is dead"— can be read as a commentary on the death of patriarchal society.

The Late 1960s

By the end of the decade, America's youth was energized in their opposition to the Vietnam War and their exploration of new sexual freedoms, the increasingly hedonistic and rebellious culture, and the use of drugs by the nation's youth. A growing

The narrator's sense of her family's past is nourished by tales of early America, a lush wilderness in which different cultures sometimes lived in harmony and sometimes clashed. Pictured here Shawnee Chief, Tecumseh, confronts General William Henry Harrison.

gap between the values of the older generation and the younger one became known as the "generation gap." Tension arose between these two generations as youth culture rejected many of the materialistic values and concerns of past generations.

Indian Activism in the 1960s

In the 1960s the Indian Reform Movement became a popular cause for many American people. Probably the best known activist group, the American Indian Movement (AIM), formed in Minneapolis in 1968 to protest against police brutality. After that, the group went on to lead several high-profile protests. In 1970 they occupied a portion of the land at the base of the Mount Rushmore Memorial.

At the same time, other Native American groups were drawing attention to the government's neglect of Native American people. One hundred Native Americans took over Alcatraz Island in 1969, offering to buy the former federal prison back from the government for twenty-four dollars in glass beads (the price allegedly paid to Indians for Manhattan Island in 1626).

The most infamous protest was the siege at Wounded Knee, South Dakota. The site of a fa-

mous massacre of three hundred Indian men, women, and children in 1890, members of AIM and the Sioux nation took hostages in a small hilltop church in Wounded Knee, on the Oglala Reservation, in 1973. The siege attracted international press attention. Two Native Americans were killed during the resulting gunfire, and one hundred were arrested; but as a result, the government promised to hold hearings on Indian rights. After one meeting with representatives from the White House, no further government action regarding Native American rights took place.

Critical Overview

The initial publication of *The Dead of the House* in 1972 had an immediate impact on literary critics, who lavished it with praise. These early reviews focused on two major issues: the first was the narrative techniques of the novel; and the second was to contextualize it within the social and political upheaval of the day.

Richard Elman's influential review deemed *The Dead of the House* "one of the most important works of fiction" to come out in years. He compared reading it to "falling in love," and singled it out as a "beautiful book" that was notable for its lack of "bigger issues." In fact, Green's novel is "nowhere bigger than itself, nowhere grander than its own scope or subject." L. J. Davis' review was similarly rhapsodic, calling Green's work "less a novel than a kind of dream ... a transcendental novel".

While both Elman and Davis stressed the singularity of Green's achievement, other reviewers interpreted it as a response to contemporary culture. Donald Markos drew attention to the complex ironies within the novel, focusing on the paradoxical representation of Grandfather Nye as a "mutual admirer of both Tecumseh and William Henry Harrison"— both colonizer and colonized. "Without an awareness of these ironies, " Markos maintained, "the reader is likely to mistake the novel as a nostalgic celebration of bygone America."

When *The Dead of the House* was reissued in 1996, many reviewers wrote nostalgically about the first time they read it. A *The Washington Post* reviewer referred to it as "the semi-legendary 1971 novel—remembered by all who read it for its quietly perfect evocation of a young girl's coming of age." This and other newer reviews tended to do exactly what Markos warned against in 1973—remove the text from its sociopolitical context, and read it as "a wistful reminiscence of family life and a vanished American past."

Criticism

Tabitha McIntosh-Byrd

Tabitha McIntosh-Byrd is a doctoral candidate at the University of Pennsylvania. In the following essay she analyzes the roles of language, narration, and self-creation in the formation of American identity in The Dead of the House.

The Dead of the House is a complex narrative: its story is assembled rather than told, its crisis points are implied rather than stated, and it offers very little access to simple interpretation. Early reviewers praised this dense insularity—reading it as a deliberate rejection of the social commentary and ideologically charged literary experimentation of the early 1970s. However, the very act of assem-

> " Nye is more Indian than the Indians—their true inheritor and avatar (so the self-serving narrative goes), and thus the real Native Americans can be discarded."

blage that the text enacts reveals the internal fault lines that deliberately shoot through the whole. The densely layered narrative is woven from grandfather's, father's, and uncle's voices, and is blended with extracts from histories, biographies, and autobiographies of the family's men.

From this linguistic melange of masculinity, the narrator, Vanessa, gradually emerges as the dominant speaker—a progression to a stronger female self that develops with adolescence and ends with maturity. As the narrator reaches adulthood, the novel ends and the symbolic ascendance of a new form of authority connoted by the loaded final words—"Papa is dead." If patriarchy is, as this ending implies, finished in mid-1950s Ohio, this conclusion invites a retrospective rereading of the significance of the narrative that leads to this. In fact, a close reading of the novel reveals not the simple minded nostalgia that early reviewers lauded, but a deliberate evocation of nostalgic sentiment that is carefully and thoroughly deconstructed and rejected in the closing section of the text.

The dominant voice of the novel—and the character whose death forces its closure—is Grandfather Nye, the patrician, cultured patriarch of the Nye family. Keeper of family memories and mythology, Nye's Emersonian vision of American life celebrates Western man as wilderness hero, gentleman farmer, and spiritual subject. The first section of the novel, "My Grandfather's House," is just that, his "house"—a recreation of the Nye's seductive and self-serving domestic, social, natural, and psychological space. As *The Dead of the House* progresses, the text's unquestioning alignment with Nye's transcendentalist idealism unravels, revealing a gradual explication and uncovering of the colonial, commercial, and industrial bases of the family. This is primarily achieved through a subtle

What Do I Read Next?

- Sherwood Anderson's *Winesburg, Ohio* (1919) is a collection of interlocking stories concerned with small town life in turn-of-the-century Ohio.

- John Sugden's biography of Tecumseh, *Tecumseh: A Life,* was published in 1998. Sugden presents the cultural clashes, struggles, and bloody conflicts caused by westward expansion.

- *As I Lay Dying,* the 1930 novel by William Faulkner, explores the impact and death of a family matriarch.

- Virginia Woolf's *To The Lighthouse* (1927) cemented its author's reputation as one of the preeminent novelists of the twentieth century. Woolf's novel concerns a family who travel to a holiday home before and after the death of the family matriarch.

- *A Portrait of the Artist as a Young Man* is James Joyce's experimental 1916 novel about the development of Stephen Dedalus. Like Green, Joyce uses linguistic innovation to convey the experience of maturation.

---

yet pointed elaboration on the commodification, artifact fetishism, and active absorption of Native American culture.

Not only do the Nye men trade, covet and own metonymic material indicators of native identity—arrows, vases etc.—they also are implicitly shown as part of the elision of "real" native America from the Americas. Just as Native American culture is reified and accumulated as trophies, so does the culture which produced these artifacts become decentered from the text and the country—pushed out into reservations of both narrative plot and historical ghettoes.

This process is exemplified in Grandfather Nye's relationship with Alfred McCloud, his "Indian guide" and "a gentleman and a scholar." As Vanessa relates, she learns a more rounded version of the truth from his letter stored in the Cincinnati Historical Society. "I can not," Alfred writes to Nye, "furnish you with any items from hunting as you requested for your lecture…. Today in Ontario there are ten white men hunting to one Indian … today the white man hold supremacy, and the poor Indian has to stand back and come back to the reserve." While Nye sees Alfred as a vicarious self whose function is to provide him with artifacts for his lectures, Alfred is fully aware that this process is one whereby he and his people are marginalized, overridden, and removed from the land. The fetishization of Alfred as an archetype both ignores and enables the economic realities that are restructuring the continent.

Only when Vanessa is an adult can she understand and visualize this process. Her figurative blindness is literalized as she finally sees the collection of bones in her father's study—the product of a burial site from which site the Nye boys "scrambled" to grab the tibias and craniums of the valley's prior residents. Her father explains that gathering "Indian relics" had always fascinated them: "Edward retrieved a nice shoulder and forearm. A few thigh bones and some ribs were accumulated. A further skull with an arrowhead imbedded in it was found. I don't recall much in the way of beads and pottery from that grave robbery." In a gruesome literalization of the pirate flag, Vanessa's father has an actual skull and crossed bones displayed in his room, making the Nye's pirate heritage vividly and horrifically real. Yes, Vanessa's has always known she came from pirate stock, but the piracy is here shown to be far more recent than either she or any of her family can articulate.

The colonizing self that this key scene throws into stark relief is constructed from a multiplicity of narratives—both historical and personal—that thread throughout the text. Grandfather Nye's book, known as the DeGolyer manuscript, is the oral history which ties the Nyes together—all of these act upon each other to create an assemblage of a colonizing narrative; a story of heritage and family that glorifies and edits the past, collapsing history into family in a project that justifies and elides the questionable/immoral practices that got them where they are. The transcendentalist self-creation of Grandfather Nye acts as a mythology of exploration—a mythopoetic reimagining of his alignment with an idealized Natural World, which places him within it as participant, instead of external and in hostile relationship to it.

Thus his project acts as a justification for land claims by eliding the very act of acquisition and possession. After all, if he is a man of nature, then he has just as much right to lay train lines in the wilderness and take control of Native American lands, as those native peoples to do be there in the first place. Nye is more Indian than the Indians—their true inheritor and avatar (so the self-serving narrative goes), and thus the real Native Americans can be discarded. It is important to note that Nye bears the pirate flag on his own body: the skull and crossbones tattooed permanently into his skin as an immediate iconic reminder of his true function.

Nor are Native Americans the only dispossessed and elided group within the Nye's story. Everything is narrative, and everyone is subsumed within its narrative imperatives. The latter part of the novel takes place in the 1950s—a time of social upheaval, civil rights agitation, and conflict between the old and news forms of representing and understanding race. Yet within the Nye family it is business as usual. The only African American who intrudes upon their text is the housekeeper, Eugenia.

However, there are fictional African Americans present, the representation of whom acts as a pivotal scene in the novel's closing pages. Vanessa's childhood memory of Eliza's house has double significance as both a metaphoric representation of her transition to independent adulthood, and as a commentary on the textual invisibility of black America. "Children, this is the Eliza house," their mother tells them as children. "This is where Eliza hid after she crossed the river on the ice." Vanessa explains that, "She was a little colored girl who was a slave, but now she was free." The "house" that Vanessa's mother points out is both real and fictional—a material space that has been overwritten with a textual reality. Eliza is the escaped slave girl from Harriet Beecher Stowe's *Uncle Tom's Cabin.* Her flight to safety is one of the compelling and persuasive narratives of white, bourgeoisie American womanhood in the abolitionism struggle.

The history of slavery of African Americans and—by extension—of the current civil rights struggle, has thus been completely absorbed into a self-serving literature of enabling womanhood. Real inequality is glossed by the narrative of reforming bourgeoisie women—of "good" women whose sentimental view of slaves thus becomes the preeminent justification for their failure to view and support civil rights struggles in the present. History, reality, and inequality are made textual and malleable—the subject and matter of orality and memory, not lived experience. Evidence of real iniquity is ignored by reifying the fantasies of the nineteenth century—conferring "fact" (the house)

upon fiction (the Eliza story); fictional sympathy into fine moral sentiment. Eugenia can remain in the kitchen and at her chores, as long as Eliza's house is designated as real.

The role of textuality is indicated in more (and more complex) ways than these. Not only the Nye's family history, but also his immediate personal history is subject to a literary reformation. As the revelations and dropped comments of part three reveal, the liberal arts maven of Vanessa's childhood was only the final incarnation of the man. His latter professional life is inextricably tied to storytelling; his status as a lecturer for hire acting as a reification of the narrative principle that structures his familial relations. Library patron, lecturer, author—these are the roles that structure Vanessa's perception of her grandfather.

Yet the brothers make it suddenly clear that these are the hobbies of old age, rather than vocation. In fact, the family's finances are, in essence, based on heavy industry—"iron and coal ... [and] manganese ore." Nor is this all. The Nye family business is predicated on exploitation and war profiteering—shipping resources to "a Europe devastated by war" and buying goods from cheap, nonunion Southern sources. These businesses have collapsed due to Grandfather Nye's failures as a commercial manager. As his son says baldly, "Papa didn't always handle things correctly." Just as the idyllic nature/man relationship is exploded by the decayed bodies that Vanessa can finally perceive, so too is the myth of liberal humanities life destroyed. The Nyes are not romantic self-creations but an inextricable part of the commercial and industrial expansion of Ohio.

By the end of *The Dead of the House,* the phrase, *Here Tecumseh Fell* has taken on different meanings. On the one hand, Grandfather Nye's cherished narrative of self is as a woodsman/wilderness dweller—an association of himself with the iconic figure of Tecumseh that forces the most obvious interpretation of the heading. Tecumseh is Nye, and the section shows his death—Here Nye (Tecumseh) dies (Fell). The real Tecumseh is thus absorbed into Nye's symbolic self-presentation, so that he becomes an avatar of self—a means of identifying Grandfather Nye with the DeGolyer manuscript and myths. This very absorption inevitably leads to the alternative interpretation of the title.

As the narrative thrust of the section makes clear through the bones and scattered corporeality of Native Americans that litter the house, the real Tecumseh—the scattered body of his people—is thrust insistently onto center stage. Tecumseh thus

> And it is here, perhaps, in Grandpa Nye's Emersonianism that his flaw is to be found: he lacks a sufficient sense of evil."

shifts from being the avatar, to being the victim of Nye and his fellow western explorers. This it is here—with "us" and with the Nye's—that Tecumseh fell. He fell in the process by which the Nye family rose—his descent the inevitable product of their economic, manufacturing ascent.

Source: Tabitha McIntosh-Byrd, in an essay for *Novels for Students*, Gale, 2000.

Donald Markos

In the following essay, Markos describes the novel as a chronicle "of paradise lost through innocence" as it describes the values and moral failures of figures from the American past.

One begins reading *The Dead of the House* with the curiously refreshing sense that this is not going to be a fashionably "absurd" contemporary novel. The manner is realistic. Instead of caricature and fantasy, we are introduced to characters of full dimensions with roots lying deep in a recognizable version of American history. Hannah Green, through her narrator, writes lovingly of an American family, of ancestors who throve on this continent, beginning with the first Nye who came to the New World as a minister called by God and the first DeGolyer who came as a deserter from the French army. The record of this first DeGolyer's adventures on the new continent, including his service in the Revolution and his ultimate withdrawal from white society to live out his last days among the Indians, wonderfully evokes the beauty and freedom of the original American forest which still lingers in the narrator's memories of her girlhood vacations in the Michigan woods and lakes. It may be, as Wallace Stegner says on the book flap, that "this is a novel that is going to reassure many readers who have not lost faith in the family"; yet there is a mood which runs counter to the seemingly nostalgic presentation of the traditionally admired American character. The novel turns out in the end to be a chronicle of lost innocence—or, more accurately, of paradise lost *through* innocence.

Though there are frequent shifts in time and narrator, the novel does have something of a loose plot structure controlled by the narrator's quest to identify herself with her family's past. The first section, "In My Grandfather's House," introduces the narrator's Grandpa Nye, a representative American and the narrator's chief link to her ancestral past. Through stories and written records the narrator, Vanessa, learns of her ancestors' removal to the New World, their settlement in Ohio, and her Grandpa Nye's paradisiacal boyhood along the Ohio River. This is followed in the second section, "Summer Afternoon, Summer Afternoon," by an account of Vanessa's own awkward, dreamy, painful, and ecstatic girlhood, particularly the summers spent in Michigan. We learn a good deal more about Grandpa Nye here, and also about the more exotic DeGolyer side of the family. In Grandpa Nye, as in Vanessa, the DeGolyer wildness and imagination have combined with the gentility and moral character of the Nyes.

The final third of the book deals with the condition of the Nye family during Grandpa Nye's declining years in the early 1950s. The younger Nyes are admirable, but lesser men than their forefathers. A breakdown in family structure has begun to show, but the author does not simply play off the present against the past, for the structure had developed a crack long ago. Grandpa Nye, now in his senility and removed to a hospital by his second wife who fails to appreciate his stature or the roots that go back so deep in American history, is presented as lost and terror-stricken. All his sense of failure seems to have centered in the memory of his first wife, who went mad. Vanessa, in a significant passage, imagines him pondering over what externally seems to have been a rich and rewarding life: "What was it [I] failed to understand?"

In the preface, Hannah Green states that she had attempted to write "a very real book, which is, in fact, a dream." The record of the fabulous Nyes and DeGolyers as filtered through their troubled and nostalgic contemporary descendant, can indeed be read as a dreamlike American fable. Grandpa Nye, respected by governors and presidents, is "connected to History," and his failure of awareness is an American failure.

Grandpa Nye's ninety years cover a rich variety of experience as Latinist, historian, Chautauqua lecturer, outdoorsman, storyteller, wine-maker, and businessman; but the novel makes a particular point of identifying him with the Indian. In his privately published *Memories of My Boyhood,* Grandpa Nye wrote of his idyllic boyhood: "It was our ambition to be as nearly savage as possible." Aside from boyhood, his happiest memories are of canoe trips into the Canadian wilderness with his friend and Indian guide, Alfred. The third section of the book, "And Here Tecumseh Fell," explicitly identifies Grandpa Nye with the great Indian leader. Grandpa Nye's love of nature and his outlook in general are strikingly Emersonian: "… one can never be lonely when he has the fields and the forest, the rivers and lakes for his companions. They never seemed to be inanimate things; rather they are living things." And it is here, perhaps, in Grandpa Nye's Emersonianism that his flaw is to be found: he lacks a sufficient sense of evil. For one thing, his culture has not provided him with this sense. His Chautauqua lectures included picturesque topics like "Washington, City of Magnificent Distances" and "Emerson and Concord." His enthusiasm for reading includes Macaulay, Southey, Milton, and Shakespeare, but no mention of Melville, Crane, Hemingway, Faulkner, or Eliot. Nor is Grandpa Nye capable of learning much about the nature of evil from reading Shakespeare or Milton.

The result of this genteel cultural background is that Grandpa Nye lives in a compartmentalized world. The most striking evidence of this is his mutual and uncritical admiration for both Tecumseh and William Henry Harrison who defeated the Indian forces under Tecumseh and later made use of his popularity as an Indian fighter in his campaign for president. Grandpa Nye is, in fact, an expert on Harrison, yet never once in the book does he indicate any sense of the social injustice which drove Tecumseh into organizing resistance. Grandpa Nye's blindness comes out in the unconscious tone of condescension in speaking of his Indian friend, Alfred: "not only a superior Indian, but a superior man … with an appreciation of Nature that was unusual in an Indian. I verily believe that his delight in the beauty of the land and water was as great as mine." A further ironic discrepancy in this vein is his love of his annual Canadian canoe trips and his ownership of a company which sells pig iron, coke, and coal. Grandpa Nye welcomes the Canadian National Railroad which makes it possible to penetrate to the heart of the Canadian wilderness (and to leave comfortably in a Pullman car), unaware that the extension of technology is also deadly to the very thing he loves. The reader may discover further discrepancies for himself, though they are not as obvious as they seem to be here, for the author's

> "Memory, record, and imagination," closely linked in experience, are often indistinguishable from one another. So it is in *The Dead of the House,* where the creative power of the imagination operates on fact to generate memory, which in turn makes imagination inseparable from fact."

method is not the traditional modern one, fostered by *The Waste Land,* of using immediately opposed juxtapositions; but the discrepancies are there and are available to reflection. Without an awareness of these ironies, the reader is likely to mistake the novel as a nostalgic celebration of a bygone America.

The novel does have its faults. Some of the historical accounts are insufficiently integrated into the fictional narration. The author too often relies on hints where important matters of motivation are concerned (was Joab Nye's death a suicide or accident? What is the significance of Grandmother Nye's madness? And did both of them have a perception of evil that was lacking in the other Nyes?). Some of the symbolism is too easy and intrusive (the "filth" discovered in cleaning Grandpa Nye's abandoned house or the wine that has "soured" as his spirit declines). Yet *The Dead of the House* is an important book for its evocation and implicit judgment of the American past—the enduring values and virtues of some of its best men, as well as their ultimate moral failure.

Source: Donald Markos, "Of Grandfathers: Hannah Green's The Dead of the House," in *Southern Review,* Vol. 9, No. 3, Summer, 1973, pp. 713–16.

Patricia Meyer Spacks

In the following excerpt, Spacks discusses the influence of memory on the creation of Green's novel.

> **❝** Like most works of fiction, it is about life as it is lived on earth; unlike so many, it has something of importance to say on the subject, with a touch that is as light and dry as a blown leaf or the touch of an old man's hand.❞

...The narratives of self-revelation that seem to issue from and speak to the vital imagination are marked by their air of restraint. Understatement can be as clichéd as its opposite, but one must welcome a book that limits its opportunities for self-indulgence, assuming that in private as well as public life surfaces may suggest interiors more accurately than mindless introspection, and that form means more than starting somewhere and stopping some arbitrary distance further on. Two comparably compelling examples of fictional reminiscence are *The Lizards*—about an inarticulate Italian girl with an efficient lawyer mother—and *The Dead of the House,* a tale of a young American girl and her relation to a complex family tradition. In a prefatory note, Hannah Green comments explicitly on the novelistic relation between fiction and fact: "I got the idea from life, but I have proceeded from vision. I have made use in equal parts of memory, record, and imagination." The intimate mystery of memory is the source of the book's power. Green's episodes have the air of being recalled, not created, and they conquer the imagination as one's own memories do, true both to the consciousness that recalls them and to an imaginable world outside that consciousness. "Memory, record, and imagination," closely linked in experience, are often indistinguishable from one another. So it is in *The Dead of the House,* where the creative power of the imagination operates on fact to generate memory, which in turn makes imagination inseparable from fact.

"Memory," in this novel, is both individual and collective, existing in the minds of the family as a whole as well as in the narrator's consciousness. It is a formative power. Listening to family reminiscences, Vanessa comments: "I felt as if I were beautiful. I felt as if I were growing, harmonizing, settling into a form filled long ago in turn by these women, my great-grandmother and her daughter." Reminiscence creates both the old form and its new content, shaping and expanding the personality of the listener. It may be in detail inaccurate: Vanessa recalls that her sister won the pearl in their father's oyster, Lisa remembers Vanessa as winner. But the pearl's possessor is irrelevant. That the sisters recall events differently helps to define their natures. Memory, creating character, generating truth, is the subject and technique of the book. Its benignity incorporates misunderstanding, hostility (Lisa confessing that she always hated her sister), violence, death, without sentimentalizing them. When it avoids direct recollection of emotion, the avoidance is itself a statement.

> "Good-bye, Vanessa. You're swell," he said, and hung up, and three weeks later, out in the Pacific where he stood on the deck of his ship, he was hit by a shell. He was buried at sea, May 7, 1944. I shut the door of my room; I drew down the blinds and doubled over.
>
> Mama was home from the draft board. I heard her outdoors in the drive talking to Helen Foster.
>
> "And Derek Monroe, his uncle whom he was named for, was killed in France in the *First* World War," Mama said, an awful pleasure wincing in her voice.

The naive sentence structure and vocabulary, the reportorial detail, intensify the reader's awareness that the narrator—not at all naive, by no means merely a reporter—fails to state her own feelings at a crucial moment. The complexity and intensity of her intolerable emotion are suggested by the girl's actions and by the unstated effect of her mother's "awful pleasure." The interstices of memory are as revealing as its densities. *The Dead of the House* offers remarkable variety of emotional texture within its prevailing atmosphere of nostalgia.

Source: Patricia Meyer Spacks, "Fiction Chronicle," in *Hudson Review,* Vol. XXV, No. 3, Autumn, 1972, pp. 500–01.

L. J. Davis

In the following excerpt, Davis describes Green's novel as a dream, a prose poem, and a transcendental novel.

The Dead of the House is less a novel than a kind of dream, a protracted prose poem of singular delicacy, filled with generosity, love, and wisdom, and steeped in lore.... [It] is a deeply felt, uniquely American fiction....

How strange it is to come upon a transcendental novel in the last third of the 20th century. Like most works of fiction, it is about life as it is lived on earth; unlike so many, it has something of importance to say on the subject, with a touch that is as light and dry as a blown leaf or the touch of an old man's hand. It is a book to make its readers feel fortunate.

Source: L. J. Davis, "An Accumulation of Time Past," in *Book World—Washington Post,* February 27, 1972, p. 4.

Richard Elman

In the following excerpt, Elman praises Green's novel for its quality as a fictional memoir and for its imagination.

[*The Dead of the House*] is one of the most important works of fiction I have read in quite a while. It is not "major," propounds no theories, participates in neither rear nor avant-garde maneuvers. Hannah Green's novel simply *is,* a family chronicle and a fictional memoir—always spontaneous, rich in atmosphere, its feelings specified, felt, projected. A beautiful book, nowhere bigger than itself, nowhere grander than its own scope or subject. It has been shaped with the caressing skill of a lover of people and words, but the words do not take over and perform a sideshow, and the people aren't always *that* lovable, and Hannah Green is aware of that, too....

I mean to say that I was not simply reading about childhood, or girlhood, or adolescence, about Ohio families and Indian forebears. I was also given a wonderful opportunity to get close to the imagination of another living person, an intelligence that was both gracious and funky, witty and charming. It was like falling in love. I was, for as long as it took, able to surrender my own callowness and smugness to the ecstasy that is fiction, is art.

Source: Richard Elman, "Great Antidote for Self-Contempt," in *New York Times Book Review,* February 13, 1972, p. 5.

Sources

Davis, L. J., "An Accumulation of Time Past," in *The Washington Post,* February 27, 1972, p. 4.

Elman, Richard, "Great Antidote for Self-Contempt," in *The New York Times Book Review,* February 13, 1972, p. 5.

Markos, Donald, "Of Grandfather's: Hannah Green's *The Dead of the House,*" in *The Southern Review,* Vol. 9, No. 3, Summer, 1973, pp. 713-16.

Publishers Weekly, Vol. 243, No. 13, March 25, 1996, p. 78.

The Washington Post, July 21, 1996, Book World, p. X12.

For Further Study

Meyer Spacks, Patricia, *The Hudson Review,* Vol. XXV, No. 3, Autumn, 1972, pp. 500-01.
    Offers a stylistic examination of Green's novel.

Thomas, Robert M., "Hannah Green, 69, an Author Who Pursued Perfection, Dies," in *The New York Times,* October 18, 1996, Section D, p. 21.
    Essentially an obituary, Thomas's article reveals many interesting biographical details about Green, as well as some of the history of the book itself.

House Made of Dawn

N. Scott Momaday

1968

When it was first published in 1968, N. Scott Momaday's *House Made of Dawn* garnered scarce critical and commercial attention. Yet within a year, it won the prestigious Pulitzer Prize for fiction, and had received international critical acclaim.

During the early 1970s America became interested in the plight of Native Americans as the truth about reservation life was exposed and publicized by Native American activists. By chronicling the struggles of a young Native American man named Abel, Momaday was able to explore some of the issues and conflicts that faced the Native American community in the twentieth century. *House Made of Dawn* was a crucial link in teaching the general public about the real lives and beliefs of Native Americans.

Although most critics admire the poetic beauty of his narrative style, Momaday's indirect way of storytelling—weaving together past, present and myth with no apparent order—may prove challenging to some readers who are used to a linear progression of events. Most critics, however, consider this style necessary for understanding Abel and his culture.

Author Biography

Momaday was born on the Kiowa Reservation in Lawton, Oklahoma, on February 27, 1934. His father, Alfred Morris, was an artist and teacher; in

N. Scott Momaday

fact, his artworks are used to illustrate several of Momaday's books, including his history of the Kiowa people, *The Way to Rainy Mountain.* His mother, Mayme Natachee Scott, taught and wrote children's books.

Momaday spent his childhood on a succession of Native American reservations, learning the cultures of the Pueblo Indians. The family eventually settled in Jemez, New Mexico, which is the model for Walatowa in *House Made of Dawn.*

Momaday attended military school in Virginia, and then went to college at the University of New Mexico. After graduation, he taught at the Apache reservation in Jicarilla for a year. He won a poetry scholarship to Stanford, where he studied under famed poet and literary critic Yvor Winters, who became his mentor and greatly influenced his poetic style. In 1963 he received his Ph.D. from Stanford.

House Made of Dawn, his first novel, was published in 1968. Although not commercially successful, it received the Pulitzer Prize for fiction in 1969. After that, Momaday moved to the University of California at Berkley, where he designed a graduate program in Indian Studies. In 1982 he became a professor at the University of Arizona. He has published several books of poetry, short sto-

ries, and essays. In addition, Momaday has often displayed his drawings and paintings in galleries throughout the country. He is an active member of the Gourd Dance Society, where he has succeeded his grandfather, Mammedaty.

Plot Summary

Prologue

The very first section of *House Made of Dawn* creates the mood for the story. Set in a canyon at sunrise, the protagonist of the novel, Abel, is introduced. Thematic issues that will appear throughout the book are also presented: Abel's isolation and his struggle to communicate, as well as the communion of man and nature. In addition, it introduces the image of Abel running, which will also be the final image in the novel.

The Longhair

In 1945, Abel's grandfather, Francisco, rides his horse-drawn wagon into town and picks up Abel from the bus station. The young man is returning from his service in the army during World War II. So drunk that he does not recognize his own grandfather, Abel stumbles off the bus and into his grandfather's wagon.

Waking the next day at Francisco's house, he recalls frightening images from his early life on the Native American reservation: the mournful sound of the wind blowing over a hole in the earth; the sight of a snake carried up into the sky by an eagle and then dropped, wriggling in its fall to the hard ground. He then reflects on his wartime experiences.

The story shifts to Father Olguin, the Catholic missionary assigned to the reservation at Walatowa. He is visited by Angela St. John, a pregnant white woman from Los Angeles. Mrs. St. John is pregnant and has come to bathe in the local mineral baths to soothe the soreness in her back. She asks Father Olguin to recommend a local person looking for work who can chop wood for her. A few days later, Abel comes to her house. He chops the wood, but does not talk to her.

At the feast of Santiago, Abel participates in a competition that is based on a folk story about Santiago, who founded the town by sacrificing a rooster. The townspeople believe that the discarded feathers and blood of the rooster produced plants and animals from the ground. At the feast, contestants ride horses toward a rooster that is buried up to its neck in the ground, trying to reach down and pull it out. Abel does poorly at the competition. The winner is an albino on a black horse, who takes the rooster over to Abel and beats him with it.

A few days later, Abel walks to Angela St. John's house. She invites him in, gives him coffee, and asks if he would like to make love to her. He accepts, and the two become lovers. Father Olguin comes to talk to her about her sin a few days later, but she does not regret her actions.

After a festival in town, Abel sits in a bar and has a few drinks with the albino. They leave together, and, while walking up the street, the man puts his arm out to Abel. Abel pulls out his knife and stabs the man, killing him.

The Priest of the Sun

Seven years later, the story shifts to Los Angeles. Reverend John Big Bluff Tosamah, the pastor of the Holiness Pan-Indian Rescue Mission and the Priest of the Sun, preaches to Native Americans in the city. Tosamah is a Kiowa, and he recalls stories told him by his grandmother, who had been present for the last of the Kiowa tribe's sun dances in 1887. He passes these Indian stories along to those in his congregation, many of whom arc from other native groups.

Abel has served his jail time for the murder of the albino. He is trying to start a new life in Los Angeles at the urging of the Indian Relocation Service. Abel has a close friend, Benally, who is an Indian also transplanted from the reservation to the city; Abel also has a girlfriend named Milly, who is the social worker assigned to his case. He struggles to stay out of trouble and survive in a white man's world.

The Night Chanter

Benally clarifies some of the details of Abel's life in Los Angeles. He is familiar with many of the members in the Native American community and mentions their names in the process of telling the story. He remembers that after his release from prison, Abel was brought to the factory where Benally worked. Feeling sorry for him, Benally gave him a place to live and went out to bars and to the beach with him.

One night they are stopped by Martinez, a local police officer. When Abel does not respond appropriately, Martinez hits his hands with his nightstick. His bones are not broken, but Abel's pride is—soon he stops going to work, and spends his days drinking and wandering the streets:

He went downhill pretty fast after that. Sometimes he was here when I came in from work, and sometimes he wasn't. He was drunk about half the time, and I couldn't keep up with him ... Pretty soon I wouldn't give him any more, but you know what he did? He started asking Milly for money.

He loses a succession of jobs, and eventually is attacked and beaten up on the street.

Benally contacts Angela St. John. She visits Abel in the hospital and tells him that she has told Indian stories to her son Peter about a man born of a bear and a maiden. Benally puts Abel on a bus back to the reservation.

The Dawn Runner

When he returns to the reservation, Abel discovers that his grandfather is dying. Abel listens to him murmuring in his delirium for six days about a bear hunt from his youth. The old man dies on the seventh morning.

Abel wakes Father Olguin before dawn and makes arrangements for the old man's funeral service. He takes off down the road south of town. When he spots the figures of men running, he strips off his shirt and runs after them.

Characters

Abel

The protagonist of the story, Abel is a Native American war veteran who struggles to find his place in the world. Some critics have interpreted Abel's behavior as being caused by the strain of trying to balance the expectations of white culture with Indian culture. Others assert that the novel's flashbacks indicate that Abel was estranged and uncommunicative even before he left the reservation for the army.

The story begins when Abel returns to the Walatowa reservation on a bus, so drunk that he can hardly stand or recognize where he is. Shortly after his return, Abel is hired by Angela St. John to chop wood. The two quickly start an affair. After being humiliated in a festival competition, Abel drinks in a bar with his chief rival, the albino. As they leave the bar, the albino takes a step toward him and Abel stabs him. Tosamah later explains that Abel testified in court that he thought the albino was turning into a snake.

After spending seven years in jail for the murder, Abel moves to Los Angles. He takes a job at a factory and meets Benally, who becomes his friend. He also becomes romantically involved with Milly, the white social worker assigned to his case. Much of the story told in Los Angeles is interspersed with sights of Abel wandering around, severely injured from a beating, with his thumbs broken—the book does not explicitly say what happened, but an earlier encounter with a brutal police officer named Martinez implies that it was he who inflicted the damage.

In the end, Abel leaves the city and returns to the reservation. A week after his return, Francisco dies. After arranging his funeral, Abel goes running to the point of exhaustion.

The Albino

The albino (also called The White Man) is a mysterious but important person in this story. He is frequently called "the white man." At the feast of Santiago, the albino beats Abel in a competition, humiliating him. A week later, Abel drinks with the albino in a bar. They leave together, and Abel hallucinates that the man is turns into a snake. He takes out his knife and stabs the albino to death.

Ben Benally

Benally is a Native American man and a good friend to Abel. Raised on a reservation, Benally adapts to life in Los Angeles and appreciates the benefits of urban culture. He asks little more of life than to keep his job and to have a room to stay in without any interference. He is sympathetic to the way life is on the reservation, but he also recognized the benefits of assimilation: "You know, you have to change. That's the only way you can live in a place like this. You have to forget about the way it was, how you grew up and all."

Francisco

Francisco is Abel's grandfather. A believer in the traditional ways, he is described as a "longhair." The novel opens with him trying to capture a sparrow so that he might have its feathers to use for ceremonial purposes. An elderly man, Francisco is mentioned in an old journal, written by Fray Nicholas. He wrote in an 1888 entry, "Listen I told you about Francisco [and] was right to say it. He is evil [and] desires to do me some injury [and] this after I befriended him all his life. Preserve this I write to you that you may make him responsible if I die." There is no indication that Francisco had done anything violent to Fray Nicholas.

Francisco recalls taking part in the Winter Race and has a page in his ledger with a drawing of himself running the race and the caption "1889."

Media Adaptations

- *House Made of Dawn* was adapted as a film by Richardson Morse in 1987. It starred Larry Littlebird, Judith Doty and John Saxon. The screenplay was written by N. Scott Momaday and Morse. It was released straight to videocassette by New Line Cinema in 1996.

- The unabridged audio book of the novel, read by Scott Forbes, is available from Books On Tape, Inc. It was recorded in 1976.

In the 1940s, when the novel begins, Francisco is a farmer working on the communal land owned by the reservation. Francisco was instrumental in raising Abel, and has been his only relative since his mother died when he was five. As such, he holds an important place in Abel's life and acts as a role model for the confused young man.

Martinez

Martinez is the brutal, sadistic police officer who ambushes Abel and Benally. Martinez accosts them in an alley when the two men are drunk, attempting to intimidate them. When Abel does not cower before him, Martinez cracks his knuckles with his nightstick. It is that senseless and brutal act that alienates Abel from white civilization. Benally also asserts that Martinez would stop in at the bar sometimes to pick up bribes—sometimes a free bottle of liquor, sometimes money.

Milly

A white social worker, Milly becomes Abel's girlfriend. Eventually, he drives her away with abusive behavior.

Father Olguin

Father Olguin is the Roman Catholic priest at the mission at Walatowa. He is a confused man, torn between the traditions of his religion and those of the society around him. He lives with a physical handicap as a result of a childhood illness.

Because of his unique position, Father Olguin functions as an intermediary between the outside culture and the people of the reservation. When Angela St. John arrives at Walatowa, she asks Father Olguin to help her hire an Indian worker. On first meeting her, he "regarded his guest discreetly, wondering that her physical presence should suddenly dawn upon him so." As the story progresses, he develops strong feelings for her.

A large part of the book is devoted to the pages that Father Olguin reads out of the diary of Fray Nicholas, a priest who was at the reservation in the 1870s. At the end of the novel, when Abel comes to him at dawn to arrange the funeral of his grandfather, Father Olguin does not hesitate to accept the responsibility, but he is disturbed that he has been waken up so early. He reprimands Abel for waking him, but then has a sudden realization of how unimportant time is to Abel and his people. This leads to a greater understanding of his place in the community and Native American culture in general. "'I can understand,' he said. 'I understand, do you hear?' And he began to shout. 'I understand! Oh, God! *I understand —I understand!*'"

Angela St. John

Angela is the white woman who comes to the reservation for health reasons and ends up having an affair with Abel. Although she is pregnant, her husband never visits her at the reservation. Seven years after their affair, Abel sees her walk by on the street in California and tells Benally about her. After Abel is beaten and hospitalized, Benally contacts Angela, and she goes to visit him in the hospital. She explains that she has raised her son with an awareness of Indian culture, telling him a story about a bear and a maiden that resembles the story that runs through Francisco's mind as he is dying.

John Big Bluff Tosamah

As pastor of the Los Angeles Holiness Pan-Indian Rescue Mission and Priest of the Sun, Tosamah gives sermons on both Biblical stories and Indian folklore, often mixing the two. Like N. Scott Momaday, he is a Kiowa, and some of the stories he tells of last days of the Kiowa people are repeated in Momaday's history of the Kiowa, *The Way to Rainy Mountain.*

Tosamah has a vast knowledge of Indian folklore and Bible stories, but he was raised in the city; therefore, his knowledge of the Indian ways is mostly theoretical. Tosamah expresses scornful admiration for the ways in which white society has controlled and obliterated the Indian: "They put all

of us renegades, us diehards, away sooner or later. They've got the right idea. They put us away before we're born. They're an almighty wise and cautious bunch, these cats, full of discretion." Once, when Tosamah ridicules the Indians who stay with the old traditions, the "longhairs," Abel becomes so angry that he almost starts a fight, driving him to a two-day drinking binge that almost costs him his job.

The White Man
See The Albino

Themes

Prejudice and Tolerance
Strangely, for a novel about Native American suffering in the white world, there is not a lot of overt prejudice on the parts of the characters in *House Made of Dawn.* The most brutal character in the novel, Martinez, says nothing to indicate that his action is racially motivated; he has a Spanish name himself, making him no more a representative of the white culture than Abel. The two white women, Angela and Milly, treat Abel well and respect his heritage.

The only character to really point out racial differences is Tosamah. He sarcastically declares his respect for the whites for the way they have oppressed the Indians. This prejudice is mirrored in Tosamah's prejudice against Native Americans that follow traditional beliefs. In talking about "longhairs," or the people who follow the traditional way and do not adapt to urban life, Tosamah is so negative that he alienates Abel.

Culture Clash
Some critics interpret Momaday's novel as a statement about the difficulty faced by Native Americans as they are forced to assimilate into the outside world. This struggle is reflected in the experiences of the protagonist, Abel, as he returns home after a stint in the army during World War II.

Late in the book, Abel recalls a culture clash between his Native American world and the white world during his time in the military. While under fire and faced with an advancing tank, Abel stood up, whooped, danced, sang, and gave an obscene gesture to the tank. Momaday is not clear about whether this monologue is meant to be testimony in a court marshal (it ends with Abel running off into the trees), but it is clearly not normal behavior under fire.

When he arrives back at Walatowa drunk, it is clear that he has not assimilated the standards of the white culture; yet after a short time, it becomes obvious that he is not comfortable with Native American culture either. While his grandfather, Francisco, remembers trying to instill "the old ways" into Abel, Abel remembers his advice as, "You ought to do this and that." He makes "a poor showing, full of caution and gesture" when he tries at the rooster-grabbing competition during the festival. Later, he kills the competition champion when he sees turning into an animal—the sort of transformation common to Native American stories such as Benally's story about a Bear and a Snake.

After his release from prison, Abel lives in the Native American community in Los Angeles. He attends the services of Tosamah, who is both pastor and Priest of the Sun. While Abel's friend, Ben, is able to mix his native culture with his new white culture, Abel is unable to bring the two elements together in harmony. When his heritage and pride is insulted, he quits work, drops out of society, and spends his days drinking. In the end, he finds some balance between the two cultures: he is able to memorialize his grandfather's death with both a Christian ceremony and an Indian race at dawn.

Return to Nature

Native American culture is closely associated with elements of nature in the novel. Native American customs are concerned with natural objects: the sparrow feathers Francisco gathers for a prayer plume, and the rooster used in the competition. When there is harmony between people and nature, the world is working as it is intended.

Examples of this harmony can be found with the characters in the novel. Francisco, an old farmer, is said to have "an ethnic, planter's love of harvest, and of rain." Abel chops wood in a way that indicates a special understanding of the inanimate object, a relationship that the white woman Angela wonders about. "He gave himself up to it," she thinks, admiring the beauty of his action. Milly, making love to Abel, is described as moving her mouth "like a small animal."

The problem with Abel is that just as he becomes disconnected from his native culture, so too he becomes detached from nature. He recalls having seen an eagle carry a snake off into the sky with mixed emotions: "It was an awful, holy sight, full of magic and meaning." He remembers an eagle caught in a ceremonial hunt: "The sight of it filled him with shame and disgust."

Topics for Further Study

- Investigate the tribal customs of Native Americans from different parts of the United States, such as the northern or southeastern regions of the country. Report on how their practices differ from those of the Pueblo peoples of the Southeast.

- Explore one of the American Indian Movement protests of the late 1960s or 1970s, such as the armed siege at Wounded Knee in 1973 or the standoff at the Oglala Reservation in 1975. What were the demands of the protesters? Did the protesters get what they wanted?

- Richard Nixon, a president often associated with corruption in government, is considered a hero by many Native Americans. Why? Prepare a report on Nixon's policies and how they benefited Native Americans.

- Examine the statistics of Native American participation in World War II. Discuss the ways in which this participation significantly changed the structure and expectations of Native American life.

- Talk to someone from a Native American group, either on the phone or through one of their websites. Identify the challenges facing Indians in the twenty-first century.

In the end, Abel returns to the reservation and reestablishes his relationship with nature by running, opening his lungs and his whole being to where he is: "He could see at last without having to think."

Style

Point of View

In this novel, Momaday often shifts from one point of view to another; as a result, it is not always clear whose thoughts are being related, or when, or what they have to do with the overall story. At first it seems that Abel will be the focus of the novel, but soon the point of view shifts to Francisco. Moreover, there is little consistency in the point of view: while it seldom shifts from one person's perspective to another within one scene, it does not follow a pattern of staying with any one point of view for a whole chapter, or even a section.

For example, Father Olguin gains perspective about what the reservation was like in the last century from the diary that he reads that was written by his predecessor. Momaday is able to relate his ideas about the relationship between Native American religion and Christian religion through the sermons of Tosamah. The incidents of Abel's life in Los Angeles are not related through his point of view, but from Benally's perspective.

By shifting point of view frequently and sporadically, it is possible for Momaday to have Abel be the central character in the book without delving deeply into his thoughts and to present the communal point of view that is more characteristic of Native American thought than of the European tradition.

Setting

More than most novels, the setting of *House Made of Dawn* is integral to its purpose. Because the story is about a man torn between his Native American world and the white world, the reservation is rendered quite differently from that of Los Angeles. At times, the story goes beyond obvious, rational differences and considers fundamental ways in which people of the different settings think differently.

Folklore

One reason that *House Made of Dawn* made such a powerful impact when it was published was for its treatment of Native American folklore and the values these tales passed on to subsequent generations. In Western culture, readers look for the "moral" of a story, especially one that is told in the context of a religious lesson. In the case of the folklore, interpretation for an audience of outsiders is almost impossible, so it is hard to explain the culture that values them. On the contrary, the fact that Western myths can be made so accessible is one of the factors that has helped Western culture dominate the globe during the age of colonization.

Historical Context

The Postwar Reservation

As with many other minority groups in America, Native American populations became more connected with the mainstream culture as a result of World War II. Prejudice and discriminatory policies did not disappear overnight, but the fact that people from ethnic subcultures were thrown together in barracks in the war led to some softening social boundaries. Many whites met real Indians for the first time, and many Indians met their first whites.

Like Abel in *House Made of Dawn,* many Native Americans came back to the reservations they had lived on with conflicted views, having been forced to align their own beliefs with American culture. Unfortunately, what little progress was made in human understanding was very quickly overruled by developers, who soon tried to exploit reservation land for their own profit.

Historically, the U. S. government dealt with the problem of taking land from indigenous peoples by providing land and services at limited locations: the reservations. From the start, the concept of reservations was divided between two general schools of thought. Some people considered them as sanctuaries, where the Indians could relax, free from persecution. Others, however, viewed them as prisons where Indians were left isolated, cut off from progress, and dependent on government charity.

During the Great Depression of the 1930s, the Roosevelt administration, and particularly his Commissioner of Indian Affairs John Collier, determined that it would be best for Native American groups to take control of their own situations. The Indian Reorganization Act of 1934 included many provisions leading toward this end: it set up reservation schools that ended the practice of shipping Indian children out to boarding schools; created tribal governing organizations that would deal with the federal government and control order; and encouraged economic development.

After World War II, the resources on Native American reservations became economic assets. Some politicians in the government argued that it was wasteful to allow Indians to keep such valuable property when they were not using it. Support grew for a plan to move Indians off of the reservations, to assimilate them into society. Some Native Americans supported this idea, lured by quick profits to be made from selling the reservations.

Compare & Contrast

- **Late 1940s:** After Europe is decimated as a result of World War II, America becomes an economic superpower, creating a thriving economy and a population boom.

  1968: The generation of Americans born in the late 1940s and early 1950s is dubbed the Baby Boom generation. Many members of this generation reject the materialistic culture and emphasize spiritual values.

  Today: America has experienced the longest economic expansion in its history.

- **Late 1940s:** The Indian Relocation program uses government money to move Native Americans off of the reservations. The aim was to assimilate them into mainstream culture and provide economic and social opportunities.

  1968: The American Indian Movement addresses the issue of police brutality against Indians in Minneapolis and soon becomes a nationwide organization advocating Indian rights.

  Today: Government efforts strive to make Native American groups economically self-sufficient.

- **Late 1940s:** Segregation laws across the country prohibit blacks from using the same public services as whites, and permits exclusion of different races from private establishments.

  1968: After more than a decade of civil rights protests, the fight for equality turns violent on a national scale in the mid-1960s, with race riots in major cities across America.

  Today: Federal laws against discrimination are generally enforced, and abusers are subject to civil suits.

- **Late 1940s:** Television starts to become widespread and influences popular culture.

  1968: National awareness increases as television broadcast color footage of the summer's racial riots and the police actions at the political conventions into people's living rooms.

  Today: The growing number of homes connected to the Internet resembles the postwar growth of television ownership.

Yet most recognized this as a blatant attempt by the U.S. government to exploit the Native American population once again.

After Collier resigned in 1945, the Senate pressured his successor, William F. Zimmerman, to devise a plan for moving Indians off of the reservations. In 1947, the Relocation Service Program, with field offices in Los Angeles, Denver, and Salt Lake City, was established. In 1953, Congress passed HCR 108, a bill that removed all special status for Native Americans. Whereas they had previously been exempt from federal, state, and local taxes, HCR 108 made them liable. Reservations became accountable to the jurisdictions of local law enforcement instead of tribal or federal laws, which allowed racial tensions to dominate control issues.

Healthcare facilities on reservations, which had been run by federal agencies, were abruptly turned over to Native American groups. When they were unable to manage, they were shut down, leaving Indians to travel off reservations when they needed medical care. HCR 108, presented as a step toward Indian freedom, has gone down in history as one of the greatest follies in U.S. / Indian relations. In 1970 President Richard Nixon pushed Congress to overturn HCR 108.

Indian Activism in the 1960s

As the Civil Rights movement raised America's consciousness about the oppression of African Americans, it also raised awareness about the treatment of other groups. For example, the Indian Reform Movement became a popular cause for many American people. Probably the best known activist group, the American Indian Movement (AIM), formed in Minneapolis in 1968 to protest against

N. Scott Momaday's writings reflect his Kiowa Indian heritage in structure and theme, as well as subject matter. Depicted here is Chief White Bear of the Kiowas.

police brutality. After that, the group went on to lead several high-profile protests. In 1970 they occupied a portion of the land at the base of the Mount Rushmore Memorial.

At the same time, other Native American groups were drawing attention to the government's neglect of Native American people. One hundred Native Americans took over Alcatraz Island in 1969, offering to buy the former federal prison back from the government for twenty-four dollars in glass beads (the price allegedly paid to Indians for Manhattan Island in 1626).

The most infamous protest was the siege at Wounded Knee, South Dakota. The site of a famous massacre of three hundred Indian men, women, and children in 1890, members of AIM and the Sioux nation took hostages in a small hilltop church in Wounded Knee, on the Oglala Reservation, in 1973. The siege attracted international press attention. Two Native Americans were killed during the resulting gunfire, and one hundred were arrested; but as a result, the government promised to hold hearings on Indian rights. After one meeting with representatives from the White House, no further government action regarding Native American rights took place.

Critical Overview

House Made of Dawn did not receive much attention from the mainstream press when it was first published. For one thing, Momaday was relatively unknown in literary circles. Another obstacle was the fact that it had been written by a member of a distinct social minority, and reviewers felt uncomfortable addressing its artistry because they did not want their criticism to seem like criticism of Native American culture: as William James Smith asserted in his review in *Commonweal,* "it seems slightly unAmerican to criticize an American Indian's novel."

Other critics found fault with the writing but suggested that the narrative problems might be necessary in order to capture the Native American mindset. Marshall Sprague, in *The New York Times Book Review,* thought that the "haze" that surrounds the telling of the story might be a natural byproduct of rendering "the mysteries of a culture different than our own." When the novel won the Pulitzer Prize in 1969, the novel's literary merit was called into question less often.

John Z. Bennett, writing in *Western American Literature* shortly after the Pulitzer was awarded, expressed his concerns that *House Made of Dawn* would be valued as a social statement rather than for its artistic achievements. Bennett recognized that it used the clichés that are often used in novels about an alienated social group—the "Indian hero's ruinous journeys into the white man's world and apparent redemption" upon returning to the ways of his people; the white woman who comes to accept the tribe; the descriptions of ceremonies; and the wise grandparent representing tradition. Still, Bennett found the book a "remarkable synthesis of poetic mode and profound emotional and intellectual intellect." His concern regarding the overemphasis of the book's cultural aspect were not very far off, as some reviewers ignored the artistic weaknesses and strengths and focused almost entirely on what it could teach the dominant culture about the Native Americans view of life.

In 1972 Marion Willard Hylton maintained that *House Made of Dawn* was "the tragic odyssey of a man forcibly removed from the psychic environment and placed within a culture light-years away from the attitudes, value and goals of his former life. His anguished ordeal, heightened by his encounter with a white woman, endows him at last with courage and wisdom.... " While Hylton's analysis of the book is accurate, it also reflects the emphasis on this as a novel primarily about the victimization of Native Americans.

Since the 1970s, critics have accepted the novel as a part of our literary culture. They concentrate on the overall themes and their relationship with one another. For instance, as Martin Schubnell wrote in *N. Scott Momaday: The Cultural and Literary Background,* the book can be interpreted as an exploration of both tribal and personal identity.

Howard Meredith has credited the book with beginning "a literary tradition of those prose narratives which previously had circulated almost exclusively within specific tribal contexts." He contends that the time was ripe for these stories to be recorded and published. "He brings American readers to a new sense of maturity through the use of the traditions of America," Meredith maintained.

Since the publication of *House Made of Dawn,* Momaday's literary reputation has rested on his work as a poet and critic, and he has been praised for his ability to blend Kiowa sensibilities with Western literary methods.

Criticism

David Kelly

Kelly is an instructor of Creative Writing and Literature at Oakton Community College and College of Lake County in Illinois. Here, he explores ways that Father Olguin can be a useful character for readers who have trouble understanding House Made of Dawn.

The best approach one can take to an unfamiliar text is to burrow into it at any point of access possible, like a termite forcing an attack upon a tree. I will admit that there is much I find perplexing and uninviting about N. Scott Momaday's *House Made of Dawn.* At times it seems pointlessly convoluted, while at other parts it seems painfully simplistic. There were some points in my first reading where I wanted to put the book aside, to write it off as a case of weak writing masquerading as a work of substance.

> Father Olguin initially appears as he is dressing for mass. One of the first things we find out about the priest is that he has one bad eye, clouded over with a film and almost closed. In fiction, any abnormality like that *has* to have a symbolic level, especially when it has to do with something as important as sight. Father Olguin has only half of the vision that he should."

Yet then I see another connection, then another, and the faith rises within me that I *might* make sense of all of this, if only I knew more about the traditions of the Pueblo Indians or if I had studied Spanish nuance. With that faith in mind, I can walk through this story, looking at it from the inside, by inhabiting the character most like me. I am not a Native American. The culture that is not only described but also actually lived out through the book's structure is foreign to me. I cannot pretend to know it, and I can't dismiss it just because it is new.

I can, however, experience it through the eyes of Father Olguin—the man who comes to the reservation just as I have come to Momaday's world through the book, and tries to understand.

Father Olguin actually turns out to be a very useful guide. Though Mexican, his Catholic training has accustomed him to Western thought; as a result, he is as curious about Native American customs as I would be in his position. At the same time, I find that Father Olguin's story provides a parallel version of the book's main story.

Father Olguin is introduced in the same scene as Angela St. John, and it is his connection to the protagonist, Abel, through her that solidifies his position in the story. She appears first, disrupting the natural serenity of the reservation with a car that is noticeable from a great distance.

What Do I Read Next?

- One of Momaday's best-known works is *The Way to Rainy Mountain* (1969), his history of the last days of the Kiowa people.

- Momaday's childhood on the Jemez reservation and at Shiprock in the Navajo country is hauntingly recounted in *The Names,* published in 1976. More than a memoir, it blends genealogy and folklore with personal reminiscences.

- Like Abel, the protagonist of the novel *Ceremony* (1977) is also a Native American returning home after service in World War II. It was written by Leslie Marmon Silko, one of the most respected contemporary Native American novelists.

- James Welch is a Native American novelist who writes about the American West. His first book, *Winter in the Blood* (1974), is set in the early 1970s.

- A summary of Indian perspectives can be gathered from *Native American Testimony: A Chronicle of Indian-White Relations from Prophecy to the Present, 1492–1992* (1991), edited by Peter Nabokov and published by Penguin.

- Published in 1970, Dee Brown's *Bury My Heart at Wounded Knee* was an international best-seller. Subtitled "An Indian History of the American West," it presents an interesting, readable story.

- Among memoirs by Native Americans, *Black Elk Speaks* holds a place of high esteem. Written by poet and novelist John G. Neihardt in 1932, it was neglected until psychologist Carl Jung's interest sparked a revised edition in the 1950s.

Father Olguin initially appears as he is dressing for mass. One of the first things we find out about the priest is that he has one bad eye, clouded over with a film and almost closed. In fiction, any abnormality like that *has* to have a symbolic level, especially when it has to do with something as important as sight. Father Olguin has only half of the vision that he should.

Moreover, Angela is staying at Los Ojos, translated as "The Eyes." Father Olguin is aware of her from the time that she walks into his church. Certainly, she would have been a curiosity in that setting. Readers could take his curiosity to mean that he is a man of the reservation—that his way of thinking is not like that of the outside world.

This is clearly not what Angela thinks. She approaches him to act as an intermediary between her and the Native American, as if she assumes that Father Olguin is part of both the white and Indian worlds—in other words, a member of neither. Her assumption is correct: he is certainly separated by language from his young acolyte Bonifacio, addressing him in Spanish, and he is not enough part of the community to quickly come up with the name of someone to chop her wood.

It is this function as a middleman between Indian and white societies that makes Father Olguin such an appropriate stand-in for the reader. Rather than being a part of both societies and thereby providing readers with an entrance into each one, he is actually alienated from each and unable to communicate in either environment. The bad news is that this prevents readers from learning much about either world; the good news is that this alienation mirrors what Abel is going through, and it therefore takes us closer to the soul of the story.

Father Olguin's love for Angela is represented by bees. Bees swarm at the window the first time that her physiological presence "dawns" on him and he considers how her physical features make her "nearly beautiful." Later, after Abel and Angela have made love (although it is doubtful that the priest could have known about it), and after he himself has taken honey from the beehive, he is able to think about her "without the small excitement that she had so easily provoked on him at first." He relishes the thought that she will be envious of his having better things to do than sit around thinking of her—this idea might be effective in suppressing his lust, but it raises three or four other cardinal sins that do not seem to bother him.

At least in Father Olguin we can see the struggle to suppress his feelings; moreover, we can understand them better because Momaday has given his feelings an external symbol—the bees. Knowing Father Olguin helps us know Abel, even though the latter keeps his own internal struggles pushed down much more deeply within him.

When Abel is in Los Angeles, Father Olguin is still present: he is represented in the figure of his opposite, The Right Reverend John Big Bluff Tosamah. It is as fair to use Tosamah to read Father Olguin as it is to guess that the shape of one side of a cloth will follow the other, so exact are they in their oppositeness.

The distinction goes beyond the obvious fact that one is a Catholic priest in Native American territory and the other a Native American priest living in the big city. Tosamah has friends, while Father Olguin delegates to his subordinates; Tosamah embraces mysteries while Father Olguin seeks the consolation of solving mysteries; Father Olguin is reticent—like Abel—while Tosamah's speeches ramble. Readers who have trouble perceiving the connection between Father Olguin and Abel must at least concede how unlike Abel Tosamah is.

Both priests are drawn to the distant past, which is something that Abel is trying to forget. For Tosamah, it is the stories that his grandmother shared with him about the last days of the Kiowa tribe in Montana. Father Olguin studies the same period of time in the journals left by his predecessor, Fray Nicolas. Abel's grandfather, Francisco, remembers these days, and is in fact mentioned in Fray Nicolas' journal, where he is represented as evil and dangerous. Abel could possibly avert tragedy in his own life by listening to what the old man has to say and learning from it, but he doesn't.

Tosamah grew up with stories of the distant past, and so theology comes easy to him. Abel is resistant to the past until the end of the novel. Father Olguin looks to the past to make sense of the present. He steps outside of his role as a priest and takes up the journal with a cigarette and a cup of coffee in his hand, as if whatever he hopes to find is beyond the consolations of religion, in that same very human realm as his attraction to Angela St. John's body. In the journals he finds a complete person, one who is disabled like he is, as religious as he would like to be, but who is still dissatisfied with himself, writing:

> Some days He comes to me in a sourceless light that rises on His image at my bed [and] then I am caught of it [and] shine also as with lightning on me…. He does bid me speak all my love but I cannot for I am always just then under it the whole heft of it [and] am mute against it as against a little mountain heaved upon me [and] can utter no help of the thing that is done to me.

In these words Father Olguin finds comfort because he recognizes himself. They are ideas that Abel might find comfort in too.

In the end, Abel and Father Olguin find their fulfillment. Whatever old Francisco carried within him passes on to Abel at his death. This understanding sends him out to run in the canyon at dawn, as Francisco had done long before. By carrying on this tradition he accepts his past and perhaps himself.

Father Olguin's enlightenment finally comes in the simple realization that to the Indians, as to death, the question "Do you know what time it is?" is irrelevant. The lesson of his predecessor, the temptation of the flesh, the humbling experience of his crippling illness all lead him toward this moment, just as Abel is guided to it by Angela, the albino, Benally, Tosamah, and all the rest.

Source: David Kelly, in an essay for *Novels for Students*, Gale, 2000.

Bernard A. Hirsch

In the following essay, Hirsch analyzes the characters of Martinez, Tosamaah, and Benally and their relationships with the protagonist, noting that for these characters Abel is a symbol of contempt and a reminder of their Native selves.

N. Scott Momaday, referring to his protagonist Abel, has said, "None but an Indian, I think, knows so much what it is like to have existence in two worlds and security in neither." True as this is of Abel in *House Made of Dawn*, it is truer still of Martinez, Tosamah, and Benally because they, unlike Abel, try earnestly to conform to Euro-American social values. Indeed, the strong responses Abel generates in each of these characters indicate their perception of something unyielding and incorruptible in him, something which throws into stark relief the humiliating spiritual compromises they have felt compelled to make. In his suffering Abel is both a sorry example and stinging rebuke to them, a warning and a goad, someone both to fear and reverence, for he reminds them of who and what they are—of what they find most contemptible in themselves and most holy. Martinez, Tosamah, and Benally have been spiritually corrupted to varying degrees by the white world, and to the extent that they have, they make Abel their scapegoat and regard him as an evil to be exorcised.

This scapegoating is most apparent in the case of Martinez who, Ben tells us, is "a cop and a bad

> ... as regards Tosamah and Benally, it is indeed painful to watch them disparage that which they most love and most need—their Indianness."

one." [The critic adds in a footnote: "Most readers assume that Martinez is white, but given his name and the fact that a number of the novel's Indian characters have Spanish names and/or surnames, it seems more likely that he is at least part Indian or Chicano—if the latter, his situation would nonetheless parallel to a significant extent that of the urban Indians. Moreover, to regard Martinez as white is to reduce him to an overworked stereotype—the sadistic white cop—of the sort that Momaday, in his portrayal of every other white character in the novel, has scrupulously avoided."] He derives his sense of self from the power and authority vested in him by white society. That power, in his eyes, makes him superior to his "brothers" in the street by enabling him to identify with the oppressor and victimize them at will. He acts out his own version of the American Dream with every Indian he extorts, yet his violent response to Abel's slight resistance suggests that he has paid a price for the power he enjoys.

Martinez emerges, appropriately enough, from a dark alley as Ben and Abel are returning home from Henry's bar. Ben meekly complies with Martinez' order to hold out his hands, and he recalls that his hands "were shaking bad and I couldn't hold them still." He had just been paid and he gives Martinez "all I had left." Martinez then notices Abel:

> Martinez told him to hold out his hands, and he did, slowly, like maybe he wasn't going to at first, with the palms up. I could see his hands in the light and they were open and almost steady. "Turn them over," Martinez said, and he was looking at them and they were almost steady.

Enraged, Martinez smashes Abel's hands with his nightstick, but Abel "didn't cry out or make a sound." From Benally's description, we can see that it is Abel's attitude rather than his actions that engenders Martinez' wrath. Martinez could not

help but notice the contrast between Ben's involuntary shaking and Abel's relative steadiness, and this implied slight to his authority threatens him. His response to it indicates just how precarious his sense of self is, and the extreme viciousness of his later beating of Abel further reveals the self-hatred that is the price of the Anglo authority he covets.

By his mere presence Abel threatens the protective illusions so necessary to Martinez' emotional and psychological survival, and he poses the same threat to Tosamah and Benally. Martha Scott Trimble maintains [in her 1973 *N. Scott Momaday*] that "the suffering of the urban Indians is ... rendered painful to watch because of their reluctance to admit to themselves that they suffer." They are so reluctant because they have been conditioned by the dominant white culture to regard their very suffering as evidence of their own inferiority. Their suffering is at least as productive of guilt as of rage and therefore they have devised what Trimble calls "strategies" to avoid acknowledging that suffering to themselves. By means of these strategies, they seek not only to adapt to white society but to retain while doing so a sense of themselves as free agents making intelligent decisions. They have chosen, in Ben's words, to "go along with it" not out of fear or because they have been seduced by the false promise of the white world, but because, they would believe, it makes sense. And as regards Tosamah and Benally, it is indeed painful to watch them disparage that which they most love and most need—their Indianness.

Tosamah, for instance, tries to better his situation by assuming a superior posture toward it—as is apparent in his use of language. In his first sermon, "The Gospel According to John," Tosamah tries to convince both himself and his congregation that he understands the white man by telling them how the white man conceives of and manipulates language. He says that "the white man deals in words, and he deals easily, with grace and sleight of hand. And in his presence, here on his own ground, you are as children...." Tosamah knows what he is talking about; his assertions are verified by Abel's experience in Los Angeles and Benally's explanation of Abel's language problems. But ironically, Tosamah uses language much as the white man does, and to much the same purpose. In fact, he uses it as Martinez uses fear and violence. Like Martinez, he has carved out a little fiefdom of sorts in the Los Angeles ghetto, and language is his means of controlling it.

By manipulating a variety of verbal styles in "The Gospel According to John," Tosamah keeps his parishioners off balance, dazzling as much as enlightening them. Through an ever-shifting combination of biblical oratory, street talk, exposition, and the simple, direct narrative style of the story-teller, Tosamah tries to relate to his audience on several levels simultaneously, to establish at once his oneness with and superiority to them. He wants to be perceived as a follow Indian sharing a similar culture and values, as a ghetto brother sharing the hardship of the streets, and as a teacher in both the shamanistic and professorial senses. The sermon is full of insight, but it is a masterpiece of verbal gymnastics as well.

Tosamah is perceptive enough to know that the agonizing conflict within himself also exists to varying degrees in the other urban Indians, and he exploits their insecurity and self-doubt to shore up his own tenuous conception of self. Indeed, his need continually to assert himself over the others is one indication of his sense of inadequacy. Like them, he both loves and fears his Indianness, and this entails a roughly similar ambivalence toward the white man. Tosamah sees through the white man to a significant extent and pointedly ridicules his blindness, but like Martinez he also feels a troubling yet insistent need to identify with his oppressor. This need underlies his use of language to intimidate and manipulate the other urban Indians. But he also feels the same need with regard to his heritage and his people. When Tosamah speaks so lovingly, so evocatively in his second sermon, "The Way to Rainy Mountain," of his journey to rediscover his Indian self, we cannot doubt his sincerity. This sermon is longer than his first, and it is free of the verbal gamesmanship that characterizes much of "The Gospel." Still, he needs to be a winner. He sees in his parishioners, and even more clearly in Abel, the fate of Indians in a white world, and he cannot accept such a density. If white society has consigned him, despite his education, intelligence, and talent, to a small, severely limited space, it has at least taught him how to control that space. Like Martinez, he has learned to exalt himself by undermining others. Oppressed, he becomes an oppressor victimizing, as Martinez does, the only people he can—his own.

As Martinez batters Abel's body, so Tosamah batters his spirit, and Momaday, through his use of narrative structure, stresses the parallel between them. The novel's second chapter, "The Priest of the Sun," in effect begins and ends with a sermon by Tosamah. These sermons frame a badly beaten, semiconscious Abel whose murder trial and life in Los Angeles pass in fragments before him. Ironically, Tosamah's second sermon, which recounts his journey to the land of his people, the Kiowa, to visit his grandmother's grave, reveals the path to salvation for Abel, tells how he might be made whole again. But Abel is not there to hear the sermon. Indeed, as we later learn from Benally, it was after Tosamah had earlier humiliated Abel that, in Ben's words, "He went downhill pretty fast...," decided "to get even with" Martinez, and was beaten half to death by him. Tosamah calls himself "Priest of the Sun," and he is sufficiently imaginative, sensitive, understanding, and articulate to be that. But he lives his day-to-day life as Coyote, the trickster who is both culture hero and buffoon. Like Coyote, Tosamah has the capacity to bring spiritual gifts to his people, to be a savior of sorts, but his actions are generally self-centered and done in ignorance—in Tosamah's case, a self-imposed ignorance—of their consequences for the world, his people, and himself. Tosamah is quick to take advantage of others to satisfy his own needs, but because he is himself a slave to those needs (emotional and psychological needs as opposed to Coyote's purely physical ones), he is at times the victim of his own tricks. Coyote is a master of self-deception and, as his own ambivalence toward and treatment of Abel indicates, so is John Big Bluff Tosamah.

Despite his awareness of the beauty and value of his native culture, despite his profound understanding of the nearly overwhelming spiritual problems modern America has created for his people, Tosamah is himself tormented by his Indianness. Abel, in his view, is the incarnation of that Indianness, and as such he fills Tosamah with shame and guilt and reverence. Tosamah, for all his insight into its workings, has been conditioned by the white world and by himself in response to that world to see with two pairs of eyes and the result, at least as regards Abel, is a mélange of contradictory impressions and impulses. For example, Ben remembers Tosamah's warning him about Abel: "He was going to get us all in trouble, Tosamah said. Tosamah sized him up right away...." Perceptive as he is, Tosamah can sense in Abel the unyielding integrity that will make him especially vulnerable in urban Los Angeles, that will keep him from "fitting in"; and that integrity implicitly confronts Tosamah with his own compromising and compromised self.

When Tosamah speaks of Abel's trial, he is both ironic and envious. True, the white society that is puzzled by Abel is the target of his irony, and he ostensibly mocks its view of Abel as "a real primitive sonuvabitch" and a "poor degenerate Indian"; but his own view of Abel, as his warning to Benally and his later psychological attack on Abel make clear, parallels to some extent that of the society he ridicules. Consider in this regard his impression of how Abel's testimony must have sounded to the court:

> "'Well, you honors, it was this way, see? I cut me up a little snake meat out there in the sand.' Christ, man, that must have been our finest hour, better than Little Bighorn. That little no-count cat must have had the whole Jesus scheme right in the palm of his hand."

Tosamah's tone conveys both embarrassment and admiration here, but alone with Ben in the privacy of Ben's apartment he lets his admiration show. Of the court's verdict, he says:

> "They put that cat away, man. They *had* to. It's part of the Jesus scheme. *They,* man. They put all of us renegades, us diehards, away sooner or later.... Listen here, Benally, one of these nights there's going to be a full red moon, a hunter's moon, and we're going to find us a wagon train full of women and children. Now you won't believe this, but I drink to that now and then."

If Ben "won't believe this" it is because the sentiments Tosamah here expresses hardly parallel his actions, and Tosamah knows it. He seeks to identify with Abel, referring to "us renegades, us diehards," and to the white man as "they," but merely to wish now and again for vengeance is an empty gesture. No doubt Tosamah's desire to avenge himself on those who have poisoned his spirit is sincere, but the courage, the spirit of defiance he recognizes in Abel, lies dormant within his own heart. Ben, as he does throughout the novel, undercuts Tosamah's pretentiousness, telling us that "He's always going on like that, Tosamah, talking crazy and showing off...."

Seeing Abel through white eyes, Tosamah finds him embarrassing. Though Tosamah ridicules Anglo cultural arrogance and the stereotypes that feed it, Abel—alcoholic, at times violent, and inarticulate—seems to him to lend credence to the stereotypes; thus Tosamah, educated and articulate as he is, feels misrepresented, degraded by association. This is the "trouble" of which he warns Benally. Seeing Abel through Indian eyes, Tosamah cannot help but admire him as a kind of modern-day warrior who refuses to give in meekly to the torment and tribulations of urban Indian life. But if Tosamah as an Indian is vicariously elevated by Abel's integrity, he is at the same time humbled by the lack of his own. Viewed from either perspective, then, white or Indian, Abel engenders in Tosamah self-contempt so strong that it is beyond enduring; he is anathema to the illusory conception of his own superiority that is Tosamah's primary means of emotional and psychological survival. Therefore, because of the guilt he feels, a guilt stemming from a profound sense of his own inadequacy, he projects upon Abel his own diminished sense of self.

Tosamah needs to tear Abel down and one evening, during a poker game at his place, the opportunity presents itself. In a seemingly expansive mood Tosamah, Ben tells us, was "going on about everything … and talking big." Ben, seeing that this talk bothers Abel, wants to leave, but Abel, already drunk and becoming more so, ignores him. Ben recalls,

> I guess Tosamah knew what he was thinking too, because pretty soon he started in on him, not directly, you know, but he started talking about *longhairs* and the reservation and all. I kept wishing he would shut up, and I guess the others did, too … because right away they got quiet and just started looking down at their hands, you know—like they were trying to decide what to do. I knew that something bad was going to happen.

Abel, too drunk to seriously threaten Tosamah, lunges impotently toward him, and the others, to relieve their own discomfort, laugh at his futility. Ben tells us that the laughter "seemed to take all the fight out of him. It was like he had to give up when they laughed; it was like all of a sudden he didn't care about anything anymore." Abel's response to the laughter indicates that, though perhaps not consciously aware of it, he attacked Tosamah not merely to avenge a personal insult but to avenge all the Indians at the table and back home, to avenge the honor of his people. Tosamah, who "doesn't come from the reservation" himself, has made the others ashamed of what they are, and when they try to dispel their shame by projecting it onto Abel, Abel's rage loses its foundation and he feels empty and alone. Ben remembers "that he was hurt by what had happened; he was hurt inside somehow, and pretty bad." Tosamah, the Priest of the Sun of the Holiness Pan-Indian Rescue Mission, has lost sight of the needs of his people in pursuit of his own isolated ends and in so doing, as his attack on Abel symbolically suggests, he has violated the very essence of his own Indianness. By shaming his people he has done the white man's work.

Unlike Tosamah, Benally is compassionate towards Abel; he is, from the time of their first meeting, instinctively protective of him. He trains Abel for his new job, introduces him around, and though he has very little himself, readily shares his home, his food, and his clothing. Most important of all, he shares with Abel, and Abel alone, his dearest possession—his native religion. It is Ben's honest, profound spirituality that sets him apart from the other urban Indians. As has often been noted, Ben is the one who has the vision during the peyote ceremony, and whereas Tosamah's understanding of his native culture seems at times largely intellectual, Ben "lives his religion on a level deeper than the intellect, the level of spirit and emotion" [Carole Oleson, "The Remembered Earth: Momaday's *House Made of Dawn*," *South Dakota Review* II, No. 1 (Spring 1973)]. Yet there are definite similarities between Ben and Tosamah as well, and to ignore them is to obscure considerably the scope and horror of the spiritual compromises white society, for its own material and psychological convenience, requires of Indians.

Sincere as his religious beliefs are and sensitive as he is, Benally has compromised himself almost as severely as Tosamah has, and this is most apparent from the contradictions in his narrative. Ben is trying earnestly to sell himself on the American Dream in a vain effort to convince himself that the life he feels compelled to live is in fact better and ultimately more fulfilling than the life he knew on the reservation. His pathetic monologue on the wonders of Los Angeles is a case in point:

> It's a good place to live.... Once you find your way around and get used to everything, you wonder how you ever got along out there where you came from. There's nothing there, you know, but the land, and the land is empty and dead. Everything is here, everything you could ever want. You never have to be alone.

But for all practical purposes Ben, until Abel comes, is alone. He has drinking buddies, true, but no one with whom he can share what is most important to him. Moreover, the "radios and cars and clothes and big houses" which, Ben says, "you'd be crazy not to want" and which are "so easy to have" have managed to elude him. He lives in a leaky, dilapidated slum tenement, gets his clothes second-hand, and is a cipher in the plant where he works. He willfully mistakes the racist ridicule of his co-workers for good-natured kidding and the pseudo-amiable hustle of the salespeople in the stores for friendliness. The extent and cost of his

self-deception, however, are most painfully revealed in his comments about the land.

Ben's narrative is punctuated at several points by contrapuntal remembrances which rise unbidden in his mind, memories of growing up on the reservation, on "the land south of Wide Ruins where I come from," on the land he still loves. These recollections are full of precise, beautiful, and evocative details which belie his remark that "the land is empty and dead." The land he recalls is rich with vitality and meaning; it is the sacred center of all life and being. He remembers childhood on the land:

> And you were little and right there in the center of everything, the sacred mountains, the snow-covered mountains and the hills, the gullies and the flats, the sundown and the night, everything—where you were little, where you were and had to be.

The vision of the land inherent in his memories is that which contemporary America requires him to abandon, and he tries to do just that. After all, "That's the only way you can live in a place like this [Los Angeles]. You have to forget about the way it was, how you grew up and all." The need to "go along with it" is a recurrent motif in Ben's narrative, and all that gives his life meaning must be subordinated to it:

> If you come from the reservation, you don't talk about it much; I don't know why. I guess you figure that it won't do you much good, so you just forget about it. You think about it sometimes, you can't help it, but then you just try to put it out of your mind ... it mixes you up sometimes....

But Abel does not let Ben "forget about it." He is to Ben what he is to Tosamah, the incarnation of all that is Indian within him, and Ben intuitively apprehends this. He remarks:

> We were kind of alike, though, him and me. After a while he told me where he was from, and right away I knew we were going to be friends. We're related somehow, I think.

Abel's mere presence evokes his memories of home, and the first of Ben's "flashbacks" occurs as he recalls their first real conversation. Ben's history resembles Abel's in certain respects, and his memories [according to Lawrence J. Evers in his "Words and Place: A Reading of *House Made of Dawn*," *Western American Literature* XI, No. 4 (February 1977)] "reveal a sense of place very like that Abel groped for on his return to Walatowa." What is especially sad about these memories is that they convey a sense of wholeness and security that contrasts sharply with the fragmented, fear-ridden, tenuous existence Ben now endures. He appears to regain a modicum of that sense with Abel, however; Ben knows that his most precious treasures are safe with him:

> "House made of dawn." I used to tell him about those old ways, the stories and the signs, Beauty-way and Night Chant. I sang some of those things and told him what they meant, what I thought they were about.

Abel is wonderfully receptive, as Ben knew he would be, and "would want me to sing like that." And Abel, Ben fears, is the only one who would. Just as Tosamah finds "longhairs" like Abel an embarrassment to him in the white world, so is Benally, within the context of that world, embarrassed by his own best impulses—and that world includes the other urban Indians. He tells of a night when he and Abel, along with the others, are drinking and having fun on a hill overlooking the city:

> I started to sing all by myself. The others were singing, too, but it was the wrong kind of thing, and I wanted to pray. I didn't want them to hear me, because they were having a good time, and I was ashamed, I guess. I kept down because I didn't want anybody but him to hear.

Only with Abel does Benally feel good about being an Indian; only with Abel can he free his spirit in song and prayer, and see past and future merge into an all-inclusive present. When Abel is in the hospital recovering from his beating, Ben, to comfort him, makes up a plan about going home, about "going out into the hills on horses and alone. It was going to be early in the morning, and we were going to see the sun coming up." There, they would "sing the old songs," sing "about the way it used to be, how there was nothing all around but the hills and the sunrise and the clouds." Ben at first did not take his plan seriously, but Abel "believed in it" and "I guess I started to believe in it, too." Dream and waking reality come together for Ben in Abel's presence, albeit briefly, and the deepest impulses of his spirit are vindicated in Abel's existence. In that respect Abel is truly a blessing for Benally. But they live in a world uncongenial to these impulses, a world contemptuous of vision and song, and in that world Abel also becomes an agonizing problem for Ben.

Ben's Indianness can find expression only through his religion and his friendship with Abel, and in a world hostile to Indians both, Ben feels, must be sheltered and protected. This is one reason why he tries to shepherd Abel as he does at the factory and why he takes him into his home. That Ben truly believes he is acting in Abel's best interest is undeniable, and in a very real sense he is. Abel sorely needs the kind of support Ben provides, and

if Tosamah's attempt to isolate Abel is a denial of his own Indianness, Ben's generous inclusion of Abel in his own life is a wonderfully rich expression of his. Moreover, by telling Abel of the old traditions and teaching him the old songs, Ben not only provides him with necessary spiritual sustenance in a world unresponsive to spiritual need, but prepares him for his return to Walatowa to try again, this time more successfully, to find himself in the life of his people. But Ben's concern for Abel is motivated by fear as well as by compassion. Tosamah feared that Abel "was going to get us all in trouble," and so does Ben. He speaks to Abel of things Indian, for, as we have seen, his own spirit requires as much, but throughout his narrative he emphasizes repeatedly Abel's inability to "get along." He understands why Abel has difficulty adjusting and implies that he himself has faced similar obstacles, but he never questions the need to accommodate oneself to the white man's world, and that is why he eventually loses patience with Abel. Abel's problems, in Ben's view, go beyond those which confront every relocated Indian, severe as these problems may be. What Tosamah recognizes as Abel's unyielding integrity Benally sees as sheer obstinacy; or rather, the sustaining illusion he has constructed about the "good life" in Los Angeles demands that he see it as such. After all, Abel has a steady job, a place to live, drinking buddies—everything he needs, Ben would believe, to make it in urban America. Yet despite these advantages, he persists in being a trial to those who care for him.

Abel scares Ben. He scares him when he subtly defies Martinez in the alley and he scares him during Tosamah's harangue about "longhairs and the reservation." In both instances his actions threaten to undermine Ben's illusions by confronting him with the truth that life in urban America is incompatible with his identity as an Indian. Benally, as Carole Oleson has said, has whitened himself considerably by removing his religion from his daily life. He retains the songs and traditions within himself, and that is good, but he also compromises the old religion by confining it like a retarded child whom the family loves but of whom they are ashamed. Like Angela St. John, whose affair with Abel in Walatowa puts her in touch, if only temporarily, with her body's potential for joy and wonder, he turns off his own light, as it were, denies his own intuitive wisdom in a futile attempt to avoid emotional and psychological conflicts which might prove irreconcilable. And like Father Olguin, Benally also preaches the white man's religion—not in the form of Christianity, as Olguin does, but in its true aspects of materialism and conformity; like both Olguin and his predecessor, Fray Nicolás, he would convert the Indian to a new and alien faith for, like them, he needs converts to vindicate his own. Thus it is that when Abel ultimately proves "unregenerate," the usually mild Benally, possessed by anger but more by fear, loses patience:

> He wouldn't let anybody help him, and I guess I got mad, too, and one day we had a fight... he was just sitting there and saying the worst thing he could think of, over and over. I didn't like to hear that kind of talk, you know; it made me kind of scared, and I told him to cut it out. I guess I was more scared than mad; anyway I had had about all I could take.

As with Martinez and Tosamah earlier, Ben knew "something bad was going to happen and ... didn't want any part of it." At this point Abel goes to look for Martinez, but even after he is gone and Ben cools off, Ben nonetheless maintains that "It had to stop, you know; something had to happen."

Benally, then, like Tosamah, is a priest whose saving message, because he has divorced his religion from his everyday life, has an ironic as well as a revelatory dimension. It is especially ironic that despite his deeper, more sincere spirituality, Ben lacks Tosamah's awareness of the redemptive potential of the old ways of seeing and knowing. As the "Night Chanter," Ben, as we have seen, is essential to any hope Abel has for recovery, but Ben himself does not see the sharing of himself and his religion in this way. The road to recovery he consciously charts, as we have also seen, involves passively assimilating the values and accommodating oneself to the demands of white America, even at the cost of one's heritage and identity. Thus the role of "Night Chanter" assumes a second, and contrary, meaning. Though with the best intentions, Benally also, and quite unknowingly, chants the dark night of the soul, the tortured, fragmented, solipsistic state of being that Los Angeles comes to symbolize in the novel. Through the distorting lens of his own desperate need for some sense of meaning to his life, Ben sees an urban paradise, and it is this vision that he consciously advances as salvation.

Though it exists to differing degrees in each of them and, given their enormously diverse natures, manifests itself in various ways, Martinez, Tosamah, and Benally all share a single quality: self-contempt. Each is ashamed of being what he is, of being an Indian, and that is why Abel, when he is relocated in Los Angeles, becomes a kind of sacrifice to their fear and desperation. A "longhair"

from the reservation, he is, among other things, a constant reminder to them of how they are perceived by the dominant culture and of that which has made them wretched. They have been made to feel, against all logic and common sense, that their suffering is somehow deserved because of what they are; thus each of them projects his own diminished sense of self upon Abel and responds to that self in his own way. Martinez tries to obliterate it through violence, Tosamah tries to disassociate himself from it, and Benally tries to remake it to fit the white world he inhabits. The issue is agonizingly complicated, however, because the very Indianness within them which they have been taught to hate is that which they intuitively love. Tosamah and Benally especially know in their very depths that fulfillment and wholeness lie in the realization and free expression of their Indian selves. Tosamah has made a long journey to the land of his people to rediscover his Indianness, and Ben hoards the old songs like treasure within his heart. Therefore, their self-contempt is further intensified by a profound sense of guilt stemming from their perceived inability to live their Indianness, by what they themselves see as a personal betrayal of their heritage and of themselves. However, though it saddens him, Momaday does not condemn the urban Indians for feeling as they do. Their self-hatred is in fact his most telling indictment of a modern America which relentlessly tries to compel its native peoples to barter dignity and self-respect for material, emotional, and psychological survival.

Source: Bernard A. Hirsch, "Self-Hatred and Spiritual Corruption in House Made of Dawn," in *Western American Literature,* Vol. XVII, No. 4, Winter, 1983, pp. 307–20.

Vernon E. Lattin

In the following excerpt, Lattin emphasizes Momaday's presentation of the failure of Christianity in the Indian culture and the desire of the latter for a renewed reverence for the land in its mythic vision of wholeness.

The Native American novel *House Made of Dawn* ... presents the failure of Christianity. Further, its mythic vision of existence becomes an alternative not only to Christianity but to modern civilization based on secular, technological structures....

Father Olguin reveals the inadequacies of Christianity for the Indian. Although attempting to live within the Indian community, he meets only with isolation and failure because he cannot understand the Indian.... Near the end of the novel,

> " ... Olguin and his religion have never understood the Indian culture, and Christianity is but a futile cry."

awakened from sleep by Abel's announcement that his grandfather is dead, Father Olguin can only complain about being disturbed. After Abel leaves, the priest illuminates the irrelevance of Christianity for the Indian by crying out after Abel in the darkness: "I can understand ... I understand, do you hear? ... I understand. *Oh God. I understand—I understand!*" Olguin and his religion have never understood the Indian culture, and Christianity is but a futile cry.

Also in *House Made of Dawn,* a Native American, the Rev. J. B. B. Tosamah, Pastor and Priest of the Sun, is a more complex religious figure than Father Olguin. Living in Los Angeles among urban Indians, Tosamah represents the religious confidence man in his most subtle form: he is both critic and supporter of the white way; he is both priest and medicine man; he is both friend and foe. Ultimately, he is a religious sham, speaking the truth but never the whole truth. His full name reveals and hides him: he is "The Right Reverend John Big Bluff Tosamah."

[Tosamah] tries to span two religions and cultures; neither Christian nor pagan, he remains isolated from himself and his tribal past. A sacred vision emerges in the novel when Abel discovers himself and when ... he returns home through his grandfather and his racial memory. His quest takes him through the typical monomythic pattern of descent and death, through "loneliness and fear" ... until he is able to return to the reservation and join the ancient religious ritual, the run against evil and death.... [He] will be able to accept his place in the universe and defeat the fear that has dominated his life.

Abel's fear arises from unconscious recognition of individual, racial, tribal, and religious extinction. He cannot see the continuity, the oneness of life, because of his fragmented existence.... Like the Bahkyush tribe, which was almost destroyed by marauders and then by the plagues, he makes a

"journey along the edge of oblivion," a journey which takes him through the white man's war, a series of brief sexual encounters, prison, and finally near-death from a brutal beating by a Los Angeles policeman. Out of their suffering, the Bahkyush acquired a tragic sense, a "dignity and bearing" which made them holy, "medicine men ... rainmakers and eagle hunters." During the depth of his despair, close to extinction, Abel likewise discovers some religious truths and acquires a holy vision that returns him to himself and his tribal past.

His final vision results from pagan realities of which he has gradually become aware. During the feast of Santiago, which takes place in the Middle, "an ancient place," ... the sacred center, the "axis munde," Abel is forced to confront his fear, his enemy in the form of a huge, grotesque Albino....

[The resulting struggle between them] reenacts the spiritual confrontation between creative and destructive elements that has been going on forever. At the end of the battle, Abel appropriately kneels down to watch the white man die. During the later trial, when the white world disposes of Abel with "*their* language," Abel's defender, Father Olguin, speaks of the "psychology of witchcraft" and of "an act of imagination," ... unable to recognize the religious significance of Abel's act. Abel understands, however: "They must know that he would kill the white man again, if he had the chance, that there could be no hesitation whatsoever. For he would know what the white man was, and he would kill him if he could."

Abel's quest also takes him back to a reverence for all existence and for the land which supports this existence. Elsewhere Momaday has written of modern America's need to come to accept the land, to develop an "American Land ethic ... not only as it is revealed to us immediately through our senses, but also as it is perceived more truly in the long turn of seasons and of years. And we must come to moral terms." One of the major themes of *House Made of Dawn* is that the people will return in a new dawn to this ancient way, throwing off the invasion and conquests of the white people and their religious vision. The narrator speaks in the novel of a prehistoric civilization that "had gone out among the hills for a little while and would return; and then everything would be restored to an older age, and time would have returned upon itself and a bad dream of invasion and change would have been dissolved in an hour before the dawn.... In part, this explains the significance of the chant "House Made of Dawn" ...: it is a prayer for a return, a rebirth of the old way....

At the end of the novel, beside his grandfather's deathbed, [Abel] is for six mornings reminded of all that is; and within these six dawns of his grandfather's dying he is reunited with his individual, racial, and religious self....

Finally, Abel's life blends with his grandfather's death, and he takes up the past and runs onward.... [As] Abel joins the ancient race against evil and death, he unites himself with his sacred past. He also completes the circle of the novel, which begins and ends with his running; he completes the circle of the history of the American continent, which began with this original pagan religion, survived the Christian polemics and onslaught, and now returns to its origin; and he completes the infinite circle itself, the circle of life which all ancient people recognized and accepted. With such knowledge, the reader recognizes that the running at the end of the novel, with Abel breathing a song, is both beginning and end....

[Momaday has] created a new romanticism, with a reverence for the land, a transcendent optimism, and a sense of mythic wholeness. [His] reverence for the land can be compared to the pastoral vision found in most mainstream American literature, but the two visions contain essential differences. In Norris's *The Octopus,* for example, the wheat remains, a symbol of the vitalistic force moving everything, but this vision of cyclically renewed life is unconvincing, overshadowed by the railroad's evil....

[Many] white heroes fail or are unconvincing because their relationship to the land has been more fantasy than history and because they are conquerors and violators. Their vision must then remain either an anomaly or forlorn and tragic. This is even more true of modern Americans, whose experience as a nation, as Momaday has said, is a repudiation of the pastoral ideal, an uprooting of man from the land, and a consequent "psychic dislocation ... in time and space." In contrast, Abel ... can return and rediscover, because [he has] a land vision that preceded the white conquerors. Abel's grandfather, a farmer and holy man who lives by the organic calendar [is] ... able to sustain the shock of civilization and technology and preserve and transmit the land vision that [he has] never violated as [an individual] or as a people. The bad dream of violation may not end, but Abel ... can transcend the nightmare, and like the Bahkyush tribe, [he] can return to the land....

[Momaday is] willing to face the "silence of the transcendent" in the modern world. Rejecting

the phenomonological limitation of writers like Beckett and Kafka, where the dissolution of the hero's quest is the form, [he creates] an optimistic fiction with the protagonist returning to wholeness and mythic vision and transcending the limitations of both society and time.... This quest can be contrasted with postmodern works like Pynchon's *V,* in which Herbert Stencil's quest is undercut by a denial of form and meaning in the universe, or with *Gravity's Rainbow,* in which the hundreds of characters, appearing and disappearing, deny the possibility of individual, personal transcendence. Abel's ... pagan vision, however, is a way of viewing the world as a religious whole: it is belief. This sacred transcendence is also different from attempts at secular transcendence in novels like *Humboldt's Gift* or the popular *Zen and the Art of Motorcycle Maintenance.* [Moreover, Momaday's novel is a form of rediscovery, an attempt] to return to the sacred art of storytelling and myth-making that is part of Indian oral tradition. [It is an attempt] to push the secular mode of modern fiction into the sacred mode, a faith and recognition in the power of the word which "comes from nothing into sound and meaning ... [and] gives origin to all things."

This rediscovery of the land, of mythic vision, and of the sacred word offers modern America not only a kind of fiction seldom seen, but, if [Annette Kolodny in her *The Lay of the Land*] is correct in her analysis of America's failure to deal with the environment and in her assessment that the twentieth century demands a new pastoral vision offering "some means of understanding and altering the disastrous attitudes toward the physical setting that we have inherited from our national past," then perhaps the mythic vision and land ethic of those people our nation so brutally conquered are appropriate and even necessary at this time.

Source: Vernon E. Lattin "The Quest for Mythic Vision in Contemporary Native American and Chicano Fiction," in *American Literature,* Duke University Press, Vol. L, No. 4, January, 1979, pp. 625–40.

Lawrence J. Evers

An American critic and educator, Evers has authored several books on Native American songs and has served as president of the Association for Study of American Indian Literatures. In the following essay, he examines Momaday's focus on language, landscape, and Native American rituals and narratives in House Made of Dawn.

Native American oral traditions are not monolithic, nor are the traditions with which Momaday

> The journey advances in a series of movements from chaos to order, and each movement takes the People toward greater social and symbolic definition."

works in *House Made of Dawn*—Kiowa, Navajo, and Towan Pueblo. Yet there are, he suggests [in "A Conversation with N. Scott Momaday," *Sun Tracks: An American Indian Literary Magazine* 2, No. 2 (1976)], "common denominators." Two of the most important of these are the native American's relation to the land and his regard for language.

By imagining who and what they are in relation to particular landscapes, cultures and individual members of cultures form a close relation with those landscapes. Following D. H. Lawrence and others, Momaday terms this a "sense of place" [in his "A Special Sense of Place," appearing in *Viva, Santa Fe New Mexican,* (7 May 1972)]. A sense of place derives from the perception of a culturally imposed symbolic order on a particular physical topography. A superb delineation of one such symbolic order is offered by Tewa anthropologist Alfonso Ortiz in his study *The Tewa World* from which the following prayer is taken:

> Within and around the earth, within and around the hills, within and around the mountains, your authority returns to you.

The Tewa singer finds in the landscape which surrounds him validation for his own song, and that particular topography becomes a cultural landscape, at once physical and symbolic. Like Kosahn, Momaday's grandmother, the native American draws from it "strength enough to hold still against all the forces of chance and disorder" [" An American Land Ethic," *Sierra Club Bulletin* 55 (February 1970)].

The manner in which cultural landscapes are created interests Momaday, and the whole of his book *The way to Rainy Mountain* may be seen as an account of that process. During their migration journey the Kiowa people "dared to imagine and

determine who they were.... The journey recalled is among other things the revelation of one way in which these traditions are conceived, developed, and interfused in the human mind." The Kiowa journey, like that recounted in emergence narratives of other tribes, may be seen as a movement from chaos to order, from discord to harmony. In this emergence the landscape plays a crucial role, for cultural landscapes are created by the imaginative interaction of societies of men and particular geographies.

In the Navajo emergence narrative, for example, First Man and First Woman accompanied by Coyote and other actors from the animal world journey upward through four underworlds into the present Fifth World. The journey advances in a series of movements from chaos to order, and each movement takes the People toward greater social and symbolic definition. The cloud pillars of the First World defined only by color and direction become in the Fifth World the sacred mountains of the four directions, the most important coordinates in an intricate cultural geography. As with the Tewa and the Kiowa, that cultural landscape symbolizes the Navajo conception of order, the endpoint of their emergence journey. Through the emergence journey, a collective imaginative endeavor, the Navajos determined who and what they were in relation to the land.

The extraordinary interest in geography exhibited in Navajo oral literature then may be seen as an effort to evoke harmony in those narratives by reference to the symbolic landscape of the present world. Significantly, a major test theme in Navajo oral literature requires identification of culturally important geographic features. Consider the Sun's test of the Hero Twins in one of the final episodes in the emergence narrative [as recounted in Ethelou Yazzie's 1971 *Navajo History*]:

> He asked them to identify various places all over the surface of the earth. He asked, "Where is your home?" The boys knew where their home was. They pointed out Huerfano Mountain and said that was where they lived. The Sun next asked, "What mountain is that in the East?"
>
> "That's *Sis Naajiní* (Blanca Peak)," replied the boys.
>
> "What mountain is down here below us?"
>
> "That's *Tsoodzi* (Mount Taylor)," said the boys.
>
> "What mountain is that in the West?"
>
> "That's *Dook'o'oosíid* (San Francisco Peak)."
>
> "Now, what mountain is that over in the north?"
>
> "Those are the *Dibé Nitsaa* (La Plata Mountains)."

Because all the boy's answers were correct, the Sun said goodby to them as they were lowered down to the earth at the place called *Tó Sidoh* (Hot Springs).

Through their knowledge of the Navajo cultural landscape the Twins proved who and what they were to the Sun.

The pattern of the emergence narrative—a journey toward order symbolized by a cultural landscape—is repeated in Navajo chantway rituals. A patient requires a chantway ritual when his life is in some way out of order or harmony. In order for that harmony to be restored he must be taken through a ritual re-emergence journey paralleling that of the People. It is important to note the role of the singer and his ritual song here, for without songs there can be no cure or restoration of order. Through the power of the chanter's words the patient's life is brought under ritual control, and he is cured.

We come round, then, to another of the "common denominators" Momaday finds in oral traditions: attitude toward language. Of Kiowa oral tradition Momaday writes [in *The Way to Rainy Mountain*]: "A word has power in and of itself. It comes from nothing into sound and meaning; it gives origin to all things." It is this concept, remarkably like one text version of the Navajo origin giving "One Word" as the name of the original state of the universe, which forms the center of Tosamah's sermon on St. John's gospel in the novel [*House Made of Dawn*]. But more germane to our discussion of oral tradition generally is the related notion that "by means of words can a man deal with the world on equal terms." It is only through words that a man is able to express his relation to place. Indeed, it is only through shared words or ritual that symbolic landscapes are able to exist. So it is that the Tewa singer, the Navajo chanter, and the Kiowa "man of words" preserve their communities through their story and song. Without them there would be no community. One contemporary Navajo medicine man [Curley Mustache] suggests that loss of ceremonial words will signal the end of the world: "The medicine men who have knowledge in the Blessing Way (*Hozho ji*) will all evidently be lost. The words to the song will vanish from their memory, and they will not know how to begin to sing."

In this context we can better appreciate Abel's dilemma in *House Made of Dawn*. As Momaday suggests [in "A Conversation with N. Scott Momaday"]: "One of the most tragic things about Abel, as I think of him, is his inability to express

himself. He is in some ways a man without a voice.... So I think of him as having been removed from oral tradition."

House Made of Dawn opens and closes with the formulaic words which enclose all Jemez pueblo tales—*dypaloh* and *qtsedaba,* placing it consciously in that oral tradition. As many oral narratives, the novel is shaped around a movement from discord to harmony and is structurally and thematically cyclic. The prologue is dominated by the race, a central theme in the novel as Momaday has suggested [in an interview appearing in *Puerto del Sol* 12 (1973)]:

> I see [*House Made of Dawn*] as a circle. It ends where it begins and it's informed with a kind of thread that runs through it and holds everything together. The book itself is a race. It focuses upon the race, that's the thing that does hold it all together. But it's a constant repetition of things too.

[Elsie Clews Parsons tells us in the 1925 *The Pueblo of Jemez*] that racing is a conspicuous feature of Jemez ceremonialism. The winter race Abel runs in the prologue and at the end of the novel is the first race in the Jemez ceremonial season, an appropriate ceremonial beginning. But the race itself may be seen as a journey, a re-emergence journey analogous to that mentioned in connection with Navajo and Kiowa oral tradition. Indeed, the language echoes a Navajo re-emergence song sung in the Night Chant, from which the title of the book is taken.

These journey and emergence themes begin to unfold in the following scene as Francisco goes in his wagon to meet the bus returning Abel to Walatowa after WWII. The wagon road on which he rides is parallel to the modern highway on which Abel rides. The two roads serve as familiar metaphors for the conflicting paths Abel follows in the novel, and Momaday reinforces the conflict by parallel auditory motifs as well. As the wagon road excites in Francisco memories of his own race "for good hunting and harvests," he sings good sounds of harmony and balance. At the same time the recurrent whine of tires on the highway is constantly in the background until "he heard the sharp wheeze of the brakes as the big bus rolled to a stop in front of the gas pump...." The re-emergence theme is suggested in the passage by the presence of the reed trap—recalling the reed of emergence, and the fact that Abel returns "ill." He is drunk, of course, but he is also ill, out of balance, in the manner of a patient in a Navajo chantway.

Abel's genealogy, the nature of his illness, and its relation to the auditory motifs mentioned above are further defined in the seven fragments of memory he experiences as he walks above the Cañon de San Diego in the first dawn following his return. At the same time these fragments establish a context for Abel's two prominent encounters in Part I with Angela Grace St. John and with the albino Juan Reyes Fragua.

Abel's genealogy is complicated. He did not know who his father was. "His father was a Navajo, they said, or a Sia, or an Isleta, an outsider anyway," which made Abel "somehow foreign and strange." The ties Abel does have to Walatowa are through his mother whose father, Francisco—both sacristan and kiva participant—is the illegitimate son of the consumptive priest Fray Nicolas V. Through Francisco, Abel is a direct descendant of the Bahkyush, a group of Towan-speaking pueblos who immigrated to Jemez in the mid-nineteenth century. He is a "direct [descendant] of those men and women who had made that journey along the edge of oblivion," an experience which gave them a "tragic sense." Abel, as his Bahkyush ancestors, is on just such a "journey along the edge of oblivion" in the novel.

Abel's journey in Part I is a journey of return to Walatowa and his illness is most explicitly related to a WWII experience. At the end of his seven memory fragments in the first dawn of his return Abel recalls:

> This—everything in advance of his going—he could remember whole and in detail. It was the recent past, the intervention of days and years without meaning, of awful calm and collision, time always immediate and confused, that he could not put together in his mind.

In the confusion of war among soldiers who recognized him only as a "chief" speaking in "Sioux or Algonquin or something," Abel lost both the sense of place which characterized his tribal culture and the very community which supports that sense of place. "He didn't know where he was, and he was alone." Incredibly, he doesn't even recognize the earth: "He reached for something, but he had no notion of what it was; his hand closed upon the earth and the cold, wet leaves."

Mechanical sounds are associated with Abel's disorientation. The "low and incessant" sound of the tank descending upon him reaches back in the novel to the "slow whine of tires" Francisco hears on the highway and looks ahead to the sound of Angela's car intruding on his vision in the first

dawn above the valley as it creeps along the same highway toward the Jemez church. These are the same mechanical sounds Abel tried "desperately to take into account" as the bus took him away to the war—again on the same highway. They are the sounds that reminded him as he left the pueblo to go to war that "the town and the valley and the hills" could no longer center him, that he was now "centered upon himself."

That Angela Grace St. John, the pregnant wife of a Los Angeles physician who comes to Walatowa seeking a cure for her own ailments, will become an obstacle in Abel's re-emergence journey is first suggested by the extensive auditory motifs of Part I. Yet her perceptions of his problems and of the Indian world generally have earned the sympathy of some readers. Perhaps her most seductive perception is that of the significance of the corn dancers at Cochiti Pueblo:

> Their eyes were held upon some vision out of range, something away in the end of distance, some reality that she did not know, or even suspect. What was it that they saw? Probably they saw nothing after all, … nothing at all. But then that was the trick, wasn't it? To see nothing at all, … nothing in the absolute. To see beyond the landscape, beyond every shape and shadow and color, *that* was to see nothing. That was to be free and finished, complete, spiritual…. To say "beyond the mountain," and to mean it, to mean, simply, beyond everything for which the mountain stands of which it signifies the being.

As persuasive as Angela's interpretation of the Cochiti dancers may seem, it is finally a denial of the value of the landscape which the novel celebrates. Angela's assumption that the Cochiti dancers possess a kind of Hindu metaphysics which rejects phenomena for noumena is a projection of her own desires to reject the flesh. Her attitude toward the land is of a piece with her attitude toward her own body: "she could think of nothing more vile and obscene than the raw flesh and blood of her body, the raveled veins and the gore upon her bones." We become almost immediately aware of the implications of that denial she craves in two following scenes: the *corre de gaio* and Abel's second reflection on the Cañon de San Diego.

We view the *corre de gaio* through Angela who again projects feelings about her own existence on the ceremony. For Angela the ceremony like herself is "so empty of meaning … and yet so full of appearance." Her final impression of the ceremony is sexual. She senses some "unnatural thing" in it and "an old fascination returned upon her." Later she remarks of the ceremony: "Like this, her body had been left to recover without her when once and for the first time, having wept, she had lain with a man." In the albino's triumph and Abel's failure at the *corre de gaio* she finds sexual pleasure.

The etiological legend of Santiago (St. James) and the rooster is told by Fr. Olguin appropriately enough for his "instinctive demand upon all histories to be fabulous." The legend explains the ceremonial game which follows in the novel. Just as the sacrifice of the rooster by Santiago produced cultivated plants and domesticated animals for the Pueblo people, so too does ritual re-enactment of the sacrifice promote fertility at Walatowa. While ethnographers suggest that the *corre de gaio* is of relatively minor ceremonial importance in Pueblo societies, in the context of the novel the rooster pull affords Abel his first opportunity to re-enter the ceremonial functions of the village. It is, we are told, the first occasion on which he has taken off his uniform. Though the ceremony itself seems efficacious, as rain follows in the novel, Abel is "too rigid" and "too careful" at the game and fails miserably.

Abel's failure at the rooster pull demonstrates his inability to reenter the ceremonial life of the village, as he realizes in his second reflection at dawn, July 28, 1945. The section opens with an explicit statement of the relation of the emergence journey and the landscape: "The canyon is a ladder to the plain," and is followed by a description of the ordered and harmonious existence of life in that landscape. Each form of life has its proper space and function in the landscape, and by nature of that relation is said to have "tenure in the land." Similarly, "man came down the ladder to the plain a long time ago. It was a slow migration...." Like the emergence journeys of the Kiowa and the Navajo mentioned earlier, the migration of the people of Walatowa led to an ordered relation to place which they express in their ceremonial life. As Abel walks in this landscape in the dawn he is estranged from the town and the land as well. "His return to the town had been a failure" he realizes because he is no longer attuned to its rhythms. He has no words to express his relation to the place. He is "not dumb," but "inarticulate."

Despite his inarticulateness, the rhythm and words are still there "like memory, in the reach of his hearing." We recall that on July 21, seven days before, "for a moment everything was all right with him." Here however,

> He was alone, and he wanted to make a song out of the colored canyon, the way the women of Torreón

made songs upon their looms out of colored yarn, but he had not got the right words together. It would have been a creation song; he would have sung lowly of the first world, of fire and flood, and of the emergence of dawn from the hills.

Abel is at this point vaguely conscious of what he needs to be cured. He needs a re-emergence. He needs words, ceremonial words, which express his relation to the cultural landscape in which he stands. He needs to feel with the Tewa singer quoted earlier his authority return to him. But here out of harmony with himself and his community he needs most of all the kind of re-emergence journey offered in a Navajo chantway.

Significantly, the passage closes, as did the dawn walk of July 21, with an emblem of Angela St. John intruding on Abel's vision: "the high white walls of the Benevides house." The house itself is another symbol of Angela's denial of the land or more particularly the landscape of the Cañon de San Diego. In contrast to Francisco and the other native residents of Walatowa who measure space and time by reference to the eastern rim of the canyon, Angela measures hers in relation to this "high, white house:"

> She would know the arrangement of her days and hours in the upstairs and down, and they would be for her the proof of her being and having been.

His re-entry into the village spoiled, Abel turns not to the ceremonial structure of the pueblo for support but to Angela. And it is the Benevides house, not the land, which provides "the wings and the stage" for their affair. Abel's first sexual encounter with Angela is juxtaposed in the novel with Francisco's encounter with the albino witch in his cornfield. Indeed, Angela, who "keened" to the unnatural qualities of the albino during the *corre de gaio,* echoes the auditory symbols of evil mentioned earlier. Just as Nicolas *teah-whau* "screamed" at him, and the moan of the wind in the rocks frightened him earlier, as Angela and Abel make love "she wanted to scream" and is later "moaning softly."

Earlier in his life Abel found physical regeneration through a sexual experience with Fat Josie. His affair with Angela has just the opposite effect. Lying physically broken on the beach in Part II Abel reflects:

> He had loved his body. It had been hard and quick and beautiful; it had been useful, quickly and surely responsive to his mind and will.... His body, like his mind, had turned on him; it was his enemy.

The following couplet in the text implicates Angela in this alienation:

Angela put her white hands to his body. Abel put his hands to her white body.

Later Abel tells Benally that "she [Angela] was going to help him get a job and go away from the reservation, but then he got himself in trouble." That "trouble" derives in part from Abel's separation from his land.

Auditory symbols follow Abel directly from his affair with Angela to the climactic scene of Part I, the killing of the albino. Just before the murder the albino laughs "a strange, inhuman cry." Like the sound of Nicolas *teah-whau* it is "an old woman's laugh" that issues from a "great, evil mouth." At the very scene of the murder the only sound that breaks the silence is "the moan of the wind in the wires."

That Abel regards the albino as evil, as a witch (*sawah*), is clear enough even without the explicit statements of Father Olguin, Tosamah, and Benally later. Moreover, it is clear at the time of the murder that Abel regards the albino as a snake. He feels "the scales of the lips and the hot slippery point of the tongue, writhing." But that Abel is "acting entirely within the Indian tradition" when he kills the albino is wrong.

Abel's compulsion to eradicate the albino-snake reveals an attitude toward evil more akin to the Christian attitude of Nicolas V.: "that Serpent which even is the One our most ancient enemy." The murder scene is rife with Christian overtones. The killing takes place beneath a telegraph pole which "leaned upon the black sky;" during the act "the white hands still lay upon him as if in benediction," and after the albino's death "Abel knelt" and noticed "the dark nails of the hand seemed a string of great black beads." Abel appears to kill the albino then as a frustrated response to the White Man and Christianity, but he does so more in accordance with Anglo tradition than Indian tradition. Indeed, he has been trained in the Army to be a killer.

We recall here that the murder takes place squarely in the middle of the fiesta of Porcingula, the patroness of Walatowa, and that a central part of the ceremony on that feast is a ritual confrontation between the Pecos bull and the "black-faced children, who were the invaders." Parsons describes the bull-baiting at Jemez during the fiesta of Porcingula, August 1, 1922, as follows:

> An hour later, "the Pecos bull is out," I am told and hasten to the Middle. There the bull-mask is out playing, with a following of about a dozen males, four or five quite young boys. They are caricaturing Whites,

their faces and hands painted white; one wears a false mustache, another a beard of blond hair. "U.S.A." is chalked on the back of their coat or a cross within a circle…. They shout and cry out, "What's the matter with you boy?" or more constantly "*Muchacha! Muchacho!*" …

> The bull antics are renewed, this time with attempts of his baiters to lasso. Finally they succeed in dragging him in front of their house, where he breaks away again, to be caught again and dragged into the house. From the house a bugler steps out and plays "Wedding Bells" and rag-time tunes for the bull-baiters to dance to in couples, "modern dances," ending up in a tumble. Two by two, in their brown habit and sandaled feet, four of the Franciscan Fathers pass by. It grows dark, the bugler plays "taps" and this burlesque, reaching from the Conquistadores to the Great War, is over for the night.

The very day then that Abel kills the albino the community from which he is estranged could have provided him with a way of ritually confronting the white man. Had his return not been a failure, he might have borne his agony, as Francisco had "twice or three times," by taking the part of the bull. "It was a hard thing," Francisco tells us, "to be the bull, for there was a primitive agony to it, and it was a kind of victim, an object of ridicule and hatred." Hard as that agony was, Abel as Francisco before him might have borne it with the support of his community. Separated from that community, he acts individually against evil and kills the white man.

Momaday forces us to see the murder as more complicated and subtle in motivation despite Benally's sympathetic reflections on the realities of witchery, Tosamah's reference to the murder as a legal conundrum, and Abel's own statement that the murder was "not a complicated thing." Death has not been a simple thing for Abel to cope with earlier in the novel, as shown by his emotional reactions to the deaths of the doe, the rabbit, the eagle, as well as the deaths of his brother Vidal and his mother. More to the point is the fact that the White Man Abel kills is, in fact, a white Indian, an albino. He is the White Man in the Indian; perhaps even the White Man in Abel himself. When Abel kills the albino, in a real sense he kills a part of himself and his culture which he can no longer recognize and control. That that part should take the shape of a snake in his confused mind is horribly appropriate given the long association of the Devil and the snake in Christian tradition and the subsequent Puritan identification of the American Indians as demonic snakes and witches in so much of early American literature. In orthodox Pueblo belief the snake and the powers with which it is associated are accepted as a necessary part of the cosmic order: "The Hebres view of the serpent as the embodiment of unmitigated evil is never elaborated among the Pueblos; he is too often an ally for some desired end" [Hamilton A. Tyler, *Pueblo Gods and Myths,* 1964].

Yet, the whiteness of the albino suggests something more terrible than evil to Abel. As the whiteness of the whale does to Ishmael, it suggests an emptiness in the universe, a total void of meaning. It is an emblem complementary to Angela's philosophizing over the Cochiti dancers. The albino confronts Abel with his own lack of meaning, his own lack of a sense of place.

This reading is reinforced by the poignant final scene in Part I. Francisco stands alone in his corn field demonstrating the very sense of place Abel has lacked on his return. We recall that in this very field Francisco too had confronted evil in the shape of the albino, but that he responded to the confrontation very differently:

> His acknowledgement of the unknown was nothing more than a dull, intrinsic sadness, a vague desire to weep, for evil had long since found him out and knew who he was. He set a blessing upon the corn and took up his hoe.

Because of Abel's act, Francisco is for the first time separated from the Walatowa community. He stands muttering Abel's name as he did in the opening of the chapter, and near him the reed trap—again suggesting the reed of emergence—is empty.

Part II of the novel opens with Abel lying broken, physically and spiritually, on the beach in Los Angeles. Like the helpless grunion with whom he shares the beach, he is out of his world. Abel's problem continues to be one of relating to place. As in Part I at Walatowa he fails to establish a sense of place in Los Angeles because of a failure to find community. Not only is he separated from other workers at the factory, but even Tosamah and the Indian men at the Silver Dollar reject Abel. That rejection is a major cause of Abel's second futile and self-destructive confrontation with evil in the person of Martinez, a sadistic Mexican policeman. The pattern of the second confrontation is a repetition of the first. Just as Abel kills the albino at Walatowa after he has failed to find community there, so too he goes after Martinez, also perceived as a snake (*culebra*), after he has failed utterly to find community in Los Angeles. Implication of Anglo society in this failure is again explicit and powerful, as Abel has been sent to Los Angeles by the

government on its Relocation Program after serving time in prison for killing the albino.

On the beach Abel "could not see." This poverty of vision, both physical and imaginative, is akin to the inability of one-eyed Father Olguin to "see" and is related to Abel's prison experience: "After a while he could not imagine anything beyond the walls except the yard outside, the lavatory and the dining hall—or even walls, really." Yet it is by the sea that Abel gains the insight required to begin his own re-emergence. For the first time he asks himself "where the trouble had begun, what the trouble was," and though he still cannot answer the question consciously, his mind turns again to the mechanical auditory images noted earlier:

> The bus leaned and creaked; he felt the surge of motion and the violent shudder of the whole machine on the gravel road. The motion and the sound seized upon him. Then suddenly he was overcome with a desperate loneliness, and he wanted to cry out. He looked toward the fields, but a low rise of the land lay before them.

The bus takes Abel out of a context where he has worth and meaning and into a context where "there were enemies all around." From the cultural landscape of the Cañon de San Diego to the beach where "the world was open at his back," Abel's journey has taken him, as his Bahkyush ancestors, to "the edge of oblivion": "He had been long ago at the center, had known where he was, had lost his way, had wandered to the end of the earth, was even now reeling on the edge of the void." On the beach, then, Abel finally realizes that "he had lost his place," a realization accompanied by the comprehension of the social harmony a sense of place requires. Out of his delirium, as if in a dream, his mind returns to the central thread of the novel, the race, and here at last. Abel is able to assign meaning to the race as a cultural activity:

> The runners after evil ran as water runs, deep in the channel, in the way of least resistance, no resistance. His skin crawled with excitement; he was overcome with longing and loneliness, for suddenly he saw the crucial sense in their going, of old men in white leggings running after evil in the night. They were whole and indispensable in what they did; everything in creation referred to them. Because of them, perspective, proportion, design in the universe. Meaning because of them. They ran with great dignity and calm, not in hope of anything, but hopelessly; neither in fear nor hatred nor despair of evil, but simply in recognition and with respect. Evil was. Evil was abroad in the night; they must venture out to the confrontation; they must reckon dues and divide the world.

We recall that as Abel killed the albino "the terrible strength of the hands was brought to bear only in proportion as Abel *resisted them*" (emphasis added). The murder is an expression of Abel's disharmony and imbalance. As Abel here realizes "evil is that which is ritually not under control" [Gladys A. Reichard, *Navajo Religion: A Study of Symbolism,* 1974]. In the ceremonial race, not in individual resistance, the runners are able to deal with evil.

Tosamah's description of the emergence journey and the relations of words and place serve as a clue to Abel's cure, but the role he plays in Abel's journey appears as ambiguous and contradictory as his character. He is at once priest and "clown." He exhibits, often on the same page, remarkable insight, buffoonery, and cynicism. He has then all the characteristics of Coyote, the trickster figure in native American mythologies. Alternately wise and foolish, Coyote in native American oral tradition is at once a buffoon and companion of the People on their emergence journey. As Coyote, a member of "an old council of clowns," the Right Reverend John Big Bluff Tosamah speaks with a voice "full of authority and rebuke." As Coyote, "he likes to get under your skin; he'll make a fool out of you if you let him." Note how Momaday describes Tosamah:

> He was shaggy and awful-looking in the thin, naked light; big, lithe as a cat, narrow-eyed, suggesting in the whole of his look and manner both arrogance and agony. He wore black like a cleric; he had the voice of a great dog.

The perspective Tosamah offers Abel and the reader in the novel derives not so much from his peyote ceremonies, for which Momaday seems to have drawn heavily on La Barre's *The Peyote Cult,* but rather from the substance of the two sermons he gives. The second sermon, "The Way to Rainy Mountain," which Momaday has used in his book by the same title and several other contexts, addresses the relation of man, land, community, and the word. In it Tosamah describes the emergence of the Kiowa people as "a journey toward the dawn" that "led to a golden age." It was a journey which led the Kiowa to a culture which is inextricably bound to the land of the southern plains. There, much in the manner of Abel looking over the Cañon de San Diego in Part I, he looks out on the landscape at dawn and muses: "your imagination comes to life, and this, you think, is where Creation was begun." By making a re-emergence journey, Tosamah is able to feel a sense of place.

That coherent native relation to the land described so eloquently by Tosamah is counterpointed in the novel not only by Abel's experiences but also by the memories of Milly, the social worker who becomes Abel's lover in Los Angeles. Milly, like Tosamah, is from Oklahoma. There her family too had struggled with the land, but "at last Daddy began to hate the land, began to think of it as some kind of enemy, his own very personal and deadly enemy." Even viewed in the dawn her father's relation to the land was a despairing and hopeless one:

> And every day before dawn he went to the fields without hope, and I watched him, sometimes saw him at sunrise, far away in the empty land, very small on the skyline turning to stone even as he moved up and down the rows.

The contrast with Francisco, who seems most at home in his fields, and with Tosamah, who finds in that very landscape the depth of his existence, is obvious. The passage also recalls Angela's denial of the meaning of the land and Abel's own reflections on "enemies."

In his first sermon in the novel, Tosamah addresses the crucial role of words and the imagination in the reemergence process. The sermon is a bizarre exegesis of St. John's gospel which compares Indian and Anglo attitudes toward language. As participants in oral traditions, Indians, Tosamah tells us, hold language as sacred. They have a childlike regard for the mysteries of speech. While St. John shared that sensibility, he was also a white man. And the white man obscures the truth by burdening it with words:

> Now, brothers and sisters, old John was a white man, and the white man has his ways. Oh gracious me, he has his ways. He talks about the Word. He talks through it and around it. He builds upon it with syllables, with prefixes and suffixes, and hyphens and accents. He adds and divides and multiplies the Word. And in all of this he subtracts the Truth.

The white man may indeed, Tosamah tells us, in a theory of verbal overkill that is wholly his own, "perish by the Word."

Words are, of course, a problem for Abel. On the one hand, he lacks the ceremonial words—the words of a Creation song—which properly express his relation to community and place. He is inarticulate. On the other, he is plagued by a surfeit of words from white men. The bureaucratic words of the social worker's forms effectively obscure his real problems. At the murder trial, he thinks: "Word by word by word these men were disposing of him in language, *their* language, and they were making a bad job of it." Again when Benally takes him to the hospital after the beach scene bureaucratic words get in the way. Indeed, Benally perceives

Abel's central problem as one of words, as he equates finding community with having appropriate words:

> And they can't help you because you don't know how to talk to them. They have a lot of words, and you know they mean something, but you don't know what, and your own words are no good because they're not the same; they're different, and they're the only words you've got.... You think about getting out and going home. You want to think that you belong someplace, I guess.

Tosamah perceives a similar dislocating effect of words on Abel, though he relates it to religion. Scorning his inarticulateness and innocence, he sees Abel as caught in "the Jesus scheme." Beyond his sermons, there is a special irony in the fact that Tosamah doesn't understand Abel and his problems, for he is described several times in Part II as a "physician." Though they put Abel's problems in a broader and clearer perspective, Tosamah's words are of little use to Abel.

Part III is told from the point of view of Ben Benally, a relocated Navajo who befriends Abel in Los Angeles. Roommates in Los Angeles, Ben and Abel share many things in their backgrounds. On his one visit to Walatowa, Benally finds the landscape there similar to that in which he grew up. Like Abel he was raised in that landscape without parents by his grandfather. Benally even suggests that he is somehow related to Abel since the Navajos have a clan called Jemez, the name of Abel's pueblo. Moreover, we recall that Abel's father may have been a Navajo, and that Francisco regards the Navajo children who come to Walatowa during the Fiesta of Porcingula as "a harvest, in some intractable sense the regeneration of his own bone and blood." This kinship gives Benally special insight into Abel's problems and strengthens his role as Night Chanter.

Benally's childhood memories of life with his grandfather near Wide Ruins reveal a sense of place very like that Abel groped for on his return to Walatowa.

> And you were little and right there in the center of everything, the sacred mountains, the snow-covered mountains and the hills, the gullies and the flats, the sundown and the night, everything—where you were little, where you were and had to be.

Moreover, this sense of place gives him words: "you were out with the sheep and could talk and sing to yourself and the snow was new and deep and beautiful."

In Los Angeles, however, Benally's sense of place is lost in his idealism and naïveté. Return to the reservation seems a pale option to the glitter of Los Angeles. "There would be nothing there, just the empty land and a lot of old people, going no place and dying off." Like Milly, Benally believes in "Honor, Industry, the Second Chance, the Brotherhood of Man, the American Dream...." Theirs is a 50's American Dream of limitless urban possibilities. Benally believes you can have anything you want in Los Angeles and that "you never have to be alone." Yet in the very scene following his reflection on this urban cornucopia, we find Benally excluded even from the community of The Silver Dollar, counting his pennies, unable to buy a second bottle of wine. Idealism obscures Benally's vision, even as Tosamah's cynicism obscures his.

Nevertheless, Benally is the Night Chanter, the singer who helps restore voice and harmony to Abel's life. In the hospital having realized the significance of the runners after evil, Abel asks Benally to sing for him:

> "House made of dawn". I used to tell him about those old ways, the stories and the songs, Beautyway and Night Chant. I sang some of those things, and I told him what they meant, what I thought they were about.

The songs from both the Beautyway and the Night Chant are designed to attract good and repel evil. They are both restorative and exorcising expression of the very balance and design in the universe Abel perceived in the runners after evil. Ben's words from the Night Chant for Abel are particularly appropriate, since the purpose of the Night Chant is to cure patients of insanity and mental imbalance. The structure and diction of the song demonstrate the very harmony it seeks to evoke. Dawn is balanced by evening light, dark cloud and male rain by dark mist and female rain. All things are in balance and control, for in Navajo and Pueblo religion good is control. Further note that a journey metaphor is prominent in the song ("may I walk....") and that the restorative sequence culminates with "restore my voice for me." Restoration of voice is an outward sign of inner harmony. Finally, note that the song begins with a culturally significant geographic reference: *Tségihi*. One of its central messages is that ceremonial words are bound efficaciously to place. No matter how dislocated is Benally or idiosyncratic his understandings of Navajo ceremonialism, the songs he sings over Abel clearly serve a restorative function.

Angela also visits Abel in the hospital and offers him words. She tells Abel the story her son likes "best of all." It is a story about "a young Indian brave," born of a bear and a maiden, who has many adventures and finally saves his people. Benally marvels at the story which reminds him of a similar story from the Mountain Chant told to him by his grandfather. Yet unlike the Navajo legend and the Kiowa bear legend told by Tosamah earlier, both etiological legends tied firmly to cultural landscapes, Angela's story is as rootless as a Disney cartoon. Abel seems to realize this, if Benally does not, for he does not respond to Angela. Benally "couldn't tell what he was thinking. He had turned his head away, like maybe the pain was coming back, you know." Abel refuses to play Angela's game a second time.

Part IV opens with a description of a grey, ominous winter landscape. Olguin is reflecting on his seven years' service at Walatowa. He claims to have grown "calm with duty and design," to have "come to terms with the town." Yet he remains estranged from the village; it is not his place. He measures his achievement in the language of commerce, noting with his predecessor Nicolas V. what good works "accrued to his account." Like Angela who was offended that Abel "would not buy and sell." Olguin seeks to at least make good the "investment" of his pride.

Whereas Abel looks to Benally's Night Chant for restoration Olguin seeks and claims to find restoration from the journal of Nicolas. In that same journal we recall Nicolas V. himself sought restoration of his Christian God:

> When I cannot speak thy Name, I want Thee most to restore me. Restore me! Thy spirit comes upon me & I am too frail for Thee!

The passage leaves off in a fit of coughing and seems a singularly ineffectual request.

At the same time Abel sits with his dying grandfather. Though Francisco's voice had been strong in the dawn, it now grows weaker and fades as it has on each of the six days since Abel's return to Walatowa. The few words Francisco does speak, in Town and Spanish, juxtapose in the manner of Parts I and II the memory fragments which Abel seeks to order in his own mind. Francisco is here, as Momaday suggests [in the 1973 *Puerto del Sol* interview], "a kind of reflection of Abel." The passage translates:

> Little Abel ... I'm a little bit of something ... Mariano ... cold ... he gave up ... very, very cold ... conquered ... aye [exclamation of pain], Porcingula ... how white, little Abel ... white devil ... witch ... witch ... and the black man ... yes ... many black men ... running, running ... cold ... rapidly ... little

Abel, little Vidal ... What are you doing? What are you doing?

As the seventh dawn comes these words grow into coherent fragments in Francisco's memory and serve as a final statement of the realizations about the relation of place, words, and community Abel has had earlier in the novel.

Each of the fragments is a memory of initiation. In the first Francisco recalls taking Abel and Vidal to the ruins of the old church near the Middle to see "the house of the sun."

> They must learn the whole contour of the black mesa. They must know it as they knew the shape of their hands, always and by heart.... They must know the long journey of the sun on the black mesa, how it rode in the seasons and the years, and they must live according to the sun appearing, for only then could they reckon where they were, where all things were in time.

This is the sense of place Abel lost in "the intervention of days and years without meaning, of awful calm and collision, time always immediate and confused." As he is instructed to know the shape of the eastern mesa like his own hands, it is appropriate that in the *corre de gaio* the albino should first attack his hands, that in the murder scene (and Abel's memory of it) hands should be so prominent, and finally that as he lies on the beach after Martinez's brutal beating of his hands, Abel should think of Angela's effect on him in terms of hands. The relation to place taught him by Francisco is broken by each, as are his hands. Now through Francisco's memory Abel is retaught his ordered relation to place and how it is expressed in "the race of the dead." Abel similarly participates in Francisco's memories of his initiation as a runner (in the race against Mariano), as a dancer (from which he gained the power to heal), as a man (with Porcingula, "the child of the witch"), and as a hunter (as he stalks the bear).

All signs then point to a new beginning for Abel as he rises February 28, the last day of the novel. His own memory healed by Francisco's, for the first time in the novel he correctly performs a ceremonial function as he prepares Francisco for burial and delivers him to Father Olguin. He then joins the ashmarked runners in the dawn. Momaday comments on that race in his essay "The Morality of Indian Hating" [in *Ramparts* 3 (1964)]:

> The first race each year comes in February, and then the dawn is clear and cold, and the runners breathe steam. It is a long race, and it is neither won nor lost. It is an expression of the soul in the ancient terms of sheer physical exertion. To watch those runners is to know that they draw with every step some elemen-

tary power which resides at the core of the earth and which, for all our civilized ways, is lost upon us who have lost the art of going in the flow of things. In the tempo of that race there is time to ponder morality and demoralization, hungry wolves and falling stars. And there is time to puzzle over that curious and fortuitous question with which the people of Jemez greet each other.

That very question—"Where are you going?"—must ring in Abel's ears as he begins the race. The time and direction of his journey are once again defined by the relation of the sun to the eastern mesa, "the house made of dawn." Out of the pain and exhaustion of the race, Abel regains his vision: "he could see at last without having to think." That vision is not the nihilistic vision of Angela— "beyond everything for which the mountain stands." Rather, Abel's "last reality" in the race is expressed in the essential unity and harmony of man and the land. He feels the sense of place he was unable to articulate in Part I. Here at last he has a voice, words and a song. In beauty he has begun.

Source: Lawrence J. Evers, "Words and Place: A Reading of House Made of Dawn," in *Western American Literature*, Vol. XI, No. 4, February, 1977, pp. 297–320.

Martha Scott Trimble

Trimble is an American educator and critic. In this excerpt, she briefly analyzes some major themes and symbols in House Made of Dawn.

Invited to submit to Harper & Row some poetry for publication, Momaday instead submitted the prose manuscript of *House Made of Dawn* for the Harper Prize Novel Contest, even though he had missed the deadline. Harper & Row published the book in 1968; Signet followed with a paperback edition in 1969. "*Three Sketches from House Made of Dawn*" had appeared in the October 1966 issue of *The Southern Review,* with a footnote announcing the pending publication by Harper & Row, and with a statement by the author:

> The novel is about an Indian who returns from World War II and finds that he cannot recover his tribal identity; nor can he escape the cultural context in which he grew up. He is torn, as they say, between two worlds, neither of which he can enter and be a whole man. The story is that of his struggle to survive on the horns of a real and tragic dilemma in contemporary society....

The three sketches were incorporated into *House Made of Dawn:* "The Sparrow and the Reed" principally as the first chapter; "Homecoming" as the first part of the second chapter; and "The Albino" as part of the fourth chapter. A comparison of these sketches in their journal form with the form

> **The book, then, is a pool, circular in structure, not a rising-action-climax-falling-action-all-from-the-same-point-of-view piece of fiction."**

they have in the novel shows that Momaday had carefully revised them to achieve greater clarity and precision.

The seminal forms of other chapters were also printed in a literary journal before the novel was published. "*Two Sketches from House Made of Dawn*" appeared in the *New Mexico Quarterly* (Summer 1967): "The Bear and the Colt" was incorporated into the next to the last chapter of the novel; and "The Eagles of the Valley Grande" was placed just after what had been "Homecoming" in the first chapter.

House Made of Dawn, a novel of only sixty-five to seventy thousand words, appeared on the editor's desk. It was not a book of poems as the editor had anticipated. Frances McCullough was the editor who saw the literary value of the book and backed it. *House Made of Dawn* was dismissed casually by some reviewers, and sadly misunderstood by others. Only a handful recognized its merit. Then to the surprise not only of the author but also of numbers of incredulous reviewers and others in the publishing world, the judges for the Pulitzer Prize for Fiction named *House Made of Dawn*—a first novel by an unknown author—the 1969 winner....

House Made of Dawn opens with a brief prologue that describes Abel running in an early spring dawn on the reservation. Abel's running with the dawn at the end of the last chapter, however, emerges as a religious act leading to self-realization. The intervening chapters describe the events that help explain Abel's run. Momaday divides these chapters, each one headed by a specific date, into four parts of varying lengths. The first part, entitled "The Longhair," contains seven chapters having dates ranging from July 20 to August 2, 1945. It is set in a pueblo at "Walatowa, Cañon de San Diego." Parts two and three take place in Los Angeles in 1952—the former, "The Priest of the Sun," occurring on January 26 and 27, and the latter, "The Night Chanter," on February 20. The final part, "The Dawn Runner," returns the reader to Walatowa and contains two chapters dated February 27 and 28, 1952.

Momaday's combination of specific chronological ordering with the circular repetition of the scene showing Abel's run emerges as a key to understanding the novel's essential nature. The book contains oppositions arising from two points. One relates to the point of view Momaday expressed in his [January 31, 1971 lecture at Colorado State University entitled *The American Indian in the Conflict of Tribalism and Modern Society*]: the differences between the white's and the Indian's view of the world and the need to reveal to each culture the knowledge possessed by the other.

The haunting descriptions of the always acutely present landscape contained in the novel spring from Momaday's background. As he says in "What will happen to the land?": "Landscapes tend to stand out in my memory. When I think back to a particular time in my life, I tend to see it in terms of its setting, the background in which it achieves for me a certain relief. Or, to put it another way, I am inclined closely to associate events with the physical dimensions in which they take place … my existence is indivisible with the land."

The other opposition has something of the same nature, is, if one likes, a concretization of the first opposition. What the reader initially thinks he knows about what happens in the novel, and why, sometimes turns out later to contrast with what he actually does know. As a minor illustration, ask what theater Abel served in during the Second World War, and then ask what is the basis of that knowledge.

As the novel continues, the effect of these oppositions grows more profound. At least with reference to the book, if the contrasts between actual knowledge and apparent knowledge can be reconciled, it will be clear that the materials Momaday presents have not been merely organized into unity by the artistic conventions available for that purpose but rather have become fused into unity through the combined efforts of both author and reader. These efforts might eventually yield cultural results also.

Plotting the events of this novel has some conventional aspects. In *House Made of Dawn* specific dates stand at the head of the chapters. But the events Momaday depicts are forced into an apparently plotted order by those dates. In actuality, they explode out of their chronological patterns, and not only because Momaday depicts them more than once. Many have taken place at some period before the date on which we see them described. We are sometimes not clear about the specific time of their occurrence. We are not sure, for example, how old Abel was when he captured the eagle as a member of the Eagle Watchers Society, nor how old "old enough" was when Francisco took Abel and his older brother, Vidal, to explain to them the movements of the sun along the silhouetted rim of Black Mesa.

In one sense, it is important that we not be sure when such events occur; their having happened becomes more pervasively influential that way. Their mystery, part of their significance, increases.

The book, then, is a pool, circular in structure, not a rising-action-climax-falling-action-all-from-the-same-point-of-view piece of fiction. Momaday patently does not use a consistent point of view, for example. In Part Three, "The Night Chanter," Momaday presents Benally, Abel's Navaho friend in Los Angeles, as a conventional first person narrator. The other three parts are not so conventional. For example, Part Two, "The Priest of the Sun," utilizes an essentially omniscient point of view, but one noticeably modified by stream-of-consciousness when it portrays Abel's agonized return to a hazy awareness after his severe beating by Martinez, a Los Angeles policeman who took pleasure in tormenting the Indians he came into contact with.

A strong sense of the mystery of what goes on in the novel emerges most clearly from Momaday's characterizations. As there seems to be no likely cause-effect pattern in parts of the plot, so there is no fully graspable sense of motive behind the characters' behavior. In fact, the vivid descriptions of the land are balanced by a vagueness, a mysteriousness in the descriptions of the appearances and behavior of the characters, with only a few exceptions. Momaday describes Angela St. John thoroughly, and the Albino. The others, even the central figure, Abel, are not thoroughly described. However, even the detailed descriptions of Angela and the Albino add to the novel's sense of mystery. Especially bewildering are the motives behind their conduct—conduct having extremely important consequences in Abel's life. The scene during which Abel kills the Albino provides the most striking instance of Momaday's refusal to give an explicit explanation of motives, Abel's as well as the Albino's.

Generally speaking, those figures whom we meet at Walatowa, including Francisco (Abel's grandfather), and the Catholic priests, Father Olguin and his distant predecessor, Father Nicolás, remain in deeper shadow than do people like Milly and the "relocated" Indians Tosamah and Benally, all of whom we see in Los Angeles.

If we as readers remained in shadow, the novel could not challenge us so deeply as it does. Before we can grow enlightened about the sometimes mysterious characters in the book and their sometimes bewildering conduct, we have to recognize that, as in his poetry, Momaday writes with symbolic intent. When we look for symbolic significance, we no longer need be discomfited by the lack of information about, for example, the disease that had "stiffened" one of Francisco's legs. Instead, we can hypothesize about the significance of the disease and its bearing on the novel's themes. Then if we wish to guess which disease had afflicted Francisco, we have a basis to use. We work backward from the significance of the crippled leg to what might have been its literal cause rather than the other way around.

The Indian subject matter of the novel contributes a source of symbolism external to but complementing the symbolism created within the context of the novel by such things as Abel's and Angela's names and the Albino's sickly whiteness. We may resolve many of the mysterious things unique to *House Made of Dawn,* but Momaday, in making his points about the range of relationships possible between cultures, wishes to leave at least the non-Indian reader with an abiding sense of what he does not know. The novel's many scenes depicting Indian religious activities are the primary means of presenting the mystery that must remain. The activities associated with the feast of Santiago, a Catholic saint who metamorphosed into the originator of the pre-Christian Pueblo culture, provide one example, for one has only a general idea of the dynamics of the "rooster pulling" ceremony, even after reading Father Olguin's tale exposing the possible origin of the ceremony; and the ancient ceremony enacted seven days later, on August first, remains as essentially mysterious to the reader as it is unsettling to Father Olguin. As Momaday says of the people of the town: "after four centuries of Christianity, they still pray in Tanoan to the old deities of the earth and sky."

Of course this sort of symbolism connects to the symbolism unique to the novel. The song Benally sings ("House Made of Dawn": hence the novel's title) to his battered friend the night before Abel leaves Los Angeles to return to Walatowa is one version of the last song of a formal nine-day purification ceremony in which the major participants are a priest and a patient. Within the context of the work, Benally would be serving as a symbolic priest preparing Abel for his return to the reservation and his subsequent ability to make the ritual run in the dawn after Francisco's death. Abel makes the run either despite or because of his great physical and psychological anguish.

In the recurring ritual running, the themes of the novel most intensely fuse with the traditional symbolism of the Indian religious beliefs. As Abel resumes consciousness after his beating at the hands of Martinez, a beating ultimately arising from his refusal to fear Martinez, he remembers what he saw after knifing the Albino. He was hiding and saw one group of runners, the "runners after evil," go by "with great dignity and calm, not in the hope of anything, but hopelessly; neither in fear nor hatred nor despair of evil, but simply in recognition and with respect. Evil was."

The mystery still remains, for although Momaday explains that Abel "suddenly saw the crucial sense in their going," he does not say whether the insight came as Abel watched from hiding on the night of August 1, 1945, or as he remembered the event during his struggle back to life on the night of January 26, 1952.

Whichever the case, the insight implies a recognition of the need for forgiveness that a neutral or resigned response to the presence of something negative or evil involves. This process also includes the forgiveness of those who called him from his life to fight a war he did not grasp and who put him in prison for six years for killing a being he considered a snake, and therefore evil, *i.e.,* the Albino. Perhaps he could run, finally, because he recognized that the snake, too, should continue to exist—a recognition that goes beyond the Christianity which for so many years in the Pueblo preached forgiveness.

In addition to Momaday's treatment of evil, other themes appear in the book. Perhaps the suffering of the urban Indians is the most noticeable of these, rendered more painful to watch because of their reluctance to admit to themselves that they suffer. Their strategies for avoiding such recognition make up much of the material in Parts Two and Three of the novel. Momaday does not assert that suffering is an Indian prerogative, of course, for all the non-Indian characters of any importance to the novel also suffer. What he does suggest is that Indians may have ways to overcome suffering which others might profit from knowing about. These others might risk the loss of some of their own culturally determined portions of their sense of self, but that risk would be no more than that which cultures subordinate to Western Civilization were forced to take. Growth to maturity requires some such risk for every individual anyway. Benally, however, sometimes yearns rather sentimentally for the tribal way of life. We see this longing in his description of the night before Abel returns.

In-depth scholarly evaluation of *House Made of Dawn* has been slow in appearing. The complexity of the novel and the layers of possible interpretation may delay what will be a growing body of evaluative work. Hopefully, if studied for sociological or anthropological reasons, the book will not be dismissed without adequate attention to its literary value. So, too, if studied as literature, it should not be accepted as art only but also as a recreation of unique human experience....

[*House Made of Dawn*] is a complex, symbolic expression of how language and culture tend through their own territorial imperatives to encompass one, sometimes to a point of isolation. If one voluntarily or forcedly intermixes with another culture and its language, he may find that in the interim he has lost both cultures and must become reacculturated. *House Made of Dawn* transcends any Indian problem; that the novel is a universal statement does not make the effect of Momaday's portrayal of the deculturation of an Indian youth any the less lamentable. If man is the archetypal Adam, in the archetypal Eden, year by year, society by society, generation after generation—if he is the "house made of dawn," the regeneration comes about.

Source: Martha Scott Trimble, *N. Scott Momday,* Boise State College, 1973.

Marion Willard Hylton

In the following essay, Hylton presents a thematic analysis of House Made of Dawn, *relating "the tragic odyssey of a man forcibly removed from [the Native American] psychic environment and placed within a culture light-years away from the attitudes, values, and goals of his former life."*

Abel was the land and he was of the land; he was a long-hair and from that single fact stemmed the fearsome modern dilemma explored by N. Scott Momaday in *House Made of Dawn.* Abel is an Indian of the American Southwest, a member of a culture for whom Nature is the one great reality to which men's lives are pegged, the only verity upon

which men may rely. Within this massive concept lie all the religion, all the mores and ethics, all the spiritual truth any man may require. To shatter the concept is to shatter the man. Momaday describes the tragic odyssey of a man forcibly removed from this psychic environment and placed within a culture light-years away from the attitudes, values, and goals of his former life. His anguished ordeal, heightened by his encounter with a white woman, endows him at last with courage and wisdom; he comes to know who he is and what he must do to maintain that identity.

In the Indian view, the universe or Nature is a great cosmological unity characterized by a harmony and oneness of all living things. Religion is not a thing apart from life, it is life itself. Oral communication is minimal; words are not needed between people sharing a common culture whose limitations and capabilities are known to all. Abel growing up in this timeless tradition is endowed with an understanding that transcends the ordinary limits of the word: "the boy could sense his grandfather's age, just as he knew somehow that his mother was soon going to die of her illness. It was nothing he was told, but he knew it anyway and without understanding, as he knew already the motion of the sun and the seasons."

After four centuries of Christianity, the essential way of life is unchanged. The people still pray to the old deities in their own language. They have assumed the names and some of the habits of their enemies but have kept their own souls and their own secrets: "in this there is a resistance and an overcoming, a long outwaiting." Evil spirits as well as good are a part of the pantheon, and Momaday uses both in the unfolding of his remarkable novel. Slowly, by means of fragmentary glimpses into the lives of Abel, Ben, Francisco, and others, Momaday leads to an understanding not only of the Indian's dilemma in the modern world, but of Abel's particular torment and what brought it about.

Francisco, Abel's grandfather, has lived all his life on the reservation, within and a part of this culture. The important events of his life are totally alien to outsiders: the ritual killing of the bear to symbolize the coming of age, the marks of pollen made above the eyes of the bear, the arduous period of instruction preliminary to his participation in a sacred ceremony, and the healing powers he later acquires as a result of his growing "understanding." In many ways, Abel and his grandfather are much alike and only a very careful reading of some passages will make clear which of them is being referred to.

One is reminded that the diminutive of Abel, "Abelito", is much like "Abuelito", the affectionate term for grandfather. The resemblance is not accidental, of course; in a sense, his close attachment to his grandfather and the old ways is the burden Abel must struggle with during the course of the novel.

Abel is not a superficial human being. His suffering is profound and moving, as is the catharsis wrought by that suffering. In a striking passage describing the shoes Abel wears when he leaves the reservation, Momaday points up the differences in attitude: "they squeaked when he walked. In the only frame of reference he had ever known, they called attention to themselves, simply, honestly ... but now and beyond his former frame of reference, the shoes called attention to Abel. They were brown and white and they were conspicuously new and too large ... they shone; they clattered and creaked ... and they were nailed to his feet. There were enemies all around, and he knew that he was ridiculous in their eyes." Years later, after a stint in the army, he returns, reeling drunkenly from the steps of the noisy bus into the arms of his weeping grandfather: "everything in advance of his going—he could remember whole and in detail. It was the recent past, the intervention of days and years without meaning, of awful calm and collision, time always immediate and confused, that he could not put together in his mind." Fully twenty-four hours elapse before Abel begins to realize where he is, both geographically and culturally. Not until he walks out, just before dawn, to a high and distant hill where he sees the vast beauty of the valleys and remembers incidents from his youth, does a kind of peace come to him. But it does not last. Less than two weeks later, during the feast of Santiago, an evil spirit reveals himself to Abel, who, acting entirely within the Indian tradition, kills him.

The albino or, significantly, the white man, has been seen earlier as a figure of evil when Francisco heard whisperings from the corn and was afraid; after he left, the albino emerged or rather seemed to materialize from the green leaves. Since corn is life itself to the Indian, to hear an evil spirit breathing in the corn is a dangerous thing. A snake, or culebra, is likewise a symbol of evil, and when the albino threatens to turn into a snake, Abel's course is clear. Significantly, after his years in prison his attitude is unchanged. "They must know," Ben says, "that he would kill the white man again, if he had the chance ... for he would know what the white man was, and he would kill him if he could. A man kills such an enemy if he can."

> **His anguished ordeal, heightened by his encounter with a white woman, endows him at last with courage and wisdom; he comes to know who he is and what he must do to maintain that identity."**

Abel's real suffering and purgation begin after he leaves prison and wanders to Los Angeles. There he meets Ben, Milly, and Tosamah. Ben, like Abel, has been raised on the reservation but has managed to make an adjustment of sorts. Ben can compromise; he is willing to overlook evil or unkindness and is able to see good in most situations: "You know, you have to change. That's the only way you can live in a place like this. You have to forget about the way it was, how you grew up and all ... You wonder how you can get yourself into the swing of it, you know? ... And you want to do it, because you can see how good it is ... it's money and clothes and having plans and going someplace fast." Because Ben wants to be a part of it, he is willing to live on the fringe of white society, like a child outside a candy store window. When he speaks, one can clearly hear the voice of a lonely man: "this place is always cold and kind of empty when it rains," "you never have to be alone. You go downtown and there are a lot of people all around and they're having a good time." Ben has not yet admitted to himself that he is only an outsider; he feels the American Dream is his, too, and he is committed to pursuing it. "I could find someplace with a private bathroom if I wanted to, easy. A man with a good job can do just about anything he wants."

Tosamah (John Big Bluff Tosamah) is a very different sort of man. Like Ben he acknowledges his heritage but is not chained to it like Abel. "Priest of the Sun" is a key section for understanding the Indian concept of "The Word" as opposed to the Christian. Tosamah begins by stating in Latin, "In Principio erat Verbum." Caught up in the mystery of the words, he continues, "in the darkness ... the smallest seed of sound ... took hold of the darkness and there was light; it took hold out of the stillness and there was motion forever … it scarcely was; but it was and everything began." But at this point, his voice and attitude abruptly switch from that of a priest to that of a huckster, as he tells how this mystery was corrupted by a Christian interpretation: "But it was more than the Truth. The Truth was overgrown with fat; the fat was John's god and God stood between John and the Truth … and he said, 'In the Beginning was the Word …' and man, right then and there he should have stopped … Old John was a white man and the white man builds upon [the word], he adds and divides and multiplies the Word and in all of this he subtracts the Truth." Tosamah's bitterness can be heard in his parting words to his "parishoners": "Good night and get yours."

Tosamah, the Priest of the Sun, is as much an outsider in white society as Father Olguin is in Indian society. The dry, mechanical Mass which Father Olguin conducts contrasts interestingly with the peyote ritual at which Tosamah presides, where the mysticism each participant comes to feel is translated into a moving and spontaneous prayer without the embarrassment of spoken prayer; it is part of the old tradition. The tears of one of the participants are not despised, they are accepted; weeping is no disgrace if the occasion calls for weeping. The Mass has the bread, the wine, the incense, the bell; the peyote ritual has the peyote buttons, the prayer sticks, the "makings," and the drummer. The Indian's ritual marking is with pollen, and the priest's with ashes. Tosamah reverts to a caricature of American speech in explaining the impact of peyote: "that little old woolly booger turns you on like a light, man. Daddy peyote is the vegetal representation of the sun," recalling the transformation of the bread and wine into the body and blood of Christ.

Where the Indian view is at one with Nature, one might say the Catholic view, as typified by Father Olguin and Angela Grace St. John, exists in spite of Nature; the basic difference would seem to doom in advance any hope of accord. Reflecting the missionary zeal which is characteristic of his faith, Father Olguin tries over the years to enlarge his small flock and to urge his parishioners away from the old ways. In the end, he comes to recognize tacitly that some old and final cleavage still exists which he can never bridge. He tries, however, to make the legal authorities understand, as best he can, what prompted Abel to kill the albino. Once again we see the clash of the two cultures: "I believe that this man was moved to do what he did by an act of imagination so compelling as to be inconceivable to us…. Yes, yes, yes. But these are the facts: he killed a man—took the life of another human being…. Homicide is a legal term, but the law is not my context; and certainly it isn't his…. Murder is a moral term. Death is a universal human term."

Both the parole officer and the Relocation people attempt to keep Abel out of trouble, but his problems only deepen. "They have a lot of words," as Ben says, "and you know they mean something but you don't know what … Everything is different and you don't know how to get used to it." Ben understands Abel's plight, and is compassionate. Tosamah understands and is contemptuous.

Ben and Milly literally keep Abel alive in his darkest hours. Where he has understanding based on knowledge, she has understanding based on love. "She was a lot like Ben. She believed in Honor, Industry, the Second Chance, the Brotherhood of Man, the American Dream and him—Abel; she believed in him." She also loved him; she gave him money, a place to stay, and ministered to his needs out of love. On a few rare occasions, she could even make him laugh. But Milly is gentle and vulnerable. And Abel is possessed by an evil spirit. They are drawn together by their awful loneliness, but it is not enough. All her experience had been a getting away from the land where his had been a returning. At the height of his suffering, her name echoes through his mind; only her name, and a question mark. Sadly, the name is remembered, but not the identity.

Abel sinks ever deeper in the white world's web. One night, too drunk and helpless to answer Tosamah's taunts, he sets out to seek some kind of release, to kill the evil spirit, the culebra, that has brought about his misery. Instead of exorcising the evil, he undergoes a mortal combat (presumably at the hands of Martinze, the sadistic cop) that leaves him broken and near death. "He had lost his place. He had long ago been at the center, had known where he was, had lost his way, had wandered to the end of the earth, was even now reeling on the edge of the void … The sea reached and waned, licked after him and withdrew, falling off forever in the abyss."

Abel, badly beaten and lying on the beach, is unable to see because of his swollen eyes. We remember that Father Olguin's vision is also poor and that the albino masks his weak sight with small dark glasses. All, in one way or another, "see" with difficulty. The albino's vision is clouded by evil, Father Olguin's by his Christian beliefs, and Abel's by not accepting his birthright. If Abel's suffering suggests that of Oedipus, then we might say that the grunion form a chorus, and it is no mean comparison. Momaday's evocation of the grunion metaphor seems singularly appropriate for the situation. They, like Abel, belong to the natural order of things; they respond from the tradition of centuries, only to fall victim to the wanton ways of the white man. Abel, too, has been beaten by an evil spirit of the white world and must somehow get back to his own environment in order to survive. "His body was mangled and racked with pain. His body, like his mind, had turned on him; it was his enemy." He has tried to do what seemed to him must be done: extirpate evil. But he has failed; in the white man's world, right and wrong are not the same, and the old values somehow do not apply. He remembers seeing, in his youth, the old men running after evil. Here, it is not the same. He knows at last that he must survive beyond his pain, and return to the life he understands.

Abel has indeed, "lost his place." A reason for his particular suffering lies in the ancient Indian belief that all secrets, even those of sorcery and evil, are divulged during sexual intercourse. Abel had lain with a woman, Angela Grace St. John, and both were altered by the experience.

When Angela comes to live at Los Ojos (The Eyes), she is a distant, disturbed woman. Her attitudes are as far as possible from the Indian's. She keeps herself coldly apart from human contact and "would have her bath and read from the lives of the saints." She despises her body and the child growing within her: "She could think of nothing more vile and obscene than the raw flesh and blood of her body, the ravelled veins and gore upon her bones. And now the monstrous fetal form, the blue, blind, great headed thing growing within and feeding upon her ... at odd moments she wished with all her heart to die by fire, fire of such intense heat that her body should dissolve in it all at once." To the suggestion of disharmony is added the hint of evil: Abel would not bargain, hence, "it remained for her to bring about a vengeance."

Their coming together is an epiphany for each of them; she draws from him a kind of vision she has never experienced before, a "knowingness" of who she is, and of her relationship to other living things and to life itself. But the evil spirit which has hitherto clouded her days now descends upon him. "Angela put her white hands to his body. Abel put his hands to her white body."

Father Olguin is the first to sense the change in her. He has seen her as an ally with whom he can share his world of words; a fellow outsider in the Indian world. But "she listened through him to the sound of thunder and of rain that fell upon the mountains miles away, ... she had a craving for the rain ... 'Oh, my God' she said, laughing, 'I am heartily sorry ... for having offended Thee.'" Her laughter horrifies him almost as much as her confession.

When the sky darkens and the storm breaks, Angela no longer fears nor shrinks from Nature: she "stood transfixed in the open door and breathed deep into her lungs the purest electric scent of the air. She closed her eyes, and the clear aftervision of the rain, which she could still hear and feel so perfectly as to conceive of nothing else, obliterated all the mean and myriad fears that had laid hold of her in the past." From that moment on, evil stalks Abel's steps; the disharmony and alienation that had characterized Angela's life now infects his.

Not until years later, when she visits Abel in the hospital and, in effect, releases him, does the evil finally begin to ebb. As she speaks of her son, Peter, and the Indian tales he loves to hear, Ben remembers the stories told by his grandfather who spoke from the legends of his heritage. Abel understands; he does not speak, nor refer to her visit afterwards. Hearing Angela and seeing how she has changed has at last made clear to him just how and why he has lost his way.

House Made of Dawn is an intricately structured novel, and difficult to analyze. Time, for the Indian, is conceived not as a rigidly divided set of days, months, and years, but as experience and wisdom and knowledge, occurring today or yesterday or many yesterdays ago. Memory is the only immortality. Through memory history is transmitted from generation to generation. Memory, too, presents the novel; events from Francisco's past, or from Abel's, Ben's, or Tosamah's, are juxtaposed with events of the present moment, giving the reader a dimensional montage of thought and attitude.

Few of us suffer from our pasts as Abel must suffer. The Abel who comes back to the reservation to tend his dying grandfather is broken in body but healed in spirit. Wordlessly, he attends the last hours until death, then dresses the body according to the ancient ways. Summoned at night, the priest, significantly, is indignant over the time: "Good Heavens, couldn't you have waited until—Do you know what time it is?" By then, Abel indeed knows what time it is as far as his life is concerned, and he knows, too, that the particular hour of the day or night is of no consequence. Father Olguin, for all his good intentions, understands the Indian no better than his late nineteenth-century predecessor, Fray Nicholas, who, we learn from the old journal, was called on a similar occasion only after the Indian rites had been performed on a body.

After a long and bitter odyssey and much suffering, Abel has come home. He knows at last where he belongs in the scheme of things. During the long vigil before Francisco's death, he begins once again to feel a peace and a kinship with his heritage: "it was the room in which he was born, in which his mother and his brother died. Just then, and for moments and hours and days, he had no memory of being outside of it." When Abel leaves the mission, rubs himself with ashes, and goes on to join the other dawn runners, he is not only assuming his role as male survivor of his family, but also completing the final phase of his own spiritual healing. As he runs, as he becomes a part of the orderly continuum of interrelated events that constitute the Indian universe, Abel is the land, and he is of the land once more.

Source: Marion Willard Hylton, "On a Trail of Pollen: Momaday's House Made of Dawn," in *Critique,* Vol. XIV, No. 2, 1972, pp. 60–69.

Sources

Bennett, John Z., review, in *Western American Literature,* Volume V, Number 1, Spring, 1970, p. 69.

Meredith, Howard, "N. Scott Momaday: A Man of Words," in *World Literature Today,* Vol. 64, No. 3, Summer, 1990, pp. 405-07.

Schubnell, Matthias, "The Identity of Crisis: *House Made of Dawn,*" in *N. Scott Momaday: The Cultural and Literary Background,* University of Oklahoma Press, 1985, pp. 109-39.

Smith, William James, review, in *Commonweal,* Vol. LXXXVII, September 20, 1968.

Sprague, Marshall, "Anglos and Indians," in *The New York Times Book Review,* June 9, 1968.

Willard Hylton, Marion, "On a Trail of Pollen: Momaday's *House Made of Dawn,*" in *Critique,* Vol. XIV, No. 2, 1972.

For Further Study

Mayhill, Mildred, *The Kiowas,* University of Oklahoma Press, 1962.
    Mayhill presents a well-documented sociological account of the Kiowa people.

Nelson, Robert M., *The Function of Landscape in Native American Fiction,* Lang Publishers, 1993.
    Examines works by Momaday, Silko, and Welch.

Nelson Waniek, Marilyn, "The Power of Language in N. Scott Momaday's *House Made of Dawn,*" in *Minority Voices,* Vol. 4, No. 1, 1980, pp. 23-8.
    Addresses the importance of language in the novel.

Scarberry-Garcia, Susan, *Landmarks of Healing: A Study of House Made of Dawn,* University of New Mexico Press, 1990.
    A rare book-length consideration of the novel that touches upon all of the varied theories, offering an excellent overview of critical opinion.

Sharma, R. S., "Vision and Form in N. Scott Momaday's *House Made of Dawn,*" in *Indian Journal of American Studies,* Vol. 12, No. 1, January 1982, pp. 69-79.
    Discusses the roles of vision and narrative form in the novel.

Zachrau, Thekla, "N. Scott Momaday: Towards an Indian Identity," in *American Indian Culture and Research Journal,* Vol. 3, No. 1, 1979, pp. 39-56.
    An overview of Momaday's career, including his attempts to use varied storytelling techniques to bring the Kiowa vision of reality to a broader public.

Howards End

E. M. Forster
1910

When *Howards End* was published in 1910, critics generally agreed it surpassed E. M. Forster's earlier novels. Forster had arrived as an important author, and the public and critics eagerly anticipated his next novel. But fourteen years would elapse before the publication of *A Passage to India,* which would also be the last novel published during his lifetime. Forster's novels are all considered classics, with *Howards End* and *A Passage to India* regarded as his best works. Like all of Forster's early novels, *Howards End* concerns itself with Edwardian society. As a member of the upper-middle class, Forster had keen insight into its attitudes and social mores, which he expertly rendered in *Howards End.* His humanistic values and interest in personal relationships inform all of his novels, and are revealed in the major themes of *Howards End:* connection between the inner and outer life and between people, the future of England, and class conflicts. *Howards End* has been called a parable; indeed, its symbolism reaches almost mythic proportions at various points in the novel. Although elements of the plot construction have been problematic for some critics, opinion of his character creation and development is almost unanimously given the highest praise. With Margaret Schlegel, Henry Wilcox, Helen Schlegel, Leonard Bast, and Forster created some of the most unforgettable and complex characters in English literature.

E. M. Forster

Author Biography

Edward Morgan Forster was born on January 1, 1879, in Coventry, England. His father died when he was only a year and a half old, leaving him to the care of his mother and a devoted circle of female relatives. He and his mother lived at Rooksnest, their beloved country house near Stevenage in Hertfordshire. After a rather unhappy adolescence as a student at Tonbridge School, Forster enrolled at Cambridge University, where he flourished.

At Cambridge the emphasis was on liberal arts and individual expression; Forster found freedom to pursue both intellectual development and personal relationships. It was here that he began developing many of the humanistic ideas and values that would come to dominate his literary works. He became a member of the Cambridge Apostles, an intellectual discussion group. Many Apostles were later active in the Bloomsbury Group, which began informal salons in London about 1905. Several in the Bloomsbury circle later became famous: Lytton Strachey as a critic, biographer, and historian; Leonard Woolf as political activist and theorist and man of letters; John Maynard Keynes as a political and economic theorist; Roger Fry and Clive Bell as art critics; Grant and Vanessa Bell as painters;

and Virginia Woolf and Forster as novelists. The Bloomsbury Group was influenced by Cambridge philosophers, especially G. E. Moore, who believed in the value of social interaction and cultural stimuli, and possessed a passion for the truth and a skepticism toward moral tradition.

After Forster graduated from Cambridge in 1901, he traveled abroad for a year. Between 1902 and 1910, he wrote four novels: *Where Angels Fear To Tread* (1905), *A Room with a View* (1908), *The Longest Journey* (1907), and *Howards End* (1910). With *Howards End,* Forster achieved status as a major writer, receiving high critical praise. Forster's novels were recognized for their precise character portrayal, their concern with the complexities of human nature, and their detailed, comical descriptions of Edwardian society. His next novel, *A Passage to India,* did not appear until 1924, and was the last novel published during his lifetime. A posthumously published novel, *Maurice,* tells the story of a young man's growing awareness of his homosexuality and is based on Forster's own experiences. The publication of *A Passage to India* firmly established Forster's reputation as a master novelist. Drawn from Forster's experiences in India during visits there in 1912 and 1921, *A Passage to India* portrays the social and political realities of colonial India.

For the rest of his career, Forster focused on writing short stories, essays, biographies, and travel books. He also became quite politically active, and wrote essays in which he spoke out against many of the political and social ills of his time. In the mid-1940s he was offered a resident fellowship at Cambridge University, which he enthusiastically accepted. He became one of the most celebrated figures at the university, and remained active in university life and continued to write and publish well into the early 1960s. He died on June 7, 1970, in Coventry at the home of friends.

Plot Summary

Howards End begins with Helen Schlegel's brief affair with Paul Wilcox. In its wake, Helen's Aunt Juley travels to Howards End, the Wilcox home, to discuss the relationship with the Wilcoxes, not knowing that it has already ended. The Wilcoxes react with horror to news of the affair, believing, unlike the Schlegels, that Paul must make his fortune before he marries.

Helen, her romance with Paul and the rest of the Wilcox family over, returns to the Schlegel house, Wickham Place, and she and her sister Margaret resume their old life together. They attend a concert of Beethoven with other family members, and Helen accidentally walks off with the umbrella of Leonard Bast, a poor clerk teetering on the edge of respectability. After accompanying Margaret to Wickham Place to retrieve his umbrella, Leonard accepts her card, and returns to his own shabby flat, where he lives with Jacky, a woman much older than he.

The Schlegels learn that the Wilcoxes are taking a flat across the street from Wickham Place, and Ruth Wilcox soon calls on Margaret. Margaret writes a rude note suggesting that they should not meet because of the possibility of an encounter between Helen and Paul, and Mrs. Wilcox replies to her that they should meet, because there is no possibility of an encounter between the two former lovers. The two women strike up a friendship, in spite of Mrs. Wilcox's discomfort in Margaret's world. Mrs. Wilcox feels that Margaret understands her attachment to Howards End, and after a day of shopping together, she impulsively proposes they go there. Margaret wavers at first, but they leave for the train station, where they meet Henry and Evie Wilcox, Mrs. Wilcox's husband and daughter. Mrs. Wilcox is spirited off by her family, and Margaret's visit is postponed. Soon after, Mrs. Wilcox dies.

The Wilcoxes are alarmed to discover that Mrs. Wilcox has left a note leaving Howards End to Margaret. They decide to burn the note, and not speak of it to Margaret.

Two years pass. The Schlegels are about to lose their house at Wickham Place, which will be destroyed so that flats may be built there. Leonard Bast's wife, Jacky, comes round to the house looking for him. Leonard has disappeared for an evening, and Jacky thinks he is with the Schlegels. The next day, Bast appears at Wickham Place, explaining that he has taken an all-night walk outside of London. When he notes that the dawn was gray and not at all romantic, the Schlegels are charmed by him. When they mention Bast to Henry Wilcox, he tells them Bast's company is in danger of going under, and they resolve to warn Bast of this eventuality. They invite Bast to tea, and he is suspicious of their desire to talk business when he wants to talk poetry. The tea is interrupted when Evie and Henry Wilcox arrive at the house, and as Bast is leaving, he tells the Schlegels he will not call again.

Mr. Wilcox thinks that Margaret is attracted to Leonard Bast, and feels an attraction for her as a result. Soon after, at a lunch with Evie, Mr. Wilcox offers to lease the Wilcoxes' Ducie Street flat to the Schlegels. While Margaret tours the flat, Mr. Wilcox asks her to marry him, and she accepts.

Margaret wants to live at Howards End, but her fiancé is against it. Meanwhile, Helen has had a letter from Leonard Bast, who is leaving his company for another post at lower pay. When Margaret mentions this to Henry, he says that in fact Bast's company is a very stable firm. Though the Schlegels blame Henry for Bast's predicament, he shrugs off their criticism.

Margaret and Henry make a trip to Howards End, where she is frightened by Miss Avery, who mistakes her for Ruth Wilcox. Margaret loves the house, but believes that she and Henry will live at Oniton, where they attend Evie's wedding to Percy Cahill. Helen, who has refused to attend the wedding, arrives there unexpectedly with Leonard and Jacky Bast, saying that she has found them starving. Margaret is planning to ask Henry to give Bast a place in his company, but before she can do so, Jacky recognizes Henry as her former lover. Helen takes the Basts to a hotel, where she and Leonard have an intimate conversation. Margaret, who believes Henry's unfaithfulness is the late Mrs. Wilcox's tragedy rather than hers, refuses Henry's offer to release her from their engagement, and they reconcile. Before Margaret can speak with any of them, Helen and the Basts leave their hotel.

Before she goes to Germany, Helen attempts to give the Basts a substantial monetary gift, but they refuse. They are soon evicted and forced to rely on handouts from Leonard's family. Wickham Place is destroyed to make way for flats, and Margaret and Henry marry. With the family scattered, the Schlegels' furniture is stored at Howards End. When Margaret hears that Miss Avery has unpacked the Schlegels' things, she goes to Howards End. She is amazed to see how well her furniture fits in the house, but is soon called away to Swanage when she gets news of her aunt's illness. Margaret and her brother Tibby contact Helen, who has been in Germany for eight months, to tell her Juley is gravely ill, and Helen agrees to come to Swanage. When Helen hears that Juley has recovered, she refuses to see her family, but will get some books from Howards End. Believing her sister to be unwell, Margaret reluctantly agrees to Henry's plan to surprise Helen at Howards End.

As the plan is carried out, Margaret realizes that "[t]he pack was turning on Helen, to deny her human rights," and it seems to Margaret "that all Schlegels were threatened with her." When she sees her sister, who is pregnant with Leonard Bast's child, she pushes her into Howards End, and bids her husband and the doctor to leave them. Helen, on seeing their furniture and other things, asks to spend the night in Howards End. When Margaret asks Henry if they may stay at Howards End, he refuses on the grounds that it would be immoral. Margaret is disgusted by his hypocrisy and she defies his wishes, spending a peaceful night at Howards End with her sister.

Leonard Bast has been looking for Margaret, and Tibby tells him she is at Howards End. As Leonard approaches the house, he is filled with happiness, but when he enters the house, Charles strikes him, and he dies. In the wake of Bast's death and her own quarrel with him, Margaret tells Henry she will go to Germany with Helen. But Henry is broken by the certainty of Charles's conviction for manslaughter, and Margaret takes him to recover at Howards End. In the final scene of the novel, fourteen months have passed, and Helen, her child by Leonard Bast, Margaret, and Henry have become a loving family. In the presence of his children, Henry deeds Howards End to Margaret, who will leave it to her sister's son. When Dolly remarks that Margaret has gotten Howards End after all, Margaret realizes that she has conquered the Wilcoxes without even trying.

Characters

Miss Avery

Miss Avery is Ruth Wilcox's old friend and the caretaker of Howards End. She unpacks and arranges the Schlegels' furniture in Howards End, even though it is only supposed to be stored there.

Jacky Bast

Jacky is Leonard's dull, uneducated wife who was once Henry Wilcox's mistress.

Leonard Bast

Leonard is the lowly clerk who wishes to educate himself by reading books and attending concerts. "Such a muddle of a man, and yet so worth pulling though," says Helen Schlegel. He is described as being on the "abyss" of poverty, and is very self-conscious about his position in society.

Suspicious of the rich, he will not be patronized by them, which is part of the reason he refuses Helen's offer of money. His two unfortunate mistakes are leaving his job on the advice of the Schlegel sisters (and Henry Wilcox), and becoming involved with Helen. The scene in which he dies, which includes a dramatic fall into a bookcase that showers him with books, has been criticized for its heavy-handed symbolism.

Frieda Mosebach

Frieda Mosebach is the Schlegels' German cousin, who attends the performance of Beethoven's Fifth Symphony with them.

Juley Munt

Juley Munt is the Schlegels' beloved but interfering aunt, whose famously comic scene in the novel occurs when she travels to Howards End for the purpose of convincing Helen to break off her engagement to Paul Wilcox.

Helen Schlegel

The charming sister of Margaret, Helen is high-spirited and hopelessly idealistic. Beethoven's Fifth Symphony affects her most profoundly, and reveals an interesting theme in the novel. She hears a "goblin footfall" in the music, which she imagines to represent the "panic and emptiness" of life, but she also hears a repetitive motif that she imagines as the heroism, magnificence, and triumph of life. These two aspects of life intrinsically bound together echo the highs and lows of Helen's own experiences. Her short-lived love affair with Paul at the beginning of the novel is indicative of her behavior throughout—heady excitement followed by disillusionment. Ruled by passion, she seldom considers the reality of a situation until it is too late. At first she is quite taken with all of the Wilcoxes, but the ill-fated love affair with Paul colors her feelings afterwards, and she is disappointed when Margaret and Henry Wilcox announce their engagement. Her liaison with Leonard Bast is the result of her sympathy for him and her anger at Henry, who will not help Leonard. Her anger at Henry also occasions a break with Margaret. Helen eventually reconciles with Margaret and Henry, who accept her and her illegitimate child (from Leonard Bast) at Howards End.

Margaret Schlegel

Margaret is the cultured, intelligent, and sympathetic protagonist of the novel. Although idealistic like her sister Helen, she is also very sensible and realistic. "Not beautiful, not supremely brilliant, but filled with something that took the place of both qualities—something best described as a profound vivacity, a continual and sincere response to all that she encountered in her path through life" is Forster's description of her. Some critics have found it hard to believe that Margaret would marry Henry Wilcox, a man most definitely her opposite. But Margaret sees things "whole," and although aware of Henry's faults, she also recognizes noble qualities in him. By the end of the novel, Margaret has had some effect on him. While it could be said that Helen reaches out to help Leonard, Margaret does the same for Henry. Indeed, Margaret is the connecting force between the Schlegels and the Wilcoxes; by the end of the novel, Henry seems less "muddled" and Helen seems less impulsive. But this does not occur until after Margaret nearly leaves Henry because of his refusal to allow Helen to stay the night at Howards End with her. In her famous speech to him, she implores him to connect his infidelity with Helen's transgression: "You shall see the connection if it kills you, Henry! You have had a mistress—I forgave you. My sister has a lover—you drive her from the house. Do you see the connection? Stupid, hypocritical, cruel—oh, contemptible!—a man who insults his wife when she's alive and cants with her memory when she's dead. A man who ruins a woman for his pleasure, and casts her off to ruin other men. And gives bad financial advice, and then says he is not responsible. These, man, are you. You cannot recognize them, because you cannot connect."

Tibby Schlegel

Tibby is Margaret and Helen's younger brother, the Oxford undergraduate. Although intellectual like his sisters, he is not interested in personal relationships as they are. His placid demeanor plays comically against their more passionate personalities, and is particularly evident in the scene where Helen visits him at Oxford to let him know of her plans to go to Germany.

Charles Wilcox

Charles is the philistine elder son of Henry Wilcox. Not especially fond of the Schlegels and their "artistic beastliness," he ridiculously suspects Margaret of scheming to get Howards End. His fierce sense of class superiority leads him to beat Leonard when he finds out that he is the father of Helen's child. Charles is convicted of manslaughter for Leonard's death.

Media Adaptations

- *Howards End* was adapted for the stage by Lance Sieveking and Richard Cottrell and was produced in London in 1967.

- The BBC production of *Howards End,* adapted by Pauline Macaulay, was broadcast in 1970.

- A film adaptation of *Howards End* was released by Merchant Ivory Production in 1992, starring Emma Thompson and Anthony Hopkins. The film garnered nine Academy Award nominations, winning for Best Actress (for Thompson), Best Screenplay Adaptation, and Best Art Direction. It is available from Columbia TriStar Home Video.

Dolly Fussel Wilcox

Dolly is the chattering, good-hearted wife of Charles Wilcox. Like her husband, she foolishly believes Margaret is scheming to get Howards End.

Evie Wilcox

Evie, the daughter of Henry Wilcox, is a rather silly, superficial woman. Although she dislikes Margaret, she humors her father's interest in Margaret.

Henry Wilcox

Henry is the head of the Wilcox clan, who marries Margaret Schlegel after the death of his wife, Ruth. Critic Rose Macaulay describes him this way: "He has the business mind; he is efficient, competent, unimaginative, practically clear-headed, intellectually and spiritually muddled, uncivilized, a manly man, with firm theories about women, politics, the Empire, the social fabric." He is not given to self-introspection, a trait that almost costs him his marriage to Margaret. She insists that he acknowledge the connection between his affair with Jacky Bast and Helen's involvement with Leonard Bast. But his flaw is that he lacks the ability to connect his actions with the pain they might cause in another person's life, thus his indifference to

Leonard's loss of employment. Furthermore, he cannot relate his own transgressions in life to another person's similar transgressions; therefore, he cannot sympathize with Helen. He cannot "connect the prose with the passion." By the end of the novel, Henry is broken by the imprisonment of his son, Charles, which forces him to reevaluate his life.

Paul Wilcox

Paul is the younger Wilcox son with whom Helen briefly falls in love. The incident sets the tone for conflict between the Wilcoxes and the Schlegels.

Ruth Wilcox

Henry's first wife, Ruth, is a kind, unselfish woman whose family adores her. However, she completely mystifies her family after she bequeaths Howards End to Margaret. She does so because she intuitively senses that Margaret will appreciate its "personality" and significance. The critic Lionel Trilling has written that Howards End represents England and its agrarian past, and that Ruth, while not intellectual, possesses ancestral wisdom that will be passed on to Margaret. Ruth is almost like a spiritual guide, or as critic Rose Macaulay states, a bridge between the unseen and the seen, and Margaret believes herself and the others "are only fragments of that woman's mind."

Themes

Connection

The major theme of *Howards End* is connection—connection between the private and the public life, connection between individuals—and how difficult it is to create and sustain these connections. *Howards End* focuses mainly on two families: the Schlegels, who represent intellectualism, imagination, and idealism—the inner life of the mind—and the Wilcoxes, who represent English practicality, expansionism, commercialism, and the external world of business and politics. For the Schlegels, personal relationships precede public ones and the individual is more important than any organization. For the Wilcoxes, the reverse is true; social formalities and the rules of the business world reign supreme.

Through the marriage of Margaret Schlegel and Henry Wilcox, these two very different worlds are connected. Margaret, unlike her wildly idealistic sister Helen, moves toward an understanding of the Wilcoxes. Helen's initial encounter with the Wilcoxes proves disastrous, but Margaret begins to realize that many of the things she values, such as art and culture, would not exist without the economic and social stability created by people such as the Wilcoxes. "More and more," she says, "do I refuse to draw my income and sneer at those who guarantee it."

Margaret and Henry's marriage nearly comes to an end, however, when Henry is unable to make an important connection between his sexual transgression with Jacky Bast and Helen's liaison with Leonard Bast. Margaret and Helen want to spend the night together at Howards End before Helen returns to Germany to have her baby. But the hypocritical Henry cannot tolerate the presence of a "fallen woman" on his property, and refuses to allow Margaret and Helen to remain there for the night. As the critic Malcolm Bradbury has written, Margaret insists on the "primacy of the standard of personal sympathy" while Henry emphasizes "the standard of social propriety." Margaret and Helen defy Henry by staying the night at Howards End, where they reestablish their relationship. By the novel's end, events force Henry to reconsider his values. He is reconciled to Helen, and along with Margaret and Helen's illegitimate son, they live together at Howards End under Margaret's guardianship.

Class Conflict

Another important theme in *Howards End* concerns struggle and conflict within the middle class. The aristocracy and the very poor do not make an appearance in this novel; the novelist states that "[w]e are not concerned with the very poor," but instead with the "gentlefolk, or with those who are obliged to pretend that they are gentlefolk." The three families in *Howards End* each represent different levels of the middle class. The Schlegels occupy the middle position, somewhere between the Basts, who exist at the lower fringes of the middle class, and the Wilcoxes, who belong to the upper-middle class. Leonard Bast, the clerk, lives near the "abyss" of poverty, while the Schlegels live comfortably on family money, and Henry Wilcox, the wealthy business man who grows steadily richer, has money for "motors" and country houses.

Leonard Bast is somewhat obsessed by class differences, and tries to improve himself by becoming "cultured." He reads books such as Ruskin's *Stones of Venice* and attends concerts. He meets the Schlegel sisters at a concert performance of Beethoven's Fifth Symphony, and becomes interested in them mainly because they seem to take his intellectual aspirations seriously. The Schlegels are fascinated by Leonard and his situation, but Leonard's connection to the Schlegels ultimately proves fatal. When Margaret and Helen hear from Mr. Wilcox that the company Leonard works for is about to go bankrupt, they advise him to find another position. The information proves to be unsound, but Leonard follows it, taking and then losing another position. As a result, he and his wife Jacky are left nearly penniless. In the scene where Leonard, Jacky, and Helen storm into Evie's opulent wedding, Forster illustrates the huge social and economic gulf between the nearly destitute Basts and the wealthy Wilcoxes. This scene, as the critic Frederick P. W. McDowell has noted, "suggests that the impersonal forces by which the Wilcoxes prosper have operated at the expense of Leonard and his class."

Leonard is destroyed by a combination of the Wilcox's indifference and Helen's sympathy. Helen tries to convince Henry that he has a responsibility to help Leonard, because his advice essentially caused Leonard's ruin. When that proves futile, Helen's sympathy for Leonard overwhelms her and she sleeps with him. Upon discovering that Leonard is Helen's "lover," the brutish Charles Wilcox beats Leonard with the flat of the Schlegel family sword. Leonard dies not from the beating, but from a weak heart. He sinks to the floor, knocks over a bookcase and is buried in an avalanche of books, seemingly a victim of his own desire for self-improvement.

Future of England

Closely related to the themes of connection and class conflict in *Howards End* is the theme of inheritance. The novel concerns itself with the question of who shall inherit England. At the time *Howards End* was published, England was undergoing great social change. The issue of women's emancipation, commercial and imperial expansion, and the possibility of war with Germany were all factors that contributed to a general feeling of uncertainty about the future of England.

According to the critic Lionel Trilling, Howards End itself symbolizes England. It belongs to Ruth Wilcox, who descends from the yeoman class, and represents England's past. Before Ruth dies, she befriends Margaret Schlegel, and on her deathbed she scribbles a note leaving Howards End to Margaret. She cannot leave it to her family because the only feeling they have for it is one of ownership; they do not understand its spiritual im-

Topics for Further Study

- Research the career of the famous German composer, Ludwig van Beethoven, focusing especially on his composition of the Fifth Symphony.

- Trace the evolution of the British Empire from 1910 to the Commonwealth of Nations today. What are some key differences between imperialist Britain of the Victorian and Edwardian eras and Britain now?

- What were the forces that led to WWI, and what was Britain's involvement?

- Analyze the history of the class structure in Britain. What were some of the political, social, and economic issues facing the proletariat class and the middle class in 1910? Can you relate them to Forster's depiction of Leonard and Jacky Bast?

portance as she knows Margaret will. The Wilcoxes dismiss Ruth's note as impossible, and disregard it completely, ignoring the rightful heir. But Margaret's connection with Ruth Wilcox in the novel is strong. Not only is she Ruth's spiritual heir, but she actually becomes Mrs. Wilcox and, ironically, inherits Howards End through her marriage to Henry.

Foster's answer to the question of who shall inherit England seems to suggest a shared inheritance. As the novel draws to a close, the intellectual Schlegels and the practical Wilcoxes are residing together at Howards End, and its immediate heir, Helen's illegitimate son, seems to symbolize a classless future.

Style

Setting

The various locales represented in *Howards End* are related to the theme of inheritance and which of England's landscapes—countryside, city, or suburbs—will claim the future. During the Edwardian era, a great migration from the countryside to the city transpired, mainly because England was shifting from an agrarian nation to an industrialized nation. London, in particular, was growing at an alarming rate, and a great deal of rebuilding and restructuring of the city occurred. New modes of transportation, such as the automobile, tramcars, autobuses, and the subway, allowed people more mobility than ever before. Urban and suburban development, or "sprawl," followed the subway and tramway lines. The novel is wary of this type of progress and movement, preferring the stability of the country life and homes like Howards End versus the impersonal, chaotic world of London.

The three families in *Howards End* occupy three different locales: the Schlegels live in London, the Wilcoxes split their time between homes in London and the countryside (easily facilitated by their "motor"), and the Basts live in suburbia. A great deal of movement occurs between country and city, and moving house is a major activity in the novel. For Ruth Wilcox, nothing is worse than being separated from your home. When she hears that the Schlegels' lease on Wickham Place will expire and they will be forced to move, she is greatly distressed. "To be parted from your house, your father's house—it oughtn't to be allowed.... Can what they call civilization be right, if people mayn't die in the room where they were born?" she says to Margaret.

Symbolism

Howards End is a highly symbolic novel; many critics have described it as parable with archetypal or mythic characters. The Wilcoxes symbolize the practical, materialistic, enterprising sort of people who have contributed to England's prosperity and strengthened the empire. The Schlegels symbolize the intellectual and artistic types who possess humanistic values and recognize the importance of the spirit. Margaret and Henry's marriage demonstrates the relationship between these two personalities, emphasizing a balance between the two.

Of all the Wilcoxes, Ruth is the only one who does not fit the Wilcox "mold." She is withdrawn from modern life, intuitive, spiritual, and not at all intellectual, but as Lionel Trilling states, representative of traditional values and ancestral knowledge. Along with Miss Avery, the caretaker of Howards End, Ruth Wilcox symbolizes the importance of the human connection to nature and the earth. The wych elm tree with the pig's teeth, the

vine, and the hayfield at Howards End also emphasize this connection. The movement of the seasons and the rhythms of nature are contrasted to the senseless movement of the modern, industrialized city, symbolized by the motorcar. The motorcar is never portrayed in a very attractive light: chaos and confusion seem to follow it everywhere, as in the scene where Charles hits the cat.

Other important symbols include the Schlegel books and bookcase and family sword at Howards End, which play so significantly in Leonard's death. When Leonard falls from Charles's blow with the sword and literally buries himself in books, it appears that the culture and intellectual sophistication he so desperately sought become his ruin. It is noteworthy that the sword and books belong to the Schlegels, however. Ostensibly, it seems that Leonard dies at the hand of the Wilcoxes—Henry, by giving him bad advice, and Charles, by actually dealing the final blow with the sword. But if Helen had not been overwhelmed by her sense of injustice, her anger toward the Wilcoxes, and her pity for Leonard, he would at least still have his life. The novel's bitter irony is that the person who tried to help Leonard the most effectively destroyed him.

Humor

Forster received high praise for his use of humor. Many situations in the novel are quite satirical or ironic. One of the earliest comic scenes in the novel involves Aunt Juley's trip to Howards End on Helen's behalf. When Aunt Juley mistakes Charles for Paul, the comedy begins. The discovery of the error only leads to an argument over Helen's behavior, which progresses to an argument over which family is better, the Schlegels or the Wilcoxes. The silly argument betrays the well-mannered facade of two supposedly well-bred gentlefolk. It also foreshadows the more serious conflict that will arise between the two families.

Another humorous scene involves Margaret trying to engage Tibby in a discussion about his future. She wants Tibby to think seriously of taking up a profession after he graduates. Of course, her reasons have nothing to do with the need for money. Rather, she believes it would build character. When she mentions a man's desire to work, Tibby replies, "I have no experience of this profound desire to which you allude." The aesthetic Tibby has no reason to consider a profession because he is financially secure. One of his satirical comments is that he prefers "civilization without activity."

Another semi-comic scene is the Wilcox family meeting concerning Ruth's bequest of Howards End. The Wilcoxes operate the meeting in an impersonal, business-like manner that reflects their style. Their mistrust of personal relations leads Charles to suggest that perhaps Margaret manipulated his mother into leaving her Howards End. Dolly irrationally fears that Margaret, as they speak, may be on her way to turn them all out of the house. The scene illustrates how suspicious and ill-mannered the Wilcoxes can be, and how they always suppose people are trying to get something out of them.

Historical Context

The Influence of King Edward VII

The Edwardian Era is so named after King Edward VII of England. Although King Edward's reign spanned only nine years, from 1901-1910, many historians extend the period to the start of the First World War in 1914. King Edward's personality had a major influence on the attitude of the day; his hedonism characterized the era. He loved ceremonial and state occasions and enjoyed extravagant entertaining; in fact, one of his first undertakings as king was to redecorate the Royal Palaces. An avid sportsman, King Edward particularly enjoyed horse racing, hunting, and "motoring." Motoring, essentially viewed as a sport in the early years of Edward's reign, quickly became an indispensable part of everyday life. In *Howards End,* the Wilcoxes rely quite heavily on their motor.

The king surrounded himself with wealthy people, befriending those who had made their fortunes in new ventures like the railway and steamship industry, and the South African diamond mines. They conducted themselves in a crude, ostentatious manner, which the king enthusiastically embraced. King Edward was also a notorious womanizer, and his wife, Queen Alexandra, eventually resigned herself to his numerous affairs. Such behavior did not endear him to the old nobility, and inevitably King Edward's rakish ways came to symbolize a certain reaction against the primness of Victorian sensibilities. The pursuit of pleasurable diversions were the hallmark of the period, with outings to musical halls, theaters, sporting events and weekend parties in the country considered fashionable. In *Howards End,* Evie's weekend wedding at Onitron represents the Edwardian flair for lavish entertaining.

Despite his flamboyant social life, King Edward took an active part in important political issues. Well-traveled and fluent in several languages, the king participated in international affairs and helped establish better relations with France. The alliance with France became crucial as England felt increasingly challenged by the German economy in world markets. The threat of German dominance in Europe seemed real as Germany built up its navy and formed alliances with Austria-Hungary and Italy. The battle lines were being drawn for World War I, and an uneasy atmosphere pervaded all of Europe.

On the domestic front, one issue that captured the king's attention was the acute, widespread poverty in England. High unemployment plagued the urban areas, and welfare did not yet exist. Only a relatively small percentage of the population could live the opulent, glamorous lifestyle made fashionable by the king and his friends. The gap between the rich and the poor grew rapidly during this time; the rich were getting richer by investing in various moneymaking schemes in overseas markets throughout the Empire. Many people were troubled by the fact that poverty should be so common during a time of unprecedented prosperity. King Edward drew public attention to the issue by personally visiting some of the worst slums in London and reporting his experience to the House of Lords. He became a dedicated member of the Royal Commissions, whose task it was to alleviate the problems of the poor, and he supported the idea of state aid for the aged poor, which later became one of the first forms of welfare.

Social Change during the Edwardian Era

The Edwardian Era was a time of great social and political change. Industrialization, which had begun in the nineteenth century, forced many people to leave their farms for employment in the cities. By 1910, the majority of the population lived in urban areas. London, particularly, was expanding rapidly, and urban sprawl became a problem. The new tramway system and "tube train," which partly alleviated traffic congestion in downtown London, facilitated the growth of suburbia. A dramatic restructuring of downtown London occurred to accommodate more people and more new businesses, and many old buildings were torn down in the process. When the Schlegels' lease expires on Wickham Place, Margaret tells Ruth Wilcox that

Compare
&
Contrast

- **1910:** The British Empire includes India, Australia, New Zealand, Canada, Ireland, parts of Africa and Indonesia, and many islands scattered across the globe.

  Today: Many countries formerly a part of the British Empire have achieved sovereignty but hold membership in the Commonwealth of Nations, an association of independent and dependent nations which recognize the United Kingdom of Great Britain as Head of the Commonwealth.

- **1910:** The cost of a Rolls Royce is approximately 1,100 British pounds; less expensive motorcars can be had for approximately 200 British pounds.

  Today: The cost of a Rolls Royce is approximately 125,000 British pounds; less expensive cars can be had for approximately 6,000 British pounds.

- **1910:** A college education at Oxford or Cambridge University is reserved only for the wealthy.

  Today: Scholarships and aid from state funds have made an Oxford or Cambridge education much more affordable.

- **1910:** For the first time in British history, a majority of the population lives in urban areas.

  Today: Approximately 80 percent of the British population lives in urban areas.

she supposes Wickham Place will be torn down and a new apartment building will be built in its place.

At the same time, many new inventions, such as the telephone, typewriter, electric motor, and the automobile, revolutionized daily life. Labor-saving devices such as the gas cooker and the vacuum cleaner allowed more time for leisure activities. In the growing business economy, the typewriter and the telephone were great assets, and opportunities for office workers grew. Many women filled these jobs, happy to leave the labor-intensive, low-paying jobs in the garment industry. Even well-to-do women began to pursue work outside the home. No longer content with only their embroidery or painting lessons, many wealthy women began opening their own businesses.

A dominant issue during the Edwardian Era was the issue of women's suffrage, and many women became involved in the movement. Early on, the suffrage campaign split into two factions, one group more militant than the other in its methods. The militant group, led by Emmeline Pankhurst and her daughters, employed tactics designed to attract widespread attention to the cause. Known as the "suffragettes," they began by heckling political meetings, breaking windows, and chaining themselves to railings. After 1911, however, women still had not received the vote, so the suffragettes initiated more violent strategies. The nation was shocked when they resorted to committing arson, cutting telephone wires, slashing paintings in public galleries, and throwing bombs. Imprisoned suffragettes held hunger strikes, which led to forcible feedings, which in turn led to fierce public debate. Finally, in 1918, women over 30 were given the right vote; women 21 and over were finally extended the same right in 1928. In *Howards End,* the Schlegel sisters are keenly interested in the suffrage issue and believe in equality for women, while the Wilcoxes dismiss the idea of women voting as pure nonsense.

Critical Overview

Howards End was critically very well received in England upon its publication in 1910. Critics declared it the best of Forster's novels, with some proclaiming it Forster's masterpiece. An unsigned review in *The Times Literary Review* stated that Forster's "highly original talent" had found "full and ripe expression" with *Howards End.* Forster

Emma Thompson and Anthony Hopkins, from the film version of Howards End.

had begun to emerge as one of the greatest English novelists of his day.

In general, reviewers praised Forster's highly detailed and accurate portrayal of Edwardian society in the novel. "In subtle, incisive analysis of class distinctions, manners, and conventions, he is simply inimitable," proclaimed the *Morning Leader* in an unsigned review of *Howards End.* Forster also gained recognition for his creation of believable, compelling characters; his considerable powers of perception and imagination, especially concerning the complexity of human nature and relationships; and his keen wit and sense of humor, which he employed to great effect in his sometimes satirical depiction of England's upper classes. His poetical style and beautiful descriptions were singled out for praise, also. *The Times Literary Review* noted the "odd charming vein of poetry which slips delicately in and out of his story, showing itself for a moment in the description of a place or a person, and vanishing the instant it has said enough to suggest something rare and romantic and intangible about the person or the place."

Although the majority of reviews were extremely favorable, some critics felt certain aspects of plot development in *Howards End* seemed unrealistic. General criticism was expressed over whether Margaret would actually marry Henry, or whether Helen, a cultured Edwardian lady, would submit to a sexual encounter with a lower-middle class man like Leonard Bast. Others cited the sequence of events beginning with the highly coincidental death of Leonard, the resulting imprisonment of Charles, and Henry's subsequent "breakdown" as too convenient. Many reviewers found the resolution of the story somewhat artificial, "not representative," but "rather melodramatic." They questioned whether the Wilcox and Schlegel families could indeed come together at Howards End and live happily ever after. But even critics who found these plot developments implausible still endorsed the novel as a whole, with some admitting they were nitpicking at an otherwise great work.

Howards End remains one of Forster's most important novels, along with *A Passage to India.* Even though Forster published no more novels after *A Passage to India,* his popularity grew steadily in England and expanded to America with the publication of Lionel Trilling's book of criticism, *E.M. Forster.* Forster's novels, established early as classics, concern themselves with the mythic and archetypal aspects of human experience and all its complexities. His formidable talents as a writer include his realistic, yet ironical and satirical portraits of Edwardian society, a talent that aligns him with such great novelists as Jane Austen, and marks his novels as descendants of the English "novel of manners." Forster's novels are distinguished by their intense personal quality, their poetical style, their humor, insight, and intelligence as well as their committed humanism. Frederick P.W. McDowell has written that readers are attracted to Forster's works because of "a fascination exerted by characters who grip our minds; a wit and beauty present in an always limpid style; a passionate involvement with life in all its variety; a view of existence alive to its comic incongruities and to its tragic implications; and a steady adherence to humanistic values."

Film adaptations of Forster's work, including the Merchant Ivory production of *Howards End,* have widened Forster's audience. The posthumous publication of his letters, two short story collections, and a novel, *Maurice,* has continued his legacy. Widely considered a literary genius, Forster's works place him in the company of other great modern writers such as Virginia Woolf, Ford Madox Ford, Joseph Conrad, and D. H. Lawrence.

Criticism

Jane Elizabeth Dougherty

Dougherty is a Ph.D. candidate at Tufts University. In this essay, she discusses Forster's depictions of the characters' relationships to their dwelling places in Howards End.

Daniel Born notes that "discussion of values in *Howards End* is never … pursued apart from a material context of physical living space." In *Howards End,* a novel which takes its name from the Wilcox family's country house, the "material contexts" of the characters and their relationships to these material contexts defines each of the three families: the Schlegels, the Wilcoxes, and the Basts. As Michael Levenson notes, *Howards End* is a novel "not of three classes, but of three households." Throughout the novel, each of the three families is defined by their relationships to their physical living spaces. These differing relationships are, in fact, shown to be in conflict in the novel, and this conflict is resolved only uneasily by the novel's end.

The novel begins with Helen's descriptions of Howards End, where she has gone to visit the Wilcoxes. In the opening paragraphs of her first letter to Margaret, she writes:

> It isn't going to be what we expected. It is old and little, and altogether delightful—red brick…. From hall you go right or left into dining-room or drawing-room. Hall itself is practically a room. You open another door in it, and there are the stairs going up in a sort of tunnel to the first-floor. Three bedrooms in a row there, and three attics in a row above. That isn't all the house really, but it's all that one notices—nine windows as you look up from the front garden.
>
> Then there's a very big wych-elm—to the left as you look up—leaning a little over the house, and standing on the boundary between the garden and meadow. I quite love that tree already. Also ordinary elms, oaks—no nastier than ordinary oaks—pear trees, apples trees, and a vine…. I only want to show that it isn't the least what we expected. Why did we settle that their house would be all gables and wiggles, and their garden all gamboge-coloured paths? I believe simply because we associate them with expensive hotels—Mrs. Wilcox trailing in beautiful dresses down long corridors, Mr. Wilcox bullying porters, etc.

Helen's letter to her sister shows that the Schlegels have spent some time speculating on what Howards End was going to be like, based on their acquaintance with the house's owners. Clearly, the Schlegels believe that one's house is, or should be, a reflection of one's personality, of one's personal relations. Howards End does not seem the type of house that Wilcoxes would live in, and it is true that only Mrs. Wilcox has a personal relationship with Howards End. The house has stood for centuries, sheltering Mrs. Wilcox's ancestors, who worked the land and lived in close relationship to it. The romanticized and pastoral Howards End stands in contrast to the ever-changing landscape of London. Of the Schlegels' house, Wickham Place, the narrator says

> Their house was in Wickham Place, and fairly quiet, for a lofty promontory of buildings separated it from a main thoroughfare. One had the sense of a backwater, or rather of an estuary, whose waters flowed in from the visible sea, and ebbed into a profound silence while the waves without were still beating. Though the promontory consisted of flats—expensive, with cavernous entrance halls, full of concierges and palms—it fulfilled its purpose, and gained for the older houses opposite a certain measure of peace. These, too, would be swept away in time, and another promontory would arise upon their site, as humanity piled itself higher and higher on the precious soil of London.

The sea is a recurring metaphor in the novel: as when Margaret says that they "stand upon money as upon islands," the sea represents the ever-changing and threatening reality of modern life.

The Schlegels, in their house on Wickham Place, are protected from the roiling sea of modern life, and their house is another island upon which they stand. Yet the Schlegels' house is constantly threatened by the "sea" around it: they will eventually lose their lease, and their house will be torn down to build more flats. The ever-increasing London masses have lost their relationship to the "precious soil" on which they live, and as a result lost what Frederick Crews calls "the last fortress of individualism in a world of urban sameness." Mrs. Wilcox reacts with horror when Margaret tells her the Schlegels will lose their house:

> "It is monstrous, Miss Schlegel; it isn't right. I had no idea that this was hanging over you. I do pity you from the bottom of my heart. To be parted from your house, your father's house—it oughtn't to be allowed. It is worse than dying. I would rather die than—Oh, poor girls! Can what they call civilization be right, if people mayn't die in the room where they were born? My dear, I am so sorry—

It seems that Mrs. Wilcox is about to say that she would rather die than be parted from her house, but in fact she has been parted from it, because her husband has decided they should take a flat in London. The forces of "civilization," in the person of Mr. Wilcox, are stronger than the forces of continuity and individualism. The other Wilcoxes do not have Mrs. Wilcox's reverence for Howards End, and at the end of her life, Ruth chooses to leave Howards End to Margaret, believing Margaret to be her spiritual heir. Ruth's husband and children do not understand this decision, seeing Howards End solely as a piece of property—not a very useful or valuable one, but one which legally belongs to them. They decide to disregard their mother's wish, and do not inform Margaret of Mrs. Wilcox's bequest.

Two years after the novel's action commences, the Schlegels do lose their house, and become subject to the threatening sea of modern life. In this, they become like the Basts, of whose flat the narrator says that "it struck that shallow makeshift note that is so often heard in the modern dwelling-place. It had been too easily gained, and could be relinquished too easily." The Basts, who are always barely able to survive financially, do not have any islands on which to stand. When they are financially ruined, they lose their flat and do not have the means to let another one. The Schlegels feel spiritually and emotionally bereft when they lose their house, but they can get another one; the Basts do not have the luxury of ever living in a house that is meaningful to them, though Leonard would

> **It is the history they share, represented by what they have jointly owned and jointly experienced, that binds them together. Because they value this common history, they also value Howards End ..."**

like to. Perry Meisel notes of Bast that he is "a grossly thematic reminder that the state of one's psyche and of one's economy are disastrously intertwined." Bast's tentative hold on financial solvency is echoed in his tentative interest in, and acquisition of, culture: like his flat, Bast's quest for meaning in his life can also be all-too-easily lost in the Basts' struggle for survival.

Like the Basts' flat, the various dwelling-places of the Wilcoxes have all been easily gained and can be easily relinquished, with the exception of Howards End. Henry Wilcox values property not for its meaning, but for its use, and he often decides that property he has acquired is unsuitable for his needs. As Levenson notes, Wilcox, unlike Leonard Bast, is a beneficiary, rather than a victim, of the ever-changing nature of modern life. When Henry and Margaret are engaged, Margaret keenly wants to settle into a house of her own, but they never seem to find one to which she is allowed to become attached. The differences in their attitudes toward Oniton, a house Henry has acquired, completely sum up the differences in their characters. Henry's attitude toward Oniton is perfectly prosaic:

> Oniton had been a discovery of Mr. Wilcox's—a discovery of which he was not altogether proud. It was up towards the Welsh border, and so difficult of access that he had concluded it must be something special. A ruined castle stood in the grounds. But having got there, what was one to do? The shooting was bad, the fishing indifferent, and women-folk reported the scenery as nothing much. The place turned out to be in the wrong part of Shropshire, damn it, and though he never damned his own property aloud, he was only waiting to get it off his hands, and then to let fly. Evie's marriage was its last appearance in public. As soon as a tenant was found, it became a house for which he never had had much use, and had less now, and like Howards End, faded into Limbo.

What Do I Read Next?

- In *Bloomsbury Recalled* (1996), Quentin Bell, son of Clive and Vanessa Bell, offers one of the most recent memoirs recounting the personalities and adventures of that famous literary group.

- Joseph Conrad's 1899 novel, *Heart of Darkness,* reveals the injustices of British imperialism in Africa.

- In Forster's first novel, *Where Angels Fear To Tread,* (1905) he contrasts the vibrant, free life of Italians with the artificial, hypocritical and bourgeois life of the suburban Londoners who visit an Italian village.

- Forster's novel, *The Longest Journey,* published in 1907 tells the story of two half brothers, one of them illegitimate.

- *A Room with a View* is Forster's 1908 novel about a young woman's love affair and her struggle with Victorian conventions.

- Forster's last and most highly regarded novel, *A Passage to India* (1924) details the social and historical milieu of colonial India, and one Englishwoman's experience there.

- Forster's posthumously published novel, *Maurice* (1971) tells the story of a young man's discovery of his own homosexuality.

- Fellow Bloomsbury Group member Lytton Strachey revolutionized the genre of biography with his *Eminent Victorians,* offering unusually unflattering portraits of four British cultural heroes, including Florence Nightingale. Critics suggest that his incisive criticisms take on the difference between mere "moral righteousness" and "true humanitarianism."

- Virginia Woolf's 1925 novel, *Mrs. Dalloway,* is at once the story of Clarissa Dalloway's party and a critique of the British social system.

- Woolf's 1927 novel, *To the Lighthouse* focuses on the inner life and experiences of an English family.

Henry bases his opinion of Oniton on the property's use to him: whether he can entertain business guests in it, whether it increases his status, whether it offers him sufficient recreation. When he decides not to live at Oniton, he does not give it up, but lets it to a tenant so he can derive an income from it. It is as if actually living in a house is a poor investment, when one can rent it out and get money from it. The narrator notes that the Wilcoxes are an imperial family, always looking for new parts of England to conquer, as the English have conquered the globe. Henry's attitude towards his home at Oniton contrasts sharply with Margaret's:

> Margaret was fascinated with Oniton. She had said that she loved it, but it was rather its romantic tension that held her. The rounded Druids of whom she had caught glimpses in her drive, the rivers hurrying down from them to England, the carelessly modelled masses of the lower hills, thrilled her with poetry. The house was insignificant, but the prospect from it would be an eternal joy, and she thought of all the friends she would have to stop in it, and of the conversion of Henry himself to a rural life. Society, too, promised favourably. The rector of the parish had dined with them last night, and she found that he was a friend of her father's, and so knew what to find in her. She liked him. He would introduce her to the town.

Margaret is stirred by the poetry of Oniton, and moreover, the community surrounding it links her to her father, because the rector had been a friend of his. Though she recognizes that the house itself is insignificant, she thinks not at all of the property's value in the real world, but only of its personal meaning to her. The Schlegels are interested in poetry and personal relations, the Wilcoxes in prose and investments. Yet, as for the first Mrs. Wilcox, her husband's wishes take precedence over Margaret's. They do not settle at Oniton. Margaret becomes estranged from her sister Helen because she has allied herself with the Wilcoxes: she no longer tries to influence Henry, but acquiesces to his wishes. It is only when Margaret and Helen meet at Howards End that Margaret sees that the Schlegels are threatened in a world run by Wilcoxes. She and Helen are reconciled to each other at Howards End, surrounded by their furniture and other possessions, when they realize that "they never could be parted because their love was rooted in common things." It is the history they share, represented by what they have jointly owned and jointly experienced, that binds them together. Because they value this common history, they also value Howards End, which is linked to the history of Mrs. Wilcox's family, to organic relationships rooted in a rural life. As Wilfred Stone notes, "[t]hough the Wilcoxes hold the 'title-deeds' and the 'door-keys,' these evidences of ownership do not impress the Schlegels," who instead value the meanings they can create from the physical space in which they live, meanings which can be more easily created at Howards End than in the impersonal and temporary dwelling-places of London.

The conclusion of the novel sees Howards End rescued from limbo: it becomes a home in which Henry Wilcox, the Schlegel sisters, and the child of Leonard Bast can live together in a life rooted to the precious soil and contained in a house which has witnessed the births and deaths of generations. Yet as Born notes, "that Forster interrupts his final scene with awareness of the encroaching London mass suggests he is not entirely happy with this one-sided vision of serene, private, poeticized culture." Though the Schlegels have conquered the Wilcoxes, the forces of "civilization" still loom in the distance. Though Howards End may represent an idealized solution to the problems of a modernizing England, the sea still threatens the island on which the new family stands.

Source: Jane Elizabeth Dougherty, in an essay for *Novels for Students,* Gale, 2000.

Duke Maskell

In the following excerpt, Maskell evaluates Howards End *for Forster's beliefs found in Forster's "What I Believe" and finds that Forster fails to embody his beliefs in the novel.*

Mr Forster's place in the canon is an unusual one. He enjoys, securely, a reputation of the most insecure kind—that of a major figure—definitely that—who falls just short—but clearly short—of true greatness. A reputation which might be expected to stimulate objections from all quarters stimulates them from virtually none. No one, apparently, wants to see him promoted into the ranks of the acknowledged masters and hardly anyone wants to see him pushed out of the canon altogether. He is the occasion of no very serious or very interesting debate. When he is praised, he is praised extravagantly but harmlessly.... Mr Forster's peculiar reputation rests, it might be guessed, not so much on what he's done as on what he's been taken to represent; and it would be a mean spirit indeed who, given what he *has* been taken to represent, would look with an unfriendly eye upon what he's done.

Looked upon so, Mr. Forster has done little more than generate in himself and others an en-

> Talk, for the novelist even more obviously than for the essayist, won't suffice. He must deliver the goods. And if he can't, if he doesn't really own the feelings he lays claim to, his novel will betray him...."

thusiasm for platitudes. Let us consider two documents, 'What I Believe', Mr Forster's personal manifesto, and *Howards End,* the novel in which he tries most directly to embody the values of the manifesto.

In the essay he says he's in favour of private decencies, personal relationships, people who are sensitive and creative—the lovers, artists and homemakers—good temper, good will, tolerance, loyalty, sympathy, friendship and Love the Beloved Republic and against public affairs, Great Men, force and violence and people who see life in terms of power.... We have to take Mr Forster's word for it that he knows not only the words for love and sympathy, but the things themselves. It's only by turning to the novel that we have any chance of bringing the essay's claims into question; it's there we are forced to turn for the knowledge that will make good these claims. And, turning and looking, what we find is not quite a vacancy but yet more fine sentiments and, dominating the palpables of tone, characterization and plot, an assortment of snobberies and a pervasive self-satisfaction.

The intentions of *Howards End* are explicit and impeccable. It urges its readers to 'only connect ...' to build within themselves 'the rainbow bridge that should connect the prose in us with the passion' for then 'love is born, and alights on the highest curve, glowing against the grey, sober against the fire' and, like the essay, the novel insists 'it is the private life that holds out the mirror to infinity; personal intercourse, and that alone, that ever hints at a personality beyond our daily vision'. Its heroes and heroines are those who 'attempt personal relations', its villains 'the hurrying men who know so much and connect so little'; its triumphs occur when 'truer relationships gleam'.

But fine sentiments and would-be noble phrases don't even make good feelings let alone good novels. And if, in an essay, a writer can't get away with just naming the things he believes in, how much less so can he in a novel, when his 'beliefs' must be acted out as particular, concrete instances? Talk, for the novelist even more obviously than for the essayist, won't suffice. He must deliver the goods. And if he can't, if he doesn't really own the feelings he lays claim to, his novel will betray him.... *Howards End* betrays Forster. He preaches in it love and sympathy and is caught furtively practising the everyday, casual snobberies of any other upper-class Cambridge don of the turn of the century.

The part of the novel that offers the most direct (but by no means the only) challenge to his sympathies is the story of his near working-class figure Leonard Bast. From an essay, 'The Challenge of our Time', one might think him well-equipped to present class relations in England. He says of his own education, for instance, that though it was humane 'it was imperfect, inasmuch as we none of us realized our economic position. In came the nice fat dividends, up rose the lofty thoughts, and we did not realize that all the time we were exploiting the poor of our own country and the backward races abroad, and getting bigger profits from our investments than we should'. But, again as Lawrence said, trust the tale not the teller. It is one thing to describe a case of social injustice in an essay, and in terms which were, after all, even in 1910, fairly common property, another thing entirely to write a novel in which the characters are seen, have to be seen, not just as illustrations of a thesis but as creatures who, whatever their circumstances, have the same human identity and physiognomy as their author. But Forster, for all his good intentions, can't see that the Basts and he do share a common condition. They are objects to him, objects to feel things for and to have attitudes towards—it makes no difference whether he sympathizes with them, feels sorry for them, condescends to them or sneers at them. These apparently divergent feelings belong to a single paradigm, one governed by the powerful unconscious assumptions of an upper-class world-view which divides the world into 'us' and 'them'. Whatever Forster 'feels for' the Basts he feels securely as one of 'us' regarding 'them'. The Basts are nothing, have nothing, represent nothing that could bring into question for Forster himself and his world. And having no authority over their author they are dead as characters.

Forster's good intentions are, on their own terms, genuine enough. But the good intentions only work as a leavening upon the snobbery. The 'facts' of Leonard Bast's 'case' are obviously meant as social criticism but, as presented, they draw our attention, not without creating a certain risibility, to Mr Forster as commentator rather than to society as commented-on. Leonard, Mr Forster tells us, was 'inferior to most rich people, there is not the least doubt of it. He was not as courteous as the average rich man, nor as intelligent, nor as healthy, nor as lovable' and his wife Jacky is 'brutally stupid'. Not only is Leonard deprived of his livelihood by an unjust and all-powerful social machine and not only is he without the cultivation of the Schlegels but, additionally, he has none of the rude vigour, physical or psychological, of the middle-class barbarians like Charles Wilcox, without whose spirit 'life might never have moved out of protoplasm'.

The other boundary of [Bast's] social world, the proletarian 'abyss' where his origins are among the 'submerged', is only a threat and a teror to him.... Somehow, he has entirely escaped being influenced by his family background. We are told certain things about it—that a grandfather was a Lincolnshire farm-labourer, his father a Cockney tradesman, a brother a lay-reader and that two sisters married commercial travellers—but none of this information is active *within* Forster's characterization of him. It is only supplied at all because Forster thinks he ought to give him a genealogy. Once he has given it he promptly forgets it because he doesn't know how to use it. Leonard isn't seen as a son or brother at all let alone one born into a particular class. The point isn't that Leonard is presented as one thing when he ought to have been presented as another, that his presentation is 'unrealistic', but that what is missing from him as a person isn't presented by Forster *as* missing. Properly speaking, it isn't missing from the character but from the book. *Howards End nowhere* contains any sense of what the alternative to Leonard might be. Leonard doesn't have merely an incomplete relation to his family and class presented as such but no relation at all.

He is without any moral or emotional history because Forster, although he would like to be writing about 'a real man', can't help running off another version of that comic Cockney stereotype which is (perhaps 'was') so indelibly printed on the middle-class imagination.... Forster wants to be generous towards Leonard, wants to present a young man with a sense of honour and of self, but the materials available to him are woefully inadequate. Leonard's would-be Cockney is stilted and inanely self-preoccupied, the sense units short and repetitive and the vocabulary picked up from the 'Music Hall' or a dictionary of Cockney English, picked up and thrown down in a heap without any sense of how, when or where the words are used. It's a fair measure of Forster's linguistic insensitivity that it's not clear whether 'in trouble' does or does not mean 'pregnant'.

Forster's tone, characteristically, is condescending, and at its worst when he is paying Leonard compliments: 'the naive and sweet-tempered boy for whom Nature intended him', 'no one felt uneasy as he tittupped along the pavements, the heart of a man ticking fast in his chest', 'within his cramped little mind dwelt something that was greater than Jefferies' books—the spirit that led Jefferies to write them'. The trouble with these remarks is not, perhaps, so much their snobbery as their simple fatuity:

> it is an adventure for a clerk to walk for a few hours in darkness. You may laugh at him, you who have slept nights out on the veldt, with your rifle beside you and all the atmosphere of adventure pat. And you also may laugh who think adventures silly. But do not be surprised if Leonard is shy whenever he meets you, and if the Schlegels rather than Jacky hear about the dawn.

This from someone who is supposed to be a major modern English novelist, preceded in importance only by Conrad, James, Lawrence and Joyce, someone often compared to Lawrence and Jane Austen. It's difficult to say what is most ridiculous about the passage, its sloppiness about the darkness and dawn, its willingness to take adventures on the veldt seriously, its arch pretence that we might meet Leonard Bast or, what we are presently concerned with, its condescension for clerks.

[Forster's] dominant attitude to the Basts is made up of a distaste for the unattractive surfaces of working-class life and an amused superiority at its bad taste....

The presence in the tone of the condescension and the contempt is, of course, bound up with the absence from the characterization of any 'solidity of specification'.... Forster condescends towards the Basts because they are stock figures for whom condescension is the stock response. His compassion and concern for people such as they is nothing more than feeling sorry for them for not being like himself. He both pities and admires Leonard but he pities him for lacking his own spiritual and

moral advantages and admires him for wanting them. It is not Jane Austen whom he resembles but Emma Woodhouse: she too, thinks 'a very narrow income has a tendency to contract the mind, and sour the temper. Those who can barely live, and who live perforce in a very small, and generally very inferior, society, may well be illiberal and cross'. At bottom, Forster's response to the Basts is the same as hers to the poor cottagers of Highbury: 'These are the sights, Harriet, to do one good'....

That Forster's concern for the victims of social injustice is make-believe is evidenced not only by his presentation of the Basts but also by the relationship their story bears to the rest of the novel. What really matters to Forster is not the fate of the Basts but that of the Wilcoxes and Schlegels. The Basts are just a side-show. The imaginative centre of *Howards End* is the division between and reconciliation of its two middle-class families. Whether the reconciliation between Wilcox and Schlegel, 'prose' and 'passion', that Margaret Schlegel works for and the novel welcomes is seen as one between social groups, the entrepreneurs and the intelligentsia, or psychological types, or whether it is read as a command to the individual to lead a whole life, it is equally irrelevant to the problems of the Basts, which are caused by an unfair division of wealth and labour and which cannot be solved without upsetting the life led by the Schlegels and, one might add, the public of *Howards End.*

Far from wishing the removal of the injustices the Basts suffer from, *Howards End* wants to see preserved a world that permits the kind of 'personal' life enjoyed by Margaret Schlegel—even if the price is being reconciled to the necessity of the Wilcoxes and the injustices attendant upon the circumstances in which they flourish. Margaret in an argument with her sister Helen says,

> If Wilcoxes hadn't worked and died for thousands of years, you and I couldn't sit here without having our throats cut. There would be no trains, no ships to carry us literary people about in, no fields even. Just savagery. No—perhaps not even that. Without their spirit life might never have moved out of protoplasm. More and more do I refuse to draw my income and sneer at those who guarantee it.

In these remarks, as in so many others, it's hard to sort out the bad faith from what is merely inept. Margaret avoids (and Forster avoids) having to comment on the morality of the social relationships that subsist under capitalism by appealing in a very general way to the desirability of 'progress'; she

Forster and his mother at Rooksnest, near Stevenage, Hertfordshire, around 1885. Rooksnest became the model for Howards End *in Forster's 1910 novel.*

gives the credit for 'progress' to the entrepreneur class and measures 'progress' by the security of existence enjoyed by 'us literary people'. Her last sentence could be anybody's recognition of what side his bread was buttered on but it's presented to us as the mark of her moral lucidity. Forster puts no distance between himself and this would-be clear-headedness; on the contrary, he shows it triumphing over Helen's muddy-minded liberalism. Helen not only gets worsted in the argument but by the end of the book has come round to 'appreciating' Henry Wilcox just as Margaret does.

Forster *is* critical of the Wilcoxes (that is to say, he often sneers at them) but he is critical not so much of their social role as of their personal inadequacies. Yet were Henry and Charles Wilcox the most loving-hearted and cultivated of men, their economic relationship with the Basts would still be a suspect one. Denying the Wilcoxes any likeable personal qualities isn't a social criticism; it's merely an intellectual's snobbery. It *obscures* the social significance of business, is an evasion of those very issues which, pursued, might have led Forster to see the role of the Schlegels, his rentier figures, as a parasitic one. As it is, he has it both ways. He sneers at the Wilcoxes for lacking the cultivation he's got and admires them for having a cer-

tain kind of confidence and power which he's without but which makes his kind of life possible—and admires them for this, moreover, in the language of *Room at the Top:* Charles is 'dark, clean-shaven and seemed accustomed to command', Henry is 'one of those men who know the principal hotel by instinct' and whose 'management' of practical things is always 'excellent'. As people, the Wilcoxes may be unattractive but as representatives of the capitalist spirit they *are,* as Lawrence said in a letter to Forster, 'glorified'.

Forster's failure with the Basts and the social issues their story raises is hardly attributable merely to a lack of firsthand experience. Nor is it necessary to explain it in Marxist terms as a 'necessary' consequence of his 'objective' class position. It seems to me a failure of intelligence and imagination, a failure to be a good enough novelist. Forster's presentation of his middle-class characters is just as coarse as that of his lower-class ones.

Forster's authorial comments regularly show only a perverse pleasure in scoring off his characters. It is one thing to dramatize a character who is 'rubbishy', say Mrs Elton in *Emma,* which requires both that one be a novelist and have a grasp of the possible other case, quite another to invent characters only in order to call them names.

In Forster's account of the Basts his lack of curiosity in the lower classes creates a moral vacuum which is filled by the stock snobberies of a rich man; in his account of the Wilcoxes his lack of curiosity in businessmen creates a vacuum which is filled by the stock snobberies of an intellectual and aesthete. The Basts and the Wilcoxes are unreal. And Forster's sympathy and respect for them are unreal. But the moral failure isn't *additional* to the artistic one. The possession of sufficient moral imagination to put oneself in the place of the unfamiliar and to deal with it generously ... is the very condition of being able to give it an air of reality.

Forster's failure with his middle-class characters isn't limited, though, to the morally unfamiliar, to the Wilcoxes. He fails just as badly with the Schlegels too. The Schlegel sisters and Mrs Wilcox are just as unreal as the Basts and the other Wilcoxes. Forster can no more give the air of reality to upper-class decency and cultivation than he can to upper-class business or lower-class aspiration. And in this instance the failure to cope with the supposedly familiar, the supposedly humane and sensitive Schlegels, is identical with the failure to cope with the unfamiliar, with the Basts and Wilcoxes. Not himself having a sufficiently sensitive and generous imagination to render the Basts and Wilcoxes decently, how could Forster ever have successfully embodied sensitivity, decency and imagination in the Schlegels? His failure with the Schlegels is not so much a failure to recognize the place of private decencies and personal relations in the larger social context (his is *not* the case of Jane Austen) but a failure to represent them at all, a failure to know what they really are. Forster's grasp of the private life as embodied in the Schlegels and Mrs Wilcox (the very heart of his book) is every bit as unsure as his grasp of business life and the life of the lower classes. There is no more knowledge of love, sympathy, affection, etc. in the portrait of the Schlegels than in 'What I Believe'. There are merely gestures on a larger scale, gestures whose import has equally to be taken on trust, gestures that are hopelessly inadequate for the job they are asked to do.

Put to the test of embodying his 'beliefs' in a novel Forster is too much the creature of his upbringing, and not enough of a novelist, to do more than display, side by side, the aimless good inten-

tions and the incurable snobberies of a no-doubt kindly but fundamentally self-regarding, upper-class English intellectual of the turn of the century. *Howards End* has the interest of a social document but none, that I can see, of the interests of a novel. The most interesting question about it is how it got its reputation, and particularly its reputation as a novel which embodies a spirit concerned with what is 'decent, human, and enlarging in daily conduct'. A large part of the answer must be, presumably, that its American readers are typically innocent of English life, particularly our class system, and are often infatuated with our upper classes, and that its English readers, being exclusively middle-class, find their own world-view mirrored in it. One enjoys reading a fairy-story, the other enjoys looking at a flattering portrait of himself. Both, no doubt, find agreeable the mildness of its social criticism and the generous vagueness of its solutions—only connect, let truer relationships gleam, build that rainbow bridge, and all may be well.

A Passage to India seems to me equally unreal, equally as factitious and unnecessary a novel. Its characters are equally stereotyped and its incidents just as merely illustrative of the stereotyped. Reading it, I have the impression, as new characters and incidents are introduced, of watching a series of *exempla* pass by, of listening to a succession of 'points' being made in illustration of the double thesis that the principled Anglo-Indians are coarse and the unprincipled Indians sensitive. Neither side seems to me to be dealt with any greater understanding than the Wilcoxes and Basts. Aziz seems to me just as insensitive and prejudiced a portrait of a member of a subject race as Leonard Bast is of a member of a lower class. He even shares Leonard's taste in paintings: 'Aziz in an occidental moment would have hung Maud Goodmans on the walls'. Robust, self-sufficient Indians have as little place in Forster's world as robust, self-sufficient Cockneys. Forster's Indians 'are deprived of their adulthood, live in a perpetual childhood'. The phraseology of his 'positives' in *A Passage to India* is just as empty and unfulfilled as of those in *Howards End:* 'the sanctity of personal relations', 'the fire of good fellowship in their eyes', 'the divine lips of beauty', 'centuries of carnal embracement', 'a sense of unity, of kinship with the heavenly bodies', etc. *A Passage to India* seems to *me* as comprehensively *not* a novel as *Howards End,* fully as much a thing of unrealized intentions.

Source: Duke Maskell, "Mr Forster's Fine Feelings," in *Cambridge Quarterly,* Spring, 1971, pp. 222–35.

Sources

Born, Daniel, "Private Gardens, Public Swamps: *Howards End* and the Revaluation of Liberal Guilt," *Novel: A Forum on Fiction,* Vol. 25, No. 2, 1992, pp. 141-159.

Bradbury, Malcolm, "Howards End," in *Forster: A Collection of Critical Essays,* edited by Malcolm Bradbury, Prentice-Hall Inc., 1966, pp. 131.

Crews, Frederick, *E.M. Forster: The Perils of Humanism,* Princeton University Press, 1962.

Levenson, Michael, "Liberalism and Symbolism in *Howards End,*" in his *Modernism and the Fate of Individuality,* Cambridge University Press, 1990, pp. 78-93.

McDowell, Frederick P. W., "'Glimpses of the Diviner Wheels': Howards End," in *E. M. Forster,* revised edition, Twayne Publishing, 1982, pp. 82.

———, "'Unexplained Riches and Unused Methods of Release': Nonfictional Prose and General Estimate," in *E. M. Forster,* revised edition, Twayne Publishing, 1982, pp. 149-159.

Meisel, Perry, "Howards End: Private Worlds and Public Languages," in his *The Myth of the Modern: A Study in British Literature and Criticism after 1850,* Yale University Press, 1987, pp. 173-182.

Morning Leader, *"The part and the whole,"* October 28, 1910, pp. 3.

Review, in *The Times Literary Supplement,* No. 459, October 27, 1910, pp. 421.

Stone, Wilfred, "Howards End: Red-Bloods and Mollycoddles," in his *The Cave and the Mountain: A Study of E.M. Forster,* Stanford University Press, 1966.

For Further Study

Forster, E. M., *Aspects of the Novel,* E. Arnold, 1963.
    A collection of lectures delivered by Forster on the art of the novelist.

Forster, E.M., *Marianne Thornton: A Domestic Biography, 1797-1887,* Harcourt Brace, 1956.
    This biography of Forster's paternal aunt, Marianne Thornton, is also a study of Forster's own intellectual origins and family lineage.

Furbank, P. N., *E. M. Forster: A Life,* Harcourt Brace Jovanovich, 1978.
    The definitive biography of E. M. Forster.

Gardner, Philip, ed., *E.M. Forster: The Critical Heritage,* Routledge and Kegan Paul, 1973.
    This book is a collection of mostly early criticism on Forster's works.

Lago, Mary, and P.N. Furbank, eds., *Selected Letters of E.M. Forster,* 2 Vols., Belknap Press, 1983-1985.
    A collection of E. M. Forster's letters.

The Naked and the Dead

Norman Mailer

1948

Published in 1948, *The Naked and the Dead* earned overwhelming popular and critical acclaim. Most reviewers deemed the novel to be one of the best war stories ever written, praising Mailer's realistic depiction of men at war. The novel focuses on the adventures of a fourteen-man infantry platoon stationed on a Japanese-held island in the South Pacific during World War II. In the course of the novel, the men struggle to survive and find meaning in their lives.

In his introduction to the fiftieth-anniversary edition of the novel, Mailer asserted that *The Naked and the Dead* reflects what he learned from Tolstoy: "compassion is of value and enriches our life only when compassion is severe, which is to say when we can perceive everything that is good and bad about a character but are still able to feel that the sum of us as human beings is probably a little more good than awful. In any case, good or bad, it reminds us that life is like a gladiators' arena for the soul and so we can feel strengthened by those who endure, and feel awe and pity for those who do not." Mailer's deft and evocative portrayal of the characters' heroic struggle to retain their dignity as they experience the horrors of war provides the book with its enduring value.

Author Biography

A self-proclaimed philosophical "existentialist" and political "left conservative," Norman Mailer has

Norman Mailer

led a colorful and notorious life. He was born on
January 31, 1923 in Long Branch, New Jersey, to
Isaac (an accountant) and Fanny (owner of a small
business) and moved with his family to Brooklyn at
the age of four. When he was sixteen, he began his
studies in aeronautical engineering at Harvard University and developed an interest in writing.

In 1944, Mailer was inducted into the United
States Army and served in the Philippines. He recounted his experiences there in his first novel, *The
Naked and the Dead,* which gained much critical
and popular acclaim. In the introduction to the fiftieth-anniversary edition of the novel, Mailer contends that "it came out at exactly the right time
when, near to three years after the Second World
War ended, everyone was ready for a big war novel
that gave some idea of what it had all been like."
After *The Naked and the Dead,* Mailer earned more
praise for his nonfiction. In 1959 he achieved national attention for *Advertisements for Myself,* a
collection of essays and writings that chronicled his
career and personal life, and in 1980 for *The Executioner's Song,* an account of the life and subsequent execution of notorious murderer Gary
Gilmore.

Mailer earned several awards for his literary
achievements. They include the National Book
Award for nonfiction for *Miami and the Siege of
Chicago* (1968); National Book Award for nonfiction, Pulitzer Prize in letters general nonfiction, and
George Polk Award in 1969 for *Armies of the
Night.* He also won the Pulitzer Prize for *The Executioner's Song;* an Emmy nomination for best
adaptation of the for screenplay for the movie version of *The Executioner's Song;* and the Emerson-
Thoreau Medal for lifetime literary achievement
from American Academy of Arts and Sciences in
1989. Mailer has also produced, directed, and acted
in films. He has been a candidate for democratic
nomination in two mayoral races in New York City
in 1960 and 1969 and was the co-founding editor
of *Village Voice* in 1955.

Plot Summary

Wave

Mailer introduces the novel's major characters
in the opening scene as the assault of Anopopei, a
mythical Pacific island, is about to begin. The platoon is part of a 6,000–man force poised to take the
Japanese-held island in order to clear the way for
a larger American advance into the Philippines. The
story of the invasion is interspersed with vignettes
that provide background information on several of
the men. As they wait for their rush onto the beach,
many of them address and try to overcome their
fear of death.

Argil and Mold

The American soldiers advance quickly during
the first few days of the campaign, with little resistance from the Japanese. Soon they realize just
how oppressive the heat and moisture of the jungle is. Lieutenant Robert Hearn feels dissatisfied
with his position as aide to General Cummings and
"contemptuous" of the other officers. He enjoys his
almost nightly talks with the general, even though
he acknowledges that he is a "tyrant." The general
is a complex character who enjoys complete power
over his men, and Hearn is attracted to that power.

One day, Hearn becomes upset when the officers get more than their share of rations. In response, the general provides him with a lesson on
the politics of war: "Every time an enlisted man
sees an officer get an extra privilege, it breaks him
down a little more." As a result the "enlisted man
involved is confirmed a little more in the idea of
his own inferiority" and he grows to fear his superior officers. The general explains, "The army functions best when you're frightened of the man above
you, and contemptuous of your subordinates."

The troops grow restless as they wait for orders to advance. When they eventually get orders to carry guns inland, they are soon exhausted by the arduous trip through the jungle. As enemy fire stops them at a river, a Japanese bullet shatters Private Toglio's elbow. Later, Croft, Red, and Gallagher come across some wounded Japanese soldiers and Croft orders them killed. Red experiences a mixture of disgust and excitement as he shoots one. Croft taunts another—allowing him to think he will be spared—and then kills him.

One night, the men get drunk and decide to hunt for Japanese souvenirs. After they come across several dead Japanese, the stench and sight of the maggot-infested bodies overcome them. They are suddenly aware of their own fragility and vulnerability. When they return to the main camp, Gallagher is told his wife died during childbirth; as a result of this news, he goes into shock. Minetta is sent to the Division Clearing Hospital for a minor wound. Fearful of further combat, he attempts to feign insanity so he can stay in the hospital longer. Eventually, he becomes restless and afraid of the other patients and returns to the platoon.

During one of their talks, the general confides to Hearn about his troubled relationship with his wife. Revolted by his display of self-pity, Hearn responds coldly, which humiliates the general. In retribution, the general reassigns him to a tedious post. After Hearn leaves a cigarette butt on the floor of the general's quarters, the general decides to flex his power and forces Hearn to pick up a cigarette that he throws on the floor. As a result, Hearn suffers an "excruciating humiliation." To avoid any further interaction with Hearn, the general assigns him to lead the platoon on a scouting mission behind the enemy troops.

Plant and Phantom

Croft resents Hearn's presence; he determines that the Lieutenant is a threat to his leadership over the platoon. During a skirmish with the Japanese, Wilson gets hit in the stomach and Hearn sends Ridges, Goldstein, Stanley, and Brown to take him back to the beach. Later, Roth finds an injured bird, which Croft grabs and crushes with his hand. After Hearn forces Croft to apologize to Roth, Croft determines to make him pay for his humiliation.

Croft convinces Hearn to send Martinez out on a reconnaissance mission to discover where the enemy troops are located. Martinez reports back to Croft that a company of Japanese soldiers is occupying the pass ahead of them. Croft, however, informs Hearn that Martinez found no evidence of

Japanese troops in the pass. As a result, Hearn, without the proper precautions, leads the platoon right into the enemy and is killed. Croft happily resumes control of the men and orders them to climb Mount Anaka.

The trek up the mountain weakens him as well as his men. After an exhausted Roth falls to his death, Red refuses to go any further. Croft stands his ground and warns Red that he will shoot him if he doesn't continue up the mountain. Realizing at that moment what Croft did to Hearn, Red ashamedly backs down. As the men continue their arduous trek up the mountain, Croft stumbles into a hornet's nest. After the stinging hornets force the men back down the mountain, Croft finally admits defeat and leads his men back to the beach.

While the rest of the men are making their way up the mountain, Ridges, Goldstein, Stanley, and Brown struggle with the task of carrying an injured Wilson through the jungle. Halfway to the beach, Stanley breaks down from exhaustion and, seizing a chance to rest, Brown agrees to stay with him. Goldstein and Ridges continue alone with the backbreaking task. After several agonizing hours, Wilson eventually dies.

Back at the main camp, the general's departure for Army Headquarters forces Dalleson to take command of the invasion. The decisions Dalleson makes, along with a good measure of luck, result in the destruction of the Japanese forces. The next day during the boat ride back to camp, the men feel "no hope, no anticipation. There would be nothing but the deep cloudy dejection that overcast everything." Yet when they see the mountain, they experience a sense of pride about almost making it to the top.

Wake

When General Cummings returns, he discovers that the Japanese were almost out of food and ammunition and so would not have been able to hold out much longer. He admits that he had little to do with the American victory and that the reconnaissance mission had been useless. The novel ends with Dalleson musing on the pride he would feel when future map-reading classes used his new teaching materials.

Characters

Sergeant William Brown

Brown is an insecure young man who doubts his abilities as a soldier. He is obsessed with the thought of his wife cheating on him while he is at war.

Staff Sergeant Sam Croft

Croft leads the Intelligence and Reconnaissance platoon of Headquarters Company of the 460th Infantry Regiment and is considered by the men to be "the best platoon sergeant in the Army and the meanest." He is "efficient and strong and usually empty and his main cast of mind was a superior contempt toward nearly all other men. He hated weakness and he loved practically nothing." Croft kills for pleasure: on Anopopei he shoots a Japanese prisoner after allowing him to think he was safe, crushes a bird that one of his men had found, and coldly plans Hearn's death in an effort to regain control of the platoon. Croft loves the war for it allows him to unleash his hatred and thirst for power. He explains, "I hate everything which is not in myself."

General Cummings

Cummings is the commander of the invading American forces on Anopopei and has an "almost unique ability to extend his thoughts into immediate and effective action." A brilliant and ambitious fascist, he believes that totalitarianism is preferable to communism because "it's grounded firmly in men's actual natures." He insists "there's never a man who can swear to his own innocence. We're all guilty, that's the truth." In order to obtain victory, he attempts to break his men's spirits. He explains: "there's one thing about power. It can flow only from the top down. When there are little surges of resistance at the middle levels, it merely calls for more power to be directed downward, to burn it out." Beneath his austere surface, however, lies self-pity and paranoia.

Casimir Czienwicz

Czienwicz (also known as Polack) is a cynical, shrewd member of Croft's platoon. His rough life growing up on the streets of Chicago prepared him for the rigors of life in the army.

Major Dalleson

After Hearn's death, Dalleson takes over the American invasion of Anopopei. A thorough and adequate leader, he feels "a little overwhelmed" in his dealings with officers because he "feared the slowness of his mind." Sometimes his responsibilities depress him. "He was always afraid that a situation would develop in which he would have to call upon the more dazzling aptitudes that his po-

sition demanded, and which he did not have." A few good decisions—coupled with a lot of luck—enables him to take credit for the defeat of the Japanese army on Anopopei.

Roy Gallagher

A member of Croft's platoon, Gallagher is a hotheaded, racist, working-class guy from South Boston. He continually feels sorry for himself, insisting "everything turned out lousy for him sooner or later." His prediction is realized when he gets news that his wife Mary died in childbirth.

Joe Goldstein

Goldstein is another member of Croft's platoon. While occasionally the target of anti-Semitic slurs, Goldstein fares better than Roth because of his religious faith, dogged courage, and essentially trusting nature. He is one of the men that carries the wounded Wilson through the jungle.

Lieutenant Robert Hearn

Hearn is General Cummings' young Harvard-educated aide. His wealthy background and slightly aristocratic air are at odds with his tyrannical supervisors as well as the enlisted men. Therefore, he does little to make friends on the island. He admits he feels "blank … superior, I don't give a damn, I'm just waiting around." He initially enjoys the general's company, but is eventually alienated by his mind games and self-pity.

Hearns' reserve is shattered when the general humiliates him by forcing him to pick up a cigarette he has tossed on the floor. The incident leaves him "burning with shame and self-disgust … suffering an excruciating humiliation which mocked him in its very intensity." When the general gives Hearn command of the reconnaissance mission, Hearn enjoys the sense of power his position affords him. Yet he tries to treat his men fairly and humanely before he is killed.

Hennessey

A young soldier in Croft's platoon, Hennessey is killed on their first day on the island. His death fills the other men with a sense of doom.

Japbait

See Sergeant Julio Martinez

Sergeant Julio Martinez

Martinez (also known as Japbait) is an excellent scout for Croft's platoon. He sometimes becomes nervous about giving orders to the other men, afraid that they would not listen to a Mexican American. Yet his role in the platoon gives him "a quiet pride that he was the man upon whom the safety of the others depended. This was a sustaining force which carried him through dangers his will and body would have resisted."

Steve Minetta

Minetta is another member of Croft's platoon. When he is sent to the Division Clearing Hospital for a minor wound, his fears about returning to combat prompt him to feign insanity so he can stay there longer. Eventually, though, he becomes restless and goes back to the platoon.

Polack

See Casimir Czienwicz

Oscar Ridges

A member of Croft's platoon, Ridges is a dull-witted and good-tempered religious Mississippi farmer.

Roth

Roth is a member of Croft's platoon. A well-educated Jewish man, he considers himself superior to the other men in the platoon, which effectively isolates him from them. Yet he experiences feelings of self-pity when he acknowledges his inability to be as good a soldier as the others are. His weakness and overwhelming fatigue cause him to fall to his death on Mount Anaka.

Stanley

When Stanley is promoted to corporal, he develops authority and begins to bully the men. Eventually though, he wonders "how he could lead men in combat when he was so terrified himself." He breaks down during the trek back to the beach with Wilson and has to be left behind.

Toglio

Toglio is a member of Croft's platoon. A Japanese bullet shatters his elbow shortly after they arrive. The other men envy the good fortune of his "million-dollar" injury.

Private Red Valsen

A rebellious member of Croft's platoon, Red is an embittered, itinerant laborer from the coal mines of Montana. His hard life leaves him feeling old at twenty-three. Although he enlists as a way out of the cycle of poverty and boredom, he experiences "the familiar ache of age and sadness and

Media Adaptations

- *The Naked and the Dead* was adapted for the screen by Denis Sanders, in a movie directed by Raoul Walsh and produced by RKO Studios in 1958. Cliff Robertson starred as Hearn, Aldo Ray as Croft, and Raymond Massey as General Cummings. It is available from United Video.

wisdom" on the island. While determined to be a loner in an effort to shield himself from the suffering of others, he periodically feels "sad compassion" for the men "in which one seems to understand everything, all that men want and fail to get." Red resists authority and often clashes with Croft. His cynicism results from his feeling that "everything is crapped up, everything is phony, everything curdles when you touch it."

Woodrow Wilson

A member of Croft's platoon, Wilson is a wild, fun-loving man from Georgia who is suffering from venereal disease. He gets shot in the stomach and eventually dies after an arduous trek through the jungle.

Buddy Wyman

A twenty-eight-year-old soldier in Croft's platoon, Wyman has "vague dreams about being a hero, assuming this would bring him some immense reward which would ease his life and remove the problems of supporting his mother and himself." The war, however, does not live up to his romantic visions.

Themes

War and Peace

The Naked and the Dead focuses on both war and peace as its narrative moves back and forth between the battle on Anopopei and the lives of many of the men prior to the war. The reader is able to

Topics for Further Study

- Look up the history of the battles between the American and Japanese armies that took place on the Philippine Islands. Were any similar to the ones that took place in the novel? Research this battle and describe it to your classmates.

- The essay included in this entry refers to Stephen Crane's "The Open Boat." Read the story and compare it to the novel. Describe the naturalistic style of both. Are the themes of these works similar or different?

- Pick a character in the novel and create a timeline of the character's life from the information in the novel. What impact did this character's past have on his behavior during the novel? How has your past influenced the person you are today?

- Investigate the psychological and/or sociological nature of power. What causes the desire for power? What are its effects on its perpetrator and victims? Do you see this desire for power in your own life? Describe a situation that you have observed or experienced. Where you the victim or victimizer?

---

discern how the war has changed the lives of these men and the ones that they have left behind in the United States.

Victim and Victimization

In a war novel, it makes sense that the theme of victimization would be a recurring one throughout the story. On the island, General Cummings and Sergeant Croft are victimizers; they are so insecure and power-hungry that they will risk the lives of their men to insure their absolute power. This results in the victimization of their men and ultimately causes the death of some.

The brilliant and ruthless General Cummings exercises a tyrannical control over his men. He maintains:

> There's one thing about power. It can flow only from the top down. When there are little surges of resis-

tance at the middle levels, it merely calls for more power to be directed downward, to burn it out.

Cummings continually tries to "burn out" his men's resistance, including that of Lieutenant Hearn, who makes the mistake of challenging Cummings' control. As a result, Cummings first humiliates him and then sends him on a useless reconnaissance mission around the back of the island. Hearn dies during this mission.

Croft, who "had a deep unspoken belief that whatever made things happen was on his side," joins in Hearn's victimization. When Hearn is assigned to Croft's platoon and therefore threatens Croft's absolute control over his command, Croft sadistically manipulates Hearn into a dangerous position behind enemy lines where he is soon gunned down. Croft also victimizes Private Valsen, who continually rebels against authority in an effort to maintain his personal dignity. Croft eventually breaks Valsen's spirit, forcing him to back down from his attempts to save himself and the other men on Mount Anaka.

Mailer reinforces the theme of victimization and in many different ways throughout the novel. Many of the men feel powerless within the constraints of American society: for example, Red Valsen abandoned his family in order to flee the impoverished and dangerous life in the coalmines of Montana. The stratification of American society has also victimized Lieutenant Hearn, who was born into an upper-class family in the Midwest. His domineering father pushed him to emphasize his "masculine" qualities, producing a "cold rather than shy" young man. As a result of their experiences, Valsen and Hearn experience similar feelings about life: Valsen is governed by a "particular blend of pessimism and fatalism," while Hearn insists that "if you searched something long enough, it always turned to dirt."

Courage and Cowardice

Valsen and Hearn exhibit courage when they struggle to preserve their personal dignity and the lives of the men around them—even when faced with personal vendettas and impossible circumstances. Valsen does not back down from his challenge to Croft on Mount Anaka until the Sergeant threatens to shoot him. Hearn accepts the challenge of leading the men into dangerous territory. The other soldiers in the platoon must also struggle with feelings of courage and cowardice. Some, like Goldstein and Ridges, successfully combat their overwhelming fatigue and sense of insecurity as they continue the arduous task of returning the wounded Wilson to the beach. Others find any way they can to avoid the terrors of war and preserve their sanity in such a chaotic situation.

Style

Structure

Mailer structured *The Naked and the Dead* to include not only the story of the armed conflict on the mythical Japanese-held island of Anopopei during World War II, but also the stories of each of the main characters involved in the struggle. He often breaks his main narrative with "Time Machine" vignettes of the past history of these men to provide readers with important information about their characters. This episodic structure illuminates character motivation and development; as a result, it also helps set up the novel's central conflicts and thematic concerns.

Weltanschauung

The episodic structure of the novel functions to sustain its *Weltanschauung,* or "world view"—in this case, a naturalistic impression of the forces that continually frustrate human will and action. Naturalism is a term used for a group of writers, including Stephen Crane, Frank Norris, and John Dos Passos, whose works reflect a pessimistic view of the nature of experience. The naturalistic view proposes that humans are controlled by their heredity and environment and so cannot exercise free will.

The Naked and the Dead expresses this literary naturalism in its story of the battle on Anopopei as well as in the histories of the men. Cummings and Croft are governed by their lust for power and violence. In an institution such as the military, these men are rewarded for what seems to be a biological impulse. Therefore, they succeed when more sensitive, less brutal men are killed or injured.

The soldiers that make up Croft's platoon feel like pawns in a large game that they have no control over; even worse, they are at the mercy of cruel and manipulative leaders. Even the officers, however, eventually learn that they do not have absolute control. After luck plays a large part in the takeover of the island, Cummings must admit that his careful strategic planning did little to help win the campaign. As a result, he will probably not get the promotion he coveted. A swarm of hornets thwarts Croft's monomaniacal drive to climb Mount Anaka, and he eventually must also admit defeat.

The landscape constantly interferes with all the men as they struggle to survive. The jungle's heat, humidity, and rugged terrain exhaust them and impede their progress. At home, poverty, class, race, as well as other factors such as alcoholism and violent tendencies, determine the men's choices and future. As they come to acknowledge their inability to control their destinies, their prime motivation becomes a personal battle for dignity.

Symbolism

The jungle and Mount Anaka are important symbols in *The Naked and the Dead.* The oppressive heat and primitive nature of the jungle reflects the animalistic, primal nature exhibited by some of the men, especially Croft. His cruel desire for power causes him to coldly shoot an unarmed Japanese soldier, kill a small bird with his bare hand, and plan Hearn's death for his own ends. Mount Anaka proves a formidable obstacle to the exhausted and traumatized men, and so symbolizes a barrier to human progress.

Historical Context

The Great Depression

The stock market crash in 1929 triggered the Great Depression, the most severe economic crisis in U.S. history. The impact on Americans was staggering. In 1933 unemployment rose to sixteen million people, about one-third of the available labor force. During the early years of the Depression, men and women searched eagerly and diligently for any type of work. However, after several months of no sustained employment, they became discouraged. President Franklin Roosevelt's New Deal policies, which offered the country substantial economic relief, helped mitigate the effects of the Depression. Full economic recovery was not complete until the government channeled money into the war effort in the early 1940s.

World War II in the Pacific

In 1940 two events occurred that exacerbated the growing tension between the United States and Japan: Japan invaded Indochina and signed the Tripartite Pact, which created an alliance between Japan, Germany, and Italy against Great Britain and France. As a result Washington drastically increased economic sanctions by withholding oil and freezing all Japanese assets. In retaliation, Japan bombed Pearl Harbor, a naval base on Oahu, Hawaii on December 7, 1941; eight battleships and thirteen other naval vessels were destroyed and three thousand naval and military personnel were

Compare
&
Contrast

- **1948:** In the aftermath of World War II, Japan is occupied by American forces. American occupation aims to put in place a democratic form of government and reestablish a successful and stable peacetime economy. Under the supervision of General Douglas MacArthur, Supreme Commander of Occupying Forces, Japanese war criminals are tried and convicted; democratic elections are held in 1946; and a new constitution goes into effect in 1947. However, economic reforms are more difficult to implement and it will take years for Japan to stabilize their economy.

  Today: Japan remains a stable democratic power in the South Pacific and is a staunch ally of the United States. Despite recent economic setbacks, Japan is also a formidable economic power in the world community.

- **Late 1940s:** After Europe is decimated as a result of World War II, America becomes an economic superpower, creating a thriving economy and a population boom. A whole generation of Americans born in the late 1940s and early 1950s will become known as the Baby Boom generation.

  Today: America has experienced the longest economic expansion in its history. The impact of technological progress propels the stock market and encourages economic expansion.

- **1948:** Although more and more women work at manufacturing jobs formerly held by men, most women remain in traditional roles in the domestic sphere.

  Today: Because of economic circumstances, many women are forced to work outside the home. In addition, the stigma of the working woman is a thing of the past; women are encouraged to educate themselves and excel in the workplace. Increased opportunities mean that women can be found at all levels of the corporate structure, yet many people feel that sexual discrimination and sexual harassment are still problems that inhibit the progress of women in the workplace.

---

killed or wounded. As a result of this surprise attack, United States entered the war and battled Japan on the sea (most notably at Midway in 1942) and on Japanese-held islands, and through a bombing campaign on the Japanese mainland.

In 1942 Japanese forces occupied much of the southeastern Pacific: the Philippine Islands, Indonesia, and New Guinea. That same year the Americans launched their counterattack. The Coral Sea naval battle prevented the Japanese from gaining access to Australia and the U.S. Marines regained Guadalcanal. After U.S. forces took control of the Solomon Islands in 1943 and New Guinea in 1944, they advanced on Japanese-held island groups: the Philippines, the Marianas Islands, Okinawa, and Iwo Jima. After protracted fighting, Allied forces took Birmania in October 1944, Manilla and Iwo Jima in March 1945, and Okinawa in June of 1945. Japan resisted until 1945; but after atomic bombs were dropped on Hiroshima and Nagasaki in August of that year, Japan reluctantly accepted the terms of an unconditional surrender, which was the dissolution of the Japanese Empire and the release of all seized territories.

Women during World War II

After American men went off to fight in World War II, jobs became available for women in many different fields, including manufacturing. By 1945, approximately nineteen million women held jobs. Women benefited from the employment in several ways: economically, as the income helped to support their families and the economy itself; and emotionally, as they knew that they were contributing to the war effort. As a result, women were independent and fulfilled; this was difficult to relinquish when, at the end of the war, the men came home and demanded their jobs back. Most wives returned to their traditional roles in the home.

Aldo Ray as Sergeant Croft in the 1958 film version of The Naked and the Dead.

Critical Overview

When *The Naked and the Dead* was published in 1948, the novel earned Norman Mailer overwhelming popular and critical acclaim. In fact, it claimed the top spot on the *The New York Times* "Bestseller List" for eleven consecutive weeks. Most critics, like *Atlantic* reviewer C. J. Rolo, considered the novel to be "the most impressive piece of fiction to date about Americans in the Second World War."

David Dempsey asserted in *The New York Times* that it is "undoubtedly the most ambitious novel to be written about the recent conflict, it is also the most ruthlessly honest and in scope and in integrity compares favorable with the best that followed World War I." Richard Match contended in his review in the *New York Herald Tribune,* "With this one astonishing book … [Mailer] joins the ranks of major American novelists."

Several reviews focused on the novel's realistic account of the war. *Time* considered it "distinguished primarily for simple realism, a forthright, almost childlike honesty, a command of ordinary speech, a cool and effortless narrative style." Some commentators deemed the language and subject matter shocking. A reviewer for *Kirkus Reviews* maintained that the novel was:

a brilliant book—but one that makes such harrowing reading, and which is written with such intensity, such bald realism, such unrestrained accuracy of detail in speech and thought, that all but the tough-skinned will turn from it, feeling reluctant to look again on the baring of man's inner beings under stress of jungle warfare.... [*The Naked and the Dead* is] an unpleasant experience, but one that makes an unforgettable impression.

In the *Library Journal,* Donald Wasson contends: "This is an exceptionally fine book.... the language employed is very strong and so accurately reported that it probably will offend many and may create problems in handling."

While some critics deride the novel's length and wordiness, most praise what Ira Wolfert in the *Nation* calls Mailer's "remarkable gift for storytelling." Moreover, Wolfert insists that the novel proves Mailer has "poetry in him and ideas."

A few critics, however, offer mixed reviews of the novel, finding fault most often with Mailer's execution of the novel's themes. In the *New Yorker* John Lardner agrees that Mailer "tells a good story powerfully and well," but finds that it "shares the tendency of most current novels toward undersimplification—it is too long and it is too complicated ... [while] its dialogue is true and straightforward." Dempsey points to an "overanalysis of motive" and a "failure of reach." While he considers the book "substantial," Maxwell Geismar, writing in the *Saturday Review of Literature,* maintains that there is "no real balance of the dramatic forces in it, just as there is a final lack of emotional impact."

As Dempsey notes, the publication of *The Naked and the Dead* "bears witness to a new and significant talent among American novelists," an opinion that has prevailed, for the most part, throughout Mailer's career. The novel's critical reputation remains strong, but the response to his subsequent works has been mixed. Mailer had a difficult time living up to the promise and popularity of *The Naked and the Dead.* In his autobiographical *Advertisements for Myself,* published in 1959, Mailer admits to the pressures he faced after the success of his first novel: "I had the freak of luck to start high on the mountain, and go down sharp while others were passing me."

In the years following the publication of *The Naked and the Dead,* Mailer earned notoriety as a dissident, a social critic, and a celebrity. He did garner praise for his forays into nonfiction, evidence with the highly acclaimed *The Armies of the Night* (1969) and *The Executioner's Song* (1980). Mailer's experiments with different literary forms,

his engrossing studies of human nature and American society, and his realistic prose style have cemented his reputation as one of the major American writers of the twentieth century.

Criticism

Wendy Perkins

Wendy Perkins, an Associate Professor of English at Prince George's Community College in Maryland, has published articles on several twentieth-century authors. In this essay she examines how the narrative structure of The Naked and the Dead *reinforces the novel's naturalistic themes.*

> [The wind-tower] was a giant, standing with its back to the plight of the ants. It represented in a degree ... the serenity of nature amid the struggles of the individual—nature in the wind, and nature in the vision of men. She did not seem cruel to him then, not beneficent, not treacherous, not wise. But she was indifferent, flatly indifferent.

This famous passage from Stephen Crane's short story "The Open Boat," which focuses on four men in a small dinghy struggling against the current to make it to shore, is often quoted as an apt expression of the tenets of naturalism, a literary movement in the late nineteenth and early twentieth centuries in France, America, and England. Writers included in this group—like Crane, Emile Zola, and Theodore Dreiser—expressed in their works a biological and/or environmental determinism that prevented their characters from exercising their free will and thus controlling their destinies. Crane often focused on the social and economic factors that impacted his characters. Zola's and Dreiser's work often mixed this type of environmental determinism with the influences of heredity in their portraits of the animalistic nature of men and women engaged in the endless and brutal struggle for survival.

Many critics have noted the same type of naturalistic tendencies in Norman Mailer's *The Naked and the Dead,* which takes place on a mythical South Pacific island. The novel's "Time Machine" sections, which provide histories of several of the men, also help reinforce the novel's naturalistic themes. These vignettes, along with the story of the island battles, present a bleak portrait of the nature of war and of American society, a vision tempered by the heroic endurance of his characters.

The jungle is a formidable obstacle as the soldiers struggle to advance on the enemy in *The Naked and the Dead*—much like "indifferent nature" continually impedes the men's efforts in the "The Open Boat" to reach the safety of the shore. The oppressive heat and humidity sap the men's strength as they engage in skirmishes with the Japanese. Their climb up Mount Anaka is completely exhausting: so much that Red acknowledges that his health has been ruined and Roth falls to his death. Like the wind-tower in the "Open Boat," Mount Anaka stands "with its back to the plight of the ants." Philip Bufithis in his critical study of the works of Mailer notes how the mountain "taunts" Croft with its "purity" and "austerity." He asserts:

> The mountain becomes for Croft what his troops are for Cummings: the "other" that resists his control and must be molded to serve his will. Like Cummings, however, Croft is unable to control the circuits of chance. When he stumbles over a hornets' nest, the men flee down the mountain and the march abruptly ends.

Thus the mountain becomes a symbol of indifferent nature as well as a barrier to human progress.

Another type of environmental determinism results from the hierarchical structure of the military. General Cummings explains the necessity of this structure when he tells Hearn, "the army functions best when you're frightened of the man above you, and contemptuous of your subordinates." Cummings controls the lives of his men with an iron fist and plays out his theories of power on Hearn. Sometimes Cummings treats Hearn as an equal, "and then at the proper moment jerked him again from the end of a string, established the fundamental relationship of general to lieutenant." Hearn acknowledges:

> [he had] been the pet, the dog, to the master, coddled and curried, thrown sweetmeats until he had had the presumption to bite the master once. And since then he had been tormented with the particular absorbed sadism that most men could generate only toward an animal. He was a diversion for the general. And he resented it deeply with a cold speechless anger that came to some extent from the knowledge that he had acquiesced in the dog-role, had even had the dog's dreams, carefully submerged, of someday equaling the master. And Cummings had probably understood even that, had been amused.

Hearn understands Cummings' desire for power, since he has lived within the same kind of class structure all his life. Born into an upper-class family, Hearn was shaped by "the emotional prejudices of his class…. Although he had broken with

> Initially he is proud to make sergeant, which proves that "any man jack can be a hero." He later admits that his position, unfortunately, "does not make you white Protestant, firm and aloof."

them, had assumed ideas and concepts repugnant to them, he had never really discarded the emotional luggage of his first eighteen years." His privileged status had produced his overwhelming sense of boredom and alienation, especially after viewing "all the bright young people of his youth [like himself who] had butted their heads, smashed against things until they got weaker and the things still stood. A bunch of dispossessed … from the raucous stricken bosom of America."

Mailer continues his critique of American society in his depiction of the other soldiers' lives back in the States. Red must abandon his family to escape the dangerous life in the coalmines, which killed his father when Red was thirteen. Yet he, like several of the other men, cannot escape the poverty of the Depression years that makes him feel old at twenty-three. As a boy, Polack is sent to an orphanage when his mother can't support him after the death of his father. As a result, he grows up on the streets of Chicago where he becomes connected with the mob.

Prejudice also impacts the lives of the soldiers before they reach Anopopei. When he is a boy, Martinez decides he will fly planes when he grows up, but there are no opportunities for a Mexican American. Initially he is proud to make sergeant, which proves that "any man jack can be a hero." He later admits that his position, unfortunately, "does not make you white Protestant, firm and aloof." Roth and Goldstein have suffered all their lives from anti-Semitic slurs, which continue on the island. As a result the two feel alienated from the other men.

Biological determinism appears most notably in the relationship Cummings and Croft have with

What Do I Read Next?

- *The Thin Red Line* (1962) was written by James Jones and focuses on the pointlessness of war in a fictional account of the battle between American and Japanese troops on Guadalcanal.

- Stephen Crane's *Red Badge of Courage* (1895), set during the Civil War, also explores the nature of courage and the brutal devastation of war.

- In the *The Executioner's Song* (1979), Norman Mailer presents a chilling look into the mind of Gary Gilmore, who in 1977 was executed for murder.

- *Going After Cacciato,* written in 1979 by Tim O'Brien, chronicles the story of an American soldier in Vietnam. The young man deserts his post so he can walk eight thousand miles to Paris to be present at the peace talks. The other soldiers in his squad are given orders to find him.

---

their men. Each man's sadistic nature and thirst for power contribute to Hearn's death. After Cummings becomes embarrassed by his display of vulnerability in front of Hearn, he determines to punish the lieutenant in an effort to regain the upper hand. Cummings concludes, "there's one thing about power. It can flow only from the top down. When there are little surges of resistance at the middle levels, it merely calls for more power to be directed downward, to burn it out."

In an effort to recoup complete control of his platoon, Croft arranges for Hearn to lead them straight into enemy territory; Hearn is almost immediately gunned down by enemy fire. Croft's sadism also emerges in his dealings with the other men in the platoon. For example, he forces Red to shoot a wounded Japanese soldier and crushes a bird Roth had found with his bare hand. Both events help to defeat the men's spirits. In the "Time Machine" sections, Mailer provides background information on Croft and Cummings that illuminates the impetus for their cruel natures. The sections suggest each inherited traits from his father and suf-

fered under their tyrannical, harsh treatment. In fact, the section titled "The Education of Samuel Croft" portrays the brutal life Croft endured with his Texan father, who abused women and African Americans and then bragged to his son about it.

Ironically, forces beyond their control ultimately defeat both of these men. Cummings must admit that he had little to do with his company's takeover of the island: "it had been accomplished by a random play of vulgar good luck larded into a causal net of factors too large, too vague, for him to comprehend." As a result he knew he would be bypassed for more honors and promotions. Croft is ultimately defeated in his monomaniacal quest to climb Mount Anaka by a swarm of hornets and learns that his reconnaissance mission has been useless to the campaign.

In his article on the novel, Chester E. Eisinger maintains that Mailer's naturalistic universe results in "a world in which nobody wins." After Wilson dies during their agonizing trek back to the beach, Ridges "wept out of bitterness and longing and despair; he wept from exhaustion and failure and the shattering naked conviction that nothing mattered." At the same moment, Goldstein acknowledged that "there was nothing in him at the moment, nothing but a vague anger, a deep resentment, and the origins of a vast hopelessness." The rest of the men come to feel this same sense of hopelessness and vulnerability to the forces that are beyond their control. When Red sees piles of rotting Japanese bodies and notes their overpowering stench, he comes to a similar conclusion. Suddenly he is "sober and very weary," recognizing that the bodies of "men" surround him. Standing over one such body, he reflects:

> Very deep inside himself he was thinking that this was a man who had once wanted things, and the thought of his own death was always a little unbelievable to him. The man had had a childhood, a youth and a young manhood, and there had been dreams and memories. Red was realizing with surprise and shock, as if he were looking at a corpse for the first time, that a man was really a very fragile thing.

Ultimately, the novel's power results from the compassionate response of readers to the characters' courage in the face of this overwhelming sense of meaninglessness. As Mailer pushes his characters to their limits and beyond, he celebrates the indomitable nature of the human spirit.

Source: Wendy Perkins, in an essay for *Novels for Students,* Gale, 2000.

Gabriel Miller

Miller is an American critic and educator who often contributes to film and literature journals. In the following essay, Miller delineates social and political themes in Mailer's early fiction.

In one of the *Presidential Papers* Mailer wrote, "Our history has moved on two rivers, one visible, the other underground; there has been the history of politics which is concrete, practical, and unbelievably dull ... and there is the subterranean river of untapped, ferocious, lonely and romantic desires, that concentration of ecstasy and violence which is the dream life of the nation." Much of Mailer's writing, like much of the American writing from which he consciously borrows, is concerned with such dualities. As he declared in "The White Negro," Mailer finds the twentieth century, for all its horror, an exciting time to live because of "its tendency to reduce all of life to its ultimate alternatives." This fascination with dynamic polarities is reflected in Mailer's style as well, as he has struggled in his modeling of language and form to fuse the real, political/social world with the world of dream and myth. In reading his novels chronologically, one can trace Mailer's process of borrowing and merging different styles, then discarding them, and experimenting with others in quest of a voice that will be most compatible with his own recurrent themes and emerging vision. Mailer's central subject is the relationship between the individual will and a world that attempts to overwhelm and extinguish it. Intimately connected with this spiritual warfare is the subject of power, particularly political power, and the individual's need to resist the encroaching forces of totalitarianism. Mailer's early fiction clearly warns that modern man is in danger of losing his dignity, his freedom, and his sense of self before the enormous power of politics and society.

These concerns are already apparent in his first novel, *The Naked and the Dead* (1948), which despite its brilliant, evocative scenes of men at war, is ultimately a political novel. Mailer describes his attitude about the Second World War in "The White Negro":

> The Second World War presented a mirror to the human condition which blinded anyone who looked into it.... one was then obliged also to see that no matter how crippled and perverted an image of man was the society he had created, it was nonetheless his creation, his collective creation ... and if society was so murderous, then who could ignore the most hideous of questions about his own nature?

> Mailer's early fiction clearly warns that modern man is in danger of losing his dignity, his freedom, and his sense of self before the enormous power of politics and society."

The Naked and the Dead elaborates this harrowing perception of the individual who exemplifies and perpetuates what is wrong with the society he inhabits. In this first novel Mailer equates the army with society and thereby explores the fragmented nature of that society, which has militated against social development, revolutionary or otherwise. In so doing, Mailer demonstrates his own loss of faith in the individual's ability to impose himself creatively, perhaps redemptively, on the oppressive condition of the post-war world.

The novel exhibits a hodgepodge of styles and influences: the works of James Farrell, John Steinbeck, and John Dos Passos inform its structure and form. Herein the thirties novel, with its emphasis on social engagement and reform, collides with a pessimistic, even despairing world view, as Mailer blends naturalism with symbolism, realistic reportage with nightmare images and hallucinatory dream landscapes, documentary portraits with political allegory. The dramatic thrust of the novel, however, springs from Mailer's fascination with his three central figures: General Cummings, Sergeant Croft, and Lieutenant Hearn.

Cummings is presented as a despotic fascist, wholly preoccupied with the power he wields over the island which his troops occupy. When Hearn accuses him of being reactionary he dismisses the charge, claiming that the war is not being fought for ideals but for "power concentration." His plan to send a patrol to the rear of the Japanese position to determine the validity of a new strategic theory is prompted by raw opportunism, and it results in the death of three men. Croft, on the other hand, is a brave but illiterate soldier who embraces the war cause to satisfy his lust for killing and conquest. He is Cummings' collaborator, carrying out the general's orders without question. It is Croft who

President Franklin D. Roosevelt signs the Declaration of War against Japan, December 8, 1941.

leads the men through jungles and swamps to pit them and himself against Mt. Anaka, even after the Japanese have surrendered (though the patrol does not know it), to further his own ambitions.

Hearn is the character who bridges the gap between the soldiers and command. Although he represents the liberal voice in the novel and so seems ideally positioned to embody the moral center in this desperate society, he emerges as a rather vague and empty character, even less sympathetic than most in Mailer's vast array of characters. This surprising deficiency in Hearn is surely intentional, as Mailer introduces an intelligent and sometimes outspoken man only to emphasize how ineffective he is. Resented both by the commanders and by the soldiers, he is eventually killed for no purpose; such is the fate of liberalism in Mailer's universe.

The political argument develops primarily in dialogues between Cummings and Hearn, whom Cummings is trying to convert to his autocratic views. This overt confrontation of ideologies, a staple of the political novel and a device Mailer would repeat less successfully in his next novel, provides an abstract gloss on the narrative, while the use of the "Time Machine" episodes to delineate the lives of the men more subtly equates the structure of so-

ciety with the army. America is thus portrayed as a place of social privilege and racial discrimination, as exploitive and destructive as the military organization that represents it. Mailer presents the individual as either submitting to these repressive forces or attempting to maintain some spiritual independence. The fates of Hearn and, to some degree, Red Valsen, a Steinbeckian hobo and laborer who struggles to preserve his private vision, indicate that defiance is fruitless. Both men are destroyed, while Cummings and Croft, in their ruthless drive to power, prevail and triumph.

However, this schematic simplification does not reflect the complexity of Mailer's view, conveyed in some aspects of the novel that undercut the apparent political formula, most notably his narrative style. Mailer recounts his tale in a tone of complete objectivity, his authorial voice remaining detached and disinterested. Considering the moral dimensions of his story, this lack of anger or indignation is disorienting, and the effect is strengthened by Mailer's unsympathetic treatment of Hearn and the vibrant images of Cummings and Croft, who seem to fascinate him. Clearly Cummings' egoism repels Mailer, but it also attracts him, for in this island tyrant he perceives also the individualistic impulse to reshape and recreate an environment and in so doing, to form a new reality. Cummings thus possesses a kind of romantic aura as a dreamlike projection—which Mailer will recast in different forms in his subsequent fiction—of the active response to life which Mailer advocates in principle, if not on Cummings' specific terms. Croft, too, seeks a channel in which to funnel his powerful drives. Both men see evil as a vital force and their apprehension of it (not only in people, but in nature as well) provides them an energy and a decisive manner that the weaker, idealistic characters lack.

Still, at this point in his career Mailer did not want to exalt Cummings and Croft at the expense of Hearn. Therefore, in his climb up Mt. Anaka, Croft is left finally with feelings of despair: "Croft kept looking at the mountain. He had lost it, had missed some tantalizing revelation of himself. Of himself and much more, of life. Everything." At another point Mailer sums up Croft thus: "He hated weakness and he loved practically nothing. There was a crude unformed vision in his soul but he was rarely conscious of it." This man has energy but no form. Mailer the novelist is himself searching for the kind of form necessary to shape his vision. The liberal philosophy of a Hearn is rejected as insufficient to the challenges of modern history. It lacks the energy and daring of Croft and Cummings, but they still frighten Mailer, and he refuses to align himself with their authoritarian methods. Concluding the novel with Major Dalleson, a mediocre bureaucrat, enjoying the monotony of office details, Mailer instead pulls back from taking a definite position on the struggle he has chronicled. As Richard Poirier points out, he "has not yet imagined a hero with whose violence he can unabashedly identify himself."

Source: Gabriel Miller, "A Small Trumpet of Defiance: Politics and the Buried Life in Norman Mailer's Early Fiction," in *Politics and the Muse: Studies in the Politics of Recent American Literature,* Edited by Adam J. Sorkin Bowling Green State University Popular Press, 1989, pp. 79–92.

Paul N. Siegel

In the following excerpt, Siegel focuses on the figures of General Cummings and Sergeant Croft who see "that there is a pattern, [and that] it means ... the presence of a malign supernatural power...."

In a *New Yorker* interview published after *The Naked and the Dead* had scored its sensational success, Norman Mailer said of his novel: "It has been called a novel without hope. I think actually it is a novel with a great deal of hope. It finds ... that even in man's corruption and sickness there are yearnings and inarticulate strivings for a better world, a life with more dignity." This statement is a remarkable example of how erroneous an artist can be about his creation.

The yearnings and inarticulate strivings of men for a better world of which Mailer speaks are shown in *The Naked and the Dead* with a sense of hopelessness about their achieving it. This is conveyed in a passage of startling beauty. As the platoon approaches the island of Anopopei in its landing craft, the men look upon it in the sunset with a strange rapture. "The island hovered before them like an Oriental monarch's conception of heaven, and they responded to it with an acute and terrible longing. It was a vision of all the beauty for which they had ever yearned, all the ecstasy they had ever sought." But this vision cannot last, and, as the sunset fades, the men are left with the reality of the terror and blackness of life....

The island of Anopopei, which presented itself as a bright vision, proves to be a nightmare. It is the mysterious world in which men live, working in unfathomable ways to confuse, terrify, and destroy them.

The only ones to whom Anopopei is not terrifying are the reactionary General Cummings, a

> The action and dialogue as well as the setting and atmosphere suggest ... that there is a pattern, [and that] it means ... the presence of a malign supernatural power...."

coldly calculating machine, and Sergeant Croft, his enlisted-man counterpart, who finds in killing the satisfaction of his powers. Each believes that life contains a pattern that he can either control or identify with, not a vaguely perceived sinister cosmic conspiracy.

The action and dialogue as well as the setting and atmosphere suggest ... that there is a pattern, [and that] it means ... the presence of a malign supernatural power.... God, it seems, is like General Cummings, unconcerned with the personalities and fates of individual men and reducing them to the point where they cease to be individuals. As the cynical petty racketeer Polack responds to the question, "Listen, Polack, you think there's a God?" with "If there is, he sure is a sonofabitch."

The climb up the mountain and the long haul of carrying Wilson bring to the men an epiphany in which they attain a fleeting vision of a cruelly indifferent God. It is this experience which gives the title to the novel. Mailer had used the word "naked" several times earlier to mean open, vulnerable.

Source: Paul N. Siegel, "The Malign Deity of 'The Naked and the Dead,'" in *Twentieth Century Literature,* Hofstra University Press, October, 1974, pp. 291–97.

Randall H. Waldron

In the following excerpt, Waldron argues that Mailer's novel "underlines ... the function of the machine as the controlling metaphor in World War II novels," and the "central conflict ... is between the mechanistic forces of the "system" [personified by General Cummings and Sergeant Croft] and the will to individual integrity."

[The] informing influence of the machine [as the force of anonymous brute mechanism] can nowhere be studied with greater interest or reward

> The principal burden of
> the novel is to explore the
> condition of man struggling
> against the depersonalizing forces
> of modern society...."

than in Norman Mailer's *The Naked and the Dead.* To reread *The Naked and the Dead* in these terms is important on two counts. First, it views the book in a light that has not been trained on it before, and that illuminates and enriches our understanding of it as a novel. Second, it underlines and clarifies the function of the machine as a controlling metaphor in World War II novels by demonstrating the organic importance of that metaphor in the first really significant, probably the best, and certainly the most imitated of those novels....

The Naked and the Dead has been interpreted in a number of ways. Mailer himself has maintained that it is an ultimately hopeful "parable about the movement of man through history." Admitting that it sees man as corrupt and confused to the point of helplessness, he insists that it also finds that "there are limits beyond which he cannot be pushed, and it finds that even in his corruption and sickness there are yearnings for a better world." Most readers have denied these positive elements, making the book a pessimistic, bleak, and hopeless account of men defeated before they start by all sorts of deterministic forces. Some see it as a roughly existential document in which the horror and absurdity of war are presented as normal in the context of the human condition at large, which is itself essentially absurd. Still others—perhaps taking Mailer at his word—put it in the class of novels in which war is horrible enough, but still an educational, broadening experience in which the soul is tested and purged by adversity, and positive values triumph. Each of these interpretations is defensible; the book is by no means clear in its thematic conclusions.

The central conflict in *The Naked and the Dead* is between the mechanistic forces of "the system" and the will to individual integrity. Commanding General Cummings, brilliant and ruthless evangel of fascist power and control, and iron-handed, hard-nosed Sergeant Croft personify the machine. Op-

posing them in the attempt to maintain personal dignity and identity are Cummings' confused young aide, Lieutenant Hearn, and Private Valsen, rebellious member of Croft's platoon. Mailer fails to bring this conflict to any satisfying resolution: at the novel's end Hearn is dead and Valsen's stubborn pride defeated, but likewise Croft is beaten and humiliated and Cummings' personal ambitions thwarted. But while the resolution of the conflict may be ambiguous, the nature of it is not. The principal burden of the novel is to explore the condition of man struggling against the depersonalizing forces of modern society....

Cummings is a man so imbued with the machine, its language, its power, its values, that he not only defends it as the instrument of military and political control, but has allowed it to penetrate to the very depths of his being. It is his aphrodisiac; the object of his lust and passion. He confounds its forces with those of life and regeneration, its objects with human beings. Thus Cummings' function as symbolic character has crucial implications for the central theme of the novel: that the machine is capable of extending its domination to the most fundamental levels of man's existence, of becoming a threat to his very nature and to his humanity.

Source: Randall H. Waldron, "The Naked, the Dead, and the Machine: A New Look at Norman Mailer's First Novel," in *PLMA,* March, 1972, pp. 271–77.

Walter B. Rideout

In the following excerpt, Rideout argues that Mailer presents hope for humankind, in the figure of Lieutenant Robert Hearn.

Mailer's radicalism is of an indeterminate sort, the kind that expresses itself preëminently, perhaps, in images and fictional constructs rather than in abstract schema.... [His] dislike [for any kind of collective action] lies at the heart of his first novel and has often been interpreted as making his critique of capitalist society an entirely negative one; nevertheless *The Naked and the Dead* is a radical novel which affirms and does so within its own logic as a literary work.

Mailer's novel has a number of faults, not the least being that it sounds at times like a pastiche of the novels about World War I. The echoes of Dos Passos, another individualist rebel, are especially insistent: the interchapter biographies in *The Naked and the Dead* combine the techniques of the biographies and the narrative sections in *U.S.A.,* and the fact that all of these individual soldier lives are thwarted and stunted by a sick society seems clearly

> " ... these qualities particularly express the personality of that key figure, Lieutenant Robert Hearn, a confused liberal intellectual who, like the middle class in Marxist theory, is caught between the hammer and the anvil of great antagonistic forces."

reminiscent of the social vision at the base of the trilogy....

If, as Mailer himself has stated, the book "finds man corrupted, confused to the point of helplessness," these qualities particularly express the personality of that key figure, Lieutenant Robert Hearn, a confused liberal intellectual who, like the middle class in Marxist theory, is caught between the hammer and the anvil of great antagonistic forces. In him Mailer skillfully fuses form and content, for Hearn partakes in and thus links both of the power struggles which operate simultaneously in the book, in each holds a kind of ideological middle ground, and in each is defeated. In order to understand Mailer's radical purpose, however, it is necessary to see that the same alternative to defeat exists in both struggles....

Mailer seeks to demonstrate the inability of power moralists to manipulate history in opposition to mass will. If *The Naked and the Dead* is taken as the accurate sum of all its parts, it must be considered, as Mailer himself has declared, a positive and hopeful book rather than a negative and pessimistic one.... More skillfully than most radical novelists Mailer has solved the problem of the ending which with artistic inevitability affirms the author's belief. Incident flowers organically into idea.

Source: Walter B. Rideout, *The Radical Novel in the United States, 1900–1954: Some Interrelations of Literature and Society,* Harvard University Press, 1956, pp. 270–73.

Sources

Bufithis, Philip H., *Norman Mailer,* Frederick Ungar, 1978.

Dempsey, David, review, in *The New York Times,* May 9, 1948, p. 6.

Geismar, Maxwell, review, in *The Saturday Review of Literature,* Vol. 31, May 8, 1948, p. 10.

Kirkus Reviews, Vol. 18, March 1, 1948, p. 126.

Lardner, John, review, in *The New Yorker,* Vol. 24, May 15, 1948, p. 115.

Match, Richard, review, in *The New York Herald Tribune Book Review,* May 9, 1948, p. 3.

Rolo, C. J., review, in *The Atlantic,* Vol. 188, June, 1948, p. 114.

Time, Vol. 51, May 10, 1948, p. 106.

Wasson, Donald, review, in *The Library Journal,* Vol. 73, May 1, 1948, p. 707.

Wolfert, Ira, review, in *The Nation,* Vol. 166, June 26, 1948, p. 722.

For Further Study

Alter, Robert, "The Real and Imaginary Worlds of Norman Mailer," in *Motives for Fiction,* Harvard University Press, 1984.
    Alter discusses the novel's political themes.

Begiebing, Robert J., *Acts of Regeneration: Allegory and Archetype in the Works of Norman Mailer,* University of Missouri Press, 1980.
    Examines the allegorical and symbolic elements in the novel.

Bufithis, Philip H., *Norman Mailer,* Frederick Ungar, 1978.
    Bufithis studies the "naturalistic universe" of the novel.

Eisinger, Chester E., "The Naked and the Dead," edited by Jim Kamp, St. James Press, 1994, pp. 1019-020.
    Eisinger argues that naturalism "directs the progress of the story from the beginning to the preordained end."

Leigh, Nigel, *Radical Fictions and the Novels of Norman Mailer,* St. Martin's Press, 1990.
    Explores the novel's depiction of American society.

Merrill, Robert, "The Naked and the Dead: The Beast and the Seer in Man," in *Norman Mailer Revisited,* Twayne Publishers, 1992, pp. 11-29.
    Merrill divides his study into an examination of the novel's documentary, social, and dramatic action.

Pizer, Donald, "The Naked and the Dead," in *Twentieth-Century American Literary Naturalism: An Interpretation,* Southern Illinois University Press, 1982, pp. 90-114.
    Pizer finds a naturalistic symbolic structure in the novel.

Pigs in Heaven

Barbara Kingsolver

1993

When *Pigs in Heaven* was published in 1993, Barbara Kingsolver was already a well-established and successful author. Her third novel garnered critical and popular success and earned her a nomination for an ABBY award, the American Library Association award, the *Los Angeles Times* Fiction Prize, and the Cowboy Hall of Fame Western Fiction Award. As in many of her other works, *Pigs in Heaven* focuses on the complexities of families, relationships, and communities.

In this novel, the protagonist, Taylor Greer, finds herself embroiled in a custody battle with the Cherokee Nation over her adopted Cherokee daughter named Turtle. As she struggles to keep her daughter and at the same time provide a nurturing and safe environment, Taylor is forced to reexamine and redefine her views on family and community. During the course of the story, Kingsolver introduces the issues of single motherhood, adoption, abuse, ethnic identity, and poverty. Her intermingling of politics and human drama results in a satisfying tale of love and understanding. Reviewers applaud the novel's realistic and compelling characters, its topical themes, and her insight into the complex inner workings of the human heart.

Author Biography

Celebrated author, journalist, and human rights and environmental activist, Barbara Kingsolver

Barbara Kingsolver

was born in Annapolis, Maryland on April 8, 1955, but grew up in rural Kentucky. As she watched her father, a country physician, minister to the poor and working class, she began to develop a sense of social responsibility and devotion to community that would later be expressed in her writing. When she was in the second grade, her father accepted a medical position in the Congo and moved his family there. At that time, Kingsolver began her lifelong habit of writing in a journal.

During her junior year at DePauw University, where she was studying biology, she took time off to work in Europe as an archaeologist's assistant. After eventually earning a degree at DePauw, she lived for periods of time in Europe and America, supporting herself with a diverse array of job titles including typesetter, x-ray technician, copy editor, biological researcher, and translator. In 1981 she earned a master's degree in ecology and evolutionary biology from the University of Arizona and soon began working as a technical writer and freelance journalist.

By 1987 she decided to devote her time to writing fiction; the following year, her first novel, *The Bean Trees* was published to national acclaim. The novel earned her an American Library Association award. In 1993, the sequel to *The Bean Trees, Pigs in Heaven,* was published. Kingsolver continues to write in such diverse genres as poetry, nonfiction, short stories, and novels as well as book reviews.

Plot Summary

Part I: Spring

The novel opens in Kentucky with Alice, Taylor's mother, considering leaving her couch-potato husband, Harland. She acknowledges that "he's a good enough man," but that the marriage "has failed to warm her," and besides, "women on their own run in Alice's family." The narrative then shifts its focus to Taylor and Turtle and their trip to Hoover Dam. Taylor had found Turtle in her car three years ago and adopted her. The two live in Tucson with Taylor's boyfriend, Jax, a keyboard player in a band called the Irascible Babies. While at the Dam, Turtle sees Lucky Buster, a middle-aged retarded man, fall into a spillway. Turtle informs her mother and they are able to summon help for Lucky.

After Lucky is rescued, the story is splashed across newspaper headlines and Taylor and Turtle end up on the *Oprah* show as part of a program called "Children Who Have Saved Lives." Annawake Fourkiller, a lawyer for the Cherokee Nation, watches the show and hears the story of Turtle's abandonment and subsequent adoption. Annawake decides that Turtle's adoption is illegal according to the Indian Child Welfare Act, which guarantees that a Native American child cannot be adopted without tribal permission. As a result, she begins to make a case for vacating Turtle's improperly conducted adoption and then finding "a proper placement" for her, where she will learn about her heritage. Soon after, Annawake arrives in Tucson to discuss Turtle's adoption with Taylor. Their conversation so alarms Taylor that she grabs Turtle and a few belongings and flees, leaving Jax.

Part II: Summer

This section opens with Cash Stillwater, who bags groceries at a health food store in Wyoming and makes bead jewelry; his girlfriend, Rose Levesque, sells the jewelry to tourists at the Cheyenne Trading post. Cash is homesick and lonely, and so decides to go back to his home and relatives in Heaven, Oklahoma.

Alice joins Taylor and Turtle in Las Vegas, where they pick up a new traveling companion: Barbie, who has made it her "career" to look and dress like a Barbie doll. When Jax reads a letter from Annawake over the phone to Alice, detailing the harsh treatment her brother endured after being adopted by a white family, Alice decides "there's another way to handle this" and leaves for Heaven to try to talk things out with Annawake. Alice stays in Heaven with her cousin Sugar Hornbuckle, telling her that she has business with the Nation, but without explaining the details.

Part III: Fall

Taylor and Turtle end up in Washington, where they have rented a gloomy apartment. Soon after they arrive, Barbie steals the money Alice gave Taylor to help with expenses, which leaves Taylor and Turtle destitute. Taylor has trouble finding someone to watch Turtle while she works; as a result, she cannot work many hours. She admits that she misses Jax terribly and that she feels like she is failing to provide a good environment for Turtle.

In Heaven, Alice and Annawake discuss Turtle but cannot come to any resolution about what would be best for her. As a result, Annawake hatches a plot to get Cash and Alice together. After the two begin dating, Cash takes Alice to a Stomp Dance, a traditional Cherokee ceremony that involves the whole community. Alice notes the closeness of the inhabitants of Heaven, all of whom seem to be related. As she joins in the Stomp Dance, she feels, "entirely alive … for the first time she can remember, [she] feels completely included."

When Alice discovers that she and Taylor have Cherokee ancestors, she tells Annawake that she will use that fact to help Taylor keep Turtle. Annawake explains that since Alice and Taylor don't know the culture and they look white, Turtle would suffer if she stayed with them. One evening Cash tells Alice about his past. He explains that after his eldest daughter, Alma, killed herself, his youngest child took Alma's baby to live with her and an abusive boyfriend. In an effort to protect the child from the boyfriend's abuse, she gave it away to a stranger who was passing through Oklahoma. Alice realizes the child he is talking about is Turtle and that Annawake has tried to engineer a relationship between Alice and Cash in order to try to hold onto Turtle.

When Annawake threatens to serve Taylor with a subpoena, Taylor comes to Heaven. Soon after they arrive, Turtle recognizes Cash as her "Pop-pop." The Cherokee Nation determines Cash to be Turtle's legal guardian, but assigns joint custody to Cash and to Taylor, and asks that they come up with a plan to have Turtle on the Nation at least three months out of the year. Cash then proposes that Alice marry him so that she will be with Turtle in the summers. Alice, however, insists she doesn't want a husband "that's glued to his everloving TV set." Taylor decides to marry Jax, and informs Turtle that she will now have two families. After Cash takes them all back to his house to watch him shoot his television set, Alice admits that "the family of women is about to open its doors to men. Men, children, cowboys, and Indians."

Characters

Alice

Alice is Taylor's mother and Turtle's grandmother. At the beginning of the novel, she is stuck in an unhappy marriage. Since "women on their own" tend to run in her family, she decides to leave her husband. She worries, though, that all the women in her family are "in danger of ending up alone by their own stubborn choice." Yet she is a caring and supportive mother to Taylor, who insists that she "always knows what you need." When she participates in the Stomp Dance in Heaven, the sense of connection she experiences makes her feel "entirely alive," and for the first time, completely included. She also is able to form a romantic connection with Cash and thus declare her "family of women" ready to "open its doors to men."

Sugar Boss

See Sugar Hornbuckle

Barbie

Barbie works as a waitress in a Las Vegas casino when Taylor, Turtle, and Alice meet her. After Barbie gets fired, Taylor begrudgingly decides to take her with them on the road. A shallow and insecure woman, Barbie makes it her "career" to look and dress like a Barbie doll. Moreover, she is a criminal: Taylor soon discovers that she stole money from the casino before she left, and that she was caught counterfeiting in her home in Bakersfield. Shortly after they arrive in Washington, Barbie steals money from Taylor and disappears.

Angie Buster

Angie is Lucky Buster's mother. A kind, loving woman, Angie lets Taylor and Turtle stay in her motel when they first start out on the road.

Lucky Buster

A mentally-challenged man, Lucky Buster falls into a spillway and is rescued after Taylor and Turtle get help. He and Turtle become fast friends.

Annawake Fourkiller

Annawake Fourkiller is a lawyer who has returned to Oklahoma to intern on an Indian Lawyer Training grant. After seeing Turtle on *Oprah,* she concludes that according to the Indian Child Welfare Act, Turtle's adoption is illegal. Initially, the pain over the memory of the tragic consequences of her brother's adoption causes her to take a firm stance against Taylor's position. After considering Turtle's close attachment to her mother, Annawake softens and tries to engineer some kind of compromise.

Gabriel Fourkiller

Gabriel is Annawake's twin brother. Sent to live with a white family after their mother was hospitalized, she explains the hardships he subsequently endured:

> He failed in school because they put him in the Mexican classrooms and so the teachers spoke to him in Spanish, which he didn't understand. The Mexican kids beat him up because he didn't wear baggy black pants and walk with his hands in his pockets…. When he was 13 … his new Mom … told him he was letting his new family down. When he was fifteen, he was accessory to an armed robbery.

As a result, he is serving time in prison. Annawake feels it is her job to protect the Nation's children from what happened to her brother. Her description of Gabriel's life touches Alice. Subsequently, she decides to go to Heaven and talk to Annawake about Turtle.

Ledger Fourkiller

Ledger is Heaven's medicine chief. He leads the ceremony at the Stomp Dance and offers Annawake sound advice about Turtle's fate. In an effort to get her to think about what is best for Turtle, he tells her an old Indian legend, which turns out to be the Bible story of King Solomon.

Taylor Greer

Taylor adopted Turtle soon after she found the young girl abandoned in her car three years ago. She is a loving and attentive mother, but has been unwilling to commit to her boyfriend, Jax. Her fierce devotion to Turtle prompts her to flee with her daughter. However, her inability to provide a good home for Turtle makes her feel like a failure.

Media Adaptations

- No film versions of *Pigs in Heaven* have been made, but an audio version was produced in 1993 and read by Kingsolver.

Taylor's love for her daughter eventually makes her realizes that she alone cannot provide a suitable environment for her.

After she is told that she must share custody of Turtle with Cash, she understands that the "absolute power of motherhood" has been taken away from her—"that force that makes everyone else step back and agree that she knows what's best for Turtle." She admits that the responsibility of motherhood at one time "scared her to death. But giving it up now makes her feel infinitely small and alone."

Turtle Greer

Turtle (also Turtle Stillwater) has "been marked in life by a great many things." Abandoned and then found by Taylor, it was discovered that the little girl was severely abused. As a result, Turtle became very attached to Taylor—it was said she gripped her like a snapping turtle, and the name stuck. Not surprising, she has a fear that she will be abandoned. Taylor remembers that when she found her, "Turtle gazed out at the world from what seemed like an empty house." With Taylor's devotion and encouragement, Turtle has been able to emerge from her protective shell and form relationships with others, such as Alice and Jax.

Gundi

Gundi is an eccentric, locally famous artist in Tucson. She owns the "little colony of falling-down stone houses in the desert at the edge of town" where Taylor lives with Jax. Gundi will not let people rent there unless she approves of them. She and Jax have a brief affair after Taylor leaves.

Letty Hornbuckle

Letty is Sugar's sister-in-law and is described as "the nosiest person in three counties." Letty is

Cash Stillwater's sister and conspires to get Cash and Alice together.

Sugar Hornbuckle

Sugar (also known as Sugar Boss) is Alice's second cousin and friend. She became the most famous citizen in Heaven after her picture appeared in *Life Magazine*. She and Alice spent their last years of childhood together at Alice's farm during the Depression.

Steven Kant

Taylor meets Steven Kant, a disabled air traffic controller, while driving a handicapped van in Washington.

Kevin

Kevin is a young man who works with Taylor in Washington. After she goes on a date with him, she decides he would have been a better match for Barbie, since "the two of them could jabber at each other all day without ever risking human conversation."

Rose Levesque

Rose is Cash's girlfriend in Wyoming. Since she is "shorter and heavier than she feels she ought to be, she clacks through her entire life in scuffed high heels, worn with tight jeans and shiny blouses buttoned a little too low. You can tell at thirty paces she's trying too hard."

Boma Mellowbug

Boma is Heaven's resident eccentric. She "sees things no one else does."

Lou Ann Ruiz

Taylor's friend, who is like a "second mother" to Turtle. Taylor and Turtle lived with her before they moved in with Jax.

Turtle Stillwater

See Turtle Greer

Minerva Stranger

Alice's mother, Minerva, was "a tall fierce woman" who ran a hog farm alone for fifty years. She instilled an independent spirit in her daughter, who passed it on to Taylor.

Cash Stillwater

Cash Stillwater bags groceries and makes bead jewelry. He is homesick and mourns the deaths of his wife and daughter and the disappearance of his granddaughter. When he recognizes that he is "simply dying of loneliness," he decides to go back to his hometown of Heaven, Oklahoma. When Alice meets him there, she can feel "sadness rising off him in waves." The two become lovers. When faced with the problem of Turtle's custody, he expresses his love for Alice and his granddaughter through a marriage proposal.

Jax Thibodeaux

Jax is Taylor's boyfriend and a keyboard player in a band called the Irascible Babies. Taylor does not feel very connected to him before she leaves with Turtle, but he is passionately in love with her. After she leaves, Jax notes "how clearly these days he can hear the emptiness inside things." He supports Taylor's desire to keep Turtle, but tries to get her to consider Annawake's point of view. By the end of the novel, Taylor decides to establish a firmer connection with him and tells Turtle that he will be her new "Daddy."

Franklin Turnbo

Annawake works in Franklin's law office. '[L]ike many his age, he's a born-again Indian," who didn't think about being Cherokee until he began to study Native American law.

Themes

Justice and Injustice

One of the main thematic concerns in the novel is the issue of justice and injustice. At the heart of the story is the following question: should an adopted child be taken away from a mother who provided her with the only comfort and love she has ever known, so that the child can gain a sense of her cultural identity? In response, both sides have valid and relevant points; as a result, it is difficult to come up with a definitive answer.

Annawake Fourkiller answers yes to the question; "as a citizen of Turtle's nation, as the sister of Gabriel Fourkiller," she provides a strong explanation why Turtle "can't belong" to Taylor. She insists that Native American children who have been taken away from their homes in the past "have no sense of themselves as Native Americans, but live in a society that won't let them go on being white, either. Not past childhood." Yet, Taylor finds Annawake's position unjust, since it would separate her from her daughter. Likewise Annawake finds Taylor's attempts to hold on to Turtle unjust, claiming that Turtle would suffer if she never gained an awareness of and acceptance by the Cherokee Nation.

Individualism

The women in the Greer family possess a sense of individualism and thus feel that their own views are just. Alice acknowledges that "women on their own run in [her] family." Neither she nor Taylor feel the need for a husband or a traditional family, at least until they face losing Turtle. Both have had men come and go in their lives and have learned to live independently.

Taylor's sense of individuality prevents her from establishing a stronger relationship with Jax. She reveals her own tendency to cut herself off from others in her observation that there is "one thing about people you can never understand well enough: how entirely inside themselves they are." Jax's conversation with Gundi at one point in the novel illustrates the problematic nature of individuality: Jax asks, "How can you belong to a tribe, and be your own person, at the same time? You can't. If you're verifiably one, you're not the other." Gundi, however, foreshadows the compromise that will be reached at the end of the novel when she responds, "Can't you alternate: Be an individual most of the time, and merge with others once in a while?"

Alienation and Loneliness

Several characters experience loneliness in the novel. Alice feels alienated from her husband Harland and so decides to leave him. Jax suffers excruciating loneliness after Taylor flees with Turtle. Eventually, Taylor also admits to feeling lonely on her own with just Turtle. As the characters experience these emotions, they are forced to redefine their notions of individuality and family.

Custom and Tradition

Annawake insists that Turtle must learn the customs and traditions of her race for her to gain a satisfying sense of who she is and where she belongs. She argues that Taylor would not be able to help her gain this knowledge on her own. When Annawake tries to explain this to Taylor, she focuses on the differences between white and Native American culture. Native Americans are "good to their mothers. They know what's planted in their yards. They give money to their relatives, whether or not they're going to use it wisely." They have extended families that share in the upbringing of the children. Eventually it is that strong sense of

Topics for Further Study

- Research the adoption of Native American children by white families in America in the past. How many children did this involve? How many others became wards of the state or were forced into boarding schools? How do Native American groups handle this situation today?

- Some experts insist that interracial adoptions are damaging to the children involved. Investigate the sociological and psychological effects this kind of adoption can have on a child. What is your opinion on the matter?

- Research the cultural aspects of the Cherokee people. What other customs are typical of this tribe besides the ones mentioned in the novel?

- What other laws besides the Indian Child Welfare Act have been passed to help establish Native American rights? Has this legislation been beneficial for the Native American community? In what ways?

community that becomes Annawake's most compelling argument for Turtle to be reunited with her relatives.

Style

Point of View

Kingsolver employs the third-person point of view throughout the novel. As a result, she is able to give a balanced portrait of each faction of the argument for custody of Turtle. Sybil Steinberg in her review of the novel in *Publishers Weekly* writes that one of its strengths is Kingsolver's ability to "make the reader understand and sympathize with both claimants on Turtle's life, the Cherokee Nation and Taylor."

Structure

Kingsolver effectively shifts between characters and their stories. This structure, coupled with the use of the third-person narrator, allows the author to present many perspectives so the reader can see all sides of the issue.

Symbol

Kingsolver often uses storytelling to symbolize the novel's conflicts and themes. For example, the story of "Six Pigs in Heaven" is told twice in the novel, each with a different interpretation. The story, an old Native American myth, involves six boys who would not do their chores, which included work for the tribe. As a result, their mothers cooked their leather balls and served them for lunch. When the boys complained to the spirits that their mothers treated them like pigs, the spirits agreed. The spirits then turned them into pigs and pulled them up into the night sky where they remain to this day.

Annawake informs Jax that "Six Pigs in Heaven" illustrates the importance of "do[ing] right by your people," while Americans learn to "do right by yourself." When Annawake is able to understand Taylor's point of view, she finds a different moral when she tells the story to Alice. Then she explains that the point is "to remind parents always to love their kids no matter what, I guess, and cut them a little slack." When she and Alice look up into the night sky and see seven stars, Annawake calls them "the Six Pigs in Heaven, and the one mother who wouldn't let go."

Annawake's Uncle Ledger tells the final story about two mothers fighting over a child and of the medicine man who makes a wise decision that will identify the mother who loves the child the most. When Annawake recognizes the "old Indian legend" as the Biblical story of Solomon, she understands that the power of a mother's love for her child is as strong in white as well as Native American cultures.

Denouement

Some critics have found the resolution of Turtle's custody issue too sentimental and unrealistic; others find it a satisfying compromise. The denouement does not, however, provide a happy ending for all. While the decision to split Turtle's time between Taylor and her grandfather (and now Alice) will be beneficial for Turtle, Taylor will be separated from her daughter for a few months each year. She admits that having to give up exclusive custody of Turtle "makes her feel infinitely small and alone."

Historical Context

The Trail of Tears

After years of pressure from white settlers who urged the government takeover of Native American land, Congress passed the Indian Removal Act in 1830. Prior to that time, the Cherokee had developed a strong agricultural economy and political system in the American Southeast; moreover, they were determined to keep their land. In 1827 the Cherokee Nation formulated its own constitution, which called for total jurisdiction over its own territory.

However, Congress soon determined that Native Americans had only temporary rights to the property. As a result, eight years later they were forced to evacuate their homes in Georgia, Alabama, North Carolina, and Tennessee and travel 800 miles along the Tennessee, Ohio, Mississippi, and Arkansas Rivers to reservations west of the Red River. The arduous journey, which came to be known as "The Trail of Tears," started in March 1838 and took one year to complete. En route approximately 4,000 Cherokee—mostly children and elderly—died after contracting measles, whooping cough, pneumonia, pleurisy, tuberculosis, and pellagra. Today approximately 4,500 Cherokee live in North Carolina, descendants of some members of the tribe who successfully resisted removal from their homes in 1838 as well as those who later returned after being relocated.

Native Americans Push for Civil Rights

In the late 1960s and early 1970s, many Native Americans, including members of the American Indian Movement (AIM), actively protested the treatment of Native Americans in the United States. During those years, groups of Native Americans seized the federal prison at Alcatraz Island and the Bureau of Indian Affairs, which garnered much media attention. Their protests against government policy reached their peak in 1973: in February of that year, the Movement, led by Russell Means and Dennis Banks, occupied Wounded Knee, South Dakota, where three hundred Sioux had been massacred by federal troops in 1890. The group held eleven residents of the town hostage and determined to keep them until certain demands were met.

As a result of subsequent negotiations, encouraged by extensive media coverage, the American government created a task force to investigate past injustices, including broken treaty agreements. In 1978 a more peaceful demonstration occurred during "The Longest Walk," a 3,000-mile march across the United States that ended five months later in Washington, D.C. Native Americans from eight different tribes participated in this event, which helped them gain a stronger sense of solidarity.

Critical Overview

A popular novelist, Barbara Kingsolver's fiction has garnered much critical and commercial success. Since its publication in 1993, most reviewers and literary critics have responded positively to her third novel, *Pigs in Heaven*. In fact, it was nominated for an ABBY award and received the American Library Association award, the *Los Angeles Times* Fiction Prize, and the Cowboy Hall of Fame Western Fiction Award.

Many commentators have praised Kingsolver's appealing characters and insightful and sympathetic portrait of familial bonds. Victoria Carchidi suggests "we read her for the homey quality of her writing. The characters are like someone we know, or would like to know, living on the interstates and small towns we grew up in or drive through." She maintains that "Kingsolver teaches her readers the language of tolerance and negotiation through characters with human failings and human nobility."

Travis Silcox contends in *Belles Lettres* that despite "a midpoint flatness … Kingsolver's supporting characters enrich the story." Some critics, however, fault Kingsolver for avoiding the novel's more unpleasant characters. A reviewer in *Kirkus Review* argues that while "all will be amicably, hilariously, and heartwarmingly settled to everybody's satisfaction," it is not "the truly wonderful book it might have been—characters who seem important disappear; carefully marked trails turn out to be merely picaresque, leading nowhere." The reviewer concludes that the novel is "a terrific read nonetheless."

Other critics praise the novel's focus on social issues like adoption, abuse, poverty, and ethnicity. The reviewer for *Publishers Weekly* comments:

> Kingsolver's intelligent consideration of issues of family and culture—both in her evocation of Native American society and in her depiction of the plight of a single mother—brims with insight and empathy…. In taking a fresh look at the Solomonic dilemma of choosing between two equally valid claims on a child's life, Kingsolver achieves the ad-

In Pigs in Heaven *Taylor Greer and Turtle witness a man fall into the spillway of the Hoover Dam.*

> mirable feat of making the reader understand and sympathize with both sides of the controversy…. In the end, both justice and compassion are served.

A *Los Angeles Times Book Review,* critic asserts: "That rare combination of a dynamic story told in dramatic language, combined with issues that are serious, debatable and painful … [*Pigs in Heaven,*] is about the human heart in all its shapes and ramifications."

In her review for *The New York Times Book Review,* Karen Karbo claims that Kingsolver "somehow manages to maintain her political views without sacrificing the complexity of her characters' predicaments." She continues: "Possessed of an extravagantly gifted narrative voice, she blends a fierce and abiding moral vision with benevolent, concise humor. Her medicine is meant for the head, the heart and the soul and it goes down dangerously, blissfully, easily."

However, some commentators deride the novel's sentimental predictability. Maureen Ryan refers to Karbo's review in her *Journal of America Culture* essay, insisting that Karbo

> unconsciously articulates the unease that Kingsolver's books inspire. Her medicine is meant for the

head, the heart, and the soul and it goes down dangerously, blissfully, easily. The dangers in Kingsolver's novels are not the challenges and perils that her characters all too easily overcome; they are the soothing strains of that old-time religion, lulling us into oblivion with her deceptive insistence that if we love our children and our mothers, and hang in there with hearth and home, the big bad world will simply go away.

Ryan concludes that Kingsolver's work to be "contemporary American fiction *lite.* It's what we're supposed to eat these days, and it's even fairly tasty, but it's not very nourishing and we go away hungry." Most critics, however, would agree with Wendy Smith's assessment of the novel in the *Washington Post Book World:* "There is no one quite like Barbara Kingsolver in contemporary literature. Her dialogue sparkles with sassy wit and the earthy poetry of ordinary folks' talk; her descriptions have a magical lyricism rooted in daily life but also on familiar terms with the eternal."

Criticism

Wendy Perkins

Perkins is an Associate Professor of English at Prince George's Community College in Maryland and has published several articles on British and American authors. In the following essay, she examines how the characters in Pigs in Heaven *struggle with the concepts of individuality and community.*

In an interview with critic Robin Epstein in *The Progressive,* Barbara Kingsolver explains:

In *Pigs in Heaven* I wanted to choose a high-profile event in which a Native American has been adopted out of the tribe and in which that adoption is questioned and challenged. Because it brings into conflict two completely different ways of defining good, of defining value. The one is that the good is whatever is in the best interest of the child; the other is that the good is whatever is in the best interest of the tribe, the group, and the community. What I really wanted to do in that book was not necessarily write about Indians. I wanted to introduce my readers to this completely different unit of good and have them believe in it by the end, have them accept in their hearts that that could be just as true as the other.

This conflict between the individual and the community lies at the heart of the novel. As Taylor Greer and Annawake Fourkiller each insists on her own notion of what is "good" for Turtle, Taylor's adopted Cherokee daughter, each delineates

boundaries and constructs borders that separate and isolate one from the other. When they are forced eventually to cross those borders, as they struggle to determine Turtle's fate, they begin to redefine their concepts of self and family.

After Taylor and Turtle help rescue Lucky Buster from a Hoover Dam spillway, his mother Angie explains that Lucky often wanders away from the house: "He just don't have a real good understanding of where home ends and the rest of the world takes up." At the beginning of the novel, Taylor and Annawake, unlike Lucky, know the boundaries of their own individual worlds and determine to keep within them. Taylor's boundaries delineate her individualism while Annawake's mark her sense of tribal community. Taylor has defined herself and Turtle as a family unit and has only allowed Jax to exist on the borders. Annawake divides her world into two parts—Cherokee and white—and sees little need for any border crossings.

Kingsolver foreshadows the border disputes that will soon arise in the novel in three symbolic scenes. In the opening scene, Alice, whose independent spirit and love for her daughter will prompt her to help Taylor retain custody of Turtle, complains that her garden is constantly overrun with her neighbor's pigs eating her flowers. Desert birds infest Taylor's apricot tree in Tucson. She finds inventive ways of chasing them away, including blasting Jax's music at them, but inevitably "one by one the birds emerge from the desert and come back to claim their tree." Cash notes before he leaves that pigeons from the city have been swarming in his town in Wyoming. These incidents foreshadow Taylor's and Annawake's movement into each other's territory. Jax's conversation with Gundi reflects this struggle between individual and community that lies at the heart of the custody battle over Turtle. Jax asks, "how can you belong to a tribe, and be your own person, at the same time? You can't. If you're verifiably one, you're not the other." When Gundi responds, "can't you alternate: Be an individual most of the time, and merge with others once in a while?" she proposes a compromise that Taylor and Annawake will eventually come to embrace.

Initially, both Taylor and Annawake refuse to consider the other's point of view. Taylor values the independence she gained as a young child when she had to accept the departure of her father. This independent spirit also resulted from the sense of otherness she developed when she was a young girl, during the time that Alice supported the two of them by cleaning houses. One afternoon while Taylor was helping her mother clean, she overheard a boy say to his friend, "you don't have to talk to her, that's the cleaning lady's girl." Taylor admits she grew up that day. As a result, she has learned to keep a part of herself detached from others, especially men, since as she notes, they often leave.

When she decides that there is "one thing about people you can never understand well enough: how entirely inside themselves they are," she reflects her own feelings of separateness. Taylor, however, has been able to forge a special bond with Turtle and as a result considers the two of them to be a family unit. Alice observes that they "share something physical, a beautiful way of holding still when they're not moving. Alice reminds herself that it's not in the blood, they've learned this from each other." Taylor's independent spirit, though, prompts her refusal to broaden her concept of family to include Jax or especially Turtle's Cherokee ancestors.

Annawake is equally committed to her sense of community. She becomes adamant about Turtle's return to the Cherokee Nation, citing the illegal nature of her adoption and the necessity of helping Turtle gain a sense of her heritage. In a letter to Taylor, she writes that the Cherokee children who have been taken from their homes "have no sense of themselves as Native Americans, but live in a society that won't let them go on being white, either. Not past childhood." After sharing the tragic story of her brother, Gabriel, who was sent to live with a white family after their mother was hospitalized, she ends the letter with "as a citizen of Turtle's nation, as the sister of Gabriel Fourkiller, I want you to understand why she can't belong to you."

Annawake constructs borders between the Cherokee and white worlds when she points out their differences. As she defines her tribe's sense of community, she creates a hierarchical value system. Cherokees, she claims are "good to their mothers. They know what's planted in their yards. They give money to their relatives, whether or not they're going to use it wisely." She also finds their sense of family, which actively involves relatives in the process of raising children, superior to the white version. She insists that the entire Cherokee nation is Turtle's family: "We don't think of ourselves as having extended families. We look at you guys and think you have *contracted* families."

The old myth "Six Pigs in Heaven" that she relates to Jax reflects the importance she and the Nation place on the concept of community. In this story, six boys refuse to do their work, are thus

> **" I wanted to introduce my readers to this completely different unit of good and have them believe in it by the end, have them accept in their hearts that that could be just as true as the other."**

transformed into pigs, and then become the constellation known as the Pleiades. Annawake explains that like other Native American myths, this one teaches children to "do right by your people" unlike American stories that teach children to "do right by yourself." When Alice and Annawake meet to discuss Turtle's future, Kingsolver offers a symbol of Taylor's and Annawake's inability to venture outside the borders they have each constructed around themselves. As Alice tells Annawake about Turtle's relationship with Taylor, she draws a pig with fences around it in the sugar that has spilled on the table. At that point Alice and Annawake admit that they each have trouble communicating with the other. When Annawake declares, "words aren't enough," Alice responds, "if we could get [our views] across, we wouldn't be sitting here right now."

After Alice spends time in the community of Heaven, she becomes a bridge between the two sides of the argument over Turtle. She encourages Taylor and Annawake to expand or redefine their concepts of family and community in order to effect a compromise. Taylor had already been prompted to reevaluate the "family" she has created on the road with Turtle. She acknowledges that she had trouble supporting the two of them and that she missed Jax. She admits to Alice, "I thought that … the only thing that mattered [was] keeping the two of us together. But now I feel like that might not be true. I love her all right, but just her and me isn't enough. We're not a whole family." This change of heart prompts her decision to take Turtle to Heaven and try to settle the custody dispute.

Alice also helps Annawake redefine her vision of community and family when she describes the strong bond that exists between Taylor and Turtle. Uncle Ledger encourages Annawake to consider

What Do I Read Next?

- In her first novel, *The Bean Trees* (1988), Kingsolver chronicles the beginning of the relationship between Taylor Greer and her adopted Cherokee daughter Turtle. Their story continues in the sequel, *Pigs in Heaven*.

- Kingsolver's *Homeland and Other Stories*, published in 1989, contains twelve short stories focusing on various characters who struggle to form and maintain meaningful relationships.

- *The Great Arizona Orphan Abduction* (1999), by Linda Gordon, narrates the harrowing real-life story of the abduction and relocation of forty Irish orphans by Catholic nuns, and their subsequent adoption by Mexican American families in Arizona.

- Jacquelyn Mitchard's best-selling novel, *The Deep End of the Ocean*, was published in 1996. It focuses on the devastating consequences suffered by a family after the disappearance of a three-year-old child.

Taylor's point of view when he tells her a story about two mothers fighting over a child and of the medicine man who makes a wise decision that will identify the mother who loves the child the most. When Annawake recognizes the "old Indian legend" as the Biblical story of Solomon, she understands that the power of a mother's love for her child is as strong in white as well as in Native American cultures. As a result, Annawake is able to find a different moral when she tells the "Six Pigs in Heaven" story to Alice. She explains that the point is "to remind parents always to love their kids no matter what, I guess, and cut them a little slack." When she and Alice look up into the night sky and see seven stars, Annawake calls them "the Six Pigs in Heaven, and the one mother who wouldn't let go."

When Taylor and Annawake begin to tear down the borders that have separated them, they are able to agree to a compromise that will be in Turtle's best interests. Taylor decides to provide a more secure sense of family for Turtle by making Jax her "official daddy" and by allowing her to spend vacations in Heaven with Cash, her grandfather, and her Cherokee relatives. Annawake realizes that the strong familial bond established between Taylor and Turtle should not be broken.

Maureen Ryan, in her essay on *Pigs in Heaven*, writes: "each of the protagonists in Kingsolver's novels must come to acknowledge the authority of seasoned customs, which is variously embodied in an appreciation for continuity, a sense of place, and family values that prevail over danger and instability in their fictional world." Thus, by the end of the novel, Alice recognizes that "the family of women is about to open its doors to men. Men, children, cowboys, and Indians."

Source: Wendy Perkins, in an essay for *Novels for Students*, Gale, 2000.

Wendy Smith

An American critic, editor, and journalist. Smith is the author of Real Life Drama: The Group Theatre and America, 1931–1940 *(1990). In the following review, she provides a highly favorable assessment of* Pigs in Heaven.

There is no one quite like Barbara Kingsolver in contemporary literature. She writes about working-class lives with an exhilarating combination of grit and joy that only Lee Smith among her peers can match, and Smith's work is more firmly rooted in a specific region (Appalachia), while Kingsolver engages the whole of American culture in novels and short fiction—*The Bean Trees, Homeland and Other Stories, Animal Dreams*—that sympathetically explore the worlds of people from many different backgrounds. She is the equal of any bestselling author in her gift for engaging, accessible storytelling, and she illuminates her themes through imagery woven into her plots with a technical aplomb that would delight any English professor. Her dialogue sparkles with the sassy wit and earthy poetry of ordinary folks' talk; her descriptions have a magical lyricism rooted in daily life but also on familiar terms with the eternal. Her political sophistication is as impressive as her knowledge of the human heart. It seems there's nothing she can't do.

Pigs in Heaven, her third novel, resoundingly reinforces that impression. Even the ungainly title, at first glance a startling lapse for someone as careful with words as Kingsolver, turns out to be a key metaphor, drawn from a Native American myth about the stars we know as the Pleiades, that encapsulates the book's most important theme: the delicate, often painful balancing act any society must perform between the needs of the community and the rights of the individual. But that's a dry way of describing an issue Kingsolver has embodied in a dramatic, emotionally complex story that sets up a powerful situation—a mother threatened with the loss of her child—and proceeds to gently thwart our preconditioned response to it.

Taylor Greer, heroine of Kingsolver's first novel, returns here with her adopted daughter, Turtle, the Indian girl who was abandoned in Taylor's car in *The Bean Trees*. While visiting Hoover Dam, the 6-year-old sees a man fall into the spillway; the ensuing nationwide media coverage of his rescue attracts the attention of Annawake Fourkiller, a lawyer for the Cherokee Nation in Oklahoma, who travels to Taylor's home in Tucson to warn her that the adoption of a Native American child without the consent of her tribe is illegal.

The reader's sympathies, of course, are immediately with Taylor, who rescued a girl who had been tortured and sexually abused. Smart, angry Annawake comes across as obsessed with the desire to avenge the disastrous adoption of her twin brother by a white family; her explanation of the 1978 Indian Child Welfare Act appears abstract compared with Taylor's love for Turtle. When the panic-stricken adoptive mother takes off with her daughter to avoid submitting to the Cherokee Nation's judgment, it appears that *Pigs in Heaven* will be a tale of a courageous individual defying interfering authorities.

But Kingsolver would never make things so simple. People's hunger for a meaningful place within a loving community has been a central subject in all her books; she has a working-class person's understanding of the ways in which the ideal of individualism can be twisted into a justification for the strong to oppress the weak and the victims to blame themselves. In her perfectly calibrated narrative, which juggles several simultaneous storylines, she prompts us to see the need for collective justice as well as personal fulfillment—not, as Annawake misguidedly does, by making blanket statements, but by showing how these issues work themselves out in particular lives.

Taylor's mother, Alice, goes to visit a cousin on Annawake's reservation (it's typical of Kingsolver's craftsmanship that this development was set up in *The Bean Trees*), allowing the author to give emotional weight to the Cherokee Nation's claim on Turtle by painting an attractive portrait of

> She is the equal of any bestselling author in her gift for engaging, accessible storytelling, and she illuminates her themes through imagery woven into her plots with a technical aplomb that would delight any English professor."

a neighborly environment in which everyone looks out for each other and by bringing to light the girl's grieving grandfather. Even the forbidding Annawake becomes human when viewed through Alice's shrewd, tolerant eyes.

At the same time, Taylor's life on the run with Turtle heartbreakingly demonstrates how impossible it is to be a good mother when you're totally cut off from any support system. Barely scraping by in a series of low-paying jobs, forced to leave Turtle with a flaky, larcenous ex-waitress named Barbie who is hardly the ideal babysitter, Taylor finally despairs when she learns the milk she's been urging her daughter to drink is actually making Turtle sick; like many Native Americans, she's lactose intolerant.

Those who see political correctness lurking behind every bush will doubtless be irritated by Kingsolver's careful, warmhearted denouement, which asserts that conflict between the individual and the collective can be resolved to everyone's benefit. But within the context of her sensitive story replete with appealing people who deserve to find happiness, her conclusion is both dramatically and emotionally satisfying. Like all of Kingsolver's fiction, *Pigs in Heaven* fulfills the longings of the head and the heart with an inimitable blend of challenging ideas, vibrant characters and prose that sings.

Source: Wendy Smith, "The Mother and the Tribe," in *Book World—Washington Post*, June 13, 1993, p. 3.

Rhoda Koenig

In the following review, Koenig offers a negative assessment of Pigs in Heaven, *faulting the novel's political implications and reliance on tidy resolutions.*

Cherokee girl in costume.

The six pigs in Heaven, explains a character in Barbara Kingsolver's [*Pigs in Heaven*], are the American Indian version of the Pleiades, or the seven sisters (one more example of Indians' being shortchanged). Originally six naughty boys who complained about being punished, they were turned into a constellation by the gods as a warning to other children. But if the moral of that story is the novel's stated theme—"Do the right thing"—the title unfortunately suggests its tone, a cute, dreamy mindlessness that subverts the issues of conflict and choice it propounds. Starting with charm, Kingsolver drifts into ingratiation.

Two years into a dismal second marriage, Alice feels she has made another mistake. Her silent, uncompanionable husband "has no words for Alice—nothing to contradict all the years she lay alone, feeling the cold seep through her like cave air, turning her breasts to limestone from the inside out." Ripe for flight, Alice takes off when she gets a call from a daughter in distress. Taylor has adopted a little Indian girl, Turtle, who had been sexually molested, beaten, and abandoned. Turtle's help in saving a life gets her on the *Oprah Winfrey Show,* where she attracts the attention of Annawake Fourkiller, an aggressive defender of Indian rights. Annawake tells Taylor that Turtle was improperly adopted, since the necessary tribal consent was never obtained, and that she is bringing an action to return Turtle to the Cherokee. Taylor's response is to scoop up her kid and head, with her mother, for the open road.

Barbara Kingsolver has a lovely eye (and nose) for details: the "face-powder" scent of peonies, a "quilt-cheeked" crowd pushing against a wire fence. In Alice and Taylor she creates women who are decent and good-natured, with a sisterly camaraderie and a tart sense of reality (though suspiciously articulate for, respectively, a housecleaner and an auto-parts saleswoman). But television seems to provide not only the motor for Kingsolver's plot but the tone of her characterization and prose. A sticky cloud of niceness soon envelops all but one of the main characters and most of the minor ones, too. I would be far more interested in Annawake's determination to take a child from the woman who has mothered her for half her life if she were envious or demented or pursuing the case out of a desire for personal gain. But Annawake is merely the kind of character we can easily forgive (and patronize): A Bright Girl Who Is Too Hard on Herself.

The prevailing coziness dissolves any chance of suspense: Who can envision a tragic ending for any of these sweet people, all of them terribly concerned about doing the right thing? (The ramshackle narrative, with characters roaming here and there and settling down for picnics and Kaffeeklatsches, doesn't help, either.) Split between real life and literature on one hand and soap opera and sitcom on the other (the dialogue is part honest talk, part TV banter), *Pigs in Heaven* introduces a number of serious problems (failed marriage, child abuse, ethnic identity), then resolves them with a dopey benignity and a handful of fairy dust.

The one rotten apple is Barbie, a waitress who has legally changed her name to match the doll's and has a Barbie hairstyle as well as an identical wardrobe of "thirteen complete ensembles and a lot of the mix-and-match parts." Barbie is fired for her obsession ("They say I tell people too much about my hobby. This is, like, so stressful for me, that choice of words. Barbie is not a hobby, do you understand what I mean? This is a *career* for me, okay?") and goes off with Turtle and the two women for a while, eventually proving to have not only the mental equipment of a Mattel toy but the morals of Klaus. But why, one wonders, would the sensible Alice insist on taking up with someone who is clearly inflammable plastic from the neck up? (It is perhaps best not to think about such things as consistent characterization in a novel like this; you might then start thinking, Why, if Alice is so nice, does she abandon a husband merely for being dull, and why does he make no attempt to find her?)

What is most dismaying is that Kingsolver, clearly a nice, well-meaning woman herself, with a large and affectionate public, has no idea of the appalling implications of her work. Having seen what passions Turtle inspires, Taylor decides to marry her adoring live-in boyfriend, who thinks she's "the Statue of Liberty and Abbey Road and the best burrito of your life." She has come to realize that children feel more secure if their parent figures are married and, come to think of it, heck, she would feel things were more permanent herself. ("When you never put a name on things, you're just accepting that it's okay for people to leave when they feel like it.") After a generation of the greatest freedom and opportunity women have ever known, we're supposed to feel a warm glow at one of them emotionally reinventing the wheel? I don't know about the pigs in Heaven, but the naïve self-congratulation here is enough to make the angels weep.

Source: Rhoda Koenig, "Portrait of the Artists' Friend," in *New York (magazine)*, Vol. 26, No. 24, June 14, 1993, pp. 99–100.

Karen Karbo

Karbo is a novelist. In the review below, she praises Kingsover's blending of political commentary and emotional insight in Pigs in Heaven.

Barbara Kingsolver's terrific new novel, *Pigs in Heaven,* picks up where her highly acclaimed first novel, *The Bean Trees,* left off. In this heart-twisting sequel, her feisty young heroine, Taylor Greer, is faced with the possibility of losing her 6-year-old daughter, Turtle. Taylor, an outspoken, self-professed hillbilly from Kentucky, had headed west to avoid the poverty and despair that were snagging her former schoolmates. Passing through Oklahoma, she was snagged instead by a child.

In the offhand way that can lead a person in a whole new direction, Taylor stopped at a bar on the edge of the Cherokee Nation; there, an Indian woman deposited a little girl on the front seat of Taylor's Volkswagen and promptly disappeared. The tiny, silent toddler, whom Taylor called Turtle for her fierce snapping-turtle grip, had been beaten and abused. Taylor kept on driving, and when the car broke down in southern Arizona, she

> " The prevailing coziness dissolves any chance of suspense: Who can envision a tragic ending for any of these sweet people, all of them terribly concerned about doing the right thing?"

decided just to stay put. Thus Taylor Greer became a single mother.

When *Pigs in Heaven* opens, three years have elapsed since Taylor officially adopted Turtle. Not surprisingly, their household in Tucson is a happy specimen of the kind of family life that could never be described as traditional. Taylor has found love of sorts with a musician named Jax, who plays keyboard for a group called the Irascible Babies. Turtle is doing well, considering her devastating past. Together, the three live in a dilapidated stone house at the Rancho Copo, an eccentric low-rent community owned by a local artist. This is deep Kingsolver territory, familiar to readers of her previous novels and short stories, a frowzy stretch of desert where modern-day absurdity, occasional beauty and grinding injustice (usually perpetrated against Indians and Central Americans) intersect.

Early in the book, when Taylor and Turtle are on a visit to the Hoover Dam, Turtle is the only witness to a freak accident: reaching over a wall to grab a soda can, a man falls off the dam and into a concrete spillway. When he's rescued as a result of their efforts, Turtle and Taylor make national headlines and are asked to appear on *Oprah*, as part of a program called "Children Who Have Saved Lives."

It goes without saying that *everyone* watches *Oprah*, even a brilliant, beautiful attorney for the Cherokee Nation, Annawake Fourkiller, who begins a campaign to investigate Turtle's adoption. According to the Indian Child Welfare Act, if an Indian is adopted without the consent of the tribe, the adoption is invalid. Soon thereafter, Annawake pays a visit to Tucson, where she has an awkward conversation with Taylor's boyfriend:

"You think Taylor's being selfish," he states.

Annawake hesitates. There are so many answers to that question. "Selfish is a loaded word," she says.

> It goes without saying that *everyone* watches *Oprah,* even a brilliant, beautiful attorney for the Cherokee Nation, Annawake Fourkiller, who begins a campaign to investigate Turtle's adoption."

"I've been off the reservation, I know the story. There's this kind of moral argument for doing what's best for yourself."

Jax puts his hands together under his chin and rolls his eyes toward heaven. "Honor the temple, for the Lord hast housed thy soul within. Buy that temple a foot massage and a Rolex watch."

"I think it would be hard to do anything else. Your culture is one long advertisement for how to treat yourself to the life you really deserve. Whether you actually deserve it or not."

Annawake is right, of course. Still, when I read this, visions of the long-suffering Cherokee who knows the value of kith, kin, sacrifice and every other noble thing missing in American society trudged through my head. And when it turned out that Turtle has relatives in a town on the reservation called Heaven, Okla., I almost despaired, foreseeing a thinly disguised morality play in which Taylor would be forced to give up Turtle simply because Taylor's skin color was politically incorrect.

I couldn't have been more wrong, which attests to Ms. Kingsolver's resounding achievement. For as the novel progresses, she somehow manages to maintain her political views without sacrificing the complexity of her characters' predicaments.

Ms. Kingsolver not only respects Taylor; she also understands a single mother's greatest fear—that her lack of resources can be used against her in an effort to take her child away. (When Annawake Fourkiller visits Taylor's house, she notes that it "is truly rundown by social-service standards … and accepts that this could be used to her advantage.") But Ms. Kingsolver also respects the virtues that Annawake sees in the Cherokee Nation: the rare sense of really belonging and, even

rarer, the privileged place held by young girls in the spiritual life of the community.

If the novel falls short, it is in its consideration of the people who gave Turtle away in the first place. This child has, after all, suffered a great deal, yet even though Taylor repeatedly attests to the abuse inflicted on Turtle before she came into her care, the actual perpetrators remain offstage, dismissed as alcoholics who left the reservation and moved to Tulsa. Near the end of the novel, one of Turtle's relatives, acknowledging his suspicions that the little girl was being beaten, admits that "I should have gone and got her. But my wife was dead and I didn't have the gumption." To which Taylor replies, "I've let her down too." But this exchange seems pat and perfunctory.

On the other hand, the solution to the question of whether Turtle would be better off with her mother or her people, while answered in a way that is fanciful, is also satisfying and just. That it is gained by way of a few suspiciously happy coincidences does little to diminish the many pleasures of Ms. Kingsolver's novel. Possessed of an extravagantly gifted narrative voice, she blends a fierce and abiding moral vision with benevolent, concise humor. Her medicine is meant for the head, the heart and the soul—and it goes down dangerously, blissfully, easily.

Source: Karen Karbo, "And Baby Makes Two," in *New York Times Book Review,* June 27, 1993, p. 9.

Laura Shapiro

In the following positive review, Shapiro provides a thematic analysis of Pigs in Heaven.

Turtle Greer, 6 years old, with a lifetime of memories her adoptive mother can only guess at, got her name from the way she holds on. She has a grip like a clamp, and when she clutches Taylor's hand, or her hair, or her sleeve, there's no dislodging those fingers. Turtle was shoved into Taylor's car three years earlier while she was parked by a highway in Oklahoma. Later, Taylor saw that the little Cherokee girl had been beaten and abused. "This child is the miracle Taylor wouldn't let in the door if it had knocked," writes Barbara Kingsolver in her fine new novel *Pigs in Heaven.* "But that's what miracles are, she supposes. The things nobody saw coming."

Pigs in Heaven is full of miracles, especially the kind that start out—like Turtle's life—as disasters. At the beginning of the novel, Turtle and Taylor are on a trip to the Hoover Dam, where Turtle is the only person to see a man fall over the side. Taylor finally persuades someone to believe her daughter, and the rescue makes Turtle a heroine. But becoming a heroine, which culminates in an appearance on *Oprah,* engenders a new disaster. Annawake Fourkiller, an Indian-rights lawyer, sees the white mother with her Cherokee daughter on TV and decides the child must be returned to the Cherokee Nation. Fourkiller has a personal stake in the issue: years earlier her brother was adopted by a white family. She also has the law on her side, for according to a recent Supreme Court ruling, no Indian child can be adopted out of the tribe without its consent. But Taylor isn't about to let go of the little girl who clings to her mother's hand as if to life itself. They pack up and run.

Kingsolver's fans will remember Taylor and Turtle from her wonderful first novel, *The Bean Trees* (1988). Her equally wonderful second novel, *Animal Dreams* (1990), took up a different cast of characters—two visionary sisters from tiny Grace, Ariz.—but retained the savvy wit, the political edge and the unabashed sentiment that make her books so satisfying. With *Pigs in Heaven* Kingsolver takes a risk she hasn't taken before: she challenges her own strong, '60s-style politics by pitting its cultural correctness against the boundless love between a mother and child. For all its political dimensions, this is no polemic but a complex drama in which heroes and villains play each other's parts—and learn from them. Fourkiller, though passionate in her belief that Turtle belongs with her own people, understands the damage that would be done if the law had its way. And Taylor, for her part, begins to understand the power of Turtle's connection to her past.

There are no perfect solutions to the conflict Kingsolver sets up here, and the denouement relies on a somewhat unwieldy coincidence. But while it is less deftly plotted than her first two novels, *Pigs in Heaven* succeeds on the strength of Kingsolver's clear-eyed, warmhearted writing and irresistible characters. There's Barbie, for instance, a waitress obsessed with Barbie dolls. She even dresses like one, in grown-up doll clothes she makes herself. And Alice, Taylor's mother, who has gone through two marriages wondering if there are any men at all who talk. Her current husband is so devoted to silence that he not only ignores her, he watches TV all day with the sound off. And there's Taylor, as smart and funny this time around as she was in *The Bean Trees* but with a new vulnerability born of her devotion to Turtle. Taylor is wonderfully tough-minded—too much so for her own good, perhaps,

> **Very few novelists are as habit-forming as Kingsolver, so if her work is new to you, go ahead and get all three books."**

but she doesn't know how to be any other way until Turtle teaches her. Very few novelists are as habit-forming as Kingsolver, so if her work is new to you, go ahead and get all three books. Read them in any order; they bloom no matter what.

Source: Laura Shapiro, "A Novel Full of Miracles," in *Newsweek,* Vol. CXXII, No. 2, July 12, 1993, p. 61.

Merrill Joan Gerber

An American novelist, short story writer, educator, and author of children's books, Gerber was one of the judges on the committee that awarded Kingsolver the 1993 Los Angeles Times *Book Award for Fiction. In the following essay, she offers a stylistic and thematic analysis of* Pigs in Heaven.

Talk shows have recently made their way to the center of our culture: the media has declared the media its subject—we hear and read impassioned debate about talk show hosts, their guests, their content. These shows are not just a reflection of our times but have become a major force—a public forum, a judge, a hanging jury. While there used to be a respectful separation between subjects and categories, we now see presidential candidates and heads of state on the same couch and in the same setting where only the day before sat cross-dressers and male exotic dancers. In an excess of democracy, we have allowed issues to become mixed up, we don't quite know what attitude to take toward any issue. Is this serious stuff, or entertainment?

Early in Barbara Kingsolver's energized novel, *Pigs in Heaven,* Turtle, the adopted Cherokee child of Taylor, a single mother, finds herself on the *Oprah Winfrey Show.* She has saved the life of a man who tumbled into Hoover Dam. Her appearance seems an innocent enough moment of recognition: Turtle appears as one of a group of "Children Who Have Saved Lives." The talk show, seen by millions, turns out to be the instrument not of

> The subject of the novel coincides with what brings high ratings to talk shows: adoption, ethnicity, child abuse, single motherhood (you name it, *Pigs in Heaven* has it)."

Turtle and Taylor's happy notoriety, but of their possible ruination. As soon as Turtle is noticed by Annawake Fourkiller, a Cherokee Indian activist/attorney, the talk show provides the stage on which the electronic village meets the Indian village. When Annawake Fourkiller is alerted to the fact that the child may have been illegally adopted by Taylor, who found Turtle in her car (details of this discovery are told in Kingsolver's earlier novel, *The Bean Trees*) she becomes determined to wrest Turtle from her mother and return her to her tribe.

The subject of the novel coincides with what brings high ratings to talk shows: adoption, ethnicity, child abuse, single motherhood (you name it, *Pigs in Heaven* has it). In fact, the "talk show" concept becomes a metaphor for the book's structure. On a talk show, people with Big Problems get to tell their stories straight from the heart. We hear their voices, see the tears on their cheeks, can judge firsthand the sincerity of their confessions, listen to the logic (or illogic) of their reasoning. By then we're thoroughly invested in the outcome and are willing to stay tuned through the commercials, the arguments of the experts, the prissy righteous statements or the passionate and sometimes violent outbursts of those who have been wronged—or feel they have been. Finally, the bit players come in, the speakers from the audience step forth and add their opinions, interpretations, their judgments and their praise. In fact, every character in *Pigs in Heaven* stands for some philosophical point of view, some political idea, some standard of behavior, and many of the situations operate, likewise, on a symbolic level.

Because Taylor and Turtle are soldered together by an accident of fate, by love, by a powerful psychic bond and by the rightness of their union, we want it to come out right for them. In *Pigs in Heaven*, Kingsolver asks us to hear everyone out, wait till all the evidence is in. We're happy to. She's an expert entertainer, is supremely able to command our attention, involve our opinions, arouse our sense, engage us—and what better combination of responses can a novel call forth in any reader?

Pigs in Heaven is that rare combination of a dynamic story told in dramatic language, combined with issues that are serious, debatable and painful. Kingsolver knows the world well, she's compassionate, she's smart, she can get into the skin of everyone from the airhead baby-sitter to the handicapped air-traffic control worker, to Taylor's mother who is having a late-in-life romance.

On a recent radio interview, I heard Kingsolver discussing *Pigs in Heaven.* She said that in 11th grade she learned what fiction had to be about: "Man against Nature, Man against Man, and Man against Himself." "Why all this against-stuff?" she said, suggesting how puzzled she was about this way of looking at the world. It certainly wasn't her way. Barbara Kingsolver is for, not against, and her fiction is about getting people together, getting them to live in the global village (not just the Indian village or any other exclusive fenced and guarded fort). When the interviewer asked her if her ability to understand all her characters was something like Flaubert's saying "Madame Bovary, *c'est moi,*" she replied: "I think he knew what she felt like and it wasn't like female-anatomy-stuff. It was the human heart."

That's what *Pigs in Heaven* is about—the human heart in all its shapes and ramifications.

Source: Merrill Joan Gerber, "Those Ideas in the Air," in *Los Angeles Times Book Review,* October 31, 1993, pp. 10, 12.

Sources

Carchidi, Victoria, "Barbara Kingsolver: Overview," in *Contemporary Popular Writers,* edited by Dave Mote, St. James Press, 1997.

Karbo, Karen, "And Baby Makes Two," in *The New York Times Book Review,* June 27, 1993, p. 9.

Kirkus Reviews, April 15, 1993.

Los Angeles Times Book Review, July 4, 1993, pp. 2, 8.

Ryan, Maureen, "Barbara Kingsolver's Lowfat Fiction," in *Journal of American Culture,* Vol. 18, No. 4, Winter, 1995, pp. 77-82.

Silcox, Travis, review, in *Belles Lettres,* Fall, 1993, pp. 4, 42.

Smith, Wendy, "The Mother and the Tribe," in *Washington Post Book World,* June 13, 1993, p. 3.

Steinberg, Sybil, review, in *Publishers Weekly,* April 5, 1993, p. 62.

For Further Study

Demarr, Mary Jean, *Barbara Kingsolver: A Critical Companion,* Greenwood, 1999.
This reading is a critical study of Kingsolver's novels which provides insight into her background as a both journalist and feminist.

Epstein, Robin, "An Interview with Barbara Kingsolver," in *The Progressive,* Vol. 12, No. 9, February, 1996, p. 337.
In this interview, Kingsolver discusses the novel's defining themes.

Lyall, Sarah, "Termites Are Interesting But Books Sell Better," in *The New York Times,* September 1, 1993, pp. C1, C8.
Lyall examines the book's thematic concerns and asserts that it reveals "a droll wit and an intricate understanding of the almost imperceptible subtleties of relationships."

Shōgun: A Novel of Japan

James du Maresq Clavell

1975

Although not considered great literature by most critics, *Shōgun: A Novel of Japan* made its author, James du Maresq Clavell, one of the most widely read twentieth-century novelists. The novel contains war, trade disputes, cultural clash, passion, death, and descriptions of beauty that have kept readers up until dawn. Such features make Clavell an "old-fashioned storyteller" who spins captivating yarns rather than an *artiste* like Virginia Woolf or Thomas Pynchon. Clavell's survival of a Japanese death camp gave him unique insight into human behavior and cultural differences, enabling him to produce a truly gripping story. In addition to penning a good book to curl up with, Clavell built a bridge of understanding from West to East by fictionalizing a historical encounter between them.

Shōgun tells the story of an English pilot, John Blackthorne, in charge of five Dutch ships whose purpose is to break the Portuguese monopoly on Japanese trade. Instead, the pilot becomes embroiled in Japanese politics as Lord Toranaga Yoshi employs him as his secret weapon. *Shōgun* uses straightforward storytelling techniques to keep readers riveted as they imagine themselves in the position of the English pilot. By the end, the reader has learned about Japan alongside Blackthorne as he attempts to survive.

That the West is interested in the East is proved by *Shōgun*'s success. In the first five years of its printing, 7 million books were sold. NBC did not risk much in sponsoring a film extravaganza. For twelve hours of prime time, 130 million people

watched *Shōgun.* The miniseries prompted sales of another 2.5 million books. Since the movie, even more people have read the book or watched the shorter 2.5-hour-long film.

Author Biography

A successful producer, director, screenwriter, and novelist, James du Maresq Clavell was also a war hero, carpenter, and political conservative who conversed with Roger Moore and corresponded with William F. Buckley. Clavell also contributed to arts and letters a bridge of understanding between the West and the East. Novels like *Shōgun* enabled the West to gain an understanding and respect for Japan at a time when Japan was emerging as an economic world power.

Clavell, born on August 10, 1924, in Sidney, Australia, was the son of British colonists Richard Charles and Eileen (Collis) Clavell. Clavell grew up hearing sea stories from his father and grandfather, both careerists in the Royal British Navy. They instilled in him a sense of pride and obligation for being British. Consequently, Clavell described himself as a "half-Irish Englishman with Scots overtones," not an Australian. The family moved to different Navy stations, such as Hong Kong, where Clavell spent much of his boyhood.

Clavell attended high school in England. After graduation, he enlisted in the British Royal Artillery the year World War II broke out. Like Peter Marlowe, in Clavell's 1962 *King Rat,* Clavell was wounded in Malaysia. He was captured by the Japanese and spent the rest of the war as a prisoner. He spent three and a half years in the notorious death camp Changi, where one in fifteen men survived. Clavell told an interviewer from the *Guardian* that in surviving he was conscious of living on "forty borrowed lifetimes."

The experience of Changi informs all of Clavell's fictions. At Changi, Clavell found he could no longer believe in the idealist code of his father. It was replaced by an Objectivist code: the individual is paramount, loyalty is given to a small interdependent group, capitalism and free enterprise guarantee freedom. The lessons he learned at Changi about human nature and the importance of bridging cultural gaps lay at the heart of his novels.

In 1946, back in Britain, a motorcycle accident ended his military career. With a disability discharge, he entered the University of Birmingham. April Stride, a friend of Clavell's sister, married Clavell on

James Clavell

February 20, 1951. They had two daughters, Michaela and Holly. Through Stride, Clavell discovered film. Soon, the family immigrated to the United States where he had his first film success, *The Fly,* in 1958. He won a Screen Writers Award for his 1960 film *The Great Escape.* He achieved cinematic fame by writing and directing *To Sir with Love* in 1969. Clavell became a naturalized citizen in 1963.

A screenwriters strike in 1960 gave Clavell time to follow his wife's suggestion and write a novel about Changi. Writing proved difficult but Clavell received help from Herman Gollub, editor for Little, Brown and Company, and his blue pen. The result was *King Rat,* and a discovery that Clavell could write about the East in a way that made it accessible to Western readers.

Clavell wrote several novels after *King Rat,* including *Shōgun* in 1975, and worked on a few more film projects. He died from a combination of cancer and stroke at his home in Vevey, Switzerland, in 1994.

Plot Summary

The Shipwreck

At the opening of *Shōgun: A Novel of Japan,* John Blackthorne, English pilot of a Dutch ship named Erasmus, arrives in Japan hoping to break the Jesuit trade monopoly on the Far East. Instead, he becomes embroiled in the feudal politics of a war-torn nation. His involvement begins as soon as he reveals his dislike for a Jesuit priest. Lord Omi and Lord Yabu see that Blackthorne may be the key to getting rid of the Jesuits. In addition, Blackthorne has the knowledge necessary to create a musket regiment for Yabu—so he can be Shōgun.

Before Yabu can secure Blackthorne, Lord Hiro-matsu, the trusted aid of Lord Toranaga Yoshi, persuades Yabu to give the ship, its contents, and its pilot to Toranaga. Hiro-matsu then takes them all to Osaka aboard a galley piloted by Vasco Rodrigues, a Portuguese merchant. He tries to kill Blackthorne, but Blackthorne saves his life instead.

Osaka

For Blackthorne, Osaka makes the "Tower of London look like a pigsty." Inside the castle, Blackthorne meets Toranaga, President of the Council of Regents and overlord of the Kwanto. Father Alvito is present to interpret and to negotiate with Toranaga about the Black Ship—the trading vessel under Jesuit control whereby the Japanese obtain goods from China. Toranaga decides Blackthorne could be his secret weapon if he learns to be Japanese. Lady Mariko will be his teacher.

In order to keep Blackthorne from his rival Ishido, Toranaga has Blackthorne thrown in prison. There, Blackthorne learns the history of the Jesuits in Asia from Father Domingo, a Franciscan and enemy of the Jesuits. After a few days with Father Domingo, Ishido's guards kidnap Blackthorne. While they attempt to steal Blackthorne away, Toranaga's men in disguise steal him back. By coincidence, Yabu arrives and rescues Blackthorne. Ishido, consequently, loses face, while Yabu and Blackthorne feel closer to Toranaga. Hiro-matsu and Toranaga get a good laugh.

The Escape

With information from Blackthorne, Toranaga begins to understand how European affairs impact Japan. More immediately, Ishido is ready to orchestrate the political demise of Toranaga. Therefore, Toranaga disguises himself as Lady Kiri and sneaks out of Osaka, but Blackthorne notices the trick.

As the party nears the last checkpoint, Ishido stops them. Blackthorne risks his life to prevent Ishido from noticing Toranaga. He succeeds, and

the party makes it to the galley, which is barricaded in the harbor by samurai in fishing boats. Toranaga cuts a deal with the Jesuits, and they take him out of the harbor. Rodrigues repays Blackthorne a life by allowing him to pilot the galley alongside the Portuguese vessel as it leaves. As a result of enabling Toranaga's escape, Blackthorne is made Hatamoto—a high-ranking samurai.

Blackthorne's Education

Back in Anjiro, Toranaga avoids Yabu's traps. He does this by honoring Yabu in front of all his men, who cheer "Toranaga!" Then, Toranaga quickly exits before Yabu realizes he has been manipulated.

That night, Blackthorne attempts suicide to protest Yabu's order that the entire village be killed unless he learns Japanese. To their surprise, Blackthorne was not bluffing, but Omi stops his arm. The Japanese now see Blackthorne as a true samurai.

While working to train Yabu's musket regiment, Blackthorne falls in love with Mariko, who is teaching him Japanese. Blackthorne discovers that to progress in his studies, and to survive, he must become Japanese.

The Game Begins

Toranaga returns to Anjiro and begins to implement his war strategy. First, he develops a false personality—one that is indecisive and weak—in order to make everyone think he is beaten. Second, he does everything in his power to gain time.

After speaking with his officers, Toranaga tells Mariko she must go to Osaka with an order for his ladies to join his procession to the castle. Then he converses with Blackthorne about the Black Ship. An earthquake disrupts the meeting, and Blackthorne saves Toranaga again. As a reward, Blackthorne receives a fief and several declarations of friendship.

Yokose

Lord Zataki meets Toranaga, on behalf of the Council, at Yokose. Toranaga tricks Zataki into revealing both of the Council's messages. First, the Council asks Toranaga to come to Osaka and declare obedience. If the invitation is refused, the second message orders him to commit *seppuku*—suicide. Toranaga promises an answer tomorrow. Toranaga now knows that Ishido has an alliance, and he has gained a day through the rules of diplomatic ceremony. Yabu also accepts a scroll and must go to Osaka without delay. At noon the next day, Toranaga says he will accept the invitation. Toranaga gains more time this way because he must arrive in Osaka with all the trappings of his societal position.

Back to Yedo

Toranaga orders everyone back to Yedo by different routes. Toranaga travels quickly by way of Anjiro to collect his men and use the galley. Back at Yedo, he begins to probe Ishido's alliance for weaknesses. Mariko and Blackthorne, meanwhile, take a lingering route overland to Yedo. On the way, they consummate their affair. When they arrive at Yedo, the love affair ends.

At Yedo, Toranaga blackmails the Jesuits by openly encouraging Blackthorne's plan to steal the Black Ship. Goyoko, a madam who is trying to create a red-light district, gives Toranaga several secrets to use against Zataki and the Christian Lords. Toranaga immediately offers Zataki a deal. While waiting for a response, Toranaga continues to act as a defeated man. He tests the loyalty of his son and heir, Lord Sudara, and then disinherits him to thwart treason plans. When he hears that Zataki accepts his offer, he sends Sudara to Zataki as a hostage. Coincidentally, Yabu succeeds in killing Lord Jikkyu—thus taking both Zataki's and Jikkyu's armies out of the field.

With things falling into place, Toranaga brings Hiro-matsu into his confidence. A relieved Hiro-matsu stops the disintegration of the officer ranks. Next, Toranaga releases Mariko, Yabu, and Blackthorne to open up Osaka. As they prepare to leave, Mariko gives information to the Jesuits in order to keep Blackthorne safe should Toranaga lose.

Mariko's Poem

Toranaga cannot act until Ishido is forced to give up the hostages in Osaka and every lord, free of coercion, can choose sides. Mariko, according to Toranaga's directions, disrupts Lady Ochiba's birthday party by demanding that Ishido allow Toranaga's people to obey his summons to join his procession to Osaka. He refuses. Citing the laws of tradition, Mariko ignores Ishido and the Council and attempts to escort Toranaga's ladies out of Osaka. They are prevented from leaving and Mariko declares she will commit *seppuku* at sunset. As a result, all the other ladies take Mariko's side because she was prevented from following the order of her liege lord.

The Council cannot allow Mariko to commit seppuku, so they publicly give in. Secretly, they

plan to disarm Mariko and keep her at Osaka. To do this, Yabu opens a secret door for Ishido's ninja, but Blackthorne prevents them from disarming Mariko. During the battle, Mariko is killed. As Toranaga will later reflect, in this game of chess, he sacrificed his queen, "but Ishido lost two castles." The deed is done; the Council has to let everyone leave or Ishido will be admitting to murder. Proof that the alliance is weakening comes when Lord Kiyama's men provide a safe exit for Blackthorne. Blackthorne learns his ship has been burned and he races back to Yokohama.

War

Blackthorne, who thinks the Jesuits burned his ship, receives a note from Mariko telling him to build another. Some day he will learn that Toranaga burned Erasmus to neutralize the Jesuits. For betraying Mariko, Yabu is ordered to commit *seppuku*.

Mariko's sacrifice unlocks Osaka and disperses Ishido's alliance. It is now clear that Toranaga was never entirely defeated, and when Ishido comes out of Osaka to fight, Toranaga launches his battle plan. He wins and becomes Shōgun.

Characters

Lady Mariko Akechi

The Dictator Lord Goroda was assassinated by General Lord Akechi Jinsai. As a punishment, the entire family was killed or ordered to commit *seppuku*. Lady Mariko, daughter of Akechi, was not allowed either privilege. Instead, Buntaro sent her to a province far to the north for eight years. There she studied Latin, Portuguese, and Catholic doctrine with the Jesuits. Even so, she is first and foremost a samurai and one of the most admired women in all Japan.

In Toranaga's falconry terms, Mariko is a prize peregrine falcon. Such a falcon is to be enjoyed and hunted with for a time but then released. Like Toranaga's prize falcon, Mariko, once released, will appear to soar away but then come back and masterfully kill her prey. Throughout the novel, Toranaga trains Mariko on Buntaro and on Blackthorne. Then he releases her on Osaka. There she performs beautifully and wins the release of hostages from Osaka.

Media Adaptations

- *Shōgun,* produced by Shogun Productions, appeared in 1980 as a television adaptation of twelve hours and five parts. The NBC-sponsored film was made in Japan for $22 million. Eric Bercovci and Clavell wrote the script. Orson Welles narrated and Jerry London directed Richard Chamberlain as the Pilot, Toshiro Mifune—as classic an actor in Japan as John Wayne or Clint Eastwood in America—as Toranaga, and Yoko Shimada as Lady Mariko. Clavell was also paid one million to be executive producer. It is estimated that 130 million viewers watched the five parts when they aired. One of the most surprising features of the film was the lack of subtitles during the first part of the series. This feature forced viewers into the position of Blackthorne until he had learned Japanese. In 1981, a 2.5-hour movie was cut from the longer series.

- In 1989, *Shōgun* provided enough material for Infocom to make a computerized adventure game. While the characterization and graphics of the product were rated highly, as an adventure game it was not received very well.

- In 1990, with investment from Clavell, the novel was adapted to the stage under the direction of Michael Smuin. "James Clavell's *Shōgun,* the Musical," with lyrics and script by John Driver, bends the novel's around Shakespeare's *King Lear.* Instead of a struggle for power, Taiko divided his realm between rivals. The play was unsuccessful both commercially and critically.

Father Martin Alvito

Father Alvito (also known as Tsukku) is a Jesuit priest who has spent most of his life in Japan and understands Japanese culture. He has the highest respect for Japanese culture but still views the Japanese as inferior people who can never be ordained priests. Father Alvito, due to his understanding of the Japanese, always gives the correct advice to his superiors, but he is not always followed. Toranaga respects Father Alvito but knows that his Catholicism and his vows of obedience to the Pope cloud him. He is working on a dictionary that will rival previous dictionaries. He gives one to Toranaga for Blackthorne's use. For his efforts, Toranaga allows him to build a cathedral in Yedo.

Father Alvito should be the hero when the novel is viewed in terms of Clavell's Objectivist philosophy. He is a capitalist who knows the Japanese and who knows how to expand trade. But he is defeated and, eventually, exiled. Meanwhile, the Englishman who wants trade becomes the hero and a samurai who will never leave Japan.

Anjin

See John Blackthorne

John Blackthorne

John Blackthorne (also known as Anjin) is an Englishman who received a complete education in sailing and war from Alban Cardoc. He left his family to become the greatest English pilot. Instead of realizing that dream, he becomes the Anjin-san, advisor on foreign trade and shipping to the Shōgun Lord Toranaga. The process is not easy. Blackthorne dies to himself as a European in his suicide attempt and is reborn a samurai.

Blackthorne immediately impresses everyone by defying the Jesuit priest. Then he wins respect by his sailing ability. Everyone notices how he laughs at death and challenges the sea when at the helm. He makes the Japanese wonder about other Europeans and how strong they might be. However, while he sticks to his European ways he is clumsy on land. It is only his education in the ways of the Japanese that makes him a man again. Blackthorne's mind is very methodical. It is the mind of a European at the earliest stages of the New Science and Enlightenment.

Toranaga realizes that Blackthorne is a special bird and sets him apart from his other falcons. Blackthorne is "a short-winged hawk, a hawk of the fist, that you fly direct from the fist to kill anything that moves, say a goshawk." It is the fierceness of the goshawk with a mix of unpredictability that makes Blackthorne such a fun bird for Toranaga to fly. While Mariko was his favorite bird, Toranaga hunted with a peregrine falcon, but in the end, Toranaga is hunting with a goshawk. This symbolizes that Blackthorne has become the friend and advisor Toranaga needs in the first years of his Shōgunate.

Lord Buntaro

Mariko's husband is the son of Hiro-matsu and a ruthless war general whose loyalty to Toranaga is beyond question. Buntaro is desperately in love with Mariko but he has never come to terms with the shame her father brought on the Akechi family. Due to this torment, Buntaro has become an abusive husband. Buntaro, except for his anger, complements the perfection of his wife by being the perfect samurai. As a display of his warrior ability, he performs the Tea Ceremony and flower arranging with perfection.

Friar Domingo

Toranaga keeps Father Domingo alive in prison until he can find a way to get information from him. Blackthorne easily extracts information from Father Domingo on the Jesuits doings and other matters of Japanese politics. For this help, Blackthorne wins his release, but when the cell guards call Father Domingo's name, he thinks it is for execution and dies of fright.

Captain Ferriera

Captain Ferriera is the military commander of the Jesuits. He wants to put Blackthorne to death immediately. He nearly does so against the wishes of his superior. Ferriera is for the Catholics what Buntaro or his father are to Toranaga, an absolutely dependable killer.

Lady Fujiko

The widow of Uragi, who was killed for insulting Ishido, is denied permission to commit *seppuku* from Toranaga. Instead, she is ordered by Toranaga to be Blackthorne's consort. In this capacity, she runs his household. She proves her samurai mettle when she has a showdown with Omi over Blackthorne's guns. From that point on, against their wills, Fujiko and Blackthorne grow fond of each other, although Fujiko's wish to die at the end of six months is honored.

Goyoko

The woman who holds Kiku's contract is madam Goyoko. Her societal position gives her access to a realm of secrets. She trades several of these to Toranaga in exchange for his support in creating a red-light district and a new class of entertainment girls, called *geishas*.

Hiro-matsu

Hiro-matsu is "very good at killing" and one of the reasons Toranaga has never lost a battle. He is not just Toranaga's first general but his most trusted vassal. Hiro-matsu, for his part, chose to serve Toranaga because he believes in Toranaga and he does not want to lose.

Hiro-matsu is the perfect warrior and the perfect samurai. His son, Lord Buntaro takes after him, except for Buntaro's uncontrollable rage. Toranaga loves Hiro-matsu so much that he must keep Hiro-matsu at a distance lest he tell him what the real strategy is. Finally, when Toranaga is satisfied his plan is working, he brings Hiro-matsu into his confidence. The old soldier is so happy that his master is doing precisely the opposite of rumor that he feigns illness lest he be unable to control his smile. Renewed in his faith, Hiro-matsu is the ideal man to carry out the battle plan, with his son, Lord Buntaro, leading the men directly.

Lord Ishido

Ishido is a peasant who has risen to be a powerful lord. He is in charge of the emperor's guard and the castle of Osaka. At first glance, he to have the upper hand against his rival, Toranaga. He gradually marginalizes Toranaga and uses every means in his control to bring him down. Ishido's downfall comes as a result of not knowing when to break the rules. His second problem is his love for Lady Ochiba, who has always loved Toranaga. Lastly, he thinks that the game for Shōgun and the game with the Jesuits are separate.

Brother Joseph

When Brother Joseph (also known as Uraga) is denied ordination, he rebels against Father Alvito. Uraga sees that the Jesuits have no intention of ordaining any Japanese and this sets him against the Catholics. He leaves Alvito's service and Toranaga gives him to Blackthorne as an aid. Fearing that Uraga will give away all their secrets, the Jesuits have him assassinated.

Lord Yabu Kasigi

Lord Yabu is overlord of Izu, which sits next to the Kwanto, where the barbarian ship is towed. Thanks to his wife, Yuriko, Yabu has a large army of samurai, and he dreams of being able to create a musket regiment. Further, he dreams of using a musket regiment to become Shōgun. "Equally dangerous as ally or enemy," Yabu is a man of contradictions incapable of sticking to an agenda unless Yuriko or Omi are there to guide him. He is willing to prove his courage or defend his honor at the drop of a hat. This rashness puts him at Blackthorne's mercy several times. Although he betrays

Toranaga in the end, he more often protects him—he carries out orders regarding the Anjin-san, he sees to it that one of Toranaga's key rivals is poisoned, and he defends Toranaga with his life. He is an opportunist hoping to wind up as Shōgun, but until he does, Yuriko tells him to be Toranaga's best vassal.

Yabu enjoys the Night of the Screams given him by the boiling of Pieterzoon. The character of Yabu is an extreme character. Omi, for example, merely does his duty when he kills. Killing, on the other hand, sexually arouses Yabu—nobody else in the novel takes such pleasure. His pleasure in killing and his betrayal of Mariko make him appear the embodiment of evil, but that is to misunderstand samurai. Except for his sexual perversion, Yabu is every bit the samurai Buntaro is, but he has too much ambition. His keen knowledge of swords proves this.

Kiku

Kiku is the woman that every man desires. Toranaga eventually buys her contract for pleasure and to put an end to Omi's distraction. Finding that Kiku is too much of a distraction except for a man who needs to be distracted, Toranaga gives her to Blackthorne.

Mura

The headman of the village and keeper of Blackthorne when he first arrives. He is a Christian and former samurai who now spies for Toranaga in hopes of regaining samurai status. He relays information about the villagers and the doings of Omi and Yabu.

Naga

Naga, another son of Toranaga, is not as smart as Sudaru but he is a good son. Naga is a good warrior who helps Omi with the musket regiment. Toranaga, in order to appease the Jesuits, tells him that he will convert. This infuriates him but he will do it. He is loyal to his father but he is easily provoked.

In terms of falconry, Naga is a falcon who is being flown at the wrong bait. Naga's game is combat. Situations of intrigue, as with Omi and Jozen, are too complex for Naga. Still, his father loves him for his good heart and his combat abilities.

Lady Ochiba

The mother of the heir, Yaemon, and former consort of the Taiko. She is a bitter woman who has always loved Toranaga. When Yodoko, widow

of the Taiko, dies she makes a request of Ochiba that she marry Toranaga. Ochiba cannot refuse such a request and, therefore, will do everything in her power to see Toranaga victorious, such as prevent Yaemon from arriving at Osaka.

Lord Omi

Lord Omi has the brains in the Kasigi clan, and although he wants to take his Uncle Yabu's place, he bides his time. It is Omi who recognizes that the real value is in Blackthorne's head, not his ship's hold. Therefore, he persuades Yabu to keep Blackthorne alive. It is also Omi who tames Blackthorne, by pissing on his back. Omi is also the mastermind behind the musket regiment. He leads the regiment with Naga.

Omi becomes a great leader by the end of the novel, but only after several distractions are removed. He is in love with and distracted by the courtesan Kiku—Toranaga takes her away and gives her to Blackthorne. His parents are also a stumbling block. When Yabu is ordered to commit *seppuku*, he orders—as his death wish—that Omi's parents be killed and that Omi take charge of the clan.

Vasco Rodrigues

Although a merchant at heart, Rodrigues knows who holds the power. He will not openly defy the Jesuits and risk losing the commission to pilot the Black Ship. His attempt to drown Blackthorne fails, as does his other murder plot. Instead he is tossed overboard, but he does not die because Blackthorne makes Yabu save him. Later, Rodrigues returns the favor by helping Blackthorne escape. Rodrigues also represents the assimilated European and a counterweight to Blackthorne's crew. He has a Japanese wife that he sincerely loves. Like Alvito, his Catholicism prevents him from total assimilation.

Jan Roper

Of the crew members, Jan Roper stands out for being a religious fanatic, a bigot, and incredibly angry. He goes far beyond Father Alvito's racism to denounce all Japanese as animals or demons.

Lady Sazuko

Toranaga's most recent consort. She might not be as brilliant as Mariko, but her convincing acting and her loyalty to her master cause everyone to face her when Toranaga and Kiritsubo switch places. It is her presence in Osaka that prevents

Toranaga from attacking. After Mariko's "poem," she can leave Osaka.

Father Sebastio

The first European Blackthorne meets is Father Sebastio. He tries to present the Dutchmen as heretics and pirates who should be executed at once. Blackthorne breaks his crucifix in order to show that he views Jesuits as his enemy

Lord Sudara

Sudara's love for his wife, Lady Genjiko, stands in marked contrast to the rest of his personality. Except when he is thinking of her, Sudara is the perfect heir to Toranaga—cold and calculating like his father.

Lady Kiritsubo Toshiko

Toranaga's number one consort is Lady Kiri. She mothers Toranaga's consorts and Mariko. She is also an information conduit for Toranaga. Mariko wins her release from Osaka.

Tsukku

See Father Martin Alvito

Uraga

See Brother Joseph

Lord Toranaga Yoshi

He has said a thousand times that he has no desire to be Shōgun but that is exactly what Lord Toranaga Yoshi will become. Toranaga, the favorite of the Taiko when he was alive, is the Lord of the Kwanto—the wealthiest province of Japan. He is also the President of the Council of Regents. Toranaga is "the greatest falconer in the realm" and a brilliant maker of noh plays who has never lost a battle. Toranaga is a master of human character and strategy who hates to waste money or the lives of his vassals. As Father Alvito puts it, "we're all clay on the potter's wheel you spin."

Toranaga sees immediately that Blackthorne would make a good friend and advisor in all matters dealing with the outside world but not in his current state. Thus, Toranaga, amid all his other operations, makes sure that Blackthorne becomes the civilized Ajin-san. Only then can the barbarian help him become Shōgun.

Toranaga, as designer, nearly approaches the status of a god. At the height of his knowledge, when only he knows the truth of the situation, he is sequestered in the highest tower of Yedo. Knowing he is there brooding, his men fear him. At other times, he startles his closest advisers with his knowledge and his ability to predict the way people will behave. His enjoyment of prediction and knowing make Blackthorne, in all his unpredictability, special to Toranaga. In the end, all his scheming brings him the Shōgunate.

Lady Yuriko

Yabu's wife, Yuriko, guides Yabu as much as she can. By economizing, Yuriko has been able to afford more samurai for Yabu than should be possible on paper. This makes him a very desirable ally. Yuriko figures out that Toranaga is playing a game, and she tells Yabu how to use the situation to his advantage.

Themes

Heroism

Clavell's *Shōgun* is a celebration of heroic deeds that changed the course of history for people all over the world. Heroes in this context are those figures who withstood the aggressions of Spain or bravely sailed into the unknown oceans to discover new lands, people, and riches. Such historic figures as Queen Elizabeth are thus described in glowing terms. The Portuguese of the past—those who belonged to the first Age of Exploration under Prince Henry the Navigator—are praised for braving the unknown and connecting the entire world in the minds of sailors and governments. Clavell contrasts these European heroes with Japanese notions of heroism.

In Clavell's Japan, winning money, plundering cities, and destroying weaker cultures are not considered heroic. Instead, heroism in samurai terms consists of fulfilling one's duty, being loyal, fighting bravely and well against a worthy opponent, and being a master of strategy. Thus, Yabu is a hero because he is brave and a good swordsman. Buntaro, the master archer, is renowned for his ability as master of the Tea Ceremony. Toranaga, a legend in his own time, epitomizes Sun Tzu's *Art of War* with his mastery of strategy as well as his accomplishments in the techniques of peace and governance.

Yet there is similarity between the two notions of heroism. To be a hero, whatever the standard, takes grit. Blackthorne's performance piloting a ship leaves spectators in awe. Lady Mariko's incredible performance at Osaka shows the heroism of great determination; she comes close to canon-

Topics for Further Study

- Under the Tokugawa Shōgunate, the Japanese rejected the attempt to modernize samurai techniques with guns and continued to fight with swords. During World War II, the Japanese proved they could fight very well with guns. After the war, the Japanese established a constitutional government, which prohibited them from having offensive military capabilities. What is the role of technology in war? What is the current attitude in Japan towards the use of the military and sophisticated weapons systems?

- Research the Tea Ceremony and the art of flower arranging in Japanese culture. How do these two arts function in Clavell's novel and why is Buntaro's mastery of them so important?

- Clavell is an advocate of Objectivism. What is this theory of social relations? Does *Shōgun* support this way of viewing society or not? How does the samurai code challenge Objectivism?

- The Japanese in 1600 were intolerant of other nations and ethnicities; they preferred to exist in isolation from the world. Is it possible to behave this way today? What economic and technological developments have affected a culture's ability to remain isolated? Give specific examples.

- Free trade, without religious or governmental interference, is championed in the novel. What do you think Clavell would say about debates over U.S. trade with China and the protests against the World Trade Organization in early 2000?

izization for her deeds. Heroism can also be shown in a small person like Mura who faces the much larger Blackthorne in order to do his duty—give the barbarian a bath. And everyone respects a woman of lesser stature than Mariko, like Fujiko, who bravely defends Blackthorne's honor against Lord Omi. The comparison of heroic ideals in the novel is one of many ways Clavell encourages multicultural understanding.

Cultural Exchange

There are two levels to the theme of cultural exchange and multiculturalism in *Shōgun*. On the first level, the cultural clash between the Japanese and the Europeans provides a litmus test of intelligence. The smartest and most successful characters are those who both understand cultural differences and try to utilize them. The second level is for the reader. Clavell gives the reader insight into the Japanese perspective in order to facilitate cross-cultural understanding.

The many scenes of information exchange build a bridge of understanding between Blackthorne and Japan, the physical exchange matters more. When Blackthorne insults Omi by saying he will piss on him, Omi pisses on Blackthorne instead. In any situation this would be insulting. However, when Yabu asks why he did not piss in Blackthorne's face, Omi proves he is an intelligent man: "to do it in his face—well, with us, to touch a man's face is the worst of insults, neh? So I reasoned that I might have insulted him so deeply he would lose control." In this very charged moment, Omi has recognized that Blackthorne is different, but has engaged with him in a memorable, reasoned way. Yabu, on the other hand, would have ruined any future relations with Blackthorne.

Another physical means of cultural exchange occurs when Blackthorne breaks the Jesuit's crucifix. Whereas Blackthorne totally assimilates to the Japanese way of life, in return the sole change of the Japanese is an end to being dominated by the Jesuits. As a result, Clavell's decidedly pro-Japanese book suggests that European culture was more elastic. That is not to say that the Japanese could change, for Mariko becomes nearly European in attitude. But in political terms, Japan chose isolation instead of openness after a very limited experience with outsiders. The Europeans, on the other hand, set out to explore the entire globe, and then fought to conquer it.

Education

A unifying theme in *Shōgun* is the importance of knowledge acquisition and the ability to pass on knowledge. Two models of education are presented in the novel: those of Toranaga and Ishido. Ishido believes in learning necessary skills and insists that his samurai learn the arts of war, how to fight and follow orders. Toranaga believes that "samurai should be well versed in the arts of peace to be strong for the arts of war." Thus, his samurai are accomplished poets, swimmers, writers, and warriors. Blackthorne's teacher, Alban Caradoc, agrees with Toranaga. He teaches Blackthorne the skills of a pilot-navigator as well as the more important lesson that "when the storm's the worst and the sea the most dreadful, that's when you need your special wits. That's what keeps you alive."

The Jesuits also use Ishido's model. They set up schools, write grammars, and teach religious values in order to maintain control. Their art of war is to split allegiances through religious indoctrination so that they maintain their monopoly on trade. Although the Jesuit dictionary comes in handy for him, Blackthorne rejects their tutelage in preference for Toranaga's star professor, Lady Mariko, whose most valuable lesson to Blackthorne is inner peace through meditation.

Those in Toranaga's camp, and Toranaga himself, are also open to learning from Blackthorne. He teaches the hornpipe dance to Toranaga and the ladies, he teaches the generals about war tactics, and he tells anyone who is interested about geography and European politics. In exchange, Blackthorne learns how to be a samurai. To do this requires mastery of two lessons: patience and transformation. Education, in the novel, is not simply the means of learning information but the process of changing and broadening one's perceptions.

Ceremony

Ceremony is both a theme and a structural element of the novel. In Japanese culture, ceremony governs every aspect of life, from simple greetings to important matters of diplomacy. Bowing, for example, is a frequent ceremonial occasion for expressing displeasure and disrespect for others. Toranaga utilizes ceremony to win the chess game but he also begins to change the ceremonies. One form of ceremony that governs the samurai is *bushido*. This is the warrior's code by which he fights and obeys his liege lord. Yabu wishes to change the code by introducing guns into warfare. When Toranaga shows disgust, Yabu replies, "a new era requires clear thinking about the meaning of honor." Unwittingly, Yabu has described Toranaga's strategy—change Japan and ready it for a new era. To do this he will bend ceremonial lines or follow them to the letter, as he does with Zataki and as he instructs Mariko to do in Osaka. Toranaga's mastery of ceremony, an art of peace, is his best weapon against Ishido.

Style

Historical Fiction

Shōgun belongs to the genre of historical fiction. This genre of literature arose in the early nineteenth century when Sir Walter Scott wrote the first historical novel, Waverly, in 1814. Scott's novel attempts to interest readers in history by showing how historical events affect private lives and individuals. One of the greatest works of this genre is Leo Tolstoy's War and Peace, which was written in the mid-nineteenth century about Russian experiences in the war with Napolean. Works of historical fiction are not always literary masterworks. Rather, historical fiction can simply be a work which is costumed by a historical setting but pays absolutely no attention to historical accuracy.

The strength of historical fiction is not in its accurate rendition of events but in its faithful portrayal of the historical moment. Thus, *Shōgun's* narrative is faithful to the reality of 1600—a rather barbaric Europe meets a highly civilized and wartorn Japan—even if it strays from accurate chronology. Clavell researched his subject exhaustively. For four years, he read accounts of visitors to Japan in the sixteenth and seventeenth century, as well as historical studies. He visited Japan. He fleshed out his novel by adding descriptions of the art of gardening and the tea ceremony. Some of the descriptive phrases used in the novel are actually paraphrases of the accounts he read. For example, much of what Rodrigues says about the Japanese can be found in the writings of the Jesuit Father Joao Rodrigues, who visited Japan in the late seventeenth century. This Rodrigues said the Japanese are "so crafty" they have "three hearts." Finally, the inspiration for the novel came from the story of Will Adams, who actually did shipwreck in Japan in 1600 and became a samurai.

Narrative

Shōgun's narrator is a straightforward example of third-person omniscient: the narrator is all-knowing. However, the narrator has some interesting limits. For example, the positions of the Portuguese forts or other Jesuit matters are never revealed, nor are the real workings of the Council against Toranaga. In fact, the narrator only reveals information that Toranaga would have known. Toranaga has spies everywhere, and he receives detailed reports from his generals, his ladies, and Lady Mariko. Furthermore, he has orchestrated all the major events of the book as if he were the director of a noh play. The idea that Toranaga is in fact the narrator is supported by the narrative shifts throughout the novel to first person when he is alone. An example of this occurs at the end of the novel. The paragraph begins with "he thought" and ends with Toranaga saying, "this is the chance I've been waiting for." Toranaga is thus revealed as the narrator, and the book is therefore the book he has been writing to advise future generations.

Structure

Clavell uses several structural elements to connect events and characters into a disciplined narrative. One structural element is chronology. The novel proceeds from the spring of 1600 to November 21, when Toranaga launches his battle plan, Crimson Sky. Along the way, flashbacks to previous events fill in the past. The novel, accordingly, is a historical account. Abetting the chronological structure are the motifs of chess and falconry. The two metaphors are used to explain how the past is mixed with the present by Toranaga as he maneuvers to become Shōgun.

Clavell's division of chapters into six books is also a structural element. Each book ends with a significant development in Blackthorne's education or Toranaga's plan. Book One establishes the situation in Japan and ends with Blackthorne saving lives. At the end of Book Two, Blackthorne is saved in return. This trading of lives ties the characters together and builds loyalty between them. In Book Three, Blackthorne dies and is reborn a samurai. From this point, Toranaga plays a larger role as he begins to implement his strategy to become Shōgun. Blackthorne's hopes to use his ship, Erasmus, in Book Four are part of Toranaga's plans, and the ship is destroyed in Book Five. Book Five also contains the climatic "poem" of Mariko, which unlocks Osaka and kills a several samurai. Book Six wraps up the loose ends and ends in Toranaga launching Crimson Sky.

A third pattern in the book is the cultural reciprocity between Toranaga and Blackthorne. The two men educate each other in the ways of the world. Toranaga takes time out of his battle plans to make sure Blackthorne is properly educated in the ways of the Japanese. In return, Blackthorne tells Toranaga about Europe. This new knowledge enables Tornaga to deal with the Jesuits and, eventually, to evict them from Japan.

Another organizing pattern concerns the characters and their love affairs, which are either reflective or codependent. The illicit love affair of Mariko and Blackthorne is matched by Omi's affair with Kiku. Both affairs must be resolved for Toranaga to win. Toranaga's light-hearted affairs with his ladies, especially Kiri, can be contrasted with the lustful courtship of Lord Zataki and Lord Ishido for Lady Ochiba. More positively, the relationships of Lord Sudara and Lady Genjiko and Rodrigues and his wife represent the ideal of pure love. All of these structural elements interlock to form the novel.

Historical Context

Early Modern Europe

Portugal, due to the efforts of Prince Henry the Navigator, had a jump start on Europe in the race for colonies. The Pope, during the fifteenth century, further aided Portugal by repeatedly renewing its monopoly on African trade. The Spanish, who had finally unified their nation, were eager to join the race and asked the Pope where they should go. As a result, the Pope drew the Papal Line of Demarcation dividing the world between Spain and Portugal in 1493. Spain was able to make better use of its colonial efforts and soon became the most powerful nation in Europe. In 1580, Spain absorbed Portugal and all her colonial possessions. Spain's zeal for colonies and the inflationary spirals produced by the continuous influx of gold and silver from the New World soon led the superpower into decline.

The first signs of Spanish decline resulted from bad luck and obstinacy. The King of Spain, Philip II, was determined to defeat the English and Queen Elizabeth. Philip II commissioned a series of Armadas—naval assaults—against England. Each Armada was beleaguered by storm and then trounced by the faster and smaller English vessels assisted by the Dutch. The Armadas bankrupted the Spanish crown. After the Armadas failed the British and the Dutch began to steal colonies.

Jesuits

In 1540, after treading through papal red tape and a vote of confidence from his followers, nobleman and war veteran Ignatius of Loyola became leader of the Jesuits, the Society of Jesus. The Jesuits vowed absolute obedience to the Pope and placed their work ahead of prayer. The group became renowned for its learning and its universities. Due to their unique governing rules and their learning, the Pope used Jesuits as emissaries to European courts and sent them to explore the world,

Compare
&
Contrast

- **1600:** Europeans rarely, if ever, take baths, thinking that it leads to illness. The Japanese, on the other hand, bathe often and prize cleanliness.

  Today: It is normal in all industrial nations for people to bathe often. Body odor and dirtiness are disapproved of by most people.

- **1600:** Japan is a wealthy nation with a vast supply of silver and other commodities. Due to political strains, it cannot trade with China directly. Europe, except for the inflationary economy in Spain, is doing everything it can to increase its trade and gain wealth.

  Today: Japan (despite a recession in the early 1990s), Europe, and the United States are the most powerful economies in the world. They meet on a regular basis to iron out trade issues for their mutual prosperity.

- **1600:** Technology, in the form of weapons, printing, and navigation, are dynamic forces facilitating change in society. Governments are still capable of allowing technology to thrive or be stifled. European governments, who are competing among themselves, take advantage of any technological edge they can. The Japanese decide to reject the onslaught of new technologies.

  Today: Japan is one of the leading producers and users of information technologies. Both in Japan and in the West, technology has become a necessary component of economic vitality.

---

make converts, and open up trade. Thus, Jesuits quickly took over the cause of the Catholic Church in Spanish and Portuguese colonies.

According to Church records, the Pope sent the Jesuits to take over trade in Japan because he realized that only the no-nonsense Jesuits would have a chance at success. Contact with Japan was made with the arrival of the Portuguese in 1543, who brought guns, knowledge of fortifications, and the pox in exchange for money and silk. Not until the Jesuit St. Francis Xavier arrived in 1549, however, did the trade become profitable. Xavier won converts everywhere he went. In his wake, the Jesuits established schools and threatened traditional Japanese thought. Xavier died while attempting to enter China. The Jesuits took command of trade in Asia and soon had 300,000 Japanese converts to Catholicism.

Will Adams

The adventures of John Blackthorne are loosely based on the story of Will Adams. He was an English pilot who shipwrecked on the coast of Japan in 1600. By 1603, he had become a samurai and an advisor to the Tokugawa Shōgun. Adams, who changed his name to Anjin Miura, was allowed to establish a Dutch trading post. As advisor to Tokugawa, Adams enabled the removal of religion from trade. This pleased Tokugawa, who wanted to curtail the influence of European religion on the Japanese. The Dutch, therefore, came as merchants—without priests—and gained access to Nagasaki. The Jesuits and everyone else were barred. Just as the Jesuits feared, this enabled the persecution of Christians to flare up on several occasions over the next two centuries. Like Toranaga, Tokugawa allowed Adams to build a ship, but not wanting to return to the days of naval battles that marked the civil wars, he gave the ship away and ordered a larger one. Adams was made a samurai—the only westerner to be so honored—and a monument was erected to him at his death in 1620.

Japan

Shōgun is a portrait of Japan as it transitioned from feudalism to a nation-state ruled by an enlightened warlord. This moment occurs in the quarter-century of jostling for power that occurred after the end of the Ahikaga Shogunate, which had ruled since 1336. The Ahikaga reign ended when Yoshiake, the Shōgun, lost a battle against Oda

A scene from the TV version of Shōgun.

Nobunaga. Yoshiake shaved his head and became a Buddhist priest.

The civil wars that followed during the sixteenth century began to end when Oda Nobunaga, whose military strategy relied on guns, was assassinated in 1582. His ablest general, the peasant Hideyoshi Toyotomi, unified the country in 1590. With a unified Japan following him, Toyotomi invaded Korea twice: 1592-93 and 1598. He died during the second invasion and Japan withdrew from Korea. Five years of uncertainty followed his death before Ieyasu Tokugawa completed Toyotomi's attempt to make Japan one nation.

Tokugawa defeated his rivals in October 1600, at the Battle of Sekigahara. He became Shōgun in 1603. Tokugawa insured the survival of his accomplishment by resigning in 1605 and helping his son carry on the Shōgunate. Tokugawa's Shōgunate established a peaceful kingdom for 250 years. Then the Americans, in 1853, forced the Japanese from isolation. In 1868, the emperor was restored and the reign of Shōguns ended. Under the emperor, the previously isolationist country took part in world affairs energetically. Its attempt to create an empire brought the country into World War II. Defeated by the United States in August of 1945, much of Japan came under US supervision for almost 30 years.

1975

By the mid-1970s, Japan had regained its sovereignty. Although it would be asked to apologize for various war atrocities committed during WWII, Japan by 1975 controlled all its islands, renewed a treaty of mutual defense with the United States (1970), and rebuilt its economy into one of the top non-communist industrial economies of the world. Soon the Japanese economy would be second only to the United States. The oil crisis of the 1970s hit Japan particularly hard. The Japanese responded by creating programs to reduce Japan's dependence on foreign oil through conservation and alternative energy sources.

Critical Overview

Critics often responded to Clavell's *Shōgun* with begrudging admiration, as if compelled by the force of the story to take the book seriously. An early book review in the *New York Times Book Review,* by Webster Schott, began "I can't remember when a novel has seized my mind" like *Shōgun.* According to Schott, "Clavell is neither literary psychoanalyst nor philosophizing intellectual. He reports the world as he sees people—in terms of power, control, strength.... He writes in the oldest and grandest tradition that fiction knows." Common themes in later criticism of Clavell tended to focus on three themes: Clavell's brilliant storytelling, the work as a historical novel or fiction, and the work's multiculturalism. It is easy to point out the historical inaccuracies of the novel, but its entertainment value and its understanding of broader historical themes to light led most critics to forgive Clavell's manipulation of historical fact.

A reviewer in *The New Yorker* desperately wanted to disparage the book, going so far as to say Clavell's novel was a throwback to the "derring-do" of Errol Flynn. But the review shifted to admiration in a blink with the recognition that "Clavell does have a decided gift for storytelling, and he makes a heroic effort to provide the right atmosphere." Still, the reviewer sneered at the anachronism of modern slang in the novel given the effort to render the atmosphere with veracity.

D. J. Enright, in the *New York Times,* was somewhat condescending in calling *Shōgun* "a tourist guide to medieval Japan." Yet Enright noticed some of Clavell's achievements in the book. noting that Clavell in some ways captured a sense of Japan's literary art in his massive work. Noting that the Japanese "are masters of the miniature," he suggested that Clavell was doing them an honor by writing his novel with such massive amounts of detail—from the way to wear a sword to a description of a Tea Ceremony. Julian Barnes, in the *New Statesman,* also commented on Clavell's attention to minutiae, noting that "Each page" of the novel "is the length of a short story, and scarcely a one passes without some new extravagant delight." Nonetheless, Barnes also criticized Clavell's sometimes clumsy attempt to mix Elizabethan English with modern slang.

Henry Smith, an educator and historian of Japan, took an evenhanded approach. He pointed out where Clavell bent fact and discussed the numerous problems with Lady Mariko being a real person—someone of her stature in 1600 would have been sequestered, not cavorting with a barbarian. But historical accuracy, for Smith, was not nearly as important as plausibility. After all, Clavell set out to write an entertaining tale through which Westerners could learn something about Japan in 1600. Smith determines that despite the inaccuracies, Clavell succeeded in contrasting the East and West. However, Smith noted, "[Clavell] is in effect delivering a polemic against the Christian church for instilling in Western man his (in Clavell's view) distorted attitudes to sex, death, and cleanliness."

Terry Teachout focused on Clavell's literary intentions. Teachout quoted Clavell saying that his goal was to "be a bridge between East and West" though writing stories that entertain and "pass on a little information." Teachout noted that between the incredible success of his novels and the huge viewing of the television miniseries, Clavell succeeded in being a bridge. Clavell, said Teachout, "is now among the most widely read authors of the century." As Susan Crosland, using material from an interview with Clavell, notes, Clavell's position as a bridge comes honestly. After purging himself of the horror of Changi in *King Rat,* Clavell began an investigation into his captors' history and psychology, discovering that his former enemies shared with him a common humanity.

In Book Two of *Shōgun,* a phrase from Edgar Alan Poe's 1849 poem "A Dream within a Dream" appears. The poem recurs amidst the crucial scenes in Osaka castle and on the last page of the novel. These literary references led Burton R. Pollin to observe a great subtlety on the part of Clavell in terms of the novel's structure. Pollin suggested that Clavell masterfully complicated the position of Toranaga as choreographer through the use of highly charged lines from a great writer. Each time the poem is referred to, said Pollin, "we are being informed about a key" to the mystery of the overall strategy of the book. Pollin's article is the nearest a critic has come to treating Clavell's novel as serious literature.

Clavell, as many critics admit, wanted to entertain and impart information to his readers. In that he succeeded, but few critics have wanted to treat his work as a serious literary effort. The popularity of the novel has not changed that opinion.

Criticism

Jeremy W. Hubbell

Hubbell is a graduate student in History at the State University of New York, Stony Brook. In the following essay, he discusses the usefulness of Clavell's insight into the historical problems of the scientific mind and the intricacies of societal adoption of technology.

A list of historical inaccuracies in Clavell's *Shōgun* would include the following: Will Adams, the model for Blackthorne, did not actually play such a large role in the formation of the Tokugawa Shōgunate. Though Adams did become samurai and an advisor to Tokugawa, it was not until 1603. Soap, a very expensive item in 1600 Japan, would not have been used with such abandon nor on a barbarian. Birthdays were not celebrated, thus making the climatic scene at Lady Ochiba's birthday party implausible. Ishida Mitsunari, Tokugawa's rival, was not as powerful as the fictional Ishido, and he was defeated in October of 1600. His execution was typical for the time, not the gruesome and lingering death in the novel. Lady Mariko was modeled on Hosokawa Gracia, whose husband was Tadaoki. Together, they were the most cultivated pair of the time. She was the most famous of all Christian converts, but he was not a brute. High-ranking ladies lived somewhat sequestered lives, and it is not imaginable that she would sleep with a barbarian such as Blackthorne. The Jesuits brought guns and cannons in 1543, not with Adams. In fact, naval battles played a part in the Japanese civil wars of the 1570s (one side even had ironclads with gun accompaniments). With the establishment of the

Tokugawa Shōgunate, such barbaric practices ceased, and Japan did indeed isolate itself from the world rather than forge ahead with industrialism.

But what do these historical inaccuracies matter? Insight into historical periods and persons are of greater value than details. An understanding of history by a society is crucial to the formation of its future direction. Clavell, who was writing in the 1970s when Americans were getting nervous about a reascendant Japan, provides a work of cross-cultural experience which helps in that formation. Facilitating understanding of self and others is within the purview of the historian, but historians, unlike novelists, are too often uninterested in playing this role.

Simon Schama, a historian of Dutch culture, reflects on this problem in "Visualizing History." There he does not lament the limited knowledge of history held by most people but urges today's historian to be less reclusive; he suggests that historians are to blame for the widespread lack of interest in history. He writes, "if [historians] want history to have real resonance in the public world, they had better start learning how to practice their trade in the noisy bazaar of contemporary culture, in the museum ... in the cyberarchive ... and in the worlds of film and television." Schama also reminds us that history writing, historically, has not always been boring. In the hands of Sir Walter Scott or Thomas Carlyle, history was enjoyable to read. And in the enjoyment of reading history both the past and present are understood.

Indeed, Thomas Carlyle, in his 1829 essay "Sign of the Times," says much the same thing. He offers his contemporaries insight into their times not, as the title suggests, to be a doomsayer but to take stock of where the society is and where it is going. In doing this, he characterizes nineteenth-century Europe as a Mechanical Age where society is mechanic rather than dynamic. For Carlyle, man in a mechanical society believes that only in "Mechanical contrivances did any hope exist for him." Opposed to this is the dynamic society, which focuses on "the divine and spiritual" and refuses to calculate life in terms of "Profit and Loss." Either position alone would be extreme. Carlyle suggests that by understanding the present time and the history behind it, it is possible to form a society in between the dynamic and the mechanic. This problem is not too far from the problem faced by Clavell's Toranaga.

Clavell's *Shōgun* gives the historian insight into a historical moment. More specifically, Clavell

What Do I Read Next?

- The challenges of adapting Clavell's novel to film are documented in a 1980 book, *The Making of James Clavell's 'Shōgun.'* The book furthers understanding of the novel by explaining the decisions made during filming.

- Henry Smith edited a book in 1980, which helps clarify the relation of the novel to the understanding of Japanese history. *Learning from 'Shōgun': Japanese History and Western Fantasy,* shows how Clavell unmasks the myths that the West has of Japan and clarifies the history Clavell fictionalizes.

- *King Rat* (1962) is based on Clavell's experiences in the death camp Changi. The story records one day in the life of an American prisoner of war, Peter Marlowe.

- In 1963, an increasingly successful Clavell returned to his boyhood haunts in Hong Kong to research his next book. Published in 1966, *Tai-Pan* tells the tale of Hong Kong's strange establishment as one of the most successful centers of trade in the world through the fictional character Dirk Struan's attempt to build a trading dynasty. An apparently poor booty of the Opium Wars for the British, Hong Kong blossomed almost immediately after its founding in 1841 to profit from a third of all imports into China.

- Published in 1993, *Gai-Jin* is Clavell's story of Japan in 1862, when it came out of isolation. The novel picks up where *Tai-Pan* leaves off. In this novel, a descendant of *Shōgun's* Toranaga reviews the history of 1600 for clues on how to deal with foreigners, the establishment of Hong Kong, and trade in the 1860s.

- Gina Macdonald's *James Clavell: A Critical Companion* (1988) provides a guide to Clavell's novels. Macdonald gives an in-depth biography and places Clavell within the literary tradition of adventure writers like Daniel Defoe and Robert Louis Stevenson. She then devotes a chapter to each of Clavell's novels.

- First published in 1719, Daniel Defoe's *Robinson Crusoe* follows its hero as he confronts other cultures and uses his technical abilities in ways remarkably similar to John Blackthorne.

- The Japanese noh play has been warmly embraced in the West, with such notable writers as William Butler Yeats and Bertolt Brecht writing their own. This form of drama began in the fourteenth century with the family of Kanzea. Nobuko Albery has fictionalized the struggle to establish one of Japan's most cherished art forms in her 1986 novel *The House Of Kanzea: Saga of Fourteenth Century Japan.*

- Clavell's Toranaga is based on Tokugawa Ieyasu, whose final victory in 1600 established the Tokugawa Shōgunate as ruler of Japan for 250 years. In 1988, Conrad Totman published a biography of this historical figure, *Tokugawa Ieyasu: Shōgun.* Although written by a Westerner, the work is an honest treatment of one of the great leaders in Japanese history.

- James A. Michener, an admitted fan of Clavell, wrote several novels about Japan. One of them, *Sayonara* (1990), tells the story of Major Lloyd Gruver, who is stationed in Japan during WWII. Gruver falls in love with a Japanese woman and encounters great difficulty as a result.

---

provides a persuasive demonstration of the differences between three mentalities struggling for dominance. First, Toranaga continues to channel the brilliance of his nation toward a pursuit of the noble ideals of the samurai code. Father Alvito, also a brilliant mind, exerts his reason and deploys technical schemes for the furtherance of the Church. Blackthorne's mechanistic mind represents the man who will eventually triumph over the other two—the rational economic man who pursues the application of the best technique for the ultimate end, profit.

> First, Toranaga continues
> to channel the brilliance of his
> nation toward a pursuit of the
> noble ideals of the samurai code.
> Father Alvito, also a brilliant
> mind, exerts his reason and
> deploys technical schemes for the
> furtherance of the Church.
> Blackthorne's mechanistic mind
> represents the man who will
> eventually triumph over the other
> two—the rational economic man
> who pursues the application of
> the best technique for the
> ultimate end, profit."

Putting these three minds together in a struggle illuminates a historical problem for the technological historian seeking an explanation for industrialization. Why did industrialization take off in Europe in the seventeenth century, and why was it victorious? The key component to understanding the rise of industrialization is noticing the increasing tendency amongst people to value the exclusively rational mind. For example, Blackthorne repeatedly pulls back from being overwhelmed by a scene or by the confusion of a moment. Faced with the incredible spectacle of Osaka he struggles to force his mind to rationalize what he observes. Blackthorne repeatedly says to himself, "Concentrate. Look for clues." Again and again, Blackthorne is the empirical scientist taking stock of details and gathering information. It is his presence of mind and search for details that always allows him to see the right thing—like Toranaga switching with Kiri.

Blackthorne developed this mental technique out of his training as a pilot, where alertness and attention to detail could mean life or death. But his ability to adapt this as a technique of survival is a sign of a mechanistic mind. Such a mind is essential to the world of industry, which requires the adaptation of ideas to reality in order to work more efficiently.

Complicating the notion of the mechanical mind is Father Alvito, representative of the Jesuits, who has a mind just as capable as Blackthorne. Jacques Ellul, writing in *The Technological Society,* says that the Jesuit mind was trained to work like Blackthorne's; they had "a precise view of technical possibilities, the will to attain certain ends, application in all areas, and adherence of the whole of society to a conspicuous technical objective." The objective of the Jesuits, however, was dynamic—to borrow Carlyle's term—not mechanic. The Jesuits aimed to please the Pope and to please God. They were interested in rendering technique—and eventually machinery—into existence not for the sake of creating the most efficient systems but for the Church.

Toranaga is similar to Father Alvito. He, more than anyone, knows what is technically possible. Yet he is locked into conserving his society's samurai code and stopping its advancement of technology. The samurai were so well-trained that had Toranaga pursued Yabu's plan of making a mechanized army of samurai, he would have had a truly awesome military. However, Toranaga preferred to maintain his dynamic society and bring to fruition the development of the samurai's art.

Clavell's novel gives us a means of seeing these three minds interact, demonstrating that the scientific mind is not "natural" but comes into being through a historical process that involved collision with other cultures. First, there are the Jesuits, whose technology and ability was a huge breakthrough in terms of European institutions. The only thing preventing the Jesuits from being a stock trading corporation was its vows. Second, there is the pilot, Blackthorne, who employs his to claim power over a situation. Clavell consistently shows how Blackthorne forces himself to focus on the situation rather than give into fatigue, fear, or overwhelming novelty. Because Blackthorne can do this, he will survive all his crewmembers. Vinck, for one, loses his mind because he had not sufficiently developed his mind—he dies, like a computer dividing by zero, because he cannot compute the loss of Erasmus. The type of mind that Blackthorne exhibits will become the ideal for the Europeans. Lastly, Toranaga could have industrialized Japan and thus joined the colonial race by leaping ahead of Europe but he did not. He saw that the Europeans, for all their technical gadgets and aptitude, were hampered by money. Alternatively, Japan—purged of outside influence—possessed ample opportunity for self-perfection within its very technical samurai code.

The idea that Europe's only contribution to the world was its trove of machines or its obsession with technical thinking is not Clavell's invention. In Sir Thomas More's *Utopia* of 1517, the author presents a perfect society, and these people provide Europe with an ideal societal model. In return, the only thing of value Europe can offer is the printing press. Clavell's *Shōgun* has a similar paradigm. The highly advanced civilization of the Japanese views Europe as useless except for its few technological advances. In terms of daily refinement and *culture,* the barbarians, well, stink. But their ships and their weapons—muskets, fortifications, cannon, fire arrows, and soldier formations—must be reckoned with. The historian's problem grows worse: must a society be either dynamic or mechanic? This was Carlyle's question of 1829, and we made much progress with it since.

Clavell's fictionalization of the founding of the Tokugawa Shōgunate is not historically accurate, as any glance at a history of Japan will confirm. However, as a piece of historical fiction, Clavell could be ranked with the nineteenth-century novelists whose purpose was to bring the past alive. For the historian, this is an effort that, like the guns of the barbarians, must be considered and used. The historical issues so crucial to the age of European imperialism, and the geometry of war as well as the decline of religion and the philosophy surrounding technology, are all present in *Shōgun.* Clavell's historical accuracy lies there—discerning the issues of a particular epoch.

Clavell's novel must also be seen in the context of the mid-1970s. Without trying to call attention to itself, the success of the Japanese economy reminds the West that its industrial dominance is about to be questioned. As in the novel, the East conquers the man from the West and domesticates him quite happily.

Source: Jeremy W. Hubbell, in an essay for *Novels for Students,* Gale, 2000.

Henry Smith

An American educator and historian, Smith has written widely on Japanese history and was the editor of Learning from "Shōgun": Japanese History and Western Fantasy *(1980). In the following essay, Smith relates Clavell's sources and manipulation of Japanese culture and history in Shōgun.*

> These charges raise some difficult questions. As a novelist, is Clavell not free to transform his characters as he pleases?"

When confronted with an extremely popular modern novel which is based on historical themes the first instinct of the historian, naturally enough, is to ascertain the 'historicity' of the work. The models for the major characters in James Clavell's *Shōgun* are easy to recognize but Clavell has considerably rearranged and refashioned the events and personalities of the time about which he writes.

These changes can be summarized briefly. The model for Blackthorne, the protagonist of *Shōgun* is Will Adams (1564–1620), the circumstances of whose arrival in Japan in April 1600 as pilot of a Dutch ship correspond closely to those of Blackthorne. Blackthorne's eventual rise to the position of adviser and retainer of Yoshi Toranaga roughly parallels the career of Adams; a key difference is that Clavell telescopes these events into a single summer, whereas in reality the intimacy of Adams and the historical Tokugawa Ieyasu grew over a matter of years. Clavell also inflates the heroic stature of the historical Adams by having Blackthorne actually save Toranaga's life, by having him introduce effective warfare with guns to Japan (something which had been accomplished several decades before), and above all by having him fall in love with the wife of one of the great feudal lords of Japan.

The depiction of the military struggle for national supremacy in *Shōgun* corresponds to historical fact in broad outline, although the intricate subplots of the novel are wholly of Clavell's invention. Toranaga's scheming rival 'Ishido' is vaguely modelled after the *daimyo* Ishida Mitsunari (1560–1600), who did in fact organize the coalition against Ieyasu that was defeated at the Battle of Sekigahara in October 1600. The historical Ishida however, was not nearly so powerful as his counterpart in *Shōgun,* nor was his execution in 1600 anything like the gruesome punishment meted out to Ishido at the very end of the novel. Similar and even greater liberties have been taken with the other *daimyo* who appear in *Shōgun,* for many of whom it is even difficult to locate a specific model.

The model of Blackthorne's lover, the Lady Toda Mariko, is Hosokawa Gracia (1563–1600), whose husband Tadaoki (1563–1645) was one of the most cultivated men of his time and is done somewhat of a historical disservice by being transformed by Clavell into the boorish 'Buntaro.' The historical Gracia was one of the most famous of all the Christian converts in Japan of her era, and is revered to this day as a saint by Japanese Roman Catholics. While she was indeed versed in both Portuguese and Latin, the historical Gracia never served as an interpreter for Ieyasu. Nor did she even meet Will Adams, and she certainly would never have had a love affair with him or any other European seaman.

It is this transformation of a chaste Catholic heroine of the sixteenth century into a modish Madame Butterfly that has tended to shock and sometimes offend the sticklers for historicity. Edwin Reischauer, the distinguished American historian of Japan, has written indignantly that Clavell 'freely distorts historical fact to fit his tale' when he stoops to having such an 'exemplary Christian wife' as Hosokawa Gracia 'pictured without a shred of plausiblity as Blackthorne's great love, Mariko.'

These charges raise some difficult questions. As a novelist, is Clavell not free to transform his characters as he pleases? The author himself has claimed that there were really no exact 'models' for the characters in *Shōgun,* simply 'sources of inspiration' drawn from the pages of history. He did, after all, change the names of virtually all the historical characters (one notable exception being Gracia's maiden name, Akechi). 'I thought, to be honest,' Clavell has said, 'that I didn't want to be restricted by historical personality.'

The more serious charge against Clavell is that of historical plausibility. Granted that the historical Will Adams never laid eyes on the historical lady Gracia, was that sort of liaison conceivable in Japan of the year 1600? Here the answer would certainly be that it was not. The *daimyo* ladies of sixteenth-century Japan were strictly sequestered and rarely had the chance to meet any men other than immediate family. Nor can one imagine any Japanese woman of good breeding entering the bath so casually with another man—much less a 'barbarian.' The only sort of woman who would have behaved with the sexual candor of Mariko in that era

would probably [have] been a prostitute (such as *Shōgun*'s 'Kiku').

The issue of historical plausibility arises on other occasions in *Shōgun.* A number of these relate to details about Japanese customs. The careful historian might insist, for example, that such a rare imported luxury as soap would not have been used to bathe a captured barbarian, or that traditional Japanese never celebrated birthdays (as Lady Ochiba does late in the novel), or that the Japanese did in fact eat meat from time to time (contrary to Mariko's claim of total avoidance). In these and other small ways, *Shōgun* will strike the historian as a somewhat flawed depiction of Japanese customs in the year 1600.

Rather more of a problem is the question of Japanese psychology and behavior as represented in *Shōgun.* Were samurai in fact given to beheading commoners on a whim and the hacking the corpse into small pieces? Were all Japanese of that era (or any other era, for that matter) so utterly nonchalant about sex and nudity? Would a peasant really have been summarily executed for taking down a rotting pheasant? Was '*karma*' in fact such an everyday word among the Japanese of the year 1600? Although precise answers to these questions are not always easy, it can certainly be said that in every case Clavell exaggerates and often distorts the historical reality.

But the real problem is to understand *why* James Clavell has depicted the Japanese in ways that occasionally strike the historian as implausible. Most of the errors of detail were surely unintentional, and probably reflect nothing more than the inadequacy of the English-language materials on which Clavell, who reads and speaks no Japanese, was obliged to depend for his information. As a practical matter it must be admitted that such authenticity is probably of little concern to the average Western reader of *Shōgun,* who knows almost nothing about Japan or its history.

But the exaggeration of Japanese behaviour, particularly with respect to attitudes about such matters as love, death, food and bathing, is clearly intentional on the part of Clavell, since in every case he strives to contrast the values of the Japanese with those of Blackthorne and his fellow Europeans. Even more importantly, the final message of the author is that, as the confused Blackthorne comes to realize, 'much of what they believe is so much better than our way that it's tempting to become one of them totally'. Whereas Western man, as symbolized by Blackthorne, is depicted as rid-

Triptych showing all the shoguns during the Tokugawa period 1603-1867.

den with shame over sex, obsessed with a fear of death, raised on an unwholesome diet of animal flesh and alcohol, and terrified of bathing, the Japanese are represented as paragons in each particular. They view sex and nudity as wholly 'natural', are able to face death with composure and even eagerness, eat only fish (preferably raw), rice, and pickles, and of course are wholly addicted to the pleasures of the hot bath.

It is precisely this rather didactic contrast that gives *Shōgun* so much of its interest, both for the average reader and for the historian. Clavell is in effect delivering a sermon on the errant ways of the West. More specifically, he is delivering a polemic against the Christian Church for instilling in Western man his (in Clavell's view) distorted attitudes to sex, death, and cleanliness. This anti-christian tone runs throughout *Shōgun* and manifests itself most clearly in the depiction of the European Jesuits. Although no responsible historian would claim that the Jesuits were without their faults as missionaries in Japan, it is hard to find the priests of *Shōgun* as anything but caricatures. While the Jesuits did indeed for a time rely on the silk trade to finance their mission, they were scarcely the greedy villains of *Shōgun,* ever ready to stoop to crude assassination plots to thwart their rivals.

The preferable religious attitude, *Shōgun,* insistently implies, is the meditative and fatalistic posture of the Japanese samurai, as epitomized by the great warrior Toranaga. About halfway through the novel there appears a description of Toranaga in a state of religious reverie; it is an effective summary of the type of mysticism which Clavell seems to advocate:

> Now sleep, *Karma* is *karma.* Be thou of Zen. Remember, in tranquility, that the Absolute, the Tao, is within thee, that no priest or cult or dogma or book or saying or teaching or teacher stands between Thou and It. Know that Good and Evil are irrelevant, I and Thou irrelevant, Inside and Outside irrelevant as are Life and Death. Enter into the Sphere where there is no fear of death nor hope of afterlife, where thou art free of the impediments of life or the needs of salvation.…

While drawing freely on elements of Asian mysticism (*karma,* Zen, Tao), this sermon is a personal statement by James Clavell. A more authentically Japanese Zen Buddhist, for example, would certainly be far more respectful of 'teachers' and the idea of 'salvation'. Yet the Zen spirit is certainly there, and the message is that the West has much to learn from Asian meditational practice—an idea to which many of Clavell's devotees would seem to be hospitable.

In a sense, then, *Shōgun* is a story of a spiritual quest. It is of course skillfully woven in among other stories—that of a tragic love affair and that of a ruthless power struggle—so that the sermon never becomes obtrusive. But it is a very important element in the overall logic of *Shōgun*. Even less apparent to the normal reader is the fact that this 'quest' is closely related to James Clavell's personal experiences with the Japanese. As a young soldier in the British army, Clavell was captured by the Japanese in Southeast Asia in 1942 and spent the remainder of the war in Changi prison on Singapore. While his experience understandably left him with many hostile feelings about the Japanese, he grew in time to respect his captors, for much the same reasons that Blackthorne does. In short, the story of Blackthorne's progress, from horror over his captors' 'barbarity' to respect for their 'civilized' values as even more 'civilized' than those of the West, is also the story of Clavell himself.

It is in order to dramatize this theme of spiritual quest in *Shōgun* that the author tends in various ways to idealize, over-simplify, and sometimes distort Japanese values and attitudes. And it is here that the historian can perhaps step in to right the balance a little.

One common form of exaggeration in *Shōgun*, is the depiction of values which were historically limited to a certain segment of Japanese society as though they were universally 'Japanese'. Take the simple example of eating meat. Mariko tells Blackthorne that the Japanese never eat meat. This was in fact true at the time only of the Buddhist clergy and the Kyoto aristocracy; the samurai class of which Mariko was a member was in fact fond of meat and frequently consumed wild game. One hastens to add that in terms of contrast with the Europeans, Clavell's depiction is still basically valid. Even samurai ate only wild game, and never raised animals or even fowl for consumption; and never did their level of meat consumption even approach that of the highly carnivorous Europeans of all but the lowest classes.

Another type of simplification which the historian is anxious to pick out is anachronism. An appropriate example here might be that of sexual attitudes, a matter of fundamental East-West contrast as depicted in *Shōgun*. Here the problem lies primarily in the characterization of European seamen as squeamish about sexual matters as Blackthorne is. The depiction of Western sexuality in *Shōgun* conforms instead to the stereotype known as 'Victorian'—although many people now question whether such prudishness was in fact typical of the nineteenth century.

In this process of trying to 'deidealize' the sharp Europe-Japan contrasts that appear in *Shōgun*, however, the historian soon learns two important lessons. The first is that we still do not really know the answers to many of these questions about the historical evolution of Japanese attitudes to sex, love, death and other such basic human preoccupations. Nor, for example, do we really know what the Japanese of different classes ate in the sixteenth century. Nor indeed can we give a satisfactory explanation of the historical development and psychological workings of the peculiar samurai practice of ritual disembowelment (*seppuku*). The lament of French historian Lucien Febvre in 1941, would certainly still apply to Japan: 'We have no history of Love. We have no history of Death. We have no history of Pity or Cruelty, we have no history of Joy.' We cannot, quite simply, answer the hard historical questions about the stuff of which a popular novel like *Shōgun* is made.

The second realization provoked by *Shōgun* is that no matter how much the historian seeks to qualify the rather stark contrasts between Japan and the West that run through *Shōgun*, there remains little doubt that in many ways Japan had by the year 1600 evolved customs and attitudes that really do seem to have been at sharp variance with those in the West. One has only to peruse some of the fascinating reports of European visitors to Japan to realize this. As the Italian Jesuit Alessandro Valignano (the model for Father Carlo dell'Aqua in *Shōgun*) wrote in 1583, 'The things which they do are beyond imagining and it may truly be said that Japan is a world the reverse of Europe'. This metaphor of Japan as a 'topsy-turvy' land, where everything is done in precisely opposite manner, is one that has appeared again and again in Western descriptions of Japan ever since.

Western understanding of Japan has, we may hope, reached the point where we can dismiss the 'topsy-turvy' argument as Europocentric nonsense. This is not, however, to deny the reality of general differences between Japan and the West—provided of course that one remains alert to the wide diversity among different classes in Japan and among the many cultures that make up 'the West'. It is precisely the general differences that make Japan such a fruitful and fascinating object of study for the West; by understanding Japan, we come to understand ourselves. It was the genius of James Clavell to mobilize this learning process as a central theme of *Shōgun*. It remains the task of the historian to probe the roots and refine the limits of Blackthorne's lessons.

Source: Henry Smith, "Reading James Clavell's Shōgun," in *History Today,* Vol. 31, October, 1981, pp. 39–42.

Sources

Barnes, Julian, review, in *New Statesman,* November 21, 1975, p. 650.

Carlyle, Thomas, "Sign of the Times," in *London Magazine,* 1829.

Crosland, Susan, "Maybe I'm James Clavell," in *The Sunday Times,* London, November 2, 1986, pp. 41, 43-4.

Ellul, Jacques, *The Technological Society,* Alfred A. Knopf, 1965.

Enright, D.J., review, in *The New York Times Book Review,* The New York Times, July 28, 1975, p. 5.

Interview, in the *Guardian,* October 4, 1975.

More, Thomas, *Utopia,* Wordsworth Editions, 1998.

Pollin, Burton R., "Poe in Clavell's *Shōgun: A Novel of Japan,*" in *Poe Studies,* Vol. 16, 1983, p. 13.

Review, *The New Yorker,* September 18, 1975, pp. 44-5.

Schama, Simon, "Visualizing History," in *Culturefront,* Vol. 7, No. 1.

Schott, Webster, review, in *The New York Times Book Review,* June 22, 1975, p. 5.

Smith, Henry, "Reading James Clavell's *Shōgun,*" in *History Today,* Vol. 31, October, 1981, pp. 39-42.

Teachout, Terry, "James Clavell, Storyteller," in *National Review,* Vol. XXXIV, 1982, pp. 1420-22.

For Further Study

Alden, Dauril, *The Making of an Enterprise: The Society of Jesus in Portugal, Its Empire, and Beyond: 1540-1750,* Stanford University Press, 1996.

> Dauril Alden's *The Making of an Enterprise* tells how the Jesuits were instrumental in the consolidation of the Portuguese Empire. First for Portugal and then for the Spanish, the Jesuits perfected the technique of colonial exploitation to the benefit of the investors and the Church.

Rand, Ayn, *Atlas Shrugged,* Plume, 1999.

> Clavell believed in the philosophy of Objectivism. This philosophy was codified by Ayn Rand in *Atlas Shrugged,* originally published in 1957, as a theory holding that all individuals operate out of self-interest. This theory is explicated in the story of Dagny Taggart's encounter with a libertarian group seeking an end to government regulation.

Roberson, John R., *Japan Meets the World: The Birth of a Superpower,* Millbrook Press, 1998.

> Roberson details the Japan's interaction with the world from the arrival of the Portuguese in 1543 to the Nagano Olympic Games. Roberson focuses on the internal politics of those 400 years as Japan made decisions about how to deal with the rest of the world.

Sun Tzu, *The Art of War,* edited by James Clavell and translated by Thomas Cleary, Delcorte Press, 1983.

> Sun Tzu's 2,000-year-old classic contains the philosophy of the warrior, such as "To win without fighting is best." Although written for the Chinese warrior, Sun Tzu's book has been used by warriors of all nations and has recently found a readership amongst businessmen.

Tames, Richard, *Servant of the Shōgun: Being the True Story of William Adams, Pilot and Samurai, the First Englishman in Japan,* St. Martin's Press, 1987.

> Tames's biography of William Adams gives the full story of the English pilot who shipwrecked off the coast of Japan in 1600. Adams eventually became a samurai and married a Japanese woman. Although he went on a few trading expeditions, he lived out his life as advisor to the Tokugawa Shōgun until he died in 1620.

Tracy, James D., *The Political Economy of Merchant Empires: State Power and World Trade, 1350-1750,* Cambridge University Press, 1991.

> Tracy presents an in-depth analysis of the role played by merchants and their shipping expeditions in early modern state formations in Europe.

Summer of My German Soldier

Bette Greene

1973

Summer of My German Soldier, Bette Greene's first and best-known novel, chronicles one summer in the life of a twelve-year-old Jewish girl in the rural South. First published in 1973, it was an over-whelming critical success and has gone on to become a classic of juvenile literature. The book was nominated for the National Book Award, and won the New York Times Outstanding Book Award, the Golden Kite Society's children's book writer's award, and the American Library Association's Notable Book Award. In 1978 Greene published a sequel, *Morning Is a Long Time Coming.*

The novel takes its inspiration in part from the author's own childhood. Like her heroine, Greene grew up in a small Arkansas town at the end of World War II. Her parents owned a country store, and they were the only Jewish family in a Protestant community. The story explores the tensions created by these kinds of ethnic and religious differences. Published the year that the Vietnam conflict ended, her book also acts as an allegory about the prejudices and fears of late 1960s and early 1970s America.

Author Biography

Born in Memphis, Tennessee on June 28, 1934, Bette Greene's childhood was very similar to that of Patty Bergman, the protagonist of *Summer of My German Soldier.* Like Patty, she was a

Bette Greene

young girl living in a rural Arkansas town at the end of World War II. Her parents also owned a country store, and—just like the Bergmans' situation—theirs was the only Jewish family in a Protestant community.

In 1950 Greene worked as a reporter for the *Memphis Commercial Appeal.* A few years later, she attended the University of Alabama, and then transferred to Memphis State University. During these years she worked for United Press, but left in 1954. She spent the next two years at Columbia University in New York City. In 1965, she attended Harvard University in Cambridge, Massachusetts.

In 1973, she published her first book, *Summer of My German Soldier.* It was an overwhelming success, both critically and commercially. The novel was nominated for the National Book Award, and won the *New York Times* Outstanding Book Award, the Golden Kite Society's children's book writer's award, and the American Library Association's Notable Book Award.

Greene has published several other juvenile novels as well as nonfiction and adult fiction. A member of both P.E.N. and the Author's Guild, Greene resides in Tennessee with her husband Donald Sumner Greene, a physician.

Plot Summary

The Arrival of the POWs

Patty's life changes when a group of German POWs arrives by train to be taken to the new prison camp just outside of town. She is struck by the fact that they look no different from anyone else. When the soldiers are brought into town to purchase hats to shield them from the "formidable Arkansas sun," Patty hurries to her parents' store to help out. There is one prisoner who speaks English, and he is singled out to make their purchases. After procuring hats for the men to wear while working in the fields, he approaches the stationery counter to buy writing supplies. Patty is at the counter, and he introduces himself to her. His name is Frederick Anton Reiker. Besides the stationery, he also buys a piece of costume jewelry, seemingly on a whim.

Anton Hides Out

News circulates that one of the prisoners has escaped. The men of the town form a mob, each being told to go home and gather firearms if they have not already brought them. A reporter named Charlene from the *Memphis Commercial Appeal* comes to Jenkinsville to get the story. Patty offers to guide her to the prison camp. She accepts the offer, and on the way to and from the camp Patty impresses Charlene with her intelligence.

One night, Patty hears a train approaching. She looks out the window of her room and sees someone hiding in the bushes, apparently about to jump onto the train. She goes outside and recognizes the shadowy figure as Anton. She offers to hide him the family's garage apartment. He accepts, and confides that he used the costume jewelry he bought at the store to bribe a guard. Patty begins stealing food for him. Her father notices the food disappearing; he assumes that Ruth is stealing it. Patty tells him that she has been eating it. She and Anton become friends.

After being caught by her father for disobeying him, her father begins beating her with his belt and knocks her to the ground. She looks up to see Anton outside. He has left his sanctuary and is going to stop her father's abuse, despite what his discovery will mean for him. Patty screams "go away" several times. Luckily, her father thinks it is directed at him. Anton returns to his hiding place, but not before he is seen by Ruth. The next day, Ruth tells Patty that she will not reveal Anton to the authorities.

A pair of FBI agents comes to Jenkinsville to investigate Anton's escape. They question everyone, and Patty tells them that she waited on him at the store. Other than his hair color and appearance, the only thing Patty tells them is that he was very polite. When they question her more closely, her father intervenes, accusing them of bullying her.

Caught

Eventually, Anton tells Patty that he must leave town. He realizes that he cannot hide out in the garage forever. The family has missed the extra food, and both he and Ruth are convinced that eventually someone will see him. Patty does not want him to leave. He gives her his great-grandfather's gold signet ring, his only personal possession, and she gives him a monogrammed shirt that she had bought for her father's birthday. He leaves. With his ring hidden, she resolves to some day find him in Germany.

Patty's need for attention is too great for her to protect her secret. She begins showing off the ring, claiming she got it from a tramp. Her father fears that the mysterious tramp may have been a child molester and calls in the sheriff. After questioning her, the sheriff decides that nothing untoward has gone on. Eventually, the two FBI agents return to question Patty again. First questioning her about the mysterious tramp who gave her the ring, they attempt to lead the conversation to Anton, asking about the tramp's age. They ask her if she gave him anything in return. She tells them that she did not, but remarks on how polite the tramp was—the same thing she pointed out about Anton. The two FBI agents show her the monogrammed shirt and she sees a stained round hole in it. Knowing that she has given up, they give her a newspaper clipping, detailing Anton's death.

Patty's father is shocked that his daughter, a Jew, would betray him for "a goddamn Nazi." The FBI men tell him that she will be charged, tried, and prosecuted, possibly for treason. The townspeople greet her with cries of "Jew-Nazi." Patty refuses to implicate Ruth and tells her parents, the sheriff, and the FBI that she did it alone, "because he was nice to me." Because of her age, she is not tried for treason, but for delinquency. She is sentenced to reform school.

Patty Imprisoned

Patty is taken to the Jasper E. Conrad Arkansas Reformatory for Girls. The other girls in the school call her "Spy" or "Nazi"—"Natz" for short. She gets a note and newspaper subscription from Char-

lene Madlee, encouraging her to "keep smiling!" Hoping for a hint of friendship in the note, Patty writes back.

When Ruth visits, she gives her the news from home: Patty's parents are closing the store and leaving. Patty cries, and insists that there is "something wrong with" her, but Ruth assures her that it is nothing "a few years and a few pounds won't take care of." When visiting hours are up, Patty breaks down and clings to Ruth not wanting her to go. After Ruth leaves, Patty expresses her feeling of helplessness:

> For moments or minutes I stood there. Not really moving. Barely managing to tread water. Was it possible for a beginning swimmer to actually make it to shore? It might take me my whole lifetime to find out.

Patty has lost Anton, alienated her parents and home town, and managed to get herself imprisoned. Yet she still has hope for a happy future.

Characters

Honey Babe

See Patty Bergen, Patricia Ann Bergen

Harry Bergen

Harry is Patty's abusive, ill-tempered father. A violent man full of repressed rage and self-hatred, he takes his frustrations out on Patty. As the only Jewish merchant in a Protestant town, Harry is constantly under pressure to underplay his ethnicity and to go along with his neighbors.

Harry is a complex character who encourages his family to be silent and go along with the majority view. He despises his own roots, and reacts with rage when his brother talks about their childhood poverty. His childhood has led him to become obsessed with the value of money, and he hates his father-in-law because he had to ask him for money to start his store. His history of violence goes back to his very early childhood, when his father had to hold him down on his bed, repeating "you will not be violent" over and over again.

Max Bergen

Max is Harry's brother. A good-humored man, he tells the important story of how their father had tried to make Harry less violent. Although he tells the story in an amused manner, it only serves to make Harry angry. Max is not embarrassed about his poor childhood, and he is the brother who remembers family history.

Patty Bergen

See Patricia Ann Bergen, Honey Babe

Patricia Ann Bergen

Patricia (also known as Patty and Honey Babe) is the young protagonist of *Summer of My German Soldier*. Lonely and frustrated, she shelters an escaped German POW and ends up being put on trial for treason. She is an outcast in multiple ways: because she is Jewish; her family is wealthy; and she is perceived as a failure by her parents. By the end of the novel, Patty has also become an outcast from her country—her unpatriotic harboring of a POW is judged to be treason.

Patty strongly feels this isolation. She copes with her boredom, frustration, and loneliness by escaping into her own world of make-believe, exaggeration, and lies. These practices lead her into even more trouble, isolation, and parental disapproval.

By the end of the novel, Patty has gained an understanding of the consequences of her actions, the reality of family relationships, and the racial prejudices of her society. However, she still has a long way to go. *Summer of My German Soldier* is a study of Patty's developing mind, and the novel ends before she has completely matured.

Pearl Bergen

Pearl is Patty's selfish and uncaring mother. She is a born saleswoman who is especially good at talking poor women into spending too much money. The pet of her own family, she refuses to grow up and still expects constant gifts and special treatment from her parents, Grandma and Grandpa Fried.

Patty feels that she is unattractive compared to her mother, and her mother does nothing to dissuade her of that. She is constantly comparing her to other girls her age as well as her younger sister, faulting her for her lack of femininity. She sometimes talks to people about her in her presence while acting as if she were not there.

Sharon Bergen

Sharon is Patty's little sister. She is too young to play an active part in the story, but is used repeatedly as an example of everything that Patty is not. Quiet, beautiful, and well-behaved, Sharon spends much of the book out of the arena of action playing in her sandbox with friends of the same age. Unlike her mother, Sharon is an extremely affectionate child and adores Patty and Ruth.

Media Adaptations

- *Summer of My German Soldier* was adapted for television in 1978. The film starred Kristy McNichol as Patty, Bruce Davison as Anton, and was directed by Michael Tuckerbook. Greene co-wrote the script. An audio book version of the novel is available from Recorded Books. Published in 1995, this unabridged recording is read by Dale Dickey, and covers six audio cassettes.

Sheriff Cauldwell

Sheriff Cauldwell is one of the few sympathetic adults in Patty's life. Initially believing Patty's story about the way she got the ring, Cauldwell forbids her father from taking it away from her. It is apparent that he knows about Patty's home life and wishes to do what he can to make her life more bearable.

Freddy Dowd

Freddy is "poor white trash" who tries his best to befriend Patty. Her father forbids her even to speak to him, as Freddy is considered too poor to be a suitable companion.

Grandma Fried

Grandma Fried is Patty's maternal grandmother. She is most concerned with feeding and caring for her family. She expresses her love for Patty through secret gifts of money and day trips, since Patty's parents live too far away for daily visits. Patty briefly thinks that her Grandma will be the caring mother figure that she so desperately wants, but feels angry and rejected when she does not fulfill this role.

Grandpa Fried

Grandpa Fried is a retired and prosperous businessman. Fond of his family and happy to receive visitors, he has, by the admission of his own family, gotten much "more nice" after his exit from the business world. His face has gone from "resolute to gentle," and he "still has his hair." While he does not particularly trust or like Patty's father, he does lend him the money to start his business.

Ruth Hughes

Ruth is the housekeeper and nurse for the Bergen family and a substitute mother for both Patty and Sharon. She is a proud woman who tries to instill a sense of personal pride into Patty. As an African-American woman in the old South, her pride is, as she says, "all she's got." Ruth is protective of Patty, and senses a microcosm of her own place in society in Patty's own treatment by her parents. Ruth is sympathetic to Anton's plight—both because he is Patty's friend and because he reminds her of her son fighting overseas.

Charlene Madlee

A reporter from Memphis, Charlene first comes into Patty's life after Anton escapes. She appears ready to befriend Patty, and remarks on her precocious intelligence. Charlene gives Patty a subscription to her newspaper, *The Commercial Appeal,* and covers the story of Patty's trial. She later writes to her in prison.

Phil McFee

McFee is one of the FBI agents who questions Patty.

John Pierce

John Pierce is one of the FBI agents investigating Anton's escape. He threatens Patty, and later shows her both the shirt she gave Anton and the newspaper clipping about his death.

Anton Reiker

See Frederick Anton Reiker

Frederick Anton Reiker

A German POW, Frederick Anton Reiker (also known as Anton Reiker) escapes from the prison camp and hides in Patty's garage apartment. He is found and shot while resisting capture. Anton first meets Patty in her parents' store and surprises her by speaking perfect English. This, combined with his civility and charming nature, causes Patty to think of him as a person rather than a German soldier.

Anton is well-educated and unsympathetic to the Nazi cause. He was destined to be a doctor before the war destroyed his plans, and is an attractive and well-spoken man. Just as Patty doesn't think of him as a "real" German, the novel is care-

ful to show that he is, in fact, not entirely German: one of his parents is English. His character breaks stereotypes about German citizens.

At first, it seems that Anton is taking advantage of Patty. However, he redeems himself when he risks his own life to save Patty from her father's beating.

Mary Wren

A middle-aged woman who works at the Bergens' store, Mary Wren (also known as Sister Wren) is described as "the gossip."

Sister Wren

See Mary Wren

Themes

Race and Ethnicity

The most important theme of *Summer of My German Soldier* is the separation of racial and ethnic groups. Patty's religion, Ruth's race, and the prejudices of Jenkinsville all play against each other to illustrate the problematic racial politics of rural Southern culture in the 1940s.

Racial Relations

The inherent racism of the South is illustrated most obviously through the character of Ruth, the family's maid. She rarely talks about the daily prejudice she faces, but the reality of her situation is revealed in several key scenes. In one such episode, a neighbor demands that the family fire Ruth for her "uppityness." Even Patty initially thinks in these racist terms, as shown by her later rejection of them. As she says, "Ruth isn't one bit uppity. Merely prideful." As the descendant of slaves and the potential victim of lynch mobs and crowd hatred, Ruth already knows more than enough about violence and the corruption of power. Because of this, Ruth is immediately drawn to Anton's plight. He is hunted, imprisoned, and cast out from the world for being German, just as Ruth is despised for being black.

Anti-Semitism

Initially, the Bergen family's Judaism is not an obvious issue in either the novel or the town. At times this seems to be deliberate, as when the family discusses the fate of their relatives in Nazi-occupied parts of Europe. When Grandmother Fried says she worries because she has not heard from their relatives in quite some time, there is only silence in response. Any intimations of anti-Semitism in their town are subtle. Most obviously, her father is not granted extra rations of gas to go to a synagogue forty miles away since it is deemed a waste of resources.

More subtly, Harry's minority status forces him to go along with the majority opinion. For instance, Harry does not try to stop the townspeople from evicting a Chinese-American storekeeper after war with Japan is declared. However, when Patty is revealed as the one who sheltered Anton, suddenly her and her family's Jewishness becomes a factor. Her father expresses outrage that she, as a Jew, would help a Nazi. Moreover, the townspeople deride her with cries of "Jew-Nazi." In an ironic parallel with earlier events, her parents are forced out of their store.

Patriotism and Identity

Anton, Patty, and Ruth have complex personal identities that are in conflict with national identity and patriotism. Anton Reiker is a divided character: both a Nazi and a German, the book serves to humanize him and define him in much broader terms. Educated, polite, and a speaker of perfect English, Anton cannot be seen as simply a German Nazi soldier. By hiding him, Patty is considered as treasonous and subversive; her Jewish heritage exacerbates the public outcry against her.

Ruth is not patriotic, which stems from her treatment as a second-class citizen; because of her feelings toward the dominant culture and the way that it has treated both herself and her son, Ruth feels no particular loyalty to it. This enables Ruth to help Anton when she finds out that Patty is hiding him, so that she too is guilty of "collaboration with the enemy."

Throughout *Summer of My German Solider,* morality is often indicated by a character's ability to see beyond stereotypes. Many of the business leaders of Jenkinsville are identified as immoral through their "patriotic" act of evicting a *Chinese* grocer in response to *Japanese* aggression. The POW camp doctor, on the other hand, is demarcated as a morally sound character through his sensitive understanding of Anton. As he says of the German POWs, "not all are rabid Nazis … Reiker wasn't cut from that mold … [H]e seemed like a decent man." This lesson is one that Patty must learn over the course of the summer. In learning it, she goes from being a patriotic young woman to being guilty of treason.

Topics for Further Study

- *Summer of My German Soldier* was published the year that the United States withdrew its forces from Vietnam. To what extent can the novel be read as an allegory about this war?

- Research the history of anti-Semitism in America. Is it fair to say that the American South was more prejudiced than the North? Why might Greene have set the story in Arkansas?

- Race and ethnicity play very important roles in the novel. How is the situation of Jewish Americans presented as the same as and different from that of African Americans?

Style

The Juvenile Novel

Summer of My German Summer is typical of the literary genre known as the juvenile, or young adult, novel. The juvenile novel is typically a first-person narrative, told from the point of view of a character trying to find his or her place in the world. This type of "coming of age" fiction is often concerned with a single large event and its repercussions on the life of the protagonist. The function of this kind of novel is to enable the audience to experience the maturing process vicariously. Targeted mainly at an adolescent audience, the juvenile novel often concerns a single issue relevant to the process of maturation. In the case of *Summer of My German Soldier,* the topic is loyalty.

The idea and responsibility of loyalty is explored through Patty's relationship with Anton, as well as Ruth's relationship with both Patty and Anton. At the same time, these personal loyalties are contrasted with the antagonistic forces of national and family loyalty. At the beginning of the novel, Patty's loyalty is to her country and her family, and her life is spent trying to fit into the demands that they place on her. As the plot develops, she gradually replaces this sense of duty with one based on emotions and personal responsibilities instead. In this way, her loyalty to Anton means that she is disloyal both her country and her parents: she must decide if friendship or patriotic duty is more important.

Unreliable Narrator

An unreliable narrator is one whose version of events cannot be accepted at face value. This can be for a variety of reasons. If the narrator is very young, or involved in the action, the narrative will not be objective. In some novels, such as *Moll Flanders,* by Daniel Defoe, the narrator is actively engaged in conning the reader—making up events and providing false interpretations in order to create a specific effect. Patty Bergen, the narrator of *Summer of My German Soldier,* falls into the former category. Because she is unaware of many of her own feelings, Patty is unable to give a full account of her motives throughout the novel.

The reliability of Patty's version of events is complicated even more by her active imagination. She lies to herself and the people around her, and her perceptions of the world are filtered through fantasies and wish-fulfillment. This is her mental defense against the reality of her violent and neglectful home life. Patty is open about her need for exaggeration and outright fabrication, recounting events and conversations, and then immediately passing them on to others in completely different forms. By the end of the novel, Patty has learned to tell the truth. Moreover, she can finally express her disappointment at, and anger with, her parents. However, she is still unaware of some key facets of the world around her, especially the facts of the Holocaust, so her narrative reflects a distorted worldview. The narrative "holes" created by this distortion make the novel more powerful by forcing the reader to complete Patty's story for her. The half-way house of the correctional facility in which she waits at the novel's conclusion thus becomes symbolic of her growing awareness.

Historical Context

World War II at Home: POWs and Rationing

World War II had a great impact on daily life in America. Like the Bergens, Americans were subjected to rationing of supplies such as milk, butter, and gasoline. The shortage of able-bodied male workers forced industry to hire previously marginalized workers, which opened up career opportunities for women. The heroic American working woman was idealized as "Rosie the Riveter." At the same time, many jobs lost to the war effort on agriculture and industry were filled by POWs like Reiker. The government contracted out POW labor to private citizens, with over half of the contracts going to farm work. In the South, POWs picked cotton, cut sugarcane, and harvested tobacco.

Nearly 372,000 Germans were held in U.S. prison camps during World War II. Conditions in the POW camps were relatively pleasant, allowing the prisoners to cook for themselves and spend limited amounts of money at their own discretion. Some POWs made friends with Americans from the surrounding communities. However, there was great tension surrounding such relationships, and frequent panics about escapes. There were 2,803 escapes during the war, and fifty-six prisoners were shot while attempting to escape. Thirty-four of them died.

Anti-Semitism at Home and Abroad

The German government seized property and businesses from Jewish citizens in the 1930s; in addition, laws were passed to take away their civil liberties and rights. After the invasion of Poland in 1939, this systematic destruction of rights turned into an attempt to exterminate Judaism in Europe. As the Nazi forces invaded Belgium, Denmark, France, Norway, the Netherlands, and the Soviet Union, Jewish people were gathered into ghettoes, and then imprisoned in labor camps, concentration camps, and death camps. Six million European Jews had been killed by the end of the war in 1945.

During the 1930s, many famous industry leaders and public figures supported the Nazi Party in the United States. Henry Ford was one of these men sympathetic to anti-Semitic views. On September 16, 1941, aviation hero Charles Lindbergh blamed Jews for trying to get the United States into a war with Germany. His views were similar to those of many Americans who are cynical about the war, angry at the loss of American life, and sick of rationing. A 1945 poll revealed that fifty-eight percent of Americans believe that Jews hold too much power in the United States—a two-hundred percent increase in the results of the same poll taken in 1938. In Patty Bergen's Arkansas, Jews make up a very small fraction of the population.

War in the Early Seventies: Vietnam

After achieving independence from French control in 1954, Vietnam was split north and south of the 17th parallel. The most organized resistance group, the Viet Minh, went to North Vietnam, where they formed a communist state. South Viet-

Compare & Contrast

- **1940s:** Many American men are drafted into the military services to fight in World War II.

  1970s: The final years of the Vietnam War are marked by intense opposition and protests. Many young men eligible for the draft find ways to avoid military service.

  Today: The draft has been abolished, and the United States has not been involved in a major military action—except the Gulf War—since Vietnam.

- **Early 1940s:** Germany conquers much of Europe by invasion and occupation.

  1970s: Germany is separated into East (communist) and West (democratic) Germany, and Berlin is partitioned by the infamous Berlin Wall. Anyone found trying to escape East Germany is imprisoned or shot.

  Today: A reunified Germany is a powerful industrial and financial powerhouse.

- **1940s:** Racial segregation in the American South is not only common, but enforced by law.

  1970s: Following two decades of turmoil and the passage of the Civil Rights Act, segregation is illegal.

  Today: The "New South" has many African-American elected officials, yet the Confederate flag still flies on the capitol of South Carolina, and affirmative action programs have been struck down in some Southern states.

---

nam remained a non-communist state. Under the Geneva Accords, free elections were due to be held on the issue of unity. The Viet Minh fully expected to win, but the leader of South Vietnam, Ngo Dinh Diem, refused to hold the election, which was in violation of international law but with the support of the United States. The North Vietnamese decided to unify Vietnam by force. The United States supported the increasingly unpopular regime in South Vietnam with military and financial aid.

As the numbers of South Vietnamese insurgents increased, President Kennedy committed more and more American troops to the region, and by the end of 1962 there were 11,000 U.S. military advisers in the country. In 1964, after North Vietnamese forces fired upon a U.S. destroyer, Congress ratified the Gulf of Tonkin Resolution, and America began full-scale intervention. The conflict escalated: American troop strength was 389,000 by 1969. In the United States, resistance to war mounted steadily. Troop withdrawal began in 1969, but the conflict widened. Under President Nixon, U.S. Forces invaded Cambodia, sparking an intense wave of antiwar action. The remaining U.S. forces did not leave until March 29, 1973. More than 47,000 Americans died during the war.

Critical Overview

As is the case with many great works of children's literature, *Summer of My German Soldier* was largely ignored by the critics upon its publication. In fact, despite being nominated for multiple awards, Greene's book received only one major review. However, *Summer of My German Soldier* has become a popular favorite and a classroom staple.

In his *New York Times Book Review* review, Peter Saurian highlights both the strengths of the novel and the possible reasons that it escaped critical attention at the time. He asserts that "in some ways Bette Greene's material is not promising. Her characters could easily have come out of a melodrama." However, Saurian does not stop at this observation, pointing out instead that "the writing is fresh" and causes the reader to see these simply presented issues "in a fresh and unexpected light."

Saurian reads the novel as a "finely hewn" presentation of emotional complexity, suggesting that the characters who surround Patty offer multifaceted foils against which her character can define itself. Anton gives her "the delicately conveyed gift

German prisoners of war in a re-education class taught by an anti-Nazi prisoner of war.

of her own value." At the same time, the review notes the major themes of the novel, calling attention to the association of Harry Bergen with Adolph Hitler. Arguing against a dismissive reception of the novel, Saurian summarizes the impact of the novel with the conclusion that "the stuff of it is fine, like the texture of Patty herself. The detail is too meaningfully specific, too highly selective to be trite."

While Saurian's review focused on the new emotional density that Greene brought to a relatively simple story, a later review dismissed the novel to such an extent that it got the basic facts wrong. The 1973 Christmas books round-up in *New York Times Book Review* summarized the plot of *Summer of My German Soldier* as the story of "a German POW in Arizona." The novel is, of course, set in Arkansas.

Despite this lack of critical reception, the novel has remained a favorite of both the classroom and the home, and some of the richest reviews of Greene's work can be found in student responses as well as lessons plans. Osayimwense Osa's lesson plan from *English Journal,* for example, compares a junior novel from the United States with one from Nigeria: Greene's *Summer of My German Soldier* with Buchi Emecheta's *The Bride Price.* Osa contends that the similarity of the two novels can inspire children from a variety of backgrounds to an awareness and appreciation of different cultures.

Summer of My German Soldier is also a key work in many online learning programs and home school plans, for the same reason that Saurian's review singled it out for praise—it combines fine writing with an accessible, "issue-based" historical plot that lends itself easily to thematic and cultural analysis.

Criticism

Tabitha McIntosh-Byrd

Tabitha McIntosh-Byrd is an English Literature instructor at the University of Pennsylvania. In the following essay she analyzes the themes of racial, social, and self-awareness in Greene's Summer of My German Soldier.

Silence and deferred knowledge—both historical and personal—play crucial roles in *Summer of My German Soldier*. That which is unsaid, or unrealized, lies at the heart of Greene's novel. Just as Patty is slowly adding to her vocabulary word by word, day by day, so the book gradually adds to her consciousness. Significantly, her favorite words—those she will share with her little sister—include the key psychological term, "ego." Patty is building her sense of self, her ego, through language. Her first-person narrative becomes structured as an infinite series of epiphanies that culminate in key revelations, the most obvious of which is her realization that she doesn't like her parents. Her thought processes leading up to this revelation are carefully laid out—the unconscious anger, harsh language, and continual self-editing creating the outlines of an emotion that Patty cannot bring herself to name until the final pages of her story.

In the same way, the more pointedly social unconscious links and drives of the world inside and around her are densely crowded on Patty, her town, and the text. Throughout *Summer of My German Soldier,* historical and social silence are elevated to such a degree that the town of Jenkinsville becomes, finally, devoid of all meaning. When the townspeople shout, "Jew Nazi!" they compound two concepts that can only be connected in conditions of willful blindness—thus revealing themselves as participants in a hypocritical cultural and linguistic system.

What Do I Read Next?

- *The Diary of A Young Girl* was written by Anne Frank and first published in 1947. Frank's diary is the record of a Jewish family's life in hiding in Nazi occupied Holland during World War II.

- The sequel to *Summer of My German Soldier* was published in 1979. *Morning Is a Long Time Coming* follows an eighteen-year-old Patty as she leaves for Germany to find Anton's mother. On the way she stops in Paris and experiences her first love affair.

- Greene's *Philip Hall Likes Me, I Reckon Maybe* (1975), chronicles the trials and tribulation of a young woman named Beth as she slowly realizes that she's been changing to win over a guy named Philip Hall. She decides to be her smart, strong self instead.

- Judy Blume's 1977 novel, *Starring Sally J. Freedman as Herself,* traces the life of Sally Freedman as she begins to grow up. Like Patty Bergen, Sally is a Jewish girl living in the South during and after World War II.

- S. E. Hinton's *Tex* (1979) remains a popular novel for young adults. Like Patty, Tex must learn how to cope with the mounting expectations of adulthood while addressing his own family issues.

The story tracks the operations of Patty's mind perfectly, revealing an embryonic self that attains greater and greater autonomy as her narrative moves forward. The gradual accretion and collection of word associations and thought patterns is stressed and illustrated throughout the novel. Patty's silences are deliberately and carefully constructed defenses against true recognition of the world. The issues about which she cannot bring herself to think, speak, or provide comment are connected to race and prejudice.

An early example in the novel sets up this paradigm of simultaneous recognition and silence. In

> When the townspeople shout, "Jew Nazi!" they compound two concepts that can only be connected in conditions of willful blindness—thus revealing themselves as participants in a hypocritical cultural and linguistic system."

her memory of the Chu Lee grocery story—whose owners have been evicted in a quasi-lynching—she evinces a careful and fragile reconstruction of the palpable reality of hatred in front of her, saying, "there's probably a simple logical explanation. It couldn't be what I think." What she thinks is of course what actually happened, and her textual self-silencing—the process by which she indicates her knowledge of the real while removing it from her linguistic reality—is abetted and caused by her parents, especially her father. In response to her questions about the incident, he tells her that she is "never in [her] life to mention it again."

This simultaneous presence and absence of "what Patty thinks" is the key element in her evolving relationship with Ruth. Patty's immersion in a world of racial division and prejudice is worked through most clearly by her gradual reshaping of the language associated with Ruth, and the linguistic boundaries of cultural vision. The most critical instance of this comes early in the novel, when Ruth explains why she should dress neatly to visit her mother at work: pride. Patty thinks to herself: "Pride. Maybe that's what it is, what Ruth has. What makes her different ... Ruth isn't one bit uppity. Merely prideful." Her previous interpretation of Ruth's behavior is here signified through its negation. Patty does not reveal her racist understanding of Ruth (the active application of the racially loaded signifier "uppity") but her reformed racism instead. Ruth is not uppity but prideful—the racial signifier unpacked, deconstructed, and reassigned in a positive linguistic pattern from which can be formed a new interpretive paradigm.

The associations that Patty is unaware of are as equally apparent from her linguistic associations as they are from her deliberate self-silencing. In a technique very similar to the narrative experimentation of stream of consciousness, the operations of Patty's mind reveal themselves through free association and pattern making of images, thoughts and words. Just as Ruth's comments on pride spark the reorganization of linguistic and racial paradigms, so Patty's observations change over the course of her narrative as she develops.

At the very beginning of the novel, her perception of the world is filtered through a semiotic set of cultural determinants, images, and pressures. This is evident in the style of her descriptions, and the way in which they connect to each other. Patty's unthinking acceptance of her culture's constructed norms is expressed primarily through the notion of patriotism. The first line of the text reveals the unthinking and naive immediacy of that acceptance: "When I saw the crowd gathering at the train station," she says, "I wondered what President Roosevelt would think ... we're as patriotic as anybody." This thought leads to a more elaborate description of "the people" whose patriotic duty is in doubt. Jimmy Wells, for example, is "wearing the same expression Dane Clark wore as the Marine sergeant in *Infamy at Pearl Harbor*."

Explicitly, Patty's anxiety over correct social form is put to rest by reading and rereading the crowd through a defining visual vocabulary of the patriotic war film. At its simplest level, Jenkinsville is patriotic because it resembles representations of patriotism. On a much more complex level, this association of idea and image carries a radical interpretation that is entirely at odds with its more immediate meaning. The linkage of patriotic feeling with cinematic trope suggests that the former is a product of the latter—that Hollywood is *creating*, instead of reflecting, national pride, and that both are, therefore, equally false.

This is, of course, the lesson that Patty has learned by the end of *Summer of My German Soldier*, but there is ample evidence from her own inconsistent presentations that this knowledge has been present from the beginning. When Sister Parker suggests that Roosevelt himself chose Jenkinsville as a POW prison site, for instance, Patty laughs at the absurd self-importance of such a claim—only several pages after she herself expressed identical ideas. Patty never explicitly connects these two passages or perceptions, but her narrative is carefully constructed to present and represent key ideas such as these in a technique that illustrates, rather than relates, her personal evolution.

At the same time, evidence of Patty's indoctrination in Jenkinsville's racial attitudes is equally important to the opening pages of the text, and is illustrated in equally complex ways. The white bystanders are referred to by their full names, such as "Mary Wren,'" and "Reverend Benn." Conversely, the only African American spectator is called, "old Chester, the colored porter." Patty's own prejudice is thus revealed through slight but important semantic differentiation. As with the Roosevelt example, this scene is paralleled later in the novel. In a moment that both underscores and then rejects her earlier prejudice, Patty observes that "the colored" always use titles when addressing each other, "to give each other the respect that the rest of the world holds back."

This retrospective, albeit implied, realization of her disrespect is presaged in the earlier scene. In an extremely telling association of images, Patty describes Chester, "the only Negro" on the platform, "in arm-touching contact with whites." Immediately after this the prisoners arrive: "Then amid hissing, steamy clouds of white, the train braked, screeched, and finally came to a halt." The "hissing, steamy clouds of white" by which Chester is surrounded gain major connotative power by being juxtaposed with him in this way. The "white" becomes not steam, but the people of Jenkinsville themselves—a pervasive, inescapable, amorphous presence that defines itself through color. Again, this interpretive move is prompted by the association of key words and images, suggesting both that the larger pattern of meaning is present in Patty's mind, at the same time as it requires reassembly by the reader. She does not, and cannot yet have access to the ramifications of the connections that her language creates.

However, some major associative linguistic patterns that appear throughout the novel have not crystallized at its conclusion, leaving certain revelations suspended—just as Patty herself remains suspended in the limbo of the correctional facility. Anti-Semitism, Judaism and the Holocaust remain almost entirely unarticulated—though Patty's growing sense of these connections is revealed by her wry comments on the preacher at the prison who describes "the method the Jews used when they killed Jesus." In fact, the expression of their religion has been systematically and literally denied to the Bergen family, by the refusal of gas rations needed to get them to synagogue. In a grotesque association of words, Jenkinsville's Jewish people have been prevented from experiencing their culture by gas, just as, a continent away, the Nazi party is using gas to remove Judaism from Europe.

The disappearance of Jewishness from the Bergen family maps onto and follows a progressively widening series of correlations. The Bergens are symbolically de-racinated/unacculturated by their inability to go to synagogue, causing their prayers to be silenced, and thus effectively silencing them. This is associatively correlated with the situation in Europe. The silencing of the Bergens functions as a paradigmatic miniature of the programmatic destruction of Judaism from Europe, represented in this text by one specification silence—the sudden cessation of letters from relatives in Germany. These two symbiotic processes—local silencing and wider cultural extermination—are reenacted on a metatextual level by the silence which lies at the heart of Greene's text: the topic of the Holocaust itself.

That at least some of the adult characters of *Summer of My German Soldier* are aware of the reality of war is made clear in several places, as is Patty's own partial awareness. Anton, for example, is entirely knowledgeable about the situation, indicated by his disbelief and amusement that "a Jewish girl has rescued [him]." More tellingly, the Fried and Bergman families touch upon the issue at dinner. As Patty notes, one of the subjects discussed is "The fate of the Jews." Yet this topic, like the silence from German relatives that Grandma Fried worries about, is entirely glossed by both families. Mary Bergen wants to talk about clothes, Harry is happy to cover the topic in silence, the grandparents are happy to be reassured, and Patty relates the conversation entirely without comment. Nor does she return to it, either explicitly or implicitly for the rest of her narrative. The effect of this is to create a metacommentary on the reality of Jenkinsville—a paradoxically "resounding silence," whose echoes can be heard only through their absence. Patty's epiphanic understanding of Reiker's shock at her religion is thus left in suspense at the end of the novel—forcing the reader to construct it. In doing so, the text forces its readers to re-imagine the novel's key symbolic operations with the benefit of a historical hindsight which Patty lacks.

Patty's uneasiness about the appearance of her conversation with Reiker is only imaginable in a pre-Holocaust World War II, an iconographic world in which the reality of Nazi Germany is ignored or unrealized. The war effort in whose service the citizens of Jenkinsville are engaged is thus a deracinated one, stripped of its compelling ethnic anxiety, and replaced with geopolitical maneuvering. This is a process whereby the delusory unity of the *American* people is promoted through a nationally experienced, monolithic sense of patriotism. The inherent fascism of this approach is drawn in vivid colors by both the final insults thrown at Patty as she is driven away, and by the "stage setting" of the POWs' arrival.

In *Summer of My German Soldier*, it is the American people who are the Nazis. They are the ones who wait for cattle cars full of prisoners to arrive so they can spit at them. They are the ones who lynch, persecute, and kill on the basis of race. Their hypocritical status as patriots and citizen killers, freedom fighters and segregationists, culminates in the fundamental oxymoron that lies at the center of the text: "Jew Nazi!" In this repeated phrase, Greene entirely deconstructs the unity of patriotic Jenkinsville—showing it to be predicated on the very acts of silencing and denial that enable the program of extermination in Europe.

Source: Tabitha McIntosh-Byrd, in an essay for *Novels for Students*, Gale, 2000.

Susan F. Marcus

In the following excerpt, Marcus compares characteristics of Them That Glitter and Them That Don't *and* Summer of My German Soldier.

[In *Them That Glitter and Them That Don't* Greene] once again places her young heroine in a family too occupied with their own lives to love or care about her. But this time, unlike Patty Bergen [the central character of *Summer of My German Soldier*], the girl manages to emerge not unscathed by circumstances, but strengthened by facing up to them. Because everyone in Bainesville, Arkansas, distrusts her conniving Gypsy mother and disdains her drinking father, Carol Ann Delaney must endure her own lonely life. When she is unexpectedly called upon to sing before her high school class, her classmates finally begin to pay attention to her and to appreciate the talent that she has always dreamed would take her to Nashville and to fame. But her high school graduation day brings to Carol Ann the realization that most of her so-called friends and, more cruelly, Mama have abandoned her after all and that she must in turn leave her little brother and sister now if she is ever to improve any of their lives. As she leaves Bainesville for

Nashville, Carol Ann calls upon those same Gypsy instincts which she has resented in her Mama to help her survive…. [Carol Ann] will keep her readers turning the page (pulling for her) as she honestly faces, and overcomes, her painful situation.

Source: Susan F. Marcus, Review of "Them That Glitter and Them That Don't," in *School Library Journal,* Vol. 29, No. 8, April, 1983, pp. 122–23.

Michele Slung

In the following review, Slung argues that Greene's presentation of people from Arkansas is inaccurate and affected by a "cosmopolitan awareness" uncharacteristic of real-world counterparts.

[In *Them That Glitter and Them That Don't,* Greene] shouts through her characters' conversation, bringing a sophisticated, wise-cracking tone and a cosmopolitan awareness that doesn't match up with the folk of Dexter County, Arkansas. Carol Ann Delaney, not surprisingly, wants to flee her surroundings and better herself, and the way she envisions doing it is by becoming a country singer, "all aglitter in a gown of sequins and feathers," lavishly praised by "the country and western music critic for *The New York Times*." Or, singing some of her favorite songs, Carol Ann thinks of herself as "there inside those batty Beatles' world within a world. Their zany, joyful world of 'The Yellow Submarine.'" None of this thought or language rings true. Bette Greene may have grown up in Arkansas, but she's East Coast now, through and through. And there are dozens of similar examples scattered around the book: it's like dress-up in reverse, with a grown woman hunched down, trying to fit her shoulders into a child-sized jacket.

Source: Michele Slung, "Adolescent Heroines," in *Book World—Washington Post,* 1983, p. 14.

Mary M. Burns

In the following review, Burns praises Green for the skilful construction and persuasive realness of her characters.

Skillfully constructed, [*Them That Glitter and Them That Don't*] is persuasively real. And while Carol Ann as narrator is undoubtedly the central character, the personality of her mother—half child, half con artist—is a brilliant creation, demonstrating that the parents' uncaring attitude toward their daughter should be understood as dependence rather than malice. Humor rising naturally from the circumstances transforms the grim details of Carol Ann's life into an optimistic chronicle. As she proudly tells her music teacher, she is, like most Gypsies, a survivor—and her argument is convincing.

Source: Mary M. Burns, A review of "Them That Glitter and Them That Don't," in *Horn Book Magazine,* Vol. LIX, No. 4, August, 1983, p. 453.

Judy Mitchell

In the following excerpt, Mitchell focuses on Greene's presentation of how Jewish reaction to the Holocaust caused by Germany creates more Jewish victims.

No one would accuse *The Summer of My German Soldier* of being an upbeat story. It seems, first of all, to operate on the principle of reversing some standard elements of holocaust literature: the American child is a Jew, but she offers safety to a fugitive German prisoner-of-war.

Her father and mother are terrible people, and Patty's isolation from everyone else in Jenkinsville, Arkansas, is so palpable that some of the children who suffered through the war in Europe seem fortunate by contrast. Patty loved Anton, gave him what help she could, and mourned his death when that help was not enough. For this she is repudiated by her family and persecuted by the townspeople. Her Jewishness is an embarrassment to other Jews.... *Summer of My German Soldier* catches the despair of the Holocaust and its aftermath by indicating that one sensitive, loving little girl and one gentle German boy are no match for the times in which they live. They make a symbolic commitment to reaching out, and because of this they swell the list of victims....

Source: Judy Mitchell, "Children of the Holocaust," in *English Journal,* Vol. 69, No. 76, October, 1980, pp. 14–18.

Kevin Wilson

In the following review, Wilson praises Greene for her use of first person narration and accurate portrayal of the speech of a nineteen-year-old girl.

The story [in *Morning Is a Long Time Coming*] is predictable enough and so is the heroine's situation, but the novel is saved from banality by the effectiveness of the narrator's technique. By telling the story in the first person the novelist succeeds admirably. The story could have become over-burdened with the bitterness and the adolescent preoccupations of a very unhappy young woman. It does not.

The author also succeeds in mimicking the speech of a nineteen year old. As a result the story

is quite realistic and not overly melodramatic. The reader cannot help but empathize with the alienation of the heroine.

Source: Kevin Wilson, Review of "Morning is a Long Time Coming," in *Best Sellers,* Vol. 38, No. 9, December, 1978, p. 291.

Jack Forman

In the following review, Forman evaluates the sequel to Summer of My German Soldier, *finding the depiction of the relationship of the same heroine to her new love-interest Roger to be strained, but the depiction of a "Southern Jewish family in the 1940s" to be "strong and honest."*

[*Morning Is a Long Time Coming,* an] autobiographical novel four years after the author's *The Summer of My German Soldier* ... opens in the same small Arkansas town. Still alienated from her father, mother, and grandparents, Patty Bergen graduates from high school, then sets out for Europe instead of going to college. In France, Patty has her first love affair with a young teacher, Roger, but feels torn between him and her need to find the parents of the German POW she once unsuccessfully hid (recorded in Greene's first novel). Wracked by a bleeding ulcer brought on by the tensions with her family and her lover, she finally leaves Roger to go to Göttingen, Germany in search of the POW's family.... Having come to terms with her anxieties, she returns to France for a rapproachment with Roger. Green's portrayal of a Southern Jewish family in the 1940s is strong and honest, but the depiction of Patty's relationship with Roger is strangely forced and detached. Despite this central flaw, however, the novel will attract teens because of its sensitive treatment of the loosening of familial bonds.

Source: Jack Forman, Review of "Morning is a Long Time Coming," in *School Library Journal,* Vol. 24, No. 8, April, 1978, p. 93.

Audrey Laski

In the following review, Laski suggests that the explicit violence and bitterness and the implicit sex in Summer of My German Soldier *would be disturbing to a twelve-year-old (the age of the heroine in the novel).*

[*Summer of My German Soldier* seems to me likely] to disturb a reader as young as its 12-year-old heroine, because of the domestic violence and bitterness it records. And though sex does not happen in it, the heroine's vicious father is convinced that it must since his daughter has done the unthinkable for a Jewish girl and helped a German soldier to escape.

Source: Audrey Laski, "Partridge in a Pear Tree," in *Times Educational Supplement,* No. 3261, December 9, 1977, p. 21.

Sources

Osayimwense, Osa, "Adolescent Girls' Need for Love in Two Cultures—Nigeria and the United States," in *English Journal,* Vol. 72, No.8, December, 1983, pp. 35-7.

Review, *The New York Times Book Review,* December 2, 1973, p. 73.

Saurian, Peter, "Summer of My German Soldier," in *The New York Times Book Review,* November 4, 1973, p. 29.

For Further Study

Buck, Anita, *Behind Barbed Wire: German Prisoner of War Camps in Minnesota,* North Star Press, 1998.

   Buck chronicles the history of fifteen POW camps in Minnesota, illustrating the occasional friendships between town and camp, and the fair living conditions for the prisoners.

Carlson, Lewis H., *We Were Each Other's Prisoners: An Oral History of World War II American and German Prisoners of War,* Basic Books, 1997.

   A wide-ranging collection of interviews and oral histories from both German and American POWs and captors during World War II.

Dinnerstein, Leonard, *Anti-Semitism in America,* Oxford University Press, 1994.

   Dinnerstein traces the history of anti-Semitism in the United States, showing its development from the early colonial period to the present day.

Lemaster, Carolyn Gray, *A Corner of the Tapestry: A History of the Jewish Experience in Arkansas, 1820s–1990s,* University of Arkansas Press, 1994.

   A comprehensive history of the Jewish people who helped settle Arkansas and stayed to become a significant cultural factor in the state's development.

McGuire, Phillip, ed., *Taps for a Jim Crow Army: Letters from Black Soldiers in World War II,* ABC-Clio, 1983.

   McGuire collects letters written home by African American soldiers in World War II, who faced discriminatory practices in the draft and combat assignments.

Shandley, Robert R. ed., *Unwilling Germans? The Goldenhagen Debate,* University of Minnesota Press, 1998.

   This essay collection responds to the best-selling book, *Hitler's Willing Executioners,* a 1996 work that argues that ordinary German citizens were complicit in the Holocaust. These essays argue both sides of the case, and the questions they raise are central to Greene's sympathetic portrayal of Anton in *Summer of My German Soldier.*

Soderbergh, Peter A., "The Dark Mirror: War Ethos in Juvenile Fiction, 1865–1919," in *University of Daytona Review,* Vol. 10, No. 1, Summer, 1973, pp. 13-24.

   Soderbergh provides an overview of the patriotism and prejudices of war fiction written for children in the century before Green's novel.

War and Peace

Leo Tolstoy

1866–1869

War and Peace is a historical novel that chronicles the tumultuous events in Russia during the Napoleonic war in the early nineteenth century. Focusing on an aristocratic way of life that had already started to fade at the time that Leo Tolstoy wrote the book in the 1860s, it covers a comparatively short span of time—fifteen years—but it renders the lives of disparate characters from all segments of society with vivid, well-realized details. The story captures a generation on the brink of change, with some defending the existing class structure with their lives while others realize that the old way of life is disappearing. Part history lesson, part grand romance, part battlefield revisionism, and part philosophy lecture, *War and Peace* has captivated generations of readers with its gripping narrative and its clear, intelligible understanding of the human soul.

Author Biography

Leo Tolstoy was born to an upper-class Russian family on September 9, 1928, at the family's estate in Tula province, Russia. His father was Count Nikolay Tolstoy, a nobleman and prestigious landowner. Tolstoy's mother died when he was two years old. Tragically, his father died when Leo was nine, leaving the young boy to be raised in the home of his aunts. He went to the University of Kazan when he was sixteen, studying Oriental languages

Leo Tolstoy

and then law, but he left in 1847 without completing his degree.

In 1851 he went to the Caucasus to live with his brother, and began writing his first novel *Childhood*. Published in 1852, it was followed by *Boyhood* (1854) and *Youth* (1856). During this time he served in the army at Sevastopol, fighting the Crimean War. His experience as a soldier in that war provided much of the experience that he drew upon in writing *War and Peace*.

After the war, Tolstoy returned to his family estate. In 1859 he started a school on his estate for peasant children. In 1861, after the emancipation of the serfs, Tolstoy served as Arbiter of the Peace, a temporary local judiciary position. The following year, after the deaths of two his brothers, he married Sophia Behrs, the daughter of a Moscow physician, and began an educational magazine, *Yasnaya Polyana*, which I. S. Aksakov called a "remarkable literary phenomenon" and an "an extraordinarily important phenomenon in our social life." Tolstoy edited the journal for a little more than a year.

After that, a second phase of his literary career began, the phase that produced his two greatest masterpieces, *War and Peace* and *Anna Karenina*. He retired to his estate with his new wife, wrote, hunted, farmed and socialized with his country

neighbors. At the end of the 1960s, though, he found himself at a spiritual crisis, brought about by the deaths of several of his children and other relatives. He questioned the meaning of life and was not sure about whether he could or should go on. He drifted away from the Russian Orthodox Christianity he had been raised in and focused on a more rational world view that eliminated the need for church intervention between humanity and God. This religious conversion left him at odds with many members of his family, especially his wife.

Impacted by his evolving philosophical outlook, his later works of fiction were less ornamental and more direct. They include the novellas *The Death of Ivan Ilych, Master and Man,* and *Memoirs of a Madman.* Tolstoy also produced many philosophical works and religious tracts. His 1888 religious essay "What Is Art?" is still considered an important treatise on art and morality. Tolstoy died on November 20, 1910 of pneumonia.

Plot Summary

Book I

War and Peace is a massive, sprawling novel that chronicles events in Russia during the Napoleonic Wars, when the French Emperor Napoleon Bonaparte conquered much of Europe during the first few years of the nineteenth century. Bonaparte unsuccessfully tried to expand his dominion into Russia, only to be turned back in 1812. The novel opens in July of 1805, with Russia allied with England, Austria, and Sweden to stave off Bonaparte's aggressive expansion.

A member of a dissolute, upper-class crowd, Pierre Bezukhov is a troublemaker who criticizes governmental policies. At night he frequents drunken card parties with a fast crowd, including Anatole Kurgagin and Fedya Dolokhov, whom Tolstoy describes as "an officer and a desperado." Another member of the group, Prince Andrew, is a patriot who is determined to defend his country and aristocratic way of life. The novel soon introduces the Rostov family as they prepare a celebration for their youngest daughter Natasha.

The illegitimate son of a well-known, wealthy aristocrat, Pierre's life changes when his father dies and recognizes him as his son. Therefore Pierre is heir to his large fortune. Prince Andrew leaves to fight in the war against the French, leaving his pregnant wife with his father and sister Mary. Natasha's brother, Nicholas, gets into trouble in the army for threatening a superior officer whom he has caught cheating; later, in battle, Nicholas runs away from the enemy and realizes that he is the coward and cheat. Suddenly popular, Pierre marries Helene Kuragin. Her brother, Anatole, proposes to Mary, but her father will not allow her marriage. Prince Andrew is wounded in battle and left for dead at the end of Book I.

Book II

Nicholas Rostov is in love with his cousin Sonya, and she loves him; unfortunately, the family needs him to marry somebody with money because their wealth is dwindling. Pierre, reacting to rumors about an affair between his wife and Dolokhov, challenges him to a duel. When Pierre wounds Dolokhov he runs away, questioning his own morals, and in an inn he meets an old acquaintance who introduces him to the Freemasons, a secret society that does good deeds. Pierre becomes an enthusiastic member, separating from Helene and arranging to give away his belongings to help humanity.

Prince Andrew returns from the war on the same day that his wife dies giving birth to their son. Nicholas encourages Sonya to accept Dolokhov's marriage proposal, but she refuses. Soon after his father puts him on a budget of two thousand rubles, Nicholas gambles with Dolokhov and loses forty-three thousand rubles, which the family has to sell more property to pay. While Pierre is busy freeing his serfs from their commitment to him, in accordance with his new Masonic beliefs, Prince Andrew is setting up new economic policies that will allow them to be self-sustaining after they earn their freedom.

In 1808 a truce is called in the Napoleonic War. Prince Andrew becomes disheartened with the difficulties of dealing with the army bureaucracy and Pierre becomes disenchanted with being a Mason. In 1809, when Natasha is sixteen, Pierre falls in love with her. So does Andrew, and he proposes to the young lady. However, Andrew's father will not give his consent and tells him to wait a year before marrying. Andrew returns to the army. Meanwhile, Nicholas' mother convinces him that he cannot marry Sonya—he must marry someone rich.

Impatiently waiting for Andrew to return, Natasha lets Anatole court her, secretly giving in to his charm. He makes plans to run away with her, but fails to tell her that he is already married in secret to a girl in Poland. The elopement is broken off when he comes to fetch her and is met by a huge doorman; like a coward, he runs away. Word of this gets back to Andrew, and he breaks the engagement. Natasha tries poison herself but is unsuccessful. Pierre visits her and confesses his love.

Book III

The war begins again in 1812, when the French army moves into Russia. The novel narrates Napoleon's thoughts and impressions of the campaign, and then switches to Tsar Alexander, going back and forth between them. During the fighting, Nicholas comes to realize that his earlier cowardice was just a normal reaction to war and he forgives himself. Recovering from her suicide attempt, Natasha starts to attend morning mass and gains peace and serenity. Her younger brother, Petya, joins the army, but cannot find a way to tell his family.

As the French army advances toward their estate in the country, Mary's father has a stroke. After he dies, Mary rides into the town nearby to prepare to evacuate her household servants. When she sees the peasants starving she offers them all of the grain stored on the family estate, but they become suspicious and think it is some sort of trick to get them to leave their land. They are on the verge of rioting against her when Nicholas rides up, saves her, and falls in love with her.

People flee Moscow to avoid the oncoming French army. Pierre travels out to Borondino, which is the last place where the French can be stopped. Much of Part III is concerned with different views of the Battle of Borondino—from Napoleon, Andrew, Pierre, and Kutuzov.

After the Russian defeat, Moscow has to be evacuated. Natasha insists that the wagons taking her family's belongings need to be emptied in order to bring some injured soldiers too. One of the injured soldiers turns out to be Andrew, who, seeing Natasha for the first time since their engagement was broken off, forgives her.

In deserted Moscow, Pierre comes up with a crazed scheme of assassinating Napoleon. Taken into custody by a French captain, he saves the man's life when Pierre's servant is going to shoot him, and, after being given the comforts of good food and drink he forgets his assassination attempt. He races into a burning building to save a peasant's child, then assaults a French soldier who is molesting a woman, for which he is arrested.

Book IV

Pierre's wife dies while he is a prisoner of the French army. During a long march, Pierre becomes even more at peace with himself. He meets Platon Karataev, a peasant who owns nothing but has a joyful outlook, and decides to be more like him.

Mary finds out that her brother, Andrew, is still alive. She travels to where Natasha and her family are caring for him, and the two women take turns nursing him until he dies.

Kutuzov, the Russian general, is pressured to overtake the fleeing French and kill them, but he knows his army does not have the energy. Petya Rostov admires Dolokhov's daring when he accompanies him on a scouting party into the French camp. The next day, they attack the French: Pierre is freed when the French soldiers flee, but Petya is killed. As the French menace fades, Pierre rejoins the Rostov family and he and Natasha console each other over their grief: she has lost her brother, Petya, and her lover Andrew; he has lost many friends in the fighting. They fall in love.

First Epilogue

Nicholas and Mary marry, as do Pierre and Natasha. They all live at Bald Hills, the estate left to Mary by her father. On December 6, 1820, Pierre arrives home from a trip to Moscow, where he has been meeting with a secret organization. Pierre and Nicholas disagree about a citizen's responsibility to the state, but everyone is happy living together—especially Andrew's son Nicholas, who idolizes Pierre.

Second Epilogue

Tolstoy discusses his view of history and how the weaknesses of the historian's methods fail to distinguish between those actions undertaken by free will and those which are caused by circumstance.

Characters

Prince Andrew Bolkonsky

Prince Andrew is a dashing, romantic figure. For much of the book, he and Natasha are in love but are separated by the war. In the beginning he is married to the pregnant Anna Pavlovna, "the little princess," and is active in the army. At the Battle of Austerlitz, he is wounded and listed as dead for a while, but he shows up alive just as his wife dies while giving birth to their son, Nicholas. When he falls in love with Natasha Rostov, he asks her to marry him right away, but his domineering father tells him to wait for a year to see if their love

will endure. He is wounded at the Battle of Borodino and again news comes that he is dead, but while Moscow is being evacuated wounded soldiers are brought to the Rostov house and Andrew is one of them. Nastasha stays with him through the evacuation, but he eventually dies. In the end, he reaches a new level of spiritual enlightenment.

Elizabeth Bolkonskaya

Elizabeth is Prince Andrew's wife. She dies while giving birth to their son, Nicholas.

Mary Bolkonskaya

Mary is the sister of Prince Andrew. She is a devoutly religious woman who stays devoted to her father even though her devotion nearly ruins her life. Early in the book she is engaged to Anatole Kuragin, but her father objects, and she finds that she cannot ignore his objection. While Andrew goes off to war, Mary stays on the family estate, watching after her father and Andrew's son, Nicholas Bolkonsky. Her father, Prince Nicholas Bolkonsky, becomes more and more verbally abusive in his old age, and Mary becomes more involved with the religious pilgrims who stop at their estate. When Nicholas Rostov stops at Bolkonsky, he protects her from the peasants and they fall in love. After her father's death she is immersed in guilt, feeling that he was not so bad after all and that it was awful of her to not be with him in his last moments. She ends up marrying Nicholas.

Napoleon Bonaparte

Napolean is the Emperor of France. Napoleon mistakenly thinks that his army's progress is due to his own skill, not taking into account the role of fate. On the eve of the great Battle of Borodino, for instance, he is more concerned with a painting of his infant son than with devising an effective battle plan for his troops.

Pierre Buzekhov

Pierre is the central character of this novel and its moral conscience. When he first appears, he is a loud, obnoxious man only interested in himself and the next party. Pierre is forced to change when his father dies: after some uncertainty over the will, it is determined that the old Count did recognized Pierre as his son. Suddenly rich and titled as Count Buzekhov, Pierre finds himself very popular. He marries Princess Helene Kuragin.

After hearing rumors of an affair between Helene and Dolokhov, Pierre challenges him to a duel. After wounding him, Pierre escapes, and while he is traveling across the country he is invited by an old acquaintance to join the Freemasons, a secret society. As a Mason, Pierre releases his servants and spends millions on charitable endeavors, often without knowing that he is being swindled. He is still married to Helene, but they lead different lives, and he finds himself attracted to Natasha Rostov. As the battle is waged against the French outside of Moscow, Pierre hangs around curiously asking questions of the officers; after his return to Moscow, he plans to kill Napoleon. He is captured after saving a child from a burning building, and is taken as a prisoner when the French march back to Paris.

After the war, when he is freed, Pierre marries Natasha. They have children, and at the end of the novel he is involved in a secret society that gathers against the government's knowledge to overthrow the social structure that kept men as serfs. The society described resembles the one that led the Decembrist uprising that was to take place in Russia five years later.

Vasili Dmitrich Denisov

Denisov is the model of a professional military man. Angered at the inept bureaucracy that is not getting provisions to his troops, Denisov rides off to the division headquarters and threatens a commander, which gets his troops food but makes Denisov subject to court martial. Returning from the division headquarters, Denisov is shot by a French sharpshooter. When Nicholas Rostov tries to visit him at the hospital the place quarantined with typhus, with only one doctor for four hundred patients. Eventually, the court martial is averted, but Denisov retires from the service disillusioned. At the end of the book he is staying with the family of Count Nicholas at their estate.

Fedya Dolokhov

Dolokhov comes off as a rogue, a man of small means who manages to impress society's elite and get ahead by using his social position. As a gambler, he wins thousands off of Nicholas Rostov. As a lover, he fights a duel with Pierre Bezukhov over rumors about Dolokhov and Pierre's wife. He is wounded in the duel, but that makes him even more of a romantic figure. He proposes to Sonya, but she rejects him. While the Russian forces are chasing the French army out of the country, Dolokhov makes the bold move of riding into the enemy camp in disguise on a scouting mission; young Petya Rostov idolizes him for his courage.

Media Adaptations

- The quintessential adaptation of *War and Peace* is the six-and-a-half hour film done in Russia in 1968, which was directed by Sergei Bondarchuk. It is available on videocassette with either dubbing or subtitles from Continental Distributing.

- *War and Peace* is available on audiocassette, in a 45-tape package, from Books on Tape, Inc. The novel is read by Walter Zimmerman.

- There was another cinematic adaptation in 1956 by King Vidor, starring Audrey Hepburn, Henry Fonda, Herbert Lom, Vittorio Gassman, and Anita Ekberg.

- In 1994 the British Broadcasting Company did a six-part miniseries adaptation with Colin Baker, Faith Brook, Alan Dobie, and Anthony Hopkins. The series is available from BBC Video.

- The novel has been adapted to an opera by Sergei Prokofiev, renown for his production of *Peter and the Wolf*. The opera version of Tolstoy's story was first produced in Leningrad at the Malay Theater on June 12, 1946.

Boris Drubetskoy

Drubetskoy's rise in the military is due to the social machinations of his mother, who is a wealthy society widow and not afraid to ask, or even peg, highly-placed officers to give her son a good position in the army.

Platon Karataev

Platon is a Russian soldier who gives spiritual comfort to Nicholas.

Anatole Kuragin

Anatole is a scoundrel. His role in the book is to break up the engagement of Natasha and Prince Andrew. He starts paying attention to her out of a sense of adventure, considering her as another in his string of conquests. When he proposes to her and arranges to elope with her, even his friend and companion Dolokhov finds the scheme ridiculous. Anatole is already married in Poland, and the priest and witnesses that he arranges for the wedding are gambling friends willing to go along with a hoax. The wedding plans fail to transpire when, approaching the house, Anatole is asked in by a huge doorman, and he runs away instead. Later, at a field hospital with an injury, Prince Andrew is put on a stretcher next to Anatole, the man who ruined his wedding plans, who is having his leg amputated. Anatole later dies of complication from that operation.

Helene Kuragin

Helen is Anatole's sister, and she is every bit as devious as he is. When Pierre inherits his father's fortune, she marries him. After he fights a duel with Dolokhov over her honor, they lead separate lives. Helene is known in Petersburg polite society. She converts to Roman Catholicism, and, under the pretense that to the church her marriage to Pierre is invalid, plans to marry one of her two suitors. When she dies, it is from a botched operation to cure an illness that is not clearly described in the book, indicating that it might be an abortion: "They all knew very well that the enchanting countess' illness arose from an inconvenience resulting from marrying two husbands at the same time, and that the Italian's cure consisted in removing such inconvenience."

Kutuzov

The commander of the Russian Army, the novel follows Kutuzov through some of his decision-making process, especially focusing on his wisdom in ignoring the popular decision that he should attack the French army as it was fleeing back home.

Natasha Rostov

In the course of the story, Natasha (also known as Nataly) grows from a petulant child to a mature woman who knows the sorrows of war. Natasha is pretty and flirtatious, and the young soldiers are smitten with her. When she and Andrew are engaged, she is delighted to feel like a grown-up, but as time goes by she grows impatient. Kuragin, convincing her that she is in love with him, arranges to elope with her, even though he is already secretly married. When Andrew learns about it, he breaks up with her. She tries to poison herself, in shame.

Later, when Moscow is being evacuated, Natasha is the one who convinces her parents to leave some of their fine possessions behind so that they can take some wounded soldiers. When she finds out that Prince Andrew is one of the wounded, she writes to his sister Mary and together they nurse her until his death. Natasha marries Pierre after he is the only person who she can talk to about Andrew's death.

Nataly Rostov

See Natasha Rostov

Nicholas Rostov

Presented as a typical example of a nobleman, Rostov lived a wasteful life with little intellectual or spiritual depth. Early on he joins the army because he needs the money. He loses great sums of money gambling. Passing by the town near the Bolkonsky estate, he finds the peasants accusing Mary of trying to steal their land by making them evacuate. His aristocratic sensibilities are offended; unarmed, he makes the mob rulers quiet down and turn away. At the end of the book he is a retired gentleman, arguing with his brother-in-law Pierre that he should leave the government alone to handle the situation of the serfs properly.

Peter Rostov

The youngest member of the Rostov family, Peter is mostly forgotten in the background, playing childish games, until, at age sixteen, he enlists in the army. He is killed in the same attack that frees Pierre from the retreating French forces.

Sonya

Sonya is a pathetic figure, always in love but too meek to do anything about it. She is a cousin of and lives with the Rostov family, and early in the book she and Nicholas Rostov pronounce their love for one another. His family, in bad financial shape, object and hope that he will find a woman with a better dowry to offer. Sonya is Natasha's confidante, and stands by her during her various disastrous love affairs.

Themes

Class Conflict

Although there is not much open conflict between members of the different classes of this novel, there is an underlying tension between them.

Members of the older generation, such as Countess Rostova and Prince Nicholas Bolkonsky, verbally abuse the peasants who are under their command. In a patronizing manner, they openly discuss how lost the peasants would be without their guidance. At the same time, there are characters like Platon Karataev, a poor man who leads a simple and happy life.

The closest the novel comes to an open-class conflict is when Mary is confronted by peasants at Bogucharovo, near her family's estate, as she is planning to evacuate before the French arrive. Tolstoy is clear about the fact that they act, not out of resentment for the social privilege Mary has enjoyed at their expense, but because of their fear that they have no leader. They are starving, but will not accept the grain that Mary offers them because they fear angering the French. The greatest danger that they pose to her is blocking her horse when she plans to leave. When Nicholas arrives they automatically fall under his spell and comply with his demands without hesitation, apparently in recognition of his superior breeding and intelligence. He orders the leaders of the insurrection bound, and several men in the crowd offer their belts for that purpose. "How can one talk to the masters like that?" says a drunken peasant to his former leader as he is being led away. "What were you thinking of, you fool?"

Duty and Responsibility

The greatest motivation for the noble families in this novel is their duty to the serfs in their care. In other words, the upper classes believe that they have the responsibility to care for their serfs, looking after them as one would look after children. This assumption stems from the common perception that the serfs were not intelligent enough to survive without their help. To do this is an important part of the code of honor; any nobleman that violates this trust is recognized and punished by his peers.

In fact, this code of conduct controls almost every aspect of upper-class life. It dictates how a gentleman should act in any given situation; to deviate from it invited the censure of one's peers. After the drunken revelers at a poker party throw a policeman in the canal, the act is derided as improper for well-bred gentlemen:

> And to think it is Count Vladomirovich Bezukhov's son who amuses himself in this sensible manner! And he was said to be so educated and clever. That is all that his foreign education has done for him!

Topics for Further Study

- Compare the protests in America during the Vietnam War in the late 1960s and early 1970s to the Decembrist uprising, which Pierre is involved with at the end of the book. What were the Decembrists protesting? Were there any similarities in the way the Decembrist and Vietnam protests were organized?

- The Society of Freemasons, which is so influential in Pierre's life, is still an active organization. Investigate the modern-day Masons. Considering the fact that it is still a secret organization, how much information can you find out about them? How have their practices and goals changed from the time of Tolstoy's novel?

- During World War II, Russia was an ally of America and Great Britain. Yet for most of the twentieth century, America and Russia were bitter rivals. Research the relationship between the two countries at the time of the novel and report on it. What is America's relationship to Russia today?

Later, Bezukhov, undergoes a series of transformations that raise his sense of social responsibility. He joins the Freemasons with the idea of working among society's elite to help the poor. He visits the army at the Battle of Borondino and tours the field; half-crazed, he decides he should get a gun and shoot Napoleon. In peacetime, he works with a secret organization to rearrange the social order and free the serfs from their oppression.

Art and Experience

Any historical novel such as *War and Peace* raises questions about the interplay between fiction and reality. The battle scenes in this novel are commended for their realism, but Tolstoy did not actually experience these battles; instead, they are drawn from his exhaustive research of the war against France and his own experiences in the Crimean War. At the end of the novel, Tolstoy dispenses of the fictional story altogether and talks directly to the reader about how historians impact history. Reality is too large and complex for humans to comprehend, Tolstoy contends, and so historians cannot cover all of the diverse aspects of historical events.

Success and Failure

A large part of what drives Tolstoy in the novel is his rejection of conventional historical perceptions of the war: Napoleon, who eventually lost in Russia, is viewed as a shrewd commander today, while the Russian commander, Kutuzov, is dismissed as a blunderer. As Tolstoy perceived the situation, those detractors who considered the Russians as failures because they did not destroy Napoleon's army were not accounting for the army's weakened condition. Moreover, those who credited Napoleon with brilliant strategy were not taking into consideration his good luck. In the end, Tolstoy reminds readers of the role of chance involved in life, and the sometimes small difference between success and failure.

Style

Structure

Since *War and Peace* was first published, critics have discussed the ambiguous structure of the novel. Some contend that Tolstoy raced through the book, putting down ideas as they came to him; therefore, any structure in the story is accidental. As evidence of this, they point to the final chapters, which seem if the author's attention was distracted and he followed his interests rather than doing what the novel would require for completion. Some critics consider the free-floating structure to the appropriate device for the ideas that Tolstoy was trying to convey about free will, and they credit him with utilizing a structure that permitted him to balance necessity with chance.

Some critics perceive a clear pattern to the overall book: the alternation of chapters about war with chapters about peace; the symmetry and repetition in the amount of time spent on the march to Moscow and the march from it; in the scenes of blithe society and the scenes of existential angst; and in the scenes about love and the scenes about death. The question of whether Tolstoy planned the patterns that can be found in his book or whether they were coincidences is an issue that will be debated throughout history.

Setting

In the early nineteenth century, Russia was going through a tumultuous and transitional time. The old feudal system was disappearing. Conventional ideas of honor were losing ground to pragmatic ideas from the Enlightenment. Military victories were seen as a result of luck. Tolstoy took advantage of these unique circumstances to set his sprawling tale of love, war, and changing political and social ideas. It took genius to recognize the potential of this setting and exploit it, but his philosophical case was helped greatly by the fact that this was a situation rich in possibility.

Hero

Prince Andrew is a hero in a conventional sense: he overcomes initial fear in battle to ride bravely against the enemy, and he has a beautiful woman waiting for him at home, dreaming of his return. He has qualities, though, that are less than heroic, such as a fear of commitment. He is all too willing to accept his father's demand that he put off his marriage for a year. During that time, Natasha is drawn to another man, Anatole, who almost ruins her socially. In the end, Andrew remains an idealized hero by dying a soldier's death after he has been reunited with his beloved.

On the other hand Pierre is more of a modern hero. He is not a warrior, but a thinker: the struggle he fights is with his conscience, after he is made rich with an unexpected inheritance. He is not a dashing figure, and he bears his love for Natasha silently instead of declaring it. Yet in the end, he is the one who wins her hand.

Narrator

Toward the end of the story, Tolstoy increasingly addresses the reader directly, stepping out from behind the persona of the third-person narrator who has told the stories of the characters. Throughout the novel, there are breaks from the action where the theoretical aspects of war are discussed. Sometimes these are written like textbooks, describing troop movements; sometimes the important figures of the war are discussed as characters, describing their specific movements and thoughts. At the end, the narration directly addresses the reader, referring to thoughts presented as having come from "I," apparently abandoning the structure of the story to talk about philosophy. The narrator becomes a character who hijacks the novel by the second and last epilogue, lecturing his audience about his theories of historical truth.

Historical Context

The Napoleonic Wars

In 1789, the French Revolution swept through France, marking one of the true turning points in Western civilization. In part, this revolt was inspired by the success of the American Revolution, which had rejected the old English monarchy and established a new country based on democratic principles. Mostly, though, the French Revolution was a protest against the widespread abuses of the French aristocracy, who lived in decadence while the lower classes had to endure higher taxes and economic restrictions. When the peasants realized that the French government was going to use force against protesters, they became violent. The violence escalated as the people systematically began to eliminate anyone of aristocratic lineage. After a long fight, King Louis IX was beheaded in Paris in 1793. There followed a two-year period called the Reign of Terror, during which the revolutionary leaders executed more than 17,000 people.

During this time, France's enemies tried to take advantage of the situation. As a result, France was constantly at war. Out of all of this confusion, conservative elements in the government supported the rise of military commander Napoleon Bonaparte, whose solution to the government's instability was to take control. He was appointed First Consul by the constitution of 1799, and in 1802 he appointed himself that position for life. In 1804, a new constitution appointed him Emperor, a title which was to pass down to his heirs.

Napoleon's influence was seen in almost all aspects of French social life. However, his true interest was in waging war. As England and France had always been enemies, he aimed to conquer England; but since England was the most powerful and important country in the world at that time, his plans were foiled. He turned his attention to Russia. The Treaty of Tilsit, which he signed with Russia's emperor Alexander I in 1807, divided Europe into half: the French controlled Holland, Westphalia, Spain, and Italy. By 1809 Napoleon was the ruler of most Europe, except for Russian and England. In 1812 he invaded Russia with 500,000 troops, a situation depicted in *War and Peace*.

Emancipation of the Serfs

From the 1600s until the middle of the nineteenth century, the Russian economy had been based upon an economic principle of serfdom. Serfs were agricultural laborers, legally bound to work on large estates and farms. Moreover, serfs were owned by the people who owned the land they worked on. The serf could buy his freedom or work it off, but this happened rarely (serfs were always males; female peasants were attached to spouses or parents and, likewise, the property of the landowners). Landowners had a responsibility to take care of their serfs, and in hard times they might have to incur losses to make sure that their serfs were all adequately fed.

This social system was always fraught with tension. As in *War and Peace*, when the war broke up society and forced landlords to flee their land, open rebellion was only avoided by those serfs who felt loyalty to the tradition. In America, the slave system that was in place at the same time was justified by theories of one race being inferior to another, but the Russian system had even less justification for saying why one human had a right to rule over another. Many members of the aristocracy realized this, and in the years after the Napoleonic Wars they banded together to form the secret societies that would lead the Decembrist uprising.

The Decembrist uprising was the first real revolution of modern Russia. In 1817 landowners started forming secret societies, patterned on societies such as the Masonic Order. These societies, such as the Society of Russian Knights and the Union of Welfare, started as gentlemen's clubs; but as they grew in number their rhetoric became more revolutionary. When Tsar Alexander I died unexpectedly in December of 1825, there was confusion about who was to assume power, and in the temporary confusion about who was to be the next ruler the members of the uprising were able to gather three thousand soldiers to their cause. Alexander's successor, Tsar Nicholas, gathered fifteen thousand soldiers; the result was a massacre in Senate Square. Members of the secret societies were gathered up and jailed. After trials, the leaders were executed and over a hundred received jail sentences, but revolutionaries in Russia since then have acted in the names of the Decembrists.

Not surprisingly, Nicholas' reign was conservative in its nature and intolerant of dissent, but even he realized that the days of the old aristocracy were disappearing. He appointed commissions to study the question of serfdom. In 1855, when his son Alexander II became took power, it was clear that the country was headed for chaos, that the serf system would not survive. He had a committee work for four years on the right way for Russia to

Compare & Contrast

- **1805:** America is still developing an identity after winning its independence from England in 1783. A second war against England will be fought in 1812–1814.

  1866–1869: In the aftermath of the Civil War, America undergoes a period known as the Reconstruction.

  Today: America is a stable country. It is considered the dominant economic and military power in the world.

- **1815:** News of Napoleon's defeat at Waterloo is reported four days later by London's *Morning Chronicle,* which scooped the competing British newspapers.

  1866: Telegraph communication is the most common way to communicate over long distances. In America, Western Union controls 75,000 miles of wire, becoming the first great monopoly.

  Today: News events are available instantly from all corners of the globe, thanks to the Internet.

- **1807:** Former Vice President Aaron Burr is arrested for his part in a scheme to form an independent nation of Mexico and parts of the Louisiana Territory.

  1868: President Andrew Johnson faces an impeachment trial, charged with dismissing the

Secretary of War, a violation of a year-old law prohibiting removal of certain cabinet officers without the consent of Congress. Opposition forces end up one vote short of the number necessary to impeach him.

  Today: President Bill Clinton is impeached by the Senate for crimes related to a sex scandal. After his acquittal, his approval ratings are higher than ever.

- **1805–1815:** Napoleon Bonaparte is the Emperor of France. He assumes that position after his rise to military power during the French Revolution.

  1866–1869: Naploean III is Emperor of France, having named himself emperor in 1852. A nephew of Napoleon Bonaparte, he is elected president in 1848 and then seizes dictatorial power.

  Today: France is a republic; the people democratically elect a president.

- **1805:** The Russian population is approximately thirty-three million people.

  1866: The population of Russia has increased to approximately seventy-six million people.

  Today: Russia has a population of approximately 149 million people.

---

evolve beyond the serf structure with the least change.

The system that Alexander announced with his Imperial Manifesto Emancipating the Serfs arranged for land to be divided: landlords were to keep half of their land, and communes, or *mirs,* were to distribute the other half equally between the serfs. The peasants had a forty-nine year period to pay back the cost of their land. This proclamation was read at churches throughout Russia in February of 1861, two years before Tolstoy began writing *War and Peace.* These reforms still left the

former serfs, now peasants, under the control of a government ruled by an aristocracy. The issues of freedom and of class continued to boil in Russia, and eventually led to the Russian Revolution in 1917.

Critical Overview

Much of the earliest critical reaction to *War and Peace* focused on how well Tolstoy had accurately portrayed historical events in Russia. Al-

Vladislav Strzhelchik as emperor Napoleon Bonaparte in the 1968 film version of War and Peace.

though Tolstoy took great pains to research the historical documents, he did not feel obliged to stick firmly to the common historical interpretations. Still, since many critics had lived through the events described, while many others had grown up hearing about them, it was difficult for critics to not talk about how Tolstoy's version related to their own. In general, they found the novel to be quite accurate.

Some critics took exception with the way that Tolstoy had presented the military commanders as less instrumental in the outcome of the war. At the other extreme were those critics who faulted Tolstoy for failing to improve the social consciousness of the time. Edward Wasiolek explains that radical critic Dmitry Pisarev commented that the first half of the book, which was all that was published before his death, was "a nostalgic tribute to the gentry."

Wasiolek also relates the comments of N. K. Strakhov, whose criticism of the novel he describes as "the best criticism on *War and Peace* at the time, and possibly the best in Russian since." He credits Strakhov for his appreciation of the psychology of the novel and for recognizing the fact, which is commonly accepted today, that Tolstoy's greatness was in being able to render a full character in just

a few words. Strakhov appreciated the novel, but he could not fully account for its greatness: as he noted, "among all the various characters and events, we feel the presence of some kind of firm and unshakable principle on which the world of the novel maintains itself."

The ambiguity of that "firm and unshakable principle" was what earned the book a lukewarm reception when it was translated into English. Matthew Arnold, in his review for *Fortnightly Review,* noted that Tolstoy wrote about "life" but not "art." Perhaps the most lasting criticism by an English-speaking author was that of novelist Henry James. In his introduction to the book *The Tragic Muse,* as in the introductions to most of his works, James considered philosophical matters of art. Considering Tolstoy and Alexandre Dumas, the French author of *The Three Musketeers* and *The Count of Monte Cristo,* James wondered, "What do such large loose baggy monsters, with their queer elements of the accidental and the arbitrary, artistically *mean?*" He went on to assert that "there is life and life, and as waste is only life sacrificed and thereby prevented from 'counting,' I delight in a deep-breathing economy and organic form."

After the Russian Revolution in 1917, Tolstoy fell into favor with new Communist government.

Up until then, his literary reputation was maintained by people who had known him (he died in 1910) and a few stalwart fans. In a 1924 article, the author Maxim Gorky relates Lenin talking about *War and Peace* in the Kremlin in 1918: "'He, brother, is an artist! ... Whom could one put next to him in Europe?' Then [Lenin] answered himself 'No one.'" It was not long before Tolstoy studies went beyond personal reminiscences to intellectual scholarship in Russia. At a time when many other significant Russian authors were banned because of their views, Tolstoy was embraced as a foresighted nobleman who wrote about the value of common people and the arbitrary nature of class distinctions.

Today, Tolstoy's career is divided into two eras: the spiritualism of the later novellas and the sweeping romances of the earlier novels, such as *War and Peace* and *Anna Karenina.* Critics perceive within *War and Peace* one phase of his life leading into the other: how the prodigious novelist of the 1860s and 1870s evolved into the thoughtful spiritual man he was by the turn of the century. There is no question of Tolstoy's greatness today.

Criticism

David Kelly

David Kelly is an instructor of Creative Writing and Literature at College of Lake County and Oakton Community College in Illinois. In the following essay, Kelly discusses why the people most likely to avoid reading War and Peace *are the ones who would probably enjoy and benefit from it most.*

It would be difficult to question the quality of Leo Tolstoy's *War and Peace.* Although most critics would not go as far as E. M. Forster did in *Aspects of the Novel,* proclaiming this to be the greatest novel ever written, all would swear to its overall excellence. As with any work, critics consider different ideas about its relative merits and weaknesses, no matter how revered.

Still, with such universal acclaim, no one ever feels the need to ask why *War and Peace* isn't read more often—anyone who has ever looked at it on a bookshelf, taking up the space of four or five average novels, knows at a glance the secret of its unpopularity. It's huge. All across the world *War and Peace* is mentioned in pop culture, but usually it is discussed in terms of how difficult the speaker's education was, or would have been, if they had actually gone ahead with things like reading big novels.

Literary critics tend to skip quickly past this issue of the book's enormous size, although the general public can never get past it. In the literary world, bringing up a book's length is as tasteless as mentioning its price—both being worldly concerns, not artistic considerations. Unfortunately, the result is a huge gap between the values of critics and the values of readers, especially students. Many students find the page count intimidating, and would be just as happy reading three hundred pages of nonsense as a thousand worthwhile pages. This is where the jokes about *War and Peace* come in, reinforcing the idea that it is not only unimportant, but is ridiculous. Students end up making their decision about whether or not to read it without ever looking at a page, judging the book by the distance between its covers. To students who do not care for literature this book seems the most dreaded of all possibilities.

Actually, this is the book that students who do not like literature have been asking for. It is not too clever, too wound up in an artistic style, to be appealing to the general reader. We all feel life's pace—its mix of chance and fate—and some people find themselves particularly irritated by the way that life is compressed to fit into a book of a few hundred pages. They sorely miss the rich incidental details that are trimmed off on the edges of the writer's frame. Young readers, who are dissatisfied with books that don't represent life, need a book like this: one that can take bends, back up, or plow straight ahead, according to what happens in the world we know—not according to some literary theory. Ernest J. Simons' classic examination of *War and Peace* quoted an anonymous reader saying it best: "if life could write it would write just as Tolstoy did."

Of course, all writers write about life in their own way, but what makes this case different is that *War and Peace* is successful at reflecting a true pace of life without having to dwell upon how poignant it is or oversell its own sensitivity. It is not difficult to understand. The book has something in it to remind readers of all of their own experiences. Working with such a long form gives Tolstoy freedom to follow the lives of his characters as they zig and zag, as they live out their intentions or fall to fate's control.

Freedom is what *War and Peace* is about, although Tolstoy does not formally declare this intention until nearly twelve hundred pages are done.

By that time, after we have felt the looseness of his style, the emphasis on freedom of the mind is no surprise. The feeling of freedom takes time to establish. A novel that is tightly plotted can get to its point in a few sentences, but these are the books that raise the suspicions of those wary readers who hate the artificiality of art. For an author like Tolstoy to follow the rhythms of life, especially the easygoing lives of the leisured class, means taking time.

The idea of freedom, which Tolstoy talks about in the Second Epilogue, is evident in the way that this book came to be, having ended up a far, far different thing than it was when he first thought of it. It originally spanned over fifty years—at the pace *War and Peace* as we know it unravels, that would come out to nearly five thousand pages. When the idea first came to Tolstoy, the character Pierre Bezukhov was to be a veteran of the Decembrist uprising, returning to Moscow in 1856 after being exiled in Siberia for thirty years for his part in the uprising. That led the story back to 1825, but writing about the uprising raised the broader question: Who were these revolutionaries? They were Russian noblemen who had tried to overthrow the government to gain freedom for the country's peasants. What gave them the idea to act against their own self-interests? Searching for the answer to that question took Tolstoy even deeper into the past.

Eventually, the sections taking place in 1856 and 1825 were dropped from the novel. Instead, the action begins in 1805, when the major characters are young adults and the Russian aristocracy is first being politicized by the threat of Napoleon, and concludes in 1820, when Pierre is just starting to discuss the ideas that later led to the Decembrist uprising. This flexibility led the book in directions that could not have been anticipated when Tolstoy started it—directions that the readers do not see coming. Reluctant readers might not buy the idea that the book is a "thrill-ride," but it certainly plays out unlike any other novel, which in itself should cut short most objections to reading it.

To get the full effect readers need to take their time unraveling this book, which is not the same thing as saying that it is difficult to understand. The language is not difficult, and the situations are clear enough, but the wealth of details just will not be understood as quickly as busy people want. Of course, there will always be readers who think that any novel that does not happen in their own towns within their own lifetimes is irrelevant to their life.

> **Actually, this is the book that students who do not like literature have been asking for."**

They foolishly think that human nature has somehow become different as the times have changed, or that it is significantly different from one place to another. There isn't much that will change these people's minds, because they will always find excuses to hate reading.

It is one of the great ironies of literature that many people will not touch *War and Peace* because they do not consider themselves to be fans of history. They feel that history is not real or relevant. These people could have sat down with Leo Tolstoy and, language problems aside, gotten along just fine. He disliked history, too—at least, the way that historians present it. The novel's long, winding road leads to its Second Epilogue, where Tolstoy addresses the problems with historical interpretation of the past and how he thinks events should be recorded as time passes. It is almost beyond worth mentioning to say that anyone who feels that she or he cannot understand history has not had it presented to them in the right way before. They might have been told about "heroic" deeds that were obviously done out of desperation, not good character, or heroic figures with despicable personal lives, or "common" people who are more interesting than the focal subjects of history. Overgeneralization makes historians liars, a fact that bothered Tolstoy as much as it bothers people who feel that reading stories based in the past are not worth the effort.

Sometimes people feel that they are not qualified to read *War and Peace* because they do not know enough about its time and setting. The book certainly mentions a lot of historical detail, but it also explains the significance of the details. If it did not explain the references within the novel, it would not have to be so frighteningly long—that is what all of those hundreds of pages are for. All one should do before starting is to take out a map, find France, find Moscow, and know that in 1812 the French army marched across Europe and Russia to Moscow, then quickly turned around and marched back to France. Any further knowledge of the

Mel Ferrer and Audrey Hepburn in the 1956 film version of War and Peace.

events of the time—why they advanced, why they retreated, who the principle actors were—would be nice, but it is not necessary.

There will always be people who do not want to read—whatever their reasons, and there are millions of them, they feel that reading is not worth their time, and, if you haven't heard it all your life, *War and Peace* takes time to read. But it is not much more reader-friendly than books a fraction of its size. It is not much more difficult to figure out what is going on than it is to catch up with the characters on a soap opera, and it is, in the end, a better experience: soap operas do not consider the questions of reality and freedom that make nonreaders shun novels in the first place.

Source: David Kelly, in an essay for *Novels for Students*, Gale, 2000.

Aylmer Maude

In the following excerpt, Maude praises Tolstoy for his artistry, for "clearness of form and vividness of colour," for showing things as his characters saw them, and for presenting the soul of man "with unparalleled reality."

Nothing can be simpler than most of the occurrences of *War and Peace*. Everyday events of family life: conversations between brother and sister, or mother and daughter, separations and reunions, hunting, holiday festivities, dances, cardplaying, and so forth, are all as lovingly shaped into artistic gems as is the battle of Borodino itself. Whatever the purpose of the book may be, its success depends not on that purpose but on what Tolstoy did under its influence, that is to say it depends on a highly artistic execution.

If Tolstoy succeeds in fixing our gaze on what occupied his soul it is because he had full command of his instrument—which was art. Not many readers probably are concerned about the thoughts that directed and animated the author, but all are impressed by his creation. Men of all camps—those who like as well as those who dislike his later works—unite in tribute to the extraordinary mastery shown in this remarkable production. It is a notable example of the irresistible and all-conquering power of art.

But such art does not arise of itself, nor can it exist apart from deep thought and deep feeling. What is it that strikes everyone in *War and Peace*? It is its clearness of form and vividness of colour. It is as though one saw what is described and heard the sounds that are uttered. The author hardly speaks in his own person; he brings forward the characters and then allows them to speak, feel, and act; and they do it so that every movement is true and amazingly exact, in full accord with the character of those portrayed. It is as if we had to do with real people, and saw them more clearly than one can in real life....

Similarly Tolstoy usually describes scenes or scenery only as reflected in the mind of one of his characters. He does not describe the oak that stood beside the road or the moonlight night when neither Natasha nor Prince Andrew could sleep; but he describes the impressions the oak and the night made on Prince Andrew. The battles and historic events are usually described not by informing us of the author's conception of them, but by the impression they produce on the characters in the story.... Tolstoy nowhere appears behind the actors or draws events in the abstract; he shows them in the flesh and blood of those who supplied the material for the events.

In this respect the work is an artistic marvel. Tolstoy has seized not some separate traits but a whole living atmosphere, which varies around different individuals and different classes of society....

The soul of man is depicted in *War and Peace* with unparalleled reality. It is not life in the abstract that is shown, but creatures fully defined with all their limitations of place, time, and circumstance. For instance, we see how individuals *grow*. Natasha running into the drawing-room with her doll, in Book I, and Natasha entering the church, in Book IX, are really one and the same person at two different ages, and not merely two different ages attributed to a single person, such as one often encounters in fiction. The author has also shown us the intermediate stages of this development. In the same way Nicholas Rostov develops; Pierre from being a young man becomes a Moscow magnate; old Bolkonsky grows senile, and so forth....

In judging such a work one should tread with caution, but we think a Russian critic judged well when he said that the meaning of the book is best summed up in Tolstoy's own words: "There is no greatness without simplicity, goodness and truth."

Source: Aylmer Maude, "Life of Tolstoy," reprinted in *Tolstoy: The Critical Heritage,* Edited by A. V. Knowles, Routledge & Kegan Paul, 1978, pp. 225–32.

John Bayley

An English poet and novelist, Bayley is best known for his critical studies of Tolstoy, Alexander Pushkin, and Thomas Hardy. In the following excerpt from his Tolstoy and the Novel, *Bayley dis-*

> **"** Men of all camps—those who like as well as those who dislike his later works—unite in tribute to the extraordinary mastery shown in this remarkable production."

cusses the depiction of characters and historical events and the themes of life and death in War and Peace.

Pushkin's tale, *The Captain's Daughter,* which describes the great rebellion of Pugachev in 1773, during Catherine's reign, is the first imagined relation of an episode from Russian history, but it is no more a historical novel than is *War and Peace.* It strikes us at first as a rather baffling work, with nothing very memorable about it. Tolstoy himself commented, as if uneasily, on its bareness, and observes that writers cannot be so straightforward and simple any more. Certainly Pushkin's way of imagining the past is the very opposite of Tolstoy's. *War and Peace* has a remarkable appearance of simplicity, but this simplicity is the result of an emphasis so uniform and so multitudinous that we sometimes feel that there is nothing left for us to think or to say, and that we cannot notice anything that Tolstoy has not. The simplicity of Tolstoy is overpowering: that of Pushkin is neither enigmatic nor evasive, but rapid and light. He writes about the past as if he were writing a letter home about his recent experiences. The horrors of the rebellion cause him neither to heighten, nor deliberately to lower, his style. And he is just as prepared to "comment" as Tolstoy himself, though he does it through the narrator, who composes the book as a memoir. The Captain, Commandant of a fortress in the rebel country, is interrogating a Bashkir.

> The Bashkir crossed the threshold with difficulty (he was wearing fetters) and, taking off his tall cap, stood by the door. I glanced at him and shuddered. I shall never forget that man. He seemed to be over seventy. He had neither nose nor ears. His head was shaven; instead of a beard, a few grey hairs stuck out; he was small, thin and bent, but his narrow eyes still had a gleam in them.

> The simplicity of Tolstoy is overpowering: that of Pushkin is neither enigmatic nor evasive, but rapid and light. He writes about the past as if he were writing a letter home about his recent experiences."

"Aha," said the Commandant, recognising by the terrible marks one of the rebels punished in 1741. "I see you are an old wolf and have been in our snares. Rebelling must be an old game to you, to judge by the look of your head. Come nearer; tell me, who sent you?"

The old Bashkir was silent and gazed at the Commandant with an utterly senseless expression.

"Why don't you speak?" Ivan Kuzmich went on. "Don't you understand Russian? Yulay, ask him in your language who sent him to our fortress."

Yulay repeated Ivan Kuzmich's question in Tartar. But the Bashkir looked at him with the same expression and did not answer a word.

"Very well," the Commandant said. "I will make you speak! Lads, take off his stupid striped gown and streak his back. Mind you do it thoroughly, Yulay!"

Two soldiers began undressing the Bashkir. The unfortunate man's face expressed anxiety. He looked about him like some wild creature caught by children. But when the old man was made to put his hands round the soldier's neck and was lifted off the ground and Yulay brandished the whip, the Bashkir groaned in a weak, imploring voice, and, nodding his head, opened his mouth in which a short stump could be seen instead of a tongue.

When I recall that this happened in my lifetime, and that now I have lived to see the gentle reign of the Emperor Alexander, I cannot but marvel at the rapid progress of enlightenment and the diffusion of humane principles. Young man! If ever my notes fall into your hands, remember that the best and most permanent changes are those due to the softening of manners and morals, and not to any violent upheavals.

It was a shock to all of us.

The tone of the commentary, and the lack of exaggerated horror, are exactly right. In his late story, *Hadji Murad,* Tolstoy has the same unob-trusive brilliance of description, but—too intent on the art that conceals art—he is careful to avoid the commentary, and so he does not achieve the historical naturalness and anonymity of this narrative. He is too careful in a literary way—almost a Western way—to avoid being shocked....

[The] passage gives us an insight, too, into the reason why all the great nineteenth-century Russians are so good on their history. They feel continuingly in touch with it—horrors and all—in a direct and homely way. They neither romanticise it nor cut themselves off from it, but are soberly thankful (as Shakespeare and the Elizabethans were thankful) if they are spared a repetition in their own time of the same sort of events. Scott subtitled his account of the '45 "'Tis Sixty Years Since," and Pushkin was almost exactly the same distance in time from Pugachev, but their attitudes to the rebellion they describe could hardly be more different. Pushkin borrows greatly from Scott.... But he does not borrow Scott's presentation of rebellion as Romance, safely situated in the past and hence to be seen—in contrast to the prosaic present—as something delightful and picturesque. Nor does he see the past as something over and done with, and thus the novelist's preserve. Unemphatically placed as it is, the comment of the narrator in the penultimate chapter—"God save us from seeing a Russian revolt, senseless and merciless!"—strikes like a hammerblow. It is a comment out of Shakespeare's histories, not Scott's novels.

Tolstoy also borrows from Scott, in particular from the device of coincidence as used in historical romance ("Great God! Can it really be Sir Hubert, my own father?") without which the enormous wheels of *War and Peace* could hardly continue to revolve. Tolstoy avails himself of coincidence without drawing attention to it. It is a convenience, and not, as it has become in that distinguished descendant of Tolstoy's novel—*Dr Zhivago*—a quasi-symbolic method. Princess Mary's rescue by Nicholas Rostov, and Pierre's by Dolokhov, are obvious instances, and Tolstoy's easy and natural use of the device makes a satisfying contrast to the expanse of the book, the *versts* that stretch away from us in every direction. It also shows us that the obverse of this boundless geographical space is the narrow dimension of a self-contained class; the rulers of *War and Peace,* its *deux cents familles* ["two hundred families"], are in fact all known to one another (we are told halfway through that Pierre "knew everyone in Moscow and St Petersburg") and meet all over Russia as if at a *soirée* or a club. Kutuzov and Andrew's father are old comrades in arms; Kutuzov is an admirer of Pierre's wife; and hence Andrew gets the *entrée* to Austerlitz and Pierre to Borodino—and we with them.

Yet Tolstoy's domestication by coincidence gives us an indication why we have from *The Captain's Daughter* a more authentic feel of history than from *War and Peace* Pushkin respects history, and is content to study it and to exercise his intelligence upon it: to Tolstoy it represents a kind of personal challenge—it must be attacked, absorbed, taken over. And in "Some Words about *War and Peace*" [see excerpt dated 1868] Tolstoy reveals the two ways in which this takeover of history is to be achieved. First, human characteristics are invariable, and "in those days also people loved, envied, sought truth and virtue, and were carried away by passion"—i.e. all the things I feel were felt by people in the past, and consequently they are all really *me*. Second, "There was the same complex mental and moral life among the upper classes, who were in some instances even more refined than now"—i.e. my own class (which chiefly interests me) and which was even more important then, enjoyed collectively the conviction that I myself do now: that everything stems from and depends upon our own existence. To paraphrase in this way is, of course, unfair, but I am not really misrepresenting Tolstoy. All his historical theories, with their extraordinary interest, authority and illumination, do depend upon these two swift annexatory steps, after which his historical period is at his feet, as Europe was at Napoleon's.

Let us return for a moment to the extract from *The Captain's Daughter* quoted above. The day after the events described, the fortress is taken by Pugachev, and the old Bashkir sits astride the gallows and handles the rope while the Commandant and his lieutenant are hanged. Nothing is said about the Bashkir's sentiments, or whether this was his revenge on the Russian colonial methods the Commandant stood for, and whether it pleased him. The hero, Ensign Grinyov, is himself about to be hanged, but is saved by the intervention of his old servant; he sees the Commandant's wife killed, and finally "having eaten my supper with great relish, went to sleep on a bare floor, exhausted both in mind and body." Next day he observes in passing some rebels pulling off and appropriating the boots of the hanged men.

I have unavoidably given these details more emphasis than they have in the text: the point is that this conveys exactly what the hero's reaction to such events would have been at that time. It is

What Do I Read Next?

- Thomas Hardy was an English author who lived at approximately the same time as Tolstoy. One of the crowning achievements of his later life was a long poem, *The Dynasts,* written between 1903 and 1908. It is an epic drama with nineteen acts and 135 scenes that are impossible to produce for the stage. The work focuses on England's role in the Napoleonic Wars.

- Tolstoy's other great masterpiece is *Anna Karenina,* his 1877 novel about an aristocratic woman's illicit affair with a count.

- *Crime and Punishment* is considered to be the masterpiece of Fyodor Dostoyevsky's literary career. It was published in 1866, the same year as the first installment of *War and Peace.*

- Russian writer Ivan Turgenev was a friend of Tolstoy. Contemporary critics consider his 1862 novel *Fathers and Sons* to be his greatest work.

- Patient readers who can work their way through this novel's mass may be ready for *Moby Dick,* Herman Melville's 1851 opus about a whaling ship captain and the object of his obsession, the great white whale of the title.

- Henri Troyat's biography, *Tolstoy,* was published in 1967 by Doubleday and Co. It chronicles the life and times of this intriguing author.

not necessarily Pushkin's reaction, but he has imagined—so lightly and completely that it hardly looks like imagination at all: it is more like Defoe and Richardson than Scott—the reactions of a young man of Grinyov's upbringing, right down to the fervent plea that manners and methods may continue to soften and improve. Now let us take a comparable episode in *War and Peace,* the shooting of the alleged incendiarists by the French in Moscow. Pierre, like Grinyov, is waiting—as he thinks—for execution; and his eye registers with nightmare vividness the appearance and behaviour of the people round him. He ceases to be any sort of character at all, but is merely a vehicle for the overpowering precision of Tolstoyan detail, and Tolstoy concedes this by saying "he lost the power of thinking and understanding. He could only hear and see." But here Tolstoy is not being quite truthful. Pierre is also to feel an immense and generalized incredulity and horror, which his creator compels the other participants to share. "On the faces of all the Russians, and of the French soldiers and officers without exception, he read the same dismay, horror, and conflict that were in his own heart." Even the fact that he has himself been saved means nothing to him.

> The fifth prisoner, the one next to Pierre, was led away—alone. Pierre did not understand that he was saved, that he and the rest had been brought there only to witness the execution. With ever-growing horror, and no sense of joy or relief, he gazed at what was taking place. The fifth man was the factory lad in the loose cloak. The moment they laid hands on him, he sprang aside in terror and clutched at Pierre. (Pierre shuddered and shook himself free.) The lad was unable to walk. They dragged him along holding him up under the arms, and he screamed. When they got him to the post he grew quiet, as if he had suddenly understood something. Whether he understood that screaming was useless, or whether he thought it incredible that men should kill him, at any rate he took his stand at the post, waiting to be blindfolded like the others, and like a wounded animal looked around him with glittering eyes. Pierre was no longer able to turn away and close his eyes. His curiosity and agitation, like that of the whole crowd, reached the highest pitch at this fifth murder. Like the others this fifth man seemed calm; he wrapped his loose cloak closer and rubbed one bare foot with the other.

> When they began to blindfold him he himself adjusted the knot which hurt the back of his head; then when they propped him against the bloodstained post, he leaned back and, not being comfortable in that position, straightened himself, adjusted his feet, and leaned back again more comfortably. Pierre did not take his eyes from him and did not miss his slightest movement.

> Probably a word of command was given and was followed by the reports of eight muskets; but try as he would Pierre could not afterwards remember having heard the slightest sound of the shots. He only saw how the workman suddenly sank down on the cords that held him, how blood showed itself in two places, how the ropes slackened under the weight of the hanging body, and how the workman sat down, his head hanging unnaturally and one leg bent under him. Pierre ran up to the post. No one hindered him. Pale frightened people were doing something around the workman. The lower jaw of an old Frenchman with a thick moustache trembled as he untied the ropes. The body collapsed. The soldiers dragged it awkwardly from the post and began pushing it into the pit.

> They all plainly and certainly knew that they were criminals who must hide the traces of their guilt as quickly as possible.

The concluding comment is not that of a man of the age, but that of Tolstoy himself (it shows, incidentally, how impossible it is to separate Tolstoy the moralist from Tolstoy the novelist at any stage of life) and though the description is one of almost mesmeric horror, yet it is surely somehow not completely moving, or satisfactory. This has nothing to do with the moral comment however. I think the explanation is that it is not seen by a real character, or rather by a character who retains his reality at this moment. It is at such moments that we are aware of Pierre's lack of a body, and of a past—the two things are connected—and we are also aware of Tolstoy's need for such a person, with these assets, at these moments. If any member of the Rostov or Bolkonsky families had been the spectator, the scene would have been very different. It would have been anchored firmly to the whole selfhood of such a spectator, as are the deeds of the guerrillas which Petya hears about in their camp....

The point is that a character like this makes us aware of the necessary multiplicity of human response, of the fact that even at such a scene some of the soldiers and spectators must in the nature of things have been bored, phlegmatic, or actively and enjoyingly curious. But Tolstoy wants to achieve a dramatic and metaphoric *unity* of response, as if we were all absorbed in a tragic spectacle; to reduce the multiplicity of reaction to one sensation—the sensation that he had himself felt on witnessing a public execution in Paris. For this purpose Pierre is his chosen instrument. He never *becomes* Tolstoy, but at these moments his carefully constructed physical self—his corpulence, spectacles, good-natured hang-dog look, etc.—become as it were the physical equivalent of Tolstoy's powerful abstract singlemindedness; they are there not to give Pierre a true self, but to persuade us that the truths we are being told are as solid as the flesh, and are identified with it. We find the same sort of physical counterpart of an insistent Tolstoyan point in Karataev's *roundness*. It is one of the strange artificialities of this seemingly so natural book that Tolstoy can juggle with the flesh as with truth and reason, forcing it to conform to the same kind of willed simplicity.

For Pierre's size and corpulence, Karataev's roundness, are not true characteristics of the flesh, the flesh that dominates the life of Tolstoy's novels. The process makes us realise how little a sense of the flesh has to do with description of physical appearance. It is more a question of intuitive and involuntary sympathy. Theoretically, we know much more about the appearance of Pierre and Karataev than about, say, that of Nicholas Rostov and Anatole Kuragin. But it is the latter whom we know in the flesh. And bad characters, like Napoleon and Anatole, retain the sympathy of the flesh. Napoleon, snorting and grunting with pleasure as he is massaged with a brush by his valet; unable to taste the punch on the evening before Borodino because of his cold; above all, at Austerlitz, when "his face wore that special look of confident, self-complacent happiness that one sees on the face of a boy happily in love"—the tone is overtly objective, satirical, even disgusted, but in fact Tolstoy cannot withhold his intuitive sympathy with, and understanding of, the body. Physically we feel as convinced by, and as *comfortable* with, these two, as we feel physically uncommitted with Pierre and Karataev.

> Anatole was not quick-witted, nor ready or eloquent in conversation, but he had the faculty, so invaluable in society, of composure and imperturbable self possession. If a man lacking in self-confidence remains dumb on a first introduction and betrays a consciousness of the impropriety of such silence and an anxiety to find something to say, the effect is bad. But Anatole was dumb, swung his foot, and smilingly examined the Princess's hair. It was evident that he could be silent in this way for a very long time. "If anyone finds this silence inconvenient, let him talk, but I don't want to," he seemed to say.

Inside Anatole, as it were, we "sit with arms akimbo before a table on the corner of which he smilingly and absentmindedly fixed his large and handsome eye"; we feel his sensations at the sight of the pretty Mlle Bourrienne; and when his "large white plump leg" is cut off in the operating tent after Borodino, we seem to feel the pang in our own bodies.

But with Prince Andrew, who is lying wounded in the same tent, we have no bodily communication.

> After the sufferings he had been enduring Prince Andrew enjoyed a blissful feeling such as he had not experienced for a long time. All the best and happiest moments of his life—especially his earliest childhood, when he used to be undressed and put to bed, and when leaning over him his nurse sang him to sleep and he, burying his head in the pillow, felt happy in the mere consciousness of life—returned to his memory, not merely as something past but as something present.

We assent completely, but it is from our own experience, not from our knowledge of Prince Andrew. Like Pierre, he does not have a true body:

there is this difference between both of them and the other characters, and it is not a difference we can simply put down to their being aspects of Tolstoy himself. The difference is not total ... but it is significant, for no other novel can show such different and apparently incompatible kinds of character living together. It is as if Becky Sharp and David Copperfield, Waverley and Tom Jones and Tristram Shandy, together with Onegin and Julien Sorel, Rousseau's Emile and Voltaire's Candide and Goethe's Wilhelm Meister and many more, were all meeting in the same book, taking part in the same plot, communicating freely with one another. For in addition to drawing on his own unparalleled resources of family and class experience, Tolstoy has borrowed every type of character from every kind of novel: not only does he know a lot of people at first-hand—he has absorbed all the artificial ways of describing them.

Moreover, his genius insensibly persuades us that we do actually in life apprehend people in all these different ways, the ways imagined by each kind of novel, so that we feel that Pierre and Andrew are bound to be seekers and questioners because the one has no past and the other no roots in life, forgetting that Tolstoy has deprived them of these things precisely in order that they should conform to the fictional, *Bildungsroman,* type of the seeker. Andrew is a son from a *Bildungsroman* with a father from a historical novel, from Scott or *The Captain's Daughter.* Old Bolkonsky (who was closely modelled on Tolstoy's own grandfather, together with recollections he had heard about Field-Marshal Kamensky) is entirely accessible to us, as much in what we imagine of his old military days, "in the hot nights of the Crimea," as in what we see of his patriarchal life at Bald Hills. But his son, as does happen in life, is distant. We receive vivid perceptions through him (see the childhood passage) but they remain generalized Tolstoy: they are not connected specifically with him. What was he like as a child at Bald Hills? When did he meet the Little Princess, and how did his courtship of her proceed?

We share this uncertainty about Andrew with Natasha, and—more significantly—with her mother. Embedded in life, the Rostovs cannot really believe that the marriage will take place, any more than they can believe they will die. When Natasha sings, her mother remembers her own youth and reflects that "there was something unnatural and dreadful in this impending marriage of Natasha and Prince Andrew." It is like a marriage of life with death.

Like Death, Andrew remains a stranger to the Rostovs. They cannot see him as a complete being any more than we can—any more than his own son can on the last page of the novel. He has become a symbolic figure, by insensible stages and without any apparent intention on Tolstoy's part. Natasha fights for his life, as life struggles against death, and when he dies old Count Rostov—that champion of the flesh—has to realise death too, and is never the same again. Not only death is symbolised in him, but dissatisfaction, aspiration, change, all the cravings of the spirit, all the changes that undermine the solid kingdom of the flesh, the ball, the supper, the bedroom. Tolstoy's distrust of the spirit, and of the changes it makes, appears in how he handles Andrew, and how he confines him with the greatest skill and naturalness to a particular *enclave*.

This naturalness conceals Tolstoy's laborious and uncertain construction of Andrew, which is intimately connected with the construction of the whole plot. First he was to have died at Austerlitz. Tolstoy decided to keep him alive, but that it was a risk to do so is shown by the uncertainty and hesitations of the ensuing drafts. His attitude of controlled exasperation towards the Little Princess was originally one of settled rudeness, culminating in a burst of fury when she receives a *billet* from Anatole. His rudeness is that of Lermontov's Pechorin and Pushkin's Onegin; it must have been difficult to head him off from being a figure of that kind. When he first sees Natasha he is bewitched because she is in fancy dress as a boy (an incident later transferred to Nicholas and Sonya) but in another version he takes no notice of her at all. Tolstoy's bother is to avoid nailing down Andrew with the kinds of *aperçu* he is so good at: he must not be open to the usual Tolstoyan "discoveries." (It would be out of the question, for instance, for Pierre to perceive that Andrew doesn't *really* care about the beauties of nature, as the "I" of *Boyhood and Youth* suddenly realises about his great friend and hero Nekhludyov who is something of a Prince Andrew figure.) Such stages of illumination would be all wrong, as would be any particular aspect of Natasha (fancy dress, etc.) which would reveal something further about him by their attraction for him. Her attraction must be symbolic of life itself.

At last Tolstoy—remembering an experience of his own—hit on the way to convey this. Andrew hears Natasha and Sonya talking together at night as they lean out of the window below his, and in this way her reality—her sense of her family and her happy sense of herself that make up this real-ity—comes before him in the right abstract and ideal way, in a way that could not have been conveyed by Natasha herself in a direct confrontation with him. Natasha's own reactions presented an equal difficulty. In one version she is made to tell Sonya that Prince Andrew was such a charming creature that she has never seen and could never imagine anyone comparable! This clearly will not do, and neither will another version in which she says she doesn't like him, that "there is something proud, something dry about him." In the final version the magical ball takes over, and removes the need for any coherent comment from her. Indeed, Tolstoy ingeniously increases her reality by this method, implying her readiness for life that can take even the shadowy Prince Andrew in its stride; that is then dashed by the prospect of a year's delay; and finally pours itself helplessly into an infatuation with a "real man" (real both for us and for her)—Anatole Kuragin.

Natasha's mode of love presents a marked contrast with that of Pushkin's Tatiana, so often compared with her as the same type of vital Russian heroine. Natasha's love is generalised, founded on her own sense of herself and—less consciously—on her almost explosive expectancy, her need not to be *wasted*. Onegin, whom Tatiana loves, is like Andrew an unintimate figure, but for quite different reasons. He gets what reality he has from the delighted scrutiny of Pushkin, and the devoted scrutiny of Tatiana. His own consciousness is nothing. As Nabokov observes, "Onegin grows fluid and flaccid as soon as he starts to feel, as soon as he departs from the existence he had acquired from his maker in terms of colourful parody." Significantly, Natasha's love is solipsistic, in herself, typical of Tolstoyan *samodovolnost* ["self-satisfaction"], it does not need to know its object, and its object is correspondingly unknowable in terms of objective scrutiny. But when Tatiana sees the marks that Onegin's fingernail has scratched in the margins of his books and realises that he is nothing but a parody, a creature of intellectual and social fashion—it does not destroy her love for him, it actually increases it! Finding the loved person's underlinings in a book is almost as intimate as watching them asleep. The two heroines are alike in the vigour of their affections, but it is a very different kind of affection for all that. In Onegin, Pushkin presents an *object* for us to enjoy, and for his heroine to love. In Andrew, Tolstoy creates the symbolic figure of a spectator of life, in the presence of whom Natasha can show what life there is in herself.

Andrew is created for death. He looks towards death as something true and real at last; and after all the false starts, alterations and reprieves, he achieves his right end. Of course this is something of a Tolstoyan *post hoc ergo propter hoc* ["faulty reasoning"], but it is a fact that all the characters in *War and Peace*—from the greatest to the least—get exactly what their natures require. The book is a massive feat of arbitration, arrived at after countless checks and deliberations: though its huge scale gives an effect of all the random inevitability of life, it also satisfies an ideal. It is an immensely audacious and successful attempt to compel the whole area of living to acknowledge the rule of art, proportion, of what is "right." What Henry James deprecatingly called "a wonderful mass of life" is in fact a highly complex patterning of human fulfilment, an allotment of fates on earth as authoritative as Dante's in the world to come. It is significant that the first drafts of the novel carried the title "All's well that ends well."

In his old age Tolstoy said, "when the characters in novels and stories do what from their spiritual nature they are unable to do, it is a terrible thing." To live, as the novel understands and conveys life, is what Prince Andrew would not have been able to do. It is impossible to imagine him developing a relation with Natasha, or communicating with her as Pierre and Natasha communicate in the last pages of the novel. For him Natasha represents life. It is his destiny as a character to conceptualise what others embody. He perceives through metaphor and symbol, as he sees the great oak-tree, apparently bare and dead, coming again into leaf. A much more moving instance of this, to my mind, than the rather grandiloquent image of the oaktree, is his glimpse of the two little girls as he visits the abandoned house at Bald Hills on his retreat with his regiment.

> … two little girls, running out from the hot-house carrying in their skirts plums they had plucked from the trees there, came upon Prince Andrew. On seeing the young master, the elder one, with frightened look, clutched her younger companion by the hand and hid with her behind a birch tree, not stopping to pick up some green plums they had dropped.

> Prince Andrew turned away with startled haste, unwilling to let them see that they had been observed. He was sorry for the pretty frightened little gift, was afraid of looking at her, and yet felt an irresistible desire to do so. A new sensation of comfort and relief came over him when, seeing these girls, he realized the existence of other human interests entirely aloof from his own and just as legitimate as those that occupied him. Evidently these girls passionately

desired one thing—to carry away and eat those green plums without being caught—and Prince Andrew shared their wish for the success of their enterprise. He could not resist looking at them once more. Believing their danger past, they sprang from their ambush, and chirruping something in their shrill little voices and holding up their skirts, their bare little sunburnt feet scampered merrily and quickly across the meadow grass.

We can see from this passage exactly why Andrew "loved" Natasha—it resembles the scene where he hears the two of them talking by the window—and why the word "love" in the novel has no meaning of its own apart from the continuous demands and rights of life. He loves the idea of life more than the actuality. When he rejoins his soldiers he finds them splashing about naked in a pond, and he is revolted at the sight of "all that healthy white flesh," doomed to the chances of war. Nor do we ever have a greater sense, by contrast, of what life means, than when Andrew, after all his intimations of death, "the presence of which he had felt continually all his life"—in the clouds above the battlefield of Austerlitz and in the birchtree field before Borodino—confronts Natasha and the Princess Mary on his deathbed.

> In one thin, translucently white hand he held a handkerchief, while with the other he stroked the delicate moustache he had grown, moving his fingers slowly. His eyes gazed at them as they entered.

> On seeing his face and meeting his eyes Princess Mary's pace suddenly slackened, she felt her tears dry up and her sobs ceased. She suddenly felt guilty and grew timid on catching the expression of his face and eyes.

> "But in what am I to blame?" she asked herself. "Because you are alive and thinking of the living, while I …" his cold stem look replied.

> In the deep gaze that seemed to look not outwards but inwards there was an almost hostile expression as he slowly regarded his sister and Natasha.

I have suggested that Andrew is not subject to "discoveries," and to Tolstoy's intimate kinds of examination, but this is not entirely true. Tolstoy's genius for character, as comprehensive and apparently involuntary as Shakespeare's, and with far more opportunity for detailed development than Shakespeare has within the limits of a play, could not avoid Andrew's becoming more than a centre of reflection and of symbol. The sheer worldliness of Tolstoy's observation keeps breaking in. We learn, for example, that Andrew befriends Boris, whom he does not much care for, because it gives him an apparently disinterested motive for remaining in touch with the inner ring where preferment is organised and high-level gossip exchanged. And Tolstoy notes that his exasperated criticism of the Russian military leadership both masks and gives an outlet to the tormenting jealousy that he feels about Natasha and Kuragin. But these are perceptions that could relate to someone else: they are not wholly him. What is? I observed that the scene with the two little girls reveals his attitude to life, and so it does; but the deeper and less demonstrated veracity in it is Andrew's *niceness,* a basic quality that we recognise and respond to here, though we have hardly met it before at first-hand. In the same way the deathbed quotation above shows something else about him that we recognise—in spite of the change in him he is still the same man who used to treat the Little Princess with such cold sarcasm: The life he disliked in her he is fond of in his sister and adores in Natasha, but now that it is time to leave it his manner is much the same as of old. Though he has only grown a moustache on his deathbed we seem to recognise that coldly fastidious gesture of stroking it.

> "There, you see how strangely fate has brought us together," said he, breaking the silence and pointing to Natasha. "She looks after me all the time."
>
> Princess Mary heard him and did not understand how he could say such a thing. He, the sensitive, tender Prince Andrew, how could he say that, before her whom he loved and who loved him? Had he expected to live he could not have said those words in that offensively cold tone. If he had not known that he was dying, how could he have failed to pity her and how could he speak like that in her presence? The only explanation was that he was indifferent, because something else, much more important, had been revealed to him.
>
> The conversation was cold and disconnected, and continually broke off.
>
> "Mary came by way of Ryazan," said Natasha.
>
> Prince Andrew did not notice that she called his sister *Mary,* and only after calling her so in his presence did Natasha notice it herself.
>
> "Really?" he asked.
>
> "They told her that all Moscow has been burnt down, and that …"
>
> Natasha stopped. It was impossible to talk. It was plain he was making an effort to listen, but could not do so.
>
> "Yes, they say it's burnt," he said. "It's a great pity," and he gazed straight before him absently stroking his moustache with his fingers.
>
> "And so you have met Count Nicholas, Mary?" Prince Andrew suddenly said, evidently wishing to speak pleasantly to them. "He wrote here that he took a great liking to you," he went on simply and calmly,

evidently unable to understand all the complex significance his words had for living people.

Apart from the theme of death, the passage is full of the multitudinous meaning—like the significance of Natasha's use of the name *Mary*—which has been building up throughout the book. It is checked once by Tolstoy's remark—"he was indifferent because something else, much more important, had been revealed to him." Certainly Andrew may think so, but Tolstoy announces the fact with just a shade too much determination: the surface of almost helpless mastery is disturbed. For where death is concerned, Tolstoy in *War and Peace* was under the spell of Schopenhauer. Life is a sleep and death an awakening. "An awakening from life came to Prince Andrew together with his awakening from sleep. And compared to the duration of life it did not seem to him slower than an awakening from sleep compared to the duration of a dream." As Shestov points out, the second sentence comes almost verbatim from *The World as Will and Idea.* In Andrew, Tolstoy has deliberately created the man who fits this conception of death. With his usual confidence Tolstoy annexes death through Andrew, to show that it must *be* something because life is so much something. Yet life and death cannot understand one another.

> —"Shall I live? What do you think?"
>
> "I am sure of it!—sure!" Natasha almost shouted, taking hold of both his hands in a passionate movement.

Natasha "almost shouts" her belief because she can do nothing else—she cannot believe in anything but life. Even when after the last change in Andrew she sees he is dying, she goes about "with a buoyant step"—a phrase twice repeated. This has a deep tragic propriety, for the two are fulfilling their whole natures. Only old Count Rostov is touching. He cries for himself at Andrew's death, because he "knows he must shortly take the same terrible step"; and he knows this because his old assurance—his *samodovolnost*—has gone.

> He had been a brisk, cheerful, self-assured old man, now he seemed a pitiful, bewildered person … he continually looked round as if asking everybody if he was doing the right thing. After the destruction of Moscow and of his property, thrown out of his accustomed groove, he seemed to have lost the sense of his own significance and to feel there was no longer a place for him in life.

As Isaiah Berlin points out, Tolstoy's conception of history resembles in many ways that of Marx, whom he had never heard of at the time he was writing *War and Peace,* and this applies to his sense of personal history as well as the history of nations. His imaginative grasp of the individual life is such that freedom does indeed become the recognition of one's personal necessity, and "to each according to his needs" is not only the ideal of society but seems in *War and Peace* the law of life and death....

Source: John Bayley, *Tolstoy and the Novel,* Viking Press, 1967, pp. 66–68, 68–72, 73–82.

R. F. Christian

Christian is an English educator, translator, and critic specializing in Russian literature. He wrote Tolstoy's "War and Peace," *which is a book-length study of the work. In the following excerpt from that book, Christian analyzes characterization in* War and Peace.

The subject [of characterization in *War and Peace*] is complicated by the sheer number and variety of the dramatis personae, but we can narrow it down from the very start by drawing a general distinction between the treatment of historical and non-historical characters in the novel. It is a fact that the generals and statesmen, the great historical names of the period of the Napoleonic wars, are almost without exception flat and static figures. Little or nothing is revealed of their private lives. We do not see them in intimate relationships with other people. Their loves, their hobbies, their personal dramas are a closed book to us. This is not accidental. As Prince Andrei reflects at Drissa in 1812:

> Not only does a good commander not need genius or any special qualities; on the contrary, he needs the absence of the highest and best human qualities—love, poetry, tenderness, and philosophic, inquiring doubt. He must be limited.... God forbid that he should be humane, love anyone, pity anyone, or think about what is right and what is not.

Their thoughts are rarely scrutinized either through interior monologue or by extended description from the author. Some characters, such as Arakcheev, for example, use only direct speech. Nothing is conveyed of their thought processes or the motives behind the words they utter. Nor do they develop with the action of the story. The statesmen and the generals in *War and Peace* are either bearers of a message or bureaucratic Aunt-Sallies for Tolstoy to knock down. This fact illustrates the unity which exists between Tolstoy's ideas and their expression through his characters. Static characters generally speaking deserve static treatment. Theme and style are as one.

An exception to the rule that generals are flat characters might be made in the case of Kutuzov.

> *Their thoughts are rarely scrutinized either through interior monologue or by extended description from the author. Some characters, such as Arakcheev, for example, use only direct speech. Nothing is conveyed of their thought processes or the motives behind the words they utter. Nor do they develop with the action of the story."*

Although he is a general, he is not, as Tolstoy understands him, arrogant or self-satisfied. The Kutuzov of *War and Peace* has some claim to be three-dimensional. It is not that he is shown by Tolstoy to have grown sufficiently in stature with the course of events to justify the remark—true though it may well have been in real life—that "In 1805 Kutuzov is still only a general of the Suvorov school; in 1812 he is the father of the Russian people." But his little acts of kindness, his friendly words to the soldiers who fought with him in his earlier campaigns, his unaffected behavior in the company of his inferiors, his present of some sugar lumps to the little girl at Fili, his request to have some poems read to him—all these small things reveal positive and humane qualities which more than balance his lethargy and lechery. Again it is in keeping with Tolstoy's purpose that a general who is not a *poseur* or an egoist or a careerist should emerge as a more rounded personality than any of his professional colleagues....

[Our] remarks will be confined to the fictitious or, rather, non-historical characters. Here again the range is enormous, and in order to restrict it as much as possible we shall concentrate mainly on the men and women who figure most prominently in *War and Peace*.... Tolstoy's first step as a novelist was to draw thumbnail sketches of his future heroes and group their main characteristics together under such headings as wealth, social attributes, mental faculties, artistic sensibilities and attitudes to love. In this respect, incidentally, his rough notes and plans are very different from those left by Dostoevsky, and illustrate an important difference of approach. Dostoevsky in the preliminary stages of his work is concerned with how to formulate his ideas (a generation earlier, Pushkin had tended to jot down first of all the details of his plots). But Tolstoy was interested primarily in the personalities of his characters—in the fact, for example, that Nikolai "is very good at saying the obvious"; that Natasha is "suddenly sad, suddenly terribly happy"; or that Berg has no poetical qualities "except the poetry of accuracy and order."

The problem of actually bringing his major characters on to the stage was one to which Tolstoy attached the greatest importance, and one which, as we have seen, gave him a great deal of difficulty. Broadly speaking, the problem was tackled in a fairly uniform manner, and the technique employed is clearly recognizable, though not of course invariable. All the main characters are introduced very early on. They are introduced with a minimum of biography and with a minimum of external detail (but such as there is typical and important, and likely to recur). Attention is drawn to their features, the expression on their faces, the expression in their eyes and in their smile, their way of looking or not looking at a person. This is a fact which has attracted the notice of most critics of Tolstoy's novels, and inspired Merezhkovsky to make his much-quoted *mot* "with Tolstoy we hear because *we see*" (and its corollary "with Dostoevsky we see because *we hear*"). From the very beginning, the fundamental characteristics of the men and women as they then are enunciated. There is little or no narration to elaborate these characteristics. Almost at once the men and women say something or make an impression on somebody, so that the need for any further direct description from the author disappears. Pierre, for example, is introduced with one sentence about his appearance (stout, heavily built, close cropped hair, spectacles); one sentence about his social status, and one sentence about his life to date. He is then portrayed through the impression he makes on other people present. He is summed up by four epithets which all refer to his *expression (vzglyad)*—clever, shy, observant, natural—and which at the same time distinguish him from the rest of the company and reveal the essence of his character as it then is. Similarly Prince Andrei is given a sentence or two of "author's description"—handsome, clear-cut, dry features, measured step, bored expression

(*vzglyad*)—while the impression he makes on the company and his reaction to them is at once sharply contrasted with the mutual response of Prince Andrei and Pierre to one another. Virtually nothing is said about the earlier lives of these two men. What did Pierre do in Paris? Why did Prince Andrei marry Lisa? We are not told. Both men immediately catch the eye, for both are bored and ill at ease. They are introduced in fact into an environment which is essentially foreign to their real natures, although their way of life requires that they should move in this environment. Despite the fact that the manner of their first appearances attracts attention, there is nothing to suggest that they will be the main heroes of the novel, in the sense that no extra length or detail goes into their description.

By contrast, Natasha and Nikolai are both introduced in their own domestic environment—home-loving creatures on their home ground—integrated in the family and, as it were, part of the furniture. But again they are presented with a minimum of external description (in which facial expressions are conspicuous); again their salient characteristics—Natasha's charm and vivacity, Nikolai's frankness, enthusiasm and impetuosity—are conveyed from the very start; and again we are told nothing about their earlier lives (for example, Nikolai's student days). This lack of biographical information is important in the sense that it enables us to be introduced to the characters as we usually meet people in real life—that is to say, as they now are, and without any knowledge of the forces which shaped them before we met them and made them what they are. It could even be argued that a novelist who introduces his heroes by reconstructing their past when that past plays no direct part in the novel, actually risks sacrificing, by the accumulation of historical detail such as we do not have about people whom we are meeting for the first time, that immediate lifelikeness which, in the case of Tolstoy's greatest characters, is so strikingly impressive.

Once the men and women have made their entrances the author has to face another problem. Are they to remain substantially as they are, with the reader's interest diverted towards the details of the plot? Or are they to grow and change as the plot progresses? If they are to develop, must they do so because the passage of time and the inner logic of their own personalities dictate it? Or because of the pressure of the events which form the plot? Or because the author wishes to express an idea of his own through their medium? In *War and Peace* the main characters do grow and change, and they do so for all these reasons. In the course of the time span of the novel the adolescents grow to maturity and the mature men reach early middle age. War and marriage make their impact on men and women alike, and experience teaches them what they failed to understand before. The Pierre of the opening chapter of the novel, with his self-indulgence, his agnosticism and his admiration for Napoleon, is very different from the spiritually rejuvenated middle-aged man who has discovered a focus for his restless and dissipated energies, and who no longer has any illusions about the grandeur of power. The course of events brings Prince Andrei round from a cynical disillusionment in life, through a feeling of personal embitterment, to a belief in the reality of happiness and love; in the face of death his vanity and ambition are humbled by the realization of the insignificance of this world, and he acquires a hitherto unknown peace of mind. Natasha acquires an unsuspected strength of character after her younger brother's death, and an unaccustomed staidness as the wife of Pierre—to some readers an astonishing violation of her nature, but to others a change which is fully comprehensible in the transition from adolescence to motherhood. Even Nikolai's impetuosity is curbed and experience gives him greater solidity and stability. These changes do not result from the fact that our knowledge of the main heroes gradually increases throughout the novel, as it inevitably does, and the picture of them grows fuller and fuller with each successive episode. They are changes of substance, qualitative rather than quantitative changes. Tolstoy's achievement in contriving the development of his main characters lies in the fact that all the reasons mentioned above for their development are so carefully interwoven that the reader is not conscious of many strands but only one. The characters change because they grow older and wiser. But the events which form the plot, and in particular the Napoleonic invasion, give them greater wisdom and experience, for characters and events are organically connected. And the state to which the main heroes come at the end of the novel—marriage, and the simple round of family life—the state which is the ultimate expression of Tolstoy's basic idea—is the natural outcome of the impact on them of the events they have experienced as they have grown older and their realization of the shallowness of society and the vainglory of war. The profoundly subjective basis of Tolstoy's art may be seen in the fact that Pierre and Natasha, Nikolai and Princess Marya all achieve the state which he himself had achieved, however imperfectly, and

which he sincerely believed to be the most desirable of all states. But this does not mean that their characters are distorted in order to force them into the channels which for him were the right ones. Pierre has so much of Tolstoy in him that he needs no forcing. Natasha, we may remember, was from the very earliest draft of *War and Peace* "crying out for a husband," and needing "children, love, bed." Nikolai and Princess Marya, for all the difference between their personalities, interests and intellectual attainments, never seem likely to stray far from the family nest or to be seduced from the family estate by the allurements of *le monde* ["the world"].

Change and development are at the centre of Tolstoy's characterization, and the process is a consistent and logical one. But however great the changes in his main heroes may seem to be, it must not be forgotten that they occur within certain well-defined bounds, and that the characters themselves remain in the camp to which they have always belonged and continue to be what they have always been—some of the finest and most sympathetic representatives of the Russian landowning aristocracy.

There is no need to labour the point that Tolstoy's principal heroes change and develop. We can turn instead to the question how he achieved the effects he desired by the devices of characterization at his disposal. It seems to me that the essence of Tolstoy's technique is to show that at every stage in the life of his heroes the likelihood of change is always present, so that at no time are they static, apathetic or inert, but constantly liable to respond to some new external or internal stimulus. Very often the stimulus is provided by a person from the opposite camp—a "negative" character, a selfish, complacent or *static* man or woman. These people act as temptations to the heroes; they are obstacles in their path which have to be overcome. Pierre, for example, is momentarily blinded by the apparent greatness of Napoleon. He is trapped into marriage with Hélène, with whom he has nothing in common, and is in danger of being drawn into the Kuragin net. After their separation he is reconciled with her again, only to bemoan his fate once more as a retired gentleman-in-waiting, a member of the Moscow English Club and a universal favourite in Moscow society. Prince Andrei, like Pierre, is deceived by the symbol of Napoleon, and like Pierre he finds himself married to a woman who is as much his intellectual inferior as Hélène is morally beneath Pierre. Natasha for her part is attracted at first by the social climber Boris Drubetskoy and later infatuated by the same Anatole Kuragin who had actually begun to turn Princess Marya's head. Julie Karagina looms for a while on Nikolai's horizon. From all these temptations and involvements the heroes and heroines are saved, not by their own efforts but by the timely workings of Providence. Prince Andrei's wife dies. Pierre is provoked by Dolokhov into separating from his wife, and after their reconciliation he is eventually released by Hélène's death. Natasha is saved from herself by the solicitude of her friends. By chance Princess Marya catches Anatole unawares as he flirts with Mlle Bourienne. (Nikolai, to his credit, is never likely to obey his mother's wishes and marry Julie.) It seems as if fate is working to rescue them from the clutches of egocentricity. But it is not only external circumstances such as personal associations with people of the opposite camp which are a challenge to Tolstoy's heroes and heroines. There are internal obstacles against which they have to contend, without any help from Providence. Tolstoy made it a main object of his characterization to show his positive heroes at all important moments "becoming" and not just "being," beset with doubts, tormented by decisions, the victims of ambivalent thoughts and emotions, eternally restless. As a result, their mobility, fluidity and receptivity to change are constantly in evidence, as they face their inner problems. Princess Marya has to overcome her instinctive aversion to Natasha. Nikolai has to wage a struggle between love and duty until he finds in the end that they can both be reconciled in one and the same person. Pierre's inner disquiet and spiritual striving express his determination, now weak, now strong, to overcome in himself the very qualities of selfishness and laziness which he despises in other people. Outward and inward pressures are continually being exerted on Pierre, Prince Andrei, Princess Marya, Natasha and Nikolai, and their lives are lived in a state of flux.

And yet Tolstoy felt himself bound to try and resolve their conflicts and bring them to a state which, if not final and irreversible, is a new and higher stage in their life's development. It is not a solution to all their problems, a guarantee that they will not be troubled in future. The peace of mind which Prince Andrei attains before his death might not have lasted long if he had lived. Pierre's uneasy religious equilibrium may not be of long duration. The very fact that we can easily foresee new threats to their security, new stimuli and new responses, is a proof of the depth, integrity and life-likeness of the two finest heroes of Tolstoy's novel.

But although there is not and cannot be any absolute finality about the state to which Tolstoy's men and women are brought, there is nevertheless an ultimate harmony, charity, and sense of purpose in their lives which represent the highest ideals of which they are capable, given the personalities with which they have been endowed and the beliefs of the author who created them.

The novelist who wishes to create a vivid illusion of immediacy and mobility in his heroes must avoid exhaustive character studies and biographical reconstructions concentrated in a chapter or series of chapters in his novels, whether at the beginning, in the middle or at the end. Many novelists begin with lengthy narrative descriptions of their main heroes.... But Tolstoy by dispensing largely with "pre-history" and allowing his men and women to reveal themselves little by little as the novel progresses, avoids the necessity for set characterization pieces, static and self-contained as they often are in other writers.

Another factor which aids the illusion of reality—and movement—is the continued interaction of all the elements which make up Tolstoy's novel—men and women, nature, and the world of inanimate objects. Very seldom is a person seen or described in isolation—just as in real life, human beings cannot be divorced from the infinite number of animate and inanimate phenomena which make them what they are and determine what they do. Tolstoy is at pains, therefore, in striving after truthfulness to life in his characterization, to show the interdependence and interpenetration of man and nature. The stars, the sky, the trees, and the fields, the moonlight, the thrill of the chase, the familiar objects of the home all affect the mood and the actions of the characters no less than the rational processes of the mind or the persuasions of other human beings. That this is so in life is a commonplace; but there have been few authors with Tolstoy's power to show the multiplicity of interacting phenomena in the lives of fictitious men and women.

Movement is the essence of Pierre, Prince Andrei and Natasha and this is shown both externally and internally. Externally their eyes, their lips, their smile are mobile and infectious; their expressions continually alter. Internally their thoughts are in a state of turbulence and their mood is liable to swing violently from one extreme to another—from joy to grief, despair to elation, enthusiasm to boredom. There are times indeed when two incompatible emotions coexist uneasily and the character does not know whether he or she is sad or happy.

Princess Marya is not such a forceful or impulsive character as her brother or sister-in-law. Her qualities of gentleness, deep faith, long-suffering, humility and addiction to good works are not combined with a searching mind or a vivacious personality. But she is, nevertheless, a restless person, and as such is clearly a favourite of Tolstoy (she even quotes his beloved Sterne!). The anxieties and disturbances in her relations with Anatole Kuragin, Mlle Bourienne and Natasha are evidence that she is a rounded and dynamic figure, and not, as it were, conceived in one piece. In the presence of Nikolai she is brought to life with all the magic of Tolstoy's art. Nikolai too, for all his apparent complacency and limited horizons, does not stand still. He has his moments of doubt, uncertainty, and fear just as he has his outbursts of uninhibited enthusiasm and emperor worship. He is given his own inner crisis to surmount when at Tilsit "a painful process was at work in his mind" as he tried to reconcile the horrors of the hospital he had recently visited, the amputated arms and legs and the stench of dead flesh, with his hero the Emperor Alexander's evident liking and respect for the self-satisfied Napoleon. The crisis, it is true, soon passes after a couple of bottles of wine. But it could never have been allowed to come to a head at all by his friend Boris Drubetskoy.

By contrast, the less prominent figures in *War and Peace* are not shown in the critical stages of their change and development. Even Sonya's conflict (she is described in an early portrait sketch in typically Tolstoy fashion as "generous and mean")—the conflict between her loyalty to the family and her love for Nikolai—emerges rather through Tolstoy's description of it than through the inner workings and sudden vacillations of her mind. Vera and Berg, Akhrosimova, Bolkonsky and many other minor figures, however vital and many-sided they might be as individuals, are fundamentally static characters who are fully-grown from the beginning. The ability to respond to change, the qualities of restlessness, curiosity, flexibility and dynamism are essentially the perquisites of the main heroes of the novel, and in particular Pierre, Prince Andrei and Natasha. And one may add that it is the growth and development of precisely these three people which reflects above all the changes in Tolstoy himself and those closest to him at Yasnaya Polyana, and is a convincing proof of the personal basis of Tolstoy's art.

In examining the characters of a novel with an historical setting, three questions immediately spring to mind. In the first place, do they emerge as individuals? Secondly, do they unmistakably belong to the historical environment in which they are made to move? And thirdly, do they embody universal characteristics which make them readily comprehensible to people of a different country and a different age? If we apply these questions to Pierre, Prince Andrei and Natasha, the answer to the first is indisputably yes. There is nothing bookish, contrived or externally manipulated about their actions. They can never be confused with any other characters. They have an outward presence and an inner life which mark them off as highly individualized personalities. To the second question the answer is less obvious and critical opinion is divided. For my own part I am inclined to think that there is nothing about them specifically representative of their own age, which is not also representative of Tolstoy's own generation. They are the products of a class and a way of life which had not materially altered when Tolstoy began to write. That they experienced the impact in their homes of a great patriotic war is a fact which distinguishes their lives from the lives of Tolstoy's own contemporaries, but the development of their characters cannot be explained solely in terms of that particular war. Pierre might ask different questions from Levin or put the same questions in a different way, but his spiritual journey is fundamentally the same. Prince Andrei's reactions to war could have been those of one of the many obscure defenders of Sevastopol. Natasha's progress to motherhood, while it is not identical with Kitty's, is not peculiar to the first half rather than to the second half of the nineteenth century. The third question, however, like the first, is easily answered. In Tolstoy's heroes in *War and Peace* there is a basic denominator of human experience which is common to all men and women regardless of class, country, age and intellectual attainment. Their mental, spiritual and emotional problems, their pleasures and pursuits, their enthusiasms and their aversions are as relevant to England today as they ever were to Tolstoy's Russia. And it is ultimately this fact which ensures that *War and Peace* and especially the main heroes of *War and Peace* will always be a part of the literary heritage of the reading public throughout the world.

Characterization cannot be considered in isolation from the many other sides of a novelist's art…. First there are the changes which occur in Tolstoy's characters themselves as the successive draft versions are written and discarded. Then there are the features which they inherit from their various historical and living prototypes. There are the ideas of the novelist himself which are transmitted to his heroes and heroines, so that they in turn express his own prejudices and beliefs and in Pierre's case, the gulf between what Tolstoy was and what he wanted himself to be. There is the question of the composition of the novel which is so designed that the character development should proceed *pari passu* ["at an equal pace"] with the development of the plot, and not fortuitously or independently of the main action. Finally there are the different linguistic devices at Tolstoy's disposal which play their part in characterization—interior monologue, the contrasting use of the French and Russian languages, speech mannerisms, irony....

In the final analysis it is the characters which a novelist creates which are the greatest and most memorable part of his achievement. In *War and Peace* they range over the scale of good and evil and they are treated by the author with varying degrees of sympathy and dislike. In later life Tolstoy wrote to the artist N. N. Gay that in order to compose a work of art: "It is necessary for a man to know clearly and without doubt what is good and evil, to see plainly the dividing line between them and consequently to paint not what is, but what should be. And he should paint what should be as though it already was, so that for him what should be might already be."

This opinion was expressed some twenty years after *War and Peace* was written, but the first part of it at least is applicable to that novel. Tolstoy knew, as well as any man can, the dividing line between good and evil, although in *War and Peace* he devoted much more time to painting things as they are than as they should be. For a novelist, however, to know what is right and what is wrong is not the same thing as to concentrate virtue in one character and vice in another, or to pass an unqualified moral judgement on any of the people he creates. "The Gospel words 'judge not'," Tolstoy wrote in 1857, "are profoundly true in art: relate, portray, but do not judge." Tolstoy's purpose in his first novel, as a creator of living characters, was to entertain and not to judge. One of the most interesting pronouncements he made about the function of an artist occurs in a letter which he wrote in 1865 while actively engaged on his novel, but which he never sent.... The letter was addressed to the minor novelist Boborykin and contains some mild strictures on the latter's two latest novels. Tolstoy wrote:

Problems of the Zemstvo, literature and the emancipation of women obtrude with you in a polemical manner, but these problems are not only not interesting in the world of art; they have no place there at all. Problems of the emancipation of women and of literary parties inevitably appear to you important in your literary Petersburg milieu, but all these problems splash about in a little puddle of dirty water which only seems like an ocean to those whom fate has set down in the middle of the puddle. The aims of an artist are incommensurate (as the mathematicians say) with social aims. The aim of an artist is not to solve a problem irrefutably but to make people love life in all its countless inexhaustible manifestations. If I were to be told that I could write a novel whereby I might irrefutably establish what seemed to me the correct point of view on all social problems, I would not even devote two hours work to such a novel; but if I were to be told that what I should write would be read in about twenty years time by those who are now children, and that they would laugh and cry over it and love life, I would devote all my own life and all my energies to it.

To make people laugh and cry and love life is a sufficient justification for even the greatest of novels....

Source: R. F. Christian, *Tolstoy's "War and Peace": A Study,* Clarendon Press, 1962, pp. 167–68, 177–79.

Clifton Fadiman

In the following excerpt, Fadiman describes Tolstoy's writing as lacking in artistic style, suspense, and originality but also as clear, good, and able to express the ordinary and real.

In a way writing about *War and Peace* is a self-defeating activity. Criticism in our day has become largely the making of finer and finer discriminations. But *War and Peace* does not lend itself to such an exercise. If you say the book is about the effect of the Napoleonic Wars on a certain group of Russians, most of them aristocrats, you are not telling an untruth. But you are not telling the truth either. Its subject has been variously described—even Tolstoy tried his hand at the job—but none of the descriptions leaves one satisfied.

You can't even call the book a historical novel. It describes events that are part of history, but to say that it is about the past is to utter a half-turth. *Ivanhoe, Gone With the Wind*—these are historical novels. Kipling (a part of him, I mean) has suddenly become for us a historical novelist: Gandhi made him one. But the only sections of *War and Peace* that seem historical are the battle pieces. War is now apocalyptic; it was not so in Tolstoy's time. Austerlitz and Cannae are equally historical, equally antique, equally part of the springtime of war. Now our weapons think for us; that is the revolutionary change that has outmoded all previous narratives of conflict.

But, except for these battle pieces, *War and Peace* is no more a historical novel than is the *Iliad.* Homer is not history, not Greek history, not Trojan history, he is—Homer. So with Tolstoy.

No, you say little when you say that *War and Peace* has to do with the Napoleonic Wars, Borodino, the burning of Moscow, the retreat of 1812. As a matter of fact the vaguer your critical vocabulary, the less precisely you describe the subject of *War and Peace,* the nearer you get to the truth. It is really—yes, let us use un-twentieth-century words—about Life and People and Love: those abhorred capital-letter abstractions that irritate our modern novelists and against which they persistently warn us....

Tolstoy is not an artist at all, as, let us say, Virginia Woolf, Hemingway, Faulkner, Proust, are artists. He does not appear, at least in translation, to have any "style." There is no such thing as a Tolstoyan sentence or a Tolstoyan vocabulary. The poor chap has no technique. He knows nothing of flash-backs, streams of consciousness, symbols, objective correlatives. He introduces his people flatly and blurts out at once their dominant characteristics. He has unending insight but no subtlety. Compared to such a great master as Henry James, or such a little master as Kafka, he seems deficient in sheer brain power, the power to analyze, the power to discriminate.

He never surprises you. All his characters are recognizable, most of them are normal. Even his villain, Anatole Kuragin, seems merely an impetuous fool compared to the monsters of labyrinthine viciousness that our Southern novelists can create with a touch of the pen.

He isn't even a good storyteller, if by a good storyteller one means a master of suspense. You do not read *War and Peace* in order to see "how it comes out," any more than you live your life in order to see how it will end. His people grow, love, suffer, die, commit wise or foolish actions, beget more people who are clearly going to pass through the same universal experiences; and that's about all there is to the "story." There are plenty of events, but they are not arranged or balanced or patterned. Tolstoy is not a neat writer, any more than your biography or mine is neat. He is as shapeless as the Russian land itself.

I found myself struck with the originality of *War and Peace,* but by a kind of reverse English.

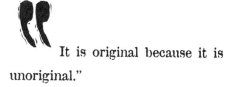

It is original because it is unoriginal."

It is original because it is unoriginal. Kafka is original. Faulkner is original. Eudora Welty is original. In fact most of our most admired modern writing is original, full of strange people, strange feelings, strange ideas, strange confrontations. But Tolstoy portrays pleasant, lively, ordinary girls like Natasha. His book is crowded with people who are above the average in intelligence or wealth or insight—but not extraordinarily so. He balks at portraying genius: he makes of Napoleon a fatuity, and of the slow-thinking, almost vacant-minded Kutuzov the military hero of the war. And when he writes about war, he does not describe its horrors or its glories. He seizes upon the simplest of the truths about war and sticks to that truth: that war is *foolish.*

Tolstoy has a genius for the ordinary, which does not mean the commonplace. It is this ordinariness that to us moderns, living on a literary diet of paprika, truffles, and cantharides, makes him seem so unusual. When we read him we seem to be escaping into that almost forgotten country, the real world.

Another odd thing—Tolstoy does not seem to have any "personality." Many fine writers are full of personality, Hemingway for instance; but the *very* finest write books that seem to conceal themselves, books like the *Iliad* or *Don Quixote* or *War and Peace.* I do not mean that Tolstoy writes like an impersonal god, but that he seems to intrude into his book only in the sense that he and the book are one and the same. I believe this effect of desingularization springs from his instinctive refusal to load any scene or indeed any sentence with more meaning than it will bear. He has no "effects." He is unable to call attention to his own mastery. He knows what he is doing, but he does not know how to make *you* know what he is doing. The consequence is that, despite the enormous cast of characters, everything (once you have waded through the rather difficult opening chapters) is simple, understandable, recognizable, like someone you have known a long time. In our own day the good novelists tend to be not very clear, and the clear novelists tend to be not very good. Tolstoy is clear and he is good....

Source: Clifton Fadiman, "'War and Peace', Fifteen Years After," in *Any Number Can Play,* Harper & Row, 1957, pp. 361–69.

Clifton Fadiman

Fadiman became one of the most prominent American literary critics during the 1930s with his often caustic and insightful book reviews for the Nation *and the* New Yorker *magazines. He also managed to reach a sizable audience through his work as a radio talk-show host from 1938 to 1948.*

I hope merely to set Tolstoy's masterpiece before the reader in such a way that he will not be dismayed by its labyrinthine length or put off by its seeming remoteness from our own concerns.

War and Peace has been called the greatest novel ever written. These very words have been used, to my knowledge, by E. M. Forster, Hugh Walpole, John Galsworthy, and Compton Mackenzie; and a similar judgment has been made by many others....

Let us ... try to discover together why it is a great novel.

The first thing to do is to read it. A supreme book usually argues its own supremacy quite efficiently, and *War and Peace* is no exception. Still, we may be convinced of its magnitude and remain puzzled by certain of its aspects—for no first-rate book is completely explicit, either.

On finishing *War and Peace* what questions do we tend to ask ourselves? Here is a very simple one: What is it about? ...

[We] are forced in the end to make the apparently vapid judgment that the subject of *War and Peace* is Life itself....

We do not know what Tolstoy had in mind as the main subject of *War and Peace,* for he stated its theme differently at different periods of his career. Looking back on it, as a fairly old man, he said that his only aim had been to amuse his readers.... More seriously, Tolstoy at times spoke of *War and Peace* as a picture of the wanderings of a people.

But whatever he thought its subject was, he transcended it. In one sense he put into this book everything that interested him, and everything interested him. That he managed to make it more than a collection of characters and incidents is equivalent to saying that in addition to being a man with a consuming interest in life he was also an artist who was not content until he had shaped that interest into harmonious forms.

Now, there are some who would demur, who feel that it is precisely in this quality of form that *War and Peace* is defective....

Suppose we admit at once that there is no classic unity of subject matter as there is, for instance, in the *Iliad....* This simple unity Tolstoy does not have. But a profounder unity I think he does have. When we have come to feel this unity, the philosophical and historical disquisitions cease to seem long-winded and become both interesting in themselves and an integral part of the Tolstoyan scheme. We are no longer disturbed as we should be if such digressions appeared in a work of narrower compass. We accept the fact that mountains are never pyramids.

Let us see whether we can get this clear. In the course of one of his digressions Tolstoy writes, "Only by taking an infinitesimally small unit for observation (the differential of history, i.e., the individual tendencies of men) and attaining to the art of integrating them (i.e., finding the sum of these infinitesimals) can we hope to arrive at the laws of history." [In] this sentence, perhaps, is concealed the theme of the book: the movement of history which Tolstoy must examine by observing "the individual tendencies of men," on the one hand, and by attempting to "integrate them," on the other. Putting it in another way, we may say that it is not enough for Tolstoy to examine the individual lives of his characters as if they were separate atoms. He must also sweep up all these atoms into one larger experience. Now, this larger experience is the Napoleonic campaign. But the campaign itself, which fuses or enlarges or focuses the lives of Andrew and Natásha and Pierre and the rest, must itself be studied, not merely as a background—that is how an ordinary historical novelist would study it—but as thoughtfully as Tolstoy studies each individual life. In order fully to understand this focusing experience he is forced to elaborate a theory of history to explain it. And so he is forced to understand the major historical characters, such as Napoleon, Kutúzov, and the others, who are the dramatic symbols of the experience.

The result of this integration may not please everyone, but the integration is there. When one reflects upon the task, one is driven to concede, I think, that Tolstoy, in his attempt to understand history through human beings and human beings through history, is undertaking the greatest task conceivable to the creative novelist of the nineteenth century, just as Milton, attempting to justify the ways of God to man, undertook the greatest poetical theme possible to a man of his century....

War and Peace is so vast that each reader may pick out for himself its literary qualities he most admires. Let us select three: its inclusiveness, its naturalness, its timelessness.

The first thing to strike the reader is the range of Tolstoy's interest and knowledge....

At first glance the inclusiveness seems so overpowering that one inclines to agree with Hugh Walpole when he says that *War and Peace* "contains everything," or with E. M. Forster who is no less sure that "everything is in it." Naturally, these statements cannot be literally true. But it is true to say that when we have finished *War and Peace* we do not feel the lack of anything. It is only when one stops short and makes a list of the things Tolstoy leaves out that one realizes he is a novelist and not a god. We get very little awareness, for example, of the Russian middle class which was just beginning to emerge at the opening of the nineteenth century. Also, while Tolstoy does describe many peasants for us, the emphasis is thrown disproportionately on the aristocratic class with which he was most familiar. Another thing: obeying the literary conventions of his period, Tolstoy touches upon the sex relations of his men and women with great caution—and yet, so true and various is his presentation of love that we hardly seem to notice his omissions. That, after all, is the point: we do not notice the omissions, and we are overwhelmed by the inclusiveness... It is Tolstoy's attitude toward his own tremendous knowledge that makes him great rather than merely encyclopedic....

The key word here is "love." One of the most penetrating comments ever made about *War and Peace* is Mark Van Doren's, "I think he can be said to have hated nothing that ever happened." This exaggeration contains a profound truth. Tolstoy's love for his characters in *War and Peace* is very different from the mystic and, some would say, morbid sentimentality of his later years. It is more like the enthusiasm of a young man for everything he sees about him during the period of his greatest vigor....

At his best Tolstoy seems to write as if Nature herself were guiding his pen....

There is no formula to explain how Tolstoy does this. All we know is that he does it....

The constant impression of naturalness one gets from reading Tolstoy comes partly from his

> Let us ... try to discover together why it is a great novel."

lack of obsessions. He does not specialize in a particular emotion, as Balzac, say, specializes in the emotions deriving from the desire for money. Perhaps we may say that if Tolstoy has an obsession, it is a passion for showing people *merely living*....

It is because his eye is always on the central current of life that his perceptions seem so inevitable....

Tolstoy's natural sympathy overleaps the boundary of sex; his women are as convincing as his men. Indeed, he has a special talent for the presentation of women at their most female....

We think of certain Tolstoyan scenes as other men would do them and then we realize the quality of his supremacy....

It is *normal*. Tolstoy is the epic poet of the conscious and the "normal," just as Dostoevski, complementing him, is the dramatic poet of the subconscious and the "abnormal." His instinct is always to identify the unnatural with the unpleasant....

This almost abnormal normality in Tolstoy makes him able to do what would seem a very easy thing but is really very hard: describe people engaged in *nothing but being happy*....

The inclusiveness of *War and Peace*. Its naturalness. Finally, its timelessness....

[Even] when his characters seem almost pure representatives of their class, they still have a permanent value as symbols....

Here is a book, too, that seems to deal with people caught in a particular cleft of history. As that limited epoch recedes, we might suppose the people should dim accordingly. Yet this is not the case. It is impossible to say just how Tolstoy manages to give the impression both of particularity and universality....

War and Peace may not have a classic form. But it does have a classic content. It is full of scenes and situations which, in slightly altered forms, have recurred again and again, and will continue to recur, in the history of civilized man....

It is as if the human race, despite its apparent complexity, were capable of but a limited set of gestures. To this set of gestures only great artists have the key....

Also the very looseness of the book's form, the fact that it has neither beginning nor end, helps to convey the sense of enduring life....

Has *War and Peace,* then, no defects? It has many. It is far from being a technically perfect novel, like *Madame Bovary....* There are also many places in the narrative where the pace lags. Certain characters in the crowded canvas tend to get lost in the shuffle and never become entirely clear.... At times, so complex is the panorama that the reader has difficulty following the story, just as we have difficulty in following everything happening in a three-ring circus. Some of these defects seem to disappear on a second or third or fourth reading. Some are permanent. But none of them is so great nor are all of them taken together so great as to shake *War and Peace* from the pinnacle it occupies. Flaubert cannot afford to make mistakes. Tolstoy can....

The insights in Tolstoy are at their best enormously moving and exactly true. But they rarely give us that uneasy sense of psychic discovery peculiar to Dostoevski....

So far in these comments I have emphasized those qualities—inclusiveness, naturalness, timelessness—that make *War and Peace* universal rather than Russian. But part of its appeal for us, I think, derives from the fact that though there is nothing in the book that is incomprehensible to the American or the Western European, everything in it, owing to its Russian character, seems to us just a trifle off-center. This gives the novel a piquancy, even a strangeness at times, that it may not possess for the Russians....

There are certain central motives in *War and Peace* that are particularly (though not uniquely) Russian. The motive of moral conversion is a case in point....

In *War and Peace,* with varying degrees of success, the characters study themselves. All their critical experiences but lead them to further self-examination....

The purpose, if we may use so precise a word, of the regeneration experience is to enable the characters to attain to Pierre's state: "By loving people without cause, he discovered indubitable causes for loving them." In this sentence, a sort of moral equivalent of the James-Lange theory, lies the

essence, the center, the inner flame, of the prerevolutionary Russian novel. It is only after one has pondered its meaning that one can understand what lies back of the sudden changes in Tolstoy's and Dostoevski's characters....

The conflict in the soul of the Russian aristocrat derived not only from the conflict of cultures within him but from the moral falsity of his social position. Although Tolstoy—and this is one of his omissions—does not lay great stress on it, the Russian upper class in varying degrees suffered from a guilt-feeling arising from the institution of serfdom....

Much of the soul-searching in *War and Peace,* though it would seem to pivot only on each individual's personal problems, is in part a result of this vague pervasive guilt-feeling. Perhaps, indeed, a large part of the genius of the prerevolutionary Russian novel comes from the conflict born of this sense of guilt.

Finally, the Russian sought spiritual regeneration because he found no outlet for his idealistic energies in the state itself....

I have made these perhaps hackneyed comments in order to show that Tolstoy is a Russian novelist first and a universal novelist only by accident of genius.... He wrote as a Russian about Russian people—indeed about his own family, for many of the characters in *War and Peace* are transcripts from reality. But he wrote about them not only as Russians but as people. And therein lies part of the secret of his greatness.

There remains for us at least one more aspect of *War and Peace* to consider—that is, Tolstoy's view of men, war, history, and their interrelationships....

Tolstoy's theory of history is that there is no theory of history. Or, to put it more cautiously, if there are grand laws determining the movement and flow of historical events, we can, in the present state of our knowledge, only guess at them. Until our vision and our knowledge are so extended that they reveal these underlying laws, the most intelligent thing for us to do is at least to deny validity to all superficial explanations of historical experience....

In *War and Peace* he attacks those theories which were popular in his own time....

It is part of the purpose of *War and Peace* to prove that there is no such thing as chance an no such thing as genius....

For Tolstoy the fate of battles therefore is decided less by prefabricated strategies than by the absence or presence of what he calls "moral hesitation," or what we would call morale....

Were Tolstoy alive today would he moderate his views because the character of warfare has changed so radically in the interim?....

Tolstoy, I think, would reply that any change is only apparent and only temporary. He would say that human nature is a constant, that it will rise to the surface despite all the deformation, the drill, the conditioning, the dehumanizing to which is may be subjected.

It is a constant, then, in war. It is a constant in peace. And it is a constant in *War and Peace....*

Source: Clifton Fadiman, reprinted as "War and Peace," in *Party of One: The Selected Writings of Clifton Fadiman,* The World Publishing Company, 1955, pp. 176–202.

"Tolstoy's 'Peace and War

In the following review, the reviewer praises Tolstoy for his accurate presentation of how people act and talk and points to Tolstoy's presentation of the moral imperfection of all and of the folly of self-will in historical events.

This book of Tolstoy's [*War and Peace*] might be called with justice 'The Russian Comedy,' in the sense in which Balzac employed the word. It gave me exactly the same impression: I felt that I was thrown among new men and women, that I lived with them, that I knew them, that none of them could be indifferent to me, that I could never forget them. I entered into their souls, and it seemed almost as if they could enter into mine. Such a power in a writer is almost a miracle. How many novels have I not read, and, after having read them, and admired many qualities—the beauty of the style, the invention, the dialogues, the dramatic situations—have still felt that my knowledge of life had not increased, that I had gained no new experience. It was not so with *War and Peace....*

It would be difficult to give a proper definition of the talent of Tolstoy. First of all, he is an *homme du monde.* He makes great people, emperors, generals, diplomats, fine ladies, princes, talk and act as they do act and talk. He is a perfect gentleman, and as such he is thoroughly humane. He takes as much interest in the most humble of his actors as he does in the highest. He has lived in courts: the Saint-Andrés, the Saint-Vladimirs have no prestige for him—nor the gilded uniforms; he is not deceived by appearances. His aim is so high that whatever he sees is, in one sense, unsatisfac-

> " I felt that I was thrown among new men and women, that I lived with them, that I knew them, that none of them could be indifferent to me, that I could never forget them."

tory. He looks for moral perfection, and there is nothing perfect. He is always disappointed in the end. The final impression of his work is a sort of despair....

[A] fundamental idea of fatalism pervades the book. Fate governs empires as well as men: it plays with a Napoleon and an Alexander as it does with a private in the ranks; it hangs over all the world like a dark cloud, rent at times by lighting. We live in the night, like shadows; we are lost on the shore of an eternal Styx; we do not know whence we came or whither we go. Millions of men, led by a senseless man, go from west to east, killing, murdering, and burning, and it is called the invasion of Russia. Two thousand years before, millions of other men came from east to west, plundering, killing, and burning, and it was called the invasion of the barbarians. What becomes of the human will, of the proud *I,* in these dreadful events? We see the folly and the vanity of self-will in these great historical events; but it is just the same in all times, and the will gets lost in peace as well as in war, for there is no real peace, and the human wills are constantly devouring each other.... We are made to enjoy a little, to suffer much, and, when the end is approaching, we are all like one of Tolstoy's heroes, on the day of Borodino....

[Tolstoy's book] is by far the most remarkable work of imagination that has been lately revealed to us....

Source: "Tolstoy's 'Peace and War,'" in *Nation,* Vol. 40, No. 1021, January 22, 1885, pp. 70–71.

Sources

Arnold, Matthew, "Count Leo Tolstoy," in *Fortnightly Review,* December, 1887.

Christian, R. F., *Tolstoy's "War and Peace": A Study,* Clarenden Press, 1962.

Fodor, Alexander, *Tolstoy and the Russians: Reflections on a Relationship,* Ardis Press, 1984.

James, Henry, "Preface to *The Tragic Muse,*" in *The Art of the Novel,* C. Scribner's Sons, 1934.

Simmons, Ernest J., *Tolstoy,* Routledge & Kegan Paul, Boston, 1973, p. 81.

Wasiolek, Edward, *Tolstoy's Major Fiction,* The University of Chicago Press, 1978.

For Further Study

Berlin, Isaiah, "Tolstoy and Enlightenment," in *Mightier that the Sword,* MacMillan & Co., 1964.
An influential assessment of the often-repeated charge that Tolstoy was a good fiction writer but a flawed philosopher.

Christian, R. F., *Tolstoy's* War and Peace: *A Study,* The Clarendon Press, 1962.
A comprehensive and recommended study of the novel.

Citati, Pietro, *Tolstoy,* Schocken Books, 1986.
Written by an Italian literary critic, this is a short biography that introduces students to the key elements in Tolstoy's life and works.

Crankshaw, Edward, *Tolstoy: The Making of a Novelist,* The Viking Press, 1974.
Traces Tolstoy's development as a novelist.

Crego Benson, Ruth, "Two Natashas," in *Women in Tolstoy: The Ideal and the Erotic,* University of Illinois Press, 1973.
Examines the conflict between Tolstoy's portrayal of Natasha as a strong complex heroine and his tendency to see women only as objects of beauty.

Debreczeny, Paul, "Freedom and Necessity: A Reconsideration of *War and Peace,*" in *Papers on Language and Literature: A Journal for Scholars and Critics of Language and Literature,* No. 2, Spring, 1971.
Debreczeny's understanding of Tolstoy's basic philosophy allows him to read the diverse aspects of the novel as one continuous, homogeneous narrative.

Greenwood, E. B., "The Problem of Truth in *War and Peace,*" in *Tolstoy: The Comprehensive Vision,* St. Martin's Press, 1975.
Explores Tolstoy's interest in the problem of historical truth.

Johnson, Claudia D., *To Kill a Mockingbird: Threatening Boundaries,* Twayne, 1994.
A book-length analysis of the novel that provides historical and literary context as well as discussion of key themes and issues.

Morrison, Gary Saul, *Hidden in Plain View: Narrative and Creative Potentials in "War and Peace",* Stanford University Press, 1987.
Discusses the structure of the novel.

Sampson, R. V., "Leo Tolstoy: 'God Sees the Truth, But Does Not Quickly Reveal It'," in *The Discovery of Peace,* Pantheon Books, 1973.
Sampson examines several key writers who have influenced the history of the moral debate about war.

Simmons, Ernest J., "War and Peace," in *Introduction to Tolstoy's Writings,* The University of Chicago Press, 1968.
In this chapter in a book about the Tolstoy's major works, Simmons provides a stylistic and thematic analysis of the novel.

Glossary of Literary Terms

A

Abstract: As an adjective applied to writing or literary works, abstract refers to words or phrases that name things not knowable through the five senses.

Aestheticism: A literary and artistic movement of the nineteenth century. Followers of the movement believed that art should not be mixed with social, political, or moral teaching. The statement "art for art's sake" is a good summary of aestheticism. The movement had its roots in France, but it gained widespread importance in England in the last half of the nineteenth century, where it helped change the Victorian practice of including moral lessons in literature.

Allegory: A narrative technique in which characters representing things or abstract ideas are used to convey a message or teach a lesson. Allegory is typically used to teach moral, ethical, or religious lessons but is sometimes used for satiric or political purposes.

Allusion: A reference to a familiar literary or historical person or event, used to make an idea more easily understood.

Analogy: A comparison of two things made to explain something unfamiliar through its similarities to something familiar, or to prove one point based on the acceptedness of another. Similes and metaphors are types of analogies.

Antagonist: The major character in a narrative or drama who works against the hero or protagonist.

Anthropomorphism: The presentation of animals or objects in human shape or with human characteristics. The term is derived from the Greek word for "human form."

Antihero: A central character in a work of literature who lacks traditional heroic qualities such as courage, physical prowess, and fortitude. Antiheroes typically distrust conventional values and are unable to commit themselves to any ideals. They generally feel helpless in a world over which they have no control. Antiheroes usually accept, and often celebrate, their positions as social outcasts.

Apprenticeship Novel: See *Bildungsroman*

Archetype: The word archetype is commonly used to describe an original pattern or model from which all other things of the same kind are made. This term was introduced to literary criticism from the psychology of Carl Jung. It expresses Jung's theory that behind every person's "unconscious," or repressed memories of the past, lies the "collective unconscious" of the human race: memories of the countless typical experiences of our ancestors. These memories are said to prompt illogical associations that trigger powerful emotions in the reader. Often, the emotional process is primitive, even primordial. Archetypes are the literary images that grow out of the "collective unconscious." They appear in literature as incidents and plots that repeat basic patterns of life. They may also appear as stereotyped characters.

Avant-garde: French term meaning "vanguard." It is used in literary criticism to describe new writing that rejects traditional approaches to literature in favor of innovations in style or content.

B

Beat Movement: A period featuring a group of American poets and novelists of the 1950s and 1960s—including Jack Kerouac, Allen Ginsberg, Gregory Corso, William S. Burroughs, and Lawrence Ferlinghetti—who rejected established social and literary values. Using such techniques as stream of consciousness writing and jazz-influenced free verse and focusing on unusual or abnormal states of mind—generated by religious ecstasy or the use of drugs—the Beat writers aimed to create works that were unconventional in both form and subject matter.

Bildungsroman: A German word meaning "novel of development." The *bildungsroman* is a study of the maturation of a youthful character, typically brought about through a series of social or sexual encounters that lead to self-awareness. *Bildungsroman* is used interchangeably with *erziehungsroman*, a novel of initiation and education. When a *bildungsroman* is concerned with the development of an artist (as in James Joyce's *A Portrait of the Artist as a Young Man*), it is often termed a *kunstlerroman*. Also known as Apprenticeship Novel, Coming of Age Novel, *Erziehungsroman*, or *Kunstlerroman*.

Black Aesthetic Movement: A period of artistic and literary development among African Americans in the 1960s and early 1970s. This was the first major African-American artistic movement since the Harlem Renaissance and was closely paralleled by the civil rights and black power movements. The black aesthetic writers attempted to produce works of art that would be meaningful to the black masses. Key figures in black aesthetics included one of its founders, poet and playwright Amiri Baraka, formerly known as LeRoi Jones; poet and essayist Haki R. Madhubuti, formerly Don L. Lee; poet and playwright Sonia Sanchez; and dramatist Ed Bullins. Also known as Black Arts Movement.

Black Humor: Writing that places grotesque elements side by side with humorous ones in an attempt to shock the reader, forcing him or her to laugh at the horrifying reality of a disordered world. Also known as Black Comedy.

Burlesque: Any literary work that uses exaggeration to make its subject appear ridiculous, either by treating a trivial subject with profound seriousness or by treating a dignified subject frivolously. The word "burlesque" may also be used as an adjective, as in "burlesque show," to mean "striptease act."

C

Character: Broadly speaking, a person in a literary work. The actions of characters are what constitute the plot of a story, novel, or poem. There are numerous types of characters, ranging from simple, stereotypical figures to intricate, multifaceted ones. In the techniques of anthropomorphism and personification, animals—and even places or things—can assume aspects of character. "Characterization" is the process by which an author creates vivid, believable characters in a work of art. This may be done in a variety of ways, including (1) direct description of the character by the narrator; (2) the direct presentation of the speech, thoughts, or actions of the character; and (3) the responses of other characters to the character. The term "character" also refers to a form originated by the ancient Greek writer Theophrastus that later became popular in the seventeenth and eighteenth centuries. It is a short essay or sketch of a person who prominently displays a specific attribute or quality, such as miserliness or ambition.

Climax: The turning point in a narrative, the moment when the conflict is at its most intense. Typically, the structure of stories, novels, and plays is one of rising action, in which tension builds to the climax, followed by falling action, in which tension lessens as the story moves to its conclusion.

Colloquialism: A word, phrase, or form of pronunciation that is acceptable in casual conversation but not in formal, written communication. It is considered more acceptable than slang.

Coming of Age Novel: See *Bildungsroman*

Concrete: Concrete is the opposite of abstract, and refers to a thing that actually exists or a description that allows the reader to experience an object or concept with the senses.

Connotation: The impression that a word gives beyond its defined meaning. Connotations may be universally understood or may be significant only to a certain group.

Convention: Any widely accepted literary device, style, or form.

D

Denotation: The definition of a word, apart from the impressions or feelings it creates (connotations) in the reader.

Denouement: A French word meaning "the un-knotting." In literary criticism, it denotes the resolution of conflict in fiction or drama. The *denouement* follows the climax and provides an outcome to the primary plot situation as well as an explanation of secondary plot complications. The *denouement* often involves a character's recognition of his or her state of mind or moral condition. Also known as Falling Action.

Description: Descriptive writing is intended to allow a reader to picture the scene or setting in which the action of a story takes place. The form this description takes often evokes an intended emotional response—a dark, spooky graveyard will evoke fear, and a peaceful, sunny meadow will evoke calmness.

Dialogue: In its widest sense, dialogue is simply conversation between people in a literary work; in its most restricted sense, it refers specifically to the speech of characters in a drama. As a specific literary genre, a "dialogue" is a composition in which characters debate an issue or idea.

Diction: The selection and arrangement of words in a literary work. Either or both may vary depending on the desired effect. There are four general types of diction: "formal," used in scholarly or lofty writing; "informal," used in relaxed but educated conversation; "colloquial," used in everyday speech; and "slang," containing newly coined words and other terms not accepted in formal usage.

Didactic: A term used to describe works of literature that aim to teach some moral, religious, political, or practical lesson. Although didactic elements are often found in artistically pleasing works, the term "didactic" usually refers to literature in which the message is more important than the form. The term may also be used to criticize a work that the critic finds "overly didactic," that is, heavy-handed in its delivery of a lesson.

Doppelganger: A literary technique by which a character is duplicated (usually in the form of an alter ego, though sometimes as a ghostly counterpart) or divided into two distinct, usually opposite personalities. The use of this character device is widespread in nineteenth- and twentieth-century literature, and indicates a growing awareness among authors that the "self" is really a composite of many "selves." Also known as The Double.

Double Entendre: A corruption of a French phrase meaning "double meaning." The term is used to indicate a word or phrase that is deliberately ambiguous, especially when one of the meanings is risqué or improper.

Dramatic Irony: Occurs when the audience of a play or the reader of a work of literature knows something that a character in the work itself does not know. The irony is in the contrast between the intended meaning of the statements or actions of a character and the additional information understood by the audience.

Dystopia: An imaginary place in a work of fiction where the characters lead dehumanized, fearful lives.

E

Edwardian: Describes cultural conventions identified with the period of the reign of Edward VII of England (1901-1910). Writers of the Edwardian Age typically displayed a strong reaction against the propriety and conservatism of the Victorian Age. Their work often exhibits distrust of authority in religion, politics, and art and expresses strong doubts about the soundness of conventional values.

Empathy: A sense of shared experience, including emotional and physical feelings, with someone or something other than oneself. Empathy is often used to describe the response of a reader to a literary character.

Enlightenment, The: An eighteenth-century philosophical movement. It began in France but had a wide impact throughout Europe and America. Thinkers of the Enlightenment valued reason and believed that both the individual and society could achieve a state of perfection. Corresponding to this essentially humanist vision was a resistance to religious authority.

Epigram: A saying that makes the speaker's point quickly and concisely. Often used to preface a novel.

Epilogue: A concluding statement or section of a literary work. In dramas, particularly those of the seventeenth and eighteenth centuries, the epilogue is a closing speech, often in verse, delivered by an actor at the end of a play and spoken directly to the audience.

Epiphany: A sudden revelation of truth inspired by a seemingly trivial incident.

Episode: An incident that forms part of a story and is significantly related to it. Episodes may be either self-contained narratives or events that depend on a larger context for their sense and importance.

Epistolary Novel: A novel in the form of letters. The form was particularly popular in the eighteenth century.

Epithet: A word or phrase, often disparaging or abusive, that expresses a character trait of someone or something.

Existentialism: A predominantly twentieth-century philosophy concerned with the nature and perception of human existence. There are two major strains of existentialist thought: atheistic and Christian. Followers of atheistic existentialism believe that the individual is alone in a godless universe and that the basic human condition is one of suffering and loneliness. Nevertheless, because there are no fixed values, individuals can create their own characters—indeed, they can shape themselves—through the exercise of free will. The atheistic strain culminates in and is popularly associated with the works of Jean-Paul Sartre. The Christian existentialists, on the other hand, believe that only in God may people find freedom from life's anguish. The two strains hold certain beliefs in common: that existence cannot be fully understood or described through empirical effort; that anguish is a universal element of life; that individuals must bear responsibility for their actions; and that there is no common standard of behavior or perception for religious and ethical matters.

Expatriates: See *Expatriatism*

Expatriatism: The practice of leaving one's country to live for an extended period in another country.

Exposition: Writing intended to explain the nature of an idea, thing, or theme. Expository writing is often combined with description, narration, or argument. In dramatic writing, the exposition is the introductory material which presents the characters, setting, and tone of the play.

Expressionism: An indistinct literary term, originally used to describe an early twentieth-century school of German painting. The term applies to almost any mode of unconventional, highly subjective writing that distorts reality in some way.

F

Fable: A prose or verse narrative intended to convey a moral. Animals or inanimate objects with human characteristics often serve as characters in fables.

Falling Action: See *Denouement*

Fantasy: A literary form related to mythology and folklore. Fantasy literature is typically set in non-existent realms and features supernatural beings.

Farce: A type of comedy characterized by broad humor, outlandish incidents, and often vulgar subject matter.

Femme fatale: A French phrase with the literal translation "fatal woman." A *femme fatale* is a sensuous, alluring woman who often leads men into danger or trouble.

Fiction: Any story that is the product of imagination rather than a documentation of fact. Characters and events in such narratives may be based in real life but their ultimate form and configuration is a creation of the author.

Figurative Language: A technique in writing in which the author temporarily interrupts the order, construction, or meaning of the writing for a particular effect. This interruption takes the form of one or more figures of speech such as hyperbole, irony, or simile. Figurative language is the opposite of literal language, in which every word is truthful, accurate, and free of exaggeration or embellishment.

Figures of Speech: Writing that differs from customary conventions for construction, meaning, order, or significance for the purpose of a special meaning or effect. There are two major types of figures of speech: rhetorical figures, which do not make changes in the meaning of the words, and tropes, which do.

Fin de siecle: A French term meaning "end of the century." The term is used to denote the last decade of the nineteenth century, a transition period when writers and other artists abandoned old conventions and looked for new techniques and objectives.

First Person: See *Point of View*

Flashback: A device used in literature to present action that occurred before the beginning of the story. Flashbacks are often introduced as the dreams or recollections of one or more characters.

Foil: A character in a work of literature whose physical or psychological qualities contrast strongly with, and therefore highlight, the corresponding qualities of another character.

Folklore: Traditions and myths preserved in a culture or group of people. Typically, these are passed on by word of mouth in various forms—such as legends, songs, and proverbs—or preserved in customs and ceremonies. This term was first used by W. J. Thoms in 1846.

Folktale: A story originating in oral tradition. Folktales fall into a variety of categories, including legends, ghost stories, fairy tales, fables, and anecdotes based on historical figures and events.

Foreshadowing: A device used in literature to create expectation or to set up an explanation of later developments.

Form: The pattern or construction of a work which identifies its genre and distinguishes it from other genres.

G

Genre: A category of literary work. In critical theory, genre may refer to both the content of a given work—tragedy, comedy, pastoral—and to its form, such as poetry, novel, or drama.

Gilded Age: A period in American history during the 1870s characterized by political corruption and materialism. A number of important novels of social and political criticism were written during this time.

Gothicism: In literary criticism, works characterized by a taste for the medieval or morbidly attractive. A gothic novel prominently features elements of horror, the supernatural, gloom, and violence: clanking chains, terror, charnel houses, ghosts, medieval castles, and mysteriously slamming doors. The term "gothic novel" is also applied to novels that lack elements of the traditional Gothic setting but that create a similar atmosphere of terror or dread.

Grotesque: In literary criticism, the subject matter of a work or a style of expression characterized by exaggeration, deformity, freakishness, and disorder. The grotesque often includes an element of comic absurdity.

H

Harlem Renaissance: The Harlem Renaissance of the 1920s is generally considered the first significant movement of black writers and artists in the United States. During this period, new and established black writers published more fiction and poetry than ever before, the first influential black literary journals were established, and black authors and artists received their first widespread recognition and serious critical appraisal. Among the major writers associated with this period are Claude McKay, Jean Toomer, Countee Cullen, Langston Hughes, Arna Bontemps, Nella Larsen, and Zora

Neale Hurston. Also known as Negro Renaissance and New Negro Movement.

Hero/Heroine: The principal sympathetic character (male or female) in a literary work. Heroes and heroines typically exhibit admirable traits: idealism, courage, and integrity, for example.

Holocaust Literature: Literature influenced by or written about the Holocaust of World War II. Such literature includes true stories of survival in concentration camps, escape, and life after the war, as well as fictional works and poetry.

Humanism: A philosophy that places faith in the dignity of humankind and rejects the medieval perception of the individual as a weak, fallen creature. "Humanists" typically believe in the perfectibility of human nature and view reason and education as the means to that end.

Hyperbole: In literary criticism, deliberate exaggeration used to achieve an effect.

I

Idiom: A word construction or verbal expression closely associated with a given language.

Image: A concrete representation of an object or sensory experience. Typically, such a representation helps evoke the feelings associated with the object or experience itself. Images are either "literal" or "figurative." Literal images are especially concrete and involve little or no extension of the obvious meaning of the words used to express them. Figurative images do not follow the literal meaning of the words exactly. Images in literature are usually visual, but the term "image" can also refer to the representation of any sensory experience.

Imagery: The array of images in a literary work. Also, figurative language.

In medias res: A Latin term meaning "in the middle of things." It refers to the technique of beginning a story at its midpoint and then using various flashback devices to reveal previous action.

Interior Monologue: A narrative technique in which characters' thoughts are revealed in a way that appears to be uncontrolled by the author. The interior monologue typically aims to reveal the inner self of a character. It portrays emotional experiences as they occur at both a conscious and unconscious level. Images are often used to represent sensations or emotions.

Irony: In literary criticism, the effect of language in which the intended meaning is the opposite of what is stated.

J

Jargon: Language that is used or understood only by a select group of people. Jargon may refer to terminology used in a certain profession, such as computer jargon, or it may refer to any non-sensical language that is not understood by most people.

L

Leitmotiv: See *Motif*

Literal Language: An author uses literal language when he or she writes without exaggerating or embellishing the subject matter and without any tools of figurative language.

Lost Generation: A term first used by Gertrude Stein to describe the post-World War I generation of American writers: men and women haunted by a sense of betrayal and emptiness brought about by the destructiveness of the war.

M

Mannerism: Exaggerated, artificial adherence to a literary manner or style. Also, a popular style of the visual arts of late sixteenth-century Europe that was marked by elongation of the human form and by intentional spatial distortion. Literary works that are self-consciously high-toned and artistic are often said to be "mannered."

Metaphor: A figure of speech that expresses an idea through the image of another object. Metaphors suggest the essence of the first object by identifying it with certain qualities of the second object.

Modernism: Modern literary practices. Also, the principles of a literary school that lasted from roughly the beginning of the twentieth century until the end of World War II. Modernism is defined by its rejection of the literary conventions of the nineteenth century and by its opposition to conventional morality, taste, traditions, and economic values.

Mood: The prevailing emotions of a work or of the author in his or her creation of the work. The mood of a work is not always what might be expected based on its subject matter.

Motif: A theme, character type, image, metaphor, or other verbal element that recurs throughout a single work of literature or occurs in a number of different works over a period of time. Also known as *Motiv* or *Leitmotiv.*

Myth: An anonymous tale emerging from the traditional beliefs of a culture or social unit. Myths use supernatural explanations for natural phenomena. They may also explain cosmic issues like creation and death. Collections of myths, known as mythologies, are common to all cultures and nations, but the best-known myths belong to the Norse, Roman, and Greek mythologies.

N

Narration: The telling of a series of events, real or invented. A narration may be either a simple narrative, in which the events are recounted chronologically, or a narrative with a plot, in which the account is given in a style reflecting the author's artistic concept of the story. Narration is sometimes used as a synonym for "storyline."

Narrative: A verse or prose accounting of an event or sequence of events, real or invented. The term is also used as an adjective in the sense "method of narration." For example, in literary criticism, the expression "narrative technique" usually refers to the way the author structures and presents his or her story.

Narrator: The teller of a story. The narrator may be the author or a character in the story through whom the author speaks.

Naturalism: A literary movement of the late nineteenth and early twentieth centuries. The movement's major theorist, French novelist Emile Zola, envisioned a type of fiction that would examine human life with the objectivity of scientific inquiry. The Naturalists typically viewed human beings as either the products of "biological determinism," ruled by hereditary instincts and engaged in an endless struggle for survival, or as the products of "socioeconomic determinism," ruled by social and economic forces beyond their control. In their works, the Naturalists generally ignored the highest levels of society and focused on degradation: poverty, alcoholism, prostitution, insanity, and disease.

Noble Savage: The idea that primitive man is noble and good but becomes evil and corrupted as he becomes civilized. The concept of the noble savage originated in the Renaissance period but is more closely identified with such later writers as

Jean-Jacques Rousseau and Aphra Behn. See also Primitivism.

Novel of Ideas: A novel in which the examination of intellectual issues and concepts takes precedence over characterization or a traditional storyline.

Novel of Manners: A novel that examines the customs and mores of a cultural group.

Novel: A long fictional narrative written in prose, which developed from the novella and other early forms of narrative. A novel is usually organized under a plot or theme with a focus on character development and action.

Novella: An Italian term meaning "story." This term has been especially used to describe fourteenth-century Italian tales, but it also refers to modern short novels.

O

Objective Correlative: An outward set of objects, a situation, or a chain of events corresponding to an inward experience and evoking this experience in the reader. The term frequently appears in modern criticism in discussions of authors' intended effects on the emotional responses of readers.

Objectivity: A quality in writing characterized by the absence of the author's opinion or feeling about the subject matter. Objectivity is an important factor in criticism.

Oedipus Complex: A son's amorous obsession with his mother. The phrase is derived from the story of the ancient Theban hero Oedipus, who unknowingly killed his father and married his mother.

Omniscience: See *Point of View*

Onomatopoeia: The use of words whose sounds express or suggest their meaning. In its simplest sense, onomatopoeia may be represented by words that mimic the sounds they denote such as "hiss" or "meow." At a more subtle level, the pattern and rhythm of sounds and rhymes of a line or poem may be onomatopoeic.

Oxymoron: A phrase combining two contradictory terms. Oxymorons may be intentional or unintentional.

P

Parable: A story intended to teach a moral lesson or answer an ethical question.

Paradox: A statement that appears illogical or contradictory at first, but may actually point to an underlying truth.

Parallelism: A method of comparison of two ideas in which each is developed in the same grammatical structure.

Parody: In literary criticism, this term refers to an imitation of a serious literary work or the signature style of a particular author in a ridiculous manner. A typical parody adopts the style of the original and applies it to an inappropriate subject for humorous effect. Parody is a form of satire and could be considered the literary equivalent of a caricature or cartoon.

Pastoral: A term derived from the Latin word "pastor," meaning shepherd. A pastoral is a literary composition on a rural theme. The conventions of the pastoral were originated by the third-century Greek poet Theocritus, who wrote about the experiences, love affairs, and pastimes of Sicilian shepherds. In a pastoral, characters and language of a courtly nature are often placed in a simple setting. The term pastoral is also used to classify dramas, elegies, and lyrics that exhibit the use of country settings and shepherd characters.

Pen Name: See *Pseudonym*

Persona: A Latin term meaning "mask." *Personae* are the characters in a fictional work of literature. The *persona* generally functions as a mask through which the author tells a story in a voice other than his or her own. A *persona* is usually either a character in a story who acts as a narrator or an "implied author," a voice created by the author to act as the narrator for himself or herself.

Personification: A figure of speech that gives human qualities to abstract ideas, animals, and inanimate objects. Also known as *Prosopopoeia*.

Picaresque Novel: Episodic fiction depicting the adventures of a roguish central character ("picaro" is Spanish for "rogue"). The picaresque hero is commonly a low-born but clever individual who wanders into and out of various affairs of love, danger, and farcical intrigue. These involvements may take place at all social levels and typically present a humorous and wide-ranging satire of a given society.

Plagiarism: Claiming another person's written material as one's own. Plagiarism can take the form of direct, word-for-word copying or the theft of the substance or idea of the work.

Plot: In literary criticism, this term refers to the pattern of events in a narrative or drama. In its simplest sense, the plot guides the author in composing the work and helps the reader follow the work. Typically, plots exhibit causality and unity and have a beginning, a middle, and an end. Sometimes, however, a plot may consist of a series of disconnected events, in which case it is known as an "episodic plot."

Poetic Justice: An outcome in a literary work, not necessarily a poem, in which the good are rewarded and the evil are punished, especially in ways that particularly fit their virtues or crimes.

Poetic License: Distortions of fact and literary convention made by a writer—not always a poet—for the sake of the effect gained. Poetic license is closely related to the concept of "artistic freedom."

Poetics: This term has two closely related meanings. It denotes (1) an aesthetic theory in literary criticism about the essence of poetry or (2) rules prescribing the proper methods, content, style, or diction of poetry. The term poetics may also refer to theories about literature in general, not just poetry.

Point of View: The narrative perspective from which a literary work is presented to the reader. There are four traditional points of view. The "third person omniscient" gives the reader a "godlike" perspective, unrestricted by time or place, from which to see actions and look into the minds of characters. This allows the author to comment openly on characters and events in the work. The "third person" point of view presents the events of the story from outside of any single character's perception, much like the omniscient point of view, but the reader must understand the action as it takes place and without any special insight into characters' minds or motivations. The "first person" or "personal" point of view relates events as they are perceived by a single character. The main character "tells" the story and may offer opinions about the action and characters which differ from those of the author. Much less common than omniscient, third person, and first person is the "second person" point of view, wherein the author tells the story as if it is happening to the reader.

Polemic: A work in which the author takes a stand on a controversial subject, such as abortion or religion. Such works are often extremely argumentative or provocative.

Pornography: Writing intended to provoke feelings of lust in the reader. Such works are often condemned by critics and teachers, but those which can be shown to have literary value are viewed less harshly.

Post-Aesthetic Movement: An artistic response made by African Americans to the black aesthetic movement of the 1960s and early '70s. Writers since that time have adopted a somewhat different tone in their work, with less emphasis placed on the disparity between black and white in the United States. In the words of post-aesthetic authors such as Toni Morrison, John Edgar Wideman, and Kristin Hunter, African Americans are portrayed as looking inward for answers to their own questions, rather than always looking to the outside world.

Postmodernism: Writing from the 1960s forward characterized by experimentation and continuing to apply some of the fundamentals of modernism, which included existentialism and alienation. Postmodernists have gone a step further in the rejection of tradition begun with the modernists by also rejecting traditional forms, preferring the anti-novel over the novel and the antihero over the hero.

Primitivism: The belief that primitive peoples were nobler and less flawed than civilized peoples because they had not been subjected to the tainting influence of society. See also Noble Savage.

Prologue: An introductory section of a literary work. It often contains information establishing the situation of the characters or presents information about the setting, time period, or action. In drama, the prologue is spoken by a chorus or by one of the principal characters.

Prose: A literary medium that attempts to mirror the language of everyday speech. It is distinguished from poetry by its use of unmetered, unrhymed language consisting of logically related sentences. Prose is usually grouped into paragraphs that form a cohesive whole such as an essay or a novel.

Prosopopoeia: See *Personification*

Protagonist: The central character of a story who serves as a focus for its themes and incidents and as the principal rationale for its development. The protagonist is sometimes referred to in discussions of modern literature as the hero or antihero.

Protest Fiction: Protest fiction has as its primary purpose the protesting of some social injustice, such as racism or discrimination.

Proverb: A brief, sage saying that expresses a truth about life in a striking manner.

Pseudonym: A name assumed by a writer, most often intended to prevent his or her identification as the author of a work. Two or more authors may work together under one pseudonym, or an author may use a different name for each genre he or she publishes in. Some publishing companies maintain "house pseudonyms," under which any number of authors may write installations in a series. Some authors also choose a pseudonym over their real names the way an actor may use a stage name.

Pun: A play on words that have similar sounds but different meanings.

R

Realism: A nineteenth-century European literary movement that sought to portray familiar characters, situations, and settings in a realistic manner. This was done primarily by using an objective narrative point of view and through the buildup of accurate detail. The standard for success of any realistic work depends on how faithfully it transfers common experience into fictional forms. The realistic method may be altered or extended, as in stream of consciousness writing, to record highly subjective experience.

Repartee: Conversation featuring snappy retorts and witticisms.

Resolution: The portion of a story following the climax, in which the conflict is resolved. See also *Denouement.*

Rhetoric: In literary criticism, this term denotes the art of ethical persuasion. In its strictest sense, rhetoric adheres to various principles developed since classical times for arranging facts and ideas in a clear, persuasive, appealing manner. The term is also used to refer to effective prose in general and theories of or methods for composing effective prose.

Rhetorical Question: A question intended to provoke thought, but not an expressed answer, in the reader. It is most commonly used in oratory and other persuasive genres.

Rising Action: The part of a drama where the plot becomes increasingly complicated. Rising action leads up to the climax, or turning point, of a drama.

Roman a clef: A French phrase meaning "novel with a key." It refers to a narrative in which real persons are portrayed under fictitious names.

Romance: A broad term, usually denoting a narrative with exotic, exaggerated, often idealized characters, scenes, and themes.

Romanticism: This term has two widely accepted meanings. In historical criticism, it refers to a European intellectual and artistic movement of the late eighteenth and early nineteenth centuries that sought greater freedom of personal expression than that allowed by the strict rules of literary form and logic of the eighteenth-century neoclassicists. The Romantics preferred emotional and imaginative expression to rational analysis. They considered the individual to be at the center of all experience and so placed him or her at the center of their art. The Romantics believed that the creative imagination reveals nobler truths—unique feelings and attitudes—than those that could be discovered by logic or by scientific examination. Both the natural world and the state of childhood were important sources for revelations of "eternal truths." "Romanticism" is also used as a general term to refer to a type of sensibility found in all periods of literary history and usually considered to be in opposition to the principles of classicism. In this sense, Romanticism signifies any work or philosophy in which the exotic or dreamlike figure strongly, or that is devoted to individualistic expression, self-analysis, or a pursuit of a higher realm of knowledge than can be discovered by human reason.

Romantics: See *Romanticism*

S

Satire: A work that uses ridicule, humor, and wit to criticize and provoke change in human nature and institutions. There are two major types of satire: "formal" or "direct" satire speaks directly to the reader or to a character in the work; "indirect" satire relies upon the ridiculous behavior of its characters to make its point. Formal satire is further divided into two manners: the "Horatian," which ridicules gently, and the "Juvenalian," which derides its subjects harshly and bitterly.

Science Fiction: A type of narrative about or based upon real or imagined scientific theories and technology. Science fiction is often peopled with alien creatures and set on other planets or in different dimensions.

Second Person: See *Point of View*

Setting: The time, place, and culture in which the action of a narrative takes place. The elements of setting may include geographic location, characters' physical and mental environments, prevailing cultural attitudes, or the historical time in which the action takes place.

Simile: A comparison, usually using "like" or "as", of two essentially dissimilar things, as in "coffee as cold as ice" or "He sounded like a broken record."

Slang: A type of informal verbal communication that is generally unacceptable for formal writing. Slang words and phrases are often colorful exaggerations used to emphasize the speaker's point; they may also be shortened versions of an often-used word or phrase.

Slave Narrative: Autobiographical accounts of American slave life as told by escaped slaves. These works first appeared during the abolition movement of the 1830s through the 1850s.

Socialist Realism: The Socialist Realism school of literary theory was proposed by Maxim Gorky and established as a dogma by the first Soviet Congress of Writers. It demanded adherence to a communist worldview in works of literature. Its doctrines required an objective viewpoint comprehensible to the working classes and themes of social struggle featuring strong proletarian heroes. Also known as Social Realism.

Stereotype: A stereotype was originally the name for a duplication made during the printing process; this led to its modern definition as a person or thing that is (or is assumed to be) the same as all others of its type.

Stream of Consciousness: A narrative technique for rendering the inward experience of a character. This technique is designed to give the impression of an ever-changing series of thoughts, emotions, images, and memories in the spontaneous and seemingly illogical order that they occur in life.

Structure: The form taken by a piece of literature. The structure may be made obvious for ease of understanding, as in nonfiction works, or may obscured for artistic purposes, as in some poetry or seemingly "unstructured" prose.

Sturm und Drang: A German term meaning "storm and stress." It refers to a German literary movement of the 1770s and 1780s that reacted against the order and rationalism of the enlightenment, focusing instead on the intense experience of extraordinary individuals.

Style: A writer's distinctive manner of arranging words to suit his or her ideas and purpose in writing. The unique imprint of the author's personality upon his or her writing, style is the product of an author's way of arranging ideas and his or her use of diction, different sentence structures, rhythm, figures of speech, rhetorical principles, and other elements of composition.

Subjectivity: Writing that expresses the author's personal feelings about his subject, and which may or may not include factual information about the subject.

Subplot: A secondary story in a narrative. A subplot may serve as a motivating or complicating force for the main plot of the work, or it may provide emphasis for, or relief from, the main plot.

Surrealism: A term introduced to criticism by Guillaume Apollinaire and later adopted by Andre Breton. It refers to a French literary and artistic movement founded in the 1920s. The Surrealists sought to express unconscious thoughts and feelings in their works. The best-known technique used for achieving this aim was automatic writing—transcriptions of spontaneous outpourings from the unconscious. The Surrealists proposed to unify the contrary levels of conscious and unconscious, dream and reality, objectivity and subjectivity into a new level of "super-realism."

Suspense: A literary device in which the author maintains the audience's attention through the buildup of events, the outcome of which will soon be revealed.

Symbol: Something that suggests or stands for something else without losing its original identity. In literature, symbols combine their literal meaning with the suggestion of an abstract concept. Literary symbols are of two types: those that carry complex associations of meaning no matter what their contexts, and those that derive their suggestive meaning from their functions in specific literary works.

Symbolism: This term has two widely accepted meanings. In historical criticism, it denotes an early modernist literary movement initiated in France during the nineteenth century that reacted against the prevailing standards of realism. Writers in this movement aimed to evoke, indirectly and symbolically, an order of being beyond the material world of the five senses. Poetic expression of personal emotion figured strongly in the movement, typically by means of a private set of symbols uniquely identifiable with the individual poet. The principal aim of the Symbolists was to express in words the highly complex feelings that grew out of everyday contact with the world. In a broader sense, the term "symbolism" refers to the use of one object to represent another.

T

Tall Tale: A humorous tale told in a straightforward, credible tone but relating absolutely impossible events or feats of the characters. Such tales were commonly told of frontier adventures during the settlement of the west in the United States.

Theme: The main point of a work of literature. The term is used interchangeably with thesis.

Thesis: A thesis is both an essay and the point argued in the essay. Thesis novels and thesis plays share the quality of containing a thesis which is supported through the action of the story.

Third Person: See *Point of View*

Tone: The author's attitude toward his or her audience may be deduced from the tone of the work. A formal tone may create distance or convey politeness, while an informal tone may encourage a friendly, intimate, or intrusive feeling in the reader. The author's attitude toward his or her subject matter may also be deduced from the tone of the words he or she uses in discussing it.

Transcendentalism: An American philosophical and religious movement, based in New England from around 1835 until the Civil War. Transcendentalism was a form of American romanticism that had its roots abroad in the works of Thomas Carlyle, Samuel Coleridge, and Johann Wolfgang von Goethe. The Transcendentalists stressed the importance of intuition and subjective experience in communication with God. They rejected religious dogma and texts in favor of mysticism and scientific naturalism. They pursued truths that lie beyond the "colorless" realms perceived by reason and the senses and were active social reformers in public education, women's rights, and the abolition of slavery.

U

Urban Realism: A branch of realist writing that attempts to accurately reflect the often harsh facts of modern urban existence.

Utopia: A fictional perfect place, such as "paradise" or "heaven."

V

Verisimilitude: Literally, the appearance of truth. In literary criticism, the term refers to aspects of a work of literature that seem true to the reader.

Victorian: Refers broadly to the reign of Queen Victoria of England (1837-1901) and to anything with qualities typical of that era. For example, the qualities of smug narrowmindedness, bourgeois materialism, faith in social progress, and priggish morality are often considered Victorian. This stereotype is contradicted by such dramatic intellectual developments as the theories of Charles Darwin, Karl Marx, and Sigmund Freud (which stirred strong debates in England) and the critical attitudes of serious Victorian writers like Charles Dickens and George Eliot. In literature, the Victorian Period was the great age of the English novel, and the latter part of the era saw the rise of movements such as decadence and symbolism. Also known as Victorian Age and Victorian Period.

W

Weltanschauung: A German term referring to a person's worldview or philosophy.

Weltschmerz: A German term meaning "world pain." It describes a sense of anguish about the nature of existence, usually associated with a melancholy, pessimistic attitude.

Z

Zeitgeist: A German term meaning "spirit of the time." It refers to the moral and intellectual trends of a given era.

Cumulative
Author/Title Index

Cumulative
Nationality/Ethnicity Index

Guest, Judith
  Ordinary People: V1
Hawthorne, Nathaniel
  The Scarlet Letter: V1
Heller, Joseph
  Catch-22: V1
Hemingway, Ernest
  A Farewell to Arms: V1
  The Old Man and the Sea: V6
  The Sun Also Rises: V5
Hinton, S. E.
  Tex: V9
  The Outsiders: V5
Hurston, Zora Neale
  Their Eyes Were Watching God:
    V3
Kerouac, Jack
  On the Road: V8
Kesey, Ken
  *One Flew Over the Cuckoo's
    Nest*: V2
Keyes, Daniel
  Flowers for Algernon: V2
Kincaid, Jamaica
  Annie John: V3
Kingsolver, Barbara
  The Bean Trees: V5
  Pigs in Heaven: V10
Kingston, Maxine Hong
  The Woman Warrior: V6
Knowles, John
  A Separate Peace: V2
Le Guin, Ursula K.
  Always Coming Home: V9
  The Left Hand of Darkness: V6
Lee, Harper
  To Kill a Mockingbird: V2
London, Jack
  The Call of the Wild: V8
Lowry, Lois
  The Giver: V3
Mailer, Norman
  The Naked and the Dead: V10
Mason, Bobbie Ann
  In Country: V4
McCullers, Carson
  The Heart Is a Lonely Hunter: V6
Melville, Herman
  Billy Budd: V9
  Moby-Dick: V7
Mitchell, Margaret
  Gone with the Wind: V9
Momaday, N. Scott
  House Made of Dawn: V10
Morrison, Toni
  Beloved: V6
  The Bluest Eye: V1
  Song of Solomon: V8
Oates, Joyce Carol
  them: V8
O'Connor, Flannery
  Wise Blood: V3

Plath, Sylvia
  The Bell Jar: V1
Potok, Chaim
  The Chosen: V4
Rand, Ayn
  Atlas Shrugged: V10
Rölvaag, O. E.
  Giants in the Earth: V5
Salinger, J. D.
  The Catcher in the Rye: V1
Sinclair, Upton
  The Jungle: V6
Steinbeck, John
  The Grapes of Wrath: V7
  Of Mice and Men: V1
  The Pearl: V5
Stowe, Harriet Beecher
  Uncle Tom's Cabin: V6
Tan, Amy
  The Joy Luck Club: V1
Twain, Mark
  *The Adventures of Huckleberry
    Finn*: V1
  The Adventures of Tom Sawyer: V6
Tyler, Anne
  The Accidental Tourist: V7
  Breathing Lessons: V10
  *Dinner at the Homesick
    Restaurant*: V2
Vonnegut, Kurt, Jr.
  Slaughterhouse-Five: V3
Walker, Alice
  The Color Purple: V5
Wharton, Edith
  Ethan Frome: V5
Wouk, Herman
  The Caine Mutiny: V7
Wright, Richard
  Black Boy: V1
  Native Son: V7

Asian American
Kingston, Maxine Hong
  The Woman Warrior: V6
Tan, Amy
  The Joy Luck Club: V1

Asian Canadian
Kogawa, Joy
  Obasan: V3

Australian
Clavell, James du Maresq
  Shogun: A Novel of Japan: V10

British
Adams, Douglas
  *The Hitchhiker's Guide to the
    Galaxy*: V7

Austen, Jane
  Pride and Prejudice: V1
Ballard, J. G.
  Empire of the Sun: V8
Blair, Eric Arthur
  Animal Farm: V3
Brontë, Charlotte
  Jane Eyre: V4
Brontë, Emily
  Wuthering Heights: V2
Carroll, Lewis
  *Alice's Adventurers in
    Wonderland*: V7
Chrisite, Agatha
  Ten Little Indians: V8
Conrad, Joseph
  Heart of Darkness: V2
Defoe, Daniel
  Robinson Crusoe: V9
Dickens, Charles
  A Christmas Carol: V10
  Great Expectations: V4
  A Tale of Two Cities: V5
Forster, E. M.
  A Passage to India: V3
  Howards End: V10
Golding, William
  Lord of the Flies: V2
Hardy, Thomas
  Tess of the d'Urbervilles: V3
Huxley, Aldous
  Brave New World: V6
Marmon Silko, Leslie
  Ceremony: V4
Orwell, George
  1984: V7
  Animal Farm: V3
Shelley, Mary
  Frankenstein: V1
Shute, Nevil
  On the Beach: V9
Swift, Jonathan
  Gulliver's Travels: V6
Tolkien, J. R. R.
  The Hobbit: V8
Woolf, Virginia
  To the Lighthouse: V8

Canadian
Atwood, Margaret
  The Handmaid's Tale: V4
Kogawa, Joy
  Obasan: V3

Chilean
Allende, Isabel
  The House of the Spirits: V6

Colombian
García Márquez, Gabriel
  Chronicle of a Death Foretold:
    V10

Subject/Theme Index